THE AMBASSADORS

Robert Cooper

Sir Robert Francis Cooper is a British diplomat and adviser currently serving as a Special Advisor at the European Commission with regard to Myanmar. He is also a member of the European Council on Foreign Relations and is an acclaimed writer on international relations. His publications, apart from a number of articles in *Prospect* and elsewhere, include: *The Post-Modern State and the World Order* and *The Breaking of Nations*, which won the Orwell Prize for Political Writing.

THE AMBASSADORS

Thinking about Diplomacy from Machiavelli to Modern Times

Robert Cooper

First published in Great Britain in 2021 by Weidenfeld & Nicolson
This paperback edition published in 2021 by Weidenfeld & Nicolson
an imprint of The Orion Publishing Group Ltd
Carmelite House, 50 Victoria Embankment
London EC4Y 0DZ

An Hachette UK Company

1 3 5 7 9 10 8 6 4 2

A CIP catalogue record for this book is available from the British Library.

ISBN (Mass Market Paperback) 978 1 7802 2836 5
ISBN (eBook) 978 0 2976 0854 7

Typeset by Input Data Services Ltd, Somerset

Printed and bound in Great Britain by Clays Ltd, Elcograf S.p.A.

www.weidenfeldandnicolson.co.uk
www.orionbooks.co.uk

Contents

Foreword: How to Read this Book

This is a book of fragments.

> Those scraps are good deeds past,
> Which are devoured as fast as they are made,
> Forgot as soon as done.
>
> (*Troilus and Cressida*, Act III, Scene 3)

History does not run in straight lines. It is made by people and by chance. The path of events and ideas does not stretch smoothly from Thucydides, through Machiavelli to Rousseau and to Kant, and thence to Perpetual Peace. This book is an attempt to think about diplomacy; the best way to do that is to focus on the concrete, on the moments when problems, people and ideas meet.

Instead of the inevitable progress that history books sometimes imply, we more often find blind alleys, random events, good intentions that go wrong and, occasionally, lucky breaks. Now and then we get glimpses of the future; but these are forgotten as the world takes another turning. Yet there is always something to learn, from success as well as from failure. The men and women who work in this world do so in the obscurity of the present, aided only by fading memories of the past, and trying to guess at the future. Sometimes, by accident or by intuition, they find a way forward; occasionally they may even half understand where it is that they are going.

This is therefore not a continuous diplomatic history. History happens in fragments; but out of these comes the world we live in. The episodes I describe are arranged more or less chronologically, but there is no reason to read them in that order. If you find Richelieu tiresome go on to Mazarin, whom I admit I like better, or to the end of the chapter – because I have the bad habit of leaving the important points to the last.

The people I have chosen to write about are those who had some insight or success. In diplomacy success is rare, and it is therefore more interesting than failure. Thus I am writing about the people that I admire: a Lives of Saints for an unsaintly world.

Whom do I, as a former diplomat, most admire? The answer may be Talleyrand. It is impossible to imagine being him – too brilliant, and the times are too different. So I include a short chapter on two lower-ranking diplomats who issued visas to Jews, going beyond the instructions from their governments, in the case of Chiune Sugihara going against them. These also are people to admire and to emulate, should the need ever come again.

Four hundred years ago, Richelieu and Mazarin inhabited a world we can hardly imagine today: the state itself was not a solid existence; its borders were subject to continuous wars and change. But this is also the beginning of modernity, and of the road to today's Europe.

Talleyrand was born in the *ancien régime*; but he understood the changing nature of legitimacy, and that the success of the state came not from conquest, but from its political strength and its economic development. The Bourbons and Napoleon both systematically ignored his ideas. So he waited for the moment of crisis, when no one was in charge, and took his own advice.

The great innovation of the Congress of Vienna – assembled to put Europe back together again after Napoleon – was multilateral diplomacy. The great powers tried to continue it afterwards in what we now call the Concert of Europe. Look at the end of Chapter Three, where Metternich's secretary, Friedrich von Gentz, reflects on what would happen if the Concert were to fail (as it does shortly after). What he gives us is an account of the origins of the First World War a century before the event.

The Congress of Vienna recognised the role of the great powers. Most writing on diplomacy, and most of this book, is about great powers. But small countries also need diplomats. In fact, they may need them more than great powers do. So among the fragments are stories of two small countries, Denmark and Finland, which against the odds survived in a world where the only guarantee of survival is strength.

Seven chapters of this book are about the people who built or rebuilt the West in the early days of the Cold War. George Kennan, one of the great diplomatic professionals, spoke truth to power; for most of his career, power was not interested. Then came men who were: George Marshall, Ernest Bevin, Dean Acheson and Harry Truman, the architects of the West. Jean Monnet, the architect of Europe, was the most creative of them all.

The high point of Cold War drama is the Cuban Missile Crisis: here we have a contrast between the open debate that Kennedy used to help him make decisions and the closed system in Moscow. Khrushchev made a colossal misjudgement, but his appeal to Kennedy was based in the end on common values. His metaphor for diplomacy – the attempt to untie the knot while the two sides are pulling at the rope – is the most powerful I know. He, for me, is, in part, a hero too.

My fantasy about Henry Kissinger is to imagine him telling Nixon, on his first day in office, that the Vietnam War is lost – he has seen that on his visits there – and that the only thing to do is to get out. Had he done that, there would have been no second day. But then imagine some more: what if Nixon had understood that this was the ultimate test of toughness and realism – and his claim was to be tough and realistic – and he had acted accordingly? He would be remembered now as a hero. He would not have won a second term, but he would not have needed one. Fantasy aside, Kissinger is the intellectual heart of the Cold War: his ideas, his successes and failures, are on a grand scale. He tried to find ways of living with enemies. That is still the most difficult task, more complicated today than ever.

The Cold War's geographical heart was Germany. In the fifty years after the war, Germany achieved a diplomatic miracle to go with its economic (and political) miracles. The credit belongs especially to three great chancellors: Konrad Adenauer, Willy Brandt and Helmut Kohl. And to America.

I have tried to write not just about what all these men did – in the nature of things they are all men, though I have worked with and for some outstanding women diplomats – but also about *how* they did it. That is not always easy. Some act by instinct, some by analysis; sometimes two people are needed to bring the package together.

When I began writing this, the title in my head was in German: *Sternstunden der Diplomatie*, after Stefan Zweig's *Sternstunden der Menschheit*. This has been translated as *Decisive Moments in History*, but that doesn't capture the meaning. One translation calls it *The Tide of Fortune*. Better, but that misses the idea of history crystallised in a moment. What I want to convey is the drama of diplomacy.

This is hard to capture. It rarely comes at the end. It is not the signing of the treaty: that is for the cameras; nor even the moment when agreement is reached. By then everyone is tired and fed up and wants to go home.

The drama is earlier: something you don't expect. In the negotiations at Westphalia, after eighty years of war with the Netherlands, the Spanish offer a truce. The Dutch reply, not with the usual proposals for amendments, but with a complete peace treaty. In modern times, after another eighty years of violence and enmity, Jean Monnet's proposal to bring Germany and France together in the Coal and Steel Community was an even bigger shock. The moment of drama is less Robert Schuman's statement in the *Salon de l'Horloge* at the Quai d'Orsay, opening the path to the European Union – though that is dramatic enough – than the moment when Monnet's idea begins to crystallise or when hears from Schuman that he'll use it: that is when the pulse begins to race.

With drama comes emotion; I invite the reader to pause now and then and imagine how the protagonists felt. The historical record does not tell us. Diplomacy is a profession in which emotions are concealed.

During the Congress of Vienna Metternich sent notes to his mistress saying that the fate of Europe depended on him. I do not think that is an exaggeration: it is how he felt. He went to the balls to relax; and his best ideas often came to him during them. That is testimony to the tensions of his work: the problems of the day never left him.

I guess at these emotions because, occasionally, I have felt them myself. Here is a small incident.

I was in Myanmar representing the European Union, the first visit by a senior official for some years. We told all the officials we met that the EU would lift sanctions if they did two things: one was to allow the National League for Democracy (Aung San Suu Kyi's party) to participate in political life. The other was to release all political prisoners. I and my colleague, a distinguished Italian gentleman, repeated this to everyone we met. But the meetings were formal and polite, full of smiles and platitudes; and I was not sure that we were getting through. So at the end of the last meeting, as we left, I shook the foreign minister's hand but then held on to it while I said to him that, if they really wanted to show that things had changed, they should release all political prisoners together, on one single day. That would make an impact across the world. He looked surprised, but said nothing.

In the evening, at a farewell dinner, his deputy asked me if I could repeat what I had said to his boss. I did so, explaining my rather implausible idea at greater length.

That was the end of the visit. We went back to Yangon. I bought some souvenirs, got rid of my suit and was getting ready to leave when I received a phone call on an extraordinarily bad line (the telephones were 1950s vintage). It was the deputy minister. Could I please tell him, he asked, exactly *who* we meant by 'all political prisoners'. I said, of course. We would send a list the next day.

No one promised or agreed anything. There was no press statement. But for twenty years we had been calling for political prisoners to be released; we had imposed sanctions for ten years. No one had ever asked who it was we meant.

Myanmar is far from a happy ending: the army is still in power, but change takes time and this was a beginning. We don't know what the ending will be.

History, especially diplomatic history, where the protagonists are hiding their motives and their feelings, leaves only fragments behind. My hope is that these may illuminate and inspire.

> The atoms of Democritus,
> And Newton's particles of light,
> Are sands upon the Red Sea shore,
> Where Israel's tents do shine so bright.

William Blake, 'Mock on, Mock on, Voltaire, Rousseau'

I

Niccolò Machiavelli

> 'Sensitive, thoughtful men realised that this was a time like none other . . . The key to their problems they knew to be rooted in the lives and actions of men, not in universal mysteries or the attributes of God. Consequently there is an astonishing freshness about the historians and the political philosophers of the Renaissance, and, as with the painters and sculptors, the greatest by far were the Florentines, and the greatest of the Florentines was Niccolò Machiavelli.'
>
> *J. H. Plumb, The Italian Renaissance*

Italy's most famous diplomat is known not for what he did as a diplomat, but for what he wrote afterwards. His life in diplomacy, working for one state and observing others, forms the essential background to his thought and writing.

His story begins as the years of the Medici came to an end in Florence. In 1494 Charles VIII of France conquered Italy 'with a piece of chalk'.[1] Arriving in Florence, his men marked with chalk the doors of houses where troops would be billeted. No one resisted.

Charles brought with him the best artillery in the world. He made himself King of Naples. He won all his battles, including the last, at Fornovo, against the League of Venice – the pope, the emperor, Spain and Milan, as well as Venice. He left with nothing, having lost his baggage train. Two years of looting wasted!

Florence was an unwilling ally of France, forced to acquiesce in the invasion when the king expelled all Florentine merchants from France. Trade sanctions work with countries that depend on trade. With the Medici gone, Florence became a purer form of republic, with wider participation. The Dominican friar Girolamo Savonarola brought extra purity. He saw Charles's arrival as a sign from God that the city must be cleansed of ostentation, usury and the Medici. But Florence needed money; to win the Vatican's consent for taxes on the clergy it accepted Savonarola's excommunication. In 1498 he was arrested, tortured and executed. His body was burned in the main square.

With this, a reshaped government comes to power. Niccolò Machiavelli is elected second chancellor and secretary of the *Dieci di Balia*, the Ten of Liberty and Peace, who are responsible for security.[2] This is an administrative position, not a political one. Niccolò's family is poor, but it has a record of service in the government of Florence. He is twenty-nine years old and has a reputation as being literate and energetic; he is untainted by the divisions that marked Florentine politics in the Savonarola period.

He is a secretary, not an ambassador. He does not have powers to negotiate with states. His first work for the *Dieci* is to negotiate with *condottieri* (military leaders) on the price for mercenary soldiers. This is what many of Florence's negotiations are about, whether the interlocutor is a military contractor or the King of France.

Niccolò is a good diplomat: he is interesting to talk to; he listens carefully, writes well, thinks ahead. His life is exciting: he deals with France, one of the great powers of the day; he sees the rise and fall of Cesare Borgia close up; he joins Pope Julius II as he conquers cities in the Romagna by force of personality. But there is not much you can achieve as a diplomat if you are working for a second-class power.

His great success is outside the field of diplomacy. When Charles VIII passed through Florence, the French encouraged Pisa to declare itself independent. Since then Florence has tried to force it to recapture Pisa, using mercenary forces. The French return to Italy in 1499, when Charles's successor, Louis XII, claims the titles of Duke of Milan and King of Naples, but they never help Florence recover Pisa.

The Pisa campaign is the dream of any mercenary commander: a rich client and a war without end, in which very few of your men die. After yet another humiliating episode – the commanders breach the walls, but decide not to risk the lives of their men by entering Pisa – Niccolò suggests, once again, to Piero Soderini, the *gonfaloniere* (chief executive) of Florence, that they create their own militia in Florence. This is controversial, but the *gonfaloniere* tells him to start recruiting.

When, in February 1506, Niccolò has his recruits join the carnival parade in Florentine colours, they are a big popular success. Piero Soderini appoints Don Michele de Corella to train the militia. He has murdered and robbed for Cesare Borgia, but he is a professional who was loyal to the last, and he does a good job.

In 1508, Maximilian, the Holy Roman Emperor, enters Italy. Venice refuses him passage through its territory; in the conflict that follows, the emperor loses important cities including Trieste before a truce is agreed. Out of this comes the League of Cambrai: a pact between the empire and France aimed at Venice. Ferdinand of Spain joins and, at the last minute, Pope Julius II: everyone except Florence is against Venice. Louis wants to secure his hold on Milan, Maximilian to regain the cities he has lost; Ferdinand wants to recapture ports in the south that Venice has occupied, Julius to end Venice's encroachments in Romagna. This is a coalition of foreign powers, plus the pope, against a single Italian state. In May 1509, at Agnadello, Venice is narrowly but decisively defeated.

Florence is absent from the League of Cambrai, but profits from it. While the big powers fight Venice, Florence deals with Pisa, which Venice is now unable to help. (It has done so in the past, hoping to extend its empire to the Tyrrhenian Sea.) Florence and the militia Niccolò has invented end the rebellion, after fifteen years and much money wasted on mercenary forces. Niccolò is one of the signatories of the peace.

Victorious coalitions turn on themselves. As this war ends, Julius starts work on a new Holy League – the papacy, Venice and Spain – to rid Italy of the barbarians: the French, that is. Now Florence is in trouble. Its nearest neighbour, the pope, is going to war with France, its protector. Florence offers to mediate: it has every interest in peace, but why should anyone listen to a weak state? Besides, Julius wants victory, not peace. To attack the pope's authority, France calls a General Council of the Church to dismiss the pope, or to split the Church, and proposes it meet in Pisa. Having done nothing to help Florence with Pisa, France now proposes that the General Council meet there, nailing their ally to the mast. Niccolò and others scramble to keep the few dissident cardinals out of Pisa, and the meeting is moved to Milan. Niccolò's friend and colleague, Biagio Buonaccorsi, quotes Livy: 'Without favour, without honour, we shall be the prize of the victor.' Niccolò tells the French that, as an ally, Florence will be more a burden than a support for France.

At first the war goes well for France, and Florence manages to stay out of it. Then the Swiss take sides against the French, and Spanish forces arrive from Naples. These attack Prato, a dependency of Florence. The Florentine militia, who did well against Pisa, are no match for the discipline and experience of the Spanish infantry. The militia flee; Prato is sacked; the republic and Piero Soderini are overthrown. The Medici return, backed by the pope, and Florence itself escapes being sacked. A year later Louis XII makes a last attempt to regain Milan. Now he is opposed by a multinational coalition including England and Leo X, a Medici pope. Louis departs with nothing, like Charles before him, after thirteen wasted years.

With this Niccolò Machiavelli's time as a diplomat ends. He is imprisoned and accused of conspiracy, he is tortured but does not confess to something of which he is not guilty. None of his friends are able to help, but the election of a Medici pope is celebrated with an amnesty and Niccolò is released.

Julius II drove the French barbarians out of Italy. But, as happened with Charles VIII, he did so by inviting others in. The next French invader, Francis I, will also leave nothing behind. But the barbarians, Spanish and Habsburg, who help drive him out will stay; and the French will continue to invade Italy once or twice a century. Italy, at this moment the richest country in Europe and a great civilisation, never takes the place that its history and its people deserve.

Niccolò Machiavelli was born for politics. No longer able to practise, he writes about it. It is for this that he is remembered: above all for *The Prince* (1513). This is the first essay in the politics of modern Europe. It is written not as a work of philosophy, but as a practical guide by a man who believed that the destiny of men is partly in their own hands. It is a starting point for the modern world.

The Prince begins not with the Bible or theology, nor with the abstract reasoning of philosophers, but with real life: history and personal experience. 'Having the intention to write something useful to anyone who understands, it seems to me better to concentrate on what really happens rather than on theories or speculations' (Chapter XV). This is not political science, but it is a step in that direction.[3] Machiavelli writes about the state – the central actor in the drama – at the moment when it is being shaped.

He writes for many reasons. He would like to return to the work he knows and has done well. *The Prince* is in part a job application. But once he starts writing he cannot help himself. The book is designed neither to flatter nor to please the Medici family. It is about princely government, but it is not difficult to guess that Machiavelli's sympathies are republican.

The Prince is meant to shock. It tells the truth about politics. It starts prosaically, but later on it is brutal: 'I shall set aside fantasies about rulers, then, and consider what happens in fact' (Chapter XV). He goes on to explain that a ruler, especially a new ruler – a category to which the Medici government may belong – 'is often forced to act treacherously, ruthlessly or inhumanly, and to disregard the precepts of religion'.

The book is for the new prince, in a new conquest, at a moment of consequence and vulnerability. He demolishes the two qualities most associated with the courtly advice in the 'Mirror of Princes' literature: generosity and mercy. Better for the prince to be cruel and miserly – if miserly means lower taxes, and cruel means that men fear punishment. Fear of punishment is the beginning of order. But 'If a ruler, then, contrives to conquer, and to preserve the state, the means will always be judged to be honourable' (Chapter XVIII).

Behind the mirror is the use of force. A good state is one that has 'good laws and good arms'. Arms are needed for internal order and external defence. The use of force is at the heart of the state. By using it early, the prince may be able to use it less. If force is needed to secure the state it is legitimate; so is fraud; the prince may, indeed must, be ready to deceive, break his word: whatever is needed.

Machiavelli is a practical man. In philosophical terms this reasoning points to the idea of the sovereign: the person, or institution to whom rules do not apply, who may use force or break laws when the survival of the state is at risk, because they are the only source of law and security. *Res publica suprema lex.* 'The survival of states is not a subject of law,' says Dean Acheson four centuries later.

The 'good arms' must be the property of the state. Machiavelli has seen the weakness of mercenary forces. If the state hires or borrows arms, they are not under its control. Florence has found this out any number of times. Mercenaries are 'useless or dangerous . . . weak and cowardly when confronted by determined enemies' (Chapter XII). Their preference is to be paid, but not to risk their lives by actually fighting. This he knows from experience. Mercenaries are the root of the weakness of Italian states (Chapter XXIV). Arms must belong to the state: in a princely state, the prince must lead his forces into battle; in a republic, the soldiers must be of its people.

He will be proved right, but not in his time. Venice managed with mercenaries; but it had long-term relationships and paid on time. Mercenaries will be a factor in war until armies become professional, in Louis XIV's France first, as part of a stronger state. Step by step, the monopoly on the use of force becomes the core attribute of the state.

If Machiavelli is cynical about the prince, he is no less so about the people. They are 'generally ungrateful, fickle, feigners and dissemblers, avoiders of danger, eager for gain' (Chapter XVII). Good government begins with fear of the law. But he also writes that if the prince is not hated by his people, he will not need fortresses.

He is not a democrat. This is the sixteenth century, and the word does not yet exist. If anything, Machiavelli is a republican. Early in

The Prince (Chapter V) he writes, 'In republics there is greater vitality . . . [T]hey do not forget, indeed cannot forget, their lost liberties.' In discussing 'civic principalities', where a prince has come to power through the support of the people – the Medici in Florence might fall into this category – he says that the ruler should aim to win over the people rather than the nobles, both because there are more of them and because their aims are more honourable: 'the latter [the nobles] want only to oppress, the former only to avoid being oppressed' (Chapter IX).

The chapter of *The Prince* titled 'What a Ruler Should Do in Order to be Thought Outstanding' brings together several themes. As the title tells us, what matters is not being outstanding, but being *thought* outstanding. His example is Ferdinand of Spain, who began his reign with the war in Granada; this kept the barons occupied and trained his army, while he pursued 'a cruel and apparently pious policy of unexampled wretchedness, that of hunting down the Moors, and driving them out of his kingdom'. Machiavelli finds the policy repugnant; but he admires the statecraft. The king 'never failed to keep his subjects in a state of suspense and amazement'. Cesare Borgia comes to a miserable end, but Machiavelli still admires his ability to surprise and amaze his audience. As Philip Bobbitt says, 'statecraft is stagecraft'.

In the same spirit, Machiavelli advises that, if you have harsh things to do, as is inevitable when you acquire a state by conquest, then you should do them all together, but 'benefits should be given out one by one, so that they will be savoured more' (Chapter VIII). This remains good political practice in the twenty-first century: after you win the election you put taxes up, hoping that by the next election people will have forgotten.

The language and the ideas of *The Prince* are brutal because this was an age of violence and danger. But the message of *The Prince* is that through politics, man can take control of the future. As a practical man, Machiavelli knows that nothing is certain. At the end of the book, he therefore asks the practical question: whether, and how far, we are in control of our destiny.

He gives a practical answer: 'I am disposed to hold that fortune is the arbiter of half our actions, but that it lets us control roughly the other half.' Machiavelli adds the observation – drawn from the successes and failures of the kings and popes he has seen – that there are times when it is right to be bold, and times when it is better to be cautious. But the character of men seems to be fixed. (Is this scientific? No, he would answer: politics is an art, not a science.)

Are we then doomed to fail half the time? One solution is to turn (as Philip Bobbitt does) to the *Discourses* (1513).[4] *The Prince* is short and shocking, and is better known; but the ideas in the two books have much in common. In the *Discourses*, Machiavelli tells the story of the defeat of Hannibal, first by Quintus Fabius Maximus, who was by character cautious. But: 'If Fabius had been King of Rome, he could easily have lost the war because he would not have known how to vary his policy as the times varied; but he was born in a republic where there were different citizens and different opinions' (Chapter III). The Senate, sensing that a different policy was needed, chose Scipio. He was bold, matching the needs of the times, and he defeated Hannibal. Does that mean that republics, being more plural, are more likely to succeed? Possibly, though Machiavelli points out in both books that republics are also slow to make decisions. He knew this only too well from his experience of Florence.

Machiavelli is right that most people are either bold or cautious, and usually are not able to change. But there are exceptions: the American jurist Oliver Wendell Holmes said of Franklin D. Roosevelt that he had a third-class mind but a first-class temperament. A feature of that temperament was an instinct which told him when to act and when to wait. He was sure from the start that the United States would have to fight Nazism, but he campaigned in the 1940 election on a platform of keeping the US out of the war. After the election he supported Britain through Lend-Lease, which he presented in a folksy and entirely misleading way. At the same time, he prepared for the moment he believed was coming. When Japan bombed Pearl Harbor he was able to expand US military capacity at an undreamed-of pace, and to take the lead in the war against Germany.

Another solution to the problem of chance and character is suggested earlier in *The Prince*, in a chapter on how to shun flatterers. This is less about shunning flatterers (not a difficult problem) than about using advisers. Choose men, Machiavelli says, who will speak to you frankly, but privately. The prince should make sure his advisers 'all realise that the more candidly they speak the more acceptable they will be'. And choose men, he might have added, who have a different temperament from yours. Here is a second example. When Winston Churchill became prime minister in 1940, he was old enough to know his weaknesses: he was resolute, eloquent and imaginative, but he was also impetuous, and he knew it. As his closest military adviser he chose Alan Brooke, a cool and methodical military professional, and also one of the few people he knew would stand up to him.

Machiavelli gives a good deal of space to the question of advisers. He underlines in two chapters close to the end of the book – which is where his most important messages are – that the prince is not shrewd because of what his advisers tell him: it is his choice of good people that marks him as shrewd.

The Prince offers advice on domestic and military affairs, but it says little on foreign policy except for one revealing passage where he sets out the mistakes that Louis XII made in Italy:[5]

- Louis allowed the pope to become too strong. Alexander VI welcomed the French intervention and saw the disruption it caused as an opportunity to extend his own power in the Papal States. Later he organised the Holy League against Louis.
- Louis overextended by taking Naples and leaving a viceroy there. Instead, he should have kept Frederick of Aragon in Naples as a tributary king, and consolidated his own position in Milan.
- To conquer Naples, Louis brought another powerful actor into Italy, namely Ferdinand of Spain. Ferdinand would later be part of the Holy League against France.
- Finally, Machiavelli says, he might have got away with these errors had he not made one more: breaking the alliance with Venice. The League of Cambrai led directly to the Holy League and to France's expulsion.

To sum up: Louis should have been content with Milan, plus indirect rule over Naples. He should have nurtured his alliances with Venice and Florence, kept watch on the pope, and protected some of the small states that he took over. A weak pope would not have been a threat. The attack on Venice unbalanced Italy and was fatal.

This is hindsight. In 1500, when Louis's minister, Georges d'Amboise, told Machiavelli that Italians knew nothing about war, he replied, rather cheekily, that France did not understand statecraft. At this point Louis had made only the first of the errors. What if Machiavelli, with perfect foresight, had warned of these risks? Would it have made a difference? Probably not: as Machiavelli suggests, each makes his own mistakes.

France is not the only guilty party. Machiavelli says that, after they had set all this in motion, 'the Venetians were able to understand the rashness of their policy. In order to gain a couple of possessions in Lombardy, they had enabled the king [Louis] to become master of a third of Italy' (Chapter III). Perhaps Venice learned from its mistake. It survived, the only independent Italian state, until Napoleon.

Machiavelli makes two more remarks on foreign affairs in *The Prince*. The first is that neutrality is a bad policy. If you do not take sides, the victor may take you as their prize. (He quotes the same sentence from Livy as Biagio Buonaccorsi did in the crisis of 1512). This may be right for his time. But after Agnadello, Venice did well as a neutral power. In a different Europe Switzerland and Finland have done so too. But in the disorderly world of his time Machiavelli has a point.

Machiavelli returns to the question of alliances (and to Florence's problem) near the end of *The Prince* (Chapter XXI), writing that 'a ruler should be careful not to ally himself with a ruler who is more powerful than himself, in order to attack other powers unless he is forced to . . . But if it is not possible to avoid such a commitment (as happened to the Florentines, when the pope and the king of Spain launched an attack against Lombardy), a ruler should then become involved, for the reasons previously mentioned.' This is a reference to the attack by the Holy League on France. He goes on: 'No government should ever believe that it is always possible to follow safe policies.' That seems to say that, for small states, sometimes there is no escape.

That is an epitaph for Florence. In the years after Charles VIII's invasion, Florence's fate became tied to France. In the past it had been close to Venice, a fellow republic, with an eye on autocratic Milan and Naples. This balance was lost through the long Pisa affair.

Machiavelli says little about Pisa in *The Prince*, though its rebellion occupied him for ten years, and its recapture was his biggest success. In Chapter V he explains the difficulty of recapturing it as the result of Pisa having been a republic: such states 'never forget their lost liberties and their ancient institutions, and will immediately attempt to recover them whenever they have an opportunity, as Pisa did after enduring a century of subjection to the Florentines'.

So, is there an alternative to conquest? Not in *The Prince*. But in the *Discourses* (Book II: XXI) Machiavelli writes that Pistoia came willingly under Florence's rule, not that they valued their liberty less, but 'with them the Florentines have always conducted themselves like brothers . . . And without doubt, if the Florentines, either by way of leagues or of aid, had tamed their neighbours and not made them wild, at this hour they would be lords of Tuscany. It is not to be understood by this that I think one never has to use arms, but they ought to be reserved for the last place.' Perhaps another future might have been possible for Florence.

That is a possibility. The reality Machiavelli lived in was a zero-sum world. The state has one supreme goal: survival. Only the big survive, so you must conquer – or you will be conquered. That is the logic of foreign policy in Machiavelli's world, and the mainstream of European politics in theory and in practice, until the Second World War.

There is no other book like *The Prince*. Everyone who reads it finds something different. Jacob Burckhardt said that Machiavelli and Renaissance Italy conceived of the state as a work of art. Friedrich Meinecke wrote that Machiavelli had plunged a sword into the body of the West.[6] Isaiah Berlin devoted fifty pages to this puzzle in 1972.[7] Since then there have been many, many more opinions.

One is Garrett Mattingly's: 'What happened in the almost three centuries between the time when Machiavelli was either praised as a daring rebel or denounced as an emissary of Satan, and the time when he began to be acclaimed as a prophet, was that all Europe had become what Italy in Machiavelli's lifetime already was.'[8]

The remainder of this book tells how others struggled with the problem Machiavelli set. The chapter that follows is about the statesman who, of them all, most resembles Machiavelli's prince.

2

Richelieu and Mazarin: the Making of the State

'One thing is certain. He who leaves the table loses the game.'

*Cardinal de La Valette**

Lyons, 30 September 1630

The king has received the last sacrament. His mother, Marie de' Medici, is by his bed. He has told her: 'I have tried to be a good son. If I have not always succeeded, forgive me.' His wife, Anne of Austria, embraces him, and they speak 'by tears rather than by voice', in the words of the king's confessor.[1] Cardinal Richelieu is there too, in tears. All kneel by the bedside.

Louis XIII has no son. His brother, the charming, irresponsible Gaston, Duc d'Orléans, Richelieu's enemy, will succeed. And the queen mother, Marie de' Medici, will be in power again.

What will happen to Richelieu? Will he be arrested, imprisoned? Cardinals are not normally executed. Whatever happens, Richelieu is done for. This is a time where ends are often violent.

Richelieu's enemies will hold him responsible for the king's death. It was Richelieu who led him into the Alps on a military adventure that has sucked in armies from both Spain and the Holy Roman

* This quotation, which appears in many accounts of the events of the Day of the Dupes, may be an invention. It is a fitting image of Richelieu's anxiety, but there are no eyewitnesses.

Empire; if the two join forces France cannot win. Their armies are massive and experienced; France's is weak and untried. Now there is plague in the mountains, and the king has returned, dying of a fever.

But it is not the plague; and the king is not dying. Richelieu writes to General Schomberg, commanding the army in the Alps: 'I saw the most excellent prince, and the best master, in such a state that I never expected to see him alive again. God in His mercy has now been pleased to relieve us of our heavy anxiety; an abscess in the king's body has burst, and his condition is so much improved that the doctors now believe he will recover.'[2]

As the king recovers, something changes. Close to death, he is once more close to his mother. Now they are again mother and son, not rival factions in the court. Louis is too sick for state business, and has no reason to see Richelieu. He is mostly alone with his mother, or with the queen. Louis tells her of his regret at their estrangement; she, quiet and feminine, says it is the cardinal's fault that they have grown apart. The king sees Richelieu once only: to instruct him to reconcile himself with the queen mother.

Behind the personal quarrels and the court intrigues is a policy choice: war with Spain, or reform at home? The king is now well enough to travel; he begins the journey back to Paris with Richelieu. Four days on the road, and the news arrives that their ambassadors in Regensburg, Brûlart de Léon and Richelieu's personal envoy, Father Joseph,* have reached a peace agreement with the emperor. In Lyons there is joy at this news. Marie de' Medici and her advisers never wanted the war with Spain, nor the expedition to Italy.

Richelieu's reaction is the opposite. Given the treaty, the cardinal, normally calm and in control, loses his temper. The ambassadors were in Regensburg to observe; they might reach an agreement on the Italian question – where Richelieu and the king have been on campaign – but on nothing more. This treaty commits France not to assist the

* Father Joseph ran Richelieu's intelligence service. As a Capuchin monk he wore a grey habit. He was the *eminence grise*, Richelieu the *eminence rouge*.

emperor's enemies. And that is exactly what Richelieu plans to do. He tears up the treaty.

Richelieu explains to the king; but he is not well enough for affairs of state. He wants to be back in Paris. Richelieu waits in Roanne for the rest of the court, so that the council can meet. When they arrive, Marie de' Medici replaces the king in the chair. The majority, led by Michel de Marillac, the Keeper of the Seals and adviser to the queen mother, want peace; but Marie de' Medici takes Richelieu's side. This is a surprise; perhaps she does not want to make a decision in the absence of the king. On the way to Paris Marie de' Medici and the cardinal seem the best of friends. But the cardinal is a courtier who can make himself agreeable; and she is a Florentine and can hide her thoughts. No one knows what will happen in Paris. The rumour is that the king has promised her that he will dismiss Richelieu.

In Paris, Richelieu's prospects look poor. The king has lodgings in Rue de Tournon, close to the Luxembourg Palace and his mother. He will not see Richelieu. He is constantly with his mother. The single theme of her conversation is the need to be rid of Richelieu. The air of Paris makes the king ill. When he can, Louis escapes to his hunting lodge at Versailles. Richelieu, who is still responsible for Marie de' Medici's household, lives in the grounds of the Luxembourg. He is in a depression; observers say he has aged years in the last weeks.

The council meets in the Luxembourg on a cold November day. It agrees the appointment of Michel de Marillac's brother to command the army in Italy. This is a victory for Marie de' Medici. Then she turns on Richelieu. She dismisses him as superintendent of her household; the friends and relations he has given jobs there will go too. Afterwards the king advises Richelieu to take formal leave of his mother the next day, hoping he can reconcile with her.

Richelieu returns to the Luxembourg the next day, as instructed. He finds the doors to the queen mother's apartments locked against him. But he has run her household for years and knows the back ways. He arrives at her private chapel. Hearing her voice inside, and the king's, he enters unannounced: 'Are Your Majesties talking of me?' 'Yes,' she says. She orders him out of her sight, and out of Paris. Some accounts say she loses control, screaming insults at him, accusing him of treason.

Richelieu, almost fainting, is on his knees sobbing, kissing the hem of her dress, begging forgiveness, asking the king's permission to resign. The king says little. His mother demands to know of her son: does the king prefer this lackey to his own mother?

The king leaves without speaking to Richelieu. For the courtiers it is the end of Richelieu. The rumours spread across Paris: Richelieu is disgraced. Michel de Marillac will replace him. Ambassadors send special couriers with the news to their capitals.

The king stops in his rooms in the Rue de Tournon, to recover his calm after the scene with his mother. Then he leaves for Versailles and the fresh air. He sends a message to Richelieu to follow him. This is unusual. The king's house in Versailles is a private place, not for business. Richelieu does not know what to do. Will he be dismissed? Will he be arrested? He is in two minds whether to go – he has prepared a place of safety in Le Havre; from there he can cross the Channel if need be. He asks advice from Cardinal de La Valette, one of his few remaining friends. La Valette tells him to go to Versailles.

In the king's modest house, Richelieu is again on his knees. He offers to resign rather than come between the king and his mother. The king will have none of this. His mother has forced him to choose. He chooses Richelieu. He sends his staff away, and they talk privately for four hours. He gives Richelieu the room directly below his own, a sign of complete trust.

Late in the evening the king calls a council meeting in Versailles, without Marie de' Medici or Michel de Marillac. The council decides on the dismissal of de Marillac. He has guessed what is happening and is already burning his papers. He is arrested and dies in prison two years later. Word is sent to Italy for the arrest of his brother. He has played no part in these events but is a relative, and close to the queen mother. Now he is in command of an army. He is tried for embezzlement before judges hand-picked by Richelieu. There is little evidence, but he is convicted by a narrow majority and beheaded; the court records are destroyed by royal order.

This day, 11 November, is known in France as the 'Day of the

Dupes'. It establishes Richelieu's domination of the court and of French policy. The man in the eye of the storm is the king. Jealous and weak, he shows he can be courageous too. 'I honour my mother,' he says, 'but my obligations to the state are greater.' He never sees her again. He decides for Richelieu and for Richelieu's policy of war with Spain. The war will last thirty years. He and Richelieu will be dead before it is over.

When it ends it is France, not Spain, that dominates Europe. The aim of the war is not just to defeat Spain; it is to remake France. Europe too will be remade, in France's image: a place of sovereign states.

The rise of Richelieu

> 'By their vocation the clergy are peculiarly fitted to hold offices of State.'
>
> *Richelieu, speaking at the Estates General* (1614)

Armand-Jean du Plessis de Richelieu is born in Paris in 1585. His father has served Henri III and has fought at the side of Henri IV. As the third son Richelieu is destined for a military career; accordingly he studies the art of war. But the diocese of Luçon, in the family's gift, falls vacant. This was intended for Richelieu's elder brother, but he has just decided to become a monk.

Luçon falls to Richelieu. His eldest brother introduces him to Henri IV, who nominates him Bishop of Luçon. Too young to be a bishop, he travels to Rome to seek a dispensation from the pope. He dazzles all, Pope Paul V included, with his intellect, charm and eloquence. He is consecrated bishop in Rome in April 1607, at the age of twenty-one.

For seven years, Richelieu sees first-hand in his diocese the weakness of France, the absence of royal authority, the ruin of the land with rebellions, the desperate peasants, the undisciplined aristocrats, the Huguenots in their fortified towns, with their private armies. The root of these ills is the weakness of the state. The king is God's representative on earth, responsible to God to protect the public interest against those who exploit it for private ends.

Since Henri IV's assassination in 1610, Marie de' Medici has been queen regent. She buys off rebellious grandees. Her Florentine favourites, Concino Concini and his sister Leonora, reward themselves. Henri IV's great minister, Sully, disgusted, leaves the court. The queen regent plans to marry her son to the Spanish Infanta to cement the alliance with Spain and ensure peace. This news brings rebellions, one by Condé, a prince of the blood but a Protestant. He demands a meeting of the Estates General. The queen regent agrees and postpones the marriage; she pays him the costs of his rebellion.

When the Estates General meets in 1614, Richelieu represents the clergy of the Poitou, and speaks for the clergy as a whole.* The misery he sees in the Poitou is reflected in the assembly. In the Auvergne men are eating grass, while the king pays millions in pensions to the nobility.

The Estates ends in spring 1615, with little by way of results. Richelieu makes the closing speech for the clergy. He praises the queen regent: 'Happy the prince to whom God has given a mother filled with love for his person, with zeal towards his state, and with experience in the conduct of affairs.'[3] She deserves to add the title 'Mother of the Kingdom' to the one she holds as Mother of the King.

The meeting of the Estates has been arranged to keep Condé quiet and to move the marriage plans forward. It fails in the first. Condé raises an army and incites the Huguenots against the marriage. The court, undeterred, travels to Bordeaux for the double marriage. Louis XIII, who has attained his majority (at the age of thirteen), marries Anne of Austria, daughter of Philip III of Spain. On the other side, the future Philip IV of Spain marries Louis's sister Elisabeth. On the way to Bordeaux the court stops at Poitiers; Richelieu pays his respects to the king and to the queen regent. After the wedding, Marie de' Medici appoints him almoner to the young queen, Anne of Austria. With this he joins the court, taking the first step on the ladder.

* This is the last meeting of the Estates General until the fateful event in 1789 when Talleyrand represented the clergy in discussion with the other estates.

Richelieu's flattery of Marie de' Medici at the Estates was just that: flattery. Rebellions by the grandees are constant, but instead of fighting, Marie de' Medici buys them off. She is in the hands of the Concinis, on whom she showers titles and pensions. Concino Concini is now a Marshal of France and one of the richest men in the land.

Nor is Marie de' Medici the good mother that Richelieu has described. The Venetian ambassador writes of the fourteen-year-old king in 1615: 'He is made to spend his time in puerilities, to devote himself to dogs, birds, and other distractions, and he can follow the hunt, his favourite sport, to his heart's content. . . . The queen mother governs his suite, and chooses them for their dullness and stupidity . . . The young monarch lives in entire obedience and dependence'; the king has a stammer; he is neglected, awkward, ill at ease.[4]

The flattery helps Richelieu's career. In November 1616 he becomes a member of the council, with responsibility for war and foreign affairs. He begins to understand how weak France is abroad. Twice he offers French mediation; and twice he is ignored.

Isolated in the court, the king finds pleasure in hunting. Out of this grows a friendship with Charles Albert, Duc de Luynes, since 1611 the Keeper of the King's Birds. In 1615 the king makes him Governor of Amboise; in 1616, Captain of the Louvre. He sleeps in the room above Louis, a staircase giving him direct access.

This is the age of the court favourite. The king has Luynes, the queen mother the Concinis. No one notices Luynes and others gathering to discuss the position of the king and the behaviour of the Concinis.

On 24 April 1617, as Concino Concini enters the Louvre, the guards close the gate behind him before his escort can follow. The guard commander seizes Concini. He and several of the guard shoot him at point-blank range. His body is buried nearby. When the story gets out the corpse is dug up by the mob, dragged through the streets, and hung upside down under the Pont Neuf. Leonora Concini is seized on the same day; she is tortured and burnt as a witch.

By Richelieu's account, after these events the king says that he wishes him well; and Luynes invites him to remain in the council. Another version has the king saying to Richelieu: 'Well, Luçon, I am rid of your tyranny. Go, monsieur, go. Leave this place.'[5] The second version is more plausible. Richelieu is seen as belonging to the queen mother.

Life changes for Marie de' Medici too. After the killing she is sent to Blois, her guard replaced by the king's men. Richelieu goes with her. Then he is sent to his diocese, and later to exile in the papal enclave of Avignon. Absence from the court is punishment; exile is disgrace.

As for the state, in the words of the Duc de Bouillon (one of the constant rebels), 'The inn remained the same. Only the sign changed.'[6] Instead of Marie de' Medici and the Concinis, it is Louis XIII and Luynes; but the style and the triviality are the same. Wherever Richelieu is, in Blois, in the Poitou or Avignon, the king and Luynes believe he is intriguing against them.

In fact, he is waiting. Other intriguers arrange Marie de' Medici's escape from Blois (she climbs down a 100-foot ladder in the dark). They gather a rebel army to support her. There follow two 'wars between mother and son'. In each, Richelieu, at the king's request, achieves the reconciliation. He is not a man of rebellions, but he is still associated in the king's mind with the Concinis; this and his all-too-visible ambition make Luynes his enemy.

Having tasted military success in the battles against his mother, the king goes south, defeats Protestant towns and incorporates Béarn, bloodlessly, into France. The next year he returns for more. But Luynes, in command of the army, bites off more than he can chew with Montauban, a Huguenot stronghold. His army of 20,000 is reduced by desertion and disease to 4,000 when he abandons the siege. After a further failure Luynes dies of a fever. On the journey home the military escort plays cards on his coffin.

The king's favourite is dead and discredited. His wife is young and full of life; but he is awkward with her. His mother treats him with disdain. She has returned to the council, and presses for Richelieu to be included. Abroad, France's reputation is so low that the Elector of Saxony enquires ironically of the French ambassador whether or not there is still a king in France. At home the pamphleteers make fun of the government. Everyone is either disloyal, like Condé, or second-rate. In the background is Richelieu, still suspect, but not second-rate. At the end of 1622, on the king's recommendation, he becomes a cardinal: a reward for his diplomacy between mother and son. A prince of the Church outranks dukes and marquises. And will now sit nearest to the king: in an age ruled by rank nothing matters more.*

In April 1624, Richelieu joins the council, with limited responsibilities for foreign and military affairs. The limits do not matter: what does is the clarity of his mind. By August he dispels the king's doubts, and it is natural that he heads the council.

What Richelieu wants, on the surface, is what everyone wants: order at home and reputation abroad. Only Richelieu is more single-minded and more ruthless. Like others he is devout; and these are steps to a larger goal, 'une paix de la Chrétienté' (peace in Christendom).[7] What he means by this is specific. The peace and liberty of other states must not be threatened by the tyranny of a universal monarchy, which he believes is the goal of the Habsburg King of Spain. Others in the court, notably the queen mother, believe that the two Christian monarchs, France and Spain, should work together. For Richelieu, his king is God's representative on earth. In serving France he is serving God.[8]

The European scene

At this time, 1624, two wars are under way in Europe. Spain's struggle against the Dutch rebellion is in its fifty-sixth year. The Spanish fight on, hoping to get better terms and save their reputation, but know it is unwinnable. When it finishes it will be named the Eighty Years War. In modern memory this is eclipsed by the Thirty Years War; the Dutch revolt is as consequent. It is the first war of self-determination;

* In foreign courts, the order in which diplomats were seated was also taken seriously. In 1661 the Spanish ambassador in London won the contest for precedence with the French ambassador by detaching the horses from the latter's carriage and getting to St James's ahead of him. This caused such outrage in Paris that Louis XIV threatened war (see Keith Hamilton and Richard Langhorne, *The Practice of Diplomacy: Its Evolution, Theory and Administration*, p. 71).

it establishes a new power in Europe and a new society, based on Calvinism, commerce and contracts. The Dutch war is small in scale, but it defeats the greatest empire since Rome.

The Thirty Years War leaves behind memories similar to those of the First World War: a great war without a great cause, an accident that led to catastrophe, with no one knowing why. Arguments about the causes and meaning of the war are still alive today. This is not a war of aggression but one of weakness, and of poorly judged policy. Once begun, the war is difficult to stop. The interventions of Sweden and France keep it going when it might have died.

France is between the wars. To the south is Spain, the greatest power in the world. To the north is also Spain – in the shape of the Spanish Netherlands. To the east is the 'Spanish Road', the route that troops from Spain take to the Low Countries and their war against the Dutch. Sending troops by sea is risky because of the Dutch navy. Spanish soldiers disembark at Genoa and pass through Milan, a Spanish possession. Thereafter a number of routes are possible. In the 1620s the Spanish army usually goes go east from Lake Como along the Valtellina towards Tyrol and Vienna.

In 1623 France has agreed with Savoy and Venice jointly to take control of Valtellina. But later the same year Spain reaches an agreement with the Vatican for papal, i.e. neutral, troops to replace the Spanish garrisons and control the valley.* Now, for the first time in years, Spain has sent 7,000 men by this route to Austria.

With Richelieu heading the council in 1624, France renews its pact with Savoy to cut the Spanish road by attacking its starting point in Genoa. At the same time Venice will attack Milan, Spain's most important possession in Italy. The operation begins with a small Franco-Swiss force taking control of Valtellina. The papal forces offer no resistance. Meanwhile an army of 30,000, one-third French and the rest funded by France, surprises Genoa in February 1625 and holds the city under siege.

* The papal forces are the equivalent, in their time, of UN blue helmets, neither intended nor equipped to deal with a military attack. The papal force includes a young captain, Giulio Mazarini.

In May 1625 Richelieu gives the king a memorandum that surveys the European scene. He concludes it is 'absolutely necessary to abandon the exterior in favour of the struggles at home'.[9] A state fighting rebellions and disorder at home – as France has been doing for the last twenty years – has neither the credibility nor the resources to act abroad. At this moment France can hardly sustain an army of 25,000 to deal with its domestic troubles; it cannot intervene outside its borders in a serious way.

Real life proves his point. The support promised by the English and Dutch for the blockade of Genoa does not arrive; in the autumn Spain breaks through and reinforces Genoa. Venice fails to attack Milan. And in France, Huguenot leaders see French involvement in Italy as a chance to regain ground, and launch a campaign in France.

Richelieu cuts his losses in Italy. He accepts papal mediation – not ideal, since the Vatican is angry at the way its forces in Valtellina have been treated. (But the Vatican, like the UN, lives by mediation and is always ready to try again.) Out of this comes the Treaty of Monzón (1626) with Spain. Papal forces replace French troops in Switzerland, restoring the status quo ante. This causes outrage in France, and with its allies. Richelieu disowns the negotiators but ratifies the treaty.

Most important of all, France fails at La Rochelle. La Rochelle is everything that Richelieu is against: it is Protestant, it is a state within the state, and it intrigues with foreign enemies. The king defeats the Huguenot army that has come to relieve it, but has to give up the siege; Richelieu negotiates peace with the Rochelais.

No one is happy. Michel de Marillac and the peace party in the council welcome the treaty with Spain, but think Richelieu should pursue the Huguenots more vigorously. The Rochelais are unhappy that the help promised by England never arrived. They have to dismantle forts and live with the massive Fort-Louis dominating the town. Richelieu has unfinished business abroad; but he can deal with that only when domestic affairs are settled. The peace with La Rochelle is no more than a truce. It is accompanied by sneers against Richelieu in the court.

La Rochelle

England does keep its promise, but a year late. In July 1627, the Duke of Buckingham arrives with eighty-four ships and 10,000 men to besiege the fortress of St Martin on the Île de Ré, held by the king's men. By October the French garrison is short of food; its commander, General Thoiras, sends a message that he will have to surrender. But under cover of night and a diversionary sea battle, the French get twenty-nine boats to their fortress unnoticed by the English, landing fresh troops and food. The next day the English besiegers are dismayed to see the garrison of St Martin waving chickens and hams on pikes, while they in turn are beginning to suffer hunger.

In November an English attempt to storm the fort fails, and Buckingham decides to go home. A new French force under General Schomberg surprises him and the withdrawal becomes a rout. Buckingham loses his artillery and 1,800 men. Forty-seven English standards are displayed in Notre-Dame when a *Te Deum* is sung.

While this action is going on, Louis XIII is seriously ill – as he often is at moments of crisis – and Richelieu is in charge of the siege. He builds a barrier that blocks access to the harbour for English ships, imitating the strategy of Alexander the Great at the siege of Tyre. The barrier has a gap in the middle to cope with the pressure from the sea; it needs constant repairs and reinforcement. Ships occasionally get through, but stakes tipped with iron are inserted to stop this. Two English fleets arrive, but neither is able to breach Richelieu's barrier.

La Rochelle is a Calvinist stronghold. A neat, well-kept town, it has prospered from trade with England, the Baltic and the Protestant towns of the North Sea. It has the highest, strongest walls in France. It is surrounded by salt marshes and can be resupplied by sea. La Rochelle survived the Wars of Religion and has never been taken by storm.

The siege ends in October 1628, after a year and four months. The barrier is maintained throughout, as is the besieging army. Unlike most armies, this one is paid regular wages (given to the men, not to their officers) – 'a soldier's pay is his soul and sustains his courage',[10] as Richelieu says.* By the end, the Rochelais are dying of hunger at a rate of 300 a day; those who live are too weak to bury the dead. When envoys come to surrender, they are 'like ghosts' – or survivors of a concentration camp – so weak they are taken by carriage to beg the king's mercy.

The surrender is unconditional. Having defeated the rebellion, Richelieu urges Louis that 'mildness and pity are the qualities in which kings should imitate God'. The king grants them their lives, and freedom of worship – in accordance with the Edict of Nantes. But the walls and towers, and the right of the city to govern itself (also in the Edict of Nantes) have to go. Its population has been reduced to a quarter of the 25,000 who were there as the siege began. Richelieu concludes that the task is 'to recover from heresy by reason those who the king has recovered from rebellion by force'.[11]

This is a great victory. War in the seventeenth century is a spectator sport and the siege has been watched all across Europe. General Spinola, famous as the victor in the siege of Breda in the Netherlands, has stopped on his way back to Spain. 'Es tomada la ciudad' – 'the city is already taken', he tells Olivares, Philip IV's minister, when he reaches Madrid.† The heroic resistance of the Rochelais is admired, but so is the king's victory. It takes Richelieu to the height of his popularity with the *Dévots* – the pro-peace, pro-Spain Catholic faction of the queen mother and Michel de Marillac. In theory Spain is in alliance with France against England; but the reality is visible in its failure to provide assistance.

* This remark is more pointed in French: *soldat* derives from *solde*, French for 'pay'.

† A siege of a major town usually took a month. Breda, which took more than a year, and La Rochelle were seen as epic struggles.

Mantua, Casale, Pinerolo – and Alais

> 'Great affairs are sometimes the matter of a fleeting moment, which, if once allowed to pass, will never again return.'
>
> *Richelieu*

After La Rochelle Richelieu sends an envoy, Bautru ('he possessed the gift of giving lies the pure colour of truth', said the Duc de Rohan),[12] to assure Olivares of his peaceful intentions towards Spain. He finds Olivares preoccupied; but it is not France, which he regards as weak, that troubles him. It is the treasure fleet, now some weeks overdue.*

In January 1629 Olivares tells the papal nuncio that if a French army crosses the Alps, Spain and France will be at war for thirty years. He is right, almost to the month. But it seems logistically impossible.[13]

At just this time Richelieu presents policy proposals at home and abroad to the king and the queen mother. His first is to follow the victory at La Rochelle by overcoming the fortified Huguenot towns in the south; strong places elsewhere will be destroyed too, unless they protect France's borders. His second proposal is to enlarge French territory, adding Strasbourg, Lorraine and the Franche-Comté, over time. Third, France should secure 'gateways' on or over the frontiers, from which neighbours can be threatened or attacked.

Olivares' remark to the papal envoy comes because of a small conflict between France and Spain, already under way in North Italy. The Duke of Mantua and Montferrat died in December 1627, naming the Duc de Nevers, from the French branch of the Gonzaga family, as his heir. Mantua is a fiefdom of the empire and the heir has to be recognised by the emperor. Nevers does not wait. His son, who married the duke's niece three days before his death, takes possession of Mantua and of Casale, a castle dominating the valley of the upper Po.

* Seized by the Dutch admiral Piet Heyn; the news arrives in December. This is a disaster for Spain.

The Spanish Governor of Milan does not want Mantua and Casale in French hands. He offers to support of Savoy, a rival claimant, taking Casale as his price. When the emperor's envoy arrives to settle the succession, he finds that the forces of Spain and Savoy have overrun the countryside and are besieging Mantua and Casale.

For some time the question has been: La Rochelle or Casale? Which siege will end first? Even if France succeeds at La Rochelle it seems too late to get forces in Italy before Casale falls.

But it is not. The king and Richelieu lead an army across the Alps in March 1629. This high-risk strategy is opposed in the council by supporters of the queen mother, but Richelieu captures the king's imagination. 'The esteem of the world is gained only by great actions,' he says. The king's presence is a decisive factor; so are his Swiss mercenaries, who go through deep snow to get behind the Savoyard forces and rout the duke's army. They arrive at Casale, end the siege and garrison it with 3,000 French.

In summer 1629 the king returns to France and brings the Huguenot towns in the Languedoc under his control. He offers the same terms at La Rochelle: freedom of worship, but not of fortification – nothing that looks like a state within his state. An explosion as it is being peacefully occupied leads to the destruction of the town of Privas, but the central fact is that the 'grace of Alais', as it is called, brings an end to seven decades of religious wars in France on terms that permit freedom of religion within the law.

At this point Spain sends its greatest soldier, General Spinola, to Milan. He thinks it a mistake. Spain should be finishing the war with the Dutch, not fighting France in Italy. But he does his duty, renewing the siege of Casale. The force inside is led by General Thoiras, who defended St Martin against Buckingham. Now Mantua is also under siege by imperial forces, arrived from Austria.

On his way back to the Alps with the king in January 1630, Richelieu meets Giulio Mazarini, now a papal envoy, for the first time. Two hours is a long time for an interview with a junior official: Richelieu must have been impressed. Papal mediation may be useful: why not make a friend of the mediator? Mazarini is dazzled: 'I had attached myself by instinct for his genius.' Shortly after the meeting, a French force of 22,000 crosses the Alps. Feinting towards Turin, Richelieu heads instead for Pinerolo, a fortress dominating a road from France to Italy – a 'gateway' and a strategic prize. He captures it in March.[14]

In summer the same year, the imperial army takes Mantua, half its population dead of plague or hunger, its art treasures looted. Casale is still under siege in October when a French relief force approaches. They are about to attack the Spanish besiegers when Mazarini arrives on horseback waving a paper, calling out '*Pace, Pace*'. Battle is averted: happily, for the Spanish are already decimated by plague and in no condition to fight. (Spinola dies of the plague the same month.)

The paper that Mazarini is waving is the agreement reached at Regensburg. The emperor's concerns are about Germany; he wants to settle matters in North Italy. He will recognise Charles of Nevers as Duke of Mantua if he compensates other claimants and allows Savoy part of Montferrat; Casale will be demilitarised, but France may keep Pinerolo. This is a good settlement for France. Richelieu's envoys, Brûlart de Léon and Father Joseph, accept it, including the standard language in imperial treaties about not assisting the emperor's enemies.

With this the Mantuan War ends. Charles of Nevers is recognised as Duke of Mantua. He promptly agrees to France garrisoning Casale. Charles Emmanuel of Savoy cedes Pinerolo to France.

The news of the settlement arrives during the crisis of Louis XIII's near-death and Richelieu's near-disgrace, as described earlier. The Day of the Dupes is the last battle of the wars between mother and son. The winner is the king, and with him, Richelieu. Marie de' Medici, de Marillac and the Catholic lobby wanted peace with Spain. Richelieu wants France to replace Spain as Europe's foremost power. That gives France two enemies: one is Spain; the other is the empire. The reason the cardinal tears up the treaty is that he is already aiding the emperor's enemies.

The Mantuan War is not a big event for Spain or the empire. It is easy to see why the emperor wanted it over. But both pay a price. Olivares guessed that Spain would finish the siege of Casale before

France got its army there from La Rochelle. He is wrong, and Spain has to divert forces from the Low Countries. And because of Mantua the emperor cancels his instruction to Albrecht von Wallenstein, his supreme commander, to assist Spain in the United Provinces.

The empire asserts its authority in Mantua, but then gives it back – in ruins – to the man it defeats. The forces deployed at Mantua then return to Germany, but too late to join the Battle of Breitenfeld in September 1631. The imperial defeat at Breitenfeld opens the way for the Swedes, who turn Germany into a wasteland. These are the enemies of the empire that Richelieu is aiding.

Richelieu has learned from his mistakes. In 1625 unreliable allies abroad and rebellion at home undermined him. In 1629–30, he secures his position at home before going abroad and uses Swiss mercenaries. His preparations bring surprise and success. He leaves mediation to others, but makes friends with the mediator.

Six months later, Mazarini reworks the Regensburg agreement as the Peace of Cherasco, omitting the commitment not to aid the emperor's enemies. France remains in Casale for twenty years, and in Pinerolo until 1696.

The challenges to royal authority

> 'I saw that those who fight the power of a legitimate state have already lost half of the battle: their imagination makes the contest uneven, for even while they fight, they see in their mind's eye the image of the king's executioner.'[15]
>
> *Richelieu*

One problem of the transition from feudalism to a stronger state and a more open society is to dealing with over-powerful aristocrats. They have a territorial base, and a local following. No one abolishes them overnight. England taxed them; Tokugawa Japan used ceremonial and took their families hostage. Richelieu believes in the executioner.

Royal authority is threatened from several quarters. One is the Huguenots. There, the king sees the problem not as one of religion but of fortifications. He has also issued an edict against the fortified chateaux of the nobility. Another royal edict makes duelling illegal. Louis is surnamed 'the Just'. As king, he will uphold the law.

The Three Musketeers portrays duels as honourable, and Richelieu's opposition as offensive. But duels are a waste of young lives and place the aristocracy above the king's justice. The king has seen friends killed in duels, Richelieu a brother and an uncle. The king's edict against duelling – which predates Richelieu's rise – says that anyone who kills in a duel must himself die.

The Comte de Bouteville is a boyhood companion of the king, but also a serial duellist. He stages a duel in the Place Royale in Paris, in a deliberate, visible challenge to royal authority. As the king sees it, he has no choice – though he needs Richelieu's support to resist the pleas for mercy from Bouteville's weeping wife. De Bouteville is executed in 1627.

A more direct form of attack on royal authority are plots against the king. All involve the king's brother, Gaston, heir apparent while Anne remains childless. Gaston is more attractive than Louis, charming, lively and fluent, while the king is awkward and tongue-tied. He is a natural focus for grandees, princes of the blood, or holders of sovereign territory inside France, who find Louis too weak and Richelieu too strong, and who think it is for them to choose which prince they serve.

The Chalais plot, in 1626, is the first. The Comte de Chalais is from one of France's oldest families, Talleyrand-Périgord, possessing a sovereign enclave in the Périgord. It is not clear who is behind the plot, but it is not Chalais. It may be the Duchesse de Chevreuse, widow of Luynes and friend of the queen. Saint-Simon, the king's favourite, wrote of her: 'Great are her grace and beauty, still greater her frivolity; but all is ruled by her mind, and above these reigns her insatiable ambition. Her head is clear, her reasoning sharp, her charm endless: full of political ideas but without scruples, she is never at a loss for a stratagem, a hundred ways to get out of trouble.[16]* Chalais, the Master of the King's Wardrobe, is infatuated with her. Or it might be Marshal Ornano, tutor to Gaston. He is urging Gaston to claim a share of his brother's power. The plan is to murder Richelieu; then the king's marriage will be declared invalid, and the throne vacant. (It helps that there is no heir). Gaston will marry Anne of Austria and become king.

Chalais's role is to reveal the plot to Richelieu, and to suffer for it. Richelieu, with foreknowledge, escapes assassination and acquires a special guard – which he retains while he lives. Ornano is the first to be arrested. He dies in prison. Royal relatives are also involved: Louis's half-brothers, César and Alexandre de Vendôme (illegitimate sons of Henri IV) are arrested at Blois. The king's cousin, Condé, makes his peace with Louis and returns to the court; the Comte de Soissons, another Bourbon plotter, flees to Italy.

Gaston's punishment is marriage. Richelieu performs the ceremony at night, as the others are rounded up. This ends the fantasy of his marrying Anne of Austria. Asked by the king if she is party, the queen says, coolly, that she would have gained too little by the exchange for her to think of blackening her name.[17]

Marie de Chevreuse is banished from the court; she goes to Nancy, where she enlivens the court of the Duc de Lorraine. Her letters to Chalais in prison, read by Richelieu, help convict him of treason.

Chalais is sentenced to torture and death, after which his body will be quartered, and his family removed from the ranks of the nobility. The king's mercy reduces the sentence to death only, but Gaston's friends make it worse by kidnapping the executioner. Instead, a condemned man does the execution return for his own life; it takes thirty blows with a blunt weapon.

Gaston learns little by this sad story. His wife gives birth to a daughter a year later, but dies soon after. Following the Day of the Dupes, he leaves France and launches a manifesto denouncing Richelieu. Then

* Richelieu sent her as an envoy to the Duke of Buckingham, known for his susceptibility to feminine charm.

he too goes to the court of the Duc de Lorraine, where he marries the duke's daughter in secret – the marriage is later annulled. He returns to France in 1632, at the head of a small army recruited in Lorraine, denouncing Richelieu as a usurper and a tyrant. He expects the people to rally to his cause, but he finds instead that the gates of the towns are barred against him. He is joined only by Henri de Montmorency, a comrade in arms of the king's in the Huguenot campaign; his name is one of the greatest in French history. He wants to raise the south against the centralising regime of king and cardinal. Schomberg defeats Montmorency, but, knowing he is a friend of the king, he tries to avoid taking him prisoner. Unfortunately he is too badly wounded to flee. Montmorency is executed in spite of his friendship with the king and the pleas for mercy from all sides. Gaston is pardoned and leaves France again.

The last plots come during France's war against Spain; and Spain is a party to them. It makes sense to turn first to that war.

The path to war

An undeclared war with Spain begins with Mantua in 1629. But when Richelieu rejects the Regensburg phrase about not aiding the enemies of the emperor, it is another project he has in mind. His agent, Hercule de Charnacé, has persuaded Poland to end its war with Sweden on terms that give Gustavus Adolphus the tolls from ships using Prussian ports. While this lasts it provides one-third of the revenues of the Swedish Crown. In 1631 Richelieu signs the Treaty of Bärwalde, giving the Swedes a further 400,000 thalers a year. This is not a large bet; it is much less than the costs the Swedes impose on those whose lands they occupy.* But the money comes at the right moment. Gustavus Adolphus arrives in Germany with cash only for one week's pay.

* Geoffrey Parker, in *The Thirty Years' War* (p. 112), cites the county of Memel, where seventeen Swedish cavalry companies were billeted. At the beginning of the year there were 154 horses, 236 oxen, 103 cows, 190 pigs and 810 sheep. At the end only twenty-six oxen and one cow remained.

This is Richelieu's way of weakening the emperor, who, like Philip IV, is a Habsburg.

De Charnacé warns Richelieu that it will be impossible to control the Swedes; this is correct, but Sweden is a useful in keeping the empire off-balance while France strengthens its position in Lorraine and Alsace.

France claims to be defending German liberties. This is its excuse for chipping away at the edges of the empire, in particular in Lorraine where the bishoprics of Metz, Toul and Verdun have been under French protection for the better part of 100 years. A number of towns in Alsace put themselves under French protection as the war gets worse. Gaston's habit of taking refuge in Lorraine gives Richelieu all the excuses he needs; and the Duc de Lorraine himself provides further material. In 1633, after Gaston's failed rebellion, the Parlement de Paris recognises France as suzerain in Lorraine. A French army of 30,000 seizes its capital, Nancy, and occupies the rest. The duke leaves for the Franche-Compté; later he negotiates his return to Lorraine, but as a fief of France. He is expelled again after failing to support France in the Soissons plot of 1641.

Richelieu has been subsidising the Dutch since 1624, so they can bleed Spain; now he does the same for Sweden, so it can bleed the empire. Having taken much of Lorraine, Richelieu offers nearby Catholic princes protection. This gives them a difficult choice: protection by France means the loss of independence, but the fear of the Swedes is real. Only the Elector of Trier accepts. He is France's main target since his lands border Lorraine.

Sweden fights its own war. The Battle of Breitenfeld establishes it as a power in 1931; but Gustavus Adolphus has fantasies of an empire that his small country could never sustain. His death at the Battle of Lützen in 1632 leaves his army – well trained but now only 10 per cent Swedish – directionless. After Gustavus's death, the League of Heilbronn brings Protestant forces together, but it is no substitute for the drive of the Swedish king. Wallenstein's guess, a few months before his murder in 1634, is that the Swedes want peace.

This would have been wise. Their defeat at Nördlingen in September that year is proof. This battle is a rare case of the imperial and Spanish armies joining forces. This is not the result of a Habsburg plot to dominate Europe but is because, at that moment, Spanish troops cannot travel along the Rhine to the Spanish Netherlands and make their way instead through Valtellina. By accident they are on hand for the battle. These are the last Spanish forces to use Valtellina.

After Nördlingen, the emperor begins a process of reconciliation with the Protestant states in Germany. Richelieu concludes that the Protestant cause is weakening and can no longer be relied on to serve French interests; France will have to fight Spain itself. He makes the case to the king for a 'vigorous open war against Spain to secure a beneficial general peace'.[15] He prepares for this by strengthening the alliance with the Dutch: they will both invade the Spanish Netherlands that year with the aim of partitioning it between them. Then he renews the subsidy for the Swedes, while he poaches their best general, Bernhard of Saxe-Weimar. He and his mostly German troops get a subsidy four times the sum France pays the Swedes. Saxe-Weimar's campaigns on the Rhine are on behalf of France, but his personal ambition is a title: Duke of Alsace, perhaps.

In May 1635, Spain seizes the Elector of Trier. He is under French protection and this brings a French declaration of war on Spain.

War

The best way to give an impression of the war is to list the most important events year by year:

1635: The Duc de Rohan, otherwise serially disloyal, leads a French army that succeeds, temporarily, in closing Valtellina.
1636: The year of Corbie: A Spanish army invades France from the Spanish Netherlands and captures Corbie, seventy miles from Paris, causing panic in the capital. Richelieu advises the king to withdraw for his safety and that of the state. Louis does the opposite. He and Richelieu ride through Paris without a guard, raising spirits; Gaston raises

an army of 12,000 to defend Paris. He retakes Roye, between Corbie and Paris. Louis takes over the siege of Corbie, an affair of mines and trenches, of laying countryside waste, poisoning wells and blocking relieving forces. It is won by determination on the French side, but also by Dutch attacks in the north that compel Spain to cut its losses.
1637: A revolt in south-west France (the *Croquants*) is defeated. The Dutch recapture Breda – a blow to Spanish morale.
1638: In December Saxe-Weimar captures the fortress of Breisach, at a critical crossroads on the Rhine.
1639: Unrest in Normandy (the *nu-pieds*) is defeated. With Valtellina closed and the route along the Rhine blocked at Breisach, Spain sends reinforcements by sea. The Dutch destroy most of the fleet in the Battle of the Downs.
1640: Some Spanish ships get through, but not enough men to prevent the capture of Arras by France. In Spain, revolts in Catalonia and Portugal bring declarations of independence.

Richelieu's age is now showing and he is afflicted with a painful illness; the king, whose first love is the army, is energised. He crosses the country on horseback, joining French forces at key moments. Spain has now been at war for seventy years. Its infantry are the best in the world, but its people are weary. The revolts in France are by starving peasants, joined sometimes by priests or local notables. But these can be defeated. In Spain the revolts take political shape as Catalonia and Portugal threaten to break up the state. The growing crisis persuades a desperate Olivares that the only way to win is by backing plots against the French state. Thus:

1641: Lorraine becomes part of France; the Soissons plot.
1642: Capture of Perpignan by France; the Cinq-Mars plot.

In 1641 Spain finances an army to invade France from the enclave of Sedan, in an attempted coup d'état. The Comte de Soissons leads the army (the Duc de Bouillon drops out since he is commanding French forces in Italy). Gaston is waiting in the background. Warned in advance, French forces block the army's path, but are defeated. By accident, Soissons shoots himself on his way back from the battle and the plot collapses.

Spain tries again in 1642, now with the help of the Marquis de Cinq-Mars. He is the last royal favourite, according to some accounts, selected by Richelieu to distract the king from a reignited passion for Marie de Hautefort, one of the queen's ladies. Cinq-Mars is young, good-looking and ambitious; for a time he attracts a strong affection from the king. By now Richelieu is bedridden, and in pain. He and the king are in the south for the siege of Perpignan, the capital of the Spanish Roussillon. Richelieu is unable to join the court and does not see the king for several weeks. The king is distracted by Cinq-Mars. Rumours that Richelieu will be dismissed are everywhere.

Close to despair, Richelieu recalls the Day of the Dupes: 'God's design was for me to find the one unlocked door, so that I could defend myself.' The unlocked door leads to the king. He gets a message from the king: 'Whatever rumours you hear, I have never ceased to love you. We have been together too long to be separated.'

It is not clear that Richelieu is reassured by this; but a few days later he receives the key document of the plot: an agreement signed by Gaston and Olivares. It sets out the plan, beginning, as usual, with his murder. After that, a Spanish army will arrive and make peace, each side taking back the territory it has lost (much to the advantage of Spain). Reading the document in his bed, Richelieu comments: 'God assists the king with marvellous discoveries.'

We do not know how 'the marvellous discovery' reaches Richelieu. It may be that Anne of Austria has a hand in it. Two days later the king sees it. He too is ill, as he often is at times of emotional turmoil; he leaves Perpignan and goes to see Richelieu in Tarascon. Their beds are placed side by side, and they talk for four hours. As the king leaves for Paris, he gives Richelieu authority over the whole of the south, including the siege at Perpignan and the investigation of the plot. Cinq-Mars is executed in Lyons on 12 July, just after Richelieu has heard church bells announcing the surrender of Perpignan.

A death and a birth

Four years earlier two important political events, not related to the war, have taken place. The first is a death. In 1638, as Breisach is captured, Father Joseph dies. In Richelieu's mind, Father Joseph has always been his successor. Following his death he asks Mazarini to work for France in Father Joseph's place. Mazarini applies for naturalisation as a French citizen.

Giulio Mazarini (now Jules Mazarin) is from a provincial Italian family. His father was major-domo for the Colonna family in Rome. Giulio is clever and charming. The Colonna connection wins him a place in the papal diplomatic service. There he is making a name for himself when meets Richelieu in Lyons in 1630. After the Mantuan crisis he sees Richelieu in Paris several times, later becoming the papal nuncio there. Then he returns to Rome to take charge of relations with France. He accepts Richelieu's invitation and joins his staff. In 1641 the king, acting for the pope, presents him with the cardinal's biretta. Mazarin is a man without family, living by his wits and used to taking risks.

Richelieu has Mazarin take on part of the investigation of the Cinq-Mars affair: 'Le Cardinal Mazarin has negotiated so cleverly, that M. de Bouillon has said enough to make our proof complete,' notes Richelieu.[19] In addition to Cinq-Mars, another conspirator, Jacques-Auguste de Thou, is executed. Bouillon saves himself by ceding his sovereign territory, Sedan, to France. It helps too that Richelieu and Mazarin both see his young brother, the Vicomte de Turenne, as a talented general.

The second event is a birth: on 5 September 1638 Anne of Austria gives birth to a dauphin, at the age of thirty-six This is a cause for great rejoicing: there are candles in windows, fireworks in the sky.

It is a strange story. The king is courageous in battle, but is awkward with women. His sexuality is uncertain: he has male favourites, but also a series of infatuations with ladies in the queen's suite: early on, the Duchesse de Chevreuse; for a long time, Mlle Hautefort; most recently, the young Louise de la Fayette. Behind the queen's conception is a curious combination of events: first the discovery that she has corresponded in secret over four years with the former Spanish ambassador in France. Four years is a long time to keep a secret from Richelieu's spies. This has been done with the help of the Val-de-Grace convent where the queen has a room for private devotion. Marie de Chevreuse has helped. (She escapes to Spain disguised as a man.) The letters contain no secrets, but they are themselves secret; and that is an offence. After an investigation the queen signs an agreement, almost a treaty – it is co-signed by Richelieu – in which Louis forgives her faults and promises 'to live with her as a good king and a good husband should'. A few months later, on 10 December 1637, the king visits La Fayette at the convent where she is a novice; in their talk (through a grille) she urges him to give Anne a child. Then a torrential rainstorm has him stop at the Louvre, where Anne's apartments are, and they spend the night together. The queen's pregnancy is announced a few weeks later.

When Mazarin returns from Sedan, after the Cinq-Mars affair, having accepted Bouillon's castle on behalf of the king, Richelieu asks him to prepare the instructions for the French negotiators in Westphalia. The negotiations are still far away, but normally Richelieu would have done this personally. He also arranges to endow Mazarin with the considerable income of the Abbey of Corbie. And he writes to his niece, 'I know of only one man who can succeed me, and he is a foreigner.'[20]

Richelieu dies a few weeks later, saying to the king that he has the consolation of leaving his kingdom in the highest degree of glory and reputation it has ever had, and to his confessor that God should condemn him if he ever had 'any intention other than the good of the State'.[21] Far from the Palais Cardinale, people light bonfires in celebration.

In death as in life, Louis XIII follows Richelieu. Early the next year it becomes clear that his tuberculosis will be fatal. Preparing for death, the king has the dauphin baptised as Louis le Dieudonné on 21 April 1643. He chooses Mazarin as a godfather. Three weeks later, Louis XIII dies. He and Richelieu were together from 1624 to 1642. In this time France has begun a transformation, both at home and abroad. The 'Bonne paix Crétienne' of which Richelieu spoke, a lasting peace for all Europe, is still far away.

Mazarin

'You will get on with Mazarini; he is like Buckingham.'

Richelieu to Anne of Austria (attributed)

In Louis's last months Mazarin takes over Richelieu's position as his adviser on foreign affairs. Louis's death makes his position precarious. The king's will makes Anne of Austria regent; but it also makes Gaston d'Orléans Lieutenant-General of the realm, and Condé head of the royal household. State policy will be approved by majority vote in the council. This means that the council, not the queen, is in charge of the regency. The queen chairs the council, but jointly with Gaston and Condé. Mazarin is a member, no more. To make sure that Anne cannot change the terms of the will, Louis has registered it with the Parlement de Paris, a last gesture of distrust towards his wife.

But the queen is now queen regent, and she is free. Her marriage has been a prison; Richelieu was the jailer. Anne is devout, but she likes lively company. With the death of the king, she can do as she pleases. She is more political than her husband: she makes friends with the princes of the blood, Orléans (Gaston), Condé and Vendôme; and with anybody else who can be useful. The Duchesse de Chevreuse returns to the court.

The queen arranges a *Lit de justice*, the most formal sitting of the Parlement de Paris, in the presence of the infant king. The chancellor, Pierre Séguier, speaks for the Crown, proposing that the Parlement amend the will so that Anne can choose ministers and decide policies on her own. Each of those present thinks she will choose them; and they give her full authority to run the regency as she pleases.

She chooses Mazarin. 'I am persuaded', she writes, 'that Cardinal Mazarin is my servant.' He understands that she is a Habsburg, 'born to govern'.[22] Richelieu succeeded with Louis because he treated him as a king; Mazarin succeeds with the queen because he treats her as a woman. Mazarin is the same age as Anne. After two years in Spain as tutor and companion to one of the Colonna sons, he speaks the same Castilian Spanish that she does. He is courtly and gallant. Where Richelieu was austere, Mazarin has a love of life and of pleasure; he is soft where Richelieu was hard; he persuades where Richelieu instructed; each evening Mazarin spends two hours with the queen, discussing foreign affairs. The most important link between them is her son and his godson, still an infant but already a king. Mazarin will be her son's mentor and tutor as well as hers.

Before the *Lit de justice*, she has allowed rumours to circulate that Mazarin will be dismissed, and that this or that grandee will replace him. The grandees are shocked at Mazarin's appointment. Things become unpleasant: as he arrives at the Louvre, a mob is waiting with pistols. The queen guesses the Duc de Beaufort is behind it.* The next time he visits her, he is arrested and spends five years in the Bastille. Vendôme is sent to his estates in the country. The Duchesse de Chevreuse returns to the Spanish Netherlands. Mazarin works with Orléans and with Condé: his son, the Duc d'Enghien, has won a victory at Rocroi in the first days of the regency. This lends reassurance that the queen has no plans to make peace with Spain.

All this is a surprise for Olivares. He reacted to Richelieu's death with a memorandum to Philip saying that peace was now within reach. A bribe for Mazarin would ease the path. He makes the mistake of all the failed conspirators, who believed that Louis was Richelieu's dupe. The war with Spain was Louis's policy as much as Richelieu's. Now it is Anne's. Instead, it is Olivares who loses office. The war lasts sixteen more years under Mazarin's direction, with unfailing support from Anne of Austria.

* The son of Vendôme. Mazarin escaped because he arrived in Gaston's carriage; assassinating him with pistols as planned would have been risky (Geoffrey Treasure, *Mazarin; The Crisis of Absolutism in France*, p. 337).

The regency is shaken by rebellions. War creates instability: the taxes that pay for it hurt the poor and provoke rebellions; the aristocrats that run the armies are a danger to the state.* Add to this the latent dissent that Richelieu suppressed, the release of grandees from prison to celebrate the new reign, and the regency itself. All these make trouble inevitable. The queen regent's style is authentic Habsburg autocrat. Mazarin is skilled in diplomacy, but not in dealing with the French *parlements*. In the end, however, it is diplomacy that matters.

The Peace of Westphalia

The point of war is peace: that is where the gains and losses of war are made permanent. Mazarin's mediation did this in a small way after the Mantuan War. Now his responsibility is to do the same after Richelieu's death in the Peace of Westphalia (1648) and the Peace of the Pyrenees with Spain (1659).

Westphalia deals with several overlapping wars: the civil war in the empire; the Dutch revolt against Spain, which began in 1568; the Swedish invasion, supposedly a defence of Protestant states but in practice a bid for empire; last, there is France's war with Spain and its defence of 'German liberties' in the empire – its war against local lords (like the Duc de Lorraine) and the emperor for territory.

The first step towards peace comes in 1635 with the Peace of Prague (just as France declares war on Spain). This settles some of the religious issues; and Ferdinand II makes peace with Saxony and Brandenburg. In 1637, the Imperial Diet in Regensburg agrees that the empire should continue the war with Sweden, whose position grows weaker as Protestant rulers make peace with the emperor; but the Diet also agrees to peace overtures. And it agrees the succession to the emperor. This is just as well, since he dies two months later. The new emperor, Ferdinand

* The backbone of the military is still feudal. Michel Le Tellier, Mazarin's great minister of defence, described the army as an independent republic in which individual corps commanders presided over autonomous cantons.

III, is deeply Catholic, but he is also determined to make peace. So is his adviser, Maximilian, Count Trauttmansdorff.

In the same year, 1637, Pope Urban proposes a peace conference of Catholic powers in Cologne: France, Spain and the empire. Richelieu appoints the Comte d'Avaux his ambassador. He goes to Germany; but to Hamburg, not Cologne. There he renews the Swedish subsidy. They agree that neither France nor Sweden will make a separate peace with the empire.

Peace is now in the air. The Cologne meeting fails because France insists that the Dutch attend. Spain, which treats them as Spanish subjects, refuses them passports. But on Christmas Day 1641 the emperor's envoy in Hamburg agrees with France and Sweden on a framework for a peace conference in Westphalia: in Münster for Catholics, in Osnabrück for Protestants. This is the first great peace conference in modern history; 194 jurisdictions are represented, 178 from the empire, mostly tiny: imperial knights as well as electors and the emperor. All the important European states are there, except for England.

Most countries have more than one plenipotentiary representative. France has three: d'Avaux, an experienced diplomat who worked with Richelieu, Abel Servien, a more gritty negotiator whom Mazarin trusts, and the Duc de Longueville, sent as a figurehead and to stop the other two quarrelling. There are some 300 assistants; Longueville has 139 bodyguards, plus servants. Sweden is more modest: two plenipotentiaries – who also quarrel – and an entourage of 165. The Dutch have eight plenipotentiaries; some provinces are represented separately. An event on such a scale has never seen before. But first the preliminaries of peace, agreed by the empire with France and Sweden, must be ratified by all the participating states. So the conference assembles only in 1644. The negotiations start in 1645.

Westphalia is a point of reference for future peace conferences, but it is different from later events in almost every way – especially in the attention given to precedence: rooms are constructed with several doors so that the question of who enters first will not arise. The Duc de Longueville, head of the French delegation, arrives in a procession led by twelve mules, each with a richly embroidered blanket showing the coat of arms of the house of Orléans: then fifty finely dressed cavaliers, after them the duke's twelve riding horses, each led by a man on a palfrey, then twenty-two pages, and twelve members of his Swiss guard. More horse and foot guards accompany the duke's carriage. The rest of his delegation, with further horsemen, follow.

The point is to impress everyone with the duke's high rank, and with the high status of France. In fact, the duke outranks his interlocutors so far that he does no business with them. What contacts he has are through mediators. This does not matter; he is there to impress, not to negotiate. The other two ambassadors are less grand, but when the Venetian mediator, Alvise Contarini, calls on him, d'Avaux comes only five steps down the entrance staircase to greet him – a deliberate slight. This, in the French view, is justified since, as a monarchy, France outranks the Venetian Republic. Contarini points out that Spain and the empire treat him as an equal; eventually the French, who need his co-operation, do so too.

This behaviour is not unique to France, though as a rising power the French may be particularly sensitive. (Trauttmansdorff, representing the emperor, who outranks everybody, arrives incognito.)[23] It is because the international system is still seen as a larger version of the domestic order.

Everything in domestic life is hierarchical: the court, the Church, the army, the family. On formal occasions, ribbons and stars make your rank clear. Civil order depends on a hierarchy. So it is easiest to imagine international order as a similar hierarchy – hence the need to insist on your high rank. In theory the pope is the spiritual leader of the world and the emperor its temporal leader, though this was never a reality. It is odd that France, against the idea of a universal monarchy, behaves as if the international order is a hierarchy. But no one is yet able to imagine the alternative: states that are sovereign and independent. That would be anarchy.*

* Shakespeare's Ulysses makes the case for hierarchy as the foundation of order in a magnificent speech in *Troilus and Cressida*, Act 1, Scene 3.

Everyone comes to Westphalia committed to ending the wars going on in Europe. The states are not all fighting each other, but the alliances make it necessary to bring them together. The collective nature of the conference is essential to its success. Nevertheless, unlike modern conferences, it is not multilateral. Treaties are signed in plenary sessions; but the negotiations and treaties are all bilateral.

Unlike the Congress of Vienna of 1814–15, or Paris after the First World War, this is a peace conference in a real sense. Its task is not to tidy up after victory but to stop the wars. That adds urgency, especially in the spring of 1646, since war is a seasonal activity.

This matters to Spain. It is under great financial strain and has made up its mind to end the war against the Dutch. It makes an opening move, on 20 February 1646, by suggesting Anne of Austria as mediator in the Franco-Spanish War. This is a surprise: she is the sister of the King of Spain and the mother of the King of France. Does that make her neutral? No: she is the Queen Regent of France.

Mazarin guesses it is a trick, perhaps intended to shake up the Dutch. If the Dutch think that something is happening between Spain and France, they may fear that they are missing their chance. He dismisses the Spanish proposal. But it stimulates him to put forward an idea of his own: that France and Spain end their war with an exchange of territory. France would take the Spanish Netherlands (Belgium, more or less) in exchange for Catalonia, then in revolt against Spain with French support. To complete the peace the infant Louis XIV would be betrothed to Maria Theresa, the Spanish Infanta.

The French team in Münster are shocked. The Catalans will see this as a betrayal. They have been in revolt against Madrid since 1640 and are protected by French forces. (In fact, they are beginning to wonder whether this is better or worse than Spanish rule.) Their Dutch allies will be shocked too. Mazarin points to the terms of their alliance of 1635, just renewed. A joint objective is to conquer and partition the Spanish Netherlands. By Mazarin's proposal France gets the territory on a plate from Spain; it could hand over some tasty morsel, Antwerp perhaps, to the Dutch. The ambassadors, d'Avaux and Servien, are not persuaded: they have been in The Hague and find the Dutch difficult.

They refuse to negotiate jointly with Spain; the most they might accept is a renewal of the alliance with France. Mazarin nevertheless decides to try out the idea of the exchange on the Dutch.

A French agent approaches the stadholder, Frederick Henry, on 26 February; he reacts positively, but insists that the French keep the discussions secret. Then, guessing that this will not remain secret for long, he takes the idea to the States General (parliament) himself. They are shocked. Dutch public opinion – and this is a country where public opinion matters – is outraged. It is one thing to conquer the territory bit by bit – war is a slow process in the seventeenth century – and then share it. A change overnight that ends Spain's war with France, enlarges France and brings it right up to the Dutch border is quite different. France finds that the Dutch, its ally against Spain, now sees it as a potential enemy. If the Dutch make peace with Spain, they will want the Spanish Netherlands as a buffer against the threat from France.

Mazarin's proposal does not get as far as Spain. It is unlikely they would have taken it seriously. Catalonia is in revolt; but it is a part of Spain. The Spanish Netherlands is under threat from France; but that too is Spain's. Giving up one to keep the other would be absurd. But Mazarin's suggestion, unintentionally, shocks the Dutch team in Westphalia into realising it is time to negotiate with Spain.

First, however, protocol has to be overcome, notably the phrasing of the Dutch letters of accreditation. These have been sent to Madrid, which is likely to object to the Dutch negotiators describing themselves as representing the 'free provinces' of the Low Countries – thus prejudging the question of their independence. (The Spanish letters refer to Philip IV, inter alia, as the King of Portugal and the Count of Flanders, both of which the Dutch will contest.)

The Dutch negotiators ask The Hague if they can get on with the negotiations with Spain while Madrid considers their credentials. This is a sensible suggestion: the Spanish State Council will not look at the credentials until June. Its advice to the king is to allow the delegation to compromise. He cuts matters short by telling the delegation to accept the credentials as they stand. He sends three copies of his letter by different routes to Münster, to make sure the message gets there by 1 July. In spite of the king's determination, the process still takes months.

Fortunately, the Dutch have permission to start talks while awaiting agreement on credentials. On 13 May the Spanish side proposes a twenty-year truce. Four days later, the Dutch reply with a full draft of a peace treaty. The Spanish tell them the next day that they can accept sixty out of its seventy-one articles.[24] As for the rest, the Dutch language on sovereignty goes beyond Spanish instructions, which is not surprising: their instructions are for a truce, not a settlement – and there are difficulties on trade and on freedom of worship. The Spanish get almost no concessions from the Dutch, but by the end of May they agree that work can start on a draft treaty.

In early July they have a joint draft treaty, which the Dutch can take to The Hague for the States General to confirm their agreement. Not all of their plenipotentiaries sign it: they represent different provinces; some do not want peace at all. But Holland does, and it pays more than half the costs of war; and Frederick Henry, the stadholder, supports it too.

This is an extraordinary success, but it is awkward for the Dutch: their treaty with France obliges them not to make a separate peace. They have insisted to the French in The Hague that they will negotiate independently, so that, except for the speed, the result is not altogether a surprise. They save face by telling the French that it is not a treaty, only elements that might be included in one.

That is clearly not true. To solve the problem of their bad faith, they offer to mediate a peace agreement between Spain and France. This is a remarkable proposal: that the Dutch mediate peace between their enemy of eighty years, with whom they have just made an agreement, and their ally for the last twenty years, with whom they have just broken an agreement. Nevertheless, they make a serious effort. But it is also clear that neither the French nor the Spanish want peace. That is bad faith too: both have come to Westphalia having pledged to negotiate a general peace.

The pace at which the Spanish have agreed a peace treaty with the

Dutch – one that recognises Dutch sovereignty and independence – shows their determination to end the Eighty Years War. Spain's financial problems have grown progressively worse, while the Dutch have become the richest people in Europe. (The guilder is now Europe's reserve currency.) Spain knows it cannot win. But now it has something in common with the Dutch: a growing fear of France. The Spanish agree whatever they need to agree: they recognise Dutch conquests in Brazil, although there are none. Brazil is Portuguese, but the Portuguese are in revolt, and Spain no longer cares.

The Dutch are reluctant to finalise the treaty with Spain because of the French problem and because of continuing arguments in The Hague. But peace is now palpable: the armies have stopped fighting.

This means that France now has an acute need to reach an agreement with the empire. The French do not want to be fighting on two fronts – Spain and the empire – while Spain is fighting only with them. And they do not want the empire to join Spain as an ally. This accelerates the negotiations with the empire; so does a Franco-Swedish campaign in Germany. (The Swedish army has to keep fighting to feed itself.) Even the pacifist Queen Christina thinks that a bit more war might bring peace more quickly. The Swedes get generous terms: a large piece of the Baltic coast (Swedish Pomerania), which they claim they need to protect themselves. From whom is not clear.

In the negotiations with the empire, the French focus on Alsace and Lorraine; they are modest in their demands compared with what the Swedes are seeking in North Germany. The emperor's offer to the French is to give them Habsburg lands in Alsace, 'in sovereignty': that is to say, full ownership, not as a fief of the emperor. (France pays him 3 million livres in compensation.) There is a good deal of ambiguity in this. Alsace is one of the most complicated areas in Europe. Its inhabitants speak German or a dialect; it is a patchwork of tiny territories, free towns and cities, bishoprics owing allegiance to the empire or to this or that lord. The regional centre, Strasbourg, is a republic. Servien advises Mazarin that there is no point in trying to be precise: 'Everyone should keep their claims and interpret the treaty as they see fit.' Isaak

Volmar, a Habsburg jurist from Alsace, takes the same view: what the treaty means in practice will depend on the strength of the contending parties.[25]

So it turns out. While the Franco-Spanish War continues, not much changes in Alsace. When France makes peace with Spain and turns its attention to the east, it establishes sovereignty in Alsace and Lorraine step by step, partly *de jure*, partly *de facto*. The Westphalia agreements with France and Sweden are written into two treaties,* concluded and sworn on 24 October 1648, accompanied by a twenty-four-gun salute.

Both France and Sweden make territorial gains. Sweden's are impressive in extent, but ephemeral. Most are gone seventy years later, and would have gone earlier without the support of France.

The empire gives up territory to France and Sweden; but it is not a territorial empire (it is better to think of it as a system of law and institutions).† On paper it loses authority in the treaties: they confirm that the emperor can make war or peace only with the consent of the Imperial Diet; and the states can act autonomously, as long as it is not against the empire.[26]

But this confirms only that the empire is not going to become a territorial state. The emperor's loss of formal powers does not make the empire weaker; a kingdom may survive better if its king concedes powers to a parliament. Ferdinand III and his successors turn to politics to maintain their system, and they prosper. The Imperial Diet meets in continuous session from 1663, and for a further century.

All the negotiations are bilateral; but the Congress of Westphalia is a collective event. Starting with the Dutch-Spanish negotiations, a reverse domino effect sets in: one peace agreement leads to another. The Dutch-Spanish settlement gives France an incentive to agree with the empire. This makes it essential for Sweden – and Queen Christina has long wanted peace – to reach an agreement too, as it is about to lose French support. The emperor wants peace in any case; he is the

* The Treaty of Osnabrück settles the empire's internal religious disputes and makes peace with Sweden; the Treaty of Münster makes peace between the empire and France.

† 'Empire' is not a good translation of Reich; 'commonwealth' is better.

prime mover of the congress. A realism grips all the parties. Count Trauttmansdorff, the emperor's negotiator, is the real hero of the negotiations. He might have taken advantage of the French need for agreement to hold out for a better deal. But after three years' negotiation, he has brought all the parties to the brink of agreement. He does not want to put this at risk in a last-minute game of bluff.

Making peace is harder than making war. When war begins, the stakes rise. It is difficult to give up unless you are victorious, or have been defeated. Peace is essential for the empire, whose function is to provide security and order – and it is failing. Ferdinand III's decision for peace probably saves it.

The last business of the Congress of Westphalia is the religious question: the origin of the Thirty Years War. The Peace of Prague began the settlement; Westphalia completes it. The emperor and Trauttmansdorff do the work. The Augsburg settlement (1555) allowed each prince to choose whether his domain should be Catholic or Lutheran; Westphalia leaves room for tolerance of individuals who make a different private choice; and it recognises Calvinism. The treaty helps reconciliation with Protestants, and the Church plays only a minor role in the congress. Neither pleases Pope Innocent X. He reacts by declaring the treaty 'null, void, invalid, unjust, reprobate, inane, empty of meaning and effect for all time'.[27] Religious tensions continue, but they never again take the form of war in Europe.

The Peace of the Pyrenees

The Congress of Westphalia ends Europe's longest war, the Spanish-Dutch or Eighty Years War – and its most destructive war, the Thirty Years War. France and Spain remain at war for eleven more years. Both are disturbed by rebellions, Catalonia and Portugal in the case of Spain, the *Fronde* in France; each aids the other's rebels. Mazarin is subject to vicious attacks and is twice exiled, but Anne of Austria sticks by him. The *Frondeurs* fail because of their disunity, the saving grace of the aristocracy.

The *Fronde* reaches its climax in 1652 in a battle in the streets of Paris. Louis II de Bourbon, le Grand Condé,* is defeated. He leaves France to join Spain. Four years later, leading Spanish forces, he beats France at Valenciennes. Mazarin decides to return to diplomacy. He says to Nicolas Fouquet, the superintendent of finances, that he thinks France will need an ally if it is to defeat Spain; probably he already has a candidate in mind.

This is England, a thought even more shocking than Richelieu's support for Sweden. England is ruled by a militant Protestant; and Cromwell is associated with the regicides who executed Charles I, Anne of Austria's brother-in-law. His son, Charles II, has taken refuge in France. It says much of Mazarin's powers that he persuades the queen to accept his idea. The alliance with England comes step by step: first, a treaty of commerce. This includes a clause saying that neither will help the other's enemies – plus a secret provision that France will arrange for Charles to leave France.

Charles II leaves France for Spain, which lends him an army to support his restoration: this means that Spain is now at war with England as well as France. The third step comes early in 1657 with a British-French treaty providing for joint operations against Spain in the Netherlands. The British will provide 6,000 soldiers, paid for by the French and under French command. If they are successful the British will get Dunkirk as part of the bargain.

And they are successful. Turenne, like Condé a Protestant and an ex-*Frondeur*, besieges Dunkirk.† In June, Condé arrives with a relieving force including an Irish regiment under the Duke of York, the future James II. The numbers are even, but Turenne has artillery support from English ships. And the battle is fought partly on the beach. Turenne, having calculated the tides, manoeuvres round the Spanish flank as the tide goes out and annihilates them. The British get Dunkirk. (After the Restoration, Charles II sells it to Louis XIV.)

* As the Duc d'Enghien he won the Battle of Rocroi for France in 1643.

† Turenne is the younger brother of the Duc de Bouillon, whom Mazarin helped save from execution. He is the only French general that Napoleon respected.

Preliminary peace talks between Spain and France begin shortly afterwards. The question in the Franco-Spanish War has been which state can endure longer. Spain did not make peace in 1648 because it thought France was about to collapse. The *Fronde* was indeed more dangerous than any rebellion Richelieu faced; but Mazarin sustained the queen's confidence through exile and abuse. These dangers are laid to rest with Louis XIV's majority and the end of the regency.

In Spain the Catalan revolt is over, but not the Portuguese War of Independence. This time, when a Spanish treasure fleet is captured, it is by Admiral Blake of the Royal Navy.

Richelieu died amid the trials and executions of traitors. As Mazarin too weakens, his preoccupation is with the Peace of the Pyrenees and the king's marriage to Maria Theresa, the Spanish Infanta. This sounds like a happy ending; but that is not entirely the case. With the Spanish procrastinating, Mazarin looks for a way to accelerate their decision. He introduces his niece, Marie Mancini, a princess of Savoy, to the king, with the idea of starting a rumour that he will marry her. This has the desired effect in Madrid; but in Lyons the king and Marie fall in love. She is attractive, clever, vivacious; he is lonely. They share a love of music, and might have been happy together. But happiness is not the objective. The interests of the state prevail.

The Peace of the Pyrenees is Mazarin's personal work. In the south, France acquires the Catalan lands north of the Pyrenees, the Roussillon and the Cerdagne; in the north, the Artois and fortresses. The people and institutions in the south remain Catalan in most respects until the nationalism of the nineteenth century turns them into Frenchmen. In the east and north of France much remains to fight over, but France secures important fortresses, still the key to warfare. The work that Richelieu began is not finished, but France is stronger than it has ever been, and it is at peace.

On Mazarin's death, Louis XIV announces that he will govern without a chief minister: this is a statement of how much he has learned, and recognition that no one can replace Mazarin.

The cardinals and their legacy

> 'I was the zero, which means something only when there are numbers in front of it.' The number was the king.[25]
>
> *Richelieu to Cardinal de La Valette*

The Europe of Richelieu is known as 'early modern Europe'. Culturally it is European; politically it is a foreign country. What we see resembles the developing world: the struggle of the state to establish its authority, the rebellions and civil wars; or it is the authoritarian world: Richelieu's spies, his trials with hand-picked judges, interrogations and torture.*

Spies, it should be noted, can also have a benign role in a world stiff with protocol. Richelieu learned from the dauphin's nurse, who sent him reports, that the king had set his son screaming by appearing in a bizarre sleeping cap. Ever distrustful, he suspected the queen was turning his son against him. When Louis next visited, the infant made a formal apology – Richelieu's suggestion probably – ending the king's threat to take him away from his mother.

But if we look through the mists of time, we can see three versions of modernity in embryo.

First there is Richelieu and his vision of a unitary, sovereign state. This is the road taken. Over time France became the pattern for most, if not all, European countries: a sovereign state responsible only to itself. Richelieu insisted on German or Italian 'liberties'; but what he meant was that France's neighbours should be weaker than France.

Richelieu studied theology and war. Theology justifies absolute monarchy – the king is God's representative on earth – and absolute sovereignty. Richelieu provided the policy; the king, the legitimacy: 'The Cardinal is the man who God has chosen to transmit His Councils

* After the murder of the Concinis, Marie de' Medici awoke to find that her guards had changed. The new guards were to keep her prisoner, not protect her. Khrushchev learned of the coup against him by Brezhnev in the same way.

to His Majesty.' Kings 'more than all other men have an obligation to act according to reason'.[29] The reason in question is *raison d'état*: the state has no immortal soul; like Machiavelli's prince, it is not subject to moral judgements.

In this world without law, states must be alert to what is happening abroad. France was the first country to create a foreign ministry; the machinery was personal and primitive, but for years to come it would be the model for other diplomatic services. Richelieu's doctrine of 'continuous diplomacy' means continuous engagement. Awareness of what others were thinking enabled Richelieu to see how Sweden might be useful to France – not obvious to many people in 1630. The same is true of Mazarin's alliance with England three decades later.

A system of dog-eat-dog is fine when you are the biggest dog. France's strength in the seventeenth century was the weakness of Spain and the weariness of the empire. France maintained its position for another 200 years. That may be as much as a statesman can hope for; the costs of failure, when it came, were large.

From Madrid and Vienna the two branches of the Habsburg family governed the looser structures of two empires. Richelieu saw the difficulties Spain had in the Netherlands, and the complications of the empire; he saw the collapse of Gustavus Adolphus's dreams of an empire in Germany. Richelieu's gains, made slowly, survive to this day.

Richelieu probably read Machiavelli, and probably agreed with him. (At his suggestion Louis Machot, secretary to the Bishop of Toul, wrote *Apologie pour Machiavel*, a study showing that his ideas can all be found in the Bible.) The policy he persuaded Louis XIII to adopt was opposite to Louis XII's, criticised by Machiavelli. He did not seek an empire abroad, but consolidated at home: sustainable gains in the Lorraine and the north; 'gateways' to give entry and influence in North Italy, without the bother of a far-flung empire. As allies he chose the Swedes, the Dutch and Bavaria, smaller than France and unlikely to become threats. And he stuck to them. He consolidated national territory within natural boundaries, the Pyrenees, the Alps, the Rhine. Places of special status, Béarn and Brittany, and sovereign enclaves such as Sedan were sucked into the king's realm.

Like Machiavelli, Richelieu understood that princes should do great deeds. The king led his troops, and great paintings memorialised La Rochelle, crossing the Alps in winter and the Grace of Alais. It is no wonder that the king chose as he did on the Day of the Dupes. But, as Machiavelli says, the credit goes not to the adviser, but to the man who chooses him.

The Peace of Westphalia restored peace in the empire, and ended the Eighty Years War. It did not establish principles for a European state system; the treaties do not mention state sovereignty. Nevertheless the congress was a step towards such a system. It brought the European states (except for England-Scotland) together in a common enterprise. After the chaos of the Thirty Years War, convoking the congress reminded everyone that a community existed among European countries.

By the time of the Peace of Utrecht (1712–13), the disputes over protocol had disappeared: in retrospect, a remarkable change. The idea of a hierarchy of states was gone. And whereas the wars that ended with the Congress of Westphalia had a variety of causes – self-determination for the Netherlands, religious differences within the empire, the pursuit of power for France and Sweden – those that ended in the Peace of Utrecht were all about one single issue: the need to defend the pluralism of the state system against French ambition. This itself was an affirmation of the principle of state sovereignty. It was not Richelieu who invented the balance of power in Europe: it was the others that built coalitions to hold back the monster Richelieu created.

The name of that monster was Leviathan,* the sovereign state. Richelieu was not its only begetter. The Dutch creation, though envied through Europe, was small and would not dominate. When Richelieu's work was done, long after his death, French power was concentrated in a unitary state. The king's ban on duelling was a part of this, the beginning of the state's monopoly on force and fortification. His refusal to accept the Lorraine as an imperial fief was of the same logic. Richelieu wanted sovereignty, not land.

* Thomas Hobbes, the author of *Leviathan* (1651), lived in exile in Paris from 1640 to 1651.

This future exists still today. As a contemporary Russian remarks: 'Sovereignty is a political synonym for competition.'* This version of sovereignty excludes co-operation, except for the temporary and the expedient.

An alternative future was set out in Richelieu's vision twenty years before the Congress of Westphalia. This proposed two treaty structures, one in Germany, one in Italy, to protect the 'German and Italian liberties' of small states. France would be the arbiter and the guarantor of both. France's 'gateways', like Pinerolo across the Alps or Breisach on the east bank of the Rhine, would enable intervention. This was Richelieu's *bonne paix de la Chréstienté.*

The German part of this plan found its way into the instructions to Richelieu's plenipotentiaries at Westphalia – and a trace of the idea can be found in the treaties. This obliged all the parties:

> to defend and protect each and any of the provisions of this peace against anyone . . . the injured party shall first of all dissuade the offending party from the use of force . . . If however the matter has not been settled by either of these procedures within the space of three years, each and every party to the present transaction shall be obliged to join forces and counsel with the injured party and to take up arms to oppose the contravention.[30]

This might be collective security, 270 years before the League of Nations, or it might be the balance of power; or is it a stronger version of NATO Article 5?

Mazarin implemented a variant of Richelieu's idea in the years after Westphalia. He built up France's relations with the German states close to its borders, starting with the archbishoprics of Cologne and Mainz, and including states on the other side of the Rhine. The League of the Rhine, a loose compact to safeguard German liberties – implicitly against both outsiders and overweening emperors – was created in 1658. Both France and Sweden joined it. Sweden had acquired

* Vladislav Surkov, sometimes described as Putin's ideologue-in-chief.

imperial territory and was a member of the Regensburg Diet; France was not – the point of taking the Habsburg lands 'in sovereignty' was to avoid being subordinate to the emperor – but it was an influential voice in Regensburg. France provided funds for a directorate in Frankfurt so it could hire mercenaries if needed. This France was a friendly, co-operative neighbour.[31]

These arrangements are more like NATO than the League of Nations. Perhaps they might have worked; but they fall under the heading of 'roads not taken', or at least not continued for long. Mazarin's diplomacy of co-operation and influence – where protection, for once, meant security, not domination – was replaced after his death by Louis XIV's thirst for glory. The soft takeover of Alsace and Lorraine was reinforced by armed force. Other European states united against France, making European politics an endless struggle for domination.

A third version of the future can be glimpsed in the Netherlands. Here it is the future of the state rather than the state system. Richelieu and Olivares envied the success of the United Provinces, and asked what they might learn from it. Copying them, Richelieu built up the French navy and proposed colonial expeditions. Both saw the United Provinces as another version of France or Spain. War was continuous, and the Dutch were good at it.

This missed the point. Dutch success came from enterprise and trade, and a new society where openness, competition, sometimes even tolerance, played a part. That was why thinkers like Descartes found their way there. This was a sovereign state, but not in the old pattern of rank and hierarchy.

The irony is that as Richelieu wondered how to learn from the Dutch, he was pounding La Rochelle. Here was the answer to his question: a Calvinist city linked by trade to similar cities in Britain, the Low Countries and on the Baltic, a commercial people who preferred trade and contract to conquest; a society not governed by rank. The France that Richelieu helped create was magnificent; but the embryo of a different, more modern, future was crushed in La Rochelle.

From the Peace of Utrecht onwards, the balance of power became an agreed principle. This was not lip service: the rules of dynastic succession – so important in the previous centuries – were set aside in favour of the balance of power. As well as Louis XIV, his brother, the Duc de Berry, renounced his rights to the Spanish crown, recognising 'la maxime fondamentale' that the strength of a kingdom should not be such as to give reason 'for fears or jealousies', and agreeing 'to maintain a certain proportion in order that the weakest might defend themselves against more powerful ones, and support one another against equals'.[32] Likewise, the Spanish-British treaty (as at Westphalia, the agreements were all bilateral) refers to a permanent separation of France and Spain for the sake of a 'iustum potentiae aequilibrium'.[33]

Behind this principle lay the idea that the 'repose of Europe' depended on all countries feeling secure. This took practical form not only in the notion of the balance of power but also in the acceptance of Dutch demands for a buffer between their rather small country and France. French instructions to their delegates recognised the need for safeguards, including that the Spanish Netherlands should be 'in the possession of a prince who has no reason on every occasion to follow the interests of France, and who is sufficiently powerful to serve as a barrier'.[34]

These principles suggest that the competing powers now accepted a common responsibility for the 'repose' of Europe. They did not yet talk of peace. 'Repose' required war. The seventeenth and eighteenth centuries were times of almost continuous war. After the War of the Spanish Succession (1701–14) – thirteen years of continuous fighting – the Peace of Utrecht was followed by a period for recovery. Then Frederick the Great took *raison d'état* to its logical conclusion: no law, except power; no order, except balance. For the moment this held; and the system returned to equilibrium.

There is something satisfying about this world: neat and tidy like Newtonian physics. This was the world of the Enlightenment, more Hume than Hobbes. War remained unpleasant, especially for the poor; but it was a world of order and of limits. Then came the French Revolution.

3

Talleyrand: the Uncorrupted Mind

Imagine that you work for the most powerful man in the world: one more powerful than any president or prime minister today. This is Napoleon Bonaparte, at the height of his power. He has returned from Spain in haste and has summoned you and other senior figures to a meeting on a Sunday afternoon. You are expecting some trouble. Moreover, Napoleon has asked you to resign one of the two offices you hold.

But what follows, neither you nor anyone else has expected. It is a tirade that goes on for thirty minutes, non-stop: Napoleon striding backwards and forwards across the room, his hands behind his back – except when he is shaking his fist at you. Those in the room are frozen by the violence of the words. They have never seen or heard anything like it: 'a thief, a coward, a man without honour, who has never done his duty in his whole life. You have cheated everyone; you have betrayed everyone. For you there is nothing sacred. You would sell your father.' Does Napoleon use the famous phrase, 'a shit in a silk stocking'? Perhaps not, but it is what he means.

All this is directed at you. What do you do?

You are Talleyrand. You do nothing. You remain immobile. You watch Napoleon as he rages, your eyes half closed. You show no emotion. You lean on a piece of furniture, because of your bad leg. Napoleon has planned this scene to intimidate you. Perhaps because of your failure to react in any way, he loses all control of himself. But he does not control you.

Most of what Napoleon has said has some truth in it, but not the accusation that Talleyrand is a coward. To listen impassive, in control of yourself, to such things from the conqueror of Europe, to remain cool – this calls for courage and control. As he limps from the room Talleyrand murmurs to the master of ceremonies: 'There are some things which one does not forgive.'[1] Later in the evening he remarks at one of the salons he frequents that it is a pity that such a great man should have been so poorly brought up.

André Suarès writes of Napoleon that he never stopped hating Talleyrand but that he could never do without him.[2] Talleyrand was his weakness: a mind that remained incorruptible, among all the rottenness of his morals and his actions. Talleyrand overcame Napoleon's scorn by the superior scorn of the egotist and the sceptic.

What do you do next? Slightly to your surprise, perhaps, you have not been arrested and imprisoned (approached soon after by Savary – who ran Napoleon's secret police and did much of the dirty work for him – Talleyrand asks: 'Ham or Vincennes?', naming two prisons). You return the next day to the court as if nothing has happened. Napoleon ignores you. A week later you are again at the court, and again Napoleon ignores you; but this time he puts a question to your neighbour. The man stammers in reply; so you interrupt and give the answer.

And what else do you do? You betray him. Actually, Talleyrand, as always ahead of the game, has begun to betray him six months before, though Napoleon does not know it.

Origins

Charles-Maurice de Talleyrand-Périgord, one of the great diplomats of his age, was born in Paris on 2 February 1754 into one of the most ancient families of the *ancien régime*. His parents decided that he should go into the Church, perhaps because his limp would be a handicap in the army. The limp may have been the result of an accident when a child, as he says in his memoirs, or, more likely, it was a club foot he inherited (his uncle had the same impediment). He did not inherit much else, except for the family name and the social position it brought. In the first sentence of his memoirs Talleyrand refers to his parents as having little money. The small amount that they did have was passed to his younger brother, along with the family title. Perhaps his parents felt that the club foot would not make their eldest son a good match and they put all their efforts into finding an heiress for his brother, to revive the family fortunes. Throughout his life the question of financial security remained a preoccupation for Talleyrand, so much so that the first sentence of an unfinished essay by Stendhal refers to him as 'a man of infinite wit who happened always to be short of money'.

As a diplomat Talleyrand lived in an age of change and had to grapple above all with the three large questions that would define the positions of the other great diplomats of his day: Klemens von Metternich for Austria, Viscount Castlereagh for Britain and Alexander I, Tsar of Russia.

The first question was the basis for the legitimacy of the state and its rulers. The divine right of kings or the sovereignty of the people? Or something in between? This question had been under the surface in Europe through the Reformation and the Enlightenment, together with the question of the relationship between Church and state. The French Revolution raised the issue of legitimacy first in debate and then in violence, as had happened in previous centuries in Britain and the Netherlands, and most recently in America. But these were on the fringes of Europe; and the French Revolution made it a central issue in European politics for the next 150 years. For Frenchmen living during the revolution it was a question that would determine the fate of their country; and the position each man took on it could be a matter of life or death.

The second question was the impact this would have on the political geography of Europe. If the people were to be sovereign, it was probably the beginning of the end for the patchwork of tiny German states and free cities in the middle of Europe. Nor could the ownership of territory and of the people living on it be so easily settled by dynastic marriages or wars. And the nature of war itself was changing. Under popular sovereignty the army would cease to be the dregs of society led by the aristocracy and instead become the nation at arms. This meant armies on a new scale: Europe had never seen anything like the 600,000 men Napoleon took with him to Russia. War was both more devastating and more expensive. And the mass army was a first step towards the mass society. The limited wars of the eighteenth century ended with the Battle of Valmy in 1792, where untrained French volunteers beat the professional forces of Prussia. That was how the story was told afterwards; as it happened, the professionally organised artillery also played a vital part in the battle, but this was less remarked on at the time. All this raised profound questions for France, for Prussia and especially for Austria.

The French Revolution shocked all Europe; but at the same time the Industrial Revolution was beginning to change lives and societies – and also the nature of power. At the end of the eighteenth century, people still regarded land and population – the peasants who were thought to make good soldiers – as the two sources of national power. But what of industry, trade and empire? Were these going to be sources of power too? This was the third question. Those who understood such things best would have the keys to the future.

Each of these questions will recur throughout Talleyrand's life, and they will be repeated in different forms for the generations that follow him. He will find himself thrust into them by war and revolution. Meanwhile the Church, one of the great estates of France, where he begins his career, is not a bad place to be. At the age of twenty-one, thanks to his birth, he is an *abbé*, and then canon at Reims Cathedral, where his uncle will later become archbishop and cardinal. At twenty-five he is ordained deacon, then priest and Vicar-General of Reims. For the next five years he works as Agent-General of the Clergy, dealing among other things with Church finances. This brings him into contact and collaboration with Charles de Calonne, Controller-General of the finances of Louis XVI; and so he begins to understand the slow crisis of the French state. The symptom of the crisis is France's massive debt – while the Church is rich. Sometime before the state collapses in the revolution, Talleyrand has recognised the financial crisis as a symptom of the chaotic, half-medieval system. De Calonne's programme is one of modernisation: a tax on land to be applied equally to all, including on the nobility. This is too much for both the nobility and the Church, and de Calonne – who has understood the problem too well – is dismissed, eventually seeking refuge in England.

Talleyrand by this time is well read and well known in intellectual circles. He has a reputation for being clever and witty. He is well received in the salons of Paris. The fact that he is in holy orders does not prevent him from having several well-known affairs. There is no reason to doubt his Christian faith, but he is a liberal thinker and an admirer of Voltaire.

At the age of thirty-four he is appointed Bishop of Autun by the pope on the recommendation of Louis XVI, which refers to his 'good life, morals, piety and other virtues'. In fact, Talleyrand is living openly with a married woman (the Comtesse de Flahaut, by whom he has a son); the king does not like it but cedes to the dying wish of Talleyrand's father. This is 1788 and the king has called together the Estates General for the following year, its first meeting for nearly two centuries. In Paris Talleyrand belongs to liberal circles, including the Committee of Thirty, among whose members are the Marquis de Lafayette, the Abbé Sieyès and the economist and mathematician the Marquis de Condorcet.

Estates General

When the Estates General meets the following year, Talleyrand has been elected one of the representatives of the Church – one of the few bishops; the majority are poor parish priests. The first business of the Estates General is a procedural question about whether the three estates will meet separately or together. Procedural questions are sometimes dismissed as secondary, but just as often they are about power. Who has a seat at the table? Who can speak? Who decides the agenda? Who can vote? These are procedural matters, but they might also be called constitutional questions: they are about power and legitimacy.

The question at issue is whether the three estates, the Church, the Nobility and the Commons, should meet separately or as a single body.

If it is together, then the Third Estate, having double representation, is likely to dominate. The decision to elect twice as many representatives for the Third Estate as for each of the other two is a concession made on the advice of de Calonne's rival and successor, Jacques Necker. But although he has persuaded the court to accept double representation for the Commons, he is equally clear that the three estates should be consulted separately by the king – affirming the principle of inequality, since this allows the other two to outweigh the third.

In his memoirs Talleyrand pours scorn on Necker. Of all his mistakes the greatest was to authorise the Third Estate on its own the same number of deputies as the other two together. The concession on double representation made no sense unless the three orders met together: it thus gave legitimacy to the insistence of the Third Estate on joint deliberation.

> There was something in Necker that prevented him from foreseeing the consequences of his own actions, and fearing the risks they might bring. He persuaded himself that he would have an all-powerful influence over the estates, that the members of the Third Estate above all, would listen to him as to an oracle, would see only with his eyes, would do nothing without his consent and would, under no circumstances, make use against his wishes of the weapons he had put in their hands.[3]

Necker is one of those who believes he can dominate events. Talleyrand, by contrast, sees that he has to deal with 'a torrent which had to be allowed to pass' and which he resolves not to fight but to be ready instead 'to run with the tide, to save what could be saved and to make use of the opportunities that it might offer.'[4]

The debate on the procedural question lasts the better part of two months and finishes with the Third Estate declaring itself to be the representatives of the nation as a whole, taking the title 'National Assembly' and refusing to disperse at the king's command.

In the course of the crisis Talleyrand advises the king, through his younger brother, the Comte d'Artois, a personal friend though at the opposite end of the political spectrum, to dissolve the Estates General. This advice is not taken and Talleyrand concludes that since he has not been able to persuade others to act, 'it was necessary, unless you were mad, to look after yourself'[5] – advice that he follows through the course of the revolution, and indeed his whole life. Accordingly, with others from the Church, he joins the Third Estate, the only reasonable course being 'to give way when one can still take credit for it, rather than to wait and do it under compulsion.'[6]

Talleyrand is a man of the Enlightenment. His inclination is towards the constitutional monarchy he admires in Britain. But he is not a great orator and speaks in the assembly on practical matters, going with the tide of events, trying to make what he can of them. After the three estates have joined together to form the National Assembly he proposes the nationalisation of Church property. This is seen by some as the first of his many betrayals. But the state is bankrupt and the Church is rich. And it is going to happen anyway (as it had, over two hundred years before, in England). He follows his rule of being ahead of events and taking credit for them. He also speaks for order in financial affairs, against the issue of the *assignats* – forced loans to the state which in a few years' time will be worthless; he speaks for citizenship for the Jewish community in Bordeaux; he delivers a report on a state system of education, some of whose features are taken up when it is reformed under Napoleon.

He is president of the assembly for a period and presents a report on its achievements. He speaks for a rational system of weights and measures (on the eve of the revolution, a quarter of a million local measures were used in France) and consults Britain and the United States with a view to establishing an international standard. An agreement with Britain on this breaks down when the monarchy is overthrown in France. (The metric system is eventually introduced in 1795 and imposed throughout France and in its conquests by Napoleon.)

On 14 July 1790, the anniversary of the fall of the Bastille, Talleyrand celebrates the Mass on the Champ de Mars as a part of a republican festival (so unfamiliar is he with the liturgy that he has to practise it the day before). He finds the event ridiculous, but manages to win enormous sums at the tables in the evening. When the festivities are over he writes to the Comtesse de Flahaut:

> I don't know who is more to be pitied, the sovereign or the people, France or Europe . . . And if, for their part, the people do not keep up their guard against the character of the Prince, I foresee frightful events: I see streams of blood . . . I see the innocent caught up with in the same devastation as the guilty . . . Far be it from me to suspect Louis XVI of being thirsty for blood, but a weak monarch surrounded by bad advisers easily becomes cruel or his weakness allows certain cruelties under the authority of his name.

This is not a perfect piece of foresight: he does not know that the king will be captured at Varennes trying to escape, nor that the cruelty will come from the elected representatives; but he understands the spirit of the times and has a sense of the way things are going, much clearer than that of many others', and he begins to play less of a part in the assembly.

In January and April 1792 he is sent to London to see if the government can be persuaded to remain neutral in the event of a war with Prussia and Austria. In fact, the British need no persuading, and have in any case made up their minds on this policy – at least until later that year, when the revolution turns violent and hostile, with the occupation of Belgium and the execution of the king. This puts France beyond the pale as far as Britain is concerned.

More significant is his third departure, which takes place before those events. With the Prussians on the frontier he can see the revolution taking a further violent turn. Arrest warrants are issued for some of his friends; others have been killed. No complaints have been lodged against Talleyrand himself but he judges that it will be dangerous to remain in Paris. He wants, however, to leave in good order and not to be seen as fleeing; and he waits a dangerous three days to obtain authorisation for a visit to London – in connection still with the negotiations on weights and measures – and a proper passport signed by Danton. He leaves on 10 August 1792, the day on which the Tuileries Palace is taken over by the mob.

After his departure, though under surveillance in London, he continues to correspond with the French government. A paper from Talleyrand dated 25 November 1792 will be found among Danton's papers after his execution. This sets out Talleyrand's reflections on the nature of power. It is written in the language of the revolution, but the ideas in it are revolutionary in a wider sense:

> We have learned, and no doubt a little late too, that for states as for individuals, real wealth consists not in acquiring or invading the domains of others but in making good use of your own. We have learned that all those extensions of territory, those usurpations by force and trickery, to which long and illustrious prejudice attaches rank, primacy, solidity and superiority among powers, are no more than cruel games of political foolishness and false calculations of power whose only result is to add to the costs and difficulties of governing, and to reduce the security and happiness of the governed to satisfy the transitory interests and vanity of the few . . . France ought to remain within her own boundaries . . .[7]

Neither the revolutionary governments nor Napoleon will follow these ideas, but Talleyrand remains constant to them throughout his life.

Talleyrand remains in exile, first in Britain and then in the United States, for four years, returning to Paris in September 1796. He is sometimes in financial difficulties, living on his wits and through his network of contacts, helping finance speculation in land in America. His return is partly owing to the efforts of Madame de Staël, who makes much of the fact that he was sent abroad on official business and has him removed from the list of proscribed émigrés.

Foreign minister

A little less than a year after his return he is appointed Minister of Foreign Affairs for the Directory. This means that he runs the ministry:

policy is in the hands of the directors themselves. But it makes him a political insider and it gives him the opportunity to make the acquaintance of Napoleon, first in correspondence and then in person when, in December 1797, he introduces him to the Directory. In July 1798 he resigns as minister amid accusations of corruption and collaboration with Britain. A little over a year later he is one of the conspirators (with Sieyès) who help organise the coup of 18 Brumaire that brings Napoleon to power.

Talleyrand becomes Napoleon's foreign minister two weeks later, on 22 November 1799. He remains in this position until late 1807, when he resigns, though he continues to be close to Napoleon and advises him on foreign affairs for a further year. During this time, the period of Napoleon's domination of Europe, Talleyrand signs more than twenty treaties, some of them redrawing the map of Europe. Little or none of this is his own policy; much of it is contrary to his instincts and his advice. He is responsible for the detail of the negotiations, not the strategy.

The work of the soldier and that of the diplomat should be complementary. Force makes sense only as part of a political strategy: war should be the pursuit of policy with the addition of other means, as in Clausewitz's definition. The methods of the military and those of the diplomat are directly opposite. The soldier operates by orders and expects obedience – his aim is to compel obedience. The diplomat's purpose is to accommodate divergent interests through negotiation and to achieve consent, since nothing else will last. One of the fundamental choices that political leaders have to make is between negotiation and compulsion. In domestic policy this is the choice between reaching an understanding and making a law; in foreign policy it is the choice between negotiation and war.

Military experience is valuable for those who make foreign policy, and some soldiers have become great diplomats, George Marshall, for example; but this is mostly when they have become sickened by war or sceptical of it as a way of solving problems. Napoleon never reached that point. By the end of his reign war seemed to have become an end in itself – this was reinforced by an army that could be sustained only when it was living off the land in someone else's country. The idea that one man could control all of Europe, with some brothers and former generals serving under him as kings, was always a fantasy. It is hard to see anything that could be described as a political strategy behind Napoleon's military policies.

It is not that Talleyrand is against war in principle. After the *coup d'état* of 18 Brumaire it was clear, as he acknowledges in his memoirs, that only further French victories will bring the other powers to the negotiating table. And this is precisely what happens following Napoleon's close-run victory at Marengo on 14 June 1800. What makes the difference is the energy of young commanders, chosen for talent, and not for family. The terms of peace following Marengo are the most generous Napoleon ever proposed. In his memoirs Talleyrand suggests that Napoleon's awareness that he had come close to defeat made him more modest in his demands. There is an additional reason: stopping the war with Austria as quickly as possible prevents his rival, General Moreau – whose victory at Hohenlinden on 3 December 1800 will leave the road to Vienna open – from delivering the *coup de grâce*. Thus, Napoleon wins the title of peacemaker for himself. His claim to legitimacy is that he has saved the nation and has brought peace; and he does not want a rival. The real spoils of war after Marengo are in France: the consolidation of Napoleon's position as First Consul.

The Peace of Lunéville with Austria (9 February 1801) is the result; Talleyrand has little to do with its negotiation. It confirms the terms negotiated by Napoleon at Campo Formio following his victories in Italy in 1797. A new independent state is created in North Italy, the Cisalpine Republic; the Venetian Republic is absorbed into Austria, which also extends its territory into Istria (modern-day Croatia). France acquires the left bank of the Rhine (the Netherlands and Belgium in today's terms). With Russia no longer a part of the coalition – the slightly crazy Tsar Paul is seduced by the glitter of Napoleon's military glory and his gift of a sword honouring the tsar's position as the Grand Master of the Knights of Malta – peace with Austria leaves Britain alone against France, and ready also to make peace.

The Peace of Amiens (25 March 1802) is accepted by the British more or less as proposed by Napoleon. This returns to France and to Holland, now under French control, almost all the colonial possessions Britain had seized.* Pitt is prepared to exchange territory for peace. Speaking for the treaty in the House of Commons (he is, however, out of office at the time), he says: 'if we had retained all our conquests it would not have made any difference to us in point of security . . . They would give us only a little more wealth but a little more wealth would be badly purchased by a little more war.'[8] An argument that Talleyrand would understand.

Talleyrand himself is more directly involved in negotiating the concordat of 1801 with Pope Pius VII. This is important for Napoleon, who understands that the French peasants are attached to the new land that they have gained from the revolution, but that they are attached also to the old religion, which the revolution has tried to overthrow. The concordat allows the state to nominate bishops, but the Church is responsible for their investiture. Talleyrand uses the occasion to renegotiate his own complicated relationship with the Church, with only partial success: his excommunication of 1791 is revoked, but the Church refuses to release him from his vows as a bishop – making his marriage shortly thereafter a further scandal in their eyes.

Talleyrand is also occupied with the follow-up to the Peace of Lunéville. This provides for mediation to rationalise the patchwork of German principalities, free cities and imperial territories in South Germany. The work of dissolving the Holy Roman Empire and creating in its place the Confederation of the Rhine will be completed after Austerlitz in 1805. But meanwhile the creation of larger units – kingdoms such as Württemberg and Bavaria – under French mediation, costs Austria influence and creates dependence on France. In the process compensation is paid to the electors, imperial knights, bishops, abbots, free cities and others who lose their powers and position. Politically this works well for France. Financially it works well for Talleyrand, who has converted the custom of giving gifts (snuffboxes, for example) to

* Another provision, not of any real significance by this time, was that the British coinage should stop referring to the 'King of England and France', a relic of the Hundred Years War.

those who negotiate important treaties into one of expecting payment in cash. Unable to make policy, he at least makes money, probably several millions of francs. Shortly after the negotiation ends he buys, or rather is obliged by Napoleon to buy, a château in the Indre for 1.6 million francs.*

The Peace of Amiens with Britain is in doubt almost from its signature. There is nothing in it that brings the two countries together, such as the renewal of the treaty of commerce that London wants and Talleyrand favours. Instead, even before the peace is signed, Napoleon starts – against Talleyrand's advice – the process of annexing the kingdom of Piedmont. He strengthens his hold over Switzerland, maintains his troops in Holland and develops the port of Antwerp, actions calculated to make both Austria and Britain uneasy. Britain uses the annexation of Piedmont as an excuse for remaining in Malta, contrary to agreement. Accusations of bad faith are justified on both sides and both assume that war will be renewed.

Another sign that France is preparing for war comes in early 1803. Under French bullying Spain has exchanged its vast, unoccupied territory in North America, then known as Louisiana, for an invented kingdom in Italy, Etruria. This alarms President Jefferson: 'There is, on the globe, only one single spot the possessor of which is our natural and habitual enemy. It is New Orleans, through which the produce of three-eighths of our territory must pass to market.'[9] Jefferson sends out feelers to see if France is willing to think of a sale, without, however, much expectation of success. But he is in luck. Napoleon wants a war chest and instructs Talleyrand to sell, and to do so quickly. Having travelled in America, Talleyrand must have some idea of the vastness of the area. The sale probably still makes sense. Unless France is going to populate and defend the land, American settlers will sooner or later take it for themselves, as they are doing with Florida and will do with Texas. But the price – 80 million francs (or $15 million) for 828,000 square miles, roughly doubling the territory of the United States – is the bargain of the century. Only under urgent need of money would

* Price comparisons are impossible; this is a princely sum for a princely chateau.

anyone accept so little. When the moment comes in the council, only Talleyrand and Napoleon's older brother, Joseph, vote for peace.

From this moment, the gap between Talleyrand's views on policy and Napoleon's never ceases to grow. Talleyrand tries in different ways to moderate Napoleon's conduct of foreign policy, but without success.

Sometimes he delays. 'If I want anything done, I do *not* employ the Prince of Benevento (Talleyrand),' Napoleon once said to Metternich, then Austrian ambassador to France. 'I turn to him when I want a thing *not* to be done.'[10] Occasionally the delay brings reflection on Napoleon's part and the action Talleyrand thought unwise is avoided. It is this method that Talleyrand describes five years later when introducing his staff to his successor as foreign minister, Champagny: 'Here are many people I can recommend to you, with whom you will be well satisfied. You will find them loyal, skilful, precise, but, thanks to my efforts, devoid of all zeal. Apart from one or two clerks who close their envelopes in a little too much of a hurry, everything takes place in the greatest calm and they have lost all habits of haste.' And a little less tongue-in-cheek: 'When you have spent a little time dealing with the interests of Europe with the emperor, you will see how important it is never to make haste to settle things or to push on too quickly with his wishes.'[11]*

Or he tries to moderate Napoleon's instructions in their execution. Napoleon's comment following Talleyrand's negotiation of the Treaty of Pressburg after Austerlitz (see below), that he was displeased with the result, means that it is not harsh enough. Metternich also concludes that it was at this moment that Talleyrand decided 'to use all his influence to oppose Napoleon's destructive plans'.

Sometimes Talleyrand sets out for Napoleon what he sees as the strategic situation in Europe. In this the constants are: a need for caution in dealing with Russia, whose relentless appetite for territory – Crimea, Poland, Georgia, Corfu – is a cause for concern and makes it desirable to

* Champagny is a disappointment to Talleyrand, who complains to Metternich that he 'does in twenty hours what the emperor tells him to do in twenty-four', whereas he, Talleyrand, 'would always have taken exactly three weeks' (Alan Palmer, *Metternich: Councillor of Europe*, p. 62).

keep them out of Europe; second, the maritime dominance of Britain. For this Talleyrand's solution is peace, a commercial treaty with Britain and the development of France's commercial and naval potential. His key point is the third one: the need for a balance between Austria and an ever more ambitious Prussia. Only Austria's continuation as a multi-national empire including many small German states prevents the formation of two German states, one northern and one southern, either of which would be a danger for France. Talleyrand, it might be said, understands the logic of the forces that the revolution released better than Napoleon even though the emperor has ridden to power on them.

These are his ideas after Marengo in 1800, and they are the same ones that he puts to Napoleon before Austerlitz in 1805: a generous peace with Austria followed by an alliance. This, he argues, will eventually oblige Britain – deprived of allies on the Continent – to make peace too. After Austerlitz he makes a final try: 'beaten and humiliated, [Austria] today needs her conqueror to offer her the hand of generosity and, by forming an alliance with her, return to her that confidence which so many defeats and disasters have destroyed. I ask that Your Majesty looks again at the draft [treaty] which I submitted earlier.'[12] Napoleon does not, and instead sets harsh terms for the Pressburg settlement.

Finally, Talleyrand sets out his views in public. He praises Napoleon as a peacemaker. Here he is before Austerlitz, speaking to the Senate in the presence of Napoleon, who has just made himself King of Italy. This is his new name for Cisalpina, the state he has carved out of former Austrian territory in (today's) North Italy: 'In your glorious expeditions and your bold undertakings was Your Majesty driven by some longing to dominate or to invade? No. Without doubt Your Majesty wanted to recall for France the idea of order, and for Europe the idea of peace . . . The time will come when even Britain, won over by the success of your moderation, will abandon its hatred.'[13] This is both an appeal to Napoleon to take what Talleyrand regards as the wise course, and – because his expectations are low – a good dose of irony.

In fact Talleyrand believes that, in taking the title of king for himself, Napoleon is already making a false step. A little while beforehand

Talleyrand has said to one of his financial friends, the banker Gabriel-Julien Ouvrard:

> Two paths are open before [Napoleon]. One is the federal system under which each prince remains master in his own house after conquest, on terms favourable to the victor, thus the First Consul could reinstate the King of Sardinia, the Grand Duke of Tuscany and so on. 'But what if on the contrary he wants to unite, to incorporate? Then he takes a path that has no end.'[14]

None of Talleyrand's delays, arguments or hints do any good. What he gets instead are the harsh terms of the Treaty of Pressburg, in which Austria loses territory to Bavaria and Württemberg and the recently acquired Venetian States to Napoleon's new kingdom of Italy, together with an indemnity of 50 million francs. The dismantling of the Holy Roman Empire is completed and the Confederation of the Rhine is formed, mostly of the states that have gained at Austria's expense, making them more dependent than ever on French protection.

In Berlin Talleyrand signs the orders setting up the Continental System, forbidding trade with Britain. If there is one thing he understands better than Napoleon it is commerce; and he knows that the Continental blockade of Britain is folly. His speech in praise of this policy is a masterpiece of irony, setting out all the problems it will cause for France.

The following year, 1806, Prussia suffers a fate worse even than Austria's: defeat (at Jena-Auerstedt) and the loss of more than half its territory, mostly to Napoleon's ally the King of Saxony, plus an indemnity of 120 million francs. Russia is defeated at Friedland in 1807, but here Napoleon takes a different course, one that is the exact opposite of Talleyrand's recommendation. Instead of an alliance with Austria, Napoleon proposes soft terms for Russia: the return of Corfu and the Ionian Islands to France (which had seized them from Venice in 1797), the evacuation of Moldavia and Walachia – and an alliance. The point of this is that Russia has to join the Continental System – economically ruinous for Russia, and eventually the cause of renewed war.

Why does Napoleon keep Talleyrand so long when he never takes his advice? He values his knowledge of what is going on in Europe; Talleyrand has an excellent network of friends (many of them are women) and informers. He admires his intelligence and efficiency. When Champagny takes three months after Wagram in 1809 to negotiate the Treaty of Vienna, Napoleon comments that Talleyrand would have taken 10 per cent but he would have done it in half the time. Talleyrand may not agree with Napoleon, but he understands him. He is the civil equivalent of Napoleon's military chief of staff, Berthier. Just as Berthier can translate a sketch-map from Napoleon into a battle plan and into orders for Napoleon's marshals, Talleyrand can turn his sketched-out ideas into a treaty and a diplomatic campaign. Talleyrand is not only amusing and clever; he is also capable and organised – as he demonstrates in Warsaw, when unexpectedly Napoleon asks him to arrange winter supplies for the army, hardly his normal business.

And on Talleyrand's side? When your advice is consistently ignored – in ways that are dangerous both for your country and for Europe as a whole – what do you do? Normally you have two choices. You can resign. This is honourable but ineffective. Or you can stay on, less honourable and probably also ineffective: why should someone who never takes your advice change his ways?

Talleyrand takes a third course. He stays on; and he systematically betrays Napoleon. He does not remain foreign minister, a role in which he would take responsibility for policies he dislikes, but he stays close enough to Napoleon to enable the betrayal.

Betrayal

The most spectacular episode of betrayal takes place at Napoleon's meeting with the tsar at Erfurt in autumn 1808, a little over a year after the alliance with Russia has been signed at Tilsit. Talleyrand has resigned as foreign minister and has become instead grand chamberlain, and Vice-Grand Elector of the Empire ('the only vice he does not already have,' says Fouché, who is responsible for police, spies and mass executions) but Napoleon still prefers to prepare the meetings with him rather than with Champagny, and relies on Talleyrand in Erfurt. In Talleyrand's own account Napoleon sets out his objectives as follows: to have his hands free to deal with Spain – where he has just begun the campaign which will prove long and unsuccessful – not to be committed in any binding way to help Russia in the south against the Ottomans, and to contain Austria. The whole construct is directed against Britain.

Two days later Talleyrand delivers a draft agreement for Napoleon to put to Tsar Alexander. This translates Napoleon's ideas as principles to govern the Franco-Russian Alliance. 'I like principles.' says Napoleon, 'They don't commit me.' In fact Napoleon likes it all, except that it is not sufficiently threatening towards Austria (Talleyrand protests that Austria, being conservative and needing peace, is not a problem for France). Napoleon says he will add some articles himself, to deal with Austria.

The ten days at Erfurt are intended by Napoleon to dazzle Alexander and to convince Vienna to put aside any thoughts of renewing the war. For culture, he has brought the entire Comédie Française with him. For display, all the South German kings and princes are invited, but not Austria. The articles that Napoleon adds to Talleyrand's treaty commit Russia to fighting alongside France if Austria restarts the war. The agreement will be secret; but they will make sure that Austria knows of it. At the last minute in Erfurt Napoleon asks Talleyrand to prepare the ground with the tsar for him to marry one of the tsar's sisters, after divorcing Josephine.

At Erfurt, Talleyrand goes with Napoleon to welcome the tsar. Returning to his lodgings in the evening, he finds a note from the Princess of Tour and Taxis – this is Talleyrand, and there is usually a woman involved – and goes to see her immediately. Fifteen minutes later Alexander arrives, and at the end of the conversation he proposes that they meet in the same way every evening. Napoleon meets Alexander during the day, sometimes for talks, often for entertainment. Talleyrand sees him in the evenings. Metternich, in his memoirs, summarises Talleyrand's proposition to Alexander as follows: 'Sire, what do you have to do here? It is to save Europe. But you can do this only if you stand up to Napoleon. The French people are civilised; their sovereign is not. The sovereign of Russia is civilised; his people are not. It is therefore the sovereign of Russia who must ally himself with the French people.'[15] Later in their conversations Talleyrand gives his view that 'The Rhine, the Alps and the Pyrenees are the conquests of France. The rest are the conquests of the Emperor of France, and we shall not hold them': this while his master is planning yet more conquests![16]

Instead of making preliminary soundings with the tsar on the proposals Napoleon is going to put to him, Talleyrand spends the time explaining to him how dangerous these are for Austria and for Europe, and suggests to Alexander how best to reject them while continuing to profess friendship and admiration for Napoleon. Before he leaves Erfurt, Alexander writes to the Austrian emperor, underlining that the meetings with Napoleon have – on his part at least – in no way been directed against his country. (True: he has avoided the trap Napoleon has set.)

As for the outcome of the meeting, Napoleon does not get what he wants: he agrees to Russia maintaining its troops in Moldavia and Walachia – a concession from Tilsit – but makes clear that he will not support the tsar in Turkey; he rejects the tsar's pleas on behalf of Prussia, though he reduces its indemnity by 20 million francs. Alexander accepts Napoleon's intervention in Spain. But on Austria the agreement says only: 'In the case of Austria declaring war against France, the Emperor of Russia undertakes to denounce Austria and to make common cause with France.'[17] This sounds well but it is moral support, not a military alliance. (We can guess that Talleyrand suggested this formula.)

As he often does, Talleyrand mixes his own interests with official business. While he is advising Alexander on how to resist Napoleon's suggestion of a dynastic marriage he is seeking his support on his own account for the marriage of his nephew to the younger daughter of the Duchess of Courland. (The Duchess of Courland later becomes Talleyrand's mistress and remains a lifelong confidante.) Her daughter, Dorothée, is a rich heiress, and this would save the fortunes of his family, Talleyrand's brother having lost most of his property in the revolution. Neither mother nor daughter like this idea, but Alexander insists, and for someone whose estates are in Russia (Courland is more or less today's Latvia) there is no refusing. Talleyrand has the ironic satisfaction of saving the fortunes of the family that has largely disinherited him.

On his return from Erfurt Talleyrand remains in contact through Nesselrode, who Alexander sends to Paris expressly for this purpose. Talleyrand also begins a collaboration with Metternich, who is now Austrian ambassador in Paris. He is paid for his services by the Austrians; Alexander never responds to his requests for money. Probably he considers that he has rewarded him enough with the marriage of his nephew. This turns out indeed, to be a more valuable gift than either of them understands at the time.

Remarkably, the attack Napoleon makes on Talleyrand in the court has nothing to do with his betrayal to the tsar; it relates instead to his suspicions that Talleyrand has been conspiring with Fouché to replace him. (There is no evidence that Napoleon is right on this: Talleyrand's style is to use events, not manufacture them, and he does not trust Fouché.) On St Helena, Napoleon, among many accusations, says that he knows Talleyrand was betraying him for six months before his abdication in 1814. In fact, the betrayal had by then been going on for six years.

At this moment in 1808, Napoleon has defeated every power on Continental Europe. Those who have opposed him have lost territory and been bankrupted by indemnities – Austria and Prussia – or, like Russia, have become allies. His brothers Louis, Joseph and Jérôme are Kings of Holland, Spain and Westphalia; his brother-in-law, the cavalry commander Joachim Murat, is King of Naples. In the German lands, kingdoms like Bavaria and Saxony, which have increased their territory at the expense of Napoleon's enemies, are now dependent on his protection.

That is one way of viewing the situation. But it is also true that enemies are everywhere. The King of Prussia, Frederick William III, is weak and his country is crushed; but the officers of his army sharpen their swords on the steps of the French embassy. Scharnhorst and Gneisenau are planning reforms for the army; others such as Clausewitz will take service with Russia, who they see as more ready to fight the French. Russia itself is ambivalent about the alliance with France and never applies the Continental System, which would be ruinous for it. Nor do countries such as Holland, although one of Napoleon's brothers is on the throne. Austria, despite two lost wars with Napoleon, is looking for revenge and (with encouragement from Talleyrand) is beginning to rearm. After Erfurt, Napoleon will defeat every Spanish army and will force the small British force under Sir John Moore to evacuate. But the British return the following year, and Spanish people never accept Napoleon's brother Joseph as their king. Meanwhile Napoleon makes no progress against Britain – rather the reverse: the Continental System is *not* bringing Britain to its knees; in fact, it is doing more damage to France and its allies.

Napoleon is a military genius without a political strategy. He ignores Talleyrand's advice. He forgets Rousseau's rule: 'The strongest is never strong enough to remain the master for ever unless he knows how to transform power into right and obedience into duty.'[18]

Six months after Erfurt, Austria renews the war against France. Napoleon defeats them again at Wagram, but only after the murderous stalemate at Aspern-Essling has shown that he is not invincible. He imposes further territorial and financial penalties. As part of the settlement Austria becomes an ally of France and Napoleon, having divorced Josephine, marries the emperor's daughter, Marie-Louise. This is the marriage and the alliance that Talleyrand has recommended, but it comes too late and it is a preparation for war with Russia, not the cornerstone of a European peace.

During this period Talleyrand has little contact with Napoleon – though, strangely, the latter helps him through some of his financial difficulties.* Before Napoleon embarks on the Russian campaign in 1812 he tries to persuade Talleyrand to accompany him to Warsaw

* Napoleon has imposed two Spanish princes on Talleyrand as prisoners in Vallençay, his château in the Indre. Entertaining two princes and their retinues in the proper style, for six years, is a massive imposition. This may be Napoleon's revenge for Talleyrand's opposition to his adventures in Spain. Eventually, Napoleon has the government pay a sum towards their upkeep. Why? Napoleon knows that Talleyrand is always short of money; he sees this as a weakness to exploit.

and from there to provide advice and to keep an eye on Prussia and Austria. Talleyrand refuses. When Napoleon returns, in early 1813, with the 'Grande Armée' defeated and destroyed, Talleyrand again puts the case for peace, suggesting that Austria might be used as a mediator. He does this in the full court, knowing that he will not succeed, but he gains support from some of those closest to Napoleon. Talleyrand makes this proposal as a step for France to take towards peace. In April 1813 Metternich makes the same proposal, but for Austria it is a step towards re-entering the war and reversing its alliance from France to Russia. Talleyrand and Metternich are not acting in concert but they are in communication.

Napoleon is now facing the Sixth Coalition, which for the first time brings together all his enemies. After his defeat at Leipzig in October 1813, Napoleon tries again to persuade Talleyrand to return to his job as foreign minister. Again he refuses: there is no sense in taking responsibility when you have no influence on policy. Many of their meetings in the court bring tirades against Talleyrand for treachery; but Napoleon never breaks with him. Instead, while returning from Russia, he has blamed the failure of the campaign on his not having had Talleyrand with him. He may warn his brother Joseph: 'Do not trust this man . . . now that fortune has deserted us he is surely the greatest enemy of our family,'[19] but at the last minute, when the coalition forces are fighting on French soil and he suspects him of treason, he tries yet again to enlist Talleyrand to represent him. He remains for Napoleon 'the most capable of the ministers I had', 'the only one who was able to understand me'. Talleyrand is not trusted but he remains indispensable.[20]

Napoleon's last request for Talleyrand's support has special significance, and so does Talleyrand's refusal: it is that Talleyrand negotiate on Napoleon's behalf at Châtillon with the four allied powers. A peace agreement is possible: both Castlereagh and Metternich are prepared to make peace with Napoleon, and they have forced a reluctant Alexander to agree on the terms. Talleyrand's refusal is not because the terms are unacceptable – he will accept exactly the same terms a few weeks later – but because he thinks that Napoleon is incapable of making peace and that the only hope for Europe is to be rid of him.

Probably he is right. Napoleon himself has repeated often enough that other sovereigns, with the legitimacy of birth and history, can lose many battles and still survive. He has to lose only one battle and he is finished. That is what Talleyrand wants. Making peace on someone else's terms is something Napoleon has never done: he has built his legitimacy on military success. Once he could have made peace on generous terms and it would have been welcomed in France and Europe; now it is too late. And even if he were to accept the terms, it is difficult to believe that he would stick to them. He is addicted to glory. At this point, restoring Europe has become synonymous with restoring the Bourbons.

Henry Kissinger in his brilliant study of this time, *A World Restored* (1957), says of Talleyrand that he failed to achieve 'ultimate stature because his actions were always too precisely attuned to the dominant mood, because nothing ever engaged him so completely that he would bring to it the sacrifice of personal advancement'.[21] This is not so. At this moment Talleyrand has rejected office several times, and is in financial difficulties as a result; he now rejects a last chance to moderate Napoleon's position – probably because he knows he will fail. Meanwhile he has been risking his life by working actively for Napoleon's overthrow. One more act of betrayal lies ahead. Talleyrand's coolness conceals the risks he is taking.*

At this moment Talleyrand's position is precarious but not uncomfortable. He remains a high dignitary of the empire – though the empire is in ruins – and is also a member of the Regency Council that advises the empress while Napoleon is out of Paris. On 28 March 1814, when coalition forces are approaching Paris, Napoleon's brother Joseph calls a meeting of the council to consider whether the empress should remain in Paris. Having heard the views of the council, almost all of whom want the empress to remain – leaving looks like abandoning the

* Kissinger's portraits of Metternich and Castlereagh are brilliant; but he underestimates Talleyrand, who was trying not just to restore the Bourbons but also to change them. He was successful only as long as the British backed him and the Bourbons needed them: Wellington trusted him more than his king did.

city – Joseph reads out a letter from Napoleon in favour of evacuation. This settles the matter. The empress and the rest of the court leave on the 29th. The day after, Talleyrand is to join them; but he chooses to leave Paris by the gate at Passy; this is under the command of a friend, Charles de Rémusat, and by prior agreement the guard politely refuses him permission to pass. Thus Talleyrand remains in Paris, in appearance at least against his will.

By this time Russian troops are approaching the city and there is fighting on the outskirts. Talleyrand goes to the house of Marmont, the marshal in charge of the defence of the capital. There he meets Count Orlov, one of Alexander's aides de camp, who he knows from Tilsit and Erfurt. Orlov is there to see if he can negotiate the surrender of the city. Talleyrand asks him to 'lay at the feet of His Majesty the Emperor of Russia the deepest respect of Prince Talleyrand'.[22] Then he meets Marmont. No one knows what passes. We can imagine Talleyrand setting out the political context for him, inviting him to think about his future. Messages go to and fro between his house and Marmont's. At 3 a.m. agreement is reached and Marmont signs an armistice that surrenders the city, allowing his forces to leave peacefully. Later on, Marmont, who defended Paris fiercely the day before, defects to the coalition with his corps.

The following morning Nesselrode, since Erfurt the contact point between the tsar and Talleyrand, arrives in Paris and goes straight to Talleyrand's house. Having been told that the Élysée Palace, the tsar's intended destination, is booby-trapped, the tsar becomes a guest at Talleyrand's house.* With the court on its way to Orleans, and Napoleon on his way to defeat, Talleyrand is the nearest thing in Paris to an official French presence, and he is on good terms with Alexander.

Talleyrand and the tsar discuss the future government of France. Until then Alexander has not been a supporter of a Bourbon restoration, finding the future Louis XVIII unimpressive. He has shown interest in other solutions: Bernadotte, one of Napoleon's less reliable

* Later Talleyrand will award himself a substantial sum from government funds to cover the costs of accommodating the tsar.

marshals, lately elected King of Sweden and fighting on the side of the coalition; another member of the Bourbon dynasty, such as the liberal Duc d'Orléans ('No less a usurper for coming from a good family,' says Talleyrand);[23] or someone designated by the people of France. Talleyrand, who has served the king, been a member of the National Assembly, worked for the Directorate, and then for Napoleon first when he is consul and then when he is emperor, puts the case that the principle of legitimacy requires the succession of Louis XVIII, but as a constitutional monarch. He persuades Alexander to issue a statement in the name of the four coalition partners that they will no longer do business with Napoleon. This is on the understanding that Talleyrand will convene a meeting of the Senate to vote the end of Napoleon's reign, recall Louis XVIII under constitutional guarantees, as the people's choice, and nominate a provisional government. On 1 April Talleyrand rounds up sixty-four senators out of 140 and persuades them to do exactly that. They nominate Talleyrand to head the provisional government.

None of this is constitutional. But at this moment there is no constitution. Napoleon has lost the war; at Fontainebleau he still has 60,000 men, but it is not clear that they will obey his orders. Paris is in the hands of a foreign army, which has been welcomed by at least some of its citizens. That welcome may not last – a reason to act quickly. The tsar cannot negotiate with Napoleon and needs someone who can deal with what is left of France without him. Talleyrand stands in the middle: he is known to the leaders of both sides; he is on the spot in Paris with the (self-appointed) representative of the coalition. Above all, he knows what he wants. He has thought it through in advance: the question of legitimacy, the position of the coalition, and the means to give his solution a coating of legitimate authority.

Nevertheless, this is a high-wire act. Unlike the other actors in the drama he has no army, no money, no authority; he depends on his personal credibility and his ability to persuade. Even so, two days after everything seems settled, Napoleon sends a delegation offering to abdicate in favour of his infant son – and the tsar, living up to his reputation for volatility, needs persuading not to accept this, in spite of his proclamation that he will no longer do business with Napoleon or his family.

In retrospect it is clear that Talleyrand's solution is the only one that would have been acceptable to the other members of the coalition, something that seems not to have figured either in Alexander's thinking or in his discussions with Talleyrand. The tsar does not consult anyone, not even Talleyrand (consultation not being a habit of tsars) when he agrees with Caulaincourt on a treaty that allows Napoleon to keep his title of emperor and be exiled on Elba, dangerously close to France. This infuriates the other allies, but it is too late.

When his brief period as head of the provisional government is ended by the arrival of the Comte d'Artois, representing the king, Talleyrand takes on the negotiations with the four coalition foreign ministers for a peace agreement. Given that these take place only days after the last battles have been fought, the results are remarkably favourable to France; Emmanuel de Waresquiel summarises them admirably as 'old regime, old frontiers'.[24]

France loses its conquests but gains a small amount of territory compared with its position before the wars, including the papal enclave of Avignon and some territory on its eastern border. French colonies seized during the wars are returned, with minor exceptions. Britain cannot give up its habit of acquiring islands: so it takes Malta, Mauritius and its dependencies; and the Cape of Good Hope from the Dutch. There is no indemnity; instead, some of France's debts are cancelled. Britain has been the paymaster of the coalition, and this is Castlereagh's treaty, notably in building up Holland so it will be strong enough to keep Antwerp out of dangerous hands.

It remains an extraordinarily generous settlement for a country that has laid Europe waste and forced punitive peace treaties on Austria and Prussia. This is less the result of Talleyrand's negotiating skills than the British and Austrian relief that Napoleon is gone, and a wish to give the Bourbons the best chance of success: the enemy is revolution and the best guarantee of peace in Europe will be stability in France. The treaty also includes liberal provisions such as freedom of navigation on the Rhine and a commitment by France to abolish the slave trade in five years. Compared with the treaties that Napoleon has forced on defeated countries – many of them negotiated by Talleyrand – it is a model of moderation. On 31 May, the day after the treaty is signed, Talleyrand writes to the Duchess of Courland that it has been done 'on the basis of the greatest possible equality'.[25]

The Treaty of Paris makes peace with France and deals with the western part of Europe. More complicated problems await in Central Europe: the tsar is becoming enthusiastic about a 'free' Poland, and the Prussians want to know what their reward is going to be. To deal with these and broader questions, such as the organisation of the German states, the four allies agree to meet in Vienna with representatives of all the countries that have been involved in the wars. Metternich expects this to last no more than a few weeks.

The Congress of Vienna

When he arrives in Vienna on 23 September 1814 for the congress, Talleyrand finds that the spirit of equality he reported to the Duchess of Courland has all but gone.

The day before Talleyrand's arrival in Vienna the four allies sign an agreement on how they will conduct the business of the congress – with some unease on the part of Castlereagh, who foresees occasions on which French support could serve his interests. The four decide to follow the argument of Hardenberg, the representative of the King of Prussia, that with France's borders already agreed in the Treaty of Paris, what they have to do is to dispose of the territories reconquered from Napoleon, and it is the four who have done the conquering. As Friedrich von Gentz, Metternich's cynical assistant and the secretary of the Congress, writes, their aim is less to re-establish peace on the basis of a fair division of power than to divide among themselves 'the booty taken from the conquered'.[26]

Talleyrand has no interest in the booty, only in returning France to the top table, where it belongs. He attacks this way the congress is proceeding on three levels. First, in a famous scene, he attacks the legitimacy of the agreement among the four. Invited by Metternich to join a meeting with them and to read their proposed communiqué, he picks up the term 'the allies', by which they refer to themselves in each paragraph, and asks them what they mean by it: 'Has peace not been made? If there is a war, against whom is it fought?' He reads them the document again, out loud, with an air of puzzlement, and repeats his inability to understand it: 'For me there are only two dates – 30 May, when the holding of the congress was agreed [in the Treaty of Paris] and 1 October, when it is supposed to meet, and there is nothing in between.'[27] At the end of this dialogue, in which the Spanish representative, the Marquis of Labrador, invited with Talleyrand, supports him, the four take their paper back and decide not to issue it.

They then attempt to persuade Talleyrand and Labrador to put their names to a separate document about the management of the congress. This is an attempt to get Spain and France to support the procedure they have agreed among themselves. In return for admitting them as members of a second circle, they want their consent to the four working on their own in an inner circle. Talleyrand again refuses and will hear nothing of the arguments the four make about the chaos that would result if everybody is allowed to participate. At the end of the proceedings von Gentz writes in his diary: 'The intervention of these two persons violently disrupted our plans, and reduced them to naught . . . They berated us vigorously for two hours: it is a scene I shall never forget.'[28]

Talleyrand not only makes life difficult for the four in private; he also responds to them in writing, complaining that they are assuming a right of decision that no one has given them. Then – and this is the second level of his attack – he leaks these notes to others in Vienna, amplifying the embarrassment for Metternich as host, and for all of the four.

A few days later there is a further scene. The plan of the four is to open the congress when they have worked out the main lines of the settlement. This turns out to be more difficult than they have expected and they need to announce a delay in the formal opening. Invited to join the four in an announcement of a further delay, Talleyrand agrees, but on the condition that a reference is made to the congress taking place 'in accordance with the principles of public law' (today we would say 'international law'). This provokes fury from Hardenberg, who, fists on the table, explodes:

'Public law! That is useless. . . . Why say that we are acting according to public law? That goes without saying.'
Talleyrand: 'If it goes without saying, it will go all the better if we say it.'
Humboldt (Hardenberg's colleague), shouting: 'What do we have to do here with public law?'
Talleyrand: 'It is why you are here.'[29]

And indeed it is. The congress has been called in virtue of an international treaty. Von Gentz, meanwhile, is making the point to Metternich that, given that this is an international congress, it is hardly possible to refuse to speak of international law. He guesses, no doubt, that the story will be around Vienna in a matter of minutes. Metternich puts the question to a vote and they accept Talleyrand's addition and get his signature.

This conversation echoes one that Talleyrand has had earlier with Alexander in which the tsar, speaking of the prospects for the congress, said that the outcome will have to follow the interests of each:

Talleyrand: 'And their rights.'
Alexander: 'I will keep what I hold.'
Talleyrand: 'Your Majesty will wish to keep only what is legitimately yours.'
Alexander: 'I am in agreement with the great powers on this.'
Talleyrand: 'I do not know if Your Majesty includes France as one of them.'
Alexander: 'Yes, but if you do not want the outcome to follow their interests, what do you want?'
Talleyrand: 'The law comes first, the interests after it.'
Alexander: 'The interests of Europe are the law.'

Talleyrand: 'Sire, this cannot be you speaking. This language is alien to you; and your heart will not accept it.'[30]

Talleyrand manipulates ideas as he manipulates people; coming from a defeated and disgraced power that has rediscovered legitimacy, he does not have many other cards to play. The law is the defence of the weak against the powerful – enabling him to use it as a standard around which to rally the smaller powers.

But there is more to it than this. Talleyrand has never liked the overthrow of old-established kings and kingdoms. He does not like the idea of the post-war settlement also taking place on the basis that might is right. He has, after all, been risking his life to oppose Napoleon, because he detested rule by conquest – the only law the emperor recognised. At just this time he is writing privately to the Duchess of Courland: 'I recognise in all the cabinets [of the allies] the principles and manner of thought of Bonaparte.'[31] And he does not like it.

What Alexander has, which he intends to hold, is Poland. He is a man capable of great generosity and of great self-delusion. He has conceived a commitment to the cause of a free and united Poland; and he has decided that he will end the partition – widely regarded as a disgraceful event – and recreate a Polish kingdom as a part of the Russian Empire. Alexander wants to be seen in Europe as a liberator; but he also has to do what the Russian army and elite expect of him, namely acquire a large piece of territory as a reward for its victory. A united Poland inside Russia is his way of squaring the circle, but it is a fantasy that this will be free: conditions in Russia will never allow that.

This also leaves the problem of how to compensate the King of Prussia for the slice of Prussia the tsar needs to reconstitute Poland in its old borders (and inside Russia). Alexander's solution is to hand Saxony over to Prussia. The King of Saxony has found himself on the wrong side at the end of the war and his country is in the hands of the Russian army. Alexander refers obliquely to this in the same conversation with Talleyrand. Neither Poland nor Saxony is mentioned by name, but he refers to 'those who have betrayed the cause of Europe'. Talleyrand replies: 'There, Sire, there is a question of dates,' and, after a pause, 'and the difficulties that circumstances may place people in.'[32] This is a striking reply. To remind the tsar that he too, after Tilsit, has been an ally of Napoleon, but to do so in a delicate and courteous way, you must be quick-witted and subtle, and also courageous.

Moreover, this is in perfect accord with Talleyrand's instructions. France does not have demands for itself at Vienna; but Louis XVIII does not want a fellow monarch deprived of his throne. (The only other concrete objective Talleyrand has been given is to secure the kingdom of Naples for its legitimate Bourbon monarch, who has been displaced by Joachim Murat.)

Talleyrand's efforts to re-establish France as one of the great powers of Europe are unsuccessful. He embarrasses the four with his logic; and he makes himself a constant source of irritation by mobilising the smaller powers against the procedure that the four have set up for themselves. But he makes no real progress. This is not just a matter of national prestige: France has an interest in the outcome. French territory may not be at stake but the nature of France's neighbours is. France's interest is a strong Austria to avoid the risk of a strong Germany: this has been a constant theme of Talleyrand's with Napoleon. Now it is the question at issue. Louis XVIII's views on legitimacy and Talleyrand's on the political geography of Europe coincide.

But Talleyrand has still not been able to stop the four excluding him and making the deal among themselves. The only people who can stop that are the four themselves. And that is what they do.

This is an ill-assorted quartet, but they are talented and powerful men. Twenty-five years of war and negotiation in Europe have brought the most skilful diplomats to power, as well as the best generals. Alexander fits poorly with the others because he is a sovereign with absolute power in his own country, used to being obeyed. And he does not delegate to Nesselrode, as the emperor does to Metternich, and Frederick William does to Hardenberg. This makes negotiation difficult. Diplomacy is designed with many escape valves. When things become tense, diplomats, even ministers, can maintain friendly relations with their counterparts by explaining that they are only following instructions; this helps prevent quarrels from becoming personal.

That does not work when the supreme authority is at the table.

As a man who knew neither exaggeration nor irony, Alexander is not well placed to deal with the subtle and serpentine Metternich, vain but with much to be vain about, a diplomatic professional, now Austria's foreign minister, always thinking two or three steps ahead.

Hardenberg, representing a weak king and the weakest of the powers, is in a difficult position. For the Prussians these negotiations are a matter of their survival as a first-rank power. Unless they recuperate the territory detached by Napoleon or acquire something similar in compensation, they will become a secondary power like Bavaria or Württemberg, not taken seriously. Prussia's recovery owes much to Russia; this is a weakness, since it makes it difficult to oppose Alexander. The only thing Hardenberg can be sure of is the strength of the Prussian army. He is an immensely courteous man: his outbursts reflect the tension he is under.

Finally there is Castlereagh, representing the superpower of the day, paymaster of the coalition. When the business is about France, Britain knows what it wants. Castlereagh has set the terms of the Treaty of Chaumont, which solidified the alliance – keeping coalitions together has been a major aim of British policy for the last twenty years. He has also drawn up terms of the offer made to France at Châtillon (where Talleyrand has refused Napoleon's request to represent him), and these are the basis of the Treaty of Paris. It is Castlereagh who, at the negotiations with Talleyrand in Paris, dismissed the Prussian demand for the repayment of the reparations they had paid to Napoleon. The Prussian demand was for 170 million francs; Castlereagh dealt with that by pointing out that Britain had subsidised the coalition to the tune of £700 million – 100 times the sum that Prussia was demanding – and was not asking for a penny of it back. Britain got what it wanted in Paris: Louis XVIII restored and Antwerp out of French hands. Castlereagh knows little of Poland or Saxony; thinking on British interests does not extend so far afield.

The structure of the Polish problem is as follows: Alexander wants all of Poland inside Russia. For the other three this brings Russia too far into Europe. If Austria, Prussia and Britain are united they might be able to persuade Alexander to back down. But the Prussian king owes his survival to Russian support; and Hardenberg wants to know what Prussia will get if it loses its Polish lands. Alexander has no qualms about handing Saxony over to Prussia – which would be a solution for Prussia. For a time, Castlereagh too is ready to agree to this as an inducement to get Hardenberg to oppose Alexander on Poland. But Austria will not accept the elimination of Saxony: for the Austrian emperor, this is not how you treat a legitimate monarch; for Metternich it makes Prussia into a dangerous rival in Germany. If Prussia supports Russian policy on Poland it will lose British support on Saxony. The problem is not complicated. It is just that there is no solution that satisfies everyone.

The discussions and exchanges of notes on this issue occupy the four from their arrival in September to the end of the year (along with balls, mistresses and Talleyrand). By December the atmosphere is so heated that Alexander tries to get the emperor to dismiss Metternich. Alexander himself has meanwhile created facts on the ground in Saxony by handing the occupation over to Prussian forces. Then Hardenberg takes the unprecedented step of showing Alexander the letters Metternich has sent him, without asking Metternich – a breach of confidence and good manners. Metternich then shows Alexander the letters he has from Hardenberg – though, correctly, first seeking his permission. The loser in these exchanges is Alexander himself, who is exposed as having misrepresented each to the other. Castlereagh is out of this, described by his own ministry as 'wandering in mazes lost' and by Talleyrand as 'a traveller who has lost his way . . . ashamed of having been the dupe of Prussia'.[33]

At the end of three months the atmosphere has become so bad that there is a threat of war among the allies. The armies have not been demobilised and Central Europe is covered with armed men. The Russian military are saying it will be better to fight sooner rather than later if Russia is being denied what it has won in the war. The Austrians have 370,000 men and are deploying into Bohemia, on the borders of Saxony. Hardenberg has consulted the military, and, finding that they would be heavily dependent on Russian support, grows increasingly nervous and unable to sleep.[34] Both Austria and Prussia are seeking allies among the smaller German states.

It is in this super-heated atmosphere that Castlereagh writes to the prime minister, Lord Liverpool, to suggest that the only way to avoid conflict would be armed mediation jointly by Britain and France. This must have been an alarming message for Liverpool: the notion of armed mediation contains an implicit threat that if an agreement is not reached the mediator will take sides against the party that has turned down their proposal. It must also have been a surprise since it puts Britain at the side of France, after they have been at war for twenty years.

The idea of armed mediation has echoes of Metternich's step-by-step method of escaping Austria's alliance with France and joining Russia and Prussia. If Talleyrand has had a hand in planning that strategy with Metternich, is it possible that he has now put the ideas into Castlereagh's head? There is no evidence, but this idea does not sound like something the conservative Castlereagh would come up with on his own.

That is no more than speculation. But it is at this moment that Talleyrand decides to join the debate, instead of sniping from the sidelines at the way the four have been handling the issue. He does this in a letter to Metternich, which he makes public on 19 December. This is a different method of operating from the secretive bilateral exchanges that have gone on among the allies and that have brought them to the brink of war. Talleyrand's timing is right – the four have run out of ideas and are talking of force, which is to say they are on the brink of a diplomatic failure. Even more impressive is Talleyrand's patience in waiting for this moment. Tracking their manoeuvres, watching them get into a mess, seeing the problem more clearly than they do – because it is not, directly, his problem – seeing where the solution will probably lie. To see all this and then to do nothing shows a high degree of confidence and control.

The problem of Poland has arisen because Napoleon created the Duchy of Warsaw, with a promise to restore Poland's independence; though under Napoleon no one was ever independent. He added to its territory each time he was in a position to punish Austria or Prussia.

Talleyrand's letter takes as its starting point the situation before Napoleon, and notes that none of the three parties to the partition of Poland – Prussia, Austria and Russia – are ready to give up their share. The status quo before Napoleon is therefore the right place to start looking for a solution.

The letter goes on to say that on this basis, the problem is to find adequate compensation for Prussia to restore it to its former status. Dispossessing the King of Saxony will not do: it is not legitimate, being contrary to European public law – the principle on which Talleyrand has insisted all along. This is correct: customarily, those who choose the wrong side in a war may lose some of their territory, but not all. It is for this reason that the partition of Poland was never regarded as legitimate. It is not, Talleyrand says, for Prussia to state what she will take, but for the legitimate king to say what he will give up.[35]

This may be sufficient for Castlereagh to see his way out of the maze; but, on its own, it is not enough to persuade Russia to abandon its claim on Poland, nor Prussia on Saxony. Both are thinking in military terms; and they will abandon their positions only if the military threat will not work. Ten days after Talleyrand has circulated his letter Hardenberg is still announcing that if Prussia is denied Saxony it will regard that as a declaration of war.

Castlereagh has meanwhile come to talk to Talleyrand about the establishment of a statistical commission to help determine exactly what territory (or population) Prussia should be granted to return it to its pre-Napoleonic size. Talleyrand turns the conversation to the question of Saxony and mentions the possibility of a 'little convention' between the two of them and Metternich, to affirm the rights of the King of Saxony.

Castlereagh: 'You are proposing an alliance?'
Talleyrand: 'We could have the convention without an alliance; but if you want, it could be an alliance.'
Castlereagh: 'An alliance implies a war or can lead to one, and we must do everything to avoid war.'

Talleyrand: 'I agree with you. We must do everything – except to sacrifice honour, justice and the future of Europe.'

Castlereagh: 'War will not be well regarded at home.'

Talleyrand: 'It will be popular if it is for a great European cause.'

Castlereagh: 'What would that be?'

Talleyrand: 'The re-establishment of Poland.'

Castlereagh – [the account is Talleyrand's] – does not reject these ideas, but only says: 'Not yet.'[36]

Two days later, on 30 December, Castlereagh argues for bringing Talleyrand into the meetings of the four powers. Only Prussia now objects. But the atmosphere is so bad that he judges that the risk of war is now real, and decides to turn Talleyrand's 'convention' into a formal defensive alliance.[37]

He does not know it but in fact, the political and military balance is shifting in the direction of the powers opposing Prussia and Russia. German states such as Bavaria are not attracted by the idea of Saxony being wiped off the map by Prussia. Talleyrand, who has been courting the smaller countries all this time, is now mobilising them to sign a petition in support of Saxony. But the biggest change is that on Christmas Eve 1814 – though no one in Vienna knows it – Britain has agreed peace terms with the United States, ending the war of 1812. This potentially frees an army of 150,000 to return to Europe. The news reaches Vienna on New Year's Day 1815. On 3 January a secret alliance is signed between Austria, Britain and France for mutual support in the event of any one of them being attacked in the context of the implementation of the Treaty of Paris. Talleyrand writes to Louis the following day, proclaiming with a keenly felt triumph that the coalition against France has been dissolved.[38]

Human stupidity should never be underestimated; but the reality is that no one wants to fight. In joining France and Austria, Castlereagh has gone beyond his instructions; France, for its part, is exhausted and tired of war – and, as the next months will show, much of the army is loyal to Napoleon rather than to France; Austria is bankrupt. On the other side too, Prussia is still awaiting further subsidies from Britain and

Hardenberg is becoming aware how much they depend on Russian support. Alexander does not want to lose his mantle as the liberator of Europe and is beginning to moderate his belligerent tone. The Russian army wants to go home.

Renewal of the war would be a nightmare on all sides. The shock of the Treaty of Alliance between Austria, Britain and France, with commitments to troop numbers for each of the allies, is needed to remind everybody of this, and to bring them back to reality.

The Statistical Commission on Prussia has begun its work on 24 December, including a single French representative – a compromise agreed between Castlereagh and Hardenberg: the other four each have two delegates. From 5 January Talleyrand joins the other four in all their meetings, re-establishing France as one of the great powers.

Talleyrand's handling of this question is a lesson in the art of seduction – especially of Castlereagh – and also in the reality of power. It is not only Talleyrand's cleverness that brings France back to the table but also the fact that France is an essential part of the European balance. The Treaty of Alliance, including troop numbers, is the proof of this. From the moment France joins the meetings, they become more formal and businesslike, and the congress begins to make progress.

As far as the Poland-Saxony question is concerned, the Treaty of Alliance of 3 January is a turning point, not an end point. Tension continues through January, especially with the Prussians. But Alexander is sobered by the news brought by the Duke of Wellington (who arrives to take over from Castlereagh) that the French government is strong and the army is in good shape. Nor is Alexander pleased to hear from Talleyrand that France would present a war as being for the liberation of Poland. This would not only expose his hypocrisy; it would also mean that most of his Polish officers and troops would change sides.

One incident among many deserves attention. In his desperation to acquire Saxony, Hardenberg approaches Talleyrand to suggest that, if he agrees to Prussia taking Saxony, he will support France acquiring Belgium.[39] Talleyrand refuses. He is not Napoleon. He does not believe that territory brings power or wealth. Having watched the return to war with Britain in 1803 and, having negotiated the Treaty of Paris six months ago, he knows that this particular piece of territory brings with it the enmity of Britain. Against this, demonstrating to Castlereagh and Metternich that he and France can be trusted is much more useful. As Henry Kissinger points out: 'he gained something much more important, the end of the isolation of France and the recognition of its equality'.[40] Talleyrand is acting on the principles he set out for Danton twenty-two years earlier.

On 6 March 1815 the five powers reach an agreement on the Saxony-Poland question, and decide that Talleyrand, Metternich and Wellington are the best placed to persuade the King of Saxony to accept it. They start discussing how all this should be presented in the Final Act of the congress.

This goes on until 3 a.m., and Metternich leaves an instruction for his valet that he is not to be disturbed. However at 6 a.m. a letter arrives marked urgent, and the valet wakes him. Metternich looks at the envelope – it seems to be from his consul in Genoa. It cannot be important. He puts it on the table and goes back to sleep. But, having been disturbed, he does not sleep well; an hour later he wakes and reads the letter. It says:

> The English Commissioner, Campbell, has just sailed into the harbour to enquire whether there has been any sighting of Napoleon, given that he has disappeared from the island of Elba. The answer being negative, the English frigate put to sea without delay.[41]

The Hundred Days*

When news comes, it is in fragments. But this is enough to turn things upside down. Now everything is at risk. Talleyrand does not wait. He nails his colours to the Bourbon mast. He drafts a statement in language of a strength rarely seen. All the sovereigns assembled in Vienna sign it and declare Napoleon an enemy and an outlaw. Any who might

* The period between Napoleon's escape from exile and the Restoration of Louis XVIII.

be tempted to make deals with Napoleon, notably the Austrians, are obliged to nail their colours to the same mast; anything else would be a disaster for France and for Europe. The campaign that follows costs 120,000 lives; it costs France the goodwill of the allies that the initial restoration had brought, and Louis XVIII a large part of his credibility.

From Talleyrand's point of view, the Hundred Days has one useful effect: it settles the last of his tasks, the restoration of a Bourbon king in Naples. This has been profitable work for Talleyrand, since he has been taking money from both sides. This might have led to an embarrassing situation, but Murat solves the problem by declaring war on Austria when he hears of Napoleon's escape from Elba. He is defeated without difficulty and Ferdinand IV returns from Sicily as king.

Talleyrand remains in Vienna with the intention of signing the Final Act of the congress – which, it seems to him, others are trying to delay, hoping that the new hostilities might bring more territory for them. But in the end the 121 Articles of the Final Act are agreed and signed at a grand ceremony on 9 June.* Talleyrand leaves Vienna on the 10th. The king has promised him that he will head his next administration. This is in spite of some reporting from Vienna, remarkable for its frankness about the mistakes the king has made following the restoration.

On his way to meet the king in Ghent, Talleyrand prepares a further report for him. Part of this is the normal ambassadorial report on the congress, and of his successes there – which are considerable; but the largest part concerns the changing nature of legitimacy and the need to take account of public opinion. It is remarkable for its clear thinking. It is as frank as anything he has written for Napoleon – and it is no more effective.[42]

Talleyrand catches up with the king, now on his way back to France, at Mons, and has a lengthy interview with him: 'I am not much satisfied with my first meeting,' he writes to the Duchess of Courland. This is an understatement, since the Comte de Beugnot's account says he saw Talleyrand shortly after, very angry. And then, it seems, there

* This returns some of its Polish lands to Prussia, and awards it almost half of Saxony (but not Dresden and Leipzig), together with territory on the Rhine.

is to be no second interview. Learning the next morning that the king is about to depart without telling him, Talleyrand hurries (for once) to see him off. Sitting in his coach, the king says to him: 'Are you leaving us? The waters will surely do you good. Be sure to send us your news.' All this in a light-hearted manner.

This is an extraordinary way to dismiss someone you have promised will lead your government. Talleyrand remains at Mons. He eats dinner with Beugnot, who later writes:

> he was an excellent companion . . . in a charming mood pouring out his wit in delightful anecdotes and striking phrases. I had never known him so open and agreeable . . . No one would have taken him for a minister who had been disgraced a few hours earlier. Was it that Monsieur Talleyrand was rejoicing to lose the burden of dealing with all the problems of France, more difficult than ever at this moment? Or was he hiding under this gaiety the anger and regret that was consuming him inside? The second is certainly the more likely. But what sort of man is he then, this Monsieur de Talleyrand?[43]

The following day a message arrives summoning both to a meeting of the Council of Ministers at Cambrai. The meeting takes place two days later in the presence of Wellington and of the ambassadors of Austria and Russia, who, it seems, have called the king to order. This transformation has been brought about by the Congress of Vienna. Until recently the British have distrusted Talleyrand so much that they have tried to settle the question of Naples behind his back, working through the king's minister in Paris. (This doesn't work anyway; the negotiations have to be in Vienna, where all the interested parties are present.) Now Wellington insists that Louis restore Talleyrand to his promised position. When the meeting opens Talleyrand takes his place as prime minister, as though nothing has happened.

In a somewhat subdued atmosphere, Beugnot reads out a draft statement which he and Talleyrand have worked on together. It says exactly the opposite of the statement the king made three days earlier: now the king admits he has made mistakes and offers an amnesty for those who have supported Napoleon. He promises guarantees of liberty and says he will govern through a united administration. This last phrase is code for the exclusion of other members of his family, notably the Comte d'Artois, from the council. There follows an exchange between him and Talleyrand.

Artois: 'This is demeaning for royalty.'

Talleyrand: 'The king has made mistakes. His attachments have led him astray. There is nothing wrong with saying that.'

Artois: 'Is it me that you are referring to – indirectly [in the word 'attachments']?'

Talleyrand: 'Yes, since Monsieur puts it that way. Monsieur has done much harm.'

Artois: 'The Prince de Talleyrand forgets himself!'

Talleyrand: 'I fear it is true. I was carried away by the truth.'[44]

And the statement is published as it is drafted.

This is a remarkable exchange between a minister, in disgrace two days before, on his first appearance at the court and the brother of the king, the heir to the throne. It is also interesting because, unlike many of the other encounters described in this chapter, the account is not from Talleyrand's own pen but from several witnesses. Henry Kissinger discounts Talleyrand's letters to Louis XVIII from Vienna on the grounds that he is trying to win the king's support and may therefore be showing himself in a light that is more flattering than truthful. As Kissinger says in *White House Years*, he has yet to read a record by an ambassador of a conversation in which the ambassador got the worst of the argument. In that spirit the reader of Talleyrand's letters is justified in wondering if he really did, for example, say to Alexander that treason was a question of dates; it would require quickness of mind and a good deal of courage to speak in this way. But if he is ready to talk in these terms to the king's brother, in front of the full court, why not also believe his account of how he has spoken to the Tsar of Russia, tête-à-tête?

As the head of the new government Talleyrand's first task is to turn into policy the liberal sentiments in the statement that he and the European powers have forced on the king at Cambrai. This is an uphill battle to limit purges (he gets rid of Fouché by sending him as ambassador to the United States) and to put through liberal legislation with a king unhappy at the way that his minister is usurping his right of initiative. The ultra-conservative faction in the background is baying for his blood.

His second task is to deal with the European powers. There is no negotiation for the second Treaty of Paris: Talleyrand is presented with the terms by the four allies and told that they do not propose to negotiate. France will lose territory to Holland, Sardinia and Prussia (though less than Prussia has been demanding); it will pay an indemnity; and there will be a seven-year occupation. Talleyrand protests, with perfect logic, that in 1814 they had been fighting France and it was correct to end that war with a peace treaty. This time they had been fighting a common enemy, namely Napoleon, and there is no reason to punish France, though it might be expected to contribute to the expenses of the campaign.

It is no longer about logic. The ease with which Napoleon has made himself the master of France and a danger to Europe, has shocked the allies and swept away the goodwill that attended the first restoration. The British water down Prussian demands; but in every capital the outcome of Vienna has been unpopular and governments are under pressure to treat France harshly. Talleyrand takes the allied proposals to the king and suggests he makes a personal appeal to his brother monarchs, saying he cannot continue on the throne under such conditions.

This might have worked: no one would have wanted the turbulence of an abdication, nor the Comte d'Artois on the throne. The advantages to the allies of the territorial changes are trivial, except perhaps for Prussia. Talleyrand says that, personally, he would rather resign than accept such terms. 'Well then,' says the king calmly after a short silence, 'I will find another minister.'[45] For once Talleyrand is taken by surprise.

The king, Talleyrand says, seems relieved. Talleyrand is too liberal for him and too independent. For the first time since 1798 Talleyrand is out of office.

Out of office

So he remains for fifteen years, Grand Chamberlain to a king who neither likes nor trusts him. At the beginning he hopes for a return to office. But as the governments become less liberal Talleyrand is increasingly identified with the opposition. Meanwhile, he completes some personal business left over from Vienna, helping Ferdinand IV of Naples secure an indemnity from the pope for lands given back to the Papal States when he returned to Naples; these include Benevento, the principality Napoleon had given to Talleyrand. In compensation for this, the pope grants Talleyrand the revenues of the estates there, and Ferdinand gives him the Duchy of Dino. He passes the title to his nephew, or rather to his nephew's wife, Dorothée, daughter of his mistress and friend, the Duchess of Courland. The Duchess of Courland herself dies in 1821; Talleyrand remains her friend to the end. Dorothée is known thereafter as the Duchess of Dino. Talleyrand has taken her with him, to act as his hostess during the Congress of Vienna, perhaps to help her recover from the death of one of her children, perhaps because she is young, beautiful and intelligent. By the end of Talleyrand's exile from power she has become his constant companion, and the great love of his life.

At the age of seventy-six, Talleyrand plays a part in the events leading up to the July Revolution that brings Louis-Philippe to the throne, his third *coup d'état*. He helps the journalist Adolphe Thiers finance his new paper, *Le National*; and he is in contact with Louis-Philippe as the revolution unfolds. When a delegation asks Louis-Philippe to accept the title of Lieutenant-General, replacing Charles X (formerly the Comte d'Artois), he sends a message to Talleyrand asking what he should do. 'He should accept,' replies Talleyrand. Later he justifies this: 'It is not I who have abandoned the king; it is the king who abandoned us.' Just as he has written earlier that he did not betray Napoleon: 'Napoleon betrayed himself.'[46]

London and Belgium

Any revolution in France makes Europe nervous. For the new regime, recognition and support from European powers are vital to its survival. Talleyrand goes to London as ambassador: this is not an honour for an elder statesman but the heart of Louis-Philippe's policy. He needs peace to consolidate his power and the key is in London. Talleyrand is respected and trusted by conservatives such as the Duke of Wellington, prime minister at the time of his appointment, but also by liberal aristocrats such as Lord Holland. The Orléanist revolution is popular among supporters of parliamentary reform in Britain. When Talleyrand arrives at Dover in September 1830 – thirty-six years since he was expelled from Britain as a refugee – he is welcomed with a six-gun salute from the government, and by an enthusiastic crowd that pulls his carriage from the quayside to his hotel.

He is almost immediately engaged in a negotiation that is a coda to the Congress of Vienna. It takes place among the same five powers, but this time Talleyrand is an equal partner from the start. Since the subject of the negotiation is Belgium, France and Britain are the main protagonists. Those who were nervous about revolution in France become even more nervous when the July Revolution in France is followed by an August Revolution in Belgium demanding independence from Holland. In France this arouses excitement among nostalgic revolutionaries and Bonapartists; in Europe it provokes both Russia and Prussia to prepare for intervention to defend the status quo. French policy – neither to intervene nor to accept intervention by any other power – has been formulated in Paris before the negotiations begin; it is an approach in line with Talleyrand's own thinking.

In fact, France intervenes twice to protect the Belgians from the Dutch army, but on each occasion with the agreement of Britain. On the second, Talleyrand negotiates an alliance between Britain and France, threatening joint action against Holland if it does not withdraw its forces. Asked what the French policy of non-intervention means,

Talleyrand replies: 'It is a word with both a metaphysical and political sense that means more or less the same thing as intervention.'[47] But the principle of non-intervention, on the condition that others do not intervene, becomes the basis of France's policy towards all its neighbours over the next half-century.

The negotiations are more complicated than the solution, which is that Belgium becomes independent, with its neutrality guaranteed by the five powers. This lasts until the First World War, when Belgian neutrality becomes the *casus belli* for Britain fighting on the side of France. The agreement is rounded off by finding a king for Belgium who has strong links to Britain – he is uncle to the future Queen Victoria – and by finding a wife for him who is daughter of Louis-Philippe. As for the barrier fortresses on the French border with Belgium, once a key policy issue and partly paid for by the indemnity in the second Treaty of Paris, Talleyrand sees them as a second-order problem. And so they are. On a border with Holland, or of a Belgium occupied by foreign troops, they might be seen as a threat to France. But, belonging to a small, friendly neighbour whose neutrality is guaranteed by the great powers, they become meaningless; and, as Talleyrand predicts, 'They will fall down because no one repairs them.'[48]

This is not a negotiation on the scale of the Congress of Vienna but it is a fitting way for Talleyrand to end his diplomatic life. Negotiations that prevent wars are as important as those that end them, though they are less celebrated. For Talleyrand it also means breaking out of the framework of Vienna and Paris, which was conceived partly without France and partly against France. The success is achieved through a partnership of the two liberal powers, Britain and France.

This partnership is not destined to last. The turbulence in Europe has far to go. France in 1830 is still torn between different ideas of legitimacy and different visions of foreign policy; Britain is no less divided between those who see its future in European terms and those who regard Europe as a source of trouble or a distraction from Britain's global destiny.

Monsieur de Talleyrand: the uncorrupted mind

As the Comte de Beugnot asks: 'What sort of man is he then, this Monsieur de Talleyrand?'

He was an extraordinary man in extraordinary times. To have been at the centre of things and to have survived was already something. But though he was at the centre and though he was one of the clearest minds of his time, for long periods Talleyrand had little influence on policy. His ideas matched neither those of Napoleon nor the Bourbons. Yet at two critical moments he served France and Europe well.

Talleyrand's life was scandalous. Even by the standards of the day his liaisons and mistresses, and even his marriage, went beyond what was normal, especially for one who started life in the Church. Having relationships with both the mother (the Duchess of Courland) and the daughter (the Duchess of Dino) was the sort of thing that excited gossip. Dorothée was a real love but she was also his niece; even this scandalous couple made an attempt to hide the fact that her last child was Talleyrand's.

Talleyrand was guilty of corruption, of betrayal of governments, perhaps also of friends, of scandalous behaviour, of breaking his vows as priest and bishop. Almost everybody in France saw him as having betrayed something: the Church, his class, the king, the emperor or the revolution. But he was loyal to France, or to a certain vision of France, one that was ahead of the times. First, a word about his qualities.

The qualities most difficult to convey are his charm and wit. Diplomacy is about people and about words: knowing people, knowing what they want, knowing how to persuade them. The witnesses to Talleyrand's charm are endless. We have seen the Comte de Beugnot describing Talleyrand as an amusing and agreeable companion even during what must have been a crisis in his life. Witty remarks are stale when recounted second-hand; charm does not come across on the printed page. The conversation that Talleyrand himself most admired was that of his mother, who spoke by nuances and never delivered a *bon mot*. They were too self-conscious; she used words that would charm and vanish as they were spoken.[49] Talleyrand's own conversation had some of this quality too.

The best witness is Madame de la Tour du Pin, a beautiful and honest young lady exiled in upstate New York to escape the revolution: 'I was out in the yard, chopper in hand, busy cutting the bone of a leg of mutton which I was about to roast on the spit for our dinner. . . . Suddenly, from behind me, a deep voice remarked in French: 'Never was a leg of mutton spitted with greater majesty'. Turning round quickly, I saw M. de Talleyrand.' And later:

> M. de Talleyrand had a grace and ease which have never been surpassed. He had known me since my childhood and always talked to me with an almost paternal kindness, which was delightful. One might, in one's inmost mind, regret having so many reasons for not holding him in respect, but memories of his wrongdoing were always dispelled by an hour of his conversation.[50]

This is a single illustration. The rest is best left to the imagination. In speech as in thought, he was a man incapable of being ordinary.

Talleyrand understood the nature of power better than either the Bourbons or Napoleon. Napoleon took the revolution abroad with armies that embodied some of its values: the career open to all talents and the *levée en masse* brought a message of equality and fraternity. But they left liberty behind; and that was the origin of their failure. In the previous century, wars had been fought with limited armies for limited objectives. In defeat the loser handed over some territory and the people who lived on it. Now it was more difficult to treat people as though they were a dairy herd (to quote Talleyrand) that went with the territory. In Russia and Spain Napoleon found himself in a new era, in which armies could be defeated but the people could not be.

Talleyrand, who had seen Napoleon's conquests evaporate, wrote in his instructions to himself for Vienna that 'sovereignty cannot be acquired by the simple fact of conquest, nor can it pass to the conqueror if the sovereign does not cede it to him'.[51] This is the principle on which he insisted in dealing with the tsar and with Hardenberg over

Saxony. It lay behind his ready acceptance of the partition of Holland, which he regarded as an artificial creation: Belgium (the Spanish Netherlands) had a history and a society too different from that of Holland to allow the two to fit easily into a single whole. Conquering territory brought not strength, but only trouble and expense, he had written in his note to Danton in 1792. It is no surprise that Talleyrand was a poor fit as foreign minister for Napoleon, a man whose great talent was for conquest.

Power, he believed, came not from war but from peace, when a nation could develop its potential. Wealth came not from plunder but from industry, trade and credit. This was already visible during the Napoleonic Wars: Britain's ability to raise money on credit was an element in the coalition's victory. Talleyrand's style was that of an eighteenth-century aristocrat, but his interest in finance and commerce could have made him a nineteenth-century bourgeois.

Napoleon, according to Wellington, was the greatest military genius of any age, but in the end, all that remained of his wars and his victories were the dead and the memories. It was the brief period of peace after 1802 – for Napoleon no more than a pause between wars – that left the lasting achievements. These included the systems of administration and of education in France, the metric system for weights and measures (Talleyrand had a hand in some of these), the Banque de France and his most enduring monument, the Napoleonic Code of civil law. Talleyrand's views were ahead of his time; the memories of glory that Napoleon left behind would remain in the French imagination for decades to come; but the real legacy was civil law.

Talleyrand believed in the legitimacy that custom and tradition conferred, hence his comments to the financier Ouvrard on the desirability of keeping existing monarchs in place and ruling through them (as the British did in India, and as Napoleon did not in Italy or Spain).

There was no need to explain this to a Bourbon king. Instead, in his report to Louis XVIII at Ghent, Talleyrand focused on the ways in which legitimacy had changed. To begin with, religion no longer sanctified kings, as it once had. Instead 'the general opinion is that governments exist for the people' and legitimate power is that which 'best assures their happiness and repose'. Because power was legitimate, that did not make it absolute. In earlier times, the powers of the sovereign had been limited by other state bodies – the Church, the nobility, the magistrates. The revolution had swept these away and now, for a king to be legitimate, he had to place limitations on himself. 'It is not enough for there to be confidence in his [the king's] virtues . . . it must be founded on the strength of institutions that are permanent.'[52] He underlined the need for guarantees of personal liberty, freedom of the press, the independence of the courts and the collective responsibility of ministers. The whole resembles a constitutional monarchy.

Louis XVIII, and especially his brother, were impervious to these ideas. After Talleyrand had succeeded in excluding him from the council, the Comte d'Artois, as Charles X then was, said to Talleyrand: 'We have you to thank that you have had us removed from the council.' Talleyrand replied, 'Monsieur will thank me when he is king.'[53] Had he listened, he might have remained king longer. Somewhere in this, not well defined, is also the idea of a European order. Talleyrand's insistence on European public law was at times self-serving; this may be true of his rejection of the tsar's 'What I have, I hold.' But he also regarded Napoleon's harsh peace settlements and seizure of territory as illegitimate and therefore sure to fail. And they did. He saw France as part of a European order, and its existence depended on that order.

Talleyrand's battles in Vienna for France to be included in the negotiations were about France's interests but they were also about international legitimacy. After France joined them, the four allies found that their work became more businesslike and proceeded faster. This was because the meetings ceased to be – in von Gentz's terms – discussions among the victors about how they shared the spoils, and instead became a collective effort to reconstruct a stable order in Europe.

Framing the question of compensation for Prussia by setting up a statistical commission (and including France in it) rather than continuing the battle of wills and of threats opened the way to a solution. This had little to do with the statistics; it was the framework, putting the problem in a practical context, that brought order to the discussion and the bargaining. Similarly, the larger meetings on constitutional arrangements in the German lands and on the questions of slavery and diplomatic precedence showed that, well managed, bodies including many states could also come to sensible agreements. Indeed, the most enduring of all the agreements of the Congress of Vienna were the rules on diplomatic precedence. These simplified diplomatic life and allowed people to get on with the real business.

Napoleon wanted to control the world. Talleyrand knew he could control neither the torrent of the revolution nor the slower changes in attitudes to monarchy. Instead he waited for opportunities to help the world return to order. What mattered was that at each stage he knew what he wanted. Through the revolution he was thinking in terms of constitutional monarchy; but he took a passive role in debate, confining himself to practical questions during that over-heated period. With Napoleon he saw the possibility of re-establishing order in France; but he could not persuade him to accompany this with peace in Europe. With Alexander in 1814 he seized the chance for constitutional monarchy and European peace; but neither lasted. He tried again in 1815, and again failed. In Louis-Philippe he found the right king and was able to resolve the Belgian question in a way that supported both internal and external peace. But by then he was old and the times would change again.

One anecdote describes a meeting between a royal emissary, the Baron de Vitrolles, and the allied foreign ministers in 1814 in which they question him about Talleyrand's position. Vitrolles begins by saying that they could be sure that, 'in his heart', Talleyrand was a royalist. At this the foreign ministers are said to have burst out laughing.[54] Such anecdotes are remembered because they contain some grain of truth.

Talleyrand's coolness was the coolness of reason. The torrent was a torrent of passion and vanity. With him, both were under control. He walked the battlefield of Austerlitz among the flayed horses and the dying men with a general who wept, but he showed no emotion himself. He wept for the death of friends but not for the tragedy of war. Tears blind the understanding; for problems to be solved they must be seen clearly. The slave of neither passion nor vanity, he accepted insults and humiliations while he waited for the moment when passions had cooled and reason could restore order.

Metternich says that when he was ambassador in Paris he found Talleyrand brilliant; but he never did anything. This is true, but it misses the point. Talleyrand was waiting for the right moment. When May 1814 came he knew what to do, and did it so fast that no one was able to stop him. He did the same briefly after the Hundred Days, but he could not change the ways of the senior branch of the Bourbons. So he waited again, for chance came to change the Bourbons themselves.

His ironic 'Surtout, pas trop de zèle' ('Above all, not too much zeal') is still not a bad motto. Decisions should be made calmly, and after thought. For that you must have the courage to wait, to speak and to act. Little in Talleyrand's life was respectable but we should respect his courage and the clarity of his uncorrupted mind.

After Vienna

The wars between 1789 and 1815 brought destruction on a scale not seen before. Five million people died in the twenty-three years of war that followed the revolution; in proportion to the population the number of the dead is similar to that of the First World War. Moscow was burnt, Spain, the Rhineland and Italy were laid waste.[55]

The Congress of Vienna marks the beginning of a new era. It took Europe's diplomatic development a stage further. The balance of power remained an objective, but Vienna also brought the first multilateral settlement. Osiander notes that Vienna established a new principle, that of great-power responsibility.[56] The great powers dominated the congress, and when they agreed, the rest accepted this. The idea of sovereign equality was retained in that all states were invited, and all agreed the final settlement; but the negotiations took place among five powers.

For a short time after the congress, the five powers continued their collaboration. Their aim was to preserve the peace they had negotiated.

This is the first of three attempts jointly to manage the peace so as to avoid future wars. When von Gentz described the system in 1818, he took it for granted that external and internal order are always linked:

> The whole group of the European powers have, since 1813, been united not by an alliance in the strict sense, but by a system of cohesion based on generally recognised principles, and on treaties in which every state great or small has found its proper place. One might deny that this state of things is what, according to the old political ideas, might be described as a federative or balanced system. But it is not less certain that, in the present circumstances of Europe – from which she will not be able to escape any time soon – the current system is the one most suited to her needs. It follows that the dissolution of this system would be a terrible calamity; for, as not one of the states included in it could remain isolated, all of them would enter into new political combinations, and adopt new measures for their security; consequently new alliances, fractures, reconciliations, intrigues, incalculable complications, which, by a thousand different chances, are all equally fatal, would bring us to a general war – that is to say (for the two are more or less synonymous), to a definitive overthrow of the social order in Europe.[57]

The Congress of Vienna is commonly seen as ushering in a century of peace. This is a false picture. It was the revolution of 1789 as much as the peace settlement that set the tone for the nineteenth century.

Von Gentz, writing after the Congress of Aix-la-Chapelle of 1818, was nevertheless right about the consequences of abandoning the system of collaboration that the powers had built up. This came to an end soon after he wrote the letter quoted above. The consequences took time to come; and the alliances, fractures, reconciliations, intrigues and complications took new forms. But they did, as he forecast, lead fatally to the First World War, which did indeed complete the overthrow of the social order of Europe.

4

Two Small Countries: Denmark and Finland

Books about diplomacy are usually about great powers. Since they are the ones that set the environment in which all countries have to operate, this is reasonable. But small countries also need diplomacy, if anything more than large ones do. Indeed, their existence may depend on it.

Getting to Denmark

A small state is one whose existence is not guaranteed. The law of the jungle says that the strong eat up the weak, and grow stronger still. This is where China, Russia and the United States come from. The reverse is true too. If you lose territory you will be at risk of losing more. That, for four centuries, was the story of Denmark, which has ended up as one of the smallest European states. And yet, as in the fairy stories, it seems to be living happily ever after.

'Getting to Denmark' comes from Francis Fukuyama's *The Origins of Political Order*. Someone once asked a Third World leader what he wanted for his country, and was told: 'I would like us to be like Denmark.' Many would say the same: Denmark is rich, peaceful, deeply democratic and modest. It looks after its own people and does not spend undue time lecturing others. It is regularly at the top of surveys of national happiness. If this is what centuries of failure in power politics brings, others should try it.

If history had taken another turning Denmark might have been a great power. In the eleventh century Cnut the Great, the King of Denmark, was also the first King of England. In the Middle Ages the King of Denmark was *primus inter pares* in a loose union of Denmark, Sweden and Norway. Then, through the Thirty Years War and after, Denmark lost a series of wars with Sweden, and with them lost territory and revenue. After that it sought protection in a friendly relationship with Russia – Sweden's enemy – and declared itself neutral. This did not work in the Napoleonic Wars: naval supplies from the Baltic were vital for Britain, and it could not risk Denmark's fleet falling into French hands. It twice attacked the Danish fleet, burning it on the first occasion, kidnapping it on the second. Unable to switch sides until too late in the war, Denmark lost Norway to Sweden – which had lost Finland to Russia. The Danish king pursued Tsar Alexander at the Congress of Vienna in the hope of getting compensation in the post-war settlement. Eventually, in exchange for Norway, he was offered Swedish Pomerania. When the Swedish king (Bernadotte, a former Napoleonic general) refused to hand it over, he passed his rights on to Prussia, which was big enough to enforce them and received the small Duchy of Lauenburg and a million thalers instead.

The disaster of 1864

Denmark's last big loss began with the revolutions of 1848. The country was caught up in the nationalist-democratic fervour that swept the continent. The king granted constitutions to Denmark and to his three duchies, Schleswig, Holstein and Lauenburg. The people of Schleswig spoke Danish in the north and German in the south. Holstein and Lauenburg were entirely German-speaking and were members of the German Confederation.

In Denmark the nationalists wanted a homeland for all Danes. That meant incorporating the Danish speakers of Schleswig. This brought a small civil war: Denmark against Holstein and the German speakers in Schleswig.

The dispute was settled not by the battles between the Danish army and local militias, but by great-power intervention. The London Protocol of 1852, agreed by Britain, Russia, France and Prussia, decided that the three duchies and Denmark would remain separate, under the Danish king, but with their own constitutions.

In 1857 national liberals in Denmark won a majority in the Folketing and set about revising the constitution to integrate Schleswig into Denmark – contrary to the London Protocol. King Frederik VII, who was dying, refused to sign the constitution presented to him in 1863. The new king, Christian IX, had fought in the war fifteen years before, on the Danish side; but he was unknown in Denmark and spoke Danish with a German accent. He knew the new constitution was a mistake, but he had no one to help him.

This time Britain and Russia did not intervene, except to warn Denmark that if it broke the London agreement they could not help it. Prussia and Austria then intervened militarily – Bismarck using the opportunity to launch the series of wars that brought German unity under a conservative monarchy. From the German perspective Denmark was collateral damage.

For Denmark it was a disaster. This time the war was not against local militia but professional armies – Prussia and Austria together. A Danish army of 40,000, poorly trained and equipped, faced a combined force of 100,000 Prussians and Austrians. The Danes were dealing with a remodelled Prussian army, led by Helmuth von Moltke, perhaps Prussia's greatest general. Ironically, he had been educated at the Copenhagen military academy.

The war was fought in winter. Inadequate clothing and medical support added to the miseries of the Danes. In one single battle at Dybbøl they lost 5,500 men. National fervour could do nothing against Bismarck's blood and iron.

The catastrophe came not from a miscalculation but from a failure to calculate at all. Denmark was swept along on a torrent of national feeling, and the belief that their cause was right and would therefore triumph. An outsider would have concluded that they were all crazy. This resembles Hans Andersen's story 'The Emperor's New Clothes':

it took a small boy, who was not part of the collective self-delusion, to talk common sense. Only one outsider tried to do this. He was the new king; but Denmark was now a democracy and he had no power.

Denmark lost the three duchies to Prussia, half its population and a third of its territory, which until then had stretched to the edge of Hamburg. It was now one of the smallest countries in Europe. By the end of Bismarck's wars Prussia had become Germany, the largest of Europe's great powers.

Denmark in the twentieth century

A book by Erik Scavenius, Denmark's foreign minister at the critical moments of the twentieth century, written to defend his record, begins with this sentence: 'There is a widespread perception in this country that Denmark's foreign policy is determined by the Danish government and parliament. . . . In fact Danish foreign policy is determined by factors over which the Danish government and parliament can exert very little influence.'[1] The crisis of 1864 ended Denmark's illusion, as a young democracy, that it was the master of its own fate. It does better in the twentieth century because Scavenius has understood that lesson.

For fifty years after 1864, Denmark has no real foreign policy. The Conservatives want to regain the lost provinces, but they do not know how. The Radical Party says that any defence capability at all would be a danger: it would give the Germans grounds to fear that Denmark has secret arrangements with their enemies. Others, such as the small but growing Social Democrat party, are mainly interested in domestic policy.

In August 1914, Germany presents an ultimatum: either Denmark blocks access to the Baltic or the Germans will do it themselves. No one knows how to respond: the Danish king and the commander of the fleet, both pro-British, settle the argument by agreeing to lay mines in the straits. This is based on the king's mistaken belief that the mines would be dummies (it is a shock when one of them blows up a fishing vessel). But it is the only realistic policy. Britain understands that Denmark has no choice but to be neutral in a way that suits Germany; it has no plans to enter the Baltic anyway. Germany respects what is left of Danish neutrality.

The defence minister, Peter Munch, a Radical and a historian of 1864, is one of those who believes that military weakness is better for Denmark's security. The foreign minister is the young Erik Scavenius, cynical but reliable. His career has been less than brilliant but he has served in Berlin, and relations with Germany are what counts now. The Radicals choose him as one of the few diplomats who shares their thinking.

Scavenius complements Munch's radical realism on defence with the belief that the foreign policy of a small country has to confine itself strictly to the realm of the possible. Denmark is so exposed that, defeated, it could disappear from the map. He spends his war in dialogue with the German government. He tells them that Denmark will defend itself against an attack by Germany's enemies. How Denmark will do this is not clear; but his assurances give the Germans an excuse not to add to their problems by making Denmark an enemy. They accept Denmark as a sort of windbreak in the north-west. What matters to Germany is that Denmark continues to supply it with food through the war.

The same is true for Britain. Scavenius persuades the Germans that imports from Britain, including fertiliser and fodder, are essential if Danish farmers are going to provide food (and horses) for Germany. He also persuades Britain that Denmark's trade with Germany is a price worth paying if it helps keep British breakfast tables supplied with Danish bacon and butter. Maintaining trade with both sides in a war in which each is trying to starve the other is a remarkable feat.

Scavenius's relations with the German authorities are so good that they involve him in some of their internal deliberations. These include discussions of a stronger German presence in Denmark, to prevent Britain seizing bases there or in Norway to combat German submarine warfare. A stronger presence would mean either an alliance or an occupation; Scavenius fends this off. But it is a close-run thing and a pointer to a future in which the battle will be for the Atlantic and not the Baltic.

The war brings changes to Denmark's overseas territories. The government sells its West Indian colonies to the United States for $25 million;* in return the US supports it in resisting British and Norwegian claims on parts of Greenland. Iceland becomes sovereign, with its own flag, but keeps the King of Denmark as its king.

The most important territorial question remains the southern border. With the defeat of 1864 Denmark lost many people who spoke Danish and considered themselves Danes. As the First World War comes to an end, the government secures unanimous support in the Folketing for a statement that Denmark will seek 'no change to the current situation in Schleswig other than one based on the principle of nationality'. This is in line with the view of the Radicals that the question is one for the people in Schleswig to answer, not the people in Denmark. The government circulates this statement to London and Paris ahead of the Paris Peace Conference. With it they send an analysis of the population, village by village and farm by farm, based on work by the historian H. V. Clausen. The peace conference in Paris agrees on a plebiscite to determine the border. The principle of national self-determination has its weaknesses; but it is a cousin of democracy and it is at least simpler than the rules of dynastic inheritance that made the Schleswig-Holstein question a nightmare over several centuries.

The plebiscite in 1920 is organised around the Clausen line; and the line is well chosen. North of the Clausen line, 75 per cent of those voting want to join Denmark; to the south, only 20 per cent. In spite of this result, and in spite of the position already laid down by the Folketing, a movement grows to include Flensburg. Until 1864 this was Denmark's second city, but it has voted 70/30 to remain German. In Denmark the movement to include Flensburg has the support of the business community, of Venstre, the party of the small farmers, of King Christian X and of a sizeable and vocal part of the population. Christensen, the leader of Venstre, persuades the king to appoint a

* They are now the Virgin Islands.

caretaker government that will reflect this 'national feeling' better than the Folketing does.

The king, who suffers from an understandable dynastic nostalgia, sets off on this course; but the prime minister, Carl Theodor Zahle, one of the founders of the Radical Party, refuses to head a caretaker government to implement it. When the king appoints an apolitical caretaker instead, some of the press call it a *coup d'état*. It is 1920, and revolution is in the air; demonstrations and calls for a general strike remind everyone of this. Some of the crowds begin to call for a republic. The king discovers that in this situation the one leader whose support he needs is the Social Democrat Thorvald Stauning. He is not in the government, but he is the man that the people on the streets listen to. Stauning insists on sticking to the previous government's policy on Flensburg, and the king gives way. When elections bring Venstre and the Conservatives to power, they follow this policy too. The king learns a lesson he does not forget; and like everyone else, he understands that the future will belong to the Social Democrats.

For a country without a useful army or a well-defined foreign and defence policy, Denmark has had a good war. It is spared the destruction that the rest of Europe suffers. In spite of the blockade it has traded with both sides. It has avoided occupation (though only just); its political system survives intact and, in the case of the king (who has discovered that he is a constitutional monarch), wiser. It regains some of its lost territory, but it manages to avoid taking too much (also only just). The foreign-policy lesson of the war years is based on what Erik Scavenius has known all along: that in war or in peace, in victory or defeat, Denmark has to have a functioning relationship with Germany. The new 1920 border is, if anything, even less defensible than the old.

The Social Democrats respond to the crisis in Europe in the interwar years in the only way they know how – domestically. In 1933 Hartvig Frisch, a member of parliament, dedicates a book to Thorvald Stauning for his sixtieth birthday. *Plague over Europe* argues that bolshevism, fascism and Nazism should be seen as a common enemy; and it outlines the programmes needed to resist them. Hitler has succeeded by painting the German Social Democrats as unpatriotic, and the Nazis as good Germans. The way to inoculate Denmark against the ideological plague is to make democracy itself into a patriotic value, and a central element of Danish identity. And this should not just be propaganda: reforms in the municipal election system, in schooling and in co-operative housing are the social expression of a democratic society. Stauning, together with his closest colleagues, Hans Hedtoft and H. C. Hansen, takes on the task of ensuring that Communists do not infiltrate the party. As Hedtoft says: 'Call us Social Democrats with the emphasis on *Democrats*.'[2]

Other leaders act against similar threats to their parties: John Christmas Møller cleans the Conservative Party of extreme nationalists; and Venstre confronts the elements in its ranks who favour a Mussolini-like system. All the leaders campaign against anti-Semitism: the idea that some citizens are second-class would be a poison for Danish society. This does not mean that Denmark keeps an open door for refugees from Germany: like other countries, it takes in very few. But in 1939 the government passes legislation against racism and xenophobia, though the conservative parties vote against. None of the other leaders spell this out with the same clarity, but these policies are exactly those advocated by Munch before the First World War. If you cannot have a strong external defence, you can still create a strong society. He is now foreign minister and Stauning's coalition partner.

Denmark defends itself against Nazi ideas; and, in line with Munch's doctrine, it reduces its military defences. The Social Democrat-Radical coalition cuts defence spending and army numbers through the 1920s and 1930s, continuing right up to 1938. At the start of the Second World War the army is down to 6,000; it might be able to deal with incursions by gangs of Nazi thugs, but nothing more. Stauning's Social Democrats talk of the need to defend the nation, but have no policies to do this militarily. The campaign for democracy, however, is a success. In the 1939 election anti-democratic parties, of which the Communists are the largest, win less than 10 per cent of the popular vote. Stauning conscripts the king for the democratic cause. The king, he says, will 'loyally follow the will of the people'.

After the autumn of 1938 and the Munich Agreement, giving in to

Hitler's demands on the Sudetenland, the expectation of war grows: the Czech crisis reminds the Danes that Germany, unlike everyone else in Europe, has never recognised the Clausen line, the 1920 border. In Germany, it is part of 'the *Diktat* of Versailles'; but it does not attract the same attention as the Sudetenland. The efforts made to follow the plebiscite strictly have probably helped prevent Schleswig becoming a Nazi cause. The danger for Denmark now is less from its 4,000 German speakers than from the German navy's plans for submarine warfare. These need bases in Norway. Once Britain and France have declared war on Germany, Denmark is at risk.

The Second World War

On 9 April 1940, Germany invades Denmark at ten separate points. Events that everyone has predicted are still a shock when they happen. The German invasion comes as a combined land–sea operation, accompanied by a show of force in the air. One of the ten points is Copenhagen harbour, where a troopship docks and lands German soldiers not far from Denmark's military headquarters before anyone can resist. Just as well: the under-manned, under-funded armed forces are in no position to do that anyway. But from that day, they send military intelligence to London – showing that the last remains of military professionalism in Denmark still have a value.

On the same day the German embassy delivers a note to the Danish Foreign Ministry explaining that the invasion is not a hostile action against Denmark but a 'peaceful occupation' – a precaution against an imminent British attack. Remarkably, Germany chooses this moment to recognise the Clausen line, although its actions have just violated all Denmark's borders. The note adds that Danish neutrality will be respected and that Danish democracy will continue, 'under German protection'; this revives a concept from the Thirty Years War.*

The Danish government orders that there shall be no resistance.

* The terminology is also used by criminal gangs.

Its reply to the German note says that co-operation will depend on Germany keeping its promise not to interfere in internal affairs and to respect Danish neutrality. Germany has just violated both, so this is not wholly convincing. The wartime relationship between Denmark and Germany thus begins with half-truths and compromises; it continues with more of the same.* Yet the need to maintain the half-truths makes this different from other occupations.

Stauning tells the two opposition parties that he will accept responsibility for government only if they share it as a national government. This is unattractive for all, but only a national government can deal with a national crisis. Co-operating with an occupying enemy power is inherently disgraceful. But it is also in the national interest: both blame and responsibility have to be shared, otherwise the Germans could play the parties off against each other. As part of the price the Social Democrats roll back some social legislation.

Stauning remains prime minister. Now Denmark is wholly dependent on Germany politically and economically. Handling relations with Germany is the government's most important and most difficult task. The debacle of 9 April is the result of Peter Munch's non-defence policy. No matter how rational this might have been, his credibility as foreign minister has evaporated. Nor is he the right man to deal with Berlin. Stauning solves the problem, with help from the king, by persuading Erik Scavenius to return. Scavenius has been absent from political life for fifteen years. He has remained active, as chairman of the board of *Politiken*, a leading Danish newspaper; his cynicism, and his sharpness of mind and tongue are also intact. When someone asks Stauning whether Scavenius was not too 'German-friendly', he replies that 'Scavenius is not friendly at all.'[3]

Scavenius writes the national government's opening statement in 1940: 'By the great German victories that have struck the world with surprise and admiration, a new era has descended over Europe.'[4] These words are agreed by the whole government; but most of its members

* On two points Denmark never compromised: it never allowed Germany to conscript Danish citizens for the *Wehrmacht*, and it never accepted Danish Nazis in the government. It did, however, intern Communists at German request.

forget this afterwards and attribute them to Scavenius. The Nazis, champions in bombastic rhetoric, may not notice, and perhaps not all the public do either, but they are written in irony. As Camus says, 'There is no destiny that cannot be overcome by scorn.'[5]

The public responds to these events with a show of national solidarity focused on the king. He, in return, rejects a proposal for an 'apolitical government' put to him by industrialists. The coalition is doing a dirty job, and it does not look good; but 'apolitical' is a euphemism for undemocratic. Instead, the king suggests to Stauning that he does the opposite and confirms that, whatever happens, Denmark will remain democratic. Accordingly, Stauning has the Folketing pass a resolution stating that co-operation with the occupier will take place only through a government appointed by democratic rules.

Danes who are outside Denmark on 9 April are freer to choose for themselves. Many Danish merchant ships, at sea on that day, take a vote on the course to follow – the habit of democracy runs deep in Danish society. All but a few choose not to return home. Some go to neutral ports but many to Britain, where they play an important part in its war effort, suffering the same losses as British merchant seamen.

In Washington the Danish ambassador, Henrik Kauffmann, takes a similar course. He cuts himself off from the government that he is officially serving. He declares that Danish sovereignty is now a fiction and that the government should be considered as being held hostage. It is for Danish diplomats abroad to serve 'Free Denmark' at their discretion. The Danish government has no choice but to reject this. However, it does not risk replacing Kauffmann since the US government leaves it uncertain whether it will accept a new representative in Washington.*

Meanwhile the US military, looking ahead, are thinking they will need bases in Greenland. They discuss this with the Danish governors of Greenland, who consider that they have authority to act in an emergency but do not want to do anything going beyond the duration of the war. Henrik Kauffmann has no such inhibitions. He believes the

* As the war went on an increasing number of Danish diplomats followed Kauffmann's example, though without such far-reaching consequences.

United States will join in the war, and will emerge from it a different country in a different world. Exactly one year after German forces begin their occupation of Denmark, Kauffmann signs an agreement with the US government allowing it to establish military bases in Greenland. The language on the duration of the agreement is deliberately ambiguous. At first Berlin refuses to believe that Kauffmann has disobeyed instructions, but they find that Scavenius is as angry with him as they are. Kauffmann is dismissed, indicted for treason, and his property in Denmark is seized. None of this stops him. On New Year's Day 1942 he broadcasts to Denmark over the BBC.

By then things are changing. Operation Barbarossa, the German invasion of the Soviet Union, begins in June 1941, but in December it stalls outside Moscow. A month earlier, when Scavenius agreed to sign the Anti-Comintern Pact for the Danish government, the Folketing insisted that Denmark would not fight outside its own borders. When Joachim von Ribbentrop tries to bully Scavenius into signing without the Folketing's reservation he refuses. Ribbentrop, agitated, backs down. These subtleties are lost on Danish citizens, who demonstrate against the pact, a warning to the government that there are limits to the policy of co-operation.

Difficulties grow throughout 1942: the formal style in which the king acknowledges Hitler's birthday greeting ('the telegram crisis') causes anger in Berlin, as does the government's refusal to agree on steps towards 'resolving the Jewish question' in Denmark. The government says that no such question exists: the Danish constitution does not accept that there are different kinds of Danes.

At just this point the Danish police, for the first time, kill a Resistance fighter – a sign of things to come. Following this, a new German civil envoy is appointed. Dr Werner Best is a high-ranking member of the SS, a committed Nazi and an anti-Semite. Stauning dies shortly before his arrival in November 1942, and Best takes the opportunity to reshape the government, with Scavenius as both prime minister and foreign minister. Scavenius, who never gives without getting something in return, secures Best's agreement to elections in March 1943, in accordance with the Danish political calendar. In these elections the

Danish Nazi Party receives less than 2 per cent of the popular vote. Over the summer, strikes and violent resistance grow; so does discontent with the occupation and a sense that the tide of war is turning.

In August 1943 Dr Best delivers an ultimatum to the government: a ban on strikes and the death penalty for sabotage, or 'co-operation' will come to an end. Scavenius, who calls the system he operates 'government by negotiation' rather than 'co-operation', is ready to negotiate; but no one else will support this. The government therefore submits its resignation. The king, by prior arrangement, refuses either to accept this or to appoint a successor government. At this point, no government exists. This brings to an end the formal relationship with the occupation authorities.

It is difficult to do without government altogether. Allowing the country to descend into chaos or into a hard occupation is not the way to defend Danish society. Without their ministers, the civil servants develop machinery for co-ordination and continue to talk to the Germans. Nils Svenningsen, state secretary at the Foreign Ministry, leads this. The state secretaries consult their former ministers informally, except for Scavenius, who sticks to the position that he will neither deal in secret, nor act without the agreement of the government as a whole.

At almost the same time, in September 1943, the different Danish Resistance movements establish the Freedom Council to co-ordinate their efforts. Communists are heavily represented on the council, as they are in the Resistance; but the young Social Democrats and Conservatives also play a role.

Also in September 1943, Best cables Berlin saying that 'the Jewish question in Denmark' has to be tackled. Instructions come on 28 September to organise the arrest and deportation of all the Jews in Denmark.

That same day, Georg Duckwitz, a maritime expert in the German mission, asks for a meeting with the leader of the Social Democrats, Hans Hedtoft. Duckwitz tells him and others what is planned. Hedtoft records that Duckwitz was 'white with shame and indignation'[6] as he delivered this message. Best knows of the meeting, and does not try to stop it. It is possible that he encourages it. We do not know Best's motives; but we can guess that he wants on the one hand to show that he is doing his duty, and that Denmark is to be free of Jews; but at the same time he wants to avoid uproar and giving a boost to the Resistance.

From the German point of view, Denmark is a model of an occupation: it supplies Germany with much-needed food and other goods; it causes little trouble and is cheap to administer (Germany manages the occupation in Denmark with seventy-nine civilian officials, compared with more than 1,500 in the Netherlands and 22,000 in France). Everyone wants to keep it that way. We can guess that Best is also thinking of his own future, and does not mind having some credit on his balance sheet in case Germany should lose the war.*

Hedtoft gives the news to leaders of the Jewish community that same day. They react with disbelief and shock – disbelief because, until then, no measures have been imposed against Jews in Denmark. In other countries deportation to the camps has come step by step. In Denmark there have been no bans on using park benches but no discrimination in employment, no seizure of property, no yellow stars.† Hedtoft's news brings alarm and fear to Jewish families throughout Denmark. Almost all pack and leave their homes before the raids take place, as forewarned, late on 1 October. Most hope, or know, that Sweden will give them refuge, but few have a clear idea how to get there. Some stay with friends; some borrow summer-holiday houses; some are given shelter by strangers or sleep rough. Most are city dwellers without contacts in the fishing communities who will eventually ferry them to Sweden.

When the Gestapo teams from Germany go to the houses of Jewish

* Best already had many debits: he joined the Nazi Party in 1930, the SS in 1931. In 1934 he oversaw the 'night of the long knives' in Munich. Then he supervised training and indoctrination in the Gestapo, explaining why it was necessary to cleanse the nation of 'diseased' elements – Communists, Freemasons and Jews. From 1939 he was responsible for appointing the leaders of *Einsatzgruppen* and *Einsatzkommandos*, who murdered thousands of Jews and others. In France, Best organised the deportation of Jews. At his trial in Copenhagen in 1948 he said he had resisted persecuting Danish Jews. He was sentenced to death, later reduced to a prison term. He was expelled from Denmark after three years in prison.

† The story that the king wore a yellow star in solidarity with the Jews is a myth, though, given the king's views, a perfectly appropriate one.

citizens, they find almost nobody at home. Their instructions are not to break down doors because this could lead to apartments being looted, and 'might give the Germans a bad name'.[7]

The Germans, sometimes aided by Danish collaborators, search boats and ports. Some of those trying to escape are captured, but most get away. German organisations do not co-operate with each other. The *Wehrmacht* do not want to disturb their good relationship with the Danish people. The German navy has no instructions to search boats heading for Sweden. A good number of patrol boats are in harbour for inspection while the operations are going on. Those trying to escape, however, know nothing of this and spend their last days or hours in Denmark in great anxiety.

While the German operation is getting under way, the Committee of State Secretaries debates whether they should involve the Danish authorities. The case against this is that the action is illegal under Danish law, and unacceptable morally. On the other hand, Nils Svenningsen and others argue, if the Danish government makes the arrests, it will have some control: it may be able to avoid deportation and its consequences. This argument wins the day, and Svenningsen takes his proposal to Werner Best. But by the time he gets there it is too late.

They are lucky to be late. One can understand the civil servants' wish to exercise some kind of control, and their feeling that doing nothing is irresponsible. But the idea that they would be in control is an illusion. If the Danish police had conducted the operation, Jewish citizens might have trusted them and assumed they would be safe. Traumatic as their departures are, especially in the first days, they will only be safe out of Denmark.

On the other hand, it is good that the state secretaries involve themselves. Svenningsen takes a continuing interest in the fate of the deportees. Two hundred of these are people who have not heard the news – often because they are elderly and isolated; they are arrested by the Gestapo on the night of 1–2 October. Others are caught trying to escape. Seventeen are killed or kill themselves. Many of those caught are refugees who, without friends or relatives in Denmark, are more vulnerable.

Six and a half thousand escape. After the confusion, anxiety and chaos of the first days, an informal organisation grows up, centred on the hospitals and churches, where many people go initially for help. Doctors and pastors play a large role. Universities are closed, and students join in. The Bishop of Copenhagen writes a pastoral letter – rare in the Lutheran Church – that is read in churches throughout Denmark on 3 October, a festival day. Churches are full; Danish flags are displayed. An eyewitness writes: 'The letter was a protest against the persecution of the Jews. One had to remember that Christ was from the Jews' land. . . . You had to obey God rather than man. Persecuting the Jews was a violation of the Danish sense of justice.'[8] The pastoral letter is a call for action and for civil disobedience. In some churches, after the letter is read, the congregation rises and says, 'Amen'.

Those deported are treated with customary Nazi brutality. They are sent to Theresienstadt in Bohemia but none are sent on to death camps, and they are allowed Red Cross food parcels. In total, 481 are deported. Of these, fifty die in the camps. There would have been more but for the constant enquiries and pressure from the Danish authorities. Svenningsen extracts a written undertaking from Best that only 'full' Jews will be deported; those of mixed blood, and Jews married to Gentiles, will be exempt. It is distasteful to deal in Nazi categories; but that is the price of saving lives when dealing with Nazis. In Denmark, the Danish local authorities ensure that the homes and property of the deportees are kept in good order. With a few exceptions, those who come back find their homes have been cleaned and looked after for their return. Nothing like this happens in any other occupied country except for Bulgaria.

For the Danish Resistance, the attack on the Jews is a galvanising event. The newly created underground press makes much of the fact that Danish police were not involved (showing again that the state secretaries were mistaken in proposing to involve Denmark in the operation). In many cases, in fact, the Danish police help Jews escape. Often, the first contact people have with members of the Resistance comes through individuals helping Jewish citizens. Over the next year resistance grows; and so does repression. Increasingly, members of the

Resistance receive training and weapons from the Special Operations Executive in Britain, though, as in most occupied countries, the impact of the Resistance is primarily political.

The Jews who survive deportation are rescued in the last days of the war by Count Folke Bernadotte* and the Swedish Red Cross, and by Danish diplomats and volunteers. They are brought home in the famous white buses. The last Danish deportees leave Theresienstadt on 15 April 1945, as the frontiers close. Nineteen days later, on the Lüneburg Heath, Montgomery receives the surrender of the German forces. (The last incarnation of the Nazi government, led by Admiral Dönitz, establishes itself in Flensburg.) Montgomery arrives there, having been ordered by Eisenhower to abandon his role protecting the flank of the US forces and hurry instead to Lübeck to prevent Soviet forces from occupying Jutland.[9]

Denmark did well in the twentieth century. It got through the First World War by luck and skilful diplomacy. In the Second World War it faced an insoluble dilemma: it could fight and lose its freedom, or it could co-operate and lose its honour. It took the second course but it was not disgraced. Scavenius was right to call this a system of negotiation; it could also be called one of delay. It was a system that recalls the story told in the Arab world of a man who, threatened with execution, tells the king that if he postpones the execution for a year he will teach the king's horse to speak. The king, who has nothing to lose, agrees. When a fellow prisoner asks him how he will teach the horse, the man replies: 'In a year many things may happen. I may die. The king may die. Or the horse may learn to speak.'

Four things saved Denmark's Jews. The first was the strength of Danish society. The doctrine of the Radicals, that Denmark could not have a strong military and therefore needed a strong society, was not empty words. It was turned into policy by the Social Democrats, with support from the other parties. What no one said out loud was that the point of a strong society was that it would have a better chance

* Count of Wisborg and King Oscar II's grandson, a descendant of Napoleon's general.

of surviving occupation. It was Danish society that saw the Jews as fellow countrymen and organised their rescue without help from the government. But it was the government and the political parties that, over many years, had helped build that society.

The second was Scavenius. He understood that this was a world of power, and that principles could be defended only by dealing with the powerful; hence his policy of negotiation and delay. When the Germans asked for something Scavenius would warn them of trouble, of risks to their relationship, of the growth of resistance. He would propose delay, half-measures, more delay. Had the attack on the Jews come earlier, the results would have been different. When it did come, Stalingrad, defeats in North Africa, the entry of the United States and the Allied landings in Sicily had changed the context. Scavenius's experience of Germany, having served there and negotiated with the Germans all through the First World War, meant he knew how to handle them.

The third factor was power – Russian and, above all, US power. The delays that Scavenius achieved meant that the sense that Germany was heading for defeat, and that a liberal order led by the United States was over the horizon, changed things. In the same way, Denmark's own story might have had a less happy ending had Eisenhower not sent the British army to get to Jutland before the Soviets.

Fourth, there was Sweden: nearby, neutral, committed to humanitarian values, but also aware of the ebb and flow of power.

Our lives are determined by the states we live in. Living in a Communist or fascist country meant facing terrible choices: in order to survive or save your family you may have to lie or to compromise. The fate of states depends on the world and the part of it they inhabit. A world in which power and force ruled gave Denmark impossible choices. It was the arrival of a liberal order backed by a liberal power that saved Denmark, as it saved also the Danish Jews.

A decent state is one that looks after the powerless. In the same way, state systems should be measured by the place they give small states. After the war, Denmark had great hesitations about joining NATO because of its tradition of neutrality; then it had similar hesitations about the EU, where its attachment to national democratic institutions and its habit of holding referendums have sometimes brought problems. But the net result of both is that Denmark has never been so secure or prosperous as it is today. And it has influence too. Big countries count more than small countries do; but around the table at NATO or the EU, who you are can be as important as who you represent. A minister or an ambassador who is respected, skilful and well liked can have a large personal influence even if he or she represents a small country. That is a mark of civilisation.

Finland: the three negotiations of Juho Kusti Paasikivi

Denmark was already an old country when it lost its head in the torrent of democratic enthusiasm that brought its national catastrophe in 1864. Finland, born democratic, but also divided, was still young when its great test came in 1939. Both are examples of the national solidarity and the strict realism needed by small states with big neighbours.

After his victory over Russia at Friedland in 1807, Napoleon, who was generous with other people's property, agreed that Alexander I could annex Finland, a Swedish territory at the time, as a present to celebrate their alliance. Alexander became Grand Duke of Finland, and this was ratified at Vienna a few years later. For roughly a hundred years, Finland remained under the authority of the tsar; but it kept its orderly Swedish administrative system and its tax revenues. It supplied officers and soldiers to the Russian army, but as volunteers, not conscripts.

Finland becomes independent through the Russian revolutions. In 1905, interpreting instructions from the Russian government liberally, it does not just propose a democratic assembly as requested, but elects one, the Eduskunta, the first in Europe by universal suffrage – the Finns take it for granted that women vote too. Then, in the revolutions of 1917, the Bolsheviks offer self-determination, and the Finns take that too. The offer is intended only as a recommendation, but the Eduskunta accepts it as final and on 15 November 1917 declares itself the sovereign power in Finland.

Civil war follows. This happens in new states. Everything is at stake; there is no machinery in place to settle fundamental questions about the state. Finland is unprepared for independence. A national police force exists in the cities, but no army. The state is there for anyone who wants to seize it. These are revolutionary times: the Bolsheviks have seized power in Russia, and strikes take place in Finland too. As in Russia, the Finnish civil war is between Reds and Whites.

The conservative forces – the Whites – win. Carl Gustaf Mannerheim, who has served most of his life in the Russian army, organises a volunteer militia (the civil guard) to disarm the 70,000 Russian soldiers still on Finnish soil. A small number of the Russians join the Reds, and a larger number turn their weapons over to them.

Two thousand young Finns who have had military training in Germany arrive to join the Whites. At the last minute the German Baltic Division joins the Whites too, invited by the government of Pehr Evind Svinhufvud, and plays an important part in the defeat of the Reds. Mannerheim resigns, uncomfortable with German influence on the government. He has a point: this intervention takes place as the Treaty of Brest-Litovsk (March 1918) marks Germany's victory over Russia in the First World War, and establishes a German sphere in Central Europe. But for Germany's collapse later in 1918, Finland would have become part of it.

The Finns have to organise their new state. The first thing is to find a sovereign. Svinhufvud, acting as regent, appoints another conservative, Juho Kusti Paasikivi, to head the government. He proposes a monarchical constitution to the Eduskunta, where there is a narrow monarchist majority (many Social Democrats have taken refuge in Russia). Paasikivi is authorised to find a suitable German prince; Germany is the best bet if Finland should need protection from Russia. Kaiser Wilhelm's family turn down the offer: Finland is too unstable. But Prince Friedrich Karl of Hesse accepts. In the Eduskunta, republicans delay the appointment.

Then, in October 1918, the German army collapses. The Paasikivi government and the regent resign. The German troops go home.

Mannerheim, who has opposed the German connection, becomes regent; and Finland becomes a republic.

The first negotiation

In June 1920, Paasikivi leads a Finnish delegation for talks with the Soviet Union to agree the border. Paasikivi studied Russian language and literature at Helsinki University and in St Petersburg. After that he worked his way through graduate school and qualified as a lawyer. Then he worked in the Treasury of the Grand Duchy of Finland. In the early years of the twentieth century he supported the movement for greater Finnish autonomy, from a conservative perspective and recognising the need for a working relationship with Russia.

The Finnish delegation he leads seeks self-determination for the people of East Karelia and makes unrealistic territorial demands there. It also asks for Petsamo, an ice-free port on the Arctic Ocean. The Soviets want islands in the Gulf of Finland to protect St Petersburg. Paasikivi's instincts are to accommodate Soviet concerns about St Petersburg; but his instructions are to stand firm, and he does. After five months the status quo, or something close to it, prevails, though Finland does get Petsamo; and some of the islands are demilitarised. The Soviet Union is fighting several wars. It needs to settle with at least one of its neighbours. Paasikivi comments later that, in this negotiation, he was *too* successful.

The Finnish civil war leaves the country shocked: 27,000 have died, three-quarters of them Reds. Many deaths occur after the fighting has ended, in camps as a result of hunger and disease. Some 10,000, mainly Reds, are executed, their bodies buried in mass graves. The civil war is brief; but the damage lasts for twenty years and is a handicap for politics through the 1920s and 1930s.

At the end of the 1930s, Finland is beginning to recover from the depression, and the political mood changes. In 1937 the right-wing President Svinhufvud is replaced by Kyösti Kallio of the Agrarian Party. He is a farmer, a devout Christian and an anti-Communist; but he has opposed retaliation against the Reds after the civil war. He is elected with the votes of the Social Democrats. The Agrarians and Social Democrats then form a series of 'red-earth' governments. Since the Agrarians have been an element in the nationalist tendency, red-earth means that the wounds of the civil war are healing.

This is not a moment too soon, as a foreign-policy crisis is approaching. The absence of a coherent foreign policy is one legacy of the civil war: the need to resolve domestic problems has overwhelmed everything else.

Finland is not the only country to fail in foreign policy in the inter-war years; many well-established European countries do no better. Broadly, Finland has a choice of three strategies. One would be a co-operative relationship with the Soviet Union. Having escaped from Russia to become independent, this would be difficult; after the civil war and the victory of the Whites, it is next to impossible. In practice, relations with Russia are poor: trade collapses; official contacts are limited; the Soviet embassy in Helsinki is cold-shouldered, or treated with disrespect. Nationalist groups, who support the 'liberation' of East Karelia from the Soviet Union, are given free rein. In a different climate a co-operative approach would have had support from men such as Mannerheim or Paasikivi who, though anti-Communist, know and understand Russia.

A second course would be an alliance with Germany, which would be seen as threatening in Moscow. For it to make sense Germany would have to be ready – and visibly ready – to defend Finland. Even then it would be risky. As it is, the Finnish government does enough to alarm Moscow, with high-level contacts and naval visits even after the Nazi seizure of power, but not enough to suggest it has German protection. This approach is associated with President Svinhufvud, who in 1937 tells a German official that 'Russia's enemy must always be the friend of Finland.'[10]

The first two options mirror the two sides in the civil war; and that makes either difficult. The third possibility is a mutual defence pact with Sweden and perhaps Norway. Finland's relations with Sweden are poor in the 1930s: nationalist groups are often hostile to Swedish-speaking

Finns. Nevertheless, Scandinavian co-operation and neutrality resonate across the political spectrum. From 1937 on, the red-earth governments try to reinforce links with Sweden; Paasikivi and Mannerheim both see this as the best way to strengthen Finland's position.

It is partly for this reason that in 1934 Paasikivi agrees to become Finnish ambassador* in Stockholm. In the late 1930s, successive Finnish foreign ministers work with the Swedish foreign minister for an agreement to co-operate on the defence of the Åland Islands (Finnish territory, but populated by Swedish speakers and lying close to Stockholm). For Finland this would be a back door to defence co-operation with Sweden. But Sweden has been neutral since the Napoleonic Wars – a reaction in part to losing Finland – and most Swedes see neutrality in national terms. In any case, when Moscow hears of the talks about the Åland Islands it demands to be consulted, and the Swedish government backs off.

The second negotiation: 1938–44

In April 1938 Boris Yartsev, a second secretary in the Soviet embassy, contacts the Finnish foreign minister, Rudolph Holsti, saying that he has an important message to deliver in person. In the Finnish diplomat Max Jakobson's phrase, 'Great events approach us often in their stocking-feet.'[11]

A direct approach from a junior diplomat to a Cabinet minister is unusual; Holsti guesses that Yartsev is neither junior nor a conventional diplomat, and agrees to see him. When they meet, Yartsev tells him that Moscow is concerned about possible German aggression, and fears an attack might come through Finland. If Finland were ready to oppose a German invasion, the Soviet Union would offer military co-operation. The Red Army does not want to wait at the border to be attacked. Holsti says he sees no cause for concern:

* Finland's relations with Sweden are not at ambassadorial level; Paasikivi is a minister plenipotentiary and heads a legation. These terms are unfamiliar and sometimes confusing, so I use 'ambassador' and 'embassy' instead.

Finland's policy of neutrality is a guarantee of its peaceful intentions.

Good intentions are not enough for the Soviet government, and it is Germany they are worried about, not Finland. Yartsev presses his message on several other members of the Finnish government as well as Holsti, always in secret. In August he gives Holsti a memorandum setting out Moscow's concerns, and offers to provide arms to Finland on favourable terms. He makes no progress.

From the Soviet point of view, the dangers increase progressively. The *Anschluss* with Austria in spring 1938 brings Germany closer to the Soviet border and puts Czechoslovakia at risk. The Munich Agreement in the autumn shows Britain and France ready to sacrifice Czechoslovakia, and perhaps to give Germany a free hand in the east. Yartsev continues his efforts. He persuades Holsti to visit Moscow, where, to his surprise, he introduces him to Anastas Mikoyan, a member of the Politburo, bypassing the foreign minister, Maxim Litvinov. Now the Russians are talking of military facilities on the island of Hogland:* vital, they say, for the defence of Leningrad. Shortly after this visit Holsti speaks dismissively of Hitler. The Germans make an issue of this and he has to resign. The Russians' campaign to engage Finland goes on with the new foreign minister, Elijas Erkko; they bring in their ambassador from Rome, who proposes Finland lease Hogland and other islands to the Soviet Union.

After Munich, Britain and France begin to talk to the Soviet government, through their ambassadors, about guarantees for the Baltic States. Both resist the idea of giving guarantees to countries that have not asked for them. Vyacheslav Molotov says there is nothing wrong with this: Russia's attitude to its neighbours is no different from Britain's towards Belgium (the Treaty of London of 1839 guaranteed Belgian independence and neutrality, in which Britain had a major interest). The analogy is apt, but it misses the point – which is about the reputation of the Soviet Union. As Churchill later writes in *The Gathering Storm*, the Baltic States had difficulty knowing which they feared more: German aggression or Russian protection.

* In Finnish, Sur Sari. It is offshore from Leningrad.

In March 1939, after Munich, Germany occupies what is left of Czechoslovakia. Two weeks later Britain and France give guarantees to Poland, then to Romania and Greece. The Soviet Union proposes a defensive alliance with Britain. Somewhat reluctantly, Britain and France agree to military talks in Moscow in August.

In fact, the Anglo-French guarantees to Poland have changed everything for Moscow. Now, if Germany invades Poland, it will be at war with Britain and France. Since Berlin will want to avoid a war on two fronts, that puts Moscow in a strong position: it can choose to work with Britain and France to save Poland, or it can join Germany to divide the spoils.

Molotov runs the two sets of talks in parallel: slow-moving military talks with reluctant Western Allies by day, and then a single night of secret talks with Ribbentrop. The second wins the competition by a distance. Officially the Molotov-Ribbentrop Pact is a non-aggression agreement, similar to many such treaties scattered through Europe, including one between the Soviet Union and Finland. But in the case of the Soviet-German treaty, as most observers guess, there are secret clauses. These contain the real substance: they provide for Moscow and Berlin to divide the space between them into spheres of influence.

On 1 September Germany invades Poland from the west; two weeks later the Soviet Union invades from the east. From 27 to 29 September Molotov and Ribbentrop sort out the territorial details: Germany takes the larger share of Poland; the Soviet Union gets the whole of Lithuania. Molotov summons the Baltic foreign ministers to Moscow, one by one, and browbeats them into granting military facilities on their territories: Estonia on 28 September, Latvia on 5 October, Lithuania on the 10th. The Baltic States are assured that, bases apart, Moscow has no intention of interfering in their affairs. They are relieved to get off so lightly.

Those who reflect further may notice that the Soviet security perimeter on the southern Baltic shore now coincides with the borders of Russia before 1914. It is no surprise, therefore, that, next, Stalin tries again with Finland. An invitation to the foreign minister to discuss 'concrete political questions' arrives on 5 October. A reply is required in forty-eight hours, this being the way great powers deal with small countries.

Finland replies on 8 October, saying that the foreign minister himself will not come; he needs to be in Helsinki to consult the Cabinet and advise the president. Both the message and its timing are intended to convey that Finland will not allow itself to be bullied. At the same time the government calls up reservists and orders its forces to the border.

The night before he sends his reply, Erkko telephones Paasikivi in Stockholm and asks him to lead the talks in Moscow. Paasikivi is now sixty-eight years old. In the early 1930s he withdrew from frontline politics to run Finland's largest commercial bank; but in 1936 he accepted the job of ambassador to Sweden. In 1939 he is a tough old man, courteous and precise but irascible, known to throw inkwells at subordinates who annoy him.

Pictures of Paasikivi leaving for Moscow show him determined and a little grim, a man aware of the threat his country faces. The government has taken military precautions. Others also fear war: Roosevelt sends a message to the Russian president. The three Nordic countries make a joint démarche in Moscow in support of Finland – or rather they try, but the Soviet ministry refuses to accept it. Paasikivi, from his time in Stockholm, knows not to expect much help. The support that matters most to him comes from ordinary Finns. They gather in Helsinki station on the evening of 9 October to see him and his delegation off. They sing the national anthem and the Lutheran hymn, 'Ein feste Burg ist unser Gott'.

At the first meeting in Moscow, on 12 October, Stalin appears in person and sets out his demands. These are for the Soviet-Finnish frontier to be moved north on the Karelian Isthmus – 'Since we cannot move Leningrad, we must move the border' – and for naval and artillery facilities on the Hanko Peninsula at the mouth of the Gulf of Finland. On both counts Stalin is following the military dispositions of the tsars. The Finnish delegation argues that a Hanko base is irrelevant under modern conditions,* but without result. After two meetings

* They are right. Germany never attacks Leningrad from the sea.

Paasikivi says that Stalin's demands go beyond his instructions; it is agreed he should return to Helsinki for consultations. Stalin neither bullies nor threatens. But he notes that Finland has mobilised its army, and that Soviet forces have moved closer to the border.

While Paasikivi is in Helsinki, the Kings of Sweden, Norway and Denmark meet in Stockholm with the Finnish president, Kyösti Kallio, to show solidarity: three tall aristocrats, and a dumpy Finn from peasant stock. This is no more than a show: Sweden is the only one that matters. The Swedish foreign minister and the general staff have argued that military support for Finland would deter Russia; but they have not persuaded the prime minister.

Paasikivi returns to Moscow on 22 October, with a mandate from the Cabinet to offer a tiny revision of the border and part of Hogland Island. He takes with him political support in the shape of Väinö Tanner, leader of the Social Democrats, the largest party in the Eduskunta.

Stalin rejects the new Finnish proposals. They are not enough. The military, he says, want the frontiers of Peter the Great. Stalin, who has not expected the Finns to negotiate, then improvises a change to his territorial demands, a concession as tiny as the one proposed by Finland; and he offers to reduce the number of troops to be stationed on the Hanko Peninsula. No agreement. By now, the feeling in the delegation is that the Soviet side may really be ready to go to war.

This mood is not shared in Helsinki. Paasikivi, returning a second time, says the choice is between a military defeat, which may mean the annexation of all of Finland by the Soviet Union, and accepting a place in the Soviet sphere of influence, but with the possibility of preserving Finnish autonomy, as they did in the nineteenth century. Mannerheim, who knows the inadequacy of Finland's defences, supports him. So does Tanner. He goes to Stockholm to seek help from his fellow Social Democrats. All without result. The Swedish government is not prepared to risk war. In Finland, Erkko points out that Moscow has not made its position public. This suggests it is bluffing.

This is a small-country misunderstanding. Great powers do not bluff. And by the time Paasikivi has arrived back in Moscow, Erkko's argument no longer holds: Molotov has set out the Soviet position in a speech in the Supreme Soviet, with one omission. Erkko responds with a defiant speech defending Finnish values and sovereignty, and receives a rousing reception. What guarantee is there, he asks, that concessions made will not be followed by demands for more?

Paasikivi and Tanner meet Molotov on 3 November – no Stalin this time – and offer the minor concessions they have brought back from Helsinki. There is little discussion. Molotov says that the civilians have made no progress, and 'it is now the soldiers' turn to speak'.[12]

As they are packing their bags to leave, a telephone call summons Paasikivi to see Stalin again. Stalin, with a map in front of him, points to three islands off the Hanko Peninsula, circled in red. He asks whether, with all its uncounted islands, Finland really needs these three. Paasikivi and Tanner then understand that Molotov's omission of the Hanko base from his speech has not been accidental. They cable Helsinki seeking instructions to offer a naval base away from the mainland, plus a further adjustment of the border in Karelia. Helsinki refuses. Paasikivi tells Stalin at a last meeting on 8 November. The two sides part without acrimony.

In his report, Paasikivi writes that an agreement could have been reached. The question is whether the Soviet Union would then have used its military facilities to attack Finland's independence. His own view is that 'Russian interests in regard to Finland have always been strategic' and that 'other considerations (economic or ideological)' have never played much part.[13] The government and public opinion, however, have taken the opposite view.

For three weeks nothing happens and it looks as though Erkko is right. Then the Soviet Union fabricates a border incident. The Finnish ambassador to Moscow tries to reach the Foreign Ministry with a proposal to resume negotiations. He is told that the Soviet Union has broken diplomatic relations and will not receive him.

The Finnish side did a remarkable job in the negotiations; they took the Russians through all their red lines. The Finnish government is right about the dangers of an agreement. The Soviet Union has not yet annexed the Baltic States; but the assumption that a Russian base could be a mortal danger is correct. Yet the Soviet Union has not handled

Finland as it did the Baltic States. Three rounds of negotiations with Stalin personally, a willingness to modify its demands, including the final offer to move its naval base offshore: this is very different from the treatment given to the Baltic States, and suggests a different attitude. An island base would have been a risk, but a much smaller one than a shore base: invading a country by sea, even from a nearby island, is not the same as moving forces out of their barracks and into your capital.

If an agreement had been reached, the government would have found it difficult to persuade the Eduskunta voluntarily to give up part of the national territory. Probably it would have failed. Persuading themselves instead that the Soviet Union was bluffing enabled them to avoid this difficulty. As it turns out, the costs of failing to reach an agreement are high.

Two wars and two armistices

The Finnish Cabinet is discussing how to react to Moscow's breaking of diplomatic relations when Soviet bombers start dropping bombs and leaflets on Helsinki. The Eduskunta passes a vote of confidence in the government. This is the right thing to do at that moment; but Väinö Tanner, whose party holds the largest block of seats in the Eduskunta, thinks that Erkko and the prime minister, Aimo Cajander, have mishandled the negotiations. He persuades Cajander to resign without a vote. Risto Ryti, the governor of the Bank of Finland, replaces him; Tanner becomes foreign minister and Paasikivi minister without portfolio. This triumvirate directs policy during the Winter War.

Soviet forces attack Finland on 30 November with half a million men and 2,000 tanks. By the end they will deploy a million, roughly a quarter of Finland's population. Opposing them are 345,000 men, 80 per cent of them reservists. Their equipment is a mixture of new purchases from Sweden and artillery pieces fifty years old; to begin with there are many shortages, including small arms and ammunition, also uniforms. Soviet forces attack at several points along the eastern border and through the Karelian Isthmus. In the east, with space to manoeuvre, Finnish forces with local knowledge, often on skis, repulse six separate attacks. Soviet columns do badly on bad forest roads. Many are cut off and their soldiers die of exposure in one of the coldest winters on record. The Finns capture a division and a tank brigade, and defeat three other divisions. In the south, on the Karelian Isthmus where the war is a trial of strength, the Finns succeed through courage and ingenuity – they use home-made grenades against Russian tanks* – in holding back the poorly organised Russian forces.

Tanner, as foreign minister, makes an immediate offer to resume negotiations. He receives no reply. The Soviet government has switched from strategic to ideological mode. The leaflets that fall with the bombs proclaim a 'People's Government of the Finnish Democratic Republic', under Otto Kuusinen. The 'People's Government' arrives with the Red Army in the Karelian Isthmus and waits in a border town for the victory that will bring it to power. Stalin, having failed to obtain his minimum objectives by negotiation, is now aiming for a full takeover. But, as is the way with ideological regimes, Moscow misreads Finnish politics: TASS reporters exaggerate labour disputes; and ideologues mistake the red-earth coalition for a united front of workers and peasants ready to welcome the Red Army and reverse the outcome of the civil war.† Few expect the Finns to fight; no one expects them to be so stubborn and effective.

Much later, Nikita Khrushchev recalled that before launching the war Stalin 'didn't even feel the need to call a meeting. He was sure all we had to do was to fire a few artillery rounds, and the Finns would capitulate.'[14] This no doubt reflects Stalin's view of small countries generally. Since Finland has no hope of winning, capitulation is the rational course. The expectation that Finland would not fight explains why many of the first Soviet troops sent to Finland were raw recruits.

Tanner pursues peace with the same stubbornness that the army resists the invasion. Moscow rejects all attempts at mediation – now

* The term 'Molotov cocktail' comes from the Winter War. It is the name Finnish forces gave to the bottles with explosives and paper fuses that they used against the tanks.

† This was the contemporary assessment of Chip Bohlen, who followed the war closely from the US embassy in Moscow (*Witness to History*, p. 93).

necessary, since diplomatic relations are broken. But Tanner finds a channel: this is through a progressive Finnish feminist, Hella Wuolijoki, indiscreet and unreliable, but a friend of the Soviet ambassador to Sweden, Alexandra Kollontai. Kollontai is a notable figure from the revolution, a feminist beauty and a liberal Marxist intellectual – too liberal for Lenin, hence her rustication to Stockholm. She is partly Finnish by birth and is sympathetic.* At the end of January 1940, after two months' fighting, she passes Tanner a message that Moscow is 'not opposed in principle to negotiating an agreement with the Ryti-Tanner government'.[15]

These bureaucratic phrases conceal a breakthrough. Moscow has dropped Kuusinen. The rest of the message says that blood has been spilled, and the terms for an agreement will be harsher than those offered before. But the point is that the Soviets are ready to talk to the Finnish government, and have given up the 'People's Government'. Kollontai's advice is that a base commanding the entrance to the Gulf of Finland will be the key to an agreement. When the triumvirate consider the position, Paasikivi is in favour of making such an offer immediately, but both Ryti and Tanner – and they are surely right – think this cannot be sold at home while Finland is still winning on the battlefield.

This military success does not continue for long. From February the Soviets deploy fifty-four divisions in the Karelian Isthmus (against six on the Finnish side), better trained and equipped than those that made the first attacks. The methods used are reminiscent of the First World War; in such a battle there is only one possible winner. Soviet victory and Finnish defeat are in any case necessary conditions for a settlement. The Soviet Union will compromise only if it is visibly the winner; Finland cannot compromise unless it has lost.

Finland's political retreat is chaotic. Tanner works on President Kallio, on Mannerheim, on the generals and then on the Cabinet to

* In a 1903 study of the working class in Finland, Kollontai wrote that the willingness of government, society and workers to work together was one reason why the 'workers question' was less acute in Finland than elsewhere (David Kirby, *A Concise History of Finland*, p. 135).

persuade them that they need to find a way to make peace, and to negotiate in a realistic frame of mind. He visits Stockholm to consult Kollontai – secretly, since diplomatic relations are still broken – and to pursue the faint hope of assistance from Sweden. Moscow, meanwhile, is insisting that Sweden act as a mediator – a way to keep it neutral. On 11 February, Soviet forces make the first breach in the Mannerheim line. With the Cabinet still unable to agree, Tanner writes (unauthorised) to Molotov offering a naval base on an island west of Hanko. On a second visit to Stockholm he receives a clear and public answer from the Swedish government that it will not help Finland; nor will it give passage through its territory to British or French forces if they decide to come to Finland's aid. While in Stockholm Tanner receives a reply from Molotov: the Soviet Union wants nothing less than the base at Hanko and the whole Karelian Isthmus – Peter the Great's frontier.

This does not reflect the military position on 13 February, but it soon will. Molotov adds that if these terms are rejected, the price will increase. The majority of the Finnish Cabinet nevertheless want to fight on, now in the hope of help from Britain and France – which Tanner thinks a chimera. On a third visit to Stockholm (on 26 February) he asks the Swedish prime minister whether, if Finland makes peace, Sweden would be prepared to guarantee her within her new frontiers, i.e. without Karelia. He does not receive a reply.

Back in Finland on 28 February, a message from Molotov demands an answer to the Soviet offer within the next forty-eight hours. Admitting defeat is not easy. By this time Mannerheim is preparing to evacuate Viipuri (the largest town in Karelia, and second-largest in Finland). Tanner argues that Allied help would be neither adequate nor in time, but just as the Cabinet is making up its mind to accept Molotov's terms a message comes from Édouard Daladier, the French prime minister, promising 50,000 men and 100 bombers. Diplomats in Paris confirm this; those in London say the opposite.

Meanwhile, on the military front Russian forces are crossing Viipuri Bay on the ice. They are being mown down by Finnish guns but are still coming, and have now established a foothold on the shore.

On 5 March the Cabinet accepts the Soviet demands. On the 7th

Risto Ryti leads a delegation to Moscow, with fighting still going on. The terms of the armistice are imposed by Molotov without negotiation; several additions make them worse than those in his messages. Finland loses Viipuri, its second city, 10 per cent of its best land, 13 per cent of its national income, and acquires 400,000 refugees.* In the war it has lost 25,000 killed and 44,000 wounded (Soviet casualties may be ten times these numbers). Two ministers from the Agrarian Party resign from the Cabinet. When the peace agreement is put to the Eduskunta, a quarter of its members absent themselves and three vote against, including the rising star of the Agrarian Party, Urho Kekkonen. President Kallio, another Agrarian, has consistently resisted giving up land. When he signs the armistice he references a verse from the Book of Zechariah, saying, 'May my right hand, which is forced to sign such a document, wither'.

From the Finnish perspective this is a bitter defeat. But what is remarkable is Stalin's decision to stop short of unconditional surrender and the imposition of Kuusinen's puppet government. He must have had in mind the need to return to the main theme of the danger from Germany, and to prepare better for that. Or it may be that he senses that the war is unpopular at home: an attack on a small neighbour is not the same as defending the motherland. Leningrad is full of wounded men and rumours of disaster. And, seeing how fiercely the Finns have fought, Stalin may have concluded that taking over the whole country would be more trouble than it was worth. Chip Bohlen, who was later ambassador in Moscow, records Khrushchev telling the Finnish ambassador (in the context of the 1956 Hungarian Uprising), 'In your country we knew the entire people were against us, and thus did not occupy Finland after the war.'[16]

One member of the Finnish delegation that conducts the peace talks remains behind in Moscow. This is Paasikivi. With diplomatic relations re-established, he becomes Finland's ambassador to the Soviet Union. He faces a stream of demands from Molotov: an agreement for Soviet

* There are no refugee camps: displaced people are billeted with Finnish families. Later they are given land and other help by the government.

troops to travel by rail to Hanko, a veto on Finnish-Swedish defence co-operation (if Sweden should respond to Tanner's suggestion of a guarantee), objections to Tanner's continued presence in the government. When President Kallio suffers a stroke in August 1940 (losing the use of the right hand that signed the armistice), Molotov gives Paasikivi a list of people who do not have the confidence of the Soviet Union and should not replace him. These include Mannerheim, Svinhufvud and Tanner.* Risto Ryti becomes president.

The peace is uneasy on both sides. Moscow seems to consider a further intervention in Finland in the summer of 1940, when it completes its occupation of the Baltic States (Mannerheim orders a partial mobilisation); but it does not act. Kuusinen has to make do with the consolation prize of heading the Karelian-Finnish Soviet Socialist Republic of the Soviet Union.†

In November 1940 Molotov asks for German agreement to a full occupation of Finland. Hitler acknowledges that Finland is within the Soviet sphere of influence, but says it is not the moment for a full takeover. This exchange foreshadows Operation Barbarossa: on the one side, the growing Russian fears of a German attack, on the other, the embryonic German plans for a thrust through Finland. Discreet contacts between the Finnish and German military have already started in the summer of that year.

Paasikivi resigns as ambassador in Moscow early in 1941. Formally this is on grounds of age (he has passed seventy). In reality it is because he has learned of the military contacts with Germany; he dislikes both the contacts and the fact that he has been kept in the dark about them. His memory of the collapse of German power in 1918, when he was prime minister, remains vivid. He retains his conviction that, to survive, Finland has to live with the Soviet Union. He retires from public service and starts work on his memoirs.

* The Soviet hatred of Tanner, who has tried to avoid the war and then to make peace, is because he is a Social Democrat who has led the workers astray.

† Kuusinen made a good career in the Soviet Union as a member of the Politburo under Khrushchev and as a Marxist scholar – his ideas are said by some to have anticipated perestroika – but he was never able to return to Finland.

In fact, Mannerheim and the military and the Finnish leadership have been briefed on Barbarossa in the spring of 1941. Germany needs Finnish co-operation; a refusal would mean fighting Germany. Ryti chooses instead to negotiate the terms of Finland's engagement: if the Soviet Union attacks Finland, it will resume the war it has broken off. Finland will not join Germany as an ally; but it will fight the same enemy as a co-belligerent.

When Germany attacks in June 1941, one thrust goes through northern Finland. Soviet air raids against Helsinki follow and Finland then begins the 'Continuation War'; the name reflects Ryti's view that this is the second instalment of the Winter War. Finnish forces win back territory in Karelia, now a neglected no-man's-land; they go beyond it to a defensible river line and stop there. They also attack across the eastern border into Eastern Karelia, where they find they are not welcomed as liberators but regarded as occupiers, burying forever the dreams of Finnish nationalists. Mannerheim refuses the Germans' offer of the supreme command in Finland, and refuses to join them in the siege of Leningrad.

The distinction between allies and co-belligerents is understood abroad. Finland breaks diplomatic relations with Britain only at the insistence of Germany; Britain declares war on Finland only in December 1941, under Russian pressure, and never fires a shot. The United States breaks relations as late as summer 1944 and never declares war. But when it comes to the terms of the peace, the Allies leave the decisions on Finland to the Soviet Union, even though they see Finland as a victim of war, not an aggressor.

After the Soviet victory at Stalingrad in 1943, Finland puts out feelers to Moscow about a peace agreement, but without success. In 1944, with the siege of Leningrad lifted, Soviet forces begin once again to threaten Finland. To maintain its position Finland needs German weapons; but it knows also that it is urgent to make peace with Moscow. Ribbentrop, smelling betrayal, flies to Helsinki and demands an undertaking from the president that Finland will not make a separate peace. He gets it. The Ribbentrop-Ryti agreement provides arms in return for guarantees that Finland will stay with Germany to the end. Ryti writes to Hitler with the same message. Both are deliberate deceptions. The Ribbentrop-Ryti agreement is invalid because the Eduskunta has not approved it; and Ryti, who is ill, makes his commitment to Hitler in a personal letter, knowing he will not remain president long.

German weapons help halt the Soviet forces' advance on the Karelian Isthmus, costing them time when their priority is to get to Berlin. The peace feelers now come from Moscow, but on tough terms, and making clear they will not make peace with Ryti as president. He resigns as he has planned and Mannerheim takes his place. An agreement to cease hostilities on 4 September follows.

A precondition of the agreement is that Finland breaks relations with Germany and drives its forces out of Finland. A thousand more Finns lose their lives in this process, in addition to the 66,000 who have already died in the Continuation War. The Germans leave scorched earth behind them: they destroy some 18,000 buildings, including churches and bridges. The civilian population has to be evacuated to southern Finland or to Sweden.

The armistice, signed in Moscow on 19 September 1944, returns the southern border to the line of 1940; in the north, Finland loses Petsamo and the corridor to the Arctic Ocean. Instead of Hanko the Soviet Union takes a twenty-year lease on a naval base at Porkkala, within artillery range of Helsinki.* The Finnish merchant marine is put at the disposal of the Soviet Union and reparations are set at $300 million – on paper, half the sum proposed by Stalin in spring 1943, but reparations are in kind and on the basis of 1938 prices, doubling their cost. This is more per capita than Germany was asked to pay after the First World War. All this, like the agreement ending the Winter War, is the result of a diktat, not a negotiation.

* This is exactly the territory that Stalin told Anthony Eden in December 1941 that he would want from Finland (*The Diaries of Sir Alexander Cadogan*, ed. David Dilks, p. 420).

The third negotiation: 1944–8

The nearest Finland comes to an occupation is the period under the Allied Control Commission after the war. Andrei Zhadanov, the former governor of Leningrad, trusted by Stalin for his loyalty and bureaucratic thoroughness, is in charge. Zhadanov sets out to create a new model: a country not under direct control, but whose government is responsive to Soviet requirements. Zhadanov's priority is the implementation of the peace treaty. He makes clear to the 'People's Democrats' – a coalition of Communists and fellow travellers* – that Moscow will not install them in power 'just for the sake of it'. He tells them not to frighten small farmers by talking about collectivisation.[17]

Two elements of the peace treaty are especially important. First, reparations: for the Soviet Union, in the ruins of war, these are an element for its survival, especially after the United States stops aid in 1946 (as it does for all Allies). The toughness of the terms is hard to imagine, as is the toughness of the Finnish government in implementing them. In 1945–8, inflation in Finland reaches 50 per cent; reparations and repayment of war debts (including to Germany!) take two-thirds of the Finnish government's budget. As reparations the Finns hand over, inter alia, the navy's flagship and their legation buildings in the Baltic States. But they are always on time.

The second important element is the punishment of so-called war criminals. For Moscow, the trials are a demonstration of the legitimacy of its war with Finland. On trial are the political leaders who co-operated with Germany in the Continuation War, notably Risto Ryti and Väinö Tanner, even though, at Moscow's insistence, Tanner was not in office at the time.

Mannerheim is not included. Zhadanov understands that his authority is needed for the transition period, and makes sure he remains president. He resigns only when the war crimes trials are over. Paasikivi,

* Trotsky coined the phrase to refer to artists and writers who were sympathetic to the revolution but not part of it. What was not known about fellow travellers, he said, was how far they would accompany you.

who Mannerheim brings out of retirement to be prime minister, replaces him, including during the last year of Mannerheim's presidency when the old soldier is ill.

Paasikivi becomes prime minister for the second time at a low point in Finland's history. As well as the armistice and the supervision of the Control Commission, Finland has displaced people and ex-servicemen to resettle. The post-war elections of 1945 make the Finnish People's Democratic League (fellow travellers) one of the largest parties in the Eduskunta. The conservative Paasikivi includes them in the government to make sure they share responsibility in difficult times. Their leader, Yrjö Leino, becomes minister of the interior.

Paasikivi's conviction is that if Soviet security interests are accommodated, Finnish independence can be preserved. Finland has therefore to implement the peace agreement in good faith. Paasikivi resists the war crimes trials; but when he concludes they have to be done, he does them thoroughly. The trials are a travesty of justice. They are based on retrospective legislation, and the Control Commission interferes to increase the sentences of those convicted. The defendants have acted in their country's best interests. But in Paasikivi's view, it is better for Finland's independence that the injustices are carried out by Finnish institutions.

In February 1947 Paasikivi signs the peace treaty with the Allies in Paris – the terms are set by the Soviet Union – and the Control Commission withdraws. In an interview following the ceremony Paasikivi says that Finland will fight any country that tries to attack the Soviet Union through Finland, and will do so with all its strength. Later in 1947 he decides not to accept the invitation to the Paris meeting to discuss the Marshall Plan, understanding that, for the Soviet Union, this is a security issue. As Max Jakobson puts it, 'The Marshall Plan was designed to save Europe from Communism, but Finland may have saved itself from Communism by saying no to the Marshall Plan.'[18]

The international environment into which Finland emerges as the Allied Control Commission closes down is tense and is growing tenser. In spring 1947 the Moscow Four Power Conference fails to agree on Germany, the main issue on its agenda. At the same time President

Truman announces his doctrine to the US Congress, prompted by Soviet activities in Greece and Turkey. In the summer Marshall's address at the Harvard Commencement proposes the Marshall Plan. And late in 1947, Zhadanov, in his role as Stalin's chief ideologue, announces to Cominform that the world is now divided into two irreconcilable camps, confirming the view now shared by both sides. By not accepting the invitation to the Marshall Plan meeting, Finland seems to place itself in the Eastern camp.

In November 1947 Finland receives another invitation. The prime minister, Mauno Pekkala,* returns from Moscow with an invitation for Paasikivi to negotiate a defence agreement with the Soviet Union. Paasikivi does not respond. Nor does he reply to the same invitation when the new Soviet ambassador repeats it on his arrival in Helsinki. In February 1948 the invitation arrives a third time, now in a letter signed by Stalin and dated the 23rd, the day of the Communist coup in Czechoslovakia.

Paasikivi handles Stalin's invitation with majestic deliberation.† First, he informs the government and the chairs of parliamentary groups of its arrival. Next, he sends Stalin an acknowledgement, noting that a treaty will need parliamentary approval. He therefore proposes to consult the parties in the Eduskunta. This takes a further week. On 9 March he replies to Stalin suggesting that the negotiations should take place in Moscow – which is where almost all Finnish-Soviet negotiations are held. On 20 March, with its instructions agreed and almost certainly known to the Soviets, the all-party delegation leaves for Moscow. Pekkala, who is to lead it, arrives by plane four days later.

Paasikivi's initial failure to respond was not play-acting: no country in the neighbourhood of the Soviet Union can feel comfortable with a proposal for a defence treaty; and Paasikivi may have hoped that the Russians would give up. But a letter with Stalin's signature commits his personal prestige. At that point it has to be handled properly. The

* Mauno Pekkala is a Social Democrat who after the war joins the Finnish People's Democratic League (SDKL). It wins a large block of seats in the 1945 elections, only one less than the SDP.

† Max Jakobson's phrase (*Finnish Neutrality*, p. 38).

Finnish government's actions are designed to make clear that it will follow its own democratic procedures. Parliament is consulted before, during and after the negotiations. In the process Moscow learns that three-quarters of the Eduskunta oppose a defence treaty: only the People's Democrats support it.

Paasikivi and Mannerheim have foreseen that Moscow will propose a security treaty and have looked at how it might be designed to protect both Russia's security and Finland's independence. Paasikivi now studies the new treaties with Hungary, Romania and Czechoslovakia. These include an obligation of mutual assistance in the event of war, and political consultations when either party wants them. In practice these are alliances. Even without Soviet interference in internal affairs through the Communist Party, they spell the end of independence. This is unacceptable to Finland. During the Second World War, attacked by the Soviet Union and threatened by Germany, it had never joined an alliance.

Paasikivi's preparations do their work. On the first day in Moscow Molotov, aware of the debate in the Eduskunta, agrees that existing models are not appropriate and offers to work on the Finnish draft. This does not mean the end of difficulties. At one point two of the delegation whom Paasikivi most trusts, Kekkonen and J.O. Söderhjelm,* return to Helsinki to consult him. Paasikivi remains in charge throughout.

The results speak for themselves: the defence agreement originally proposed becomes a Treaty of Friendship, Co-operation and Mutual Assistance. The heart of the treaty is in two articles. Article 1 states:

> In the event of Finland, or the Soviet Union through Finnish territory, becoming the object of an armed attack by Germany or any state allied with the latter, Finland will, true to its obligations as an independent state, fight to repel the attack. Finland will in such cases use all of its available forces for defending its territorial integrity by land, sea and air, and will do so within the frontiers of Finland in

* From the Swedish speakers' People's Party. His views are also close to Paasikivi's.

accordance with obligations defined in the present treaty and, if necessary, with the assistance of the Soviet Union.

This limits the treaty to cases where Finland is attacked. Finland's responsibility is to defend its own territory, on its own territory. As Paasikivi says, explaining the treaty to the public, this was what Finland would do anyway. The limitation to attacks by Germany or its allies matters less; the main point is geographical. Finland has no obligations unless the Soviet Union is attacked through Finland.

The second sentence of the article reads: 'In the cases aforementioned the Soviet Union will give the help required, the giving of which will be subject to mutual agreement between the Contracting Parties.' (I.e., no assistance without Finnish agreement.)

Article 2 states: 'The High Contracting Parties shall confer with each other if it is established that the threat of an armed attack as described in Article 1 is present.'

This has an ominous ring to it for small neighbours of the Soviet Union: for the Baltic States, a summons for consultations in Moscow was the first step to annexation. Paasikivi says he understands the phrase: 'it is established' (in Article 2) to mean that consultations are required only if both parties agree that there is a threat. In the course of the negotiations Kekkonen has cabled Paasikivi, describing the article as 'alarmingly broad and open to interpretation'. This is one of the issues that he and Söderhjelm returned from Moscow to discuss. The article obliges Moscow to point to a specific and narrowly defined threat. It does not say what happens if the parties disagree about whether a threat exists. This question will arise thirteen years later, with Kekkonen as president.

The text of this treaty is very different from those with the future Warsaw Pact countries. This includes the preamble, which recognises 'Finland's desire to remain outside the conflicting interests of the great powers'. The words, like those of most treaties, are formal and uninspiring, but they are words that confirm Finland's independence: they are what all those young men died for.

After the treaty is signed Stalin gives a dinner, as is customary on such occasions, and makes a speech congratulating both sides on the compromises they have made. One of the Finns interrupts: 'What compromises? The whole thing was dictated by Paasikivi.' After a moment of chilled silence, Stalin bursts out laughing.[19]

As the delegation leave, Molotov asks anxiously whether they are sure it will be ratified by the Eduskunta. This enquiry itself is a recognition of Finland's independence, and of its democratic institutions. Paasikivi's preparations and the confidence he enjoys among the Social Democrats and the Agrarian Party – the Finn who had interrupted Stalin was Urho Kekkonen – ensure a large majority in the Eduskunta for ratification. But the debate exposes the suspicions from all quarters about whether the Soviet Union can be trusted to act in good faith, and to stay out of Finland's internal affairs.

Tension is still in the air. One symptom is the talk in diplomatic circles of secret clauses. US diplomats believe it is only a matter of time before there is a Communist takeover; these include respected figures such as 'Doc' Matthews in Stockholm, a protégé of Dean Acheson, and Walter Bedell Smith in Moscow, later John Foster Dulles's deputy.*

While the negotiators are in Moscow, the leader of the Finnish Communists, Hertta Kuusinen, daughter of Otto, contributes to the tension by calling for Finland to follow the Czech example. A month later, during the ratification debate, rumours of a coup (from either left or right) circulate widely and the security forces are put on alert.

Another moment of danger comes after ratification. Conservatives in the Eduskunta launch a vote of no confidence in the interior minister, Yrjö Leino, on the grounds that he violated the constitution in 1945 by deporting Finnish citizens to Russia. He is the only Communist in the government (and, at that point, the husband of Hertta Kuusinen). The motion is passed but Leino refuses to resign. Paasikivi is furious with the proposers for doing this at a sensitive time, after ratification of the treaty and before a general election; but he insists that the constitution

* By contrast, Ernest Bevin, the British foreign secretary, sees the Finnish success as confirming his view that the way to deal with the Russians is to stand up to them (Alan Bullock, *Ernest Bevin*, p. 347).

be respected and fires Leino himself. Communist-controlled trade unions then begin a series of strikes and demonstrations in protest.

This would be the perfect moment for Moscow to intervene in support. And Moscow does intervene – but in the opposite sense. It orders the Communist Party to stop the strikes. Then it intervenes again, halving the reparations Finland has still to pay. It seems as if Moscow hopes to win in the elections what it has chosen not to take by force. If so, it fails. A 78 per cent turnout reduces the People's Democrats in the Eduskunta by a third; the Social Democrats and Agrarians are the big winners. Paasikivi is able to propose a minority Social Democrat government with no participation from the far left. With Paasikivi's support, the new government cleans the intelligence services of Communist influences and reorganises them around the objectives of defending the rule of law and Finland's independence. The Soviet concessions on reparations help the economy and have the useful side effect of persuading the United States to compete by offering Finland aid outside the Marshall Plan.

Now Paasikivi, with the support of the new government, pardons those of the 'war criminals' who are still in prison, including Risto Ryti, by this time seriously ill. Paasikivi writes that this partly expiated the shameful deed they were forced to do in 1945. Väinö Tanner returns to political life in the same year, and a few years later becomes chairman of his party. When Risto Ryti dies he is given a state funeral.

Paasikivi lays down at this point that he will never again accept Communists in the great offices of state, interior, defence or foreign affairs: Hertta Kuusinen aspired to the last. But by then the far left has begun its long decline and the question does not arise again.

The year 1948 is a beginning, not an end. Finland is successful in the negotiations, but its position remains precarious. Each turn of the Cold War screw impacts on it in some way. In 1948, the debate begins in Scandinavia about who should join NATO. After their experiences in the Second World War it is no surprise that Norway and Denmark choose to join; but it helps Finland that Sweden does not. In 1949, Finland's minority government has to contend with Communist-organised strikes; it arrests activists and uses the army to keep order. In

1950, the Korean War raises tensions and makes many wonder whether the Soviet Union might attack Finland.

With 1952 comes better news: the Olympic Games, held over from before the war, take place in Helsinki, for the first time with full participation from the Soviet Union. Even better, this is the year of Finland's last reparations payment. Now the West can worry instead that Finland is too dependent on trade with the Soviet Union.

Stalin's death in 1953 brings relief but uncertainty. In 1954, with the failure of the European Defence Community, which supported the formation of a supranational European army subsuming German forces, the Western Allies agree instead that German rearmament should take place in the framework of NATO membership. Responding to this 'revival of German militarism', Molotov invites all European countries to a Conference on European Security in Moscow. This time Paasikivi responds quickly, wanting to be ahead of everyone else. After three days of careful thought, Finland replies that it supports the objective of a collective security system in Europe and will attend 'if all major European nations' do so too. Thus Finland gives a positive reply but does not attend the conference, which turns out to be the first step towards the creation of the Warsaw Pact.

Paasikivi's last negotiation in Moscow takes place in 1955. He brings back two new treaties. One is a twenty-year extension of the 1948 Treaty of Friendship, Co-operation and Mutual Assistance. He and Kekkonen, who accompanies him as prime minister, want a ten-year extension; but the Soviet side has an irresistible argument for twenty. This is their proposal for the second treaty, which commits the Soviet Union to withdrawing its forces from Porkkala the following year.

With the Austrian State Treaty (February 1955), the Soviet withdrawal is part of Khrushchev's campaign for the idea of peaceful coexistence between socialist and capitalist countries. The Zhadanov-Stalin doctrine is one of inevitable conflict, a world divided into two armed camps with no space between (John Foster Dulles's view of neutrality as 'an obsolete conception . . . an immoral and short-sighted conception'[20] drew on the same logic). Khrushchev's approach makes space for neutrals. A Finland allied to the West would be a danger to the Soviet Union; a Finland allied to the Soviet Union would not be independent. The problem of Porkkala – Paasikivi has described it as 'lending a colouring to Finnish neutrality not normally found in handbooks of international law'[21] – is more about independence than neutrality. Soviet forces are there as a threat, not as allies. On his return from Moscow, Paasikivi says that, for the first time, he has come back satisfied from a negotiation with the Soviet Union.[22]

How did Finland do it?

Geography matters. Finland is not Poland. It is on the flank, not at the centre. Nine months after Soviet forces left Porkkala, Hungary declared itself neutral, with very different results. But geography is not the whole story. Of no less importance is that Finland fought. Its readiness to take on the Red Army was first a surprise, and then, when it proved effective, a shock. Surprise brings respect: when people can't be sure how you will react they treat you with caution. On a human level, Finland's courage and patriotism impressed Stalin as nothing else could. At the Tehran Conference of 1943, the first meeting of Roosevelt, Stalin and Churchill, Chip Bohlen recorded him saying: 'Any country that fought with such courage for its independence deserved consideration'.[23]

Stubbornness in negotiation is the civilian equivalent of resolution in war. A reputation for being stubborn is useful. Paasikivi had such a reputation and deserved it, including in 1939 when he was defending policies he thought unwise. Finnish stubbornness registered with Stalin personally. Speaking to Anthony Eden in 1944, he said: 'Mr Mikolajczyk (the prime minister of the Polish government in exile in London) was so obstinate I thought he must be of Finnish origin.'[24]

Stubbornness is barren without credibility. People need to believe that when you agree, you will keep your promises. Breaking the armistice agreement of 1940 lost Finland credibility, and it had ground to make up. It did this by following to the letter the terms imposed in 1947. Its exact and correct payment of the reparations left a lasting impression in Russia, a country where doing the least you can get away with is the norm ('gift-wrapped' was how Khrushchev described the materials handed over as reparations). The war crimes trials and Paasikivi's readiness to send innocent men, his friends and colleagues, unjustly to prison for the good of his country also registered in Moscow.

Behind this lay Finland's solidity as a democratic society. In 1938 it had been a state for no more than thirty years. Its people and its institutions were born in revolution, divided in civil war, then brought together in war and in defeat, in the loss of national territory, then by a flood of refugees and an unjust peace. Through all this, Finnish institutions survived. No other European country in the twentieth century has a record to equal it. Finland seems never to have looked back; instead, it did what had to be done. Kollontai's assessment of Finnish society* was right. Before independence, there was no *ancien régime* of great estates; after independence, workers were represented intelligently by the Social Democratic Party, and small farmers by the Agrarian Party, both bastions against Communism. (In the 1956 election Kekkonen for the Agrarians and Karl-August Fagerholm for the Social Democrats each presented their parties as bulwarks against the far left; and, in different ways, they were.) Finland's electoral system allowed multiple parties to represent diverse interests. It developed a political culture of coalitions, balanced by a strong presidency. Without the resilience of Finnish democracy the best diplomacy in the world would not have worked.

For diplomacy, democracy is a two-edged sword. It was critical for Paasikivi's success in negotiating a treaty that reassured the Soviet Union and preserved Finland's independence. But the Treaty of Friendship, Co-operation and Mutual Assistance of 1948 looks remarkably like the agreement Yartsev proposed in 1938. That, however, would never have been accepted in 1938, even if reliable anti-Communists like Paasikivi and Mannerheim had put it forward. The suggestion alone would have caused outrage. Similarly, the agreement Stalin offered Paasikivi

* See the footnote on p. 141.

in November 1939 at the end of four weeks' negotiation could not have been sold in a democratic political system, for good reason: there were no grounds to trust the Soviet Union in 1938 or 1939. The blood spilled on both sides in the wars that followed had the strange effect of creating a basis for mutual trust. As Henry Kissinger says in *A World Restored*, 'Nations learn only by experience. They "know" only when it is too late.'[25]

As often in diplomacy, once something is done it looks easy, even inevitable. In Finland's case, it was not; among the many things that contributed to the success, some of the credit should be given to Paasikivi personally for his insight that, in Finnish-Soviet relations, security mattered more than ideology, and for his doggedness in pursuing that logic. That doggedness brought a second asset, his reputation in Moscow as an interlocutor who listened to Russians and could be trusted to deliver. The reciprocal of Paasikivi's doctrine that being trusted by the Soviet Union was the way for Finland to preserve its independence was this: that 'as long as Stalin had Paasikivi he did not need the Finnish Communists'.[26] The Soviets were right to prefer Paasikivi: he could deliver the consent of the Finnish people and the Communists could not.* At the moment of Finland's defeat Paasikivi added a second insight: that until Finland's security – that is, its relationship with the Soviet Union – had been settled, everything else was subordinate; justice, in the shape of the war crimes trials, and the economy, in the shape of the Marshall Plan, had to take second place.

* They also trusted Paasikivi, oddly, because he was a conservative. In 1939 Tanner's views were exactly the same as Paasikivi's, but Tanner became the Soviets' bête noire.

5

George Kennan: the Foot Soldier

February, 1946. Moscow. George Kennan is sick in bed with sinusitis and other competing ailments. His ambassador, Averell Harriman, is away and Kennan is in charge of the embassy.

He is frustrated. That is not unusual: life in Moscow is frustrating. The Russians have been treating Allied diplomats as if they were enemies all through the war, and now after it too. Contact with ordinary Russians is impossible; and the Soviet bureaucracy has turned obstruction into an art form. Kennan is frustrated also because his ambassador, brilliant though Harriman is, does not seem (to Kennan) to be telling Washington the whole truth. Kennan knows Russia better than any other American. He is outraged by what it is doing; he is disgusted with the US government's unwillingness to understand the sort of country they are dealing with.

This mood has grown. In the summer of 1944, Soviet forces watched from the other side of the Vistula as the Germans crushed the Warsaw Uprising* ('a people who have been our allies, who we have saved from our enemies, and who we cannot save from our friends', Kennan writes in a note to Harriman).[1] The Russians' refusal to allow US and British planes to use Russian refuelling facilities so they can airdrop

* On 1 August 1944, as the German army prepared to retreat ahead of the Russian advance, the Polish Resistance attacked them – the largest operation mounted by any resistance movement in the Second World War. Fighting continued for sixty-three days with little outside support, until German forces had defeated the Poles and razed Warsaw to the ground.

supplies to the Poles has shocked even Harriman. But in 1944 Russia was an ally and Roosevelt wanted good relations. In February 1945, before the Yalta Conference of the Big Three, Kennan writes to his friend and fellow Russian expert Chip Bohlen advocating a tougher line. Without result.

In April 1945 Roosevelt dies, just at the moment when, perhaps, he is beginning to change his mind about the Soviet Union. Shortly after, Kennan tells Harry Hopkins – in Moscow as a special envoy for President Truman to talk to Stalin about Poland – that it would be better *not* to have an agreement with Russia than to share responsibility for its takeover of Poland. Hopkins replies that he respects Kennan's views but he is not at liberty to follow them. On Truman's instructions Hopkins reaches an agreement with Stalin to recognise the puppet government in Warsaw. In exchange he gets some concessions to break the deadlock in the San Francisco Conference on the UN – a matter of little importance for Stalin.

The Potsdam Conference comes in July with two new men, Truman and Clement Attlee, facing Stalin, but no change in US policy to match the changing situation in Europe. It is one thing to turn a blind eye to the faults, even the crimes, of allies when fighting a common enemy; but Hitler is now defeated and there is no more reason to pretend. In August Kennan sends in another resignation, referring to 'a deep sense of frustration over the squandering of the political assets won at such cost . . . and over the obvious helplessness of our career diplomacy to exert any appreciable constructive influence on American policy'.[2] But he remains in Moscow.

He is still there in late December when the US secretary of state, James Byrnes, arrives for a Three-Power Conference that he has set up without consulting the third power, Britain.* Kennan writes of Byrnes's performance: 'He plays the negotiations by ear, going into them with no clear or fixed plan, with no definite set objectives or limitations . . . his weakness in dealing with the Russians is that his

* Ernest Bevin was furious. He came only because he thought leaving Byrnes on his own with the Soviets was the worst of all options (Anne Deighton, *The Impossible Peace*, p. 46).

main purpose is to achieve some sort of an agreement, he doesn't care much what.' The visit causes Kennan to reflect that it is not just US policy towards the Soviet Union that is naïve; its methods also are all wrong. 'Perhaps it was the visit of Secretary Byrnes to Moscow that caused my pot of patience to boil over with relation to this area.'[3] As a way of dealing with his frustration he writes down a set of rules for dealing with the Stalin regime. The first three serve as a commentary on Byrnes's approach:

A. Don't act chummy with them.
B. Don't assume a community of aims with them which does not really exist.
C. Don't make fatuous gestures of goodwill.[4]

Kennan is still there in February 1946, when, sick in bed, he receives a cable asking for a commentary on a speech by Stalin to the Russian political elite announcing a series of five-year plans and calling, as usual, for sacrifices. On the one hand it is infuriating that no one seems to take any notice of his reporting on what the Soviet Union is and how it operates: 'So far as official Washington was concerned, it had been to all intents and purposes like talking to a stone.' But on the other, for once, somebody is asking for his opinion. Perhaps they will even read what he writes. 'They had asked for it. Now, by God, they would have it.'[5]

And so he writes the most famous diplomatic cable in history. The normal rule in diplomatic life is that, if you want your cables to be read, you make them short. Kennan does the opposite. He writes a telegram so long that (in a pretence of respecting the rules about cables) he cuts it up into five parts, transmitted separately, more than 5,000 words in all. Today it is still referred to as the 'Long Telegram'. It contains all his accumulated anger, frustration and wisdom. It changes his life.

In his *Memoirs* and in later articles, Kennan writes that the Long Telegram was the response to a different enquiry from the one mentioned above, one from the US Treasury expressing perplexity at the Soviet Union's not wishing to join the IMF and the World Bank. The record shows this is not the case (he answered the Treasury enquiry the previous month). Curious but not important. What matters is Kennan's response: anyone reading the telegram today can still feel the frustration and the 'Now, by God, they would have it' spirit in which it is written.

From Kennan's perspective, the Stalin speech is a routine production, repeating well-known themes – the inevitability of conflict with the capitalist world, the probability that they will fight among themselves first. But by some accident it has caught the attention of Washington and of the media, who are taking an interest in Stalin's post-war policies.

The point is that, in parallel to Kennan's mounting frustration in Moscow, a process is under way in Washington in which the Truman administration, and Truman himself, are beginning to realise that they do not understand the Soviet Union and that they need someone to explain it to them.

While the war continued, US policymakers concentrated single-mindedly on co-operation with the Soviet Union. Harriman knew that the Soviets were not to be trusted, but he also knew that it was Roosevelt's policy to ignore this. Privately, Roosevelt would quote a Balkan proverb saying that, sometimes, to cross a river you had to hold hands with the devil. With victory the crossing was done. At the beginning of April 1945 Roosevelt was infuriated by Stalin's accusations of an Anglo-American plot to make peace with Italy so as to divert German troops to the eastern front.* If Roosevelt had lived, he might have recognised the multiple instances of bad faith on Stalin's part and adjusted his policy. But, equally, he might not have. In fact, just hours before he died Roosevelt was insisting that Stalin's accusations, which a few days before had made him furious, should be treated as a minor incident. When Harriman queried this Roosevelt underlined the word 'minor'.[6] With Roosevelt's death on 12 April, Truman inherited the

* That is to say, Stalin assumed that, just as Soviet forces had watched the Germans crush the Warsaw Uprising, Roosevelt would watch happily while Germany and the Soviet Union destroyed each other.

Roosevelt philosophy of the alliance with Stalin without Roosevelt's experience and cynicism.

The first policy meeting Truman holds as president is about the Soviet Union. It remains his constant foreign-policy preoccupation for the next eight years. Truman's natural instincts pull him in opposite directions. On the one hand, as a plain-spoken middle American he believes in democracy and is used to tough bargaining and dirty politics. He is suspicious of foreigners and especially of dictators, and is a firm anti-Communist. On the other hand, as a New Deal Democrat he inherits the idealistic traditions of Woodrow Wilson; he admires Roosevelt's policies and wants to pursue his legacy. His lack of direct involvement in foreign affairs means that until he becomes president he has never had to choose between these contradictory attitudes.

In 1945 it is natural for him to follow Roosevelt's commitment to a new world order and to make the creation of the UN the centrepiece of his policy. For most of his life Truman has carried in his wallet lines from Tennyson's 'Locksley Hall':

Till the war drum throbb'd no longer, and the battle flags were furl'd
In the Parliament of man, the Federation of the world.

And he is accustomed to quote it to explain his commitment to the UN. Nor is it unreasonable, in 1945, to suppose that world peace is going to depend on co-operation between the United States and the Soviet Union, the only great powers left at the end of the Second World War. In pursuit of this Roosevelt agreed ambiguous language at Yalta about Eastern Europe, which Stalin is now implementing in an unambiguous fashion.

Truman's first direct encounter with the Soviet Union is with Molotov, the foreign minister, who stops in Washington on his way to the San Francisco Conference on the UN to talk to Edward Stettinius, the US secretary of state, about Poland. At a courtesy call on Truman they exchange pleasantries about friendship and co-operation. Then Molotov goes to the talks and, as usual, refuses to move an inch. Truman sees Molotov again when the conference is under way, and tells him that while the United States has carried out all its obligations from Yalta, the Soviet Union has not done so. He speaks of Poland as a test for US-Soviet relations, in such plain language that this is followed by:

> Molotov: 'I have never been talked to like that in my life.'
> Truman: 'Carry out your agreements and you won't get talked to like that.'[7]*

After this excursion into his personal instincts, Truman returns to Roosevelt's policy. There is little the United States can do for the countries in Eastern Europe, now occupied by the Red Army. At the San Francisco Conference on the UN, Soviet co-operation is needed. Eighty per cent of Americans think it is important to establish a world organisation to maintain the peace. So does Truman. By mid May the conference is deadlocked and he sends Harry Hopkins to make a deal with Stalin.

Hopkins's instructions, according to Truman's diary, are that Poland and other Central European countries, including Yugoslavia and Austria, 'made no difference to US interests so far as world peace is concerned'. But 'Poland ought to have "free elections", at least as free as Hague, Tom Pendergast, Joe Martin or Taft would allow in their respective bailiwicks.' (Frank Hague and Pendergast were Democratic Party bosses, Martin and Robert Taft Republican.) Finally, 'Uncle Joe should make some sort of a gesture – whether he means to keep it or not – before our public.'[8] It is for this reason that Hopkins replies to Kennan's plea that the United States should not be party to what Stalin was doing by saying that he is not at liberty to follow this line.

At the time of the Potsdam Conference in summer 1945 the advocates of co-operation with the Soviet Union at any price are in the ascendant. Truman is one of them. Political leaders choose their advisers according to the policies they want to follow, not the other way round.† At Potsdam, Truman has at the table with him his new

* There are two versions of this conversation: either way the tone is the same.
† See Machiavelli, *The Prince*, Chapter Twenty-three.

secretary of state, Jimmy Byrnes, and Joe Davies, an adviser and former ambassador to Moscow, as well as his military adviser, the sceptical but loyal Admiral William D. Leahy. Kennan, who served under Davies in the late 1930s, dislikes and despises him. He accompanied Davies as interpreter to the first of Stalin's show trials, fetching the ambassador his sandwiches 'while he exchanged sententious judgements with the gentlemen of the press concerning the guilt of the victims'.[9] At that time Davies's main preoccupation was his image in the press and his desire to present US-Soviet relations – and Stalin's regime – in the most favourable light possible. On Davies's advice, Truman does not meet Churchill ahead of Potsdam lest it give Stalin the impression that they are ganging up against him – mirroring Roosevelt's approach.

Potsdam is slow-going, but the United States secures its main objective: Soviet entry into the war with Japan. By then, this is a Soviet objective too. The Soviet Union gets the western border it wants for Poland, provisionally; but there is no agreement on German reparations.

The positive tone of US policy towards the Soviet Union continues; the exchanges at Cabinet level in Washington about the handling of nuclear technology illustrate this. Henry Stimson, the secretary of war and the member of the Cabinet most respected by Truman, argues that US possession of the bomb may create rivalry and suspicion on the part of the Soviet Union and that, working with Britain, the United States should propose nuclear disarmament and joint development of nuclear power for peaceful purposes with the Soviet Union. Stimson concludes: 'The chief lesson I have learned in a long life is that the only way you can make a man trustworthy is to trust him.'[10]

Of the heavyweights in the Cabinet, Acheson (in Byrnes's absence) and Henry Wallace (commerce) support this strongly; only James Forrestal (navy) objects. Truman also is sympathetic, and commissions Acheson and David Lilienthal (later head of the US Atomic Energy Commission) to work on a proposal for an international control regime for nuclear technology that can be submitted to the UN. During the autumn, Truman continues to refer to Stalin as someone he can make deals with.

As the year draws to a close, however, things begin to change. Discussions with Moscow over Germany go nowhere in spite of Byrnes's efforts to create a good atmosphere. Truman is becoming irritated with Byrnes, who behaves as if he, and not Truman, is making policy, giving Truman only sketchy accounts of his talks in Moscow – the ones that reduced Kennan to fury. This prompts Truman to look more closely at the results, and he concludes that Byrnes has made concessions while receiving little in return; and the 'good atmosphere' Byrnes claims to be creating is not delivering anything. At the same time Byrnes is coming under attack from senators such as Arthur Vandenberg, who fear he is preparing to give away the US nuclear monopoly. Truman is also alarmed at the continuing Soviet troop presence in Northern Iran (which the Soviet Union is trying to detach from Iran and annex), and at their demands for joint control with Turkey of the Black Sea Straits. Public opinion is becoming more sceptical, too: in mid 1945 most Americans expected co-operation from the Soviet Union; by February 1946 the number is down to 35 per cent.

The atmosphere of growing distrust means that Stalin's speech of 9 February 1946 to the Party Congress – standard rhetoric calling on the Russian people to prepare for conflict and sacrifice – is viewed in a different light. *Time* magazine, probably not having read much else Stalin has said, calls it 'the most warlike pronouncement by any top-rank leader since V-J day'.[11] Truman brushes it aside, saying to an audience: 'Well you know, we always have to demagogue a little before elections,' showing also how little he knows about elections in the Soviet Union.[12]

State Department officials who know the Soviet Union and share Kennan's views see this as an opportunity to change the thinking in Washington. They urge Kennan to send a think piece to exploit the new mood. This, from the Washington perspective, is the origin of the Long Telegram.

One of the lessons of politics and diplomacy is that nobody hears your messages unless they are listening. Choosing the moment to speak is as important as what you say. The Washington team, who sense the change in mood and see an opportunity to educate the government, choose well. They, as well as Kennan, succeed beyond their expectations.

The Long Telegram

Kennan's Long Telegram reaches Washington on 22 February 1946. It is a primer on the Soviet Union. It explains, in words of one syllable, that the Soviet Union is like nothing Americans have encountered before: hostile, secretive, seeing the world through a Marxist lens, ignoring facts that do not fit its ideological framework, believing that conflict with the West is inevitable, expecting conflict between capitalist countries and planning to play them off against each other (as it did in the Molotov-Ribbentrop Pact). The Soviet Union that Kennan describes sees itself surrounded by hostile powers. But it is weak compared with the West; so its methods will be infiltration, subversion and opportunist actions rather than a frontal assault. The weakness is important: 'impervious to the logic of reason [the Soviet Union] is highly sensitive to the logic of force',[13] Kennan writes, and it will retreat where it meets resistance.

The first step for the United States, Kennan suggests, is to understand what it is dealing with, and to educate the American people to understand it too. This includes recognising that the US stake in the Soviet Union is small, and that the Soviet Union's leverage on the United States is therefore similarly small. The second step is to understand that success in dealing with the Soviet Union depends on the United States' confidence in itself and in its own system, and its ability to project that confidence on its allies: 'Communism is like a malignant parasite that feeds only on diseased tissue.'[14] Keep the United States and its allies strong, politically, economically, morally – and the problem of Communism will look after itself.

Kennan, having broken every diplomatic rule with the Long Telegram, waits in Moscow wondering how his uncompromising picture will go down. The last senior visitor he has seen from Washington, Secretary Byrnes, does not seem likely to welcome this sort of message.

The usual response to efforts to educate has been silence, or 'the dull sound of my paper hitting the files'. To his amazement his telegram is read, it seems, by everyone from the president down. Byrnes circulates a shortened version to important diplomatic posts. Navy Secretary Forrestal makes the full version required reading for hundreds of senior military officers. Among them is George C. Marshall, who directed the US army in the Second World War and is now in China on a special mission for President Truman.

The telegram is long but its message is not complicated. Behind it lie years of experience and thought.

The education of a diplomat

George Frost Kennan was born in Milwaukee on 16 February 1904, to respectable middle-class parents (his father was a tax attorney). He shared both name and birthday with a cousin of his grandfather, who travelled in Russia and wrote and lectured on the evils of the tsarist regime. Kennan attended Milwaukee State Normal School and later St John's Military Academy. From there he passed the entrance examination for Princeton, the only pupil from his school to have made it to an East Coast college. He was not happy there but achieved decent academic results. Good at languages – the Milwaukee Normal School taught German from the first grade – and wishing to travel, he took the entrance exams for the newly established US Foreign Service.*

Passing the exams in 1926, he entered the (also newly established) Foreign Service School and was then posted abroad, temporarily in Geneva, and then substantively as a vice-consul in Hamburg. From there, in November 1927, he submitted the first of several letters of resignation. These came from the restlessness that followed him for most of his life, from the feeling that he needed to pursue his

* The 1924 Rogers Act had the objective of creating a professional Foreign Service open to all by competitive examination. It unified the diplomatic and consular functions and established salaries and career structures that allowed men (not yet women) without private means to join.

education further, and from a romantic attachment in Washington.

The romance ends with his return; and though the restlessness takes longer, his teacher from the Foreign Service School persuades him that he can continue his education without leaving the Foreign Service. He points Kennan to a new programme offering three years' postgraduate study at a European university to master languages such as Chinese, Japanese, Arabic or Russian. Kennan chooses Russian, foreseeing opportunities if the United States re-establishes diplomatic relations, and because of the elder George Kennan.

Kennan spends the next five years in Tallinn, Riga and Berlin. He works in the US missions in Estonia and Latvia (during their inter-war period of independence), studying Russian in his spare time. Then he spends two years in Berlin, where he studies Russian history and literature, having mastered the language early on. His instructions from the State Department are to acquire the education of a well-educated Russian of the pre-revolutionary period. While in Berlin Kennan marries Annelise Sorensen, whose Norwegian home remains a refuge for much of his life. They remain together until his death in 2005. Back in Riga he analyses developments in Russia for Washington by studying the press and Russian journals – the pre-revolutionary education applied to the Communist world: work, but also a continuation of his studies.

By the end of this time, his Russian and his analysis of Russia are of a high standard. In answer to a query from the head of mission about whether the Russian people are content with their government, he replies that in a country where millions have been killed or sent to prison camps, 'where the ideals, principles, beliefs and social position of all but a tiny minority have been forcibly turned upside down by government action . . . it is scarcely to be expected that most people should be as happy as in other countries'. In spite of his immersion in detail, Kennan does not lose sight of the obvious. Nevertheless, he says, some, such as the army and factory workers, have benefited from Communist rule, and young Communists in particular have the happiness of 'having been relieved of the curses of egotism, romanticism, day-dreaming, introspection and perplexity which befall the youth of bourgeois countries'. It sounds – as often in Kennan's writings – as though he is thinking of himself. He adds that if Soviet economic policies fail, anger would paralyse the regime; but if they were ever to succeed, then 'autos, radios, and electric iceboxes would drain ideological zeal'. And, 'guided neither by tradition, example, ideals, nor by personal responsibility which acts as a steadying influence in other countries, the young Russian will probably be as helpless and miserable as a babe in the woods . . . From the most morally unified country in the world Russia can become overnight the worst moral chaos.'[15]

This report, unearthed by Kennan's biographer, John Lewis Gaddis and, as he says, probably unread in Washington, is striking in its vision of the moral crisis that will afflict Russia sixty years later, after the collapse of Communism – though the young Kennan underestimates the capacity of the Russian people to suffer and to survive.

On leave from Riga, and taking Annelise on her first visit to the United States, Kennan is sucked into the preparation of the Roosevelt-Litvinov talks that will lead to US recognition of the Soviet Union in 1933. Personally, he is against: his work has convinced him that the Soviet Union will break whatever agreement it makes; but no one is interested in his opinion. He is visiting the State Department shortly after the talks finish when a friend introduces him to William Bullitt, who Roosevelt has nominated as the first US ambassador to the Soviet Union. Bullitt asks him some questions about the Soviet economy. After five years of daily study, few people could be better able to answer. Impressed, Bullitt asks if he speaks Russian well enough to interpret. Hearing that he does, Bullitt invites Kennan to go with him to Moscow.

Bullitt is a man of independence and style. In 1919, Woodrow Wilson and Lloyd George sent him from Versailles to establish contact with the Bolshevik government, but the agreement he made with Lenin to end Western support for the White Russians was dropped by those who sent him. Now he is acting for Roosevelt in the process of recognising the Soviet Union. Bullitt's independence is both financial – he is from the Philadelphia aristocracy – and intellectual: he is a former radical, now a progressive, but he remains someone who makes up his own mind. The style comes from his background. On the Atlantic crossing it is too rough to drink red wine – which will be badly shaken – so they stick to champagne, all except for Kennan, who has a bad cold and is confined to his bunk.

Kennan is with Bullitt on 11 December 1933 when he presents his credentials. For the first and last time the Soviet government is friendly. Bullitt returns to Washington, leaving Kennan behind to set up the embassy. When the State Department objects that Kennan has no administrative experience, Bullitt replies that the Russians have asked for him specifically, because of the excellence of his Russian. Bullitt takes it directly to Roosevelt and gets his way.

In the weeks that follow, Kennan shows that he is not just a thinker but can also get things done, taking advantage of a honeymoon moment of relative co-operation from the Russians.* Bullitt returns with a team of Russian specialists who the State Department has been preparing for this moment: these include Chip Bohlen, who works with Kennan on political reporting, and Loy Henderson, with whom Kennan has worked in Riga.

Kennan's work in the embassy is a continuation of what he has done in Tallinn and Riga: reporting and analysis of political events in the Soviet Union, but with the difference that he is on the spot and for the first time can travel, see the people he is writing about, 'drink in impressions of Russia itself: of its life, its culture, its aspect, its smell'. He works intensely, so much so that he falls ill and is sent by Bullitt to a sanatorium in Austria. The benefits of the work are, as he says, 'once again, primarily educational'.[16]

By the time Bullitt leaves in 1936 the US embassy is among the most highly respected diplomatic missions in Moscow, rivalled only by the Germans. Since doing business with the Soviet government is a lost cause, they have made it their task to understand them. In the winter

* To help him Kennan recruits Charles Thayer, a West Point graduate who wants to pick up some Russian and join the Foreign Service. When Bullitt instructs the staff to organise his Christmas party and 'make it good', it is Thayer who hires performing seals from the Moscow Circus to slide down the room balancing champagne glasses on their noses. Kennan misses the party, being ill. Bullitt gives another famous party – the inspiration of the ball in Bulgakov's *The Master and Margarita* – for which the Moscow Circus lends further animals, including a baby bear that gets drunk on champagne.

of 1934–5 the purges have begun, followed by the show trials. Free communication between Russians and foreigners becomes impossible; contact with foreign diplomats is life-threatening for Russian officials; and the only way to follow events is by deciphering the printed record and matching it to the atmosphere in public places. At the heart of this intellectual effort is Kennan himself, not just earning his daily bread by reporting on current developments but also writing think pieces to put Soviet policy in a wider context.

One of these, 'The War Problem of the Soviet Union', written to clear his mind and not sent to Washington, shows how clear that mind is.[17] Kennan describes the Soviets' view of themselves as surrounded by hostile, capitalist states with whom war is inevitable. He comments that the Soviet Union is in no danger from its neighbours but that its greedy and aggressive policies, driving wedges between capitalist enemies, suggest that Russia might keep out of a European war at the beginning but later, when other participants have weakened themselves, would not be able to resist the temptation to come in, 'if only in the capacity of a vulture'.[18]

Kennan, like others, underestimates Hitler; but his analysis of the Soviet Union is precise and accurate. The logic he describes underpins Soviet policy in the Molotov-Ribbentrop Pact and the Winter War with Finland.

Bullitt's farewell despatch warns of unremitting Soviet hostility towards the United States, but concludes:

> We should remain unimpressed in the face of expansive professions of friendliness and unperturbed in the face of slights and underhand opposition. We should make the weight of our influence felt steadily over a long period of time in the directions which best suit our interests. We should never threaten. We should allow the Bolsheviks to draw their own conclusions as to the causes of our acts.[19]

Kennan is Bullitt's protégé; the ambassador protects his career and his health. Kennan is his main source of advice on the Soviet government; in style and substance this passage sounds like Kennan. But

Bullitt leaves Moscow disappointed and frustrated at his inability to make a personal difference to Soviet-US relations.

Not long after, Kennan himself leaves too, happy to escape from the new ambassador, Joe Davies. He spends a year in the State Department, where the Russia division has been downgraded to a single desk. Bullitt and Henderson believe that if they have fewer resources they must maintain quality, and insist that the job is given to Kennan.

By the end of this year Kennan has spent ten years working on and thinking about the Soviet Union. What is the product? Much reporting of day-to-day events, now forgotten, some interesting think pieces, unread at any senior level. He is nevertheless beginning to make a name for himself on Soviet affairs among the professionals in the State Department.

Prague, Berlin, Bad Nauheim

Kennan is posted to Prague in September 1938. He arrives there while Chamberlain is meeting Hitler in Munich. He spends the next year watching the German army and the Gestapo dismantling Czechoslovakia. In his first days in Prague he is confronted by 'an attractive young woman . . . tossing a most magnificent head of golden hair'[20] and demanding to know what he is doing to prepare for the flood of Czech refugees likely to come to Prague as the German occupation of the Sudetenland begins. This is Martha Gellhorn, later a good friend, but at this moment a one-woman humanitarian movement.* There is nothing, Kennan rather stiffly explains, that a diplomatic mission of six people can do in a foreign country over which they have no control.

But there is something diplomats can do: they can report on what is happening, what it means, what the implications are for the United States; they can put it in a historical and a moral framework. It is not

* Martha Gellhorn was one of America's greatest war correspondents, reporting on conflicts from the Spanish Civil War to Vietnam. She also worked for Harry Hopkins, reporting to him on conditions in the United States in the great depression. Her novel *A Stricken Field* is set in Czechoslovakia in 1938.

very different from what Martha Gellhorn does as a journalist, except that diplomats, if they are lucky, are occasionally able to move governments and not just readers. Kennan remains in Prague after the diplomatic mission is closed, reporting on the German occupation from the US consulate.

When that too is closed, Kennan moves to Berlin, aiming to continue to follow developments in Czechoslovakia. But he finds the embassy in such turmoil that he volunteers to run its administration. This is now a big task: the United States is the protecting power for Britain and France, responsible for their nationals and their property. By the time Hitler declares war and the US embassy closes, it will be acting for a further nine countries. It is also doing the work of ten US consulates in different German cities, closed by the German authorities; and it is doing what it can under US law to help Jews seeking asylum. This is a mission whose principal officers are working a twelve- to eighteen-hour day. In 1940, the departing chargé d'affaires of the Berlin embassy, Alexander Kirk,* who has understood something about Kennan, passes on to him his contacts with Helmuth von Moltke and others in the circle of the anti-Nazi Prussians.

In spite of the burdens of administration, Kennan writes on. He writes about the German occupation policies, having seen them in Prague, and now in German-occupied Holland, Norway and France. In a paper on the different occupation regimes, he concludes that military success brings political problems. A permanent military occupation is almost a physical impossibility; but the creation of a collaborator regime, unloved by its own people like Vichy France, is not a solution

* In his memoirs Kennan is sparing of portraits of those he worked with. There is no pen portrait of Acheson, with whom he worked closely, nor of his friend and contemporary Chip Bohlen. But he includes a sketch of Alexander Kirk. Kennan says that later he realised he had learned much from him, more perhaps than from any other chief. Kirk is an old-style diplomat. 'I am particularly indebted to him for the impressive lesson he gave me, by example more than by precept, of the importance of the means as compared with the ends. The only thing worth living for, he once told me, was good form. He himself had little to live for; there were moments when he would have liked to leave this life, but suicide would be bad form.' He despised the Nazis, Kennan says, and held them at arm's length with a barbed irony. Something in this portrait recalls Talleyrand, for whom style was also a cardinal virtue (Kennan, *Memoirs 1925–1950*, p. 114).

either. Later he asks if the State Department found these reflections useful. The answer is that no single desk covered all the countries in Kennan's paper, and it has remained unread.*

In June 1941, Germany attacks Russia. Kennan writes privately to his friend and colleague Loy Henderson, arguing against giving Russia 'moral support in the present German-Russian conflict'. The United States should treat it as a 'fellow traveller in the Moscow sense rather than as a political associate'. Material support should be given, but not moral support; Russia is in the war not because of sympathy with the Allied cause but because its attempt to purchase security by compromising with Germany has gone wrong. He sees no reason why the West should allow itself to be identified with the Russian destruction of the Baltic States and the attack on Finland.[21]

When war comes to the United States via Pearl Harbor, Kennan hears the news on a shortwave radio. He rouses Lelan Morris, Kirk's successor as chargé d'affaires, and organises the burning of classified material while they wait to see if Germany is going to declare war. When it does, he accompanies the chargé to receive the declaration of war from Ribbentrop, who screams at them that the war is all America's fault.

Thereafter Kennan finds himself responsible for 130 Americans who are interned under armed guard in a former hotel near Frankfurt.† Cold, hungry, worried, they are cut off from home and the rest of the world for five and a half months. Kennan has to maintain morale and negotiate on their behalf with the Germans: 'Their cares, their quarrels, their jealousies, their complaints filled every moment of my waking day. . . . The details of this ordeal would alone make a book.'[22] In fact, he does a lot more than listen to complaints about food. He organises the 'Badheim University', courses given by volunteers to keep boredom at bay. Kennan's lectures on Russia are among the best-attended.

* Kennan's observations on German occupations recall Talleyrand's views on conquest, and those of François-Poncet on the French occupation of Germany recorded in Chapter Five.

† It is not clear why Kennan and not Lelan Morris, his boss, takes these responsibilities. All Kennan says is that 'poor Morris' was kept standing by Ribbentrop during the tirade.

When their repatriation via Portugal is finally arranged, and the train stops at a station on the border, only Kennan is able to leave the train to deal with formalities. There he takes revenge on his charges and their complaints about the food by eating an enormous breakfast all on his own.

Arriving in Lisbon, he is greeted with the news that the US government has decided not to pay him for the period of captivity 'since he has not been working'. Not only does the State Department not read what he writes, it has no idea what he is doing when he is not writing.* (The order stopping his pay is eventually rescinded.)

After three months Kennan is back in Lisbon, appointed number two in the US mission. After sixteen years in the Foreign Service this is the first time he has anything like a normal diplomatic posting. He has studied and observed Russia from the Baltic; he has been in the hostile territory of Russia itself, then Prague as it is invaded by Germany; then Germany at war with Europe and Russia, leaving when it declares war on the United States. Nor has his work been normal: ten years of study and political reporting on Russia, an interlude in a collapsing Prague, then looking after an embassy under stress in Berlin, and 130 Americans, also under stress, in Bad Nauheim.

Portugal and the Azores

This is wartime, so although Portugal is neutral, it too is not normal. However, neither the amiable head of mission, Mr Bert Fish, a political appointee from Florida, nor the State Department seem to have worked out how Portugal might matter to the war effort. Mr Fish takes no interest in political relations with Portugal and refuses to call on the Portuguese leader, Dr Salazar ('Ah ain't going down there and get my backsides kicked around. He's too smaht for me.')[23] Kennan tries to interest the department by sending them a paper on the

* In fact, Kennan has also been writing while in Bad Nauheim: two papers for the administration on the handling of internees and the need to strengthen the Foreign Service in wartime. He finds both of them, unread, a few weeks later in Washington.

Anglo-Portuguese Alliance, dormant at this stage in the war but with potential to be reanimated and broadened to encompass the United States. No reaction.

In the summer of 1943, while Kennan is in Washington to collect his daughter, Bert Fish dies. Kennan finds himself in charge of the US mission. Returning to Lisbon, he learns that the British are engaged in secret negotiations with Portugal for military facilities in the Portuguese-owned Azores. Here is an important US interest: a massive volume of men and war materiel is crossing the Atlantic; and it will grow. The Azores could be vital as a staging post for aircraft and a base for conducting anti-submarine warfare.

The British keep Kennan informed about the negotiations, and he in turn sends classified messages to the secretary of state, hoping that the obvious US interest in these arrangements will enable him to extract a coherent policy from the State Department. The Portuguese position is delicate: Lisbon wants to remain neutral, but does not want to reject the British request; Britain's support over 600 years has enabled Portugal to maintain its independence from Spain. The facilities are finally announced on 12 October 1943 (four days after British forces have landed in the Azores). Winston Churchill refers to them in the House of Commons as 'the latest application' of the Anglo-Portuguese Treaty of 1373. On this basis Portugal claims a rather implausible exception to the normal rules of neutrality.

The story of the Azores is complicated. From Kennan's perspective it looks like this:

- Early October: Kennan receives instructions that, *if asked*, he may give the Portuguese assurances that their sovereignty over their overseas possessions – including the Azores – will be respected.
- 8 October (the British have by now started landing in the Azores, but no announcement has been made): Kennan receives instructions to call on Dr Salazar and give him assurances (without being asked) that the United States will respect the sovereignty of Portugal's overseas possessions. He arranges the call, hinting at the subject matter.

- Sunday, 10 October: On his way to see Dr Salazar, Kennan finds new instructions *not* to give him the assurances. He embarks instead on a general discussion of US-Portuguese relations, leaving Salazar wondering why he has interrupted a Sunday for this.
- Sunday, 17 October: Kennan receives instructions, on the authority of the president, to seek military facilities in the Azores. The facilities requested are on a scale that amounts to a takeover of the islands.
- 18 October: After speaking to the British ambassador Kennan tells Washington he sees compelling reasons for not proceeding as instructed, and offers to return to Washington to explain – to the president if necessary.
- 20 October: A reply arrives saying the president sees no reason for him to return to Washington but invites him to explain his reasoning by cable. Kennan replies, saying inter alia that he needs to offer a quid pro quo.
- A reply from the State Department says that the president gives him discretion on the detail of the negotiations, including on how much he should ask for. They add that the assurances on sovereignty could be a quid pro quo. (This is like saying: if you don't give us the facilities, we'll invade.)
- 23 October: As a preliminary to seeing Dr Salazar, he calls on the head of the Foreign Ministry, who asks why, in his previous conversation with Salazar, he said nothing about guarantees of sovereignty. Understanding that without these assurances he will not get through the door of Salazar's office, Kennan offers to give the assurances in writing that day. He types a note himself and sends it to the Foreign Ministry. He cables Washington that he has disobeyed his instructions, and explains why.
- The following day he receives an invitation to call on Dr Salazar. But before he can do this, another cable arrives, instructing Kennan to return to Washington immediately.

The cable recalling him to Washington gives no explanation and makes no mention of the instructions he has disobeyed, but he assumes it is for a reprimand. He arrives in Washington after a five-day wartime journey in a somewhat nervous state. There, he is taken by the acting secretary of state, Stettinius, and 'Doc' Matthews, the head of the Europe Bureau, to see Stimson, the secretary of war, together with all the chiefs of staff.

They ask Kennan why he has questioned the instructions sent two weeks before (seeking vast military facilities). He states his arguments, and says that an agreement to use the airfield available to the British should be negotiable. The airfield is dismissed by the head of the air force as 'nothing but a goddam swamp'. The meeting concludes with the secretary of war suggesting that Stettinius appoint a proper ambassador to Portugal. (Later Kennan discovers that the chiefs of staff have seen only his first cable, with reservations about the instructions, and neither his subsequent explanation, nor the revised instructions from the president.)

Downcast by all this, Kennan, as he thinks it over, gradually becomes angry: 'What stung . . . was the realization that these various people, for all their lofty rank and enormous power, were unquestionably wrong. I knew more about Portugal and about the ins and outs of the situation than any of them did.'[24] At the suggestion of Matthews he calls on Admiral Leahy, Roosevelt's chief of staff, who, after a few questions, passes him on to Harry Hopkins. Hopkins questions him sharply and sceptically for an hour. He has little time for diplomats and puts them through a searching examination before deciding to take them seriously.

A few hours later Hopkins telephones Kennan and calls him back to the White House. He takes him to see the president. There, for the first time, someone treats him in a friendly fashion. Roosevelt, at his most affable, recalls that as assistant secretary of the navy he had personally supervised the dismantling of US bases in the Azores after the First World War, and wonders why, after that, Dr Salazar should distrust him. He volunteers to write a personal letter to Salazar. When Kennan mentions the different approach that the defence officials seem to be taking, the president – in Kennan's account – says, 'Oh don't worry,' with a debonair wave of his cigarette holder, 'about all those people over there' – thus dismissing the secretary of war and the chiefs of staff.[25]

Roosevelt's letter and backing enable Kennan to reach an understanding with Salazar. By the time this is done the State Department, responding to the secretary of war, has appointed a new head of the US mission, and by mutual consent Kennan leaves Lisbon so that his successor can take the negotiations forward. The Azores facilities prove invaluable to the war effort, and the airfield is not a swamp.

This episode is apart from Kennan's work on the Soviet Union, Germany and the Cold War. But it illustrates both Kennan's qualities and the problems he and others faced at the time.

The demands of the US chiefs of staff for massive facilities are born of the knowledge that, in war, half-measures cost lives – hence the standard military preference for a sledgehammer, no matter how small the nut. For the chiefs of staff the Portuguese were no more than a nuisance; for Kennan and for the British ambassador, Sir Ronald Campbell, they were real people who had their own interests, dilemmas and pride – and with whom one could get a reasonable result by negotiating in the right way.

This incident also illustrates the casualness of the old State Department. Kennan received three instructions in rapid succession: first to give assurances on sovereignty *if asked*, then to give them anyway, then not to give them at all – without any explanation of the changes of mind. To handle a sensitive issue without any guidance on what lies behind the instructions he would have had to be clairvoyant. (He later discovers that the third instruction, not to give the assurances at all, was a suggestion from the US ambassador in London, who knew nothing of Portugal.) Here, as with the military list of demands, the State Department seems to have regarded itself as no more than a messenger box for others to use.

Finally, there are Kennan's actions: risky but right. Lord Palmerston is quoted, probably apocryphally, as saying that what he wanted was diplomats who were prepared to disobey their instructions. If their only function was to obey, then a messenger boy would do.

The Azores are important, but in the grand scheme this is a small incident. The British had broken the back of the problem by the time Kennan became involved. Even with clumsy handling, as proposed by the US military or the ambassador in London, the result would probably have been the same, though the process would have been more difficult. But occasionally, careless handling of small countries produces a stubborn reaction. Kennan's insistence – on doing things properly and treating serious business seriously – deserves credit. So does his readiness to take responsibility when everyone else – in the State Department at least – was anxious to avoid it.

In spite of his disobedience, Kennan's career remains intact. He is sent to London to work as an adviser to Ambassador John Winant, who is representing the United States in the European Advisory Commission. This body has been set up by the foreign ministers of the United States, the Soviet Union and Britain at their meeting in Moscow in October 1943 to serve 'as a clearing house for (non-military) problems of common interest connected with the war'. It works on the terms of a German surrender and the occupation zones. Kennan finds Washington wary of it. Returning there for instructions prior to taking up his appointment, he writes:

> So far as I could learn from my superiors in the department, their attitude was dominated by a lively concern lest the new body should at some point and by some mischance actually do something . . . Uneasiness centred particularly on my own person as a result of my recent adventures in the matter of the Azores bases – adventures which, in spite of their generally favourable outcome, many in the department still viewed with a disapproval bordering on sheer horror.[26]

Kennan is warned that the State Department has only an advisory role, and that it gives advice only when asked. This means that, as was the case with the Azores, State Department officials regard their job as being to pass on whatever the Pentagon gives them. Thus, when the commission holds its first meeting the United States has nothing to say and can only pass back to Washington the British proposals for the terms of surrender and zones of occupation. The Russians are in a similar position, but a month later they propose different surrender terms and agree to the British proposals on occupation zones. Still no reaction from Washington.

Three weeks later Washington sends its own version of the terms of surrender, and then, after a further interval, its proposals on the occupation zones. Neither is accompanied by commentary or argumentation. Putting forward the new US proposal on occupation zones appears problematic: it foresees a US zone covering half of Germany and takes no account of administrative or geographical boundaries.

Unable to agree with Winant's military adviser on how to proceed – the adviser thinks they should argue for the Pentagon's map, though they do not understand its logic – Kennan proposes they go back to Washington together for clarification. As in the Azores case, he ends up taking the question to the president. Roosevelt agrees that it makes sense to accept the Russian proposal for the Soviet zone; he and the British can argue about who is going to have the northern and who the southern occupation zones in Germany.* As for the Pentagon's map, this turns out to come from something the president has scribbled on the back of an envelope on his way to the Tehran Conference. By now Kennan is again sick, and his involvement with the European Advisory Commission ends, no doubt to the relief of the State Department, which sends him back to the Soviet Union.

The European Advisory Commission does not give Kennan much to do; but it makes him think about the problems of post-war Europe. Two products come out of this: one is a memorandum to Admiral Leahy proposing that the US objective in occupied Germany should be to ensure 'that no European power acquires the possibility of using Europe's resources to conduct aggression outside the continent of Europe'.[27] With Germany and France defeated and Britain exhausted, this is about preventing a Soviet takeover of Germany.

The other is advice to a State Department committee on post-war Europe, warning that a big programme of denazification will be difficult

* In the end it is settled personally between Roosevelt and Churchill.

to administer justly and will make government itself almost impossible. In any case it will be unnecessary: with the Nazi leaders gone, the lesson of defeat itself will teach the nationalists the folly of nationalism. As usual, there is no evidence that anybody reads it.

Back to Moscow

Returning to Moscow, Kennan reflects on the situation there, setting out his thoughts in two papers for Ambassador Harriman. One is about the state of the Soviet Union as he finds it after seven years; the other is about Russia's international position at the end of the war in Europe. Both, in the Kennan style, are long; they show both why Kennan has acquired a reputation as a thinker, and also why he fails to influence policy.

The first sets the scene. The Soviet Union is now the greatest power in Europe: 200 million people under one single man, facing a collection of weak states to the west that have neither the means nor the unity to stand up to it. This does not mean it will be aggressive. In the past it has sought security in isolation. That isolation has brought with it a profound ignorance of the outside world, for the Soviet Union as a whole and for Stalin in particular. And after the purges and the war, it is only Stalin that counts. Isolation has enabled the Soviet Union to construct its own reality – over which the state has total control. It can accuse victims of the purges of being agents of foreign powers, and then a few months later ally itself with those powers. This is a country without objective truth:

> the apprehension of what is valid in the Russian world is unsettling and displeasing to the American mind. He who would undertake this apprehension will not find his satisfaction in the achievements of anything practical for his people, still less in any official or public recognition for his efforts. The best he can look forward to is the lonely pleasure of one who stands at long last on a chilly and inhospitable mountaintop, where few have been before, where few can follow and where few will consent to believe he has been.[28]

These sentences tell the reader – if he or she has got that far – that Kennan expects neither to be heard nor to be understood. He is right. If you formulate your thoughts, perceptive though they are, in essays of this length and in this baroque prose, you are challenging your masters to ignore them. And they do.

The second essay has a starker message. The war will leave the Soviet Union in control of Central Europe; the Soviets see this as necessary to strengthen their security. But it will be a weakness. Communism has lost its power to mobilise, and all that remains is Russian nationalism. The Soviet Union will be an imperial power in Communist clothing. It will have to deal with nationalist sentiment in the countries it controls; the puppets who govern there will be despised. Lacking legitimacy, the Soviet Union will want the United States to give its blessing to this division of Europe and to the fiction that the puppet governments in Central Europe are independent. The Soviets will feel confident of obtaining this because they know that the American public has been taught to believe:

> (a) That collaboration with Russia as we envisage it, is entirely possible.
> (b) That it depends only on the establishment of proper personal relationships of cordiality and confidence with Russian leaders, and
> (c) That if the United States does not find means to assure this collaboration (again, as we envisage it), then the past war has been fought in vain, another war is inevitable, and civilization is faced with complete catastrophe.[29]

As long as these views can be maintained the Soviet Union will be able to count on the United States as an auxiliary in support of its power in Eastern Europe. If, contrary to his expectations, the West refuses to legitimise Soviet rule, Kennan predicts that the Soviet Union will not be able to maintain its hold over *all* its Eastern European acquisitions.

History has too many twists and turns to make it sensible to judge Kennan or anyone else on whether their predictions are fulfilled – in fact, he is part right, part wrong.* What matters is Kennan's insight that Eastern Europe will be a problem and not a solution for the Soviet Union, a source of weakness, not of strength; so that, sensing its weakness, it will be forever on the hunt for legitimacy.

These views are at odds both with US policy and with the public mood in 1945. Policy is founded on the hope that an international organisation can ensure that war will never recur. And the UN will depend on US-Soviet collaboration.

Two of the ambassadors Kennan has worked for illustrate the illusions that he believes the Kremlin will exploit. One, Joe Davies, published his memoirs, *Mission to Moscow*, in 1942 – a bestseller, serialised by *Reader's Digest* and made into a Hollywood movie. Throughout these works and in his reports from Moscow, Davies' attitude was that the Russians were straightforward people, men of goodwill and that they were easy to do business with, absurd adjectives to describe Stalin written by someone who has been in Moscow for the purges and the show trials.†

The other is Bill Bullitt. Disappointed and disillusioned, he feels he failed in Moscow because he did not create the relationship he wanted with the Soviet Union. He reacts to difficulties at the Dumbarton Oaks Conference on the creation of the UN with an article in *Life* magazine, stating that no workable agreements can be reached with an evil, atheistic power like the Soviet Union, and the sooner the United States goes to war with it the better.[30] Joe Davies illustrates illusion (a), that collaboration with the Soviet Union is possible – as well as the degree of self-deception it requires. Bill Bullitt's conclusion supports illusion (c), that the alternative to collaboration is war. As for Kennan's second axiom/illusion, the belief that a personal rapport with Stalin is

* If one had to judge pedantically, the answer might be that Kennan is right that adjustments will be made to the area controlled – the Soviet Union allows Finland to negotiate an escape from its sphere, agrees to Austria being free in exchange for neutrality, and 'loses' Yugoslavia. On the other hand, he was wrong in that hegemony over the rest lasts for forty years – far longer than he implies.

† Like the stopped clock, Davies was not always wrong. When Hitler attacked the Soviet Union he predicted that, in spite of the evidence, they would survive and fight back. This was the view that Roosevelt listened to (Gaddis, *George F. Kennan*, p. 142).

profoundly important and can be established with a little effort – this is held by almost all US leaders. Roosevelt and Byrnes shared this fantasy (so did Churchill, sometimes). It is in pursuit of such a rapport that Truman sends the dying Hopkins to see Stalin. He is there just at the time that Kennan writes 'Russia's International Position'. It is quite likely that Hopkins has read it. Unknown to Kennan, Harriman has sent him a copy prior to his visit. Kennan's plea to him, not to give legitimacy to Soviet hegemony in Eastern Europe, reflects the advice in this paper. But Hopkins has been sent to do just that: to offer the Soviet Union legitimacy in Poland in exchange for concessions on the UN.

The damage done by US acquiescence in the Soviet takeover of Eastern Europe is not as bad as Kennan believes. Much though the Soviets want it, US approval or disapproval has no impact on their policies. But nor is the continuation of wartime collaboration as vital for peace as its advocates claim.

It is easy nevertheless to understand the logic that leads Roosevelt and others to these conclusions. Twice in a generation European power politics brought destruction to Europe and war to the United States. Something fundamental has to change. After the First World War, Woodrow Wilson proposed the League of Nations to guarantee the peace; but against the background of the Versailles Peace Conference, with the United States absenting itself and Germany excluded, and with its own design flaws, the League was never going to succeed. So the inheritors of Woodrow Wilson aim to redo what he proposed, and this time to do it properly. That means creating a universal organisation to do what the League never did – defend the peace against all comers. For this, Soviet participation and US-Soviet co-operation are essential. Co-operation with the Soviet Union was the key to victory in the Second World War; why should it not be the key to peace thereafter?

Without the rose-tinted spectacles, or viewed from Moscow, the collaboration in the Second World War looks more limited than anyone admits. There was a common enemy but, beyond Germany's defeat, no common objectives, only supplies of war materiel. This contrasts with US-UK co-operation, based on joint aims for the post-war world in the Atlantic Charter and marked by intense military collaboration

– and intense arguments – between the US and British staffs. It is something like this that Kennan advocates in his letter to Loy Henderson in 1941: an alliance of convenience with the Soviet Union, limited to the one aim of defeating Hitler. The reality of these limits is not properly understood in Washington in May 1945.

The UN was never going to be the cornerstone of peace that Roosevelt imagined. Peace in Europe is achieved by other means. Kennan is not opposed to the UN, but he does not believe that laws and votes will stop the strong dominating the weak. An international organisation, as he sees it, is no substitute for a foreign policy based on the realities of power. What disgusts Kennan is the make-believe agreements with the Soviet Union, and the illusions on the US side.

Before returning to the Long Telegram and its consequences, one further piece of writing by Kennan, from the same time, shows a different side of his personality. This is not policy analysis but an account of a Sunday excursion to a village on the outskirts of Moscow. Kennan, like everyone else, gets there clinging to the outside of a train:

> I finally found a step, a bottom step, which seemed to have room for one more single foot, and hopped onto it. A young girl, observing my success, immediately jumped up behind me and threw both arms around me to clutch the guard rails. Hanging widely out over the platform, she shouted exuberantly to an invisible companion down on the platform: 'Sonya, Sonya: I have found a seat.'

On the way he listens to the conversations going on in the train:

> Someone had read in the morning paper the new decree about marriage and divorce, and the idea of premiums for large families was giving rise to a series of hilarious comments from the women. Just above me a peasant girl was relating her own sufferings and those of her native village at the hands of the Germans. The tale began with hiding in a barrel of honey and ended with the demise of her husband and her relatives. I could hear the conclusion flung out to the sympathetic audience with all the throaty eloquence of the Russian

tongue: 'Who has need of me now? To whom am I now necessary?'

I tried repeatedly to turn around and climb up a step, in the hopes of hearing more of these discussions, but in doing so, I jostled the old peasant woman above me. She descended upon me with virulence:

'What's the matter with you anyway, comrade?' she shouted. 'Such vulgarity. After all. That's the tenth time you've jostled me. And you with the outward appearance of a cultured man.'

After a day sketching a church while listening to the service, talking to an old woman and seeing the half of a room in an old house where she lives, he returns to the railway:

Somewhere in the woods a woman was singing, in a clear strong voice, a voice you would never hear anywhere but in Russia. On the other side of the ravine two young women were working in a small potato field, and a man was lying on his back in the grass and watching them. The women had broad faces, brown muscular arms and the powerful maternal thighs of the female Slav. They laughed and joked as they worked and it was clear that they enjoyed the feeling of the sun on their bodies and the dark earth, cool and sandy under their bare feet.[31]

Kennan's dislike of the Soviet government and its policies is deep. Behind it is an equally deep sympathy for the Russian people, reinforced by his admiration for their courage during the war. It reminds us too that his ability as a Russian speaker was such that, when he could escape from his minders, ordinary people took him for an educated Russian.

Stuck at Omsk airport, and with the NKVD (the KGB of its day) having lost track of him, he reads aloud from a biography of Peter the Great to a group of fellow passengers: 'In the evening I shared their company in the little airport dormitories as though I were a common citizen like the rest of them. I felt immensely at home among them and never did the artificial barriers that separated people like myself from Soviet citizens in Moscow seem more absurd and more deplorable.'[32]

Then there is Yalta, where Roosevelt is focused on building the UN and Stalin on establishing Soviet control over Poland. Then victory in Europe; the ambassador is away and Kennan is in charge of the embassy. Thousands assemble spontaneously in the square outside. He sends someone over the roof to the neighbouring hotel – anyone venturing out at ground level is seized by the crowd and tossed in the air in celebration – to borrow a Soviet flag, which he hangs next to the Stars and Stripes. He climbs out of a window on the first floor and congratulates the crowd on their common victory. A Marine sergeant, who joins him, is captured by the crowd and returns only the next day, after the night of his life. The celebration is natural and heartfelt. (Kennan learns later that Stalin resented Soviet citizens showing warm feelings towards a foreign power.)

Then there is Hopkins's visit and the compromise with Stalin; Potsdam and the drawing of lines on maps with 'casualness and frivolity', also the beginning of deadlock on Germany, and a decision to set up the Nuremberg Tribunal including Soviet judges – fresh from Stalin's show trials – as though they represented some universal notion of justice. Then the Byrnes visit and the papering-over of differences to contrive the appearance of agreement.

After the Long Telegram

And so back to the Long Telegram, the distillation of the thoughts and frustrations of seventeen years, during which he has concluded that talking to Washington is 'like talking to a stone'. But now, in February 1946, instead of the prose style of Gibbon, Kennan writes with a brutal simplicity. The effect of the telegram, in Kennan's words, is sensational. 'My official loneliness came to an end . . . My voice now carried.'[33]

If we want to identify the moment when the United States grows up to its responsibilities in a dangerous and divided world, this would be as good as any. Big changes do not take place as the result of a single cable, however long it is. Kennan's career changes overnight. US policy takes longer; but Kennan now has an active role in making it.

The Long Telegram is a warning about the Soviet Union: what it is, how it operates, the difficulties of dealing with it. It says less about what the United States should do. But the warnings are a start. We have seen Truman, who assumes that Stalin is more or less like a Democratic Party boss; and Roosevelt, who suffered from the illusion that a personal relationship with Stalin could persuade him to change his policies. Everyone in the political class seems to share this view: none of them has been in the Soviet Union for any length of time; most of them know nothing about its history, nothing about Marxism, and nothing about the Communist Party.

The message of the Long Telegram is this: do not think these people are like us; do not think their country is like ours; do not think that we can do business with them on normal terms.

At the end of the cable Kennan makes some 'practical deductions' for US policy. These are something of an afterthought; but they contain themes that will grow into policy. He describes the Soviet Union primarily as a *political* force; this thought will recur often as he tries to resist the tendency to frame East-West relations primarily in military terms. Second, the Soviet Union does not have a plan to conquer the world; it is cautious, not adventurist: when it meets resistance it will stop or reverse. This thought develops into the idea of 'containment'. Third, the United States needs to educate itself to these realities, and educate its public too. Finally, the strength and health of US and European society is the vital factor in resisting the Soviet threat. This last recommendation seems banal – that is Acheson's reaction – but it contains a profound truth. For European countries, this is the reasoning behind the Marshall Plan. For the United States, his injunction is that 'the greatest danger that can befall us in coping with this problem of Soviet communism is that we allow ourselves to become like those with whom we are coping'.[34] These are the last words of the Long Telegram, an intuition of and warning against McCarthyism.

As for Kennan's proposal that the United States should educate itself and its public about Soviet Communism, that is what he spends much of the next year doing. Leaving Moscow in April 1946 just after the arrival of a new ambassador, General Walter Bedell Smith, he takes up an appointment as Deputy Commandant of the National Defense College, newly created to bring together the military and the political – something Kennan has argued for during the war. In the spaces between preparing curricula and lecturing, the State Department sends him on a tour of the United States to explain the Soviet Union to a wider audience.

The National Defense College provides a setting for Kennan to look beyond the questions of Communism and Moscow and to shape ideas for a new era out of his knowledge of history, of Russia and of diplomacy.

One of George Marshall's first actions as secretary of state is to create the Planning Staff. The idea comes naturally to a soldier: planning is an essential military competence. Ensuring that you have the right troops, the right weapons, that you have the vehicles to move them and that these are brought together at the right time and place – this is the art of military planning. Until Marshall no one had tried to apply the concept to foreign policy.

When Acheson asks Kennan if he would be interested in being director of policy planning, he refers to Marshall's wish for a unit to fill the role, 'or at least part of it', that belonged to the Division of Plans and Operations in the War Department. Neither Acheson nor Kennan is sure what this means. Perhaps Marshall himself is in the same position. On his first day, Kennan asks Marshall what his instructions are. Marshall (famously) replies, 'Avoid trivia': memorable, but enigmatic as the basis for founding a new operation. Marshall's aim is to stimulate advance thinking about possible crises; and to improve coherence across the State Department and the government. Kennan himself, in Lisbon and London, has discovered how badly this is needed.

The idea that brilliant minds, detached from everyday work, can plan a grand strategy is something that Kennan himself comes to doubt. But this is one of those post-war moments when the world is remade, and the United States with it. That Kennan's instructions are vague does not matter; he has been itching to remake US diplomacy for years; and he is an expert on the country that poses a fundamental challenge to the United States. Marshall has chosen Kennan not just because of the Long Telegram: as the Chief of Staff of the Army he has heard him defend himself on the Azores and knows he is not just a thinker. His interview with the chiefs of staff was not, after all, the disaster it seemed to him at the time.

Marshall has ideas too. On his first day, he tells Kennan that he wants to take the initiative, not to leave it to others. This coincides with Kennan's own governing idea, that the threat from the Soviet Union is primarily political. To deal with that, a political strategy is needed: this is the business of the State Department. Thus, for two or three years it is the Planning Staff that develops and brings together strategy for the whole government.

This new world begins with the Long Telegram and the realisation that the dreams of post-war harmony and co-operation are an illusion. It continues, and takes concrete shape, with the Truman Doctrine.

The Policy Planning Staff and 'Containment'

The big decisions come not from Kennan but from Truman, advised by Marshall and Acheson. Kennan, though still at the National Defense College, is consulted. But the Truman Doctrine is not the result of abstract thought about grand strategy; it comes out of a crisis. Britain, crippled by debt, by the burdens of occupation and by the winter of 1946–7, can no longer meet the costs of military and economic assistance to Greece and Turkey.

The actions in Greece and Turkey are in line with Kennan's themes: strengthen allies politically and the advance of Communism can be stopped. He questions, both then and later, the terms in which the Truman Doctrine is announced: 'It must be the policy of the United States to support free peoples who are resisting attempted subjugation by armed minorities or by outside pressures.' Kennan's reservations are not to the substance – which is precisely in line with the ideas in the Long Telegram. His complaint is about the sweeping nature of a doctrine that placed our commitments to Greece 'in the framework of a universal policy rather than in that of a specific decision addressed to a specific set of circumstances'.[35]

Kennan has already set out his broad ideas on US policy in a paper for James Forrestal, secretary of the navy. It is published (with the State Department's permission) in *Foreign Affairs* with the author's name replaced by an 'X', intended to preserve Kennan's anonymity. This is naïve. The quickest way for a government official to achieve fame is to publish something anonymously and be found out. With the Long Telegram and the lecture tours, Kennan's name is already known. Many people will recognise his ideas and his style – no one else knows the Soviet Union so well; and there are few who quote Gibbon.

Foreign Affairs publishes the article in July 1947; fifty years later, in an anniversary volume, two of its editors will describe it as the journal's most important article ever. By the time it appears Kennan has forgotten about it, and has been director of policy planning for several months. The article develops some of the ideas in the Long Telegram. It argues that history, geography and ideology incline the Soviet Union's rulers to authoritarian methods, and to see themselves as surrounded by enemies. At the heart of the Soviet system is the claim that the Party and the Kremlin are infallible. All who work for Party or government are thus impervious to reason, no matter who their interlocutor and how persuasive his arguments. The normal give-and-take of dialogue and diplomacy is therefore meaningless. On the other hand, the Soviet Union is weak, and if arguments will not work, facts can halt the expansion of Communism.

Here, for the first time, Kennan uses the word 'containment' in a published paper. Many of the ideas now grouped under this title have appeared in earlier lectures and writings: that Soviet expansion can be resisted – that the readiness of the Kremlin to change tactics means also that it is ready to retreat; that opposing the Soviet Union need not involve military conflict; that change will come, eventually, through the weaknesses of the Soviet system. The 'X' article brings them together.

Containment is a strategy of patience, of winning without fighting, more Sun Tzu than Clausewitz. In a lecture at the National War College in December 1949 Kennan concludes: 'I would rather wait thirty years for a defeat of the Kremlin brought about by the tortuous and exasperatingly slow devices of diplomacy than see us submit to the test of arms a difference so little susceptible to any clear and happy settlement by those means.'[36] An advocate of patience, Kennan himself is often impatient at how slowly results come; it is in the nature of containment that you are not in control.

The proper object of containment is the Soviet Union, not the global Communist movement. It is a specific policy for a specific adversary. Kennan believes that nationalism is stronger than ideology, and that the extension of Communist rule to countries not controlled by Soviet forces will be a weakness and not a strength. He advocates a selective approach in handling governments bearing a Communist label. He is consistent in his belief that a Communist China will be a problem for the Soviet Union as well as for the United States. In this respect his intellectual successor in US diplomacy is Henry Kissinger.

Henry Kissinger, in *White House Years*, says that Kennan 'came as close to authoring the diplomatic doctrine of his era as any diplomat in history'.[37] Kennan himself dislikes the idea of 'doctrine' – implying something of universal application. Universal does not work in foreign policy, where every situation is particular. It is reasonable to aid Greece; but it is also reasonable to cut American losses in China when it is clear that the Nationalists cannot win. Kennan is sceptical that 'policy guidelines' can be sophisticated enough to meet changing situations. What is needed is people who understand the situation and can make judgements as it evolves.

Yet containment is a useful idea. For Kennan it is a political concept, since he sees the threat as political. The 'X' article says that the United States should be ready to 'confront the Russians with unalterable counter-force at every point where they show signs of encroaching on a peaceful and stable world'.[38] The political commentator Walter Lippmann and others take this to mean a military response, though the word 'unalterable' suggests something else.

Taking Kennan's papers and lectures together, what he proposes represents the outline of a strategy:

- The United States cannot do business with the Soviet Union as though it were a normal country.

- The Soviet Union does not plan offensive action but it will take advantage of the weakness of others to spread Communism.
- The United States should neither appease nor make war, but should counter Soviet attempts to widen their sphere of influence.
- The United States does not need to do this everywhere but only in areas of strategic significance, notably Europe and Japan.
- The way to oppose Communism is to create the political strength to resist Soviet ideas and Soviet subversion.
- The imbalance of power arises from the collapse of Europe. A confident and united Europe would be able to contain Soviet power.
- In the long run, the spread of Communism may be a weakness for the Soviet Union, not a strength.
- This, combined with its own internal weaknesses, may eventually lead it to change, making it possible to negotiate a more sensible relationship.

These are Kennan's main themes. They outline a programme dramatically different from that foreseen by Roosevelt and Truman. The assumption that peace will be assured by co-operation among great powers in the UN framework is mistaken. Peace comes by recognising and managing the conflict between them.

Some of Kennan's points are far-sighted. The notion that Communism can be pluralistic and that independent Communist powers will be a source of weakness for Moscow is ahead of its time, intellectually and historically. Tito's break with Moscow comes in 1948; Kennan's thinking here had been influenced not by foreknowledge of Yugoslavia but by advice from his China expert, John Paton Davies, and by his observation of the Nazi occupation of European countries – as well as by his reading of Gibbon. His case for sustaining Tito in his opposition to Moscow becomes the basis of US policy through the Cold War; his insight that Beijing will one day be a thorn in the side of Moscow is ahead of events by two decades.

Kennan's immediate concern is the political weakness of Western Europe. He is already thinking about this when he is summoned by

Marshall to start work on a paper on the European crisis. This is 29 April 1947 and Marshall has just returned from Moscow. The story of the Marshall Plan is told in the next chapter. Here it is enough to say that Kennan makes two particular contributions: first he insists that the initiative should come from Europe, and should be collective. Second, it is his – and Bohlen's – confidence that the Soviets will not accept the offer of assistance that persuades Marshall to take the risk of including them among the possible beneficiaries. Together with Will Clayton, the energetic internationalist under-secretary for economic affairs, he is one of the major influences.

Kennan also works on NATO, and on Germany. On both he is, at times, a heretic.

Kennan's view is that the Soviet threat is political; the response should be to restore confidence in democracy and hope for the future. For this the instruments are the Marshall Plan and co-operation among European countries, so that they will face any threats together. He sees the military threat as more theoretical than real. The Soviet Union has no history of invading Europe except when provoked, or when quarrels among the capitalists provide easy pickings. It has played the 'role of the vulture' in the Baltic States and in Eastern Europe. In 1947 Kennan thinks it is exhausted and unready for another war. He is not against the United States and Canada giving guarantees to a European organisation for collective defence, for the sake of reassurance. But it is a mistake to focus too much on the military threat; and he opposes military guarantees for Europe: 'The suggestion . . . that an alliance was needed to assure the participation of the United States in the cause of Western Europe's defence, in the event of an attack against it, only filled me with impatience. What in the world did they think we had been doing in Europe these last three years?'[39]

One answer to Kennan's rhetorical question would be that Europeans will not forget what the United States did in the war; but they will also remember the twenty-two years between 1919 and the Japanese attack on Pearl Harbor. In a longer perspective Kennan has a point: with the United States participating, the prospect of an independent European defence disappeared, and the world and the West lost what might have been a further element of pluralism. Containment as he saw it was not just about the United States responding, but about building strong, independent countries able to resist the Soviet Union on their own.

Nor is Kennan's estimate of the risk of aggression necessarily wrong. After the Second World War the only countries the Soviet Union invaded were Warsaw Pact allies. But it did use military pressure: half a million troops moved into Bulgaria when it was proposing a plan for joint control of the Black Sea Straits with Turkey. In Korea the Soviet Union gave massive support to the North and had – unacknowledged – Soviet pilots in the air, though Soviet boots were never on the ground.

Kennan's case is reasonable, but in 1948 European countries are not going to be convinced by political and historical analysis. They are scared of the Soviet Union, with its ruthless leader and its military not yet demobilised; and they worry about Germany, whose future is far from clear. The only way to give Europe confidence is to keep US forces in Germany. Kennan is right about many things; but on this Truman, Marshall and Acheson, who make the decisions, are righter. Seventy years later, a less reliable United States is still better than an absent United States.

Kennan also produces heretical ideas on Germany. These are in response to an instruction to the Planning Staff to look at possible ways out of the Berlin blockade. This has been imposed by the Soviets in June 1948 in response to Western steps to create a West German currency and state; so it is reasonable to examine alternatives to this policy.

The vision Kennan offers is of a united Europe, independent of the United States, confident and prosperous enough to resist the political threat from Communism. Germany, embedded in this Europe, would be subject to limitations on its level of armaments. The Four Powers would guarantee these arrangements. They would end their occupation, but each would retain one military base in case the agreements should be breached. (This – see Chapter Five – is more or less the treaty proposed by Jimmy Byrnes.) With Germany united, peaceful and free there would be no justification for the Soviet occupation of

Central Europe, and, in due course, the division of Europe also would come to an end.

Kennan's proposals are stillborn. Policy has been going in the opposite direction for some time: creating a West German state is the only way to restart the German and European economy; and the Marshall Plan consolidates the division of Germany. A reversal of policy in favour of a united but neutral Germany, under quadripartite supervision, would have been a leap in the dark. Why should quadripartite co-operation, which has proved impossible so far, suddenly start to work? Would Germany be a democracy or a 'people's democracy'? If it is disarmed, who guarantees its security? Could it be part of a united Europe and at the same time neutral? The idea that the Soviet Union, having taken so much trouble to secure control of Poland, would decide that it could now leave Poland and Central Europe alone looks fanciful to say the least.

There are no good answers to these questions. By this time policy on West Germany has momentum. It is being implemented day by day, in agreement with Britain and France, and with the involvement of the Germans. It would have needed an earthquake to overturn it.

In the run-up to the Paris Foreign Ministers' Conference of 1949, Bohlen and Jessup are authorised to mention Kennan's vision to the British and the French as ideas that have been considered but not taken up. But before this can happen an inaccurate version is leaked to the press. The reaction to it makes it clear that Kennan's ideas would have sunk like a stone if they had ever been put forward: Britain and France may be ambivalent about the concept of a united Germany anyway (as they were forty years later); packaging this with US troop reductions would make rejection certain.

How is it that the hard-headed Kennan, sceptical about treaties, sceptical about co-operation with Russia, sceptical about the UN, a believer in the balance of power, comes to propose something so unrealistic? After Potsdam, he has written in his private papers that 'the idea of a Germany run jointly with the Russians is a chimera . . . Better a dismembered Germany in which the West at least can act as a buffer.'[40] And he has written to Bohlen that it would be better for the

United States to accept the division of Europe and that of Germany, with an understanding that each would keep out of the other's sphere of influence.[41]

The answer is that Kennan is for once obeying instructions. He has been asked to propose an alternative policy, and that is what he does. The paper does reflect one strain in his thinking. This is his scepticism of occupation and empires. He is disgusted at the sight of Americans lording it over Germans. Looking at children playing among the ruins, he wonders from whom they will find guidance: 'From us Americans? We were doing our best. But we had no answers . . . And our own vision was clouded by our habits, our comforts, our false and corrupting position as conquerors and occupiers.'[42]

He discards the ideas in the paper with little more than a shrug. In contrast, his dissent on NATO and the militarisation of policy are themes to which he constantly returns.

Kennan is right that the threat is primarily political. But Stalin is ready to use other means if an occasion presents itself. The Berlin blockade is not an armed attack and the air lift is not a military response in the normal sense; but the Soviet blockade is backed by military force and the air lift needs military planes and organisation.

In fact, the Berlin air lift is a good example of containment: it avoids direct military confrontation but it responds to Soviet pressure; and it continues until the Soviet Union gives up (along with a counter-blockade, embargoing trade with the Soviet zone).

Another case of containment in action is – or might have been – the Korean War. This begins just as Kennan is leaving the Planning Staff. Korea is not among the places – Europe and Japan – whose defence he considers essential for US security; and it shows that containment must sometimes be military. Neither shows that Kennan's notion of containment is mistaken, only that rigid 'doctrines' do not work in foreign policy. Kennan's instinctive reaction is to support a military response: real life takes precedence over theory.

It is just as Kennan is about to leave the State Department for Princeton that the North Koreans, backed by the Soviet Union and China, launch the attack. His successor, Paul Nitze, is on holiday and out of contact; so, at Acheson's request, Kennan stays on for the initial phase of the crisis. His assumption from the start is that the US objective should be to restore the status quo ante, with US forces and ambitions stopping at the 38th parallel. He is dismayed when this policy is overtaken by the obsession of General MacArthur with China and the enthusiasm of everyone else for a united democratic Korea – though, like others, it is Russian rather than Chinese intervention that he fears. He manages meanwhile to annoy John Foster Dulles sufficiently that he shouts at Kennan and tells a reporter that 'while he used to think highly of George Kennan, he had now concluded that he was a dangerous man'.[43] This was because he was advocating the admission of the Chinese Communists to the UN and a halt to US military action at the 38th parallel. In both cases Kennan turns out to be right.

Finding his advice neglected, and uneasy at the way policy is going, he leaves for Princeton at the end of August 1950. Much later, when the war has stabilised, the State Department asks him to approach the Soviet ambassador at the UN informally to raise the question of armistice talks. In due course these begin; ending them is another matter.

Containment meant something between war and peace – the term 'Cold War' became current in the same year as the 'X' article. It was a strategy to deal with a particular adversary at a particular moment.

Walter Lippmann criticised containment as the negation of diplomacy: an abdication of the responsibility to seek political solutions through dialogue.[44] If diplomacy was ruled out, then the use of force would come into the picture. In fact, containment was about *not* using force, a kind of diplomacy without words. Lippmann was one of many liberals who had no direct experience of the Soviet Union in the 1940s. Kennan conceived the concept of containment while Stalin was the dominant figure. After Stalin's death in 1953, when a more normal diplomatic relationship gradually became possible. Pure containment – the policy of dialogue by facts, since words were no use – was no longer the only possible approach.

By this time, however, with John Foster Dulles as secretary of state, the administration was so rigidly anti-Communist that dialogue did not figure in its agenda. Eisenhower himself was willing to try, but late in his period of office, and his attempt broke down on his bad faith over the U-2 flight. (A US spy plane was shot down over Soviet territory in 1960 after Eisenhower had given an assurance that the flights would cease.) Kennedy, after the Cuban Missile Crisis of 1962, might also have gone beyond containment had he not been assassinated. Johnson was distracted and weakened by Vietnam. Thus containment lasted, by default, far longer than its author intended and in forms that he personally opposed. Kennan's disappointment with the slowness of change is a disappointment that the United States did not probe more aggressively to see if engagement might bring better results.

Later Career

Two episodes and one incident complete Kennan's diplomatic career.

The first episode comes in the autumn of 1951. Kennan is working at Princeton, though officially he is still a member of the State Department. Acheson and Truman ask him to go to Moscow as US ambassador. In theory, this is the job for which he has been preparing all his life. In practice, it comes at an awkward moment. He is settled in Princeton and knows what he wants to do there. By contrast, no one in Washington seems interested in what he might do in Moscow. He leaves for Russia with mixed feelings.

Moscow is more unpleasant than ever. The armistice negotiations in Korea are making no progress; anti-American propaganda is at full blast. Kennan is under constant intrusive surveillance – his minders shoo Russian children away when they try to play with his two-year-old son through the bars of the embassy gate. As ambassador he cannot mix with the ordinary people as occasionally Kennan did in the past; now and then he can escape, as once to visit Tolstoy's estate outside Moscow; but such occasions are rare. For the most part he is a prisoner in a hostile country. Washington is no more interested in what he has to say as ambassador than it was when he was a second secretary. Frustrated and lonely, Kennan makes the mistake of comparing his position in Moscow to his internment in Germany ten years earlier when talking to a journalist in Germany. Comparison with Nazi Germany is the one thing that the Soviet government will never accept. A few days later, in London, Kennan hears he has been declared *persona non grata* after just four months as ambassador. This sorry end adds chagrin to his other sources of unhappiness.

Had Kennan been in Washington rather than in Princeton, he might have recognised – as he does in his memoirs – that he has been sent to fill a gap during a presidential election year. With lower expectations he could have taken his position less seriously and found survival easier. But it is not his way to take anything less than seriously. He was unlucky with the timing. Had he held out to spring 1953, he would have been there for Stalin's death and the Korean armistice, and the embassy coming back to life again.

The incident arises from a lecture given in a private capacity. This is one of the Reith Lectures that he has been invited by the BBC to deliver on radio while he is a visiting fellow at Oxford. The third of his six lectures is entitled 'The Problem of Eastern and Central Europe'. His lecture is not, as some of his critics suggest, a 'proposal' but rather a series of questions about the conditions under which a withdrawal of Soviet forces from Central Europe might be negotiable. This is 1957. The recent past has seen force used to suppress demonstrations in East Germany and riots in Poland. In Hungary, Soviet tanks have fired on civilians and overthrown the government in 1956. The question is worth asking.

The problem is that Kennan's questions about Central Europe lead to questions about Germany, and whether withdrawal of Soviet and US forces there could also be considered. This Germany could not be a member of NATO – that would not be negotiable with Moscow – but Kennan seems to envisage that it would still be aligned with the West:

> I cannot see that this sort of thing would invalidate the essential relationships of NATO. It cannot be stressed too often that NATO's real strength does not lie in the paper undertakings which underpin it; it lies . . . in the appreciation of the member nations for the identity of

their real interests, as members of the Western spiritual and cultural community.[45]

He asks whether a situation in which Soviet forces are withdrawn from Central Europe, and Germany does not create a large army, would necessarily be less stable than the (opposite) arrangements foreseen by the governments of the day.

We will never know the answer. Kennan's lecture gets a massively hostile reception from the governments of the United States and Germany. That Chancellor Konrad Adenauer should dislike anything that seems to weaken ties to the West or to reawaken dreams of neutrality and unification ought not to surprise Kennan; and that the United States should dissociate itself from ideas which upset Adenauer follows naturally – though there is some irony in Dulles's hostility to a lecture that explores a route to a 'rollback' of Soviet domination of Central Europe more realistic than anything he proposes himself. Acheson joins in, savagely, to protect the Democratic Party from contagion.

The difficulties with options of the sort that Kennan suggests have not changed from those that greeted his paper on Germany in 1949; it is easy to understand why no one wants to explore them. There is no obvious reason for a change in strategy. That does not mean that the questions he asks are absurd or dangerous. Adenauer could reply that these questions have been answered once already, at the cost of some pain, and he does not wish to repeat the process. Few voices are heard in support. That is because the people most interested in change live in Central Europe, and have no voice. To the accusation that Kennan is recycling ideas which got nowhere in the past, it could be said that times have changed. Stalin is dead and Khrushchev is more flexible: he has just negotiated the withdrawal of Soviet troops from Austria. Perhaps the fact that at this moment his ideas are *not* completely unrealistic – as they were ten years earlier – makes them more dangerous, and prompts the ferocious response.

The result is that Kennan, who, in government, complained for years that no one read what he wrote, now finds that, out of government, he attracts more attention than he wants. He retires, hurt, to a sanatorium.

It remains the case that as the President of Germany, Theodor Heuss, says – in the fairest comment on the lecture – much of what Kennan said was true, and that he was 'a cautious and profound man'.

Kennan's last episode as a diplomat comes in 1961. He is at Yale as a visiting fellow. Passing the front desk, an agitated undergraduate manning the telephone jumps up and calls out: 'Mr Kennan, the President of the United States wants to talk to you.' Kennedy offers Kennan the embassy in Warsaw or Belgrade. He accepts the second, thinking to end his career as a diplomat in a more satisfactory way than being declared *persona non grata* by Moscow. He admires Kennedy and is attracted by the idea of pursuing the policy he proposed a decade earlier of working to widen the split between Yugoslavia and the Soviet Union.

Kennan has wanted to return to the government almost since he left it. Power is a drug; even influence is addictive. Kennedy has written once or twice to him, including after the row about the Reith Lectures, taking his side against Acheson and welcoming his 'carefully formulated and brilliantly written set of alternative proposals'.

Kennan likes Yugoslavia, both the country and the people: they are Slavs and they are Communists, but they are also friendly. He has easy access to Tito, who respects him personally. But still it does not work. Hoping to improve relations between Belgrade and Washington, he tries to get Tito to chair a meeting of the Non-Aligned Movement as though it really were non-aligned. He fails. Yugoslavia's relationship with Russia, in spite of the split, matters more than that with the United States. Tito uses the meeting to demonstrate both his connections in the Third World and his alignment with the Communist bloc. He is rewarded with a visit to Moscow on his own terms. An American ambassador cannot change such realities.

Nor is Kennan able to stop the US Congress from treating Yugoslavia as though it were an ally of Moscow. This is the opposite of the policy Kennan and others tried to put in place when Tito broke with Stalin. The rhetoric of the Truman Doctrine has come home to roost, and anti-Communism is an indiscriminate crusade. Kennan tramps the corridors of Congress but fails to persuade. He has a direct line to the president, and uses it; but for the president, relations with Congress matter more than those with Yugoslavia. Since he cannot do his job as he would wish, he resigns, though without histrionics. He does not blame Kennedy but the congressmen and lobbyists who (in his view) have too much say in making US policy. He leaves without regret, but concluding that his time in Belgrade, though agreeable, has been a failure in diplomatic terms.

Kennan remains in the academic world, a respected historian, winning the Pulitzer and other prizes, and commentator. He lives to see the policies he launched succeed, but the process takes longer than he has ever imagined, and the policies are executed in such crude ways that he disowns most of them.

In 1985 Kennan tells a friend that 'this man Gorbachev has begun to dismantle the Soviet Union'. Two years later, at a reception, Gorbachev recognises him and, taking his hand, says: 'Mr Kennan. We in our country believe that a man may be a friend of another country and remain, at the same time, a loyal and devoted citizen of his own, and that is how we view you.'[46]

George Kennan: Foot Soldier and Professional

And how should we view George Kennan? What made him special?

In one respect Kennan is the least special of those in this book. He was the most ordinary kind of diplomat, a career official, one of many thousands around the world.

The big decisions in diplomacy are taken by political leaders. Kennan's ideas had influence; others made the decisions. But a book on diplomacy should say something about the bread-and-butter diplomats: their understanding of what is happening on the ground is critical to decisions made at the political level. Diplomats like Kennan spend much of their lives abroad, often in difficult or dangerous places. Like Kennan, they are frustrated in dealing with their capital. The great figures, presidents, prime ministers and foreign ministers, whether they succeed or fail in foreign affairs, are dependent on the foot soldiers. In a small post an ambassador is also a foot soldier. Kennan was one of the most distinguished of this large regiment.

He was one of a new generation of professional diplomats in the US Foreign Service. The Rogers Act of 1924 opened up the State Department. Under the *ancien régime* in France the diplomatic service, like military command, was confined to the aristocracy: since their work was with monarchs and courts this was part of the order of things. The upper classes continued to have a monopoly on diplomacy in European countries until the First World War. In Britain the requirement that candidates have a private income of £400 per year (£60,000 today) was dropped in 1919; private means were also needed in the United States until the Rogers Act.

The First World War brought the end of the *ancien régime* all across Europe, and discredited the idea that diplomacy was best conducted by Europe's transnational ruling elite. Some also drew the lesson from the war that diplomacy was too serious to be delegated to well-bred amateurs, and the intention of the Rogers Act was to improve professionalism. One part of this was the training Kennan and some of his contemporaries received in Russian language and history.

By 1945 the transition was complete. The world in which ruling families were cousins and the tsar spoke French was gone. Instead two powers, the United States and the Soviet Union, each on the margins in the inter-war years, had become twin pillars of the world system, and it was important that they should understand each other. Political leaders of the generation of Roosevelt and Truman operated on the basis that Stalin was like them, give or take the eccentricities often found among foreigners. After the Second World War this was not good enough. In fact, the Soviet Union was more different, more foreign, more difficult to understand than most of the US political class could conceive. From the Western point of view it was the first completely foreign country to become a world power. Handling it required professional knowledge that could be acquired only by study and experience. Happily, a professional Foreign Service was in the making; and one of its best products was George Kennan.

Kennan stands out; but he should be seen as a leading member of a new class of professionals. This included his friend Chip Bohlen, the other great Russian linguist and Soviet specialist of his day. Bohlen's close reading of Soviet statements enabled him to spot the opening that led to the end of the Berlin blockade; his skill in handling Soviet officials helped bring about the Korean armistice after the death of Stalin (and, unlike Kennan, he was a highly successful ambassador in Moscow).

In his memoir of the mistakes of Vietnam, *In Retrospect*, Robert McNamara writes of the administration's profound ignorance of the history, culture and politics of the people in the area, and the personalities and habits of their leaders. We might have made similar misjudgements regarding the Soviets during our frequent confrontations – over Berlin, Cuba, the Middle East, for example – had we not had the advice of Tommy Thompson, Chip Bohlen, and George Kennan.[47]*

Churchill's description of Russia as 'a riddle wrapped in a mystery inside an enigma' is not enough. Policy needs firmer ground. What is needed is people who know the Russians, how they think, what they want, what they believe, what they fear, how they react. This knowledge is the core skill of diplomats.

In personality Kennan was far from typical of the diplomatic profession. He was shy, sombre, pessimistic; he brought a moral intensity to his work, something not always associated with diplomacy. Behind his disgust at the Soviet government lay a deep feeling for Russia. Isaiah Berlin said of Kennan that he loved the Russians, and responded to Russian books and to the Russian character. Bohlen's memoirs are full of anecdotes† of the meetings he attended with Roosevelt; he was interested in the personalities: the cynicism of Roosevelt, the bellicosity

* Llewellyn (Tommy) Thompson was not part of the Russian-language programme. He served in Moscow during the war, and dealt with the Russians in the negotiation of the Austrian State Treaty (1955) that ended their occupation of Austria (where he was ambassador). He was ambassador in Moscow (1957–62) through many crises and summits. McNamara praises his role during the Cuban Missile Crisis. The record shows Thompson's advice was erratic, and his guesses about Khrushchev's motives were often wrong; but Khrushchev was unpredictable. A different type from Kennan or Bohlen.

† Some of these are remarkable: for example, a story of Alan Brooke (Chief of General Staff) in Tehran proposing a toast to Stalin's success in deceiving Hitler with the Molotov-Ribbentrop Pact (*Witness to History*, p. 149).

of Churchill and the cunning of Stalin. All of these, and especially the vanity of Western leaders, shocked Kennan. A sense of personal responsibility sharpened the edge of his analysis. It brought him frustrations with policy, together with ulcers and other illnesses. Kennan saw himself not as an observer but as an actor who had responsibilities in the drama.

Kennan's intellect demanded that he understand, and his conscience told him he must bring Washington to see the light. Hopkins, when Kennan tried to persuade him not to make deals with Stalin about Poland, said: 'You think it's just sin, and we should be agin it.'[48] This hits the nail on the head. Moral intensity brought the tortured prose of his writings on Russia: compare the sentences from his memorandum 'Russia – Seven Years Later' with the easy flow of his writing on his day in the Russian countryside.

The same moral sense lay behind his insistence on the primacy of political over military means. His intellect made him distrust the moralistic, legalistic approach to foreign policy that ignores the realities of power. His conscience gave an urgency to his speech and writing. ('You missed your vocation,' a minister of the Church said to him after one of his lectures on the Soviet Union.)[49]

Kennan's *Memoirs* are different from those of other diplomats. They say little of many of the events he lived through, and not much about the great figures of the age that he encountered or advised; instead they tell the story of his own struggles, thoughts, frustrations and failures. But of the memoirs of this time his are among the most brilliant intellectually, the most compelling and the most inspiring.

6

All the Olympians: Bevin, Marshall, Acheson

Bevin

Ernest Bevin was born in 1881 to Diana Bevin and an unknown father. He was six years old when his mother, who worked as a household servant and midwife, died; he went to live with his newly married half-sister. At the age of eleven he left school and worked in labouring jobs, on farms, in kitchens, delivering laundry, then for some time selling mineral water from a cart drawn by two horses. He joined the Bristol Socialist Society, and organised silent protests by the unemployed in churches. Later he played a part in creating a branch for carters like himself, in the Bristol Dock Workers' Union.

He has a talent for mobilising people and becomes secretary of the Bristol branch, and then, in 1914, a national organiser. After the First World War he co-founds the Transport and General Workers' Union. Bevin, as its general secretary, makes this the most powerful labour organisation in the world. He has a deep sympathy for working people: 'my people', he calls them.* His campaign for paid holidays for workers eventually (in 1938) wins holiday pay for eleven million men.

Bevin likes facts. They are the starting point for his policies and the basis of his arguments in negotiation. In 1920 his evidence at the Court of Inquiry into dock workers' wages makes him a national figure. He

* His sympathy extended to horses, having worked with them. When he could, he improved their conditions too.

supports his case with a mass of documents: extracts from government reports and statistics from every branch of the union. His case is that in the sixteen years since 1904, dockers' pay had doubled but the cost of living had gone up four times. When he finishes there are several minutes of applause; the *Daily Mail*, then as now far from left-wing, writes of '"his masterly statement" in support of increased pay, leisure and dignity of life'.

The most famous moment in the inquiry comes when the ship-owners submit statistics to show that £3 17s a week is adequate for a docker's family. This is based on the assumption that rent is no more than 6s 6d per week. Bevin calls the clerk of Tilbury Council in to explain that before the war, the cheapest house had been let at 8s a week; now rent is between 17s 6d and £1. Then, during the lunch break Bevin and his secretary go to a street market and buy food with the money that would be left after rent. They cook it and present it to the court on five plates – for the average family. The argument does not end there, but this glimpse of real life wins the day. Afterwards, speaking to his friend Francis Williams, Bevin denies that it was a stunt: 'These fellows quote statistics but they forget about human beings. I had to make 'em remember they were dealing with human lives.'[1]

It is the facts about what is happening in Germany that lead Bevin, in the 1930s, to campaign against fascism and against appeasement. At the Labour Party's annual conference in 1935 he does this in a ferocious speech attacking its leader, George Lansbury. Lansbury, who is recovering from illness, receives an ovation as he goes to the podium to speak in a debate on Abyssinia. This reflects the party's affection for a leader who cannot serve it much longer. Lansbury says he speaks knowing that his views may be rejected, and that he will resign if they are. Even so, he will oppose sanctions on Italy, because sanctions may lead to war:

> If mine were the only voice in the Conference, I would say in the name of the faith I hold, the belief I have, that God intended us to live peacefully and quietly with one another, that if some people do not allow us to do so, I am ready to stand as the early Christians did

and say: 'This is our faith, this is where we stand, and if necessary, this is where we will die.'[2]

The conference rises to its feet, some with tears in their eyes, honouring his courage, his sincerity and his service to the party.

Bevin chooses to speak immediately after this. He reminds the conference that party policy is to support the League of Nations and sanctions against aggression. Lansbury has accepted this too. Loyalty to the party means loyalty to its decisions. The middle classes have done well enough under fascism: 'The thing that is being wiped out is the trade-union movement. It is the only defence the workers have got. . . . Our Austrian brothers tried to defend themselves. We did all that we could.* It is we who are being wiped out, and who will be wiped out if fascism comes here.'[3]

Lansbury tries to defend himself, but the microphone is cut off. By the time Bevin finishes, the mood of the conference has reversed. It votes to support sanctions by two million to 100,000. Lansbury resigns and leaves heartbroken. When friends tell Bevin that his speech had been unnecessarily harsh, he replies: 'Lansbury has been going about in saint's clothes for years waiting for martyrdom. I set fire to the faggots.'[4]

On 7 May 1940, with the war going badly, the Conservative Leo Amery makes the speech that brings down the Chamberlain government. As he works up to his climax,† the House of Commons fills up; it hears him call for a national government: 'The time has come when the Hon. and Right Hon. members opposite must definitely take their share of responsibility. The time has come when the organization, the power and influence of the Trades Union Congress cannot be left outside.'[5] He is surely thinking of Bevin.

Bevin is Churchill's choice as minister of labour in his government. Later Churchill brings him into the War Cabinet. Churchill's confidant,

* The Trades Union Congress had sent them £10,000 to buy guns the year before.

† Amery finished: 'This is what Cromwell said to the Long Parliament when he thought it was no longer fit to conduct the affairs of the nation: "You have sat here too long for any good you have been doing. Depart, I say, and let us have done with you. In the name of God, go"', pointing his finger at Neville Chamberlain's empty seat.

Brendan Bracken, suggested a Cabinet of four men: Churchill himself, Clement Attlee as deputy prime minister, Anthony Eden, 'the most popular member of the Cabinet', and Bevin, 'the strongest man in the present Cabinet'. In practice the War Cabinet is larger and fluid in its composition, but Bevin is a fixture.

On his first day in office Bevin discusses the organisation of the workforce for wartime with officials. On his second day he presents his plans to the Cabinet. A week later Attlee introduces the Emergency Powers (Defence) Bill, saying: 'It is necessary that the government should be given complete control over persons and property. Not just some persons of some particular class but all persons, rich and poor, employer and workman, men and women and all property.'[6] Three hours later these powers are given to Bevin as minister of labour. Meanwhile Bevin is setting up the machinery for consultation with trade unions and the employers. He negotiates agreements with the unions to set aside established rules and allow untrained and unskilled men from the vast numbers of the unemployed – and women who had never before worked – to take their place in the industrial war effort. In the course of two weeks Bevin explains to 2,000 union delegates what is going to happen, and asks them to take the message back to their mines, factories and docks. In the next months all these begin to operate twenty-four hours a day, seven days a week.

Bevin serves both his country and his class. He uses the war to make reforms, to ensure that disabled people are able to work, and to end casual labour in the docks. He knows that 'my people' are patriots, and uses his powers only rarely. The result is that two-thirds of the working-age population contribute to the war effort – many more than in Germany – with a level of strikes half that of the First World War. When he tours the ports with Churchill to see the men embarking for D-Day, it is Bevin that they cheer, calling out, 'See they don't let us down when we come back this time, Ernie.'[7]

The cheers for Bevin are an omen: it is Bevin and Attlee's vision of post-war Britain that wins the general election in 1945. Attlee appoints Bevin foreign secretary.

Bevin is built like a tank; he is slow, but capable of great force, in speech and in personality. Something of that force is conveyed in an account by the then journalist Douglas Jay of a lunchtime lecture by Bevin, in late 1939, part of a series organised by Sir Arthur Salter:*

> Bevin was addressing the polite company as prosaically as others (including John Simon) had done in the series. Suddenly, as he spoke of the Nazi persecution of Jews and trade unionists, his great head swung this way and that, his fist struck the air like a steam hammer, and his voice rose to a roar. The words were no more than pedestrian: 'I'm not going to have my people treated like this.' But this highly respectable audience was astonished and enthralled, and sprang to their feet with unrestrained applause. Heavens, I said to myself, we shall win this war after all.[8]

Bevin's life is spent negotiating: with ships' captains on behalf of dock workers, with employers as a union leader, and then, in government, with both the unions and the bosses. As foreign secretary he and others negotiate the post-war settlement.

In one of the last conversations of his life Bevin, lying sick in bed, says to Francis Williams, his friend from his trade-union days: 'Always remember, Francis, the first thing to decide before you go into a negotiation is what you'll do if the other chap says "No".'[9] That was on 13 April 1951. He dies the following day.

Potsdam

As foreign secretary, the central question for Bevin is what to do with Germany. His problem is that he has no answer to the question: what to do when the Soviet foreign minister, Vyacheslav Molotov – known as 'Mister Nyet' – says 'No'.

As the war ends, post-war problems begin. Germany is in ruins. President Harry S. Truman, who served in France in the First World War and has seen destruction, writes in his diary that when he saw

* Who worked with Jean Monnet in the First World War: see the next chapter.

Berlin it made him think of Carthage, Baalbek, Jerusalem, Rome.[10] Civilians shuffle aimlessly, dazed from months of Allied bombing and Russian artillery fire. The canals are choked with corpses; the city is choked with refugees, many living like animals in the ruins.

The Allied commanders meet there on 5 June 1945. Eisenhower suggests to his Russian counterpart, Marshal Zhukov, that they make a start on establishing the Allied Control Commission, the body that will govern Germany. Zhukov declines: first, each occupying power must withdraw its forces into its own zone. Only then can joint activity begin. This is a sign of things to come: everything will be a negotiation; territory will be the key.

Later that day the commanders-in-chief agree two proclamations. The first announces that they are assuming supreme authority in Germany. The second states that in matters concerning Germany as a whole, the commanders will act together, by unanimity; within their separate zones each will have supreme power. This structure – vetoes on all-German policy, and freedom of action for each occupying power in its own zone – sets the pattern and the problem of the next forty-four years.[11]

Two months later, the big three – Truman, Stalin and Churchill – meet in Potsdam. This is Truman's first visit to Europe since 1918. He is not Roosevelt, but he makes a good impression on Churchill, and on his own team. Then Churchill is gone, replaced by Attlee. As for Stalin, he is at his softest, but there is no agreement on the Polish border, except that it will be provisional until there is a peace treaty with Germany; and there is no agreement on reparations. Truman thinks Stalin is 'a fine man who wants to do the right thing'. Stalin tells Khrushchev that Truman is a man of no importance.[12]*

Potsdam establishes the Council of Foreign Ministers as a joint executive to draw up the peace treaties. These will be confirmed by a peace

* The quotation from Truman is authentic, but he was a politician and knew that everything he said was on the record. More revealing was his body language at Potsdam. Robert Murphy sat behind Truman there. He writes that Stalin left Truman uneasy, impatient and finally infuriated. He never showed any interest in meeting him again. (Robert Murphy, *Diplomat Among Warriors*, p. 342).

conference, which will bring in other allies. (The defeated countries are not expected to negotiate.) The council will consist of the Potsdam three, the United States, Britain and the Soviet Union, plus France and China, mirroring the permanent members of the UN Security Council. It will meet at intervals, tackling issues one by one. The intention is to allow more time to settle the peace treaties, especially that for Germany, and to avoid the mistakes of Versailles.

The London Council

The first meeting of the council is in London in September 1945. All five members send delegations. The council is to start with the 'satellites': Italy, Romania, Bulgaria, Hungary and Finland.

The meeting is a fiasco. One article of the Potsdam Protocol lists France and China as members of the council; another says its composition will vary according to the treaty under discussion. At the first session of the council, Molotov agrees to Bevin's proposal that France and China should participate throughout. Two weeks later, on instructions from Stalin, he withdraws his agreement. Bevin and Jimmy Byrnes, the US secretary of state, refuse to accept that France and China should be humiliated in this way. Truman and Attlee send messages to Stalin asking him to agree to the French and Chinese presence. After a week of waiting for a reply, and a good deal of argument, the council breaks up without a concluding statement or a date for a further meeting.

Bevin, the host, is new as foreign secretary, but he has long taken an interest in foreign affairs. He is the first foreign secretary from the working classes,* admired by his staff for his toughness, decency and authority. The last comes from the complete confidence Attlee has in him. He has followed foreign developments as a member of the War Cabinet, and of the committee responsible for post-war planning. Alan

* Bevin remarked on this to his private secretary, Gladwyn Jebb, on his first day. Jebb reminded him that in the sixteenth century Thomas Wolsey, a butcher's son, had become Henry VIII's 'foreign secretary', and a cardinal too; 'and coincidentally, he was not unlike you, physically'.

Brooke, chair of the chiefs of staff, brooded in his diary on the committee's discussions shortly after the Normandy landings:

> Should Germany be dismembered or gradually converted to an ally, to meet the Russian threat of 20 years hence? I suggested the latter, and feel certain that we must from now onwards regard Germany in a very different light. Germany is no longer the dominating power in Europe, Russia is. Unfortunately, Russia is not entirely European. She has, however, vast resources and cannot fail to become the main threat in 15 years' time. Therefore, foster Germany, gradually build her up, and bring her into a federation of Western Europe. Unfortunately this must be done under the cloak of a holy alliance between England, Russia and America. Not an easy policy and one requiring a super Foreign Secretary.[13]

This is a diary entry, not a policy. It is more precise than anything we have from Bevin, but it is not inconsistent with his views. He is anti-Communist as well as anti-fascist; he has fought Communists in the unions for years. He makes no secret of this in his first encounters with Molotov at Potsdam. Before the London Council he tells the House of Commons that in Hungary, Romania and Bulgaria, 'the impression we get from recent developments is that one kind of totalitarianism is being replaced by another'.[14]

British policy on Germany has not yet crystallised, but it is shaped by two legacies of the war: first, Britain ends the war as the leading power in Western Europe – and Bevin is determined that this will continue. The second legacy is that Britain is bankrupt.

The self-image of Britain in 1945 – still current today – is of it standing alone against Hitler. This is only half true. In December 1940, Churchill wrote to the newly re-elected Roosevelt. He began by noting progress on the military front; but at the end of the letter he admitted that 'the moment approaches when we shall no longer be able to pay cash for shipping and other supplies'. It was following this that Roosevelt invented Lend-Lease, the lifeline that, by the end of the war, covered two-thirds of Britain's foreign-exchange costs.

All the countries of Europe, except for the neutrals, are bankrupt. But as a victor Britain has expensive responsibilities. These have been increased by Churchill's success in securing North-west Germany as Britain's occupation zone. This includes most of German industry, a big population and massive bomb damage. Unless industry recovers it will be costly to feed. As a would-be great power, it is difficult for Britain to admit its lack of money. Bevin's solution is to regard the financial problem as temporary, and to look to the empire as a source of wealth. Neither he nor anyone else sees how unprofitable the empire will be, nor how soon it will dissolve. (Like most people of his class, Bevin has seen the empire mainly in picture books.) At Potsdam, finding himself between the Russian bear and the American colossus, he has an acute sense of Britain's weakness: his response is to seek a partnership with France, and a transatlantic relationship that works in peace as it has in war.

His partners do not look promising. The background of Jimmy Byrnes, the US secretary of state, is a little like Bevin's. His father died before he was born; his mother was a dressmaker, and Byrnes left school at fourteen to help support the family. He worked as a messenger; then as a court reporter, studying law from books at the same time. Later he became clerk to a judge – having lied about his age. Elected to the House of Representatives and then to the Senate, he was a Roosevelt supporter. He expected to be Roosevelt's running mate in 1944; Roosevelt chose Truman instead, but took Byrnes to Yalta as a consolation prize. Byrnes is thus a natural choice as secretary of state for Truman, who wants to be true to Roosevelt's legacy. This legacy includes the view that world peace will depend on good relations between the United States and the Soviet Union.

At Potsdam, Byrnes has shown himself quick and clever – from the British point of view, perhaps too quick and too clever. While Churchill and Eden are gone, and before Attlee and Bevin replace them, he makes a deal in which Molotov gets the border Stalin wants for Germany – the western rather than the eastern Oder, a large difference that puts Stettin (now Szezecin) in Poland – in exchange for a reduction in Russian demands for reparations. Churchill has argued fiercely for the eastern Oder and Bevin does the same when he arrives; but it is too late. In London Byrnes makes no attempt to work with Bevin. Nor, at this point, does the United States look like an easy partner. Lend-Lease, which has kept Britain afloat for five years, has been stopped with brutal speed; equally brutal negotiations for a dollar loan have followed. Roosevelt's prediction that US troops will stay no more than two years in Europe weighs on British minds.

Neither Byrnes nor Bevin find Molotov easy to handle. They deal with this in different ways: Bevin is pugnacious in public, but tries in private meetings to understand Molotov's refusal to allow France into the conference. What is he after? But Molotov only complains about Bevin's unwillingness to give him what he wants, whether it is a base on the Black Sea Straits or 'a corner of the Mediterranean', taken from one of the Italian colonies. On all of these questions, on the procedural problem and on everything else, Molotov's attitude is that there is no hurry: he can wait; the problem will be solved over time.

Bevin's attempt to understand Molotov's policies fails because there is nothing to understand: Molotov has no policy; he follows Stalin's orders.* Bevin's view of Russia's policy, as he tells Byrnes, is that if the Soviet government sees a piece of land they instinctively want to grab it, as British admirals did in the nineteenth century when they spotted an undiscovered island.[15] These conversations do not bring Bevin nearer to solving the dispute about France. Molotov says it is a trivial matter. But it is not: Stalin is unmoved by the appeals from Truman and Attlee.

Nor does Molotov treat the issue as trivial; he insists that his agreement to France and China joining the meeting be removed from the record. Both Byrnes and Bevin refuse; Bevin, provoked by this attempt to rewrite history, makes a comparison with Hitler's methods, and has to apologise and withdraw the remark.† This, as George Kennan too discovers, is the unforgivable sin in Communist theology.[16] Since

* Stalin probably sees France as weak and treats it accordingly.

† Bevin said that he ''adn't 'eard any argument that resembled the 'itlerite philosophy as much as the one that Molotov was using'. He felt some chagrin at this loss of control. He knew well enough what Molotov was up to.

nothing is happening, Byrnes, without consulting anyone, persuades the Chinese delegate, then in the chair, to declare the council closed.

John Foster Dulles, who is in the US delegation to represent the Republican Party, provides a good account of Molotov. Molotov, he says, exercised 'an adroitness that has seldom been equalled in diplomacy'. He drew Byrnes out, asking him to rephrase and explain, hoping that his tendency to improvise would yield something he could use. Bevin, Molotov treated 'as a banderillero treats a bull, planting darts in him that would arouse him to an outburst', giving him a psychological advantage. With Georges Bidault, the French foreign minister, he 'played on the sensitiveness which is natural to the French character'. 'French feelings were still raw' from their exclusion from Potsdam. 'So Mr Molotov tried to outrage French honour by petty slights', agreeing with Byrnes and Bevin that a meeting would be postponed for an hour, and not telling Bidault, who would turn up to an empty room. Dulles thinks Molotov's objective was to get Bidault to walk out. If so, he failed.[17]

Bevin's own view of Molotov, as he tells Hugh Dalton* at the time, is that 'Molotov was like a Communist in a local Labour Party. If you treated him badly he made the most of the grievance, and if you treated him well, he only put up his price and abused you next day.'[18] His conclusion, after the failure of the conference, is that Russia has overplayed its hand and will regret it; his plan is to wait for Stalin and Molotov to see this. Byrnes takes the opposite view. Without consulting his own officials or Bevin (who is furious), he agrees with Molotov that he and Bevin will improvise a meeting with him in Moscow. (Byrnes 'ran much of foreign policy from within his head', according to his adviser, Chip Bohlen.)[19] Bevin's fear about this meeting is similar to Kennan's: because Byrnes has arranged it, he will feel obliged to bring home a success, and may make unnecessary concessions to obtain it.

* Dalton was chancellor of the Exchequer. He and Bevin had worked together in the 1930s against pacifism in the Labour Party, and for rearmament. Dalton was from the upper classes – Eton, Cambridge and the LSE – and was under-secretary in the Foreign Office in the 1920s. He was tipped as foreign secretary in the post-war government. Attlee decided only at the last minute to offer the job to Bevin.

It is ominous that Byrnes, again improvising, invites James B. Conant to join him. Conant is a scientist and the president of Harvard; he has played a role in supervising the Manhattan (nuclear bomb) Project. (Byrnes consults neither Britain, still a partner of the United States in nuclear matters, nor Truman.) The way Byrnes arranges and handles this visit enrages Kennan in Moscow; his failure to consult – not least on taking Conant with him, hinting at collaboration on nuclear matters – enrages Truman in Washington.

While in Moscow, Byrnes and Bevin raise their concerns about Soviet pressure on Iran with Stalin, but without result. Not having consulted the president in advance, Byrnes follows up by not reporting to Truman during the visit. When Bohlen, who is with him, suggests he might, Byrnes says that it is for him to judge. Bohlen: 'I was put in my place and stayed there.'[20]

The Moscow meeting has two results: one is that Stalin gives way on France; probably he would have done this anyway. The Chinese, who Molotov has treated throughout as though they were not there, disappear into their revolution and never return. The second is that Truman decides to replace Byrnes, when he has secured his successor.

The Paris Council: Bizonia

The Council of Foreign Ministers meets in Paris in spring 1946, with France as the fourth member. Bevin's preparations for the Paris conference bring the moment when British policy on Germany begins to crystallise. Bevin has grown sceptical about the chances of establishing a central government in Germany. In their zone, the Soviets have forced the Social Democrats to fuse with the Communists, creating the Socialist Unity Party (SED). Bevin fears they will do the same through the whole of Germany. On 3 April 1946 he holds a meeting with the minister responsible for Germany, John Hynd, who tells him that, under financial pressures, British occupation policy is 'purely negative, as [is] that of the Americans'. He wants to regenerate industry. The Christian Democrats and Social Democrats are losing their grip; the Communists are moving ahead. Bevin says 'he has never understood why we could not proceed with our own policy in our own zone', as the Russians do in theirs. The record continues:

> Mr Hynd . . . said that the question must be faced whether we should now establish a German government in our zone with full powers of government, including economic powers.
>
> Mr Arthur Street remarked that this amounted to a partition of Germany and Sir Orme Sargent said that such a step would be irrevocable.
>
> Mr Bevin said this meant a policy of a Western Bloc, and that meant war.
>
> Sir Orme Sargent said that the alternative to this was Communism on the Rhine.[21]

Sir Orme Sargent's reputation as an anti-appeaser makes him a powerful figure. Bevin concludes that if Britain is to go in this direction, it has to take the US administration with it. The advice from Germany is that the US representative there, General Clay, will not be enthusiastic about this course. Bevin nevertheless puts a paper to the Cabinet proposing that if Russia continues to block Four-Power government in Germany, he should explore a 'Western option' as a way to restore the economy and to make life more bearable for both the Germans and the British taxpayer.

In Paris, the four foreign ministers spend eighty working days together. The council meets in April/May and then in June/July; the wider peace conference gathers from July to October to examine the treaties proposed by the council. Much time is spent in repetitive debate on questions such as Italian colonies, Greek islands, Trieste and the treaties with the Balkan countries and Finland.

The first substantive discussions on Germany take place in Paris. There are three visions: the United States and Britain want to build a federal state, from the *Länder* up; France wants weak German states in a weak confederation, the pre-Bismarck model; the Soviets want a centralised Germany and a strong Communist Party.

At the start of the conference, Byrnes tables a draft treaty proposing that Germany be disarmed for twenty-five years and subject to inspections to verify this. He has tried out this idea on Stalin in Moscow; at that point Stalin seemed well disposed: Molotov said twenty-five years was too short, and Byrnes offered forty instead. Now Molotov rejects it, no doubt because of an allergy to inspections in the Soviet zone.* He says that the Potsdam Agreement already provides for disarmament, adding that this is not being implemented in the British and American zones. This provokes Bevin, who says he would love to know what is going on in the Soviet zone. He welcomes Byrnes's draft. This is because it means a long-term US commitment to Europe; and he wants to work with Byrnes.

After three weeks discussing other treaties, the council returns to the subject of Germany. Molotov begins with an attack on Clay's suspension of reparations deliveries. Bidault repeats French themes on separating the Ruhr and the Rhineland, Germany as a confederation, the French need for German coal. He too supports the US draft treaty.

Bevin begins with the options for peace in Europe – a balance of power, domination by one power or two blocs, or united control by the Four Powers. He goes on: 'It has been said that the seeds of all future wars are sown in the settlement of previous wars. The opposite is equally true. If we sow the right seeds, permanent peace may grow from them.' On this day and the next, Bevin will sow the seeds both of the Cold War and of peace in Western Europe.

Bevin cites the Potsdam Agreement: reparations should not leave the German people needing external assistance; and Germany should be treated as a single economic unit. The current arrangement costs the United States $200 million per year and Britain $320 million:

> I must formally state that the United Kingdom will co-operate on a fully reciprocal basis with the other zones, but in so far as there is no reciprocity from any particular zone or agreement to carry out the

* This treaty was a bad idea. It was discussed in Paris only because no one offered anything better. If Germany were disarmed for forty years, and the Four Powers were responsible for its security, sovereignty would have been restored only in 1986. But Byrnes did at least have ideas.

> whole of the Potsdam Protocol, my government will be compelled to organise the British zone of occupation in Germany in such a manner that no further liability shall fall on the British taxpayer.[22]

The following day, Bevin returns to the need to raise production, including of coal, so that their zone will not be a burden on British taxpayers; if trade between zones could resume, it would be easy to build up production in the British zone.

At the end of the conference Byrnes makes a formal statement. He says he had hoped to avoid the situation outlined by Bevin, but:

> Pending agreement among the Four Powers to implement the Potsdam Agreement requiring the administration of Germany as an economic unit, the United States will join with any other occupying government or governments in Germany for the treatment of our respective zones as an economic unit.
>
> We are prepared to instruct our military representatives in Germany to proceed immediately with the representatives of any other occupying government to establish German administrative machinery for the administration of our zones as an economic unit.[23]

Following this the meeting adjourns.

Byrnes's invitation is what Bevin was asking for. It will put Germany on the road to recovery – healthy for German politics as well as for the British taxpayer; it will be a collaborative project with the United States, potentially a way to revive the wartime relationship. There is no prospect yet of France joining the United States and Britain: it opposes anything that contributes to a centralised German state.

Bevin has first to sell this in London: it is not difficult. His paper goes to the Cabinet when it is in a state of shock from the bombing of the King David Hotel in Jerusalem – apart from Germany, Palestine is the most difficult foreign-policy issue for the government.

The merger of the two zones, 'Bizonia', is approved on 30 July 1946. That gives the signal to officials on the ground to work out the practical consequences. A memorandum of agreement between Britain and the United States is signed in December 1946. For this to function, something like a joint US/British policy will be required. Some doubt whether Bizonia will ever work – including, on occasions, General Clay.

In September 1946 Byrnes delivers a significant speech in Stuttgart, the first by a senior American to an audience including Germans. The most important point is his commitment to keep US forces in Germany so long as any other occupying power does the same. Clay persuades him with the argument that, 'We can't expect Germans to work all out, unless they have some assurance that their country will survive. The pledge of American troops serves that purpose.'[24] Here too Byrnes is making policy as he goes along; but this time he takes the advice of Clay, who by now knows Germany well. Byrnes's speech is a sign that America is beginning to see its role as protecting Germany from the Soviet Union as well as protecting Europe from Germany.

In January 1947, Truman accepts Byrnes's resignation, having secured George Marshall as his successor. In fairness it should be said that Byrnes learned as he went; by Paris his attitude was no different from Bevin's. He came to appreciate Bevin's qualities, and commended him to Dean Acheson. But by then it was late. His weakness was that, aware of his ability to charm others, he took little notice of how they saw things. It is about the time of Byrnes's departure that Bevin says in a Cabinet committee, 'I don't mind for myself, but I don't want any other Foreign Secretary of this country to be talked at or by a Secretary of State in the United States as I have just had [*sic*] in my discussions with Mr Byrnes. We have got to have this thing over here, whatever it costs. . . . We've got to have the bloody Union Jack flying on top of it.' 'This thing' is the atomic bomb. Bevin's intervention is decisive. This is how Britain's nuclear programme begins.[25]

Marshall

In a brief statement on his appointment, George Marshall says that he will continue the course taken by his predecessor. He adds, with some emphasis, that he assumes that the office of secretary of state is, in the circumstances of the day, non-political; he will work in that spirit. He has no intention of seeking or accepting political office. This means he will not compete for the presidential nomination with Truman, nor with any of the Republican grandees.

Marshall is the only leading American who could say this and be believed, even by the most cynical journalist. Churchill said of him, 'This was the greatest Roman of them all.' This catches the feeling that, in whatever age he had lived, Marshall would have embodied the old-fashioned virtues that others had forgotten.

Marshall became chief of Army Staff on the day that Germany invaded Poland; and most Americans think of him as the man who won the war for the United States. He listens a lot, remembers everything,* thinks before he speaks. He is courteous and restrained. When he does speak, others listen. Everyone addresses him as 'General Marshall'. There is a story that Roosevelt once called him 'George', and he replied: 'It's General Marshall, Mr President.' This formality protected his position as a professional soldier; he never joined the Roosevelt circle at his home, Hyde Park in upstate New York, nor allowed the president to manipulate him. Keeping this distance made it easier to be frank with his superiors when he thought they were wrong. During the war Marshall never forgot that he was dealing in men's lives. From time to time he would send the daily casualty list to Roosevelt, so he did not forget either.

Marshall's arrival transforms the State Department. He has two qualities the Department appreciates: he listens to those who work for him, and the president listens to him. When Eisenhower, now chief of Army Staff, wonders what armed forces the United States will need in the post-war world, his first thought is to consult Marshall. Now, for the first time, the State Department is at the centre of the government. Marshall has two further valuable qualities: he knows how to handle difficult people – he has spent the war managing admirals and generals

* He was said to remember the telephone numbers he used when he was Pershing's chief of staff in France in the First World War.

– and he takes decisions. When he arrives in the State Department he asks Acheson, his deputy for the next six months, if there are questions for immediate decision. Acheson says that the question whether the Department should move to a new building has been debated for six months. He explains the arguments in a few sentences. 'Move,' says Marshall.

For the past year, Marshall has been in China on a doomed mission to mediate between the Communists and the Nationalists. He has seen some material about Europe – among it, Kennan's Long Telegram – but he has not followed the negotiations on Germany. One of the first documents on his desk as secretary of state is an overview of Soviet attitudes to Germany, sent by his former chief of staff, Walter Bedell Smith, now ambassador in Moscow. Smith writes that Germany has a special place in Moscow's thinking: ideologically, Lenin regarded it as the country most suited for Communism; practically, Germany is the 'greatest potential threat, most potent potential associate' for the Soviet Union.[26]

Before Marshall can leave for Moscow and the negotiations on Germany, the US government has to face the consequences of British bankruptcy. At the end of 1946, Britain has one and a half million servicemen overseas. This is unsustainable in a country with a labour shortage at home, especially when it is up to its neck in debt. The winter of 1946–7 is the worst on record: it freezes the ships in their harbours, kills the winter wheat and keeps the coal underground. Bevin has to ignore his bad heart condition and walk up two floors to discuss the financial crisis with Dalton, because there is no electricity.

Bevin sends Marshall advance warning: the message arrives on a Friday afternoon in February 1947. Acheson, Marshall's deputy, has already heard from the US embassy in Athens of the possible collapse of the Greek government and the rumours of a British withdrawal (their 16,000 troops are vital for stability in Athens). A note from the British embassy – with an advance copy of Bevin's message to Marshall – announces that Britain will be forced to stop support for Greece and Turkey in six weeks.

Acheson calls in Jack Hickerson and Loy Henderson, responsible for Europe and for the Near East, and asks them to assemble the facts of the Greek and Turkish situations; the resources needed – people and money; the resources available; and the significance of Greece and Turkey. They are to consult the Navy and War Departments. He tells Marshall and Truman what he is doing. Through the weekend he keeps in touch with the groups working on these questions. He receives the finished products on Sunday evening. Henderson asks if they are working to prepare a decision or to execute one. Acheson: 'I said that . . . under the circumstances there could be only one decision. At that we drank a martini or two towards the confusion of our enemies.'[27]

Marshall sees the papers on Monday morning. He discusses the subject with the British ambassador and then at the Cabinet lunch with the president. After this the secretaries of war and navy meet in Acheson's office and agree the proposals to put to the president. On Wednesday the president receives and agrees the joint State-War-Navy recommendations. The problem, he says, is not of knowing what to do, but of persuading Congress to agree it. He therefore invites seven Congressional leaders to a meeting on Saturday morning.

At this meeting on 27 February, Truman gives Marshall the floor. He speaks clearly but, as always, with restraint: 'we are faced with the first of a series of crises which may extend Soviet domination to Europe, the Middle East and Asia'. The choice is 'to act, or lose by default'. The Congressional leaders respond with questions about cost, and whether this is about pulling British chestnuts out of the fire. Acheson, worrying that it is not going well, asks Marshall in a low voice, 'Is this a private fight or can anyone get into it?' Marshall turns to the president and says that Acheson has something to say.

Acheson speaks of the political and economic crisis in the Western democracies: Germany and France are under threat from Communist subversion. He describes the Soviets' tightening hold on Central Europe and the pressures they have been putting on Iran and on Turkey. He describes the situation in Greece: a Communist-led civil war, with Yugoslav, Bulgarian and Albanian forces on its borders. If Greece goes, so may Turkey.

British power is failing, and so is that in every democratic country except for the United States. Only two great powers remain: the United States and the Soviet Union. Not since Rome and Carthage has there been such a polarisation of power. The poles are opposites: liberty and dictatorship. The area now threatened by Moscow is at the junction of three continents.

There is a silence. Senator Arthur Vandenberg breaks it. He says that if the president speaks to Congress and to the people in these terms – not just about Greece and Turkey, but about the wider context – he will support him; and so, he believes, will other members.*

Truman addresses a joint session of Congress on 12 March. He has told his Cabinet that this is not just about Greece. 'It means the United States is going to be involved in European politics.' Truman says:

> At the present moment in world history nearly every nation must choose between alternative ways of life. The choice is too often not a free one . . .
>
> I believe it must be the policy of the United States to support free peoples who are resisting attempted subjugation by armed minorities or by outside pressures . . .
>
> Should we fail to aid Greece and Turkey in this fateful hour, the effect will be far-reaching to the West as well as to the East.
>
> This is a serious course on which we embark. I would not recommend it except that the alternative is much more serious.

Some in the administration find the terms too sweeping; but the Congress and the media welcome the message. Senator Vandenberg tells the Canadian ambassador afterwards that the people would rise to boldness, 'like a trout to a fly . . . to pursue a vigorous 100% American foreign policy, which would combat on a world scale the spread of Communism'.[28]

* This account of the meeting is based on Acheson, *Present at the Creation*, p. 219, Jones pp. 138–42 and Beisner, *Dean Acheson*, p. 57. Pogue, *George G. Marshall*, p. 165, differs. But Acheson is likely to have remembered well what he said and how Senator Vandenberg reacted.

Bevin's plea for help is real, as is Britain's overstretch: at the same time as the government tells the United States that it needs to share the burden of supporting Greece, Bevin announces that he will refer the Palestine question to the United Nations, and is prepared to hand over its mandate there; the Cabinet also fixes the date for Britain's withdrawal from India.

Bevin wants the United States to see itself as a European power as well as a Pacific power. Britain has guarded the eastern Mediterranean against Russia for more than a hundred years, to secure the route to India. Now it is leaving India and Palestine, and it is not able to cope with Greece on its own. And this is not the same Russia. The Soviet Union may be in ruins, but as Milovan Djilas observed 'Stalin's armies and marshals, heavy with fat and medals and drunk with vodka and victory, had trampled half of Europe underfoot, and they were convinced they would trample the other half in the next round.'[29]

Marshall leaves for Moscow after Truman's decision to take on responsibility for Greece, but before he speaks to Congress. In Moscow the prospect is bad, but not hopeless. Marshall has spent the war resolving quarrels within the US government and among allies. The peace treaties with Finland, the Balkan countries and Italy – all signed in Paris on 10 February 1947 – show that it can be done.

The Moscow Council and the Marshall Plan

For someone who has created and then managed the most powerful military machine in the world, who expects decisions from all who work for him – 'Don't fight the problem, decide it,' he says – it must have been strange and depressing for Marshall to spend seven weeks in Moscow settling almost nothing. This is what the records show.

But three important things emerge. First, the seven weeks are proof that the Four-Power Council cannot do the job it has been given. The consequences of this judgement are so important that it has to be tested to the limit. The time is anyway not wholly wasted. Along the way, Bevin learns from Molotov that Britain is still using 91,000 German prisoners of war as labour; he also discovers that the Soviet Union is doing the same with ten times that number; they agree that prisoners should be repatriated by the end of 1948.*

The second result of the seven weeks is the growing collaboration between Bevin and Marshall. Bevin remains combative with Molotov; Marshall remains restrained. Molotov never finds a weakness in him that he can work on; but Bevin and Marshall take care not to expose any differences between them. When Bevin calls on Stalin, he gives Marshall a full account, oral and written. Bevin takes the direct approach with Stalin: he raises all the difficult issues – reparations, the border with Poland, the need for economic unity in Germany; Stalin gives soothing replies, but no insight into his thinking.[30]

The Four-Power talks go round in circles. At the end of one more discussion on the division of powers between a future German central government and the *Länder*, Marshall proposes the council move to the next agenda item; Molotov opposes. Bevin says that after four weeks in Moscow he doesn't care what they discuss next. Later he and Marshall agree to try and shorten discussions, except for those on the Four-Power (Byrnes) Treaty and on Austria.

Austria is a test of Russian good faith. The Soviet Union is occupying part of Austria, in theory to secure reparations from German property there. Russia refuses to recognise that most German property in Austria is really Austrian, seized or handed over under duress. Russian forces are meanwhile stealing oil and other Austrian assets; its occupying force also gives Moscow an excuse to keep troops in Hungary and Romania, in theory to protect lines of communication to Austria.

The most substantial talks in Moscow are between Bevin and Marshall. Their relationship is illustrated in the record of their last conversation. This is a joint memorandum recording the points for action by the bizonal authorities. These cover many items on which the Four have failed to agree: levels of steel production, reparations, the division of powers between the centre and the *Länder*, locations of joint authorities. They agree to delay announcements 'to avoid the implication

* German prisoners were held in the Soviet Union into the 1950s. Bevin may nevertheless have helped start the process of releasing them.

that we have been insincere in our efforts in Moscow to agree on economic unity'.[31] Marshall stops in Berlin on his way back to Washington and meets not only Clay, but also General Robertson, the British representative.

Bevin and Marshall each try to reassure Bidault. On his way to Moscow, Bevin has signed a Treaty of Alliance with him at Dunkirk. Marshall's last conversation in Moscow is with Bidault, who asks for help with the World Bank and with the Saarland. On the issues discussed in the council, Marshall says that he understands how different the wartime experiences of Frenchmen (and Russians) have been from those of Americans. 'I was fearful of the influences their horrible experiences would have upon the Allies. It might lead us to solutions which appeal to us for the present but might be fatal for the future.'[32] Bidault replies that he understands, but that France still needs more time.

In his memoirs Bidault reflects on Marshall and on their many conversations: 'No other man since 1945 approaches him in uprightness and stature. . . . He was not vain; he spoke with great simplicity and humour . . . He was unaffected and did not pretend to be infallible. He would ask others for advice and could be unsure, even hesitant. But once he had made up his mind nothing could have made him change it.'[33]

The best summary of the three months in Moscow and the forty-three sessions of the council is in the radio address Marshall gives on 28 April, after his return to the United States. Unlike Byrnes, he has reported daily to Truman. He listens to suggestions from his team. But the product is Marshall's alone, especially in its patience and restraint. He does not say that it is impossible to make progress in the Four-Power format. But that is now his working assumption.

The questions they are tackling, he says, need concrete solutions, not 'what Lincoln called "pernicious abstractions"' that give the appearance of agreement without the substance. He takes coal as his starting point: it is needed urgently throughout Europe, especially in France. To mine coal, the mines and their equipment must be renewed; that means that steel is needed; this adds to the demand for coal; but as steel capacity grows, so does capacity for war. Marshall is a soldier and thinks in concrete terms.

Then Germany: vital for the European economy, but as it regains strength, memories of the disasters it has brought will revive. How should Germany be governed? The United States and Britain do not want anything that could easily convert into another Nazi regime, and think in terms of a federal system. The Soviet Union, by contrast, wants a strong central government. (He does not add that this includes a strong Communist Party.) Instead he mentions, in a low key, that there have been 'few, if any, reports of what has been occurring' in the Soviet zone.[34] He explains Bizonia: this will allow movement of goods; the Soviets attack this as a breach of the Potsdam Agreement, but it is their refusal to implement Potsdam that is the cause of the bizonal merger. The invitation to the Soviet Union and France to join Bizonia stands. He mentions frontiers, and concerns about whether the border with Poland is now too far to the west and might be a cause of future trouble. (Marshall's fear is that this is reminiscent of Versailles.)

Marshall refers to the Byrnes Treaty – Germany disarmed for twenty-five years under a guarantee by the United States. This would also guarantee that the United States would not repeat what it did after the First World War, insisting on the terms of peace and then withdrawing. On Austria he says that if Soviet demands are met, Austria's chances of surviving as an independent state will be in doubt. Prompt action to relieve Austria of the costs of occupation is needed. Marshall's description of the Moscow Council finishes with his meeting with Stalin.

This, for Marshall, is the moment when doubt becomes conviction. Marshall has handled it differently from Bevin. He has focused on the main question, Germany, returning to it several times, giving Stalin space to explain his thinking.* In reply, all he gets is indifference and Stalin's comment, as he doodles wolf heads in a red pencil,[35] that the weeks in Moscow are no more than 'the first skirmishes and the brushes

* This was partly accident. Stalin's invitation came at short notice, and Marshall had no talking points; so he returned repeatedly to the question most on his mind.

between reconnaissance forces'. Agreement may yet come, when the negotiators have exhausted themselves in dispute and see the need to compromise.

Marshall tells his radio audience this, concluding:

> But we cannot ignore the factor of time involved here. The recovery of Europe has been slower than we expected. Disintegrating forces are becoming evident; the patient is sinking while the doctors deliberate. So I believe that action cannot await compromise through exhaustion. New issues arise daily. Whatever action is possible to meet these pressing problems must be taken without delay.

These thoughts are the third result of the Moscow Council. On 5 June Marshall turns them into policy in an address at Harvard.

The credit for the Marshall Plan belongs to Marshall and to Truman. By this time many are advocating action to tackle the economic crisis in Europe. Acheson has trailed the thought in a speech in Mississippi on 8 May while Marshall is still in Moscow; Will Clayton, the creative assistant secretary for economic affairs, has been saying for some time that poverty and hunger in Europe are a threat to democracy. He returns from Europe on 27 May, with personal observations of the dislocation of European economies. Kennan has been working on these questions and submits ideas on 23 May. Marshall gives Bohlen, his newly appointed counsellor, the task of writing his speech for the Harvard commencement: he does this by bringing together Clayton's picture of dislocation in Europe and Kennan's proposal that Marshall ask Europe to take the initiative, and to do so collectively.

As before, Marshall puts the problem in concrete terms. On the radio he spoke about coal; at Harvard he tells of farmers unwilling to sell their produce in the cities because there is nothing for them to buy:

> it has become obvious during recent months that this visible destruction was probably less serious than the dislocation of the entire fabric of the European economy. . . . The modern system of the division of

labour, upon which the exchange of products is based, is in danger of breaking down.

The remedy lies in breaking the vicious circle and restoring the confidence of the European people in the economic future of their own countries and of Europe as a whole. . . . I am convinced this must not be on a piecemeal basis as various crises develop. Any assistance that this government may render in the future should provide a cure rather than a mere palliative.

. . . there must be some agreement among the countries of Europe as to the requirements of the situation and the part those countries themselves will take in order to give proper effect to whatever action might be undertaken by this government. It would be neither fitting nor efficacious for this government to draw up unilaterally a program designed to place Europe on its feet economically. This is the business of Europeans. The initiative, I think, must come from Europe.[36]

In Marshall's low-key way, this is as clear as it could be. He and Acheson have already warmed up Vandenberg to the thought that something like this will be needed. Marshall has considered tipping Bevin off, but does not want to create difficulties between him and Bidault. Then chance takes over. The BBC correspondent Leonard Miall has a thirty-minute commentary slot to fill. Normally he asks an American to explain some aspect of US policy. This week his guest has cried off, but he knows what Acheson has said in Mississippi, and is planning to feature that. At the last minute the press officer at the British embassy tells him of Marshall's speech, which he will deliver on 5 June, the same day as the broadcast. Copies of it are now available. Reading it, Miall understands it is a big story and devotes the whole programme to it, reading out extracts. The broadcast goes out at 10.30 p.m. UK time.

Three things are original in the Harvard address. First is the concept itself. The term 'foreign aid' does not yet exist. This is a new idea, an original one because economic means are used for a political goal. Nowadays, whatever the crisis, someone always calls for a new Marshall Plan. In 1947 there had never been anything like it before.

Second, though we talk of 'the Marshall Plan', the speech does *not* propose a plan. Instead, Marshall calls on the Europeans to produce the plan, and to do so jointly. 'The initiative, I think, must come from Europe,' says Marshall, thereby taking the initiative himself. This will also make it easier to sell in Congress: it will not be the US government asking for yet more money; it will be a united group of friends from Europe asking for help.

Third, if you are proposing assistance, normally you say who it is for. Marshall does not name the recipient countries. It is for them to decide who they are. Marshall wants as many European countries as he can get, without the Soviet Union. He does not want to take responsibility for dividing Europe, though everyone assumes that this will be the outcome. Kennan and Bohlen assure him that the Russians will exclude themselves. When asked, Marshall and Truman confirm that the offer is open to Russia.

By chance, Bevin has his bedside radio on before he goes to sleep and hears the broadcast. He arrives at the Foreign Office the next morning demanding a copy of the speech – he thought it was Marshall he was hearing on the radio – and demanding someone get him Bidault on the telephone.

No one knows anything. There is nothing in the press. The embassy has instructions to reduce cable traffic and has sent the text of the speech by diplomatic bag. Sir William Strang, the permanent secretary, suggests they ask the embassy in Washington what Marshall meant. 'Bill,' says Bevin, 'we know what he said. If you ask questions you'll get answers you don't want. Our problem is what *we do*, not what *he meant*.'* Instead he telephones Bidault and together they start the process of giving the Marshall Plan shape.

Bevin and Bidault take responsibility for organising the Europeans – as Marshall has hoped. First they invite Molotov to Paris. It would be fatal if the Soviet Union decides to join, but they cannot discourage their attendance. This sounds like a task for subtle diplomacy; in fact it is easy. Molotov comes to Paris with an entourage of eighty,

* Acheson, *Sketches from Life*, p. 12. Acheson must have had this story from Bevin.

many with links to the French Communists, on whose support the French government depends. His objective is to stop the project, not to join it.

Bidault and Bevin meet him over five days from 30 June, each giving blow-by-blow reports to the American ambassador. Bidault gives Molotov a paper on how the conference will proceed. Each participant will set out their needs and their resources. Molotov says this violates national sovereignty: each country should calculate what it needs; the conference can add these up and pass the total to the United States. Bevin and Bidault explain that it doesn't work like that, not when you are asking for a loan from the bank, nor when you want one from the United States.

To begin with Molotov is 'unusually mild', not wanting to give France and Britain a pretext to break with him. But soon he is asserting: 'All the programmes mean that small states are being subject to Big-Power domination, and interference in national sovereignty.'[37] This is remarkable from a Russian, seeing what the Soviet Union is doing in the Baltic States, in Bulgaria, Poland and Austria. In the final session Molotov warns that the process will lead not to the reconstruction of Europe, but to 'very different results'. Bevin whispers to Piers Dixon, his private secretary: 'This really is the birth of a Western bloc.'[38]

Bidault and Bevin send out invitations the next day. They go to everyone, Moscow too, and Ankara, though not Madrid. They reassure the United States that there is no risk of the Soviets accepting. Almost everyone else does, including the Scandinavians, which no one had expected – but not Finland. Three days later, Molotov advises the Central European governments to withdraw their participation; the Marshall Plan aims to create a Western bloc, including the western part of Germany. All except the Czechs comply. They are summoned to Moscow and bullied into cancelling.[39] Bedell Smith in Moscow describes the Czech reversal as 'nothing less than a declaration of war by the Soviet Union, on the immediate issue of the control of Europe'.[40]

Giving the initiative to the countries of Europe is intended to make it difficult for local Communist Parties to attack the programme. They do this anyway, on Moscow's orders, calling for strikes in France and Italy. In countries desperate for capital to repair war damage, desperate for dollars to import food, this is crazy. The French and the Italian governments take the opportunity to drop the Communists from their coalitions.

This is only the beginning. Now Europe has to create the plan; and Washington has to persuade Congress to act, out of both generosity and self-interest. And since it will take time to work out the long-term plan, Truman asks for a smaller sum in emergency finance.

A paper by Kennan identifies three critical problems in Europe: England, Germany and the political condition of Europe.[41] The condition of Europe is well understood: a mountain of problems, and governments whose political fabric is in as much need of repair as their economic systems are.

Of Britain, he says: 'her problems are deep-seated and grave, and they require for their solution, all the coolness, the realism, the energy and the unity that the British people can muster'. By early September, sterling convertibility has been suspended. But illusions still persist. Bevin assumes that Britain is different from Europe and the Marshall Plan will be a joint venture between America and Britain. That is not how Washington sees it.

Of Germany – Bizonia, that is – Kennan says that the occupation authorities have neither dealt with its internal problems, nor established the international links that prosperity requires. The chances of the Marshall Plan being able to accomplish anything for Germany are therefore meagre.

This is all true; the difficulties and mistakes are endless. But, as Bevin says two years later to the Washington Press Club, Marshall's speech 'was like a lifeline to a sinking man'. Or, as he tells the US chargé in London: the United States is in the same position as Britain was at the end of the Napoleonic Wars, when it accounted for 30 per cent of the world's wealth. For eighteen years after Waterloo Britain 'practically gave away her exports; but this had resulted in stability and a hundred years of peace'.[42]

The Second London Council and NATO

An essential step towards economic and political success in Germany comes at the London meeting of the Council of Foreign Ministers in November 1947. This is different in tone and substance from the previous councils.

In the interval between Moscow and London, the Soviet Union's order to East European countries not to attend the Marshall Plan conference cuts Europe in two. In September the Soviet Union creates Cominform (the Communist Information Bureau). At its inauguration Andrei Zhadanov announces the division of the world into two camps. Between spring and autumn, what remains of non-Communist parties, peasant or social democrat, in Central and Eastern Europe are destroyed. Their leaders are imprisoned or executed. In Paris this translates as the French Communists taking to the streets; the battle reaches its climax while the council is meeting in London.

In this new context, the Western Three concert their positions in the conference in advance. Marshall's collaborative style and the Marshall Plan have brought them together.

They go into the council anticipating failure. Bevin is direct with Molotov, asking him on the eve of the council whether he is ready to reach agreements or if he will insist that the other three agree with him. The council begins by failing to agree an agenda: when it gets past this, it continues mainly as a theatre for propaganda. Molotov attacks the United States and Britain for seeking an imperialist peace, in contrast to the Soviets' 'democratic peace'. He accuses the others of planning a government for the three Western zones: for once this is close to the truth.

In early December the conference returns to Austria. France has proposed a lump payment to the Soviet Union to cover the German property they claim. Moscow is interested but will not name a sum.* Meanwhile, Molotov accuses the United States of violating Austrian sovereignty by offering it financial assistance: this, from a state whose army is camped in Austria and stealing its oil.

* This does not prevent Molotov from offering to reduce it by 10 per cent.

On 6 December Marshall tells Bevin he wants the break to come on a point of substance that the public will understand. This proves difficult. In the final stages they reach agreements on issues where before they have made no progress, such as steel production in Germany. Molotov probably wants to keep the council alive, but dysfunctional. The next day the Western Three ask for transparency on the reparations taken by Russia from East Germany. Here Molotov cannot compromise, and the pretence of trying to work together ends in an exchange of accusations. Molotov finishes with an attack on the United States for enslaving Germany by providing economic aid. They all take a day off and return on 15 December. Molotov tries to bring in 'elected representatives' from the Peoples' Assembly (*Volkskammer*) in the Soviet zone. Marshall and Bevin refuse. Each of the Western Three makes a brief review of the council's failures; it is then adjourned without a date to reconvene.

Bevin is now beginning to know where he wants to go. When Marshall makes a farewell call, Bevin says:

> [T]he problem should not be isolated into a mere quarrel between the Western Powers and the Soviet Union. The issue, to use a phrase of the American ambassador, was where power was going to rest. His own idea was that we must devise some Western democratic system comprising the Americans, ourselves, France, Italy etc. and of course the Dominions. This would not be a formal alliance, but an understanding backed by power, money and resolute action. It would be a sort of spiritual federation of the West.[43]

Alan Bullock quotes a *Manchester Guardian* correspondent's remark that, 'like the Greek historian Thucydides, the more interesting Mr Bevin is, the more obscure he becomes'.[44] This is how it is with new ideas: they emerge as half-formed thoughts. They arrive in conversations when the main event is over and tension released. They come most often when you have just failed, and need to decide on a new course.

Bevin goes on to say that, instead of trying to deal with Germany as three powers – the Byrnes Treaty minus the Soviets – he would like to involve the Benelux countries and Italy: 'The essential task was to create confidence in Western Europe'.[45] Marshall says that the European Recovery Program deals with material aspects of the problem, but that these efforts could 'be given a greater dignity'.

This conversation continues the next day at the US ambassador's house, with the participation of Generals Clay and Robertson. They discuss the development of German institutions, and the urgency of currency reform. Here, a project is already under way; memories of German hyperinflation in the inter-war years are in everyone's mind.

The generals are going to mention currency reform in the Allied Control Commission in Berlin. Clay notes the vulnerability of the Western presence in Berlin in passing. The Western powers are already subject to harassment and could hold out against a blockade for some time. He is thinking, however, of a blockade aimed at the western military, not at the whole population of West Berlin. The main feeling is one of relief. Now that the council has broken down, they are free to act. It is high time. The British zone is in a worse condition than two years before – Bevin is much criticised for it.* Recovery in Germany depends on European recovery, and vice versa; both need capital, confidence and a reliable currency. As Marshall leaves, the news comes that Truman has signed the Bill for Interim Aid for Europe, phase one of the Marshall Plan. That makes a start on capital.[46]

As for confidence, on the voyage back to the United States Marshall tells Jack Hickerson, the head of the Europe Bureau, of Bevin's still-unshaped idea of a 'spiritual federation of the West'. He in turn discusses it with John Foster Dulles, travelling with the delegation, who is receptive.

The paper that Bevin puts to the Cabinet early in January 1948 envisages a consolidation of Western Europe, based on democratic values 'with the backing of the Americas and the Dominions'. He sees it including countries from Scandinavia to Greece, and, as soon as circumstances permit, Germany and Spain. 'This need not take the shape

* One result of Bizonia is to end British plans to nationalise industry in the Ruhr.

of a formal alliance, though we have an alliance with France and may conclude one with other countries. It does, however, mean close consultation with each of the Western European countries, beginning with economic questions.'[47]

He sends a shorter version of these ideas to Washington, and receives a warm response from Marshall: 'I want him to know', he writes to the British ambassador, 'that his proposal has deeply interested and moved me, and that I wish to see the United States do everything which it properly can to assist the European nations in bringing a project along these lines to fruition.'[48]

Then, on 25 February, comes the coup in Prague. It is a shock, but not altogether a surprise. It illustrates what Europe has to fear: not an invasion, but a local Communist Party capturing key institutions, police and internal security, and then seizing the state itself with Moscow's backing. Prague has a special resonance in London and Paris.

Bevin is conscious of the pressure being applied to Finland; and he knows that Moscow has invited Norway to negotiate a treaty. Out of this comes a message to Marshall:

> the most effective course would be to take early steps, before Norway goes under, to conclude, under Article 51 of the Charter of the UN, a regional Atlantic Approaches Pact of Mutual Assistance in which all the countries directly threatened by a Russian move to the Atlantic could participate, for example US, UK, Canada, Eire, Iceland, Norway, Denmark, Portugal, France (and Spain, when it has a democratic regime).'[49]*

This is a concept that those who remember the Battle of the Atlantic will understand. But Bevin is thinking primarily in political terms: if governments have confidence that they will be backed up by the

* Apart from Benelux and Italy, this lists all the founding members of NATO. Bevin suggests three security systems: the Brussels Pact, backed by the United States, a North Atlantic system, and a Mediterranean system including Italy. He is wrong only in including Ireland, a country that Britain often misunderstands.

United States, they will be strong enough to resist enemies both within and without.

Marshall replies the next day, inviting a British representative to Washington for consultations. In a note to the president he stresses that 'the outcome of the Anglo-French-Benelux talks should indicate the extent to which the participating states are prepared to go in mutual defence'.[50] Marshall's approach is similar to that in his Harvard address: 'The initiative, I think, must come from Europe'.

A week later Bevin signs the Brussels Treaty. Its commitment to mutual assistance is unambiguous, but it is not a duplicate of the Treaty of Dunkirk. It does not identify an enemy. Its full title is: 'Treaty on Economic, Social and Cultural Collaboration and Collective Self-Defence'. The last element is the one that is remembered, but Bevin's original idea was wider. He proposes regular meetings of the Consultative Council to discuss co-operation on questions such as clearing arrangements for foreign exchange, harmonisation of social services and co-operation against Communist subversion.[51]

On the same day, Truman makes a special address to Congress, seeking the reintroduction of limited conscription – for the first time in peacetime – so 'that we keep our occupation forces in Germany until peace is secured in Europe'. At the end he refers to the Brussels Treaty: 'This development deserves our full support. . . . I am sure that the determination of the free countries of Europe to protect themselves will be matched by an equal determination on our part to help them do so.'[52]

Exploratory talks begin a few days later: the United States, Britain and Canada. Britain suggests including the French but Washington prefers not, on security grounds. (Ironically, the British team includes Donald Maclean.)*

Senator Vandenberg, chair of the Foreign Relations Committee and an aspirant for the Republican nomination for the presidency, hears of the talks and suggests his committee should be involved. If the State

* Maclean, with Guy Burgess and Kim Philby, was one of the 'Cambridge spies'. He sent an enormous amount of material to Moscow. It is not clear if it was read.

Department asked for a resolution of the Senate, it could provide a basis for the Brussels Pact countries to seek consultations. Canada might also be involved, and at some point other European countries such as Greenland (i.e. Denmark), Iceland and Norway. Senator Vandenberg and Dulles mention the United States' association with Latin America under the Rio Treaty, setting up the Organization of American States (OAS). This has just been agreed and they have been involved in the negotiation.

The Vandenberg Resolution is passed by the Senate on 11 June. Its starting point is that peace should be assured by the UN. However, the use of the veto (unstated – by the Soviet Union) has rendered UN collective security unworkable. It recommends that the president pursue a voluntary agreement at the UN that the veto should not be used on questions involving the peaceful resolution of international disputes. It goes on to suggest, as an alternative, the development of regional arrangements for collective self-defence and 'Association by the United States, by constitutional process, with such regional and other collective arrangements as are based on continuous and effective self-help and mutual aid, and as effects its national security.' In this way the US Senate becomes one of the co-founders of NATO.

By now the Marshall Plan is becoming a reality: Congress votes an unbelievable $5 billion; this will become $13 billion over the next four years, well over $100 billion in today's money. The Plan acquires initials: 'ERP' for European Recovery Programme, a coming-of-age ritual in the world of bureaucracy. The Atlantic project (it does not yet have initials) is now Bevin's priority. A sign of this is that he sends his best man to Washington. This is Oliver Franks, another of the new men – a grammar-school boy, recruited from Oxford as permanent secretary in the Ministry of Supply during the war. Since then he has been Bevin's man on the Marshall Plan, putting the European half of it together. He now becomes ambassador in Washington, where he helps bring Bevin's next project home.*

* Franks was one of the great bureaucrats of his age. His rule when he chaired committees was: never allow them to agree on what to do, unless they also agree on how to do it.

West Germany and Berlin

Meanwhile, important work is done on Germany. Five meetings of the Four Powers (London, Paris, New York, Moscow, London again) have made no progress. From February 1948 the Three – Britain, France and the United States – meet in London and plan Germany's future: mixed teams of military and civilians, Clay and Robert Murphy for the United States, Robertson and Edmund Hall-Patch for Britain, General Koenig and Maurice Couve de Murville for France. They work until June, bringing the Benelux countries in for the final sessions, tackling the issues of governing Germany: how to fuse the three zones, what to do about reparations and dismantling, the status of the Ruhr, how to draft a German constitution.

Berlin, 20 March: the tripartite conference is meeting in London. Marshal Sokolovsky, the Russian member of the Allied Control Commission, asks for a report on its proceedings. Clay, Koenig and Robertson refuse. Sokolovsky then reads a statement saying that the Western Powers are in breach of the Four-Power Agreement and the Allied Control Commission therefore no longer exists.

This action precipitates a long-expected political crisis in France: Bidault, attacked from all sides, asks Britain and the United States for more concessions on Germany. They refuse: the concessions already made to France and the Benelux countries are unpopular in Germany. With the Russian walk-out, France has no choice. It puts the package to the Assembly, as the Three have agreed it. Bevin sends friends to Paris to stiffen the Socialist Party. In the end they and the French centre support Bidault. He and the agreement survive. The programme goes into effect, with the new currency.

This is a moment of change in Western Europe. First there were ruins; then there were plans; now, in mid 1948, the plans become action. Congress has agreed the Marshall Plan funding in July; and the national plans are now finalised. Of these, the last, signed in Berlin on 9 July, is that for US/British Bizonia.

In the East a new regime, launched with purges and atrocities, is already under way. Now order can be brought to West Germany too.

A new currency is the first step; then the Parliamentary Council will propose a constitution, so that Germans can take control of their lives in a liberal political framework.

On 22 June Sokolovsky issues an order that all Berlin authorities must recognise the new Soviet currency (the *Ostmark*) as the only legal currency in Berlin. The next day the West Berliners make their views clear. Ignoring Communist threats, the Berlin City Assembly meets in the Soviet sector and votes to reject this order: it insists that they will follow orders only from the Western Powers. The new West Mark, the *Deutsche Mark* stamped with a large 'B' (for Berlin), is introduced on 25 June. The Western Allies accept the *Ostmark* for some transactions. In the Soviet zone, possession of the Western currency is a criminal offence. An observer describes the effect of the new currency: 'Currency transformed the German scene from one day to the next . . . goods reappeared in the stores, money resumed its normal function, the grey and black markets reverted to a minor role'.[53]

Then the blockade of West Berlin by the Soviets begins. Sporadic harassment during the spring has given a warning. From 24 June the blockade is in earnest. The West retaliates immediately, stopping all traffic and all trade with the Soviet zone.

Bevin is on holiday on the Isle of Wight. A torpedo boat is sent to collect him. Anticipating a crisis, he has already set up a Berlin Committee. In practice he takes the decisions, and Attlee backs him. When the deputy military governor is pessimistic about supplying Berlin by air, Bevin demands a second opinion. When an American air force general explains the difficulties to him, Bevin says he is surprised that the United States cannot do what the RAF is planning to do. Leaving the room, the general says to Frank Roberts, Bevin's private secretary, 'I suppose we've got to do it.'

The US air force in Germany is made of sterner stuff. Clay telephones Curtis LeMay, its commander:

Clay: Have you any planes that can carry coal?
LeMay: Carry what?
Clay: Coal.

LeMay: We must have a bad phone connection. It sounds as if you are asking if we have planes for carrying coal.

Clay: Yes, that's what I said – coal.

LeMay: The air force can deliver anything.[54]

The US air force does fly anything. So does the RAF. The air lift begins on 26 June. Clay estimates that 2,000 tons a day will be needed for the civilian population. By the end of the air lift, planes are landing at two-minute intervals and are unloaded by Berlin volunteers in seven minutes. Deliveries exceed 7,000 tons a day. Two million Berliners make do on limited food and four hours' electricity a day. In the process, occupiers become protectors, and enemies become friends.

Clay would prefer to test the Soviets, sending armed convoys by road. Political leaders on both sides of the Atlantic think this too big a risk. What would they do when Soviet forces place obstacles in their way? Nobody wants to fire the first shot. In the airlift the Soviets show that this is their philosophy too.

The crisis proceeds on three levels. First, the air lift: the tonnage carried doubles between July and October as the result of more planes and better organisation. Seaplanes land on the lakes. New runways and a new airport (Tegel) are added in record time.* In July, Bedell Smith in Moscow assumes that time is on the Soviets' side.[55] But by October the Allies are building up stocks for the winter. Happily, this is mild; getting through it is another milestone.

The second dimension is diplomacy. Once Truman has said: 'We stay. Period.' the course is set. Bevin is sceptical of negotiations, especially at foreign-minister level; he does not want to revive the Four Power council. He prefers the military framework in Berlin. Eventually talks take place in Moscow between Molotov – and on two occasions, Stalin – and the United States, Britain and France, represented by ambassadors, with Bedell Smith leading. (Frank Roberts replaces the British ambassador, who is ill.) In spite of Stalin being in an amiable and co-operative mood, the talks lead nowhere.

* Tegel airport was built in ninety days.

They establish that the Russian target is the West German constitutional process, not the currency. The attack is on Berlin because that is the West's weak point. In August the Moscow talks appear, briefly, to make progress; but the moment the results go to Berlin for implementation they are blocked. The Three raise the issue at the UN in late September. This also leads nowhere; but by this time their sense is that, as Marshall says, 'In every field, the Russians are retreating.' Russia is still strong in Berlin, but 'we have put western Germany on its feet and we are engaged in bringing about its recovery.'[56]

The third dimension is the Berliners. The Russians offer extra rations for every citizen of the Western sectors who registers with them. No more than 4 per cent take this up. Then they try to take control of the police; the result is a split into a Western and a Communist force. At the end of August, a Communist-organised crowd prevents the City Assembly from meeting. When the Communists occupy the Assembly chamber a week later, a counter-demonstration of up to a third of a million Berliners takes over the main square – the numbers astonish even the bullish Clay. They hear the mayor, Ernst Reuter, speak for Berlin: 'We cannot be bartered; we cannot be negotiated; we cannot be sold.' Demonstrators pull down the Soviet flag from the Brandenburg Gate; the crowd tears it up.

Russian troops open fire. City officials ask the British liaison officer to intervene. Bevin instructs Robertson, who sends soldiers to escort the Assembly to the British sector. Meeting in the Technical University, without their Socialist Unity Party colleagues, they decide to hold new elections. On 5 December, 83.9 per cent vote for democratic parties.

Finally in the background is domestic politics. In Britain nothing changes. But in France, after weeks of turmoil, a new government emerges, stronger than its predecessor, with Robert Schuman as foreign minister. And in the United States, to everyone's surprise, Truman is re-elected president. Whether this impacts on Stalin's calculations we do not know, but it is shortly after Truman's inauguration that Stalin shows signs that he may be willing to drop the Berlin blockade. In Germany, meanwhile, work on a new constitution is close to completion.

For the moment, however, the United States, Britain and France govern Western Germany; and they continue to wrestle with four problems. The first is reparations: the US government does not understand why it should spend money to promote European and German recovery, while Britain and France dismantle industrial assets. (By 1949 the emphasis is on reducing war-related industrial capacity.) This policy is unpopular in Britain; in Germany it risks causing riots.

Second, the Ruhr: this has been difficult from the start. The Russians called for internationalisation, while they sealed off their own zone. The French wanted to separate it from Germany, but have dropped this in return for an international Ruhr authority to supervise how the Ruhr's coal and steel are allocated to buyers. Bevin considered international ownership at an earlier stage, but dropped the idea as too complicated. The Ruhr authority itself also looks complicated.

Third, to guarantee the security of France and others, a Military Security Board will verify Germany's disarmament. A directive on this is agreed but has not been implemented.

Last, the French zone has to merge with Bizonia; and the Three have to agree an Occupation Statute – their powers in West Germany, when it has a constitution and elects its own leaders. Each of these raises the question about security in Europe. The key items are the Occupation Statute and the Ruhr.

It is the arrival of Robert Schuman as foreign minister in September 1948 that changes things. He has been prime minister for a year. This is a miserable job in post-war France: trying to keep a coalition together, attacked by Gaullists in the Assembly and Communists in the streets. As prime minister, Schuman stuck to the policy of breaking Germany up, which Bidault has defended in Allied discussions. The new government also has a torrid time with the Communist unions, but by November it is over the worst. Schuman is from Moselle, a *département* of France since 1919 but German when he was a boy. Now he is one of the three foreign ministers responsible for the fate of Germany.

While this work is going on in Europe, the US government responds to the Vandenberg Resolution by inviting the Brussels Pact countries and Canada to begin consultations. A treaty will have to wait until after the elections for the president and the Congress. This means that the autumn can be used to work on it. The issues are not complicated. The most important questions are: what obligations will the treaty impose, and who will belong?

Jack Hickerson has told the British ambassador in his first discussion on the subject that the Rio Treaty of 1947 would be a good model: it contains the formula that 'an attack against one shall be considered an attack against them all'. This is language that the Senate is familiar with. It leaves the final decision on war and peace to each country. That means the Senate will have its say. It is a moral commitment to react; but there is no obligation to react in a particular way. This – Hickerson points out – could include an attack by a member of the treaty as well as by an outsider. Thus the treaty lies in territory between collective security in the League of Nations sense, and the sort of commitment that old-fashioned alliances represented.[57]

As for who joins, the United States takes the North Atlantic dimension seriously: their list starts with Norway, with its long coast, Iceland and Greenland/Denmark, Portugal, because of the Azores. Bevin is against Italy. He would prefer to stick to the North Atlantic and deal with Italy separately. The French, having been passionately against, notice that Italy is on their flank, and become passionately for; the United States sees political reasons – Italy too needs confidence to face down its Communist Party. Italy is invited. Miraculously, the French persuade the United States to include Algeria in the territory covered.

These questions and other less interesting matters are discussed by a committee of ambassadors in Washington and a working party at a lower level. The ambassadors make speeches; the working party makes drafts. It is a foretaste of life in a multilateral organisation. The birds circle overhead seemingly endlessly; then, suddenly, they land.

Acheson

The moment for this is Truman's victory in the presidential election, unforeseen and decisive. Acheson also returns; Truman appoints him secretary of state. He has been away from the Department only eighteen months and is ready to start. He takes the treaty in hand, listens to Franks' advice, talks to Vandenberg and Tom Connally in the Senate. Franks judges that a military reference will be essential on the European side; the senators want to underline their constitutional prerogatives. Acheson makes the deal. Article V of the treaty will refer to each 'party taking such action as it deems necessary, including the use of armed force', and Article XI will say that each party shall implement the treaty 'in accordance with their respective constitutional processes'.* Both state the obvious: 'such action as it deems necessary' evidently includes military action; and of course each member is going to act in accordance with its constitution. But with this the Europeans are reassured and the Senate is satisfied.

On membership, the Norwegian foreign minister knows what he wants. His personal experience of a concentration camp and a death sentence help him conclude that neutrality did not benefit Norway in the Second World War. A barrage of threats and territorial claims from the Soviet Union, demonstrating its usual diplomatic subtlety, reinforces his convictions. Acheson, by contrast, underlines that the choice is for Norway, and offers neither threats nor inducements – a mirror of the way the two alliances (when the Warsaw Pact is formed) will function over the next decades. When Norway decides to join, this tips the balance for Denmark – bringing Greenland with it; Iceland too opts for membership. This secures the position in the north. France insists on Italian membership, and the Italians themselves plead that they will be vulnerable to a Communist takeover without it; Acheson and the others give in, making the North Atlantic Treaty Organisation less northern and less Atlantic.

Truman insists that Acheson sign the treaty for the United States – paradoxical in a sense because, of all the steps taken to strengthen post-war Europe, this was the only one at the creation of which Acheson had *not* been present. Escott Reid remarks: 'He was present only on

* The story of the negotiation is told briefly in *The Birth of NATO* by Sir Nicholas Henderson, who was there, or blow by blow in *Foreign Relations of the United States, 1948*, vol. 3.

the sixth, the last day of the creation; but that was a particularly busy day.'[58]

This is a good moment for Acheson to become secretary of state. He starts with a major treaty, and has as his partners the most creative British and French foreign ministers of the post-war period.

Acheson begins his book *Sketches from Life* (1961) with portraits of Ernest Bevin and Robert Schuman. The memoir has several fine portraits, but those of Bevin and Schuman stand out; it seems as if the wish to recall his foreign minister partners from 1949 to 1951 inspired him to write it. (They are also the main subjects of the cartoons reproduced in its pages.)

This is an unlikely trio. Acheson's background – Groton and Yale – is the opposite of Bevin's; but both are men who value facts above theories and who want to get things done. They also share something close to complete control of foreign affairs: Bevin has a cast-iron relationship with Attlee. Acheson has Truman's full confidence.

Schuman, like Acheson, has studied law, but he is from a different social and intellectual tradition. Acheson and Bevin address each other as 'Ernie' and 'My lad'; but Schuman is always 'M. Schuman' or 'M. le Président'. Acheson's father was an Episcopalian bishop; Bevin has been a Baptist lay preacher; Schuman is a devout Catholic. Acheson, like Bevin, thinks in concrete terms of 'What are we going to do next?', Schuman deals in concepts, less well defined, since he is trying to look further ahead. He lives a charmed life as foreign minister, surviving as Acheson and Bevin's partner for four years while the French prime minister changes nine times.

Acheson's essays give the reader a sense of the charm he felt at discovering how much could be shared with this 'gentle, gallant and great man' so different from himself.

On policy the Three are as close as one could hope; Bevin is as tough as Acheson towards the Soviet Union; Schuman, though less belligerent, is of the same mind: he is the man who dropped the Communists from his coalition when prime minister. On Germany, which is now the central issue, Bevin understands that European recovery needs a German recovery, and he is committed to establishing a high degree of

German self-government in the West, a policy that until then has faced a long rearguard action from Paris. Here the arrival of Schuman makes the difference. He is, as Acheson writes, a man from a border region who understands, like Edith Cavell, that 'patriotism is not enough'. As a committed Catholic, he sees reconciliation as essential if countries are to live together. His appointment itself is a signal that France wants a new policy.

Bevin begins 1949 by meeting Schuman. They get on well, but differ on Europe: Schuman is a born European; he understands the emotional pull of the European movement and of a European assembly. Bevin does not like the idea of a free-floating assembly, responsible to nobody. He likes practical politics; he wants co-operation among governments, and has several times suggested a study on a European customs union. His priority at this point is to get on with NATO.

Schuman's evolving attitude to Germany is conveyed by George Kennan's record of a conversation with André François-Poncet, a diplomat who served in pre-war Germany. Schuman has sent him to Germany to look around. Kennan reports him saying that:

> This business of military government was irritating and discouraging for the vanquished, corrupting and demoralising for the victors . . . The occupation statute they were laboriously grinding out in London was over-complicated and politically deadening. Mr Schuman, who knew Germany from the old days . . . felt the time had come for a forward-looking solution to these problems which would give not only hope . . . to German political life, but also respite to the Allies from their own wearisome internal differences.[59]

Up to this point discussion with France over Germany has been a series of battles about the details of the Occupation Statute, each modification requiring exceptions and reservations, making it ever more complicated. Schuman proposes instead that the government of Germany should be civilianised, and apart from general reserve powers, the three occupying nations should keep powers only in specific fields such as denazification, anti-cartel policy and foreign affairs. The rest should be left to the Germans.

Acheson, Bevin and Schuman discuss these questions in Washington before the signature of the North Atlantic Treaty: Acheson says of the discussions that what was interesting was not so much the content,

> but how, through all the complexity and confusion, we found a way to agreement. . . . The task was to fix the broad line along which we wanted to move . . . Disagreements could be dealt with last, and would then appear not as isolated points of principle, but as items in an otherwise acceptable and workable scheme. We did not begin with papers, which so often divert readers to trivia, but with dialogue.[60]

The Occupation Statute, under which the new government will take office, is agreed in April 1949 by Acheson, Schuman and Bevin. They write it on the premise that the German government will run the country. The three Allies will retain powers in foreign and defence policy, and the right to intervene if they have to. (In short, everything belongs to the Germans except sovereignty.)

While Bevin and Schuman are in Washington, Acheson tells them of the conversations about Berlin between Philip Jessup, US ambassador-at-large, and Yakov Malik, the Soviet deputy foreign minister. These started in February, and have continued until late April. Out of them comes an agreement that in return for the Soviets lifting the Berlin blockade, the Three will attend a Council of Foreign Ministers in Paris (and lift their ban on trade with East Germany). The meeting of the council, as foreseen, achieves nothing; but the blockade is lifted and stays lifted, in spite of the usual last-minute crisis – a strike by railway workers that produces a self-imposed blockade.*

* Bohlen, who noticed the change of line by Stalin, tells the story in his memoirs (pp. 283–7). Acheson, who managed the process, tells it from a different angle in his (pp. 267–70 and 293–301). The records of Jessup's talks with Malik (*Foreign Relations of the United States, 1949*, vol. 3, pp. 355–77) are an excellent example of diplomacy between countries that do not trust each other but want to reach an agreement.

While the Three – before Schuman – have been failing to agree on Allied voting rights in the Trizone, the Germans have written a new constitution for their country. Work began on 1 July 1948. The Allied commanders mandated the minister-presidents of the eleven *Länder* to assemble a Parliamentary Council. This has met in Bonn from September 1948, choosing Konrad Adenauer as its president. By the middle of May 1949, the *Länder* have agreed the Basic Law* of the future Federal Republic. If we ask how the Three finally merge their occupation zones, the answer is that the Germans do it. The new German government takes office on the day that the Berlin blockade is lifted.

The policy of dismantling is ended by the Three at a meeting in Paris on 11 November. They agree a final list of military production plants. In return, the new civilian commissioners will ask Adenauer (now chancellor) to agree to the German government joining the Ruhr Authority, and co-operating with the Military Security Board. Neither of these bodies ever comes into being. The Ruhr Authority is absorbed into the Schuman Plan. The Military Security Board disappears in the debate on German rearmament.

After this meeting Acheson makes his first visit to Bonn, and meets Adenauer. American-German relationships, both personal and political, will become one of the pillars of transatlantic relations through the Cold War.

The unfinished business is the Ruhr. The story of the Schuman Plan, Jean Monnet's proposal for collective management of coal and steel in Europe, is told in Chapter Six. For Bevin, the news is a shock. It is not the first time that one of the Western Three has taken the initiative without informing the others – that was Byrnes's regular practice – but he, Schuman and Acheson have worked together well. That Acheson knows about it and he himself doesn't, makes him suspicious – as he is by nature: why has he been kept in the dark? Coal, steel, Germany and Europe – are all sensitive in Britain too.

It is May 1950, and Bevin is seriously ill. He is not fully recovered

* The Basic Law was the constitution of the Federal Republic. It was given this name to indicate that it is provisional pending reunification.

from an operation. Acheson describes him as 'in distressing shape', Kenneth Younger (his deputy) as 'only half alive'. His meeting with Acheson is painful in both senses, and that is before he hears the news from Paris. Acheson finds him 'in a highly emotional state', and realises he 'had been stupid in not foreseeing both Bevin's rage at his apparent exclusion from the circle of consultation, and his old socialist's difficulty with the problem the Schuman Plan presented to a socialist government'.[61] He concludes it would have been better if Schuman had authorised him to try to persuade Bevin and Attlee to give the plan their support. As it was, 'anger was added to bad judgement to ensure the triumph of the latter'.

This is a bad start for the European project in London. Bevin, it is true, did not see Britain as 'just another European country', but he has a large vision. Attlee said of him that he had 'never met a man in politics with as much imagination . . . with the exception of Winston'. In 1927 Bevin spoke at the TUC in favour of a European economic union.[62] Post-war he has raised the possibility of a customs union with France, but has not pursued it as the experts were against – except for Hall-Patch, a favourite of his in the Foreign Office. Three days later, in a more conciliatory mood, Bevin says to Schuman and Acheson that 'he always considered that the divisions caused by national frontiers made it impossible for heavy industry to function economically, and he wished to give the French proposal not only a welcome, but a helping hand'.[63]

At this particular moment, given the government's commitment to nationalisation, the European Coal and Steel Community (ECSC) does not look like a likely runner in Britain. Herbert Morrison's comment* that 'the Durham miners will never wear it' may even be right (for all that he was Bevin's number-one political enemy). But it is a pity that Bevin and Monnet did not get to know each other. Both were practical and imaginative men. Bevin was not just an old socialist: Keynes respected his understanding of economics, and he knew industry as well as Monnet – though from a different viewpoint. If Britain had

* He was deputising for Atlee at the time.

approached Monnet's first great experiment in a more open frame of mind, its reaction to the invitation to the Messina Conference on Europe six years later might have been wiser.

These decisions set Germany, and Europe, on the right track. This is just as well: Europe is by no means the only strategic issue on Acheson's mind.

Nuclear and conventional arms

In September 1949 the Soviet Union detonates a nuclear device, a warning that the US monopoly is not going to last long. The question for the United States now is whether to work on thermonuclear weapons ('super', as it is called at the time). A three-man committee is set up to advise the president: the defence secretary, Louis Johnson, who supports the programme; David Lilienthal, the head of the Atomic Energy Commission, who is opposed; Acheson, who has not made up his mind, is chair. Acheson is a friend of Lilienthal; his relations with Johnson are so bad that there are periods when they do not speak to each other.

Acheson has already asked Kennan and his successor as director of policy planning, Paul Nitze, each to prepare him a report on the issue of thermonuclear weapons, guessing they will disagree.

They do. Nitze's two-page report arrives a few days later. It says that the weapon will serve no one's interests; but the United States cannot be inferior in a vital technology. Development work should therefore go ahead. Kennan's seventy-nine-page paper reaches Acheson some weeks later. By then Kennan is at Princeton and the question has already been settled. His paper is discursive and philosophical, but it develops concepts – no first use, minimum deterrence – that will be part of the nuclear debate for the next decades.[64]

Acheson wants to make a unanimous recommendation to the president. To bring Lilienthal on board he proposes they pursue development but not yet production, with the promise that, when the paper is presented to Truman, he will be able to explain his reservations orally. Johnson needs Acheson's support on thermonuclear weapons and therefore agrees (reluctantly) to a further recommendation, that the State and Defense Departments should 're-examine national objectives in war and peace' in the light of probable nuclear capabilities in the Soviet Union.

When they have agreed the report, the Three walk to the White House and give it to Truman. Lilienthal begins to explain his reservations but is cut short by the president, who asks: 'Can the Russians do it?' 'Yes,' says Lilienthal.* Truman says, in that case, he has no choice. The meeting lasts seven minutes.[65]

Truman also agrees that State and Defense should review strategic developments. This work becomes NSC 68. Its purpose is to make the case for a conventional arms build-up. It is a call to arms, written in lurid prose: its authors intended it for publication at some point. (In practice this takes place only after the document has become history.) While it is still policy, Acheson makes its argument in a series of speeches. The paper does not put a figure on the defence budget required; but what Nitze has in mind is quadrupling the budget from $13 billion to $50 billion.

Nitze is almost an anti-Kennan. Kennan lives in words: he is a linguist and a lover of literature; he writes all the time – papers, diaries, memoirs, poems, essays. Nitze likes things quantified; he is a banker, an analyst who made his name in the Strategic Bombing Survey. Kennan's focus is on Russian intentions – and he may underestimate the risks as a result. Nitze is interested in capabilities, quantifiable facts – an approach that leads to worst-case scenarios. (The figures in NSC 68 are large overestimates.) The contrast between the two is reflected in their prose styles: Nitze instructs the team drafting NSC 68 to write 'Hemingway sentences'. Kennan's prose is more like Gibbon. Nitze emphasises the military dimension – which Kennan resists all his life. But they are good friends, and agree that nuclear weapons are unusable. Nitze and Acheson take this thought a step further and conclude that a conventional build-up is needed.

* The reason they assume the Russians can do it is the discovery that Klaus Fuchs, a British/German theoretical physicist in the Manhattan Project, has been passing information to the Russians for seven years.

In fact, the United States has just reacted on a conventional level, and with success, to the Berlin blockade. This too has drawn attention to the weakness of US conventional forces. NSC 68 is not specific on the capabilities required; it says only that they will be costly.

Much bureaucratic manoeuvring goes into NSC 68. Nitze has the work classified top-secret to keep the Bureau of the Budget out; Acheson instructs that the paper should not put a figure to the programme; but it should be written (in spite of the classification) with the aim of winning public support for more defence spending. Having kept the Treasury away, Nitze works with the service chiefs and defence officials to encircle Johnson – who is as parsimonious as Truman – provoking a scene that leaves one general in tears and Acheson concluding that Johnson is mentally ill. Johnson ends by endorsing the paper.

Could a way have been found around Truman's aversion to defence spending? His response does not endorse the paper. He asks for more information, particularly on costs, and says that the Bureau of the Budget should be involved. The paper should remain classified. It looks as if it is heading for defeat.

The bureaucratic battle is interrupted by real-world battles – in Korea. The question of rearmament is settled, like many Cold War questions, not by theories but by facts. Stalin provides them.

The Korean War

Korea is a story of the futility of war, and also of its necessity.

At Potsdam Truman pressed Stalin to declare war on Japan, expecting a long war. The success of the Manhattan Project, and Truman's decision to use nuclear bombs on Japan, changed that. The Potsdam conference finished on 2 August 1945, and the first bomb destroyed Hiroshima four days later. Russia declared war on Japan that same day. On 9 August the United States dropped the second bomb on Nagasaki; Japan surrendered on 14 August.

With the Soviet declaration of war, the United States offered to share the occupation of Korea, a Japanese colony since 1910. Dean Rusk, then a naval officer, proposed dividing the peninsula at the 38th parallel: this put the capital, Seoul, in the US zone, with two ports, Inchon, west of Seoul, and Pusan in the far south. Soviet troops were already in Manchuria – and the United States was relieved when they agreed. No one regarded Korea as important.

The United States knows nothing of Korea, unlike Japan, where it has done business for decades and which it has studied seriously.* As an occupying power in Korea it makes some bad decisions. One is the choice of Syngman Rhee to lead the local administration. He is a Korean nationalist exiled for thirty-five years in the United States, the first Korean to be awarded a US PhD. Now he is 'America's man' in Korea. Once in power, he eliminates all opposition. When the United States gives in to Rhee and holds elections in May 1948, he is able to construct a coalition of the right. Had the elections been free and fair, the Communists, who had led the Resistance against the Japanese, would probably have won.

The Soviets' man is Kim Il-Sung. Before the war he was with the Chinese underground in Manchuria against the Japanese; in the Second World War he joined the Soviet army and was decorated. Kim secures support in the North through land reform. After the elections, Rhee declares South Korea a republic; Kim does the same for the DPRK. The North and South Korean constitutions both lay claim to the whole peninsula.

The United States withdraws most of its forces soon after the elections, in spite of continuing trouble on the border. This is part of a general demobilisation. The Soviets withdraw their forces too, but they have reason to believe the North can look after itself: thousands of North Koreans fought on the Communist side in the Chinese civil war.

Kim asks Stalin's agreement several times for his plan to unify the country by force. In 1950 Stalin agrees, but he insists that Kim consult China. Stalin's decision is probably a reaction to his defeat in the Berlin blockade, perhaps with a side interest in keeping China off-balance.†

* For example, the Department of Defense commissioned Ruth Benedict's classic study, *The Chrysanthemum and the Sword*.

† Odd Arne Westad's *The Cold War* contains a brilliantly succinct chapter on Korea.

North Korean forces attack the South on 25 June 1950.

We do not know how far Stalin considered the US reaction. Truman and Acheson see the North Korean attack as part of a global Soviet challenge. They convene the UN Security Council – which, at that point, the Soviet Union is boycotting in sympathy with the People's Republic of China – and instruct General MacArthur, supreme commander in Japan, to deploy forces to Korea. Washington rejects offers of troops from Nationalist China. (But MacArthur visits Taiwan and makes an unauthorised statement of support for the Nationalist Chiang Kai-shek.)[66]

The wider international community's reaction is reflected in UN decisions. On the day of the invasion, the Security Council calls for the withdrawal of North Korean forces; later it calls on members of the UN to assist in repelling the aggressors. Bevin's last important decision as foreign secretary is to recommend that Britain contribute troops in Korea.

US combat troops arrive in Korea in small numbers from 1 July 1950. At the beginning of September they are overrun by DPRK forces with Soviet tanks. They and other Allied forces are driven down the peninsula and end penned up in a pocket around Pusan at the extreme south, while Northern forces control the rest of South Korea.

In this difficult situation, MacArthur proposes landing a force at Inchon. The port is close to Seoul and to the 38th parallel. But it is 190 miles from the main force at Pusan. Inchon is also highly unsuitable for a landing, with mudflats, high sea walls and difficult tides. The joint chiefs oppose; the army commander in Pusan does not want the Marines withdrawn from his hard-pressed defence; the navy thinks the landings are impossible. MacArthur turns their arguments around: 'the impracticalities involved will tend to ensure for me the element of surprise'. He finishes theatrically: 'I can almost hear the ticking of the second hand of destiny.'[67] Overpowered by his confidence and charisma, the navy and the chiefs agree.

On 5 September 1950, with the North Korean forces still threatening Pusan, 260 ships, many old and rusting and smelling of fish, sail from Yokohama. They arrive at Inchon ten days later. A typhoon blowing at

125mph adds to the element of surprise. The Marines take the beaches, scale the walls and seize the port. In four days they are in the outskirts of Seoul, which falls soon after. North Korean forces around Pusan, finding their supply lines cut and the enemy in their rear, collapse. The US army breaks out of the Pusan pocket.

Instructions to MacArthur envisage his forces pursuing the North Koreans across the 38th parallel into the North, but he must clear his plans with Washington if there are indications or warnings of Soviet or Chinese forces. In fact, a warning comes to Acheson via the Indian ambassador in Beijing on 5 October: if US troops cross the 38th parallel the Chinese will intervene. The Indian ambassador has cried wolf before, and the message is dismissed. But this message is from the premier, Zhou Enlai, who has called the ambassador in to deliver it. Acheson describes it as 'a warning . . . but not an authoritative statement of policy'. The first part of this is right; the second is questionable.[68]

At this moment, the United States and others are carried along on a torrent of enthusiasm. Everyone is in favour of taking over the whole of Korea. A UN resolution calls for a united, independent and democratic Korea – though the text is more nuanced than the title. Only Kennan and Nitze argue for stopping at the 38th parallel. And they are forecasting the wrong storm: a Soviet, not a Chinese, intervention.

Truman meets MacArthur for the first and only time on Wake Island, in the middle of the Pacific, on 15 October. MacArthur is dismissive of the Chinese. In fact, they have already crossed into Korea in large numbers. In early November they make reconnaissance attacks on Korean and American units. In late November they attack in force, routing the 8th Army, which retreats in disorder. Seoul is overrun for the third time. The Marines retreat too, but in better order, taking their equipment and their dead with them.

This is a failure for the Truman administration. The failure has three parts: a military failure, a diplomatic failure and a potential constitutional crisis. This chapter looks at the second and the third.*

* For the first see Max Hastings, *The Korean War*, or David Halberstam, *The Coldest Winter*. Eliot A. Cohen and John Gooch, *Military Misfortunes*, has an excellent concise analysis.

The diplomatic failure is a consequence of ignorance of China: a misreading of its intentions and an underestimate of its capacities. There is a mirror image of these failures on the Chinese side. Both pay a heavy price.

The problem is the absence of any relationship between the United States and China. No one in the government has direct contact with, or direct knowledge of, China. This is not all the fault of the United States: the Chinese Communist Party regards the United States as a capitalist, imperialist power and wants nothing to do with it. The United States has lived up to this by supporting Chiang Kai-shek. A sober analysis in the United States might have concluded that, unpleasant as the Communists are, their victory over the Nationalists – who were well funded by the United States – suggests real strength, even legitimacy. Marshall's mission to reconcile the two sides was doomed. It would have served US interests to retain a channel of communication with the Beijing government. This, however, was difficult while the United States did not recognise it.

The root of the problem is in Congress, where Acheson and the State Department are under attack from Republicans for 'having lost' China. This is absurd. China never belonged to the United States; if anyone lost China, it was Chiang Kai-shek.

Had they received Zhou Enlai's warning direct, the United States would have been better able to evaluate it. US diplomats or military on the spot would also have advised that the Korean peninsula, through which Japan has twice attacked China, was of strategic importance to China.

With US forces in full retreat MacArthur demands reinforcements – which do not exist. The alternative, he says, is to withdraw to more defensible positions, if not from Korea altogether. He proposes instead an offensive against China, a blockade of its ports, air and artillery attacks on its industry.* But while MacArthur is making these arguments, General Ridgway turns the military crisis around. He takes over when

* These proposals treat China as if it were Japan or Germany. It has little industry and its army fights on foot.

the army commander in Korea is killed in a road accident. He purges ineffective officers and changes tactics to deal with the Chinese style of warfare, and drives them back. When US/UN forces approach the 38th parallel, Acheson and Marshall* advise Truman that Ridgway slow the advance.

Then the constitutional crisis: MacArthur, who has always believed that the decisive confrontation with Communism would take place in Asia, makes a public statement threatening to take the war to China. Washington sends a mild rebuke. Then he writes to Joseph Martin, Republican leader of the House, criticising the conduct of the war and saying that Chiang Kai-shek should be allowed to attack China. 'There is no substitute for victory.' Martin releases the letter to the press. After consulting the joint chiefs, Truman relieves MacArthur of his command.

MacArthur is a hero, first from the Pacific War and now through the Inchon landings. He returns to Washington in a blaze of publicity, addresses a joint session of Congress, denouncing the appeasement of Communism in Asia; 'The voice of God,' says one Republican. Millions watch him on TV, in schools and in bars. Half a million turn out to see him at a parade through New York.

When the tumult is over, Senate hearings investigate MacArthur's proposals more soberly. MacArthur does not impress: asked what would happen if the Soviet Union joined a war against China, he replies that this is not his responsibility. The joint chiefs all reject his proposals. When the committee asks Marshall how he thinks of Korea – a police action, a large or a small war? – he replies that it is a limited war and he hopes it stays that way.

The longest testimony is Acheson's, eight days, meticulously prepared. One Republican complains that his knowledge of the subject gives him an unfair advantage. By the end, in late June 1951, everyone has lost interest in MacArthur.

Armistice talks begin in July 1951. The question of prisoners of war is a problem: many Communist prisoners do not want to be repatriated.

* Truman fired Johnson and brought Marshall out of retirement to be defense secretary.

Syngman Rhee, who gives the United States much trouble, solves this by instructing guards to open the prison gates. Agreement on the armistice comes only with the death of Stalin. Half of the US casualties occur during the negotiations.*

There are only losers. North and South Korea end the war in ruins. The dead are counted in millions, orphans in hundreds of thousands. China has fought the world's leading power to a standstill; but at a huge cost. One-third of its budget is spent on the war, plus large 'voluntary' contributions from citizens, plus several hundred thousand casualties; this while it is still recovering from its own civil war.

In the United States, as well as the cost in lives and dollars, Korea reinforces the irrationality gripping Congress – though the 'loss' of China remains the main theme. US policy, that the government in Taipei is 'the authentic representative of the Chinese people', remains frozen for two more decades.

The Korean war costs the Soviet Union little directly. But it sows the seeds of its quarrel with China. More visible at the time is the economic boom it creates in Europe and Japan, completing the work of the Marshall Plan. And in spite of everything, the war strengthens confidence in the United States as a reliable partner. It brings increases in defence spending throughout NATO, and opens the door to German rearmament. In the United States the programme of conventional rearmament that NSC 68 called for becomes a reality.

Truman

Behind the achievements recorded in these pages stands Truman. His presidency finishes on a downbeat note: stalemated in Korea, harried at home by Joseph McCarthy and the 'primitives' – as Acheson called them – and low in the opinion polls, he decides not to run again, for what would have been in practice a third term. This is a sensible

* Korea has similarities with Vietnam: the lesson the United States drew for the Vietnam negotiations was to give prisoners of war priority.

choice. Since then, Truman's reputation has only grown.

Truman was the directing spirit of the post-war settlement in the West. When he arrived back at the Union Station in Washington on a bleak November evening, following the mid-term elections in which the Democrats lost their majority in Congress, only Acheson was there to greet Truman. But now he was his own man. Liberated from the Roosevelt legacy, his State of the Union speech in 1947 did not mention Roosevelt, but did mention civil rights, as Roosevelt never would have done. And with Marshall replacing Byrnes, he set a new course for the United States.

The Truman Doctrine – the United States' readiness to support countries threatened by Communism – announced America as a world power. The Marshall Plan enabled European recovery and marginalised Communist Parties across Western Europe. In his book *The Presidents*, Stephen Graubart labels Truman 'the Creator', echoing the title of Acheson's memoir, *Present at the Creation*. The 'creation' is the Western liberal world order, which for all its faults and mistakes is still the centrepiece of today's world, unique in history, and resting on American power. For this, Truman created world-class institutions at home to manage global power abroad: the Department of Defense, making military planning a collective task, as it had been during the Second World War; the National Security Council, bringing together all the dimensions of security.

Truman set the direction, chose first-class people to execute his policies, listened to their advice and let them get on with it. If he made a mistake – Byrnes at State or Louis Johnson at Defense – he corrected it. He respected the office of president, and expected others to do the same. Grandees from the Roosevelt era, who thought they could push the unknown senator from Missouri around, were mistaken. Henry Morgenthau, Roosevelt's Treasury secretary, threatened to resign if Truman did not include him in the party for Potsdam. Truman accepted his resignation on the spot. Later, Harold Ickes, interior secretary under Roosevelt, made the same threat and got the same result.

While Truman reorganised government at home, Marshall and Acheson created the modern State Department. When Acheson arrived as assistant secretary for economic affairs in 1941 it was the same department whose aimlessness drove Kennan to distraction. The secretary of state, Cordell Hull in 1941, nominally the senior Cabinet officer, was one of its least influential members. As Acheson said, 'The old State Department' was 'closer to its nineteenth-century predecessors in both what it did and how the work was done than to the department I was later to command. Between the two, a great world change and General Marshall intervened.'[69]

So did Dean Acheson. Marshall's stature and Acheson's organisation made the State Department a fitting instrument for American power. It is America's voice abroad. It clarifies America's actions; it warns; it reassures America's allies that they are listened to, making American power acceptable to weaker partners.

How should the weaker partners behave? In late 1945 Bevin felt Britain's weakness acutely. He interrupted himself speaking in the House of Commons to say: 'I'm sorry to be so long. I cannot help it. All the world is in trouble, and I have to deal with all the troubles at once.'[70] This was after the failed London conference. In time, and especially with Marshall and Acheson, he perfected, as Douglas Hurd has written, 'the practice of acting as a junior partner to the USA . . . Bevin did what all good allies do best – he argued.' But more than that: he had ideas, and he was trusted. Navy Secretary Forrestal recorded in his diary (6 February 1946): 'Byrnes gave it as his opinion that we could not be in the position of doubting the good faith of Britain . . . as long as Mr Bevin was at the Foreign Office.'[71] He was a partner for the United States when no other was available.

Truman renewed democracy in America, not because of the Cold War, but because it was the right thing to do. His State of the Union address in 1948 called for a programme to improve civil rights, federal laws against lynching and federal protection of the right to vote. When he won the nomination later in the year – not a foregone conclusion – he called a special session of Congress and proposed legislation on housing, health and education as well as civil rights; he issued an executive order ending segregation in the armed forces.

Truman's civil-rights policy ensured that he faced a Southern

Democrat candidate in the presidential election, while his foreign policy brought Henry Wallace as a left-wing 'peace' candidate. Three Democrats on the ballot paper, plus his low poll ratings at the time made his re-election all the more improbable. But he won; his second term left America more equal and more democratic as well as stronger and more secure.

Truman's proudest boast was that America defeated its enemies and turned them into friends. That is the true meaning of victory.*

* In the conclusion of *Leviathan* Thomas Hobbes writes: 'He that is taken and put into prison or chains is not conquered, though overcome; for he is still an enemy.'

7

Jean Monnet: the Practical Imagination

The problem for France is this: five years after the war, policy on Germany is still not settled. The early post-war years have been lost trying to agree with the Russians – whose policy is that Germany should be left to rot, creating the conditions for a Communist takeover. Britain and America are now feeling their way towards reducing Allied controls and allowing Germany to govern itself. The French are joining in this, but with delays and conditions at every step. In 1949, West Germany has agreed its Basic Law and elected Konrad Adenauer Chancellor. Germany is to remain demilitarised. The Ruhr is to stay under international control – one of the French conditions – with a ceiling on German steel production.

The German position is straightforward. Adenauer wants Germany to escape from its past, to be treated as an equal, to make its own decisions. He is some way from this. The economy will not revive until the Ruhr is functioning properly. But that is not under his control. Germany is not sovereign, and is regarded with suspicion on all sides. He has no scope to take the initiative.

The first important foreign visitor Adenauer receives as chancellor is Dean Acheson, late in 1949. Adenauer tells him: 'Germans take the colour of the wall,' meaning that they change according to their environment. Adenauer wants Germany to be part of Western Europe, where 'their more liberal traditions will find strength through companionship'. It is not good for people to be isolated, he says: it accentuates their least desirable characteristics. He has reason to know. Acheson comes away convinced that Adenauer and Germany deserve American support.[1]

The American version of the problem is this: America needs Europe back on its feet economically if it is to resist Soviet ambitions; Europe has to include Germany, or as much of it as can be rescued from the Soviets. In Washington almost everyone wants to see some sort of united, federal Europe, to end its wars and to make a more solid bulwark against the Soviet Union. The United States can provide money and security – the one through the Marshall Plan and the other through NATO – but the changes implied in words like 'united' and 'federal' are political. The United States would be happy if Britain took the lead, but the line in London is that Britain's interests go beyond Europe; with the empire/commonwealth it represents a separate power centre, admittedly in temporary financial difficulty. Acheson has written to Robert Schuman, France's foreign minister, in October 1949 urging French leadership in integrating Germany into Europe.[2]

But France has no real policy on Germany. This is understandable but disturbing. It is disturbing because Germany is France's neighbour, and it has been the central issue in French foreign policy for three-quarters of a century. The first post-war instinct in Paris looks to the past: to break Germany up, returning to the world of small German states, before Napoleon or Bismarck. When this gets no support, France has fought to keep Allied controls and to continue dismantling German industry. This too is unwelcome in Washington, which finds itself supporting the European economy; it wants to restart trade, not to create new barriers. Bit by bit French policy has had to give way. The United States is the guarantor of European and French security, and it has the last word. Everything France has tried so far has failed.

The French dilemma centres on the Ruhr, the powerhouse of German industry, including the armaments industry. It is still under international control. This regime – with the Saarland, economically annexed by France – is all that remains of the French policy of dismembering Germany. These policies repeat those that followed the First World War, when the Rhineland was demilitarised and the Saar was administered, for a period, by France. They failed then and are likely to fail again now.

It is spring 1950. The Germans want to increase their steel quota from ten to fourteen million tons, well above French output. The weakness of its steel industry is a symbol of French weakness overall. Steel is the material of war. But German prosperity is also the key to French recovery – and this will come only when the Ruhr, on France's borders, is working full-time.

These dilemmas are most acute for Robert Schuman, a loyal Frenchman. He was a member of the Resistance, was captured and escaped; but he was born in the Lorraine when it was part of Germany. He was educated at a German university, and conscripted into the German army in the First World War (for medical reasons he did a desk job). He is using his position as foreign minister to do things he could never have done as prime minister: especially, to make Allied co-operation on Germany work better. But now he does not know what to do. Whatever he says causes a storm either in the National Assembly or in the Bundestag. In Bonn he finds that the Ruhr, the Saar and rearmament poison every discussion.

Adenauer and Schuman have much in common: they are both committed Catholics; they are both from the borderlands. Adenauer sympathises with Schuman. But policy keeps them apart.

Everyone is talking of a federal Europe. This is the Europe the Resistance fought for. Churchill has called for a United States of Europe in Zurich; newspaper articles are written and resolutions are passed. Some talk of 'internationalising' coal and steel; Adenauer has said that he will accept an international authority for the Ruhr, but only if it includes parts of France, Belgium and Luxembourg as well. However, Germany is not yet fully sovereign, and he may not have much choice. After he becomes chancellor Adenauer gives an interview to an American journalist, Kingsbury Smith, suggesting a complete fusion of France and Germany.

Schuman is a modest man without personal ambition. He wants to serve his country and the cause of peace. He has told the Assembly that he is foreign minister not because he wants the job, but because someone from the eastern frontier is needed to achieve peaceful co-existence with Germany. But he does not know how to do it.

The problem is now personal, because the previous autumn Schuman promised Acheson and Bevin that he would bring ideas on Germany with him when the three of them meet in London on 11 May 1950. The recollection of his chief of staff, Bernard Clappier, is that when Acheson made the suggestion,

> Bevin gave a grunt which could have signified that he was unprepared or none too pleased, but which Acheson chose to interpret as assent. As for Robert Schuman, the bald top of his head went red, as always when he was embarrassed. . . . Back in Paris hardly a week passed without Schuman pressing me: 'What about Germany? What do I have to do to meet the responsibility put upon me?' It became an obsession with him.[3]

Jean Monnet, head of the French Commissariat du Plan, is responsible for the modernisation of French industry. He is far from being a conventional public official: he has worked for the French government in the First World War, then for the League of Nations, for the British government in the Second World War, and unofficially for the US government; these in addition to the family cognac business and banking. He too believes in peace, and in co-operation across national borders. But he is sceptical of the rhetoric of the statesmen about co-operation. Experience shows that when you get down to business, each state insists on a veto. Everyone talks of union; but no one knows what that means.

Monnet has noted that in the interview with Kingsbury Smith Adenauer said that 'if the French and the Germans sat down around the same table, in the same building, to work together and assume joint responsibility, a great step forward could be taken . . . France's desire for security would be satisfied, and the revival of German nationalism would be prevented'. Monnet sympathises and agrees. But 'experience had taught me that one cannot act in general terms'.[4] Adenauer's answers are largely about the Ruhr. He talks about a global union; but it is really about coal and steel.

De Gaulle has said of Adenauer's interview that 'if one were not constrained to look at matters coolly', the prospect of combining French and German strength would be dazzling, 'giving a modern economic, social, strategic and cultural shape to the work of the Emperor Charlemagne'. This is irony. In the real world, which is a world of power and conflict, one has no choice but to look at matters coolly. For Monnet this comment falls 'like the chorus in some Greek tragedy', an ironic warning, unheard by the protagonists, leaving them to their fate.[5]

Monnet has more practical experience of international co-operation than Schuman, Adenauer or de Gaulle. He also is in charge of France's national plan, where coal and steel are major themes. He knows that Schuman needs help. It is March, and the May deadline is approaching. What does he do? He goes for a walk.

Monnet's habit is to rise early in the morning and take a long walk in the countryside. He returns with a clear head and a sense of how to tackle the problems of the day. But the problem he faces now is not one for a morning walk. He goes to the Alps, and walks alone or with a guide for two weeks, from refuge to refuge, writing down his thoughts in the evening. He returns to Paris at the beginning of April, refreshed and more convinced than ever of the dangers of war. This time Germany will be not the protagonist but the prize. In a paper circulated in the French government he writes:

> Whichever way we turn in the present situation, we see nothing but deadlock – whether it be the increasing acceptance of a war that is thought to be inevitable, the problem of Germany, the continuation of France's recovery, the organisation of Europe or the place of France in Europe.
>
> Words are not enough. Only immediate action on an essential point can change the present static situation.
>
> We must not seek to solve the German problem in its present context. We must change the context by transforming the basic facts.
>
> War is in men's minds, and it must be opposed by imagination.

But still he does not have the answer:

> The situation was tangled. What we had to do was to find a thread to pull so as to unravel some of the knots . . . But where was the thread to be found? In the confused state of Franco-German relations, the neurosis of the vanquished seemed to be shifting to the victor: France was beginning to feel inferior again as she realised that attempts to limit Germany's dynamism were bound to fail.[6]

If the French could lose their fear of German industrial domination, if they would recognise that attempts to keep Germany in check were bound to fail, and think not of domination but of relations based on equality, 'if victors and vanquished could agree to exercise their joint sovereignty over part of their joint resources – then a solid link would be forged'.[7] Monnet knows that French policy is doomed; in a message to Schuman he notes the German demand for an increase in their steel quota: 'We will refuse, but the Americans will insist. In the end we will state our reservations, but we will give in.'

He gropes towards the answer. He needs an international lawyer. By chance he hears that Paul Reuter, a law professor (who he has never met before), is in the building on other business. Monnet pulls him into his office and explains his half-formed ideas. Reuter, like Schuman, is from the Franco-German border; he reacts 'with such intelligence and enthusiasm'[8] that Monnet invites him and Étienne Hirsch, one of his colleagues at the Commissariat du Plan, to his home for the weekend. There they produce the first draft of what is now known as the Schuman Declaration.

Eight further drafts follow as Monnet tests the ideas on different colleagues with different expertise; in this process they take concrete shape. Monnet insists from the start on a joint executive, able to make decisions and not subject to vetoes. But he eliminates the word 'supranational', which he dislikes. The important thing, in his view, is to define the tasks the executive is given and the interests it will serve. Pierre Uri, a brilliant young economist, brings these into closer focus with the idea of a common market, a space without barriers and without national discrimination; Étienne Hirsch helps define the powers of the High Authority and the question of fair competition.

The draft includes the words, 'The French government proposes'. In Monnet's mind this is a document for Schuman, though Schuman himself is not yet aware of it. But Monnet has talked to Clappier and knows of Schuman's preoccupation with Germany and the deadline of 11 May.

Hearing nothing more from Clappier, Monnet sends a copy of his draft to the office of the prime minister, Georges Bidault – who has switched jobs with Schuman. A few moments later, Clappier gets in touch to ask if he has made progress, and Monnet shows him the draft (number seven). 'It's excellent,' says Clappier, and hurries to the Gare de l'Est, where he catches Schuman, in the train waiting to go to his home near Metz for the weekend. 'There is a political element', says Clappier, 'and a technical element.' The political part is Schuman's responsibility. Schuman asks if there are technical problems. 'Absolutely not,' says Clappier.[9]

This is an instance of bureaucratic heroism. Had Clappier known, he might have said that Monnet and his team had consulted neither the coal nor the steel industry, nor those in the government who knew them – fearing that they would produce a mass of technical problems to confound the political purpose of the initiative.

When Schuman returns from Metz on Sunday evening, Clappier meets him at the station. Schuman says: 'I've read the proposal. I'll use it.'

At this point the circle widens. Schuman refers to the ideas in the paper when the Council of Ministers meets on 3 May. But he does this at the end of the meeting as the ministers are leaving and in a low voice; only Prime Minister Bidault picks it up. He has put forward a different vision, an 'Atlantic High Command', to strengthen transatlantic economic relation. He hears enough of Schuman's ideas to understand that they come from Monnet. He calls him in to ask why he has not been consulted. Monnet points to the letter he sent Bidault the previous Friday. It is lying on the desk. This takes the wind out of Bidault's sails. He does not object.

The following Sunday Dean Acheson arrives in Paris to meet Schuman in advance of the London meeting with Bevin. Acheson needs a break from the hothouse atmosphere of Washington.

Schuman meets Acheson at a reception at the American ambassador's residence. He sketches out the ideas he is planning to put forward. He insists on secrecy, since he does not yet have Cabinet consent, but suggests that Acheson discuss further with Monnet and John McCloy, the American high commissioner in Germany. They meet the following day. Acheson has only half understood Schuman's explanation the day before, delivered hesitantly and through an interpreter. As he talks to Monnet and McCloy, both old friends, Acheson comes to understand that 'Monnet's apparently . . . limited and modest plan was in reality . . . imaginative and far reaching . . . Only by the patient coaching of Monnet and McCloy, and by their answers to our questions, did this come home to us.'[10]

Concerned that the US government may react in the wrong way to half-digested rumours, Acheson sends Truman a personal message, warning that an important proposal is coming from the French government, and asking that comment should be withheld until he can explain.

With Schuman and Monnet, Acheson should be remembered as one of the founders of the European Union (EU). In 1950 nothing is possible without American support; from this moment on the United States plays an indispensable role in bringing Monnet's idea to fruition.

Two steps remain. First, on 9 May, while the French Council of Ministers is in session, a personal friend of Schuman delivers two letters – one formal, one personal – from Schuman to Adenauer, explaining what he is about to propose to the French government. Adenauer interrupts his own Cabinet meeting to look at them. He sends an immediate and positive response.

When word comes of Adenauer's agreement, Schuman puts a formal proposal to the Council of Ministers. According to Monnet he is 'even more elliptical and less audible than usual', but this time political allies are ready to speak in support – Monnet has spoken to his friends – and he gets a green light to present this as a proposal from the French government and to do the same at the London meeting.[11]

The afternoon is taken up with briefing European ambassadors. At 6 p.m. a press conference is called. In the *Salon de l'Horloge* of the Quai d'Orsay Schuman reads out, in his flat, hesitant way:

> World peace cannot be safeguarded without creative efforts proportionate to the dangers which threaten it. . . .
>
> Europe will not be made at a stroke, nor according to a fixed plan. It will be built through concrete achievements . . . Bringing together the nations of Europe requires that the age-old opposition between France and Germany be brought to an end.
>
> With this aim, the French government proposes to take action at one limited, but decisive point.
>
> It proposes to put Franco-German coal and steel production, in its entirety, under the authority of a common High Authority, in the framework of an organisation open to the participation of other European countries.
>
> The pooling of coal and steel production will establish directly common foundations for economic development, a first step towards a Federation of Europe . . .
>
> . . . will make clear that war between France and Germany becomes not only unthinkable, but materially impossible . . .
>
> . . . establishing a new High Authority, whose decisions will bind France, Germany and other countries who join . . .
>
> The French government is ready to open negotiations on the following basis:
>
> The tasks of the common High Authority will be . . . the modernisation of production, . . . the supply of coal and steel on identical terms to the French and German markets and those of other member countries, the development of common exports to other countries, the equalisation and improvement of living conditions of the workers in these industries. . . .
>
> The movement of coal and steel in member countries will be freed immediately from all customs duties . . .

Five years after the war, every word is a bombshell.

As soon as he finishes reading, Schuman leaves for the station to catch his train for London, evading questions from the press, not least since he has no idea how to answer them. But one reporter says to him on the way out: 'So it's a leap in the dark?' 'That's right,' says Schuman, 'a leap in the dark.'

For Monnet this is a climax that has been in preparation through his life. Marking the occasion, he has brought with him not just those who have worked on the different drafts, Étienne Hirsch and Pierre Uri, but also his wife, Silvia.

Schuman has seen Monnet's draft for the first time eleven days earlier. He has secured agreement from Adenauer that morning, and then from his own government – but with no discussion – for a policy which will change Europe. He is speaking the truth when he says it is a leap in the dark. Schuman, who makes the leap, deserves our admiration; so does Monnet, whose practical imagination gave birth to the policy.

The family business and the First World War

Jean Monnet is born on 9 November 1888 in Cognac in the south-west of France, the son of a small cognac producer. The family is respected and bourgeois, but only a generation or two from the soil – his grandfather cultivated a small vineyard. Monnet himself seems to many of his friends to have something of a French peasant in him, with his superstitions, his interest in the weather and the soil, his down-to-earth approach, his stubbornness. Stubborn, people would say, like a peasant trying to sell a cow.

The young Monnet does not like school: 'From very early, my instincts told me that thought cannot be divorced from action . . . I could use my brains and my energy right away: why take the roundabout route of studying?' He leaves school at sixteen and joins the family business. This means going to London, to live and work with a wine merchant in the City, to learn the business and to learn English, the language of the clients of Monnet and Co.

From the age of eighteen he travels on behalf of Monnet and Co. to North America and to Sweden, Russia, Greece and Egypt. 'Don't take books,' his father tells him, 'no one can do your thinking for you. Look out of the window. Talk to people.' He does business, meets people, makes friends – including with the Hudson Bay Company. At the age of eighteen he is negotiating large contracts. He learns patience and persistence and the different ways of doing business. In the Rockies he acquires his love of long country walks.

He is twenty-five and on his way back to Cognac when, changing trains at Poitiers, he hears the news that France is mobilising for war. When he arrives home his brother is leaving to join his regiment. Monnet has a kidney complaint and is unfit for military service. He does not share the excitement of his countrymen. His travels have given him some idea of the vastness of the resources that can be poured into a life-and-death struggle. He guesses that the war will be long, and fought by industries as well as by armies. He is impressed by the industrial strength of Germany and by the vast resources of the British Empire. He concludes that co-operation in supply and shipping among the Allies, especially Britain and France, will be one of the keys to victory. Obsessed by this thought, he talks to everyone he can about it, with such conviction that a well-connected family friend introduces him to the prime minister, René Viviani.

The prime minister hears Monnet's argument for 'joint bodies to estimate the combined resources of the Allies, to share them out and to share the costs'. He does not dismiss it, but he is sceptical of joint decisions – 'we are talking about two governments and two sovereign parliaments'.[12] Still, he is impressed by Monnet's energy and his knowledge of the British. He has him sent to London in the Service of Civil Supply.

In London Monnet is struck by the anarchy of the economic war effort. Little has changed from peacetime: free trade on the British side, government control on the French. He looks for an opportunity to prove, in a practical way, that the private sector on its own is not adequate for the requirements of wartime, and that an organisation based on separate national interests does not meet the needs of an alliance.

The opportunity is some time coming. But eventually a joint committee is set up bringing together the French and Italian government purchasing authorities with a British private company, to buy wheat collectively for the armed forces of the three Allies. Even so the French government is still buying separately for civilians in competition with its allies. (Monnet himself negotiates some of the contracts with the Hudson Bay Company.) Monnet complains and comes to the notice of the French minister for commerce, Étienne Clémentel. He persuades Clémentel to negotiate the creation of an inter-Allied 'Wheat Executive'. This body comprises one member from each of the Allies; they are instructed to work as much as possible like a commercial firm, and to meet all Allied needs for grain, within the budget available. It is stated, rather obliquely, that, 'the absence of a unanimous decision should not prevent the Executive from acting'.[13]

This is something new: not a committee with national vetoes, but an executive with a common task, instructed to keep in mind the advantage of centralising purchases of wheat on behalf of the Allies. Reading between the lines, their instructions are to put the common interest above national interest. Seeing each other every day, the three men who make up the Wheat Executive find ways of acting fairly for each and efficiently for all, producing better results than could ever have been achieved separately. The war is two years old, and shortages have to become acute before such an experiment can be launched. Bit by bit the system is extended to other commodities.

Another year passes. Submarine warfare creates a crisis in shipping. Monnet returns to the concept he put to Viviani three years before, of Allied co-operation on shipping. Negotiations last until November 1917, when Clémentel threatens to walk out: 'We have sacrificed everything . . . All we are asking is to be treated as equals with our allies.' Arthur Balfour, the British foreign secretary, overrules the president of the Board of Trade, and an agreement is reached that the provision of shipping shall be a common charge among the European Allies. Clémentel instructs Monnet to work out the details with his friend Arthur Salter in the Ministry of Transport.[14] Action was beginning, Monnet concludes, at a specific but a decisive point, and it would not stop there. The initiative is confined initially to the shipment of food; it works and is extended to other cargoes.

Monnet has done the planning for this weeks earlier with Salter and with John Anderson, the minister in charge of shipping. But it is March 1918 before the full Allied Maritime Transport Executive (AMTE) comes into being.* Salter becomes the secretary general of the Executive; Monnet is the French representative.

By now shipping is a key resource. It is in ever shorter supply, not least because American armies are now on their way to France. Choices have to be made. Do you use available capacity for men, equipment or food? Should the needs of civilians or the military come first? Which of the Allies will get priority? These questions take concrete form as choices about shipping. The United States becomes a full member of the shipping pool only in September 1918; but it does so because the system works. Like the Wheat Executive, each of the representatives understands their national priorities but also the collective needs of the alliance. In his biography of Dwight Morrow, an adviser to the Allied Maritime Transport Council – the political body above the AMTE – Harold Nicolson describes the AMTE as 'the most advanced experiment yet made in international cooperation'.[15]

The Executive, and Monnet's position on it, have meanwhile become too powerful, and he attracts the attention of the French minister of armaments, who complains that 'This young man should be in the army.'[16] Monnet is summoned by the prime minister, Georges Clemenceau, to explain what he is doing. Clemenceau asks a few questions and sends him away. The minister is an old associate of Clemenceau, and Monnet expects him to get his way. A week later he is summoned again by Clemenceau, who gives him a copy of a decree signed by the Cabinet and stating that 'Lieutenant Monnet is to return at once to his post in London.' Clémentel delays his transfer to the front until mid November. Monnet is readying himself to go when the armistice settles the question. By this time shipping resources have

* It is roughly at this time that Britain and France agree to give Foch 'strategic direction of military operations' – not the same thing as supreme command – after almost four years fighting together as an alliance.

been found to transport 1.65 million American servicemen as well as food and equipment. There is no way to quantify Monnet's contribution; but the British government thinks enough of it to give him an honorary knighthood; this does not happen to many thirty-year-old civil servants.

With peace, the Shipping Executive is absorbed into the Supreme Economic Council chaired by Herbert Hoover. But as America hurries to return to free markets, the instruments of Allied co-operation are dismantled and the Economic Council closes down after a few months.

Monnet has hoped that the experience of sharing shortages among the Allies during the war might be translated into a system to handle the chaos of post-war peace, and that former enemies might be included. Instead, all hopes are poured into the League of Nations. The weaknesses of the League are already clear – guarantees without the means to enforce them, and a respect for sovereignty that translates as vetoes for all who want to use them. But there is also to be an international secretariat, the first such body ever set up. The only government officials who have experience of working together internationally at this moment are those who have been running joint executives on behalf of the Allies, Monnet, Salter and their Italian colleague, Bernardo Attolico. They are among the early appointments to the Secretariat of the League.

The League of Nations Secretariat

As assistant, and later deputy secretary general to the League, Monnet deals with two critical post-war problems: Upper Silesia and Austria.

Upper Silesia is disputed territory following the application of the Versailles principle of national self-determination. It is an industrial area, like the Ruhr, with coal and metal ores, and a mixed population of Germans and Poles – the latter have been treated as second-class citizens under the German Empire. The border is to be settled by a plebiscite; but both sides bring in paramilitary units (*Freikorps* on the

German side), and fighting breaks out. Allied forces are needed to restore order. The plebiscite takes place in March 1921 in difficult conditions, with both sides offering inducements, and the Germans transporting Silesian miners back from the Ruhr to vote. The Inter-Allied Commission, which has organised the plebiscite, is unable to agree on the border; the British are advocating a line more generous to Germany, the French want a larger territory for Poland. At this point, in August 1921, the problem is handed over – with some scepticism – to the Council of League, which sets up a commission under a Japanese chair.

The commission's report is drafted by Monnet's team. It proposes to divide the population almost equally, but gives Germany the larger share of the territory in line with the results of the plebiscite. However, some 80 per cent of the German-owned heavy industry will be in Poland. To cope with this the commission proposes institutions to resolve disputes, with equal representation from Poland and Germany, and a representative of the League in the chair. On this basis a Polish-German Convention is signed in May 1922. With more than 600 articles, it is longer than the Versailles Treaty. But it is agreed by both sides and ratified – with the Reichstag draped in black for the occasion. And the two sides accept the authority of the institutions. The interests of both German owners and Polish workers are safeguarded. The arrangement lasts until German armies enter Poland in 1939.

In the summer of 1922 people are starving in the streets of Vienna. Austria, the biggest loser in 1919, has lost 80 per cent of its territory and is at risk of being partitioned further. In August the government declares that it is without resources; and the Allied powers refuse to guarantee its borrowings. Earlier in the year Monnet has already discussed with Salter, head of the League's financial section, the possibility of appointing an impartial financial controller to preserve Austria from predatory neighbours or banks. To this he now adds a 'protocol of abstention' in which neighbours and great powers agree to respect Austria's independence. Until then each has been keeping their options open in case one of the others should decide to intervene. This provides a breathing space for a recovery plan, worked out with the banks by Salter and his staff and supervised by an independent financial controller – Monnet persuades the mayor of Rotterdam to take this on. The political and the financial solutions reinforce each other. In the absence of international financial institutions the League Secretariat, though without resources, plays the part of the role that is later taken by the IMF.

One further episode in Monnet's brief career with the League of Nations deserves mention. At the end of the war the Saarland is occupied by France and then placed under the authority of commissioners appointed by the League. Monnet goes there on behalf of the League to talk to the commissioners and to take a view on how the arrangements are working. On his return he tells the secretary general that the reality is that the Saar is governed not by the commissioners, but by what remains of the previous German administration. France has taken over the economic resources, mainly coal, but it is unable to change the sentiments of the people who remain attached to Germany. Monnet says in his memoirs: 'like all attempts at domination', this was a doomed policy. He concludes that some method is needed to ensure that the economic interests of one country do not clash with the sovereignty of another. He proposes an immediate referendum to the French government. Prime Minister Poincaré refuses. When the referendum is finally held, a decade later, the Saar reverts to Germany.

The League of Nations is remembered for its failures in the 1930s. But in the years after the First World War it played a constructive role providing, as Monnet described it, 'little solutions for big problems'. With the three greatest of the great powers absent, and the two remaining, France and Britain, pursuing opposite policies, the League's failure as a political body should not be a surprise. But its secretariat, an executive body acting on behalf of its members, often coped creatively with the problems that followed the war. After its intervention in Austria the League helped find solutions for financial problems in Czechoslovakia and Hungary, and for refugee and humanitarian crises in Greece and the Middle East. Almost all today's international bodies

– the World Health Organization, the UN High Commissioner for Refugees, the IMF – grew out of the improvised solutions of people who worked for the League. Salter's work with Monnet prefigures the post-war role of the IMF; Ludwig Rajchman, a public-health expert, did work (funded by the Rockefeller Foundation) that anticipates the WHO. Rajchman himself went on to found UNICEF after the Second World War.*

Business and banking

Monnet saw his life as a series of responses to imperatives. In 1922 the imperative is to save the family business from bankruptcy. To do this he leaves the League of Nations (taking with him his office furniture).† He also takes with him a reputation and an extraordinary list of connections – and the conviction that international co-operation is both possible and necessary. But it must be practical, based on something more concrete than rhetoric.

Monnet rescues the family business – or at least he buys it some time.‡ Then he goes into business on his own account, or rather on behalf of an American investment bank, Blair & Co., whose Paris subsidiary he runs. His work is on the frontier between business and politics, lending to sovereigns, advising governments, helping stabilise currencies so that governments can borrow; Monnet knows something of both governments and business from the inside; and he knows the right people too. Some, like Dwight Morrow of J. P. Morgan, 'the conscience of Wall Street', he met in the context of the AMTC; others, like John Foster and Allen Dulles and John Maynard Keynes, he got to know at Versailles, along with Walter Lippmann – then a bright young man in Wilson's team – and Bill Bullitt, later American ambassador in Moscow

* See Mark Mazower, *Governing the World*, Chapter Five.

† This was the same furniture he had used in his office in London, purchased at the cost of much bureaucratic aggravation from the French government.

‡ Part of the rescue comes from a loan from the Hudson Bay Company, which Monnet is not expected to repay. HBC's business with the French government during the war has been considerable; and much of it has come through Monnet.

and Paris. Through his work at the League he has met the important central-bank governors: the governor of the Bank of England, Montagu Norman, described Monnet as a magician. In the course of life on Wall Street he will get to know, among others, Dean Acheson and John McCloy, Robert Lovett and Felix Frankfurter. In the second half of the 1920s he helps refloat the Polish zloty and stabilise the Romanian leu. This last deal is sealed by a loan from the Swedish would-be match monopolist Ivar Kreuger, in exchange for a thirty-year monopoly on matches in Romania. This is early 1929, in the last days of optimism and prosperity.

It is not only Americans that Monnet gets to know in this period: one of his assistants is René Pleven, later prime minister of France. When Schuman presents his plan to the Council of Ministers on 9 May 1950, Pleven is one of the heavyweights whose support persuades Bidault to accept it.

The Blair & Co. connection brings another important meeting. Francesco Giannini, the Blair agent in Italy, comes to a dinner that Monnet gives in Paris in August 1929. He brings with him his bride of four months. Monnet writes: 'That night I saw his young wife for the first time. She was very beautiful. We forgot the other guests.'*

Some have questioned how far the *coup de foudre* Monnet describes was mutual; after all, Silvia di Bondini Giannini remains with her husband for two more years, and has a daughter, Anna, by him. Yet something happened to her that evening too. There are not many occasions for Silvia and Jean Monnet to meet in the two years that follow, and the courtship is conducted 'by cable and transatlantic phone', according to Salter.[17] For a young Italian – she is only twenty when they first meet – and an ardent Catholic to take her daughter to Switzerland and refuse to return to her husband when it is not clear whether she will be able to divorce and remarry, suggests that a powerful force was at work on her side too. But there is no doubt that Monnet pursues

* The two short paragraphs in Monnet's memoirs (p. 109) describing this scene and their subsequent marriage are the only part of the book written by Monnet himself – or rather by Jean and Silvia Monnet together – the rest was written by François Fontaine from Monnet's oral account.

Silvia with the same single-mindedness that grips him whenever he sees something as vitally important.

Their relationship brings many legal complications, but it is one of the solid foundations of Monnet's life. It anchors him in the 1930s when his business career is turbulent and his life is without a clear direction. It does the same for the rest of his life.

In 1929 Blair and Co. merges with a California bank to form a new worldwide concern; Monnet joins as vice-chairman in January 1930. Then the California partner withdraws, awarding himself a large bonus, and returns when the shares have lost 98 per cent of their value to organise a revolt to oust the Wall Street team. Later, he is accused of financial irregularities by the Securities and Exchange Commission; but that is too late for Monnet and the others from Blair & Co. At this point John Foster Dulles helps Monnet, who has lost large sums of money, to find work winding up the Kreuger Trust following Ivar Kreuger's bankruptcy and suicide.

From there Monnet is recruited by T.V. Soong, finance minister of the Republic of China and brother of Mme Chiang Kai-shek, as a consultant to the Chinese Nationalist government, which needs assistance in raising capital for infrastructure in China. Monnet travels to Shanghai and helps establish the China Development Finance Corporation, which issues a successful railway bond. But it is now 1934 and it is becoming difficult to do business in China without backing from the Japanese.

In the middle of 1934 Monnet leaves Shanghai and travels back through Moscow. There he meets the US ambassador, Bill Bullitt. Silvia, in Switzerland, has meanwhile become a Soviet citizen, so that later in the year, after she and Monnet have travelled separately to Moscow, she can obtain a divorce at the Hall of Marriage. She then crosses the corridor to marry Jean Monnet. The two then return to Paris, where Silvia's mother has been looking after Anna. Rajchman, Monnet's colleague from the League, has sent introductions to the Soviet ambassador in China; Bullitt has looked after the couple in Moscow; and the French ambassador in Moscow, René Mayer, is another friend of Monnet. The couple then go, via the United States, to

Shanghai, partly in the hope that they will be safe there from Silvia's former husband, who is seeking custody of his daughter.*

In 1936 Monnet moves from Shanghai back to New York, where he has established a new business partnership with George Murnane. The work with China continues, but the Japanese presence makes business increasingly difficult. Monnet now visits Europe more frequently, and is aware of the storms gathering there.

The Second World War

In this period Monnet gets to know Édouard Daladier, then minister of defence and acutely aware of France's weakness. By the time of Munich, Daladier is also prime minister. He returns from the meeting with Hitler and Chamberlain 'with a sense of humiliation rather than relief'.[18] At Munich, Daladier has been conscious that France has only 600 aircraft, and that Germany can bomb Paris whenever it chooses. Three days after Munich, he asks Monnet – who is not likely to be recognised – to go to talk to Roosevelt on his behalf. Bill Bullitt, now ambassador in Paris, makes the arrangements, and the three of them meet in Roosevelt's home, Hyde Park in New York. They discuss the numbers of aircraft needed, how they might be financed, where factories might be built safe from German attack. But such things cannot be done quickly. The Military and Finance Ministries on both sides of the Atlantic are slow to react. Neither Daladier's sense of crisis nor Roosevelt's instincts are enough to overcome them – at least not on the scale that they and Monnet have in mind. Eventually, as a result of their efforts, 100 American aircraft are in service with the French air force when the German attack comes in May 1940. This makes no material difference; but the failure provides an important lesson for the future.

A more immediate result is that, when war is declared in 1939, Daladier is receptive to Monnet's suggestion that a system for joint

* They may be free from lawsuits in Shanghai, but they are not safe. Francesco Giannini attempts to have Anna abducted through the Italian consulate while Monnet is away. Silvia and Anna are given refuge in the Soviet consulate.

Allied procurement should be put in place on the model of the co-operation during the First World War. Daladier writes to Chamberlain, who agrees to set up five executive committees covering armaments, food, petroleum, aircraft and shipping; these will be under the authority of an Anglo-French Co-ordinating Committee of senior officials. The committee is based in London, so it is agreed that the chairman will be French. Daladier nominates Monnet.* He sets about the work by constructing a 'balance sheet' to compare what the Allies have in the area of armaments with what they will need to defeat Germany. This involves making an estimate of German capabilities – and the two intelligence services do not communicate with each other – and then deciding on common needs; and the two administrations have never worked together. They have different procedures, even different weights and measures. But at least the work begins from the outbreak of the war rather than at its end, as in 1918.

The end for France comes all too soon. In May 1940 Britain retreats through Dunkirk as the French army collapses. In an effort to keep France in the war even when its territory has been overrun by the *Wehrmacht*, Monnet puts forward the idea of an Anglo-French union. He approaches Churchill, now prime minister, through Chamberlain. Churchill is not attracted; but later de Gaulle, just arrived in London, persuades him to take the idea seriously.† When the proposal for union is put to the War Cabinet they also support it. Churchill agrees, saying to Monnet: 'At as grave a time as this, it shall not be said that we lack imagination.'[19]

De Gaulle puts the proposal to Paul Reynaud, the new French prime minister, now in Bordeaux. At Reynaud's request de Gaulle dictates the proposed joint declaration over the telephone to him – the British

* Monnet notes in his memoirs that his instructions from the two prime ministers were to 'use [his] best efforts to smooth out differences and bring about joint decisions by adopting an Allied rather than a national point of view'. Monnet comments that this is precisely the role he later envisaged for the ECSC's High Authority.

† On the day of his arrival, 14 June, Monnet invites de Gaulle to dinner. Monnet, as usual, is late returning home and Silvia, finding herself with the general, attempts polite conversation, asking him how long his visit will be. 'Madame,' he replies, 'I am not here for a visit. I am here to save the honour of France.' (Monnet, *Memoirs*, p. 24.)

ambassador, Sir Ronald Campbell, with Reynaud at the time, says that his face lit up as he heard what was proposed. He asks: 'Has Churchill approved it?' De Gaulle says he has. Then Churchill himself comes on the line to say that de Gaulle will travel to Bordeaux immediately with the draft declaration. Churchill also proposes to meet Reynaud the next day in Brittany.

As Churchill's party starts for Brittany, the news comes that Reynaud has resigned and has been replaced by Marshal Pétain, and that armistice negotiations are under way.*

Like much else in 1940, the idea of an Anglo-French union fails; but it says something of Monnet's imagination that he conceived it, and of his powers of persuasion that he got de Gaulle and Churchill, two men for whom national sovereignty was sacred, to take it up.

With the fall of France the Alliance is dissolved, and with it the Anglo-French Co-ordinating Committee that Monnet chairs. Monnet sends his resignation to Pétain. He writes to Churchill, offering to work for the British government, 'in order to serve the true interests of my country'. Churchill replies, proposing that Monnet join the British Purchasing Commission in the United States, to continue the work he has begun at the Anglo-French Co-ordinating Committee. Churchill provides him with a British passport, which he signs personally.

This is the job Monnet wants – he has no doubt had a hand in arranging it – but his position in Washington is not straightforward. Unlike others in the Purchasing Commission he does not represent a Whitehall department; his official backing is a single letter from Churchill; and he is French – not a popular nationality in 1940. Monnet is regarded, in both London and Washington, with suspicion.† But he is well known

* De Gaulle's journey to Bordeaux is therefore fruitless, except that Pleven, who has joined de Gaulle in London, goes with him, and by accident meets his wife and family in the street in Bordeaux. They go back with him to London.

† This is true, above all, of Henry Morgenthau, secretary to the Treasury, trusted by Roosevelt for his loyalty and his hatred of fascism. His suspicion of Monnet may have originated in Monnet's connections to Dulles, whose law firm has acted on behalf of the Franco government. Morgenthau pursues an investigation of Monnet through almost the whole length of the war.

to Arthur Purvis, the head of the commission, and to Salter, who is running the London end of the operation.

In Washington, Monnet begins a programme similar to the one he initiated in London – to work out what it is that Britain will need to defeat Germany. His starting point is that, for practical purposes, the resources of the United States should be considered limitless. What matters, therefore, is not what *can* be done, but what *must* be done. Robert Sherwood, one of Roosevelt's speech writers, describes him as 'the greatest, single-minded apostle of all-out production, preaching the doctrine that ten thousand tanks too many are preferable to one tank too few'.[20]

A critical moment in this story is the re-election of Franklin Roosevelt in November 1940. Shortly after this, Monnet, in conversation with Felix Frankfurter, is expounding his view that it is only with material support from the United States that Hitler can be defeated. To explain what he means, he says that America must become an arsenal, 'a great arsenal of democracy'. Frankfurter stops him, saying that the phrase is very good; he asks Monnet not to use it again. A week later, on 29 December, Monnet hears Roosevelt use the same phrase in the most famous of his 'fireside chats', in which he calls for the United States to manufacture and supply arms for those fighting Nazism, and proposes Lend-Lease.[21]

Monnet's mission in America is to turn the words 'arsenal of democracy' into a reality. He begins, as in London, with a balance sheet comparing the resources of the enemy and those of Britain. Failing to get all the numbers they need from London ministries, Purvis and Monnet make their own estimates. The result is a requirement costing $15 billion, twice the annual defence budget of the United States. Purvis presents the estimate to Roosevelt the day after the 'great arsenal of democracy' fireside chat.

Early in January 1941 Roosevelt sends Harry Hopkins to London to meet the British government. Before he leaves, Felix Frankfurter introduces Monnet to him, as someone who has seen the British government from the inside. Monnet tells Hopkins that the only person he needs to see is Churchill: Churchill *is* the government. Hopkins, a hard-nosed, low-key man of the left from a poor family, unimpressed by romantic rhetoric and by British aristocrats, dislikes the message, but Monnet persists.

Hopkins's visit is a turning point in the transatlantic relationship; at a dinner the unrhetorical, unemotional Hopkins, addressing Churchill, quotes from the Book of Ruth: 'whither thou goest, I will go; and where thou lodgest, I will lodge: thy people shall be my people, and thy God my God. Even to the end,' moving Churchill to tears. Hopkins cables Roosevelt saying: 'Churchill is the government in every sense of the word . . . he is the one and only person over here with whom you need to have a full meeting of minds.'[22] Returning to Washington, he invites himself to dinner with Monnet. As he is leaving Monnet asks if there was something he wanted. 'Only to get to know you better,' says Hopkins, and they remain trusted friends.

In spite of their different lives Monnet and Hopkins have much in common. Both are single-minded; both cut corners and ignore established practice to get things done. In tackling social problems, first in the private sector and then working for Roosevelt to implement the New Deal, Hopkins's approach has been to ignore budgets and work only on what must be done. ('Hunger is not debatable.')[23] Monnet pursues the question of what is needed to beat Nazi Germany in this spirit. And Hopkins does the same on war production when Roosevelt gives him responsibility for that.*

Roosevelt is sufficiently impressed by the method of calculating the 'deficiency' in capability that in February 1941 he asks the Defense Department to work out what would be required for a (hypothetical) joint US/British programme. In the spring John McCloy – a friend from Wall Street days, now assistant secretary for defence – enlists Monnet's help to draft an order instructing government departments to compile a balance sheet comparing Anglo-American capabilities and those of

* When the US administration is beginning to think about increasing arms production and creates the National Defense Advisory Commission, one of its members asks General Burns of the Army Ordnance Department how much he needs. After years of difficulties with Congress the army's estimates have become modest. Hopkins advises General Burns instead to 'ask for everything' (Robert E. Sherwood, *Roosevelt and Hopkins*, p. 197).

Germany. The Monnet balance sheet becomes the 'Anglo-American Consolidated Statement', and the basis of US government planning.

This document, sixty pages long and a work constantly being updated, shows that it will be the end of 1942 before the United States can catch up with Britain and Canada in arms production. In September 1941 Roosevelt sets up what becomes the 'Victory Programme', turning the balance sheet into a programme for producing equipment for Britain (and for the Soviet Union too), and to begin rearming the United States. The plan shows that by spring 1944 production can reach $150 billion per year. The feasibility study is presented to Roosevelt on 4 December 1941. Three days later Japan attacks Pearl Harbor.

When Roosevelt addresses Congress in January 1942, he calls for production of 60,000 aircraft in that year and 125,000 in 1943. At the time such numbers are scarcely conceivable. But by the end of the war the United States is producing 300,000 aircraft a year. And instead of sacrificing civilian production, the result of the programme is that the depression finally comes to an end.

What is Monnet's contribution to this? He has mobilised and he has motivated. When no one knows where to start, Monnet proposes a method and then helps make it work. He operates at every level – letters to Roosevelt, consultation with Hopkins (who is responsible for Lend-Lease when the bill is passed in March 1941), collaboration with McCloy, and then detailed work with Stacey May, the economist and statistician, and Robert Nathan, who compiles the feasibility study. He raises the level of ambition and persuades ministries to work out the plans that enable the transformation of the United States from depression to war economy. He bridges the gap between ambition at the political level and the practical needs of those who have to deliver the results. When the British Supply Council – which has followed Monnet and moved to Washington from New York – has an insoluble problem with the US government, it is to Monnet that they turn. Keynes's view was that the production targets imposed on a disbelieving nation by Roosevelt – and inspired by Monnet – shortened the war by a year.[24]

Two witnesses closer to Monnet's work give a similar assessment: Robert Nathan in an interview described him as one of the most important contributors to the Allied victory in the Second World War. Whether on an early-morning walk in Rock Creek Park or at a dinner party at his home on Foxhall Road, Monnet stressed the urgency of America's industrial mobilisation. 'Monnet had one goal in Washington: to impress on American decision makers that American production was needed to stop Hitler.'[25]

John McCloy wrote of Monnet's work:

> [He] talks, and presses to the point almost of irritation, the United States' obligation. He spares himself no indignity or rebuff but before long he has the Army officers repeating his arguments. . . . You know the regard in which he is held among those in high places. I see his influence on the hewers of wood and I repeat, no one in the British Mission, capable as so many of them are, is near the equal of Monnet, measured in terms of influence.[26]

Vichy and de Gaulle

Monnet describes himself as a man of beginnings. As work goes forward to implement the plan he has helped create, his thoughts turn to France and to North Africa, where the Allied victories pose the question of who should represent France in liberated French territories: Henri Giraud or de Gaulle? General Giraud is on the spot in Algiers. He is an admired and courageous soldier – he has escaped twice from captivity in Germany, once in each war, and he has been appointed by the Vichy authorities as 'Civil and Military Commander' to replace the assassinated Admiral Darlan; and the United States has accepted him. De Gaulle is supported by Churchill and found unbearable by everybody (including Churchill). He is especially disliked in Washington, where he is seen as an authoritarian who brings nothing to the table except his difficult personality. Giraud is in place and commands a substantial (though under-equipped) army. The army is a Vichy army.

The US military are practical people and they see Giraud as a practical solution.

But there are also complaints about the United States being too close to the anti-Semitic Vichy regime. This is not true; Giraud is on the right, and he is working for Vichy, but he is a patriot. His defect is that he is hopelessly unpolitical. At the last moment it is decided to invite de Gaulle as well as Giraud to the Roosevelt-Churchill meeting at Casablanca in January 1943. There, an attempt is made to get the two generals to form a joint committee led by Giraud. De Gaulle rejects this, together with all the variants proposed by Churchill and Roosevelt. (Giraud accepts them all.) All that is left at the end is a handshake for the cameras.*

It is not a surprise that this sideshow at Casablanca does not come off. Such last-minute efforts rarely work. Besides, Giraud regards de Gaulle as a jumped-up junior – he was de Gaulle's commander years before, and they did not get on then either – who has betrayed the army for personal ambition; de Gaulle sees Giraud as a Vichy collaborator, and now a tool of the United States. In their writings, both men, like Caesar, refer to themselves in the third person.

During the Casablanca meeting Roosevelt sounds out Cordell Hull, his neglected secretary of state, about the possibility of inserting Jean Monnet into the French administration in Algiers to give it a civilian element. (They are uneasy about a general as 'civil and military commander'.) Hull replies that Monnet is too close to de Gaulle. This is not true. Monnet is also suspicious of de Gaulle's ambitions and authoritarian tendencies. Roosevelt's cable (it sounds like Hopkins) is closer to the mark when it describes Monnet as having 'kept his skirts clear of any political entanglements'. He has friends in the de Gaulle camp, but he also helps aides of Giraud when they come to Washington looking for arms. Giraud's generals have discovered that it is through Monnet that you get to Hopkins and McCloy.

* The French personalities concerned are summarised by Alan Brooke, the British chief of staff, in his *War Diaries*, p. 363: Darlan has ability but no integrity; Giraud has charm but no ability and is no match for de Gaulle, who has the mentality of a dictator and a most objectionable personality. (Brooke implicitly admits his ability.)

Out of this comes an invitation from Giraud to Monnet to visit Algiers. Hull acquiesces. Hopkins, in his capacity as the chairman of the Munitions Assignment Board (the body which decides who gets what), asks Monnet to go. Before Monnet leaves, he talks to Roosevelt about the question of a French government in exile. As a result, Roosevelt tells the White House correspondents on 12 February that sovereignty rests with the French people – they will choose who represents them when they are liberated. In the meantime, under German occupation, sovereignty has been suspended. This is Monnet's well-calculated answer to the question, 'Who represents France?' – for the moment, no one.

McCloy, who is responsible for military relations with Allies, visits Algiers in advance of Monnet. He is attracted by the idea of French soldiers as well as British participating in the Normandy landings, and wants to see their army. While he is there he makes it clear to both French and Americans that Monnet comes with the backing of the US government. When Monnet arrives he brings with him a letter from Roosevelt to Eisenhower saying the same.

From working for Britain in Washington, Monnet switches to working for the United States in Algeria. He arrives with instructions from Hopkins on arms procurement, but they both know he is going to play a political role. He is attached to Giraud as an adviser; his job is to make him politically acceptable. His reports to Hopkins are all about handling Giraud: 'Giraud and I have had several conversations . . . on the need for reaffirming through words and deeds, French traditional principles of democracy and liberty. . . . He also agreed on immediate action cancelling anti-Jewish decrees . . . He will speak on Sunday and I am working on a draft.'[27]

Monnet's responsibilities concerning equipment for French forces are a key card.[28] Unable to alter Giraud's personal convictions by political reasoning, he finds the argument that 'the Americans would refuse to equip an army . . . which was supporting a racist regime' is decisive with a professional soldier. Giraud's own record says: 'I had many meetings with Jean Monnet. The theme was always the same: no reforms, no equipment.' Giraud concludes that if Paris is worth a Mass, then Allied munitions are worth a progressive speech. On the Sunday mentioned in Monnet's report to Hopkins, Giraud reads out 'the first democratic speech I ever made'.[29]

He resists to the last. The night before the speech Giraud gives Monnet his final draft. Monnet decides it will not do, and works overnight on an alternative version, consulting Robert Murphy and Harold Macmillan, the American and British representatives. When Giraud wakes up the next morning he finds a note from Monnet and the new version. 'This was one of the many occasions on which I was able, at the last moment, to substitute a patiently worked out text for one that an indecisive or careless politician has failed to perfect. When Giraud got up next morning he found my note and my draft. He had no time to do anything but accept it.'[30]

The speech, made before the microphones of the world's press, is interrupted twenty-six times by applause. It does not just distance Giraud from Vichy. It contains a powerful passage on the Resistance: 'The people of France have not accepted the armistice. The heroes of the Resistance, . . . those whose faith has survived the most desperate hours, express, and still express, the true France.' And then: 'From now on there will be only one French army fighting Nazi Germany . . . Disunion is the mark of defeat; union is the sign of victory. This union . . . will gather together not only Frenchmen in France at present under the enemy yoke, but those who like ourselves are outside France. For our country this is a matter of life or death.'[31]

After the speech a number of Vichy supporters resign. In the next days Giraud annuls some of the worst Vichy decrees. Murphy and Eisenhower cable Roosevelt and Marshall that 'Monnet has done a grand job'. Macmillan gives the same message to London. The speech is welcomed in another quarter, too. Its emphasis on the Resistance brings de Gaulle back into play. He is a symbol of resistance and is associated with those in France fighting the Germans, including the National Resistance Committee, led by Jean Moulin. In Algiers, Monnet has the portraits of Pétain removed and looks for republican busts of Marianne to replace them. He finds only one. No matter, his own position is clear: he has named his daughter, born before he left Washington, Marianne.

De Gaulle sends his chief of administration, General Catroux, a general sufficiently senior for the army-minded, rank-conscious Giraud to deal with him, to Algiers. Then begins a period of manoeuvring, interspersed – after de Gaulle has arrived – with walk-outs, ultimatums, empty chairs and confrontations; but at the end, on 3 June, a joint committee is born. Monnet and Catroux are its midwives. Giraud and de Gaulle are each to nominate two further members; the seventh will be agreed jointly. The French Committee for National Liberation (CFNL) is chaired alternately by Giraud and de Gaulle; it operates by majority vote and collective responsibility. Monnet is one of Giraud's nominated members.

On the day the CFNL begins its work, it decides by majority vote to retire the two most prominent Vichy officials. Monnet votes with de Gaulle. Later, the committee is enlarged and its members take responsibility for specific areas – Monnet's is armaments and supplies. It becomes clear early on that de Gaulle is the real head of the CFNL, and that he has a built-in majority on most issues, not least because Monnet sides with him. By October Giraud, already marginalised, is with French forces in Italy, and de Gaulle persuades the committee to make him its sole chairman.

The American conception of French unity was that it would be under their man, Giraud. Their objective in sending Monnet was to make him politically acceptable. Monnet took this a step further by making Giraud acceptable to de Gaulle as well. Once he was on the spot, he did not conceal from Murphy that he was going to pursue that objective. Hopkins probably understood that too. Only a Frenchman could have brought about unity – Monnet and Catroux do this together. The achievement of unity makes the question of leadership into a purely French issue; and Washington can do nothing about it.

For Monnet, de Gaulle was the more able politician and a more authentic representative. He was sent by Roosevelt to look after Giraud. Instead he arranges for de Gaulle to replace him; yet he retains his relationship with the Roosevelt administration. He also takes care that de Gaulle does not have too much personal power: decisions in the CFNL are collegiate and there is no scope for authoritarianism. De Gaulle's takeover of the CFNL in Algiers is a key step towards his leadership of the Provisional Government in liberated France.

This story, on the surface a conflict of personalities, is more than that. It is vital for France that, when liberation comes, there should be political unity. After occupation, after collaboration, resistance, clandestine parties, profits made and lives lost, there is a risk of civil and political disorder. Lost wars bring revolutions; revolutions bring civil war. The CFNL, embracing the whole political spectrum, enables France to take its place with the victors and helps avoid the dangers of division.

The events in Algeria have moments of drama. But in between, Monnet has time for reflection. As he does later in Paris, he lives away from the centre of Algiers, fifty miles along the coast. The diplomat Hervé Alphand describes him, 'under a clear Mediterranean light, with a profusion of flowers and birds'. Monnet, in shorts, is 'talking, thinking aloud, dictating, playing a different part with each of his colleagues, trying his ideas on all of them, taking care not to limit his options'. Louis Joxe, who was the secretary of the CFNL, wrote: 'He . . . spent entire days questioning people or thinking alone by the sea, hours also writing to his wife, whose opinion mattered to him more than anyone else's. Then abruptly he would lift the telephone, and call Giraud or Bob [Murphy] in Algiers, John McCloy or Robert Sherwood in the States.'[32]

Here he is among French people for the first time in more than ten years, and he begins to think about post-war France. Many of those he will work with in the future are in Algiers: René Mayer, Robert Marjolin, René Pleven, Hervé Alphand, and Étienne Hirsch, active members of the Resistance. Alphand is interested in the idea of a European economic union, Mayer has been thinking in terms of 'Lotharingia', an economic entity bringing together the coal- and steel-producing areas of Germany, France and Belgium. Monnet himself fears a return to protectionism and alliances, and writes of a federation of European states. 'The British, the Americans and the Russians have worlds of their own into which they can temporarily withdraw. France is bound up in Europe. She cannot escape.'[33]

At a lunch with de Gaulle in October to discuss these questions,

Monnet sets out the idea of a Europe united economically on terms of equality among its members. Germany might be divided into several states, but they would be treated as equals. Coal and steel would be under an international authority. De Gaulle imagines a union, but without Germany – except for the Rhineland, which has been detached. This might include Benelux, Italy, Spain and Switzerland. On de Gaulle's side, echoes of this debate may be heard in a speech in 1945 when he speaks of integrating the Ruhr and the Saar in a European federation.[34]

In late October, when the CFNL and the re-equipping of the French army are going smoothly, Monnet returns to Washington, now working for France as the CFNL's representative there, to prepare for the administration of a liberated France. This again is about establishing priorities and identifying resources; a large part of these will be American. As the Normandy landings approach, the question of whether the CFNL should be recognised as representing France becomes urgent. In May 1944 the CFNL is widened to include representatives of the Resistance, and renames itself the Provisional Government of France.* Most of the US administration is resigned to recognising de Gaulle, much as they would prefer not to work with him, but Roosevelt resists to the last.

Alphand writes in his diary concerning this: 'Jean Monnet amazes me. It is he who drafts the memoranda handed to the President of the United States, who incites Eisenhower to send telegrams to shift the balance on our favour.'[35] He may be referring to the memorandum on recognising de Gaulle from the State Department which Hopkins is said to have put in Roosevelt's in-box; and which, whenever it got to the top, Roosevelt is said to have moved back to the bottom.

This problem is solved when, after the Normandy landings, de Gaulle visits France and is greeted by enthusiastic crowds. He then appoints prefects in liberated areas, without asking anybody's permission. The people accept them, and the US military find it useful to work with them. From this moment, political authority belongs to de Gaulle.

* Monnet ceases to be a member, but continues to represent it in Washington.

Monnet visits France in November 1944. After five years' absence he is shocked by what he finds. While others have been fighting wars of production and technology, France, under occupation, has stagnated. It is exhausted, divided, impoverished. When de Gaulle visits Washington in summer 1945 to meet Truman, Monnet talks to him about the state of France. If France is to be the great country that de Gaulle speaks of, it needs to modernise. De Gaulle, dazzled by the prosperity and productivity of the United States, is all the more conscious of the weakness of France. He asks Monnet if he would like to take on the task of modernisation.

Leaving the Supply Council in Washington to his deputy, Monnet returns to France and spends much of the autumn there. He buys Houjarray, his family house on the outskirts of Paris, by the forest of Rambouillet, where he lives for the remainder of his life. In between work on supply issues, he considers with friends such as Hirsch, Alphand and Marjolin how to take forward de Gaulle's task.

The result is a five-page memorandum entitled 'Proposals for a Modernisation and Investment Plan'. This underlines the backwardness of France – national income is half what it was in 1929; agricultural productivity is one-third of America's; its most modern steelworks was built in 1906 – and proposes a system of planning to renew the French economy. This foresees collaboration among industrialists, unions and experts, all orchestrated by the state in a number of Modernisation Commissions. A State Planning Commission would be represented on each of these: it would draw up an overall 'balance sheet' of French assets and deficiencies, and establish priorities. De Gaulle receives the paper on 5 December. Monnet then returns to Washington to complete the negotiation of a $550 million loan from the Export-Import Bank (Lend-Lease having ended). The Council of Ministers approves Monnet's proposals and on 5 January 1946 de Gaulle sets up the Commissariat du Plan and appoints Monnet its first head; this is one of his last acts before he resigns as head of the Provisional Government.

The Commissariat du Plan and the Schuman Plan

Everyone is agreed on the need for planning in post-war France. In war everything is controlled by the state; the transition to peace needs to be planned in the same way. There will be shortages, and choices will have to be made. The failures of laissez-faire economic policies in the 1930s mean that among the Resistance, the unions and most of the political parties it is common ground that planning will be needed. What Monnet does is to propose an objective and a method.

The objective is modernisation; the method is consultation and persuasion, not a rigid Soviet-style Gosplan. Monnet arranges that the Commissariat du Plan is the smallest of all government departments – no more than 100 people, including doormen and cleaners: 'that way no one will be jealous, and we shall be left in peace'. But it is attached to the prime minister's office and includes some first-class brains. He also employs American consultants: George Ball, who has worked on Lend-Lease, and Robert Nathan, with whom he collaborated on US arms production. (Nathan talent-spots the young Pierre Uri, whom Monnet takes into his staff.) The plan identifies priority sectors for investment: coal, steel, cement, electricity, transport and agricultural machinery. The Monnet Plan was also a political conjuring trick: it was a Plan – and that satisfied the left, but it was rooted in free markets, which meant it was acceptable to the right. And it worked. It was admired and imitated abroad – imperfectly and too late in the case of Britain.

The involvement of Americans is not accidental. Monnet has access to some of the best brains in Washington: Nathan, who has invented the method of calculating US GNP, provides important comments on an early draft; George Ball advises on competition policy. Monnet guesses that much of the investment foreseen in the Plan will be financed by the United States. That, however, is a year away. In 1946 France is not able to obtain the money it needs from Washington. The loan that the veteran statesman Léon Blum and Monnet negotiate is modest – $650 million, compared with the $3 billion that Keynes obtains for Britain – but Monnet succeeds in selling the idea of the Plan and getting broad agreement on its outlines.

At this stage Monnet has no radical plans for the Ruhr, in spite of the speculations in Algeria. The Plan foresees French steel output at 12.7 million tons, while German production will be held at 7.5 million; security is cited as one of the reasons for the Plan's emphasis on heavy industry. It also assumes deliveries of German coal as reparations. Monnet sees the Marshall Plan as an American way to make German reconstruction palatable to the other Allies. This is over-suspicious; it is a symptom of the way that everybody, Monnet included, has the threat from Germany on their minds.[36]

The Plan is both a framework for France to think about its future and a tool for negotiation with the United States on the use of counterpart funds.* In spite of Marshall's words about the need for the initiative to come from the Europeans, Congress insists the US government controls how the Marshall Plan money is spent. (Five per cent of counterpart funds go to pay the costs of US supervision.) The doctrine in Washington is that counterpart funds should be spent on consumer goods, affordable housing and healthcare – to win popular support away from Communist Parties. The French government's priority is investment. Having a Plan agreed by government, industry and unions – and one whose outline has been accepted in Washington – helps France get its way. Monnet's friendship with David Bruce, head of the Marshall Plan mission, helps too. As Irwin Wall puts it, 'The Marshall Plan in France became an auxiliary to the Monnet Plan in achieving the reconstruction and modernisation of the country.' Marshall himself saw his own plan as something like the Monnet Plan, but on a larger scale and involving several countries.[37] In the end a token amount is allocated to American priorities and the rest is spent in accordance with the Monnet Plan.

* The dollar credits of the Marshall Plan enabled the purchase of goods from the United States; purchasers paid for the dollars they bought in francs, which went to the French Treasury and were then available for government programmes.

Of the sectors to which it gives priority, coal and steel help prepare French industry for European competition; electricity and railways have been two success stories in post-war France.

Thus Monnet comes to the crisis of 1950 with practical experience of international co-operation, with an understanding of the failed policies of the 1930s in the Ruhr and the Saar, and with a keen awareness of American power. To this he adds a good knowledge of the French steel industry.

Monnet has worked with the British in the First World War and for them in the Second.* But they are not part of the problems of the Ruhr and of Franco-German relations that he is trying to solve. Nor, when speculating on the future of Europe in Algeria, did he include them in his ideas on a possible European federation. Perhaps the British Empire looked too solid for this to seem natural.

Nevertheless, after Schuman proposes the Coal and Steel Community in the *Salon de l'Horloge* Monnet travels almost immediately to London. There Sir Stafford Cripps, chancellor of the Exchequer, asks to see him – Bevin is ill and Monnet has met Cripps before to discuss post-war planning.† Cripps is interested in the Schuman Plan; he asks the Economic Policy Committee of the Cabinet to study it with a view to 'a practical scheme . . . not inconsistent with our essential interests'.[38] Nobody else at a senior level in Whitehall sees it this way. The British government decides it cannot accept the condition set by Monnet that those joining the negotiations should agree the idea of a High Authority with the power to act independently. By contrast the Dutch make a reservation on this precise point, but they still join the negotiations.

Apart from Cripps, the only voices to support Monnet's plan are from the opposition. Anthony Eden, the shadow foreign secretary, says it 'must not be allowed to fail', and speaks of it not as an attack on but

* Churchill offered Monnet a substantial salary as a member of the British Purchasing Commission, but he seems not to have taken it.

† Cripps was a man of intellectual scope: in the First World War he drove a Red Cross ambulance and later ran a munitions factory (he was a chemical engineer). He was also a qualified and brilliant lawyer.

a 'fusion of sovereignty'. Churchill objects to Britain absenting itself from such significant discussions. These views evaporate when they are in government. With one exception: in his maiden speech, the newly elected Lieutenant-Colonel Heath refers to the political importance of the plan and says that its supranational objectives should not be feared.[39] Meanwhile another conservative, Harold Macmillan who knows Monnet well from Algiers, attempts to neuter the Schuman Declaration by putting the ECSC under the Council of Europe, and subjecting it to national vetoes.

Monnet's view is that 'the "special problems" [of the UK], real or imaginary, present or past – the problems of the Commonwealth, sterling, or the socialist experiment – did not explain the attitude of the British'. This is 1950, a peak of Cold War anxiety in Europe and of war in Korea. 'The same fear led to contrasting reactions: unity on the continent, isolationism in Britain' – which he fears has written Europe off. Here Monnet may be wrong: the British response is not isolation, but a renewal of the position where it is most comfortable: that of the first and most dependable ally of the United States.[40]

Another explanation is provided by a senior official working for Cripps, Edwin Plowden, a man that Monnet respects, but among those responsible for the British rejection of the Schuman Plan. Later he tells Monnet why he resisted his offers of co-operation on planning: 'We'd won the war, and we weren't ready to form special links with the Continent. That prevented my understanding what you were getting at.'[41]

From London Monnet goes to Bonn. There he persuades the Allied commissioners to allow Germany to negotiate the future of its coal and steel industries as a sovereign power – which at the time it is not. But the American commissioner, McCloy, is a friend; the French, François-Poncet, has instructions from Schuman; and the two overcome the reservations of their British colleague.

To Adenauer, Monnet says:

> we want to turn what divided France from Germany – that is, the industries of war – into a common asset, which will also be European. In this way Europe will rediscover the leading role which she used

> to play in the world, and which she lost because she was divided. . . . The aim of the French proposal, therefore, is essentially political. It even has an aspect which might be called moral. . . . It has one simple objective which our government will try to attain without worrying, in this first phase, about any technical difficulties that may arise.[42]

He adds that the Schuman proposal has had a profound effect on public opinion in France. The negotiators must keep its political purpose at the front of their minds.

Adenauer replies that for him too the project is of the highest importance. 'We have a moral and not just a technical responsibility to our people . . . The German people have enthusiastically welcomed the plan, and we shall not let ourselves be caught up in details. I have waited twenty-five years for a move like this.'[43]

But, like it or not, the negotiations to establish the Coal and Steel Community have to deal with technical questions. Monnet expects them to be over by August 1950; but they go on into spring 1951. Monnet chairs the negotiations and is also the French representative; he has drafted the Schuman Declaration and made acceptance of the High Authority the entry price for any country wishing to join; the working document is his draft. Adenauer is committed, and Monnet has the all-powerful Americans behind him. He could hardly be in a stronger position. But the governments who are negotiating have managed their coal and steel industries for decades; they are suspicious; so are the mine owners and the steel magnates, who hate his proposals, and do everything they can to resist them.

The treaty that emerges preserves the essentials: a High Authority with executive powers is responsible for organising a common market for coal and steel, ensuring competition and promoting modernisation. The powers of the High Authority come under attack from the German negotiators who want them transferred to an association of producers (i.e. a cartel). This is defeated; but the High Authority will be subject to consultation with the Council of Ministers, the six member states of the ECSC, that is.

The most difficult question in the negotiations is decartelisation – a major plank of American (and French) policy towards Germany. The German industry has a history of cartels, self-regulated in its own self-interest. It opposes this part of the treaty and secures the support of German ministers. It takes an intervention by McCloy with Adenauer to get agreement. For Adenauer the treaty is a step towards peace and sovereignty. When the negotiations begin, the Ruhr is under an international authority in which Germany has no say; in the ECSC it will be an equal partner and a sovereign state.

Monnet gets what he wants in the treaty; but when it comes into force, reality takes over. No other industries could be as difficult to manage as coal and steel. All over Europe coal-mining is either state-run or organised in cartels. When the cartels are dismantled they reappear in another form. The steel industry has run cartels for years; this includes an export cartel, which is allowed to continue; as is some collaboration on pricing. Both industries have long experience of dealing with governments that try to control them. As for a common market without national distortions, this too is easier said than done: governments can employ hidden subsidies through freight charges (for example); or they can insist – as Belgium does – that employment must be protected even if the mines are inefficient. Other objectives, such as the equalisation of living conditions in different countries, are pie in the sky. Each country has had its own way of intervening in these sectors. Practice has been built up over decades, and it does not disappear overnight. The British nightmare of a supra-national authority under nobody's control and issuing orders on its own account could not be further from the truth.

Pursuing the modernisation of industry in the French planning authority, Monnet could use the post-war shortages to force decisions. In Europe, coal and steel modernisation comes not through shortages but through cheap imported coal. From the late 1950s this decimates coal-mining, but it permits steel to prosper. Trade within Europe in steel grows, and price rises are moderate. The market is not as open as intended; and the High Authority is not as strong as the treaty implies. But the results are not bad. The ECSC's achievements are sometimes at the margins: better organisation of the market for scrap metal, better systems for retraining redundant workers, lower market concentration, and an agreement to harmonise freight charges. Not perfect, but better than many of the national systems it replaces.

What matters most is the change in the way the coal and steel industries are regarded. Until the Schuman Plan, the coal and steel complex of the Ruhr was seen in France as a kind of dragon, holding the French industry captive, and threatening French security. From 1918 to 1950, control of the Ruhr was regarded as a vital interest for French national security. But when the steel boom comes in the 1950s, it is no longer just in Germany. France does well too, and Italy also shares in it, partly on the basis of scrap metal. Imported coal relativises the position of the Ruhr. Cartels are not wholly eliminated, but they are no longer a security issue. The dragon dies of natural causes; and by then it is a jointly owned dragon, and that makes a big difference.

The Coal and Steel Community is in many ways chaotic; that should not be a surprise. A new multinational body dealing with two old-established industries was never going to find its task easy. Its creation is nevertheless an act of genius. France escapes its failing policies on the Ruhr; Germany escapes from a twilight zone on the edge of European politics; it opens a path to Franco-German reconciliation, and to wider integration in Europe. Most remarkable of all, after four centuries of competition the Treaty of Paris organises Europe around Franco-German collaboration.

Monnet himself is frustrated in his role as president of the High Authority. The man who has operated through informal conversations, or in small groups, who has been most effective behind the scenes, letting others take the credit, finds himself a public figure with a large organisation to run. Those who work for him in Luxembourg find him inspiring but chaotic. He finds out how difficult the people who run the coal and steel industries can be to deal with. He has insisted on strong powers for the High Authority, and on majority voting for its decisions, but power does not suit him; his instincts are to persuade and to seek consensus, creating a culture of endless meetings that lives on in today's European Union. Monnet is right about the need for a strong joint executive – without it nothing would have changed; but it also makes him an easy target. His opponents in France make the High Authority and Monnet into an imaginary ogre, threatening French sovereignty.

His next venture is risky precisely because it does touch on matters that are close to the core of sovereignty, and to French national myths: defence and the French army.

The European Defence Community

Six weeks after the Schuman Declaration, North Korean forces cross the 38th parallel and the world is at war again. This means that, just as France is finding a solution to the problem of the Ruhr, the more difficult question of German rearmament becomes urgent. In July 1951, McCloy says in a speech that it is 'difficult to deny the Germans the right and the means to defend their own soil'.[44]

This is a reversal of policy. In May the year before, Acheson told the US Senate that recreating a German army would be 'quite insane'.[45] Monnet takes time out from negotiating the Treaty of Paris to suggest to the French government that the increases in defence spending – which Acheson now is calling for – might come through a common European budget. Churchill, who is in opposition and free to let his imagination take over, proposes a resolution in the Council of Europe calling for 'the immediate creation of a unified European army, under the authority of a European minister of defence' – as a vehicle to enable German rearmament.

When Schuman arrives in New York in September for the General Assembly he finds that Acheson is talking about sending more American forces to Europe, but only if Europe contributes too – sixty divisions, including ten from Germany. When Schuman voices reservations, Bevin, for once, does not take his side.

Monnet's answer to this problem is to transpose the concepts of the Schuman Plan into the field of defence. Working with the same team that created the Plan (plus Hervé Alphand from the Quai d'Orsay), he sends a series of notes to René Pleven, now the prime minister.* From these and from Pleven's other consultations the Pleven Plan emerges, proposed by Pleven on 24 October. This is for a European Defence Community (EDC), including a European army, 'integrated at the lowest possible level' – thought to be the battalion. Acheson, hard-headed as usual, suspects the plan is a way of ensuring that France is the predominant military power in Western Europe, or if that fails, of stalling German rearmament by setting off a never-ending debate.[46] Pleven's approach suggests the second theory is right. He insists that the ECSC treaty must be ratified before work on an EDC treaty can begin; it is the Schuman Plan, not the one that bears his own name, that he wants.

Later Acheson succumbs to the arguments of Bruce and McCloy, the two American proconsuls in Europe, that the EDC is the only way to secure French acceptance of German rearmament. These are two of Monnet's best friends; and probably he has converted them. It is certainly Monnet who converts Eisenhower: the strength of the West, he tells him, depends not on the number of divisions, but on unity and a common will:

> 'What you're proposing,' says Eisenhower, 'is that French and Germans should wear the same uniform. That's more a human problem than a military one.'
>
> 'You're right,' says Monnet, 'it's in that order that problems come up in Europe.'[47]

Monnet is responding to Eisenhower's second sentence. As for the first, Pleven has already vetoed Monnet's proposal of a single uniform.

Eisenhower is converted. He sweeps away the objections of his staff, who want to talk details. If the Allied supreme commander supports

* Monnet, in his memoirs, defends the absence of military experts in this group, saying that the Schuman Plan had not been drawn up with experts on the steel industry. 'Essentially it was a political question.' Technicians 'always make things more complicated and resist change'. There is something in this; on the other hand, his team for the Schuman Plan included economists who knew about markets, and lawyers who understood competition policy.

something, then the whole army supports it. A few days later, on 3 July in London, Eisenhower makes a clarion call for a united Europe, including in defence, and it becomes US policy. McCloy persuades Adenauer that the United States will improve the parts of the plan that are difficult for Germany.

Monnet's success in persuading Eisenhower is remarkable, since it is not clear how far he believes in the proposal himself. David Bruce, who was present at the meeting with Eisenhower, commented afterwards that 'he rose to great heights defending something he didn't really believe in.'[48] Later, when the Plan fails and a friend commiserates, Monnet replies that it was a '*mauvaise affaire*' – a bad idea, a mistake.[49]

So it was. Nothing like the intense thought and discussion that lay behind the Schuman Declaration has gone into it. Except for Eisenhower, those who go along with it do so reluctantly, especially the Germans. Everyone else will have two forces, a national army and a share in the European army; Germany alone will be confined to the European force; 'a German foreign legion' is the popular phrase. This is not the equal treatment that made the Schuman Plan attractive to Adenauer. In France, even those who have proposed it, Monnet and Pleven, are not sure that they like it. (On the morning that he launches it Pleven telephones René Mayer to ask if he thinks it is really a good idea.) The military on all sides are sceptical – but they are hardly consulted at all. It is strange that a project so hastily put together, with so few real supporters, becomes a treaty. It is signed on 27 May 1952 by six countries.

It is ratified only by five. The prospect of the treaty winning a majority in the French National Assembly grows ever fainter as time goes by. Opponents of a supranational Europe join opponents of German rearmament: Gaullists share platforms with Communists. To these are added pro-Europeans such as the strategic thinker, Raymond Aron, who do not think a European army will make sense until there is something more like a European state. It is almost a relief when, in August 1954, the French premier, Pierre Mendès-France, gives the treaty to the Assembly to administer the *coup de grâce*.

At the time, the failure of the EDC seemed a devastating blow to the idea of a united Europe. But failure brings fewer problems than success would have done; and the time spent in debate in France allows people to get used to the idea that, one way or another, German rearmament is going to happen.

After the collapse of the EDC, Monnet resigns as president of the High Authority, a position that never suited his talents. He founds the Action Committee for a United States of Europe, a lobby group for the European idea. He is consulted on the next stages of Europe; he remains respected and influential, especially in the United States and in Germany. But in France he is now a public figure, and he never regains the influence of his days of anonymity.

What he has started goes on. With the collapse of the EDC an effort is made to find a different path forward. Monnet argues for nuclear energy as an area for European integration – hoping perhaps that, by working on virgin soil, the trouble he had dealing with the deep-rooted coal and steel industries can be avoided. But it is the idea of a common market covering all sectors – that becomes the centrepiece of the relaunch of Europe after the failure of the EDC. This has been discussed on and off since the ECSC was created. The Belgian foreign minister, Paul-Henri Spaak, takes this forward, building on the experience of the Benelux union, and consulting Monnet in the process. The countries who will negotiate the Treaty of Rome, which creates the European Economic Community (EEC), are the six members of the ECSC. They have grown accustomed to working together.

This was part of the purpose of the Treaty of Paris. The common experience of trying to make the ECSC work has created the beginnings of a political community. The people working for Spaak behind the scenes include Pierre Uri – he drafts the Spaak report that leads to the Treaty of Rome – and Robert Marjolin, who persuades the French government that an open European market can be the salvation of French agriculture.

The two treaties – on the Common Market and nuclear energy - are signed in Rome in March 1957, two and a half years after the Defence Community died. This begins the most successful attempt at international co-operation ever. It is a measure of its success that four years after the Treaty of Rome comes into force, Britain, which has decided once again not to participate in the negotiations, applies for membership. The goals of the treaty are not realised quickly, but the EEC establishes itself as the core of a new Europe, with a political as well as an economic identity. The contrast between this and the Europe of the 1930s, or the Europe before the First World War, could not be greater. The EU has and continues to have episodes of difficulty, stagnation and failure – but also moments of success, especially after the revolutions of 1989, when EU enlargement became a force for stability and progress.

The Monnet method

In an interview with Kathleen Graham, the publisher of the *Washington Post*, Monnet said that all his life he had only had one idea. He did not say what it was. His memoirs suggest the answer. Monnet says of his friend Antoine de Saint-Exupéry that he would never forget one sentence that he wrote: 'Man's finest profession is that of uniting men.'[50]

That was what Jean Monnet did. He did it in London during the First World War, in Silesia and in the Austrian financial crisis on behalf of the League of Nations. In Washington in the early years of the Second World War he brought people together in pursuit of war production. In Algiers he brought the political factions of a divided France together. At the Commissariat du Plan he brought together the state, the workers, employers and experts to help modernise France. And with the Schuman Declaration he brought together enemies. Any diplomat, politician or civil servant would be proud if they had done just one of these things.

Often these were crisis situations. Monnet says (with no trace of false modesty), 'in crises people do not know what to do. I do know what to do.'[51] In normal times, too, people often do not know what to do; but it does not matter. In a crisis they do not know what to do, but they know that they have to do something. Then they become ready to try things that would normally be ruled out, and the man who has the idea has his chance. This was the position in London as the crisis of the First World War became deeper. (It says something about the instincts of the sovereign state that it is only when the state itself is at risk that it can contemplate joint decision-making with allies). In 1950 France's mounting crisis over policy on Germany was an opportunity, not just to think the unthinkable but also to do it. As Monnet said: war must be opposed by imagination.

Monnet was never alone. He had Salter with him in London, and Clémentel behind him in Paris. He worked with Purvis in the United States, not to mention McCloy and Hopkins and the many others he enlisted throughout the US administration: in Algiers, Catroux, who had to manage de Gaulle, was an indispensable partner; there Monnet built up the French network that would support the Schuman Declaration; for this not just Schuman but also Adenauer and Acheson were essential, as well as his friends in Bidault's Cabinet.

At each stage of his life Monnet added to his address book. His life was proof of his dictum that friendship was the result of joint action, not the reason for it.[52] A few of those he worked with became personal friends, the McCloys, David Bruce and George Ball among others; but many relationships were based on mutual interest. Monnet switched them on and off as required. He had nothing to do with Dean Acheson during the Eisenhower administration when he worked with John Foster Dulles, his old friend and Acheson's political enemy. But the moment Kennedy was elected he was in touch with Acheson again. Acheson, who operated in a similar way, did not mind; he always made a point of seeing Monnet when he was in Europe on other business.

Monnet operated at every level. It is not just the people at the top who matter: those close to them, the Clappiers and Catrouxes, matter too. So do those who translate political decisions into operational instructions – this is roughly the position of people such as McCloy during the war – and those who turn the instructions into plans and plans into action, such as Robert Nathan. Below them are the hewers of wood and drawers of water. Monnet knew them all.*

* This was an approach he shared with Hopkins, who also believed in the importance of the 'office boys' who decide who is going to take on a specific task. If they are convinced it is important they will give it to someone capable. (Hopkins referred to himself sometimes as Roosevelt's office boy.)

Monnet's method was to focus relentlessly on a single objective. He saw no need to invent different arguments; instead he spent endless time making his message simple and his proposal practical. Then he would repeat it to whoever might be useful in his cause. He cited his maternal grandmother, 'Marie la Rabâcheuse' (Marie the monotonous), as a family precedent for this method.[53]

Most conversations are quickly forgotten. If someone remembers one thing, it is a success. Monnet made sure there was only one thing for them to remember, and that it was simple and practical.

Murphy commented from Algiers that Monnet was loyal neither to de Gaulle nor to Giraud, but to France. This is part of the truth.[54] Monnet was loyal to France; but, like de Gaulle, it was to a certain idea of France.* Modernisation, for Monnet, included an open society and openness in foreign relations. That meant France in the context of a wider vision of Europe and the world.

Monnet was loyal to himself, too, but not in the usual way. In his memoirs he speculates that, had Bidault read his note, there might have been a Bidault Plan rather than a Schuman Plan. At no point does the idea of a Monnet Plan occur to him. (The name 'Monnet Plan' was given by others to the French national plan.) He quotes Felix Frankfurter saying of him that he was a man who wanted to *do* things, rather than one who wanted to *be* somebody. He cared only that the key insiders should understand his role, so that they would help him with his next project.

The founders of states through history have wanted to leave behind an heir so that their name will live after their death. Monnet wanted to leave behind not a name but certain ideas. He did that by founding institutions.

Speaking to the Assembly of the Coal and Steel Community, Monnet quoted the Swiss philosopher Henri-Frédéric Amiel: 'Each man's experience starts again from the beginning. Only institutions grow wiser: they accumulate collective experience; . . . men subject

* At the end of Chapter Three I make the same remark about Talleyrand. It is difficult to imagine two more different people; and yet, taking account of the changes in society, their ideas of France and of Europe were similar.

to the same rules will not see their own nature changing, but their behaviour [is] gradually transformed.'[55]

On one level the Schuman Plan failed. The Coal and Steel Community achieved few of the objectives in the Treaty of Paris. The one objective it did achieve was an unwritten one: it brought better political relations among the governments of Europe than they had ever had before. The fruit of that came in the Treaty of Rome, and the Europe we have today. This happy ending did not come from the drama of Schuman's announcement on 10 May 1950, nor from the magic of Monnet's ideas. It came out of the give-and-take of politics in the Coal and Steel Community.

The Treaty of Rome was an example of intelligent institutional lessons being learned.* It would be good if the idea of learning from institutional mistakes were taken more seriously. The EU is new, and there is no reason to expect everything to be right first time. But it might usefully ask itself, for example, how it came to adopt a plan so poorly conceived for Economic and Monetary Union, or whether the European Parliament embodies democracy in a way that ordinary people understand. As Monnet wrote: 'Europe will not be made at a single stroke, nor according to a fixed plan, but through concrete achievements.'

Monnet likened the process of building institutions to walking in the mountains: when you take a few steps forward the landscape changes. So with institutions we ought to pause, look around and see how the landscape has changed with our journey; and reflect on what works well and what does not, and be ready where necessary to change direction. Monnet believed in a federal Europe; but what he meant by that changed constantly.

It is fashionable today to discount the EU's contribution to peace in Europe over the last sixty years. But the Treaty of Paris establishing

* Those who drafted the treaty deliberately gave the commission less power than the High Authority. Its most important power is that it proposes legislation to the council: this is appropriate since its role is to identify policies that reflect the collective interest of the Union. Curiously, this was the last important power that the king retained under the French constitution drafted by Talleyrand after the second Bourbon restoration; see Chapter Two.

the ECSC was something like a peace treaty between Germany and France. Joint management of the coal and steel industries did not make war 'materially impossible', as the Schuman Declaration says. If people want to fight they will find a way. What has changed Europe is the creation of a political community among its states who are in continuous communication and negotiation with each other. The EU, for all its faults, has altered the Continent in ways that make it quite different from the Europe of 1914 or 1939.*

* And not just the Continent: joint membership of the EU by Britain and the Republic of Ireland played an essential role in reaching the Good Friday (or Belfast) Agreement that brought peace to Northern Ireland.

8

The Cuban Missile Crisis

Nikita Khrushchev (before the crisis, to his defence minister): 'Rodion Yakovlevich, what if we throw a hedgehog up Uncle Sam's pants?'[1]

John F. Kennedy (afterwards, to Kenneth Galbraith): 'Ken, you have no idea how much bad advice I received in those days.'[2]

The Cuban Missile Crisis is the most told and retold of all diplomatic stories. The story is short and exciting, and it has a happy ending. The West wins and the world is saved from nuclear war. 'We went eyeball to eyeball, and the other fellow just blinked,' as Dean Rusk said.[3] The story is full of heroes, some self-appointed: President Kennedy, his brother Robert, Defense Secretary Robert McNamara and Ambassador Llewellyn Thompson are often mentioned. Others, mostly the hawks, do not cut quite such good figures: the military and Dean Acheson, for example. And then there is Khrushchev, who backs down.

The background

Two important events mark the path to the crisis. First, Berlin: from 1958 onwards Khrushchev makes several attempts to change the status quo of Berlin. If the triumph of socialism is inevitable, how is it that the capitalist outpost of West Berlin continues to prosper and mock the dreary East Berlin? In 1958 he delivers an ultimatum to President

Eisenhower calling for Berlin to become a 'free city'; he sets a six-month deadline but then lets it slip. This is repeated several times. In June 1961 when Kennedy and Khrushchev meet in Vienna, Khrushchev threatens to sign a peace treaty with the GDR, with the implication that the Soviet Union will cease to recognise Allied rights in Berlin. Then, in August, the Berlin Wall goes up, and for the next year the situation in Berlin remains tense.

The running crisis over Berlin has a nuclear dimension: Khrushchev's initial ultimatum comes from his belief that he can blackmail the West; this is based on the missiles he has deployed in East Germany. These, for the first time, bring London and Paris within the range of Soviet nuclear weapons.

Second: Cuba. On the American side, shortly after taking office Kennedy authorises an ill-considered and incompetent attempt to overthrow the revolutionary regime of Fidel Castro in Cuba. On 17 April 1961, the CIA lands 1,400 Cuban exiles at the Bay of Pigs. In the next twenty-four hours most of them are killed or captured on the beach or near it. Kennedy, wisely – but against CIA expectations – refuses to reinforce failure. His reaction, instead, is to ask himself how he could have been so stupid, and to resolve 'never to trust the experts', especially the military. Khrushchev concludes from this fiasco, and from their meeting in Vienna, that Kennedy is weak, and in the hands of the hardliners of the American military-industrial complex.

The crisis

The facts of the Cuban Missile Crisis are simple enough. Khrushchev conceives the plan to put medium-range nuclear missiles into Cuba in the spring of 1962. In April he asks his defence minister, Rodion Malinovsky, to look into it, using the hedgehog metaphor quoted at the start of this chapter. When the question is discussed in the Party Presidium, only Anastas Mikoyan – a veteran member of the Presidium and a Khrushchev ally – questions it. He doubts, in particular, that it will be possible to get the missiles there and to install them secretly. He expects others to raise objections to the plan; but no one does, not the military, not the Cubans, not even Andrei Gromyko, who knows the United States. When Khrushchev asks his foreign minister in private what he thinks, Gromyko (or so he claims) replies that it will cause a storm in the United States. But he does not press the point. No one else with any knowledge of the United States is consulted.

The Presidium agrees provisionally in May, and a team is sent to Cuba to look at sites where the missiles might be concealed (General Biryuzov's idea is to disguise them as palm trees) and to get Castro's agreement.

Castro agrees; and in June the Soviet Presidium unanimously accepts the Defence Ministry's plan. This involves sending thirty-six medium-range and twenty-four intermediate-range missiles* with nuclear warheads to Cuba, plus 144 surface-to-air missile (SAM) launchers to defend the missiles, plus helicopters, bombers, motorised rifle regiments, tanks and a large number of ships. The military do things thoroughly. More than 50,000 men are to go with the equipment – this is later reduced to 45,000; and in the end not all of them get there. But it is a massive operation: 150 round trips by sea will be needed to ship everything to Cuba. The large concrete slabs that underpin the launchers, together with bunkers and the largest missiles, will all be visible from the air. The ships begin arriving at the end of July.

Even a mediocre intelligence service would notice this level of activity. From early 1962 the United States has been making U-2 flights over Cuba. By mid August the CIA is tracking the massive sealift to Cuba with low-flying reconnaissance planes photographing the freighters and their mysterious cargo. The missiles are too long to be stowed below, so they are on deck, covered up in various ways. Bizarrely, in early July the Russians, through the 'back-channel' of the military intelligence officer Georgi Bolshakov, ask President Kennedy to reduce the surveillance flights. He says that he will; but he doesn't. The flights go on as before.

* Medium-range missiles have a range of up to 1,200 nautical miles, intermediate range missiles up to 2,200. The latter would reach Washington.

By early September the U-2 photographs over Cuba show the SAM launcher sites. The new head of the CIA, John McCone,* is almost alone in guessing that such expensive equipment must be there to protect something valuable, probably nuclear weapons. No one else can believe that the Soviets would be so stupid. But Robert Kennedy, tense, emotional, and looking for revenge on Cuba for the Bay of Pigs fiasco, supports McCone. The president makes a statement on 4 September that 'the presence of ground-to-ground missiles or other significant offensive capability either in Cuban hands or under Soviet direction . . . would raise the gravest issues'.[4] In diplomatic terms, 'the gravest issues' is strong language.

The statement does not mention nuclear weapons, but Robert Kennedy does when he gives the Soviet ambassador in Washington advance warning of the statement. Anatoly Dobrynin, who knows nothing about the missile deployment (and cannot imagine anything so stupid), denies any possibility that nuclear weapons might be sent to Cuba.[5] Congress, meanwhile, has passed a resolution authorising the president to use force if necessary. By the end of the crisis the US side abandons back-channels in favour of Dobrynin who is much more effective.

Khrushchev's reaction to these warnings is to send yet more nuclear weapons to Cuba: submarines with nuclear-tipped torpedoes, and the short-range 'Luna' missiles, battlefield nuclear weapons. On 11 September the Soviet government makes a statement that the arms being sent to Cuba are 'purely for defensive purposes'. Bolshakov repeats the same line to Robert Kennedy on 8 October. In Moscow on 16 October Khrushchev tells the newly arrived US ambassador, Foy Kohler, that he will not do anything to embarrass the president before the mid-term elections. All these are true in a literal, logic-chopping way, but they are designed to mislead: Khrushchev's plan is to keep everything secret, and to save the embarrassment for mid November.

On the same day, 16 October 1962, before breakfast, McGeorge Bundy, Kennedy's special assistant for national security, goes to the

* Allen Dulles was fired after the Bay of Pigs, along with several others.

president in his bedroom, where he is reading the morning papers, and shows him the U-2 photographs of medium-range missiles in Cuba. Bundy has the news the evening before, but thinks it better to let the president get a good night's rest before giving him the bad news.[6] Later in the morning the president holds an informal meeting in the White House with the secretaries of state and defense (Dean Rusk and Robert McNamara) and the chair of the joint chiefs of staff. He sums up the discussion by saying, 'We're certainly going to do [option] number one', i.e. destroy the missiles, while preparing for option numbers two and three: wider air strikes, and general invasion.[7]

He cannot have been wholly comfortable with this conclusion since his next action is to establish a group of advisers, the Executive Committee of the National Security Council, 'Excom'. The name is misleading: the committee is advisory, not executive. It is the president who makes the decisions. Kennedy chooses the participants. From the way Excom works, it is reasonable to guess that Kennedy wants to hear a range of views, and to make sure that the military and intelligence agencies do not dominate. This may be a lesson drawn from the Bay of Pigs; or he may be recalling Barbara Tuchman's *The Guns of August*, and the chain reaction that led to the First World War.

The debates

Dean Acheson, who attends Excom's early meetings, later criticises its unstructured process and open debate. Foreign policy was run differently in his day.* But Kennedy is dealing with the first nuclear confrontation with the Soviet Union. No one has faced decisions like this before. As the debate in Excom shows, nobody (including Acheson) has thought through the implications of nuclear weapons in anything like the depth required. That Kennedy wants to make his choices having heard all points of view seems admirable rather than the reverse.

* As secretary of state Acheson made policy, consulting Truman. Rusk was chosen by Kennedy to execute it; this role is partially usurped by Robert Kennedy.

This is different from the way in which Khrushchev makes decisions. There is no debate in Moscow before the deployment. What little debate there is begins only when the missiles are in place. Excom, meanwhile, is trying to understand Khrushchev's motives. Probably, the most important of these is to redress the balance of power. Khrushchev is aware of the Soviet Union's strategic inferiority; bad news about the progress of his missile programme is one of the things that sets his imagination working and leads to the Cuban deployment. In February 1962 Khrushchev has learned that the only intercontinental ballistic missile deployable is the R-16, which uses liquid fuel and has to be fuelled just before it is launched (the fuel is corrosive and cannot be left in the motor). This process takes some hours. By contrast, the United States is about to deploy the solid-fuelled Minuteman, which can be launched in minutes from hardened silos. There are few R-16s, and they are not reliable. Khrushchev's boast that the Soviet Union is turning out missiles like sausages is not true; and the sausages are not very good.

The news of delays in the missile programme is the opposite of what Khrushchev needs. He is making a big bet on nuclear forces. By the end of the Eisenhower presidency, he has reduced the size of the Red Army by one million men. Putting medium- and intermediate-range missiles on Cuba – he has plenty of these, and they are reliable and accurate – is a way of achieving deterrence quickly and cheaply.

Khrushchev's ideas on deterrence are, to say the least, eccentric. His conviction is that Kennedy will never choose war. But from this reasonable premise he draws the conclusion that he can get the US president to do whatever he wants. Perhaps this might have worked if Khrushchev himself had been willing to risk war, but he is at least as averse to war as Kennedy. It is precisely because Kennedy does not want to be faced with an all-or-nothing nuclear option and no other choice that he is going in the opposite direction from Khrushchev, and is building up non-nuclear, flexible options.

Berlin is one of Khrushchev's reasons for seeking strategic parity. On paper West Berlin is a point of weakness for NATO; but it is also an everyday proof of the failure of Communism. Until the wall is built in 1961, West Berlin has been a magnet, attracting people with skill and ambition from the GDR, further weakening the GDR's economy and underlining its failure. In the end the wall is the solution, though not a glorious one. Khrushchev has put a lot of capital into solving the problem of Berlin and is unwilling to let go.

Khrushchev's analysis of Kennedy's position, delivered to the departing German ambassador, goes thus: 'Kennedy cannot be the first to say, "I agree to take my troops from West Berlin." Why? Because Adenauer and de Gaulle would be against him. Kennedy is waiting to be pushed to the brink – agreement or war? Of course he will not want to go to war: he will concede. No rational being could but agree with us.' Fursenko and Naftali name this strategy 'détente through fear'.[8]*

Strategic parity is not Khrushchev's only motive. The question of US missiles in the neighbourhood of Russia is significant, though it is of a different order of importance. The Jupiter missiles in Turkey have been operational since May that year, 1962, when Khrushchev first raised the possibility of putting Russian missiles into Cuba. In making this suggestion he speaks of making Cuba into the Russian equivalent of Turkey or Italy (where there are more Jupiters). At other times Khrushchev talks of showing the Americans how it feels to be surrounded by hostile nuclear weapons. This is not the reason for putting the missiles on Cuba; but it provides another argument.

Finally, there is the defence of Cuba and of its revolution. This is much mentioned in correspondence, but it is not central. There is sympathy for Castro in Moscow, and recognition that the Bay of Pigs could be followed by a further attack. There are also attractions in having an ally so close to the United States; and it is better that Cuba is tied to Russia than close to China. These are good reasons for a defence agreement with Cuba. But none of them points to deploying nuclear weapons.

Excom discusses all these factors. At its first meeting General Maxwell Taylor, speaking for the joint chiefs, says that the missiles in Cuba

* Taubman adds, 'This was vintage Khrushchev. The missiles were meant to frighten, not to be fired.' (William Taubman, *Khrushchev*, p. 535)

represent a major change in the strategic balance. Robert McNamara argues against this. McNamara thinks in quantitative terms, and in quantitative terms he is right: the warheads in Cuba are only a small part of those available. Nevertheless, this is not the whole picture: the Soviet deterrent is inferior in both quantity and quality – many of its missiles can be destroyed before they can be launched. US intelligence suspects that Moscow's intercontinental capability is poor; Khrushchev knows it. McNamara does not persist with his argument that the missiles have no impact on the strategic balance; we may assume that he and others do not find it convincing. The point is that the nuclear weapons in Cuba are a significant new threat to the United States; they are a cheap way to change the military balance, and that is Khrushchev's main motive.

Berlin is also mentioned early in the discussions. Llewellyn Thompson, who has just returned from Moscow to become an adviser to the president, refers to leverage on Berlin as one of Khrushchev's motives for placing the missiles in Cuba. Berlin figured prominently in a five-hour conversation with Khrushchev before he left. A couple of months earlier, in July, Khrushchev sent a message to Kennedy proposing, yet again, to make Berlin a 'free city', and demanding that half of the Allied forces be replaced by troops from smaller NATO countries or the Warsaw Pact. His plan is to turn this into an ultimatum when his missiles in Cuba are operational and the United States feels under pressure.

As it turns out, Berlin is more discussed in Washington than in Moscow. It is natural, when Kennedy has decided on quarantine for Cuba, to ask whether it might trigger another Russian blockade of Berlin. But as the crisis develops it is the Soviet Union, not the United States, that feels under pressure. The Foreign Ministry, and Dobrynin in Washington, mention using Berlin as leverage to Khrushchev. But by this stage, this is the sort of advice he can do without: he has no intention of adding fuel to the conflict. One crisis at a time is enough.[9]

Excom discusses the Jupiter missiles in Turkey and Italy on and off. Kennedy has been aware of this question even before he became president. A note written during his campaign asks whether the Soviets might possibly use Cuba as a missile base, 'to counter ours in other countries?'.[10] McCone has suggested to the president that Khrushchev might justify siteing missiles in Cuba by reference to the US Jupiter missiles in Turkey. At the second meeting of Excom on 16 October, Kennedy says: 'Why does he put these there? . . . It's just as if we began to put a major number of medium-range missiles in Turkey. Now that'd be goddam dangerous, I would think.'[11] He is speaking ironically.* Two days later he mentions, tentatively, the idea of a deal: the United States might withdraw missiles from Turkey if the Soviet Union does the same with its Cuban ones.

Protecting Cuba as a motive for deploying the missiles is little discussed. Nuclear weapons in Cuba enhance Soviet security, but they do not do much for Cuba – the reverse, in fact: they make it a target. Soviet forces with conventional weapons – and this is what Castro wanted – might deter an American attack. Fighting Cubans is one thing; clashes with Soviet forces would be another. But when these forces look like a threat to the United States, rather than protection for Cuba, they become a liability instead of an asset. Arming them with nuclear missiles does exactly that. Castro himself understood this: he refers to his acceptance of the Soviet presence as an 'act of solidarity'.[12]

There is not much discussion of Khrushchev's personality, though it is a key factor; he has driven through the decisions on his own, and the whole policy reflects his constant, sometimes creative, search for magic solutions. Oleg Troyanovsky, a close collaborator, says that 'Khrushchev possessed a rich imagination, and when an idea took hold of him, he was inclined to see in its implementation an easy solution to a particular problem, a sort of cure-all. . . . [he] could stretch even a sound idea to the point of absurdity.'[13] Hubert Humphrey, meeting Khrushchev shortly before the crisis, summed him up neatly as 'a man who is defensive in an offensive way,'[14] which describes Khrushchev well, and his missiles too. However, trying to psychoanalyse foreign leaders thousands of miles away is not the best way to make policy. Kennedy's lengthy meeting with Khrushchev in Vienna has demonstrated that he

* Bundy, being cute, replies: 'Well we did it, Mr President.' He knows that Kennedy is aware of this. From start to finish Kennedy sees the missiles in Turkey as part of a possible solution. He is almost alone in this.

is capable of charm, but his preferred method of interaction is bullying.

Each side assumes the presence in the background of 'hardliners' on the other side, who are somehow manipulating the leader. Both are wrong. On the US side, Kennedy's advisers are overwhelmingly more hawkish than he is; but Kennedy makes up his own mind. In Moscow, Khrushchev himself is the origin of the whole mess. The only person who stands up to him is Mikoyan, who, at every stage, argues for caution.

The debate on the US side is about the use of force. Like almost everybody else, Kennedy's first instinct is to use force. But as the debate goes on, he grows conscious of the risks. Air strikes are unlikely to be 100 per cent effective. Invasion of Cuba – which has the merit that you can make sure you have destroyed all the missiles and warheads – involves problems of a different order. Both risk Soviet casualties and retaliation. The Excom debate resolves into a choice between, on the one hand, air strikes and/or an invasion; and on the other hand, a blockade.

The most determined advocates of immediate military action are the chiefs of staff and Dean Acheson. Acheson makes the case that delay – a blockade, that is – gives the Soviet side time to prepare the missiles for a strike on the United States. An immediate attack on the missile sites is therefore less risky than one that follows a failed blockade. He accepts that the Soviets may respond to air strikes by using force themselves, but he argues that they are more likely to use sub-nuclear options, for example, against missile sites in Turkey. Asked how the United States should respond to that, he suggests it would have to attack a missile base in the Soviet Union:

'Then what would *they* do?' By now Acheson is becoming a little less sure of himself. 'Well,' he says with some irritation, 'that's when we hope that cooler heads will prevail, and they'll stop and talk.'[15]

Those advocating the blockade are not excluding military action: to begin with, enforcing the blockade is itself a military operation. And the blockade is not a complete answer – it does not get the missiles out of Cuba. But it gives the United States some control of the situation; it shows a readiness to use force without doing so; and it gives the Soviets time to think. It does not, however, get rid of the missiles and has to be followed by an offer to negotiate, or an ultimatum.

Decisions

At the end of the debates the president concludes, on 20 October, that they have to take action. But he wants to give the Soviets time to pull back. Therefore, after five days of debate, he chooses blockade plus ultimatum. He announces the blockade and delivers the ultimatum in his TV broadcast on the evening of 22 October.* After describing the 'secret, swift and extraordinary' build-up of missiles he says: 'I have directed that the following steps be taken immediately. First: to halt this offensive build-up, a strict quarantine on all offensive equipment being shipped to Cuba is being initiated. All ships of any kind . . . will, if found to contain cargoes of offensive weapons, be turned back.'

He says (second) that US surveillance activities in Cuba will go on. If the military preparations there continue, 'further action will be justified. I have directed the armed forces to prepare for any eventualities.' And (third) 'any nuclear missile launched from Cuba will be regarded as an attack on the United States, requiring a full retaliatory response upon the Soviet Union'.

He announces military and diplomatic steps, including through the United Nations and the Organization of American States. He ends by calling on Khrushchev to halt the build-up and to eliminate the missiles from Cuba.

Just before the broadcast the Soviet ambassador is asked to call on Rusk, who tells him what the president will say and gives him a letter for Khrushchev – the first of a series that runs through the next week. Learning of the missiles in Cuba from the American side, Dobrynin asks why Kennedy did not raise them when he met Gromyko. Rusk does not reply, but the answer is that Kennedy did not want to mention

* Excom met from 17 October; to conceal the crisis Kennedy missed one day to fulfil a previous engagement.

the subject until he has decided how to respond. Later the next day, Robert Kennedy calls on Dobrynin; this becomes a regular channel of communication in the days that follow.

Kennedy's broadcast message is an ultimatum without a deadline: Kennedy is demanding immediate action. There is no offer to negotiate; but the exchange of letters with Khrushchev begins at the meeting with Dobrynin, and is a de facto invitation to dialogue.

Success has many fathers. Some accounts attribute the idea of the blockade to Robert McNamara, and make Robert Kennedy a strong advocate. Sheldon Stern* has shown, by a painstaking examination of the tapes, that the picture is more complicated. Almost everybody takes different positions at different times. Against immediate air strikes the analogy with Pearl Harbor, stressed by Robert Kennedy, has emotional resonance – though, as Acheson points out, the comparison makes little sense. The strongest argument for the blockade is made by McNamara, though he is by no means a consistent supporter. He makes the powerful point that the 800 sorties proposed by the joint chiefs† would kill thousands of Russians and Cubans, and 'The United States would lose control of a situation which would escalate to general war.'[16] That is what is on the president's mind when he decides for the blockade.

These are the core questions. The discussions in Excom also help sort out mundane but crucial practical issues: should the blockade extend to oil as well as weapons? No: this is about missiles and is not a general blockade (which might encourage retaliation against Berlin). Should the cargo of ships not crossing the blockade line, or leaving Cuba, be examined (an idea from Robert Kennedy)? No: this is about getting rid of missiles, not gathering intelligence. This is sensible: one of the reasons Khrushchev orders his ships not to cross the blockade line is that he does not want US agents examining Soviet technology. Will the blockading ships have Russian speakers on board? Arrangements are made for this. Should the blockade be accompanied by a declaration of war (suggested by George Ball from State and Llewellyn

* In *The Cuban Missile Crisis in American Memory*. The tapes do not, however, cover some of the early discussions in George Ball's conference room at the State Department.

† The US military also do things thoroughly.

Thompson)? No – Acheson says that 'the survival of states is not a matter of law'. This is in any case an odd proposal from people who want to avoid a war. Is Pearl Harbor preying on their minds again? The president ignores the suggestion of a declaration of war, but decides to call the action 'a quarantine' – which sounds less warlike than 'blockade'. What about allies? They are informed, not consulted – that includes the Turks much later when Kennedy decides to remove the missiles from Turkey.* When McNamara speaks of the need to hold the alliance together, Kennedy says that most of the allies regard Cuba as a fixation of the United States rather than a serious military threat; 'they think we're slightly demented on this subject'.[17]

Throughout the discussions it is the president who keeps the focus on getting rid of the missiles, and not using force except as a last resort.

The debate is often confused and contradictory. That is how it is when people are grappling with new situations. But it clarifies the issues, and Kennedy – in spite of his remark to Galbraith – gets value from it. As much as voting, debate reflects democratic practice. As a way of making decisions it compares well with the Soviet method. It also compares well with decision-making on the Bay of Pigs, where Robert Kennedy opened discussion at one National Security Council meeting by saying that the president had made up his mind and did not want to hear contrary opinions.[18]

Khrushchev decides not to challenge the blockade. Mikoyan reinforces this, outmanoeuvring Malinovsky to ensure that submarines also do not cross the blockade line. On 23 October he argues in the Presidium that Soviet submarines crossing the blockade line will be detected by the Americans. Malinovsky denies this. He repeats this line in the afternoon, when Mikoyan gets Khrushchev to raise the question a second time. That should have settled it; but Mikoyan raises it a third time, suggesting at the end of the session that they call in Admiral

* A partial exception is the British ambassador, David Ormsby-Gore, whom Kennedy consults as a personal friend. On 23 October he suggests shifting the blockade line closer to Cuba, so that confrontation does not take place during Moscow's night and the Soviets have time to reflect; Kennedy overrules US navy protests and does this. As far as the British government is concerned, Macmillan's attempts to insert himself into the solution fail (Percy Craddock, *Know Your Enemy*, pp. 179–90).

Gorshov, a specialist in submarine warfare. The Presidium meets again after dinner. Admiral Gorshov shows, with maps, the danger submarines would be in if they approach Cuba, winning the argument for Mikoyan and humiliating Malinovsky.

Mikoyan and Alexei Kosygin also persuade the Presidium that Moscow must keep control of all the nuclear weapons on Cuba, including battlefield weapons (the Lunas). Meanwhile in Cuba work continues to make further missiles operational – as Acheson has suggested it would. Khrushchev's decision to observe the blockade is not yet a decision to back down. He sends a letter about the illegality and unacceptability of the blockade ('Our instructions to Soviet mariners are to observe strictly the universally accepted norms of navigation in international waters').[19] His words – 'who asked you to do this? By what right did you do this?' – suggest exasperation, or perhaps that he is rattled. But his actions speak loudest. The ships turn round. Khrushchev also pulls William Knox, the president of Westinghouse Electric Corporation, who happens to be in Moscow, into the Kremlin for a three-hour conversation to explain that his missiles are not offensive: 'If I point a pistol at you, to stop you from shooting me, it is a defensive weapon'.[20] Dean Rusk's comment when the ships turn around, 'the other fellow just blinked' is correct, but the game is not yet over.

The next day, 25 October, Khrushchev, having taken the first step by accepting the blockade de facto, receives what seems a softer letter from Kennedy. It expresses regret at the deterioration in relations, and the hope that the Soviet government will take action to restore the earlier situation.[21] He also learns from Soviet military intelligence that US nuclear bomber forces are now on DEFCON 2, the threshold of nuclear war.* Khrushchev decides to settle for what he can get. The Presidium (as usual) agrees his proposal that he should offer to dismantle the missiles if Kennedy guarantees not to invade Cuba. Khrushchev

* Since 22 October US forces outside Europe have been on Defense Readiness Condition 3. This puts them at fifteen minutes' notice to move. The decision to go to DEFCON 2 is taken by the head of Strategic Air Command without political authority. He transmits the signal uncoded so that Soviet intelligence makes no mistake (Rodric Braithwaite, *Armageddon and Paranoia*, p. 328).

writes to Kennedy on the night of 25 October, making this offer. This letter[22], the most celebrated part of their exchanges, no. 65 in the FRUS series, will be discussed later.

Washington has not reacted to Khrushchev's letter when, the next day Moscow time, Khrushchev makes a broadcast in which he adds an additional demand: the removal of the missiles from Turkey. In Washington the events come almost simultaneously: the letter dictated by Khrushchev on the 25th has to be translated; it arrives late on the 26th. The next day, before they have considered it, they hear the broadcast. For once the president's advisers all agree: any deal involving the missiles in Turkey is a bad idea. Some worry about NATO, others think Khrushchev is in bad faith after proposing something different the night before. Most are tired after eleven days of continuous strain. All the advisers agree, but not the president. He cannot see why the United States should risk a nuclear war over the missiles in Turkey. They have no military value, and he has wanted to get rid of them for a long time. In a small group, Dean Rusk suggests they offer this as part of an agreement, but not immediately and not to be made public. Robert Kennedy speaks to Dobrynin, and this is the basis on which the crisis is resolved.

Of course, it is not as simple as that: in fact, nothing is as simple as this highly compressed account makes it. October 27 is both the day when the solution is found and also the most dangerous day of all.

Khrushchev's day is disturbed. After his broadcast, early in the day, he hears of a U-2 flight in the polar region that has strayed into Siberia. Both sides have scrambled planes in response, but no shots are fired. It ends safely, but this incident is a reminder of the risks that the state of tension brings.

More worrying is a message he sees from Castro. This seems to advocate a pre-emptive strike on America to forestall an invasion. Because of the pace of events he has forgotten about the Castro factor. The air is now full of rumours of an invasion – and the largest peacetime concentration of US forces is now taking place in Florida. That is not a rumour. The last thing he wants is for Castro to intervene.

Another event on this event-filled Saturday should also be mentioned, though none of the participants hear of it until later.

McNamara has persuaded the president to let the navy send 'signals' to Soviet submarines, by way of a small depth charge. The explosion nearby does not seem small to the captain of the submarine, Valentin Savitsky, who loses his cool: 'Maybe war has already started up there . . . We're going to blast them now. We will die but we will sink them all. We're not going to be the shame of the fleet.' He orders the weapons officer to fire the ship's nuclear-armed torpedo. By chance, this particular submarine carries the chief of staff of the submarine brigade, Vasily Arkhipov. He outranks the captain, and countermands the order. Instead, the submarine surfaces. Had the torpedo been fired it would have destroyed a US aircraft carrier and a number of support ships. No one can know what would have happened then. As it is, far from becoming the 'shame of the fleet', Arkhipov is recognised as a hero in the limited circle in Russia that knows of this incident. Acheson's 'plain dumb luck' was meant to apply to Kennedy's strategy – which he regarded as hopelessly weak – but it is appropriate here.[23]

A second incident is no less dangerous. One of the Soviet SAM batteries shoots down a U-2 plane.* The US air force has standing instructions to respond by destroying any SAM site that has fired on a US plane. The military do not respond immediately because they plan to attack several batteries. Kennedy stops the action. It is the last thing he needs, now that a solution may be in sight. When Khrushchev hears of the incident the next day he too is furious. He orders a stop on all firing of missiles; Soviet planes are grounded. Two days earlier Khrushchev has said to his son, Sergei, that once the shooting started there would be no stopping it.[24]

Now he calls together the Presidium and speaks of the need to settle things – recalling Lenin's decision to agree the Brest-Litovsk peace. He reads out a new message from Kennedy – the last of the series (no.

* The pilot of this plane, Major Anderson, was one of those who took the original reconnaissance photographs on 14 October.

67). This agrees the proposal in his long and personal letter (it makes no mention of the missiles in Turkey). While the Presidium is meeting the Soviet Foreign Ministry telephones with an account of Dobrynin's conversation with Robert Kennedy, including the 'highly electric' atmosphere and the pressure from the military to respond to the killing of an American airman. The Presidium agrees.

What should we learn?

The Cuban Missile Crisis was the last great crisis of the Cold War. In the years that followed there were moments of great tension, but nothing to compare with Korea, Berlin and Cuba. This was the only crisis directly about nuclear weapons, in which they were deployed on a war footing. Had the United States invaded Cuba early on, the Luna battlefield weapons could have been fired without authorisation from Moscow.

There is nothing inevitable about the happy ending. Until the last minute Khrushchev's behaviour is a textbook example of bad strategy. He does not think about the position of his adversary, what options he will have, how it will look to him, how he may react. He does not factor the relative strength of the two sides into his strategy – though his relative weakness is one of his reasons for adopting it. When Khrushchev decides to withdraw the missiles, it is because he does not want a nuclear war. He tells the Presidium it had never been his plan to unleash a war. All he had wanted was to threaten. Had he thought further, he would have understood that both sides would be losers in a nuclear conflict; but the Soviet Union would be the bigger loser – in so far as the concept has any meaning. McNamara's initial judgement that the missiles in Cuba did not change the balance was in that sense right. That did not mean that Kennedy wanted war; but it gave the United States more room to contemplate it.

Perhaps because of this calculation, or because the United States has no recent experience of war on its own territory, Kennedy is surrounded by people advising military action. He is the *only* high-level participant of Excom who consistently gives diplomacy priority.* Had Kennedy been the weak leader that Khrushchev imagined, he might have followed the advice of the brilliant men around him.

As for the lesson Kennedy learned, he commented later that 'the first advice' he would give to his successor was 'to watch the generals' and not to think that 'just because they were military men, their opinions on military matters were worth a damn'.[25] Vice-President Johnson was present, but largely silent at Excom; it is a pity he did not draw the same conclusion.

A practical lesson that both sides not only learn but also implement is the need for stricter controls on nuclear weapons. At the time of the crisis there are few technical controls on nuclear weapons; the decision to use them in 1962 could be made by the captain of an aircraft, a ship or an infantry unit. Technical locks or special codes existed in only a few cases. This is changed.

Kennedy set up Excom to examine the consequences of using force – his own first instinct when he heard of the missiles – and he encouraged an open debate. It was for this reason too that he refused to make the missiles public until he knew what he wanted to say. There was almost a week between Kennedy learning of their existence and his broadcast.†

The big lesson was the realisation that, thousands of miles apart, the two men in charge were in agreement in wanting to avoid conflict, but did not know it. Kennedy afterwards reflected that it was 'insane for two men sitting on opposite sides of the world to be able to bring an end to civilisation'.[26] The crisis was one of communication.‡

The bad communication was partly deliberate, notably on Khrushchev's side. Dobrynin lied unwittingly, having been kept in the dark by the Kremlin. Gromyko did not lie, but did not speak the truth either.

* Chuck Bohlen and George Ball took the same view, but Bohlen was involved only briefly and Ball was outranked by Rusk, his political master.

† *The New York Times* got hold of the story the day before Kennedy's broadcast, but was persuaded not to publish (George W. Ball, *The Past Has Another Pattern*, p. 296).

‡ As well as the difficulty of communication, in the deep sense of understanding each other, communication via coded messages is very slow. On both sides the most urgent messages are delivered in public broadcasts.

He spoke in platitudes in Kennedy's office on 18 October while he wondered if the folder on the desk might contain photographs of the missiles.[27]* Lying may be normal between states; but it is dangerous. If you don't believe people are speaking honestly, what is the point of talking to them? How can you reach agreements? Kennedy did not attempt to deceive, but the way the game was played, it did not allow him to tell the whole truth either. Had he said that he, personally, thought that war would be a disaster, it would have looked like weakness; and Khrushchev might have been tempted to continue the game of chicken. The problem is that the game has no rules. Khrushchev does not lie, but defining nuclear missiles as defensive is twisting things. They are more like a sword than a shield.

On the American side, Kennedy's television statement is cool and clear. The tone is of someone who expects to be obeyed. He underlines the secrecy of Soviet actions and their false statements: secrecy is a sign of bad faith. He sets out the steps the US government will take, beginning with the quarantine. He makes only one demand of Khrushchev: the ending and reversal of the missile deployment. Thereafter, Kennedy focuses exclusively on this. Kennedy's letters to Khrushchev are short and underline the US determination to see the missiles removed. To begin with, Khrushchev does not admit the existence of the missiles and argues instead that the quarantine is illegal. Kennedy just repeats his demand.

The key moment comes with Khrushchev's letter on the night of 25 October.† A *cri de coeur*, George Ball calls it. For Curtis le May, chief of the air force staff, it is 'a lot of bullshit'. McNamara is only a little more polite: 'twelve pages of fluff' and 'not a single word in it that proposes to take the missiles out'.[28] This is not true. The letter says that if the US government undertakes not to invade Cuba, then 'the question of armaments would disappear' . . . 'and the necessity for the presence of our military specialists in Cuba would disappear'. This is an offer of a settlement. The letter is repetitive but it is also personal

* It did not: they were in a drawer.

† This is when he dictated it. It arrived in Washington the next day and is dated 26 October there.

– the copy delivered to the US embassy has Khrushchev's handwriting on it. Some parts are as vivid as any diplomatic exchange in history. To help Washington understand, the KGB warns in advance of its message.[29]

Khrushchev opens by saying that continuing the exchange as before will not get them further. Then he adopts a new tone: 'We have always regarded war as a calamity, not as a game', and later: 'but if indeed war should break out, then it would not be in our power to stop it, for such is the logic of war. I have participated in two wars and know that war ends when it has rolled through cities and villages'.

Then follow passages where Khrushchev repeats the point he made to Mr Knox, about weapons not being, in themselves, offensive or defensive, and points from earlier letters about the illegality of the quarantine, and the threat to Cuba from the United States. The heart of the letter is that:

> the preservation of world peace should be our joint concern. . . . If people do not show wisdom, then in the final analysis they will come to clash, like blind moles, and then reciprocal extermination will begin.
>
> Mr President, we and you ought not now to pull on the ends of the rope in which you have tied the knot of war, because the more the two of us pull, the tighter the knot will be tied. And a moment may come when the knot will be tied so tight that even he who tied it will not have the strength to untie it . . .[30]

He ends: 'Let us take measures to untie the knot. We are ready for this.' This is personal, and powerful. The metaphor of the knot in the rope is a perfect image of their position: distant yet joined together, unable to communicate except by pulling the rope – and that makes things worse. This is the real Khrushchev speaking to Kennedy, not as the leader of a hostile power but as a kind of partner, joined by the knot they have to untie.

The record does not show how the president himself reacted. By this time Excom is exhausted and the letter is drowned out by the broadcast about Turkish missiles – but what Khrushchev is saying is exactly what has been going through Kennedy's head over the last days, powerfully expressed. With it the way to a solution opens.

By this time the White House has improved communication by involving Dobrynin. When Robert Kennedy sees him on the evening of the 27th he can talk about the calls for retaliation by the military after the U-2 has been shot down, and deliver the message that they will say nothing about the missiles in Turkey; but they will be removed in a few months. For different reasons neither of these points can go into Kennedy's letter. Such dialogue is more useful than trying to analyse letters – which are in translation – word by word, as they do in Moscow. There, they note for example that Kennedy's letter (no. 67) does not end, 'Sincerely yours' as earlier letters do, and assume something is amiss. In fact, this looks like an oversight.

Following the crisis Kennedy works on improving communication – with the first hotline – and on agreeing some rules. The partial Test Ban Treaty of 1963 is one of the results. If Kennedy had not been murdered and Khrushchev had not been ousted, there might have been more. It is right to see the Berlin agreements of 1971 as part of the longer-term result.* The same is true of the growth of the Soviet missile programme, and search for nuclear parity, and then for arms control with Nixon and Kissinger. Ten years later, the Helsinki Final Act starts on the road to confidence-building measures, and to openness in defence matters: if you can see missiles and verify where troops and equipment are, then the risk of a surprise attack is less. All of these trace their origins in part to the Cuban Missile Crisis. The most important legacy is that there were no more crises in the confrontational style of the first decade and a half of the Cold War.

These results flowed from the realisation that there was a mutual interest in avoiding a nuclear war. Out of this grew the gradual codification of rules for the nuclear age. The post-Cold War decline in fear and in respect for international rules is deplorable. Acheson may be

* The Tutzing speech in which Egon Bahr (and Willy Brandt) set out the bases of *Ostpolitik* begins by quoting the speech Kennedy made after reflecting on the Cuban crisis.

right that the survival of states cannot be subject to international law; but mutually understood codes of behaviour, treaties, transparency – all of these make the world a less dangerous place.

Who won? The common perception is that Kennedy and the United States did. But although Khrushchev did not get the magic solution to his problems that he sought, he finished better than he started. Cuba was given guarantees against invasion – condemned vigorously by Nixon at the time, but observed by the United States since; and the Jupiter missiles were removed from Turkey. These two results were Russian wins, though the United States lost nothing by either, except the chance for further folly in Cuba.

The sentimental answer is to say that everybody won. In this episode an ugly, impulsive, ageing Communist leader, risen from poverty in the Donbass, and a good-looking, cool-headed young man who became president though charm, brilliance and family money, found that they had more in common than either of them expected. The sentimental answer is also true.

But then, look again at Khrushchev's sentence about the rope, and note the personal pronouns: 'in which you [Mr President] have tied the knot of war . . . a moment may come when the knot will be tied so tight that even he who tied it [you, Mr President] will not have the strength to untie it'. Khrushchev is recognising that Kennedy is ready to risk war, and that he is the stronger – though that does not mean he will be strong enough to control events if war begins.

This is not a unipolar moment. The Soviet Union's aim now becomes to match the United States missile for missile – though they never quite succeed. They compete in the Third World, where the stakes are smaller and everybody loses; but the Soviet Union makes no further attempt to confront the United States directly.

In both capitals a single man is making the decisions. Their styles were different, but we are lucky that each had a sense of personal responsibility. This goes with office. Acheson was more cautious as secretary of state than he is as a part-time adviser. When he consults Congressional leaders Kennedy finds they also want to go to war. There is a gap between those who have responsibility and those who do not. Only Eisenhower seems to understand Kennedy's position. He says he will support him whatever he decides. Nor should we think of Khrushchev as the man who backed down. He also saved the world.

Henry Kissinger writes that the statesman must be an educator: 'he must bridge the gap between a people's experience and his vision, between a nation's tradition and its future'.[31] In public John F. Kennedy was a hawk, as the American public was; but he had personal experience of war, and had thought about the consequences of nuclear war. When it came to taking responsibility for decisions that could lead to a nuclear exchange he followed the advice he had noted two years earlier from a book by Basil Liddell Hart: 'Keep cool. Have unlimited patience. Never corner an opponent, and always assist him to save his face. Put yourself in his shoes. . . . Avoid self-righteousness like the devil – nothing is so self-blinding.'[32]

9

Henry Kissinger: Theory and Practice

Many diplomats write well on diplomacy; this is, after all, a profession of words. Often they do so in memoirs. Some, having come to diplomacy half by chance, leave it wondering that great issues of war and peace can rest on such accidental things as the personalities of a few men. Henry Kissinger is unique: he thought and wrote about diplomacy, and did so brilliantly, twenty years before he became the most important diplomat in the world.

We should imagine Kissinger returning from Europe in 1947, asking himself how the things he had seen there came about. It must have been a strange experience to go from interrogating Nazis in post-war Germany to studying at Harvard as an undergraduate. In his thesis he pursues the question that the wreckage of Europe brought to his mind: what difference can men make in history? Was the ruin of Europe inevitable, or were men responsible? His answer is that, yes, up to a point, men are masters of their fate. Then, his doctoral thesis looks at what diplomacy can do. For this he turns not to the failed diplomacy of 1914 or 1918–39 but to an earlier century, to the stability that the Congress of Vienna brought. He is looking for clues in the past to understand the present.

This is published in 1957 as *A World Restored*. As a book on diplomacy it is a great work, one where every page contains something to make the reader think. It is so filled with ideas that it is tiring to read. Kissinger is writing about the present as well as the past. That is clear, not just from the mention of nuclear weapons in the first sentence, but also in the larger theme he announces in the paragraphs that follow.

> Those ages which in retrospect seem most peaceful were least in the search for peace. Those whose quest for it seems unending appear least able to achieve tranquillity.
>
> Whenever the international order has acknowledged that certain principles could not be compromised even for the sake of peace, stability based on an equilibrium of forces was at least conceivable. Stability, then, has commonly resulted not from a quest for peace but from a generally accepted legitimacy.[1]

The French Revolution overturned the accepted order in Europe at the end of the eighteenth century. The heroes of *A World Restored* are the conservative statesmen Prince Metternich and Lord Castlereagh, who, for a time, brought order and peace to Europe.

The themes of his book are the intellectual framework that Kissinger takes with him, through his academic career and beyond into the Nixon administration.

First, the need for an order accepted as legitimate by the main actors: this is a precondition if diplomacy – the resolution of problems by negotiation – is to function. This does not mean that all problems are solved, nor that wars never happen; but there are limits to the problems, and limits to the wars.

A revolutionary power is one that rejects the existing order. International order cannot be separated from domestic order; so it is no surprise that when an ideological revolution overthrows a state, it may also seek to overthrow the international order. After 1789, governments in France drew their legitimacy from new sources, alien to their neighbours as well as to their predecessors. This kind of regime poses a problem different from that of an actor who is disruptive, like Louis XIV or Frederick the Great, but operates within the rules of the game as it is played at that time.

Revolutionary powers do not compromise. This was true of French governments after the revolution. Of these, Napoleon's was the most dangerous because it was the most effective. If revolutionary powers negotiate, it is not by the same rules or the same logic as others. Sometimes they do not play by any rules at all. Those who do not understand this risk falling into a trap – as Neville Chamberlain did.

Politics is about dealing with the future. Kissinger's third theme is that the statesman is the man who has an instinct for the future and who sees a path, somehow, to get there safely. The statesman's problem is that he is ahead of his people: all they know comes from their memory of the past and their collective experience of the present. If the statesman is to succeed, he has to find a way to take them with him. His challenge is to secure support for a vision of the future among an audience whose ideas are based on present experience and past myths. Castlereagh failed because he could not persuade the House of Commons of the need for continued involvement in Europe once the danger from Napoleon was gone. Metternich failed because his vision of legitimacy was no more than a continuation of Austria's present, understood by his people, but sure to fail in a changing world. Together, nevertheless, their efforts secured half a century of relative peace in Europe.

His fourth theme is that bureaucracy is the enemy of imaginative policymaking: 'for the spirit of policy and that of bureaucracy are diametrically opposed'.[2] Bureaucracy longs for the safe, the familiar and if possible the routine; policy for the future must be creative and will be based on intuition and conjecture. Castlereagh's struggle was not with bureaucracy in the twentieth-century sense,* but with the Cabinet; however, the point still applies. Castlereagh's intuitions about the future came from being on the spot; this gave him insights not available to those in London, especially insights into people. Liverpool and the Cabinet wanted a policy based on facts, not on intuition; but Castlereagh was right.

A final, recurring theme is the importance of intangible factors. 'It is the essence of mediocrity that it prefers the tangible advantage to the intangible gain in position', writes Kissinger, in praise of Metternich's view that security was based on relations between states and

* In Britain the struggle against Napoleon was exactly the moment when bureaucratic government, in the Weberian sense, first began to take shape. See Roger Knight, *Britain Against Napoleon*.

not territorial holdings.[3] In the same vein, Kissinger comments on the Cabinet's reaction after Waterloo, when Castlereagh called for moderation in dealing with France: 'An impotent enemy is a fact, a reconciled enemy a conjecture. . . . It is no accident that the advocates of "absolute security" always have popular opinion on their side. Theirs is the sanction of the present, but the statesman must deal with the future.'[4]

The search for absolute security, expressed in quantitative terms as the disarmament of a defeated country rather than through the intangible quality of reconciliation, may produce the opposite of the result intended by turning the defeated country into a revolutionary power that seeks to overthrow the whole system.

Kissinger has Versailles in mind. Throughout *A World Restored*, as he writes on the nineteenth century he is thinking about the twentieth: the failure to confront revolutionary fascism in the 1930s – the age that longed too fervently for peace – and the challenge of revolutionary Communism in the post-war world.

The proof of this comes in his article in *Foreign Affairs*, 'Reflections on American Diplomacy'. This appears in October 1956, a few months before *A World Restored* is published in Britain. Kissinger's article applies the lessons he has drawn from Metternich and Castlereagh to twentieth-century America. The attack on bureaucracy, an aside in the book, becomes a larger theme in the article. Here and there we find phrases he has taken directly from *A World Restored*: 'A statesman who too far outruns the experience of his people will not be able to sell his programme at home; witness Woodrow Wilson. A statesman who limits his policy to the experience of his people will doom himself to sterility; witness French policy since World War One.' The same sentences appear in *A World Restored*,[5] except that instead of 'Woodrow Wilson' the first sentence ends 'witness Castlereagh'; the second, 'witness Metternich'.*

* Kissinger might have written 'witness Clemenceau'; perhaps he feared American readers might not know who he was. Seeing the parallels between people from different ages with personalities as different as Metternich and Clemenceau, Wilson and Castlereagh, is a piece of Kissinger brilliance. *A World Restored* stayed with Kissinger all his life; another echo comes in his summing-up of Nixon's achievement in *Years of Upheaval*, almost thirty years after the original.

The article makes explicit what the reader of *A World Restored* will have guessed: that when Kissinger writes of revolutionary powers he is thinking of the Soviet Union.

> There can be little doubt that we are living through a revolutionary period . . . And the Soviet bloc, eager to exploit all dissatisfactions for its own ends, has given the present situation its revolutionary urgency. . . . we have been reluctant to take at face value the oft repeated Soviet assertion that they mean to smash the existing framework.[6]

Kissinger's message is similar to George Kennan's in the Long Telegram: that it is a mistake to think that the West and the Soviet Union speak a common diplomatic language, or that they can do business in a normal way.

What *A World Restored* does not offer is an answer to the question of how diplomacy can deal with a revolutionary power. In the Nixon administration Kissinger had to deal with three different revolutionary powers; so the question is of importance, the more so since one of them is a nuclear power.

We do not know whether Kissinger, as he wrote *A World Restored*, dreamed of high office. He puts himself so well into the shoes of Metternich and Castlereagh that he must have imagined it. It is a series of accidents, personal and historical, that lead him to think about diplomacy at all. No other US secretary of state has a background or career as remarkable as that of Henry Kissinger.

The refugee

Heinz Kissinger is born on 27 May 1923 to respectable Jewish parents in the town of Fürth in northern Bavaria. His father is a teacher at a state-run girls' school, a respected profession in provincial Germany. With the Nazi seizure of power and the Nuremberg decrees, he loses this position. Heinz Kissinger and his younger brother, Walter, have to change their school and their friends. In 1938 his mother arranges for the family to emigrate to the United States, saving all their lives. In New York the family lives the precarious life of refugees: his mother cleans houses and Henry, as he now is, works in a shaving-brush factory, going to school after work. New language and new life notwithstanding, he excels at school and enters New York City College, where he studies accountancy, also at night, for two years until in 1943 he is called up into the US army.

The army and the war change Kissinger's life. They bring separation from family and integration into American life, as they do for many other draftees and refugees. More unexpectedly, they bring wider intellectual horizons. These come through Fritz Krämer. Krämer is a German of the old school, honourable and well educated. He has chosen exile in the United States out of hatred for the Nazi Party, and is a volunteer in the US army. While Kissinger is training at Camp Claiborne in Louisiana, Krämer addresses his regiment about the political and moral stakes of the war. He does so wearing a German uniform and a monocle, to get the audience's attention. It is the lecture, not the uniform, that catches Kissinger's imagination and he writes to Krämer, expressing appreciation and offering help. The letter is nothing special, but Krämer does not receive many letters from conscripts. He meets Kissinger and sees in him a potential that no one else has recognised. Krämer becomes a mentor who helps and inspires him for many years to come, and who awakens Kissinger's interest in history and political philosophy.

In war, young men find themselves with responsibilities they would never have in peacetime. In Camp Claiborne Kissinger's visible intelligence brings him the job of company education officer, continuing the political education of the troops begun by people such as Krämer. When his division is sent to Europe in November 1944 Kissinger begins as a rifleman on the front line, but then becomes a counter-intelligence officer, attached to divisional headquarters. Initially his job is to interrogate German prisoners. Then, when the division enters Germany, it is to identify Gestapo officers and other threats to the US military. In the course of this he encounters first-hand the results of Nazi rule, including concentration camps and their victims. A letter to his parents from this time describes the survivors of the concentration camps and shows how quickly a twenty-two-year-old can mature in wartime:

> But having once made up one's mind to survive, it was necessary to follow through with a singleness of purpose, inconceivable to you sheltered people in the States. Such singleness of purpose broached no stopping in front of accepted sets of values, it had to disregard ordinary standards of morality. One would survive only through lies, tricks, and by somehow acquiring food to fill one's belly. The old, the weak had no chance. . . . The survivors are not within the ordinary pale of human events any more.[7]

The Counter-Intelligence Corps is an elite body. Most of its members are non-commissioned officers, but they have authority that goes far beyond their rank. (And a lifestyle too: Kissinger has five domestic staff plus guards.) Kissinger's day-to-day work is to collect intelligence, mostly through informers, to sift evidence, to interrogate witnesses and suspects. Some of those he identifies will be imprisoned; some may be executed. His work is also about the administration of a large area of Germany – for example, will Herr X be reliable as the chief of police?

Letters to his parents reflect a sense that his duty is to act in a spirit that respects the United States' democratic values. He has a team of sixteen to assist him. In 1946, when he leaves this work to lecture at the Intelligence School established by Krämer in Oberammergau, he has experience of power and responsibility such as many men much older than twenty-three never acquire. He knows how to operate in a (military) bureaucracy and how to exercise authority. He has a reputation for thoroughness, toughness and efficiency. For a young man whose background is a brush factory and studying accountancy at night school, this is a new life.

When Kissinger is considering what to do next, Krämer, who has doctorates from Frankfurt and Rome and who recognises Kissinger's intellect, encourages him to set his sights higher than the College of the City of New York. Kissinger applies to Columbia, Princeton and Harvard. Harvard offers him a scholarship. Kissinger takes with him not only his experience in Germany, but also one of Krämer's themes, the primacy of the moral over the material – of the intangible over the tangible.[8]

As an undergraduate in the Department of Government, Kissinger is guided by William Elliott – to whom he dedicates *A World Restored*. His undergraduate thesis on the philosophy of history, at close to 400 pages, establishes a Harvard record.* Its subject, whether individuals can make a difference in history, is a question that comes naturally to someone who has himself played a small part in a great historical drama. His doctoral thesis takes up the same question but in a more concrete fashion, through a study of the statesmen who made peace following the Napoleonic Wars. After this, some suggest that he should join the History Faculty; but though the period of *A World Restored* is in the past, its subject is not history but politics and its purposes, including its moral purposes.

While working on his PhD, Kissinger runs the Harvard International Seminar. Elliott lends his name, his contacts and his support, but it is Kissinger who does the work, including the fundraising. The seminar brings an elite group of young foreigners to the United States and exposes them to the best that it has to offer in the academic and political world. Today such programmes are common, but at this time the seminar is unique: its participants are hand-picked and the programmes are tailor-made, both largely by Kissinger. Participants include the young Yasuhiro Nakasone and Valéry Giscard d'Estaing; among the speakers are the secretary of state, Christian Herter, and Eleanor Roosevelt. The seminar, supported indirectly by the US government, is one of the first ventures into the Cold War as an intellectual competition: soft power four decades before the term is invented.

Kissinger, his doctoral thesis finished and still attached to Harvard (though neither tenured nor elected to the Society of Fellows), becomes director of a study group on nuclear weapons organised by the Council on Foreign Relations. This puts him in the middle of the most

* After this Harvard establishes the 'Kissinger rule', setting a limit on the length of undergraduate dissertations.

important debate of the times: it takes him into the world of policy and politics, introduces him to Nelson Rockefeller, who he advises over the next ten years, and stimulates him to write his first bestseller: *Nuclear Weapons and Foreign Policy*, published in 1957. This has the merit of ease and clarity of expression. Its readership includes Richard Nixon. Kissinger gains attention and notoriety – for his argument that a limited nuclear war is conceivable, and that the United States should therefore acquire smaller warheads for tactical nuclear exchanges. His friend Thomas Schelling argues that it is a fantasy to think that a nuclear war, once started, could be controlled, a view that Kissinger himself later accepts. The book is part of the process of collective thought that leads to the doctrine of flexible response. Kissinger becomes an advocate, though he remains sceptical of easy answers; later in life he is sometimes quoted summarising flexible response as 'First we lose the conventional war; then we lose the tactical nuclear exchange; then we blow up the world.'

The most important point in his book, however, is that the nature of nuclear weapons makes diplomacy more, not less, important. This, as the next fifteen years demonstrate, is surely right. It is therefore not quite fair of Peter Sellers to model his appearance in the title role of Dr Strangelove on that of Dr Kissinger.*

The commentator

In the decade that follows, Kissinger establishes himself as a respected and readable commentator on foreign policy. Hamilton Fish,† the editor of *Foreign Affairs*, considers him the most original thinker in the field; and Kissinger has (to this day) more articles in its pages than any other author.

Kissinger is not a natural member of the Kennedy circle, not least because he is a conservative and in the orbit of Nelson Rockefeller.

* As Niall Ferguson points out, the character of Dr Strangelove (as opposed to the hair-style) is based on Wernher von Braun or Herman Kahn, not on Henry Kissinger.
† Hamilton Fish commissioned George Kennan's 'X' article. See Chapter Four.

McGeorge Bundy, who is close to Kennedy, has been elected to the Harvard Society of Fellows on the strength of his reputation at Yale, and becomes Dean of Harvard. He is a brilliant teacher and administrator, but he never does work of the distinction of Kissinger's.* In spite of the Rockefeller connection, Kennedy offers Kissinger a role in the White House. After discussion with Bundy he settles for a part-time consultancy. This is a mistake: part-time doesn't work in Washington. Perhaps he is manoeuvred into this position by Bundy, who may not want a sharp and original rival in a front-line role. For a brief period Kissinger is actively involved in work on Berlin, including discussions with Adenauer and Franz Josef Strauss. Kissinger's contribution is intelligent but marginal to the policymaking process. Foreign policy is made in day-to-day decisions; it belongs, therefore, to those who are there every day and have access to the president, not to part-timers. This may be the most important lesson Kissinger draws from the experience.† Although the venture into Washington is a failure, Kissinger's reputation as a policy intellectual grows; his seminars are packed and his stream of publications on Cold War subjects continues. His comments on the issues of the day are original and pertinent, witty but also serious.

Later, half by accident, he does significant work for the Johnson administration on Vietnam. It is now 1965, and the new assignment comes at the suggestion of George Lodge, a professor at the Harvard Business School and the son of Henry Cabot Lodge, then the US ambassador in Saigon. Kissinger jumps at the chance to see what is happening on the ground in Vietnam. Vietnam is now the number-one

* Of Bundy Kissinger writes: 'I admired his brilliance even when he put it, too frequently, at the service of ideas that were more fashionable than profound. . . . He tended to treat me with a combination of politeness and subconscious condescension that upper-class Bostonians reserve for people of, by their New England standards, exotic backgrounds and excessively intense personal style . . . Had he lived in a less revolutionary period . . . Bundy would have moved through high offices of government until his experience matched his brilliance and his judgement equalled his self-confidence' (*White House Years*, pp. 13–14). This comment is well observed; but, for once, there is also a hint of payback.

† Kissinger's appointment may have been the result of Konrad Adenauer having heard of *Nuclear Weapons and Foreign Policy*. He invites Kissinger for a talk, in the course of which the former predicts the Sino-Soviet split – prescient in 1958. Later Adenauer recounts the conversation to Kennedy, drawing his attention to Kissinger.

issue in US foreign policy, and the first doubts are beginning to surface. Even Bundy may be starting to share them. He welcomes Kissinger's support for the administration's policy – vanishingly rare at Harvard in the 1960s.

Kissinger takes leave of absence from Harvard. Before going to Vietnam he talks to all the officials, civilian and military, that matter, from Robert McNamara down. In Vietnam, too, he gets unlimited high-level access; but he spends time with soldiers on the ground as well as with generals in headquarters, asking sharp questions of them all. None of the answers he hears suggests a realistic plan to win the war. Part of Kissinger's assignment is to look at the prospects for negotiations; but he says almost nothing on this subject when he returns, having concluded that any proposal to negotiate would undermine the government in Saigon. Instead his report tells what he has seen: the ineffectiveness of US military and civilian programmes and the bureaucratic tangle surrounding them. There is too much focus, he says, on outcomes that can be 'expressed numerically', not enough on more important 'intangible qualities'. This echo of *A World Restored* is an acute observation on the United States' failure in Vietnam.[9] The analysis is penetrating, but it does not say how the problem is to be solved.

Kissinger visits Vietnam again the following year (1966), and hears General Westmoreland repeating exactly what he said the year before: give him more troops and he will win the war inside a year. Now he has the troops he asked for the previous year; but he is making just the same demand and the same promise.[10] Sceptical about the war effort in private, Kissinger continues to support it in public. He believes that a retreat from Vietnam will be damaging internationally. An article he writes in *Look* magazine on 8 June 1966 refers to the 'Impossibility of Withdrawal' and 'The Inevitability of Negotiations'. But the latter will make sense only if Hanoi's control of the countryside is reduced – and his analysis does not suggest there is much prospect of this.

Kissinger's involvement on the margins of Vietnam policy is completed by a diplomatic non-event in the summer of 1967. A Pugwash

Conference* in Paris that he attends decides to send a delegate, Hermann Marcovitch, to Hanoi with a message proposing negotiations. Marcovitch takes with him a friend, Raymond Aubrac, who knows Ho Chi Minh personally. Kissinger tells Dean Rusk and McNamara about this. Rusk is dismissive, but McNamara – who is beginning to despair of victory – urges that the opportunity be taken seriously. Marcovitch and Aubrac return from Hanoi in July with an apparently positive response. This suggests that secret talks between North Vietnam and the United States could begin quickly if the latter pauses its bombing of the North.

McNamara takes this sufficiently seriously that he and the president agree instructions for Kissinger; and at his next meeting with Marcovitch and Aubrac, Kissinger is joined by a US official. Their message from Hanoi turns out, however, to have been the high-water mark of hope, and by October the North Vietnamese consul general in Paris is refusing to receive Marcovitch and Aubrac. Kissinger concludes rather late that he has been taken for a ride.†

With that, Kissinger's involvement with the administration ends. In 1968 he works on Rockefeller's campaign for the Republican nomination. His contribution includes a plan to end the Vietnam War by negotiation. Rockefeller's campaign is doomed: he is yesterday's man; his money for advertisements is no match for the work Richard Nixon has put into winning over the delegates, one by one, for a period of years.

National security adviser

Nixon wins both the nomination and the election. One of his first appointments is Henry Kissinger as his national security adviser. Is it

* The Pugwash Conferences brought together scientists and political scientists interested in reducing the risks of the Cold War through disarmament.

† Niall Ferguson's conclusion (*Kissinger 1923–1968*, pp. 753–82) is that Hanoi was stringing Kissinger and Washington along while it prepared the 1968 Tet Offensive. McNamara's account of the episode ends with the reflection that it paved the way for the peace talks initiative of 1968 (*In Retrospect*, pp. 259–303). The formula on the bombing pause used in 1968 may come from the Kissinger episode, but not much else.

strange that Nixon chooses someone he has hardly met as the sole executor of his foreign policy? Perhaps, but Nixon is a strange man. It is not strange, however, that he chooses Henry Kissinger. By this time Kissinger is the leading man in the field, visible in print and on TV. He is also a conservative, not part of the liberal chorus on Vietnam.

Nixon invites Kissinger to his suite at the Pierre following his election victory and discusses foreign policy with him. Kissinger is impressed by Nixon's grasp of the issues. Nixon, who is shy and fears rejection, does not make it clear that he is offering him a job. It is only two days later that Kissinger learns from John Mitchell, who is acting as Nixon's chief of staff ('Jesus Christ, he screwed it up again'), that the president-elect meant to offer him the job of national security adviser. Taken by Mitchell to see him a second time, Nixon emphasises his distrust of the State Department and the CIA, and his wish to run foreign policy from the White House.

Nixon has read some of Kissinger's articles, as well as *Nuclear Weapons and Foreign Policy*. He may be aware that Kissinger dislikes bureaucracy in foreign policy as much as he does.* Kissinger is a Harvard professor; that might make him a member of the East Coast establishment that Nixon resents – but the establishment also regards Kissinger as pushy. And he is Jewish. So, like Nixon, Kissinger is an outsider. He is enough of an American to know that things do not come to those who sit and wait. He has been in touch with the Nixon team in the final phase of the campaign, with warnings of a deal between North Vietnam and the Johnson administration for a bombing pause and negotiations. This information, from people Kissinger knows from his work on Vietnam, is the kind of intelligence that those out of office and deprived of official sources value. Thus his summons to meet Nixon is not as much of a surprise as *White House Years* suggests.[11]

In spite of their different backgrounds, Nixon and Kissinger have a lot in common. Kissinger is not just a professor. He has been an

* In 'Domestic Structure and Foreign Policy', for example, *Daedelus*, vol. 95, no. 2 (Spring 1966). Kissinger's views, however, go back to *A World Restored*: 'For the spirit of policy and that of bureaucracy are diametrically opposed. The essence of policy is its contingency . . . The essence of bureaucracy is its quest for safety' (p. 326).

army intelligence officer and has interrogated Nazis. His instinct for power has developed through this experience, and has been refined by work in Washington – including being frozen out by Bundy. His intuition that foreign policy requires a creativity rare in a bureaucracy has been confirmed by his real-world work in Vietnam. Like Nixon he believes that problems can be solved by negotiation, and like Nixon he sees negotiation as a way of exercising power. Executing Nixon's policies needs someone ruthless in bureaucratic politics. Kissinger is the man: he cuts out all competitors, starting with Richard Allen, Nixon's foreign-policy adviser during the campaign. Allen makes sure that he is appointed as Kissinger's deputy by Nixon personally. But Kissinger makes sure in return that he gets almost no access to Nixon. After an interval Allen resigns.[12]

When Nixon announces Kissinger's appointment, he says that his national security adviser 'is keenly aware of the necessity not to set himself up as a wall between the President and the Secretary of State'.[13] In practice that is exactly what he becomes, and also what Nixon wants.* Bill Rogers, the secretary of state, is a decent man, but he contributes nothing to policy. It is a strange way for Nixon to treat an old friend.

Kissinger expects in any case that Nixon will be his own secretary of state. For this reason he has advised Rockefeller that secretary of defense would be a better job than secretary of state. This prediction does not need great insight: Kennedy chose Dean Rusk as secretary of state for this reason; and Nixon is more expert in foreign affairs than either Jack or Robert Kennedy.[14]

When Nixon asks Kissinger at their first meetings for a memorandum on the structure of government, he means one that excludes the people he distrusts – the East Coast establishment in general and the State Department in particular. The organisation proposed by Kissinger and agreed by Nixon gives the president control of decisions, and his national security adviser control of the options put to the president. Kissinger may dislike bureaucracy, but he certainly knows how it

* Hanhimäki quotes Peter Rodman, a Kissinger student and long-term associate: 'Nixon's doing. Henry didn't object, obviously.' (Jussi M. Hanhimäki, *The Flawed Architect*, p. 25)

works.* All advice to the president goes through him. Less than six months into his presidency Nixon stops holding regular meetings of the National Security Council – too many papers, too many participants, too many leaks. Instead, decisions are taken in dialogue with Kissinger. For the sake of form, stage-managed meetings of the National Security Council ratify the most important decisions. This brings a concentration of power greater than in any other post-war administration.[15]

The use of 'back-channel' diplomacy conducted by Kissinger and kept secret from the secretary of state and his department takes this system one step further. It also corresponds to Kissinger's views on the conduct of diplomacy; but it is Nixon who initiates the system, telling the Russian ambassador, Anatoly Dobrynin, at their first meeting, that 'all matters of special sensitivity' should be taken up first with Kissinger – who will tell him whether or not others, for example the State Department, should be involved.[16]

And what about policy? Kissinger's 3,500 pages of memoirs cover everything in detail – more detail than any other diplomat has ever given. This chapter will focus on four big themes: the Soviet Union, China, Vietnam and the Middle East.

The Soviet Union

Kissinger arrives in office with a vision not just of US policy, but also of world order. He has written that a new administration 'must recognise that, in the field of foreign policy, we will never be able to contribute to the building of a stable and creative world order unless we first form some conception of it'.[17]

Of his predecessors, only John Foster Dulles might have thought in such terms. What Dulles did in practice was to follow the Truman-Acheson line, with added rhetoric. Nixon signals a change of course. In his inaugural address he calls for 'an era of negotiation . . . Let all nations

* Under the old system the State Department chaired the committee that identified the options. They complain. Nixon ignores them; Kissinger points out that the committee in question hardly met.

know that during this administration our lines of communication will be open'. This echoes Kennedy's 'Let every nation know . . . that we shall pay any price, bear any burden, meet any hardship', but it speaks instead of negotiation: a striking message from the arch-Cold Warrior. Not so stirring, perhaps, but the United States is in the middle of the Vietnam War and is tired of paying the price and bearing the burden.

The relationship between the United States and the Soviet Union will be at the heart of any world order. Kissinger wants to go beyond containment – a policy suited to dealing with a revolutionary power – and instead create a relationship where differences are handled by negotiation.

During the transition Nixon and Kissinger agree on three principles to govern détente: *concreteness*, meaning that they want real agreements on real issues, not diplomatic fluff; *restraint*, because détente between the superpowers would not survive attempts to exploit crises for unilateral advantage; and *linkage*. The last attracts most attention: it means that the relationship should be seen as a whole. If the Russians want movement in one area they should be ready to give something in another. This idea is as old as the hills, but in Kissinger's view it has been lost in a bureaucracy where experts handle issues one by one, 'on their merits'. Everyone studies the trees; no one sees the wood. Comprehending the relationship as a whole needs someone who surveys the entire field, and holds all the threads in his hand. At his first National Security Council meeting, Nixon announces that he will be that person. He follows this up in a letter to Secretary of State Rogers, stressing that 'we must . . . make clear that we see some relationship between the political and the military'.[18] This means linking arms control, which the Soviets are thought to want, to other issues. What is unsaid is that this means Vietnam.

It starts slowly. Nixon and Kissinger don't want to be seen to be in a hurry; and the Russians are sceptical about Nixon, guided by his reputation as the toughest of the Cold War hawks. Talks on the limiting of nuclear weapons (SALT – Strategic Arms Limitation Talks) have been agreed under President Johnson but postponed because of the Soviet invasion of Czechoslovakia in 1968. They finally start in late 1969, a year after Nixon's election, delayed first by the United States and then by the Soviets.

This is the right moment for arms control: political, military and technical developments all come together. The Cuban Missile Crisis gave both sides a political shock, and they want to reduce risks. Cuba made the Soviet side conscious of their relative inferiority and they have spent the time since then catching up, so that in 1969 they are approaching parity with the United States in missile numbers. Technically, satellite technology now means that each can now monitor missiles without intrusive inspection or U-2-style violations of airspace.

The complexity of these negotiations is formidable. The negotiators must balance numbers of missiles and warheads – the United States is developing multiple independently targeted re-entry vehicles (MIRV) – sizes and capabilities of different missiles, land-based missiles and those carried by bombers or submarines, and perhaps also missiles or bombers owned by allies.

The most important of the new technologies are the anti-ballistic missile (ABM) systems. Negotiations on these are less complicated. But the arrival of defensive systems poses a fundamental question. Is the purpose of the negotiation unilateral advantage? Or is it stability?

The answer is, both. The job of negotiators is to get the best deal for their side: that means you try to finish with more missiles than the other side.* On the other hand, this is the moment both sides are beginning to think that it may be desirable that their adversary does not feel threatened. This is less evident with the Soviets, who are the weaker party. But they are now beyond Alexei Kosygin's reaction at the Glassboro Summit Conference in 1967, when he told Johnson and McNamara that: 'Defence is moral; aggression is immoral.'[19] Now the Soviets want to ban missile defences, or at least to limit them. On the US side, Nixon's defense secretary, Melvin Laird, goes further and

* This recalls a conversation in which Defense Secretary Robert McNamara is said to have asked Curtis LeMay, then head of the US air force: 'Supposing there's a nuclear war, who would be the winner?' Instead of treating this as a rhetorical question LeMay answered literally: it would be whoever was left with more missiles (Michael Dobbs, *One Minute to Midnight*, p. 267).

welcomes submarine-launched missiles as a component of the Soviet deterrent; these are the least vulnerable to a first strike. Both sides are starting to see a common interest in strategic stability.

Nixon and Kissinger add an extra layer of complexity in Washington by negotiating through a back-channel between Dobrynin and Kissinger ('the Channel', Kissinger calls it). This is asymmetrical. In Moscow, Dobrynin works with the whole Soviet machine: his instructions are cleared by the Politburo. In Washington Kissinger writes his own instructions, using a small staff in the White House, cutting out the State Department, the Pentagon and the US SALT delegation in Vienna/Helsinki.* Arms control needs a team of experts. No one would believe that one man could do it all.

Not if the man is Kissinger. Seymour Hersch, not otherwise an admirer, records: 'His staff watched in awe as Kissinger, in a dramatic show of brilliance and determination, spent hundreds of hours in the first months of the administration mastering the technicalities of arms-control negotiations. By mid 1969 he seemed to be the best-informed and most forceful voice on SALT.[20]

In most diplomatic negotiations a point comes when a back-channel is needed. Negotiations have to be confidential because an agreement can be sold only when it is complete. If the concessions proposed by one side become known without the quid pro quo of the other side, the deal will be dead before it is done. Usually, agreement is reached only when both sides have gone through their 'red lines'. They need, therefore, to do this together. Thus, within the normal confidentiality of negotiations, a further layer of secrecy is needed when important moves are made. Perhaps the two negotiators go for a 'walk in the woods' together.† Woods are a good place, because they are likely to

* The venue alternates.

† The phrase comes from another set of US-Soviet arms-control negotiations, in Geneva in 1982, about intermediate-range nuclear missiles. The US negotiator was Paul Nitze. When the negotiations neared breakdown, he and his Soviet opposite number took a walk together and agreed that they would each propose a new compromise to their capitals, going some way beyond their current positions. The US side found the ideas interesting, but Nitze's Soviet colleague never got a response from Moscow and the negotiations broke down. An agreement on the elimination of this class of missile was reached five years later after Mikhail Gorbachev came to power.

be free from bugs of the electronic variety. Or there may be direct contact between the offices of heads of government. But almost certainly, at some stage the ideas that bring the solution will be tested informally, unofficially and secretly.

What is unusual in this case is that, on the US side, the back-channel takes over the whole process. Nixon's distrust of state, Kissinger's belief that bureaucracy is fatal for diplomacy, his and Nixon's wish to keep all the threads in a single hand, and their joint wish to share the credit with as few people as possible: all of these contribute. This method delivers an agreement, and at the right moment for Nixon's re-election campaign. But it has undesirable side-effects. Sharing credit builds support; freezing others out makes enemies. When Kissinger agrees with Dobrynin that the two sides will work for simultaneous agreement on ABM systems and limits on offensive weapons – the standard solution when two sides are insisting on different priorities – Nixon deals with the problem of breaking the news to Bill Rogers, who has been told he is personally in charge of the negotiations, by telling him that the proposal came in a private letter from Brezhnev. This is a direct lie. Kissinger is more honest with the head of the official delegation, but the result is to alienate a number of loyal officials.

Another charge is that, for all his personal brilliance, Kissinger makes mistakes that a more thorough process would have avoided. Kissinger has a small and overworked staff. He uses the National Security Council committees as a sounding board to explore options – without telling them that this is the purpose of their discussion. Kissinger is right that bureaucracy often fails at creativity because its main goal is to avoid error. But if you cut it out, then you risk making errors.

The most important error concerns submarine-launched missiles. The evidence suggests that Kissinger, having accidentally left these out of his proposal, solves the problem by offering the Soviets limits so generous that they cannot refuse. The US navy is then bought off by promises of expensive programmes to counter what the Soviets are now allowed to build. Kissinger's most credible critic, Raymond Garthoff, who was deputy in the US delegation, argues that because of this, arms limitation brought more rather than fewer missiles.[21] Kissinger's reply is that 'Hell hath no fury like a bureaucrat scorned', and that 'those who are excluded from the ebb and flow of negotiation feel free to give expression to a fantasy of negotiation in which all the concessions are made by the other side'.[22] Garthoff cannot prove that a better deal could have been achieved. But nor can Kissinger show that his was the best of all possible deals, or that it could have been negotiated only by the methods that he and Nixon used.

Other evidence also suggests that SALT accelerated rather than slowed the arms race. After the Moscow summit, Defense Secretary Laird insists that the Pentagon will support the agreement only if Congress agrees new programmes: cruise missiles, the Trident missile, the B-1 bomber – bombers and cruise missiles are outside the agreement. Admiral Zumwalt, chief of navy operations, comments: 'The fact was that it was the unconscionable numbers in the SALT agreements themselves that virtually froze us into five more years of high spending'.[23] The numbers also speak for themselves: in the decade following 1972, the Soviets produced 4,125 ICBMs to the 929 of the United States (and even then they never felt they achieved strategic superiority).[24]

A second complaint (unprovable but credible) is that the coverage of the agreement might have been wider. For example, anti-satellite weapons might have been included. This was not a top priority, but it is easiest to ban new technologies at the conceptual stage, and before they have been funded. More bureaucracy might have helped.

Despite these flaws the SALT agreements are a breakthrough. The ABM and SALT agreements were something new in relations between the superpowers; they promised stability and strengthened the prospects for peace.

These two agreements should be looked at together with a third, 'The Basic Principles of Relations Between the United States of America and the Union of Soviet Socialist Republics', signed on the last day of the Moscow summit. In the Soviet Union, an ideologically based regime, ideas matter, and so does this document. The United States, preferring the practical and the concrete, sees it as a routine piece of diplomatic prose. For most of the US side it comes as a surprise. It is agreed by Kissinger on a secret visit to Moscow before the summit, and is seen by nobody else except Nixon. Kissinger's main concern with the paper is how to handle Rogers, from whom it has been concealed.

One of the principles in this document is that of 'equal security'. Some commentators see this principle as reflecting the Soviet wish to be regarded as equal to the United States. This is indeed a Soviet obsession; but the phrase is really about the interdependence of security in a nuclear age. The ABM and SALT agreements are designed to ensure not so much equal security as equal insecurity – mutual vulnerability and therefore a common interest in avoiding conflict.*

The term 'historic' is overused – especially by Nixon. But the SALT and ABM agreements are indeed something new. They are not the first agreements in the nuclear field: the ban on nuclear tests in the atmosphere was signed in 1963, the Treaty on Non-Proliferation in 1968. But these are the first limits on weapons systems since the naval agreements of the inter-war years, and the first ever on nuclear weapons. The Nixon-Brezhnev agreements accept interdependence and make stability a goal; for a world that has spent twenty years in fear of nuclear war, this is new and important. For two superpowers that still think of themselves as locked in a fundamental conflict, it is remarkable.

This is expressed in the Basic Principles in the phrase 'peaceful coexistence'. The inclusion of this piece of Communist jargon is seen as a triumph by the Soviet side. It does not mean that the ideological competition is at an end, only that it will be pursued by non-violent means. To US critics the wording seems a concession. In fact, it stands for the end of a piece of Marxist doctrine: the thesis that war between capitalism and Communism is inevitable. In Europe, though not necessarily in the Third World, the Soviet Union is announcing that it is no longer a revolutionary power.

Nixon, Kissinger and the Soviet leadership too are all conservatives. This could be an opportunity for Kissinger and Nixon to build an international order based on a common conception of legitimacy. For this the SALT and ABM agreements and the Basic Principles would

* The SALT agreements had a higher profile; but the foundation of détente was the ABM treaty. Missile defence has remained a crucial question in East-West relations ever since.

be a starting point. This is the logic that Kissinger describes on the first page of *A World Restored*.

In retrospect it seems that all the stars were aligned for the Moscow summit. The two superpowers are approaching parity in nuclear weapons; and the level of their holdings is approaching absurdity. Both have economic reasons to reduce spending on arms, or at least to slow the growth of their defence budgets. (So it is a pity that SALT did the opposite.) In the Soviet Union peace is a popular cause – the generation in power still remembers the war. Brezhnev, who has won political authority by suppressing the Prague Spring, now makes himself almost untouchable by being the first Soviet leader to sign an agreement with the United States. On the US side the Vietnam War has created a new public mood. Bringing China into the equation gives the Soviet Union an incentive to come to the table at a time when the United States is in difficulties and it might have been more natural to play a waiting game.

Nothing happens just because the conditions are right. Sovereign states are designed for competition and conflict, not for agreement. The machinery of foreign affairs and defence is organised around the assumption of hostility and duplicity on the part of other states; and domestic politics gives no prizes for being nice to foreigners. Even when a compromise is good for your country, you still have to prove that you are the winner. This is especially true of the United States, which expects to win every time. The forces that have to be overcome to reach agreement should not be underestimated. That Nixon and Kissinger get so far is remarkable. It is also not a surprise that détente does not last.

The Moscow summit that saw the birth of détente is also its high point. For a further seven years relations with the Soviet Union remain more cordial than they have ever been before – until the Soviet intervention in Afghanistan in 1979. But after Moscow, the difficulties begin; and they grow until détente is overwhelmed.

Some of the blame belongs to Nixon and Kissinger. Secrecy is needed in negotiation. But if détente is to be sustained it will need support. Nixon must have known that; Kissinger, who has written eloquently of how Castlereagh (and Wilson) failed by getting too far ahead of public opinion, knows it too.

It would have been especially useful to secure the endorsement of the defense secretary and the chiefs of staff. Kissinger admits that

> In retrospect it would have been better to have brought both [SALT] delegations to Moscow . . . Given Nixon's feelings about who should get the credit, I doubt if he would have agreed if I had proposed it. We could never know because I did not put forward the idea, not uninfluenced by vanity and a desire to control the final negotiation.[25]

The wider the circle of people involved in policymaking, the more experts there are to defend it. Détente and arms control take government into problematic territory – the normal rule is that one cannot have too many weapons; it is therefore important to have authoritative voices in support, including from the military. Handling an inherently bureaucratic subject in an autocratic way is a mistake. Kissinger himself accepts that his system could not be sustained, even in the context of a normal second term.[26] For all the talk of linkage, arms control was the heart of détente; it needed to be done well and explained widely.

The breakthrough in arms control is also undermined by the failure of the other two components. The most visible of these is in the trade dimension. Apart from trade in agricultural products (the 'great grain robbery' according to the press), the centrepiece of economic détente is the settlement of the Soviet Union's Lend-Lease debts and the return to a normal trading relationship, misleadingly known as 'most favoured nation' (MFN) status. Alongside this, the United States offers credits to restart trade. Unlike the SALT agreements, these require Congressional approval. Senator Henry Jackson holds the package to ransom. He disapproves of détente, and he is thinking of running for the presidency. His proposes that MFN status should depend on the Soviet Union easing the conditions on Jewish emigration, making a point about human rights and attracting support from the Jewish lobby, uniting, as Kissinger notes, 'the conservatives who hated Communism and the liberals who hated Nixon'.[27]

Jackson's initial demand is for the Soviet Union to drop its 'education tax' on emigrants; this supposedly reimburses the state's investment in its citizens. The Soviet government agrees to this, and Kissinger tells Jackson in April 1972, before the Moscow summit, expecting that the problem will end there. Wrong: Jackson then sets targets for Jewish emigration that the Soviet Union must meet before the commercial treaty is ratified. When it looks likely to allow 45,000 to emigrate, Jackson raises the target to 60,000.

Senator Jackson adds further amendments as he goes along, notably a ceiling of $300 million for credits by the US government. Given the Soviet Union's lack of hard currency, credits are essential to launch a trading relationship.[28] Senator Jackson has counterparts in the Soviet Union who believe it is wrong to do business with class enemies; against them, the industrial lobby's wish for access to Western capital and technology provides support for Brezhnev.[29] When the Trade Act finally passes in December 1974 the Soviet Union makes it clear that it does not regard it as reflecting what was agreed at the Moscow summit. It stops repaying its Lend-Lease debts, cancels purchases of wheat and recalls its ambassador in protest. Western Europe fills the gap. It offers $10 billion in credits and makes its own trade agreements. Jewish emigration, meanwhile, falls from its 1973 peak of 35,000; by 1975 it is down to 13,000.

Détente is more contested in the Soviet Union than Kissinger imagines. Brezhnev faces opposition on arms control from some parts of the military. His personal authority matters, and trade is one factor that helps him build support. Senator Jackson's attack is aimed at the core idea of détente, that different systems can do business together, 'peaceful coexistence' in Soviet language. The Soviet Union does not like being given orders on domestic affairs. This, together with the miserable credit ceiling, makes the Congressional version of the trade agreement too much to swallow. Summits come and go; arms control has its ups and downs; but trade, once started, can go on for a long time and help sustain a relationship in difficult times.

The third component of the failure of détente is relations in the Third World. Kissinger and Nixon insist to each other, and to Dobrynin, that arms-control agreements must be accompanied by co-operative conduct in other areas. One of the Basic Principles sets this out:

> The United States and the Soviet Union attach importance to preventing the development of situations capable of causing a dangerous exacerbation of their relations. . . . Both sides recognise that efforts to obtain unilateral advantage at the expense of the other directly or indirectly are inconsistent with these objectives.[30]

This is almost exactly the same as the Nixon-Kissinger 'principle of restraint'. But it is hardly discussed, much less put into practice. In Third World policy the United States makes no attempt at co-operation: rather the reverse.

The opening to China

After the victory of Mao Zedong's revolution over the US-sponsored Nationalists, the United States and China cut themselves off from each other. And China cut itself off from the world. Revolutionary zeal on one side matched the McCarthy frenzy on the other (see Chapter Five). Neither Eisenhower nor Kennedy nor Johnson tried to reverse this. Richard Nixon, the respectable face of McCarthyism, seems the least likely person in the world to change it.

In fact, the opening to China is his idea. Most of the Nixon-Kissinger policies are jointly conceived, but not this. Returning from Vietnam in July 1969 on the presidential plane, Kissinger comes back from a conversation with Nixon and says to 'Bob' Haldeman, the White House chief of staff: 'You know, he seriously intends to visit China before the end of the second term! Fat chance!'[31] Nixon is from the West Coast: unlike Kissinger, he knows Taiwan and Japan and sees foreign policy in Pacific as well as Atlantic terms.

In spite of his comment, Kissinger has already set work in hand on China, and is recommending some small gestures towards Beijing. The tensions in Sino-Soviet relations are already visible to China-watchers:

armed clashes are taking place on the River Ussuri. To begin with, Kissinger's interest is from a Cold War perspective. Chip Bohlen and Llewellyn Thompson, former ambassadors to Moscow, warn Kissinger against using China against the Soviet Union. He replies that he envisages nothing so crude. In fact, his consistent aim is to have better relations with each than they have with each other – which amounts to the same thing. Given how bad their relations are, this is not difficult.

At Nixon's initiative, the United States takes some small steps: trade and travel restrictions on China are eased; naval activity in the Taiwan Strait is reduced. And attempts are made to start a dialogue. The first attempt is through Romania. Nixon goes there in August 1969, the first time that a US president visits an Eastern European capital. He chooses Bucharest because the Romanians have treated him well out of office, but also because Romania has good relations with China. In a speech there Nixon refers, for the first time, to China as 'the People's Republic', and talks to Nicolae Ceauşescu about the possibility of Bucharest acting as a channel to Beijing.

Next, Warsaw. This is where US-China problems have been handled in the past, through contacts between ambassadors. Kissinger has the US ambassador approach the Chinese chargé d'affaires, who jumps out of his skin. The Cultural Revolution is still going on, and small missteps can have big personal consequences. In February 1970, at a formal meeting in Warsaw, the US side mentions the possibility of sending a special envoy to Beijing, but the Chinese do not respond. In Paris also – where China has a resident ambassador – the Americans drop hints, but without result.

At just the same moment the Chinese also are trying to signal a desire for contact. They release some American detainees, who might otherwise have been held indefinitely. In October 1970 they send what is intended to be a more public message by inviting the journalist Edgar Snow, an aged 'friend of China', to join Mao in Tiananmen Square reviewing troops on the Chinese national day. They give Snow a personal message from Mao for Nixon, saying that he will be welcome in China in whatever capacity he cares to come. This is exactly the wrong way to contact Nixon. Snow is regarded in Washington as a half-crazy socialist; he knows no one at all in the administration and fails to deliver the message.

The approach that bears fruit is through Pakistan. The process is laborious: the Pakistani ambassador in Washington takes written messages personally to Islamabad. There they are passed to the Chinese ambassador, who sends them to Beijing. The reply comes back to Washington by the same route in reverse. The message that finally produces a response is taken personally by President Yahya Khan himself. He sees Nixon in autumn 1970 and then meets the Chinese premier, Zhou Enlai, in Beijing. The reply arrives in December. It is a standard Chinese statement demanding the withdrawal of US forces from Taiwan as a condition of a meeting.

The content doesn't matter. This is the first contact in forty years between the White House and the Chinese premier. Kissinger sends a response saying that a US-China meeting can cover a range of issues, including Taiwan.

The Chinese reaction to this comes four months later, in April 1971. It is softer on Taiwan, saying full relations can be restored only when US forces have been withdrawn; but it does not make this a condition for the visit. It adds that the question can be discussed with Nixon himself or with an envoy in Beijing: in effect, an invitation to visit. On 10 May the US reply is handed over to the Pakistani ambassador in Washington, proposing a visit by Kissinger and stressing that this should be kept secret. The Chinese message has mentioned Kissinger as a possible envoy; probably he has fed this thought to the Pakistani ambassador.

According to Kissinger, the original plan had been to use someone other than himself; Nixon makes a show of considering alternatives – David Bruce, Nelson Rockefeller, Thomas Dewey (Kissinger reminds him that Dewey is dead). Kissinger is the obvious choice: he is Nixon's man and no one knows Nixon's mind as he does. A Chinese invitation to Kissinger arrives in June, twenty-two months after the effort to make contact began.

Why does it take so long? This question has two parts: why the forty-year gap? And why does it end at this particular moment?

The Chinese government is an excellent specimen of a revolutionary power in the Kissingerian sense. It has triumphed through a popular revolt, led by the charismatic Mao Zedong. It blames the miseries of the last 100 years on imperialist powers, and puts the United States at the head of its list. It stands outside the normal world order. And by mutual consent its relationship with the United States is negligible. US citizens and diplomats remaining in China at the time of the revolution were treated as enemies, i.e. very badly indeed. On the US side the fantasy that the United States, rather than Chiang Kai-shek, lost China, takes over; and the separation becomes mutual and absolute. The Korean War, Stalin's decision rather than Mao's, reinforced hostility on both sides and also helped ensure that the Taiwan question remains unresolved.

Through the 1950s the Soviet Union, the only foreign country that Mao ever visited, was China's model. Modernisation was based on the model of the Soviet Union in the 1930s, terror included. Under Khrushchev the Soviet Union became the first country to meet the 0.7 per cent of GDP target for foreign aid, all of it going to China. But Mao still saw himself as the leader of anti-imperialist forces. He resented Soviet advisers, as aid recipients often do. Hubris became megalomania in the Cultural Revolution, and then paranoia as China provoked clashes on the Soviet border.

The action that establishes Brezhnev's authority in Moscow is the crushing of the Prague Spring in 1968. In Beijing, still in the throes of the Cultural Revolution, these events are seen in a different light. The Brezhnev doctrine, that the Soviet Union has the right to act against deviant socialist countries, is a threat to China. Fears of a Soviet attack, even a nuclear attack, are sufficiently real – or paranoia is sufficiently strong – that parts of the government move out of Beijing. The Soviet Union encourages these fears, on the theory that intimidating the Chinese will make them behave better.[32]* It is at about this time that Soviet diplomats in Washington are asking how the

* This method echoes Khrushchev's theory – on which the Cuban missile deployment was based – that threatening the United States will encourage détente.

United States would react to an attack by the Soviet Union on China.

Against this background Mao commissions a study of the international situation by four retired field marshals, led by Marshal Chen Yi, a comrade from the Long March. They report to him in September 1969 that 'It is necessary for us to use the contradiction between the United States and the Soviet Union in a strategic sense and to pursue a breakthrough in Sino-American relations.'[33] The Chinese Foreign Ministry quails at such ideas (bearing out Kissinger's views on foreign ministries). But Chen Yi insists. By coincidence, it is at roughly the same time that Nixon is telling his Cabinet colleagues that it is not in US interests that China should be 'smashed' in a Sino-Soviet war.

Thousands of miles apart, China and the United States, opposite in every other way, are thinking the same thoughts. But it still takes persistence for Nixon and Kissinger to get their meeting. And why at that particular moment? The answer is partly happenstance.

In April 1971 the International Table Tennis Championship is coming to an end in Nagoya. Earlier in the week one of the US team has asked the Chinese why they are not invited to the tournament in China that follows the championship in Japan. This provokes a flurry in the Chinese Foreign Ministry. Zhou advises Mao against any change of plan. Mao has approved this recommendation, but he is sick at the time and one of his nurses tells him of another incident in Nagoya.

Glen Cowan, an American player with hippy-length hair, boards the Chinese team bus in Nagoya by mistake. Against all instructions not to fraternise with the American team, Zhuang Zedong, the world champion, speaks to Cowan through an interpreter and gives him a silk scarf. Having nothing with him to give in return, Cowan looks for Zhuang the next day and gives him a T-shirt with a peace symbol and the words 'Let it be' on it. Mao, who is at this stage permanently ill, hears of this exchange from his nurse, and reverses his decision ('Zhuang Zedong not only plays good ping-pong but knows how to do diplomacy too').[34] He instructs the Foreign Ministry to invite the Americans to Beijing.

The team ask their embassy minder what to do. He, half remembering a Nixon speech that is positive on China, tells them to accept; so they go to Beijing. (The embassy minder goes home to check that his advice was correct, wondering if his career is still intact.) Zhou Enlai makes sure the American team is well treated and that the visit – the first by any US organisation since 1949 - gets big coverage in the US media.

It is after this series of accidents that Zhou sends his reply to Nixon's message on 21 April. In *White House Years* Kissinger describes the ping-pong incident as 'vintage Zhou Enlai. Like all Chinese moves, it had so many layers of meaning that the brilliantly painted surface was the least significant part'.[35] In fact the decision is Mao's, and it is partly the product of chance.

The decision to make contact is a big one for both sides. No lobby in the United States is calling for a change of policy; many would have opposed it had they known. Neither Kennedy nor Johnson has looked at this, even though they were under growing pressure in Vietnam. If they had thought about an opening to China, they would have hesitated because of the savage attacks it would have attracted from Nixon. Nor does China look like a useful partner: its invective against US imperialism is non-stop; diplomats in Beijing during the Cultural Revolution risk having embassies burnt down like the British, or being spat on like the Soviets. At the UN the People's Republic will soon have enough votes to take the Chinese seat in the Security Council; but this is not what is on Nixon's mind. He wants to be seen as a peacemaker, a man with a global vision. The hope that China might somehow help the United States get out of Vietnam is an unspoken motive.

As they begin to look at the idea, the thought of playing China off against the Soviet Union becomes increasingly appealing. For once the secrecy makes sense, not just because of the media sensation the announcement makes, but because, if rumours get around, the Taiwan lobby will mobilise against it. The Chinese do not understand the US wish for secrecy – but in China everything is secret anyway.

The Chinese difficulty is that it is a genuinely revolutionary regime that has been denouncing US imperialism for thirty years; and the United States is fighting an imperialist war on China's borders, a war where China itself has been involved since before Dien Bien

Phu.* On the other hand, China is now threatened by the Soviet Union; this is mostly its own fault, but that does not matter: it is alone with a powerful enemy on its borders.

Without the initiative from the United States, nothing would have happened. When it comes, the Chinese tell themselves that the United States is making contact because of its weakness. This is true as far as Vietnam is concerned; but it also reflects Chinese ignorance of the United States and of the world. In Chinese eyes, however, the arrival of a US president in Beijing is public proof that China is the stronger party. Meanwhile the Chinese leadership believe that the United States is aligning itself with the real revolutionary power (China) against the Soviet Union, which has abandoned the revolution. There is some truth in this, but also some irony: within ten years China will abandon the revolution too, and it will do so as a result of the opening to the United States. But at this moment the Chinese decision requires a large effort: it grows out of strategic need but is also based on a misreading of world affairs. Such a big decision is inevitably accompanied by false starts and delays.

The message arrives in Washington on 27 April. Kissinger is about to go on holiday, but the Pakistani ambassador insists on coming to see him. Zhou Enlai's reply to the US message (sent three months earlier) proposes a public visit by a special envoy, or the secretary of state, or even the president, as the United States wishes. Kissinger finds Nixon and reads the message to him. Of all their moments in the White House, this is perhaps the most exciting. Two and a half years into the presidency they know that something is going to happen which will not be forgotten.

The secret visit to Beijing by Kissinger is well told by Kissinger himself:[36] a fake stomach upset in Islamabad, a fake convalescence in Yahya Khan's hill-station retreat, a flight across the Himalayas in a Chinese aircraft into what, in diplomatic terms, is unknown territory. Kissinger enjoys the cloak-and-dagger arrangements that enable him to dupe the

* The French defeat that brought the Communist Viet Minh to power in 1954 and ended the First Indochina War.

press, the rest of the US administration and every other government in the world. It is a last great success for secret diplomacy.

The reason that, even at an interval of fifty years, interest focuses on the mechanics of the visit rather than its content is that there is little content. Kissinger is in Beijing from 9 to 11 July, roughly forty-eight hours. Aside from questions about Nixon's visit not much practical business is done. Kissinger's priority is to establish a relationship with Zhou Enlai. They discuss global affairs, 'a conversation', Kissinger says, 'whose easy banter and stylized character, as if it were a dialogue between two professors of political philosophy, nearly obscured . . . the penalty of failure'.[37] In fact, having gone so far, the idea of turning back in failure is unimaginable for both sides. Both profit: domestically it is a stunning success for Nixon; internationally it shakes the Soviet Union and gets Nixon the Moscow summit he wants. For the Chinese, in the short term – which is all that they have in mind – the new relationship gives them security against threats from Moscow, real or imagined. In the longer term, after the death of Mao in September 1976, it changes their country and the world in ways that none of the decision-makers could foresee.

For the United States there are costs in relations with others in Asia, but these are small change. Foreign ministries all over the world go into shock on 15 July, when Nixon announces that Kissinger has been to China and that he is going there himself the following year. Taiwan and Japan feel betrayed. The Japanese ambassador in Washington resigns. But they all get on with the new reality. The Japanese embark on the commercial relationship with China that they have long dreamed of; Taiwan redoubles its lobbying in Washington to preserve as much as it can of its relationship with the United States; in time it builds its own complicated relationship with Beijing.

Kissinger goes to China again in October to prepare for Nixon's visit. The agreeable dialogue on world affairs continues; but the most time is spent on the communiqué that the two sides will endorse at the end of Nixon's visit. Zhou Enlai proposes, sensibly, that on difficult issues the two sides should not pretend to agree but instead use the statement to set out their different positions. In theory this should make drafting easy, since the bulk of the communiqué does not need to be agreed.

In practice, in spring 1972, when the visit is under way, it turns out not to be so simple: the United States cannot put its name to a document including the full Chinese anti-imperialist rhetoric. For the Chinese every word on Taiwan matters, even if it is in a statement of the US position. The first half of the problem is easily solved; but negotiations on the Taiwan language – supposedly a unilateral statement by the United States – take twenty hours of word-by-word discussion between Kissinger and Qiao Guanhua, Zhou's man in the Foreign Ministry: two hours for each line. Kissinger passes the result to Nixon, who has no problem with it. Not so Rogers and the State Department: even today the language on US ties in the region (this is how they get round the question of Taiwan) looks odd. Only Japan and South Korea are mentioned: nothing about the Philippines, Thailand, Australia. Probably someone from State could have helped get it right. Kissinger, in his memoirs, says that Nixon was against this; we can assume he was too.

The communiqué has two short paragraphs about trade and people-to-people exchanges. Kissinger delegates these to Rogers, as matters of secondary importance: 'We both know they don't mean anything,' he tells Zhou, 'there will be little impact in the real world.'[38]

The visit is seen on TV by millions of Americans. It leaves a mark on history and on public opinion. Both matter to Nixon, especially in an election year. Communiqué and photographs apart, the visit has little content. On such occasions diplomats often say that the visit is more important than the talks; for once this is true. By the end, Nixon is bored with the Chinese and the sightseeing.

Kissinger is not. His admiration for the Chinese in general and for Zhou Enlai in particular is striking. His memoirs are full of flattering portraits of the people he deals with.* Zhou tops them all. He

* Sir Michael Howard, reviewing *White House Years* in *The Times Literary Supplement* on 21 December 1979, wrote: 'Dr Kissinger's ink is quite unmixed with acid. Everyone he had to deal with were honourable men. Even his stubborn detractors in the media and academe he treats in sorrow rather than in anger. Whether this is because Dr Kissinger does not want to make unnecessary enemies at this stage of his career, or because he has absorbed at least the tedious blandness of American camaraderie in which everyone is a lovely person and all geese are swans, or because he is simply a warm-hearted and generous man, the reader must judge for himself.'

has suffered and survived; his upbringing has left him the middle-class virtue of courtesy, and his experience has given him patience and time to reflect. The Chinese people share Kissinger's respect. But Zhou is still subject to Mao's every whim.

Kissinger's admiration for China is even more remarkable. Here is a country whose domestic policies have brought a series of disasters and whose foreign policy has left it with no friends – so that it has to seek help instead from its enemy. But for a diplomat it is new and exciting. Kissinger finds the Russians crude, the Japanese boring, the Europeans tedious. The Chinese are exotic and powerful. He handles them more softly than anyone else, notably on Taiwan (Margaret MacMillan describes his approach as 'obsequious'). He explains the US position, apologetically, as a problem of public opinion. Meanwhile he deluges the Chinese with secret intelligence about Russian weapons and military deployments. The Chinese give nothing back.

Mao tells the Vietnamese that Kissinger is 'a university professor who knows nothing of diplomacy'.[39] Talking to Hanoi, Mao has reason to downplay the new relationship with the United States – they are in competition with the Soviet Union in Vietnam; but it is also possible that the Chinese see Kissinger as a soft touch. Later Mao describes him to Kim Il-Sung as 'a bad man' who used China to get better relations with the Soviet Union. That is only half true: his objective is not improved relations, but to get the better of the Soviet Union.

Kissinger returns regularly to China. He has further interesting conversations with Zhou. Nothing comes of them, except in a limited way on Vietnam, where Chinese interests coincide with those of the United States. The immediate purpose of the Nixon visit is to shake the Soviet Union, and to help Nixon and Kissinger get what they want in Moscow.*

But we should not reject Nixon's grander ideas of the visit as a

* One case where the relationship with China could have been useful but was not is in the seizure of the *Mayaguez*, a US container ship, by the Cambodian Khmer Rouge government shortly after it takes over. The United States has no relations with the new government; the Chinese are its sponsors. They could have helped with negotiations, but do not – and the United States does not press them. Instead, several US Marines are killed in a botched military operation.

step towards world peace, vague and sentimental as this sounds on first hearing.

The opening to China is a world-changing event, above all for China. It begins the Chinese retreat from revolution. It matters that it takes place while Mao Zedong is still alive. That makes it easier for Deng Xiaoping later when he wants to remove the revolutionary element in foreign and domestic policy at the same time. Nixon and Kissinger did China a service by starting the process.

Vietnam

Henry Kissinger is remembered for the opening to China, for détente and the beginning of nuclear-arms control with the Soviet Union, and for his shuttle diplomacy in the Middle East. In office, the issue that consumes both Kissinger and Nixon is the war in Vietnam. This accounts for 500 pages of *White House Years*. Kissinger ends the book with his initialling the agreement on 'Ending the War and Restoring Peace in Vietnam'. Then, he says, he was at last at peace with himself.

Nixon and Kissinger have thought about Vietnam before taking office. It is not their personal priority – neither wants Vietnam to take over foreign policy as it did under Lyndon Johnson – and both are more interested in the grand strategy of the Cold War. But Vietnam is the priority of the American people. Nixon has found that he gets the most applause in his election campaign when he promises to end the Vietnam War with honour. By the end of the campaign he has dropped the preceding sentence on the war being 'vital to America's strategic interest', which gets no applause.[40]

The big scare of Nixon's election campaign comes when Johnson announces that Hanoi has agreed that the negotiations in Paris can include the government of President Thieu, provided the United States stops bombing the North.* This is read as a sign that peace may be at

* In theory, Vietnam was a civil war; so Hanoi's readiness to negotiate with the Saigon government was good news for those who wanted to end it.

hand; with it the opinion polls give Hubert Humphrey his first lead over Nixon. (It is at this moment that Kissinger makes contact with the Nixon campaign.)

The scare does not last. Thieu refuses to go to Paris; and the last-minute effort at negotiations ends up looking more like an election stunt than a breakthrough. Nixon makes mischief by offering to go to talk to Thieu in Saigon if he wins.[41] There is no doubt about it: the 1968 election has been about Vietnam, and Nixon has promised peace with honour.

Nixon has no plans for ending the war. The nearest he comes to one is his commitment to train and equip Vietnamese forces, so that US forces can be phased out. He does not want to be the first president to lose a war. The war is about control of South Vietnam, so peace with honour means peace with the South Vietnamese government intact – not very different from peace with victory.

Kissinger has seen the war at close quarters. He writes an article in 1968 that offers many notable insights.* On guerrilla war, for example: 'A guerrilla war differs from a traditional military operation because its key prize is not control of territory but control of population.' This is now a classic formula. '[C]ontrol of population' includes intimidation; but it can also mean owning an idea that mobilises people – national self-determination. Kissinger underlines the importance of such intangible factors in assessing power; these are less measurable than the 'body-count' numbers that the Pentagon collects, but more important.

On the nature of the war Kissinger writes: 'We fought a military war; our opponents fought a political one. We sought physical attrition; our opponents aimed for psychological exhaustion. . . . [we] lost sight of one of the cardinal maxims of guerrilla war: the guerrilla wins if he does not lose; the conventional army loses if it does not win.'

This Kissinger aphorism is also received wisdom today. The point is to win the politics. For Kissinger this means negotiation. But it is not the nineteenth century, and this is a civil war. The politics that matter

* It appears in *Foreign Affairs* in January 1969, just after Kissinger has joined the administration.

are domestic politics in South Vietnam. Foreigners, especially foreign armies, are temporary; they can win battles, but not political loyalty.

After this forensic analysis of US failures in Vietnam, Kissinger dissects Johnson's attempts at negotiation. It is problematic to make a bombing pause conditional on the talks being 'productive' – not a benchmark anyone can measure objectively; but the real difficulty is that restarting the bombing would cause domestic uproar. It is also awkward to make a ceasefire the goal of negotiations in a war fought by irregular forces. At the heart of it all, however, is the disconnect between the political and the military: 'our diplomacy and strategy were conducted in isolation from each other', whereas Hanoi 'does not view war and negotiations as separate processes'.

Kissinger's analysis of the war is based on his own observation. He has no personal experience with Hanoi; so it is understandable that much of what he says about the North is wrong. It is true that the North 'could not continue the war without foreign material assistance', but Hanoi's problems in manoeuvring 'between Beijing and Moscow' are not as difficult as he suggests. Hanoi is playing the same game with the Communist giants as he is: it is encouraging them to compete – in the Vietnamese case - in support of a revolutionary cause. He describes the Soviet invasion of Czechoslovakia as a 'major setback for Hanoi'; on the contrary, it deepens the Sino-Soviet split and so works to Hanoi's advantage.

Kissinger is also wrong in the subtlety he attributes to Hanoi's negotiating methods. The politeness of Southeast Asians can mislead those unfamiliar with the region: Southeast Asians can also be stubborn and violent. Perhaps he is misled by his encounters with Vietnamese in the South, men such as Bui Diem, Prime Minister Ky's clever collaborator. South Vietnamese officials live in a semi-colonial world and are used to manoeuvring between American and Vietnamese generals. Kissinger has not yet met the very different men of Hanoi, whose iron discipline defeated the French.

Above all, it is wrong to say that negotiations are inevitable: 'We are so powerful that Hanoi is simply unable to defeat us militarily. . . . Since it cannot force our withdrawal it must negotiate about it.'

Kissinger's article itself makes the case for the opposite view. Military strength alone does not bring victory: for the United States, not winning means losing. In the next four years the United States will withdraw unilaterally. The negotiations ease the path of withdrawal; they do not cause it. He is right that 'our military strength has no political corollary: we have been unable . . . to create a political structure that would survive . . . after we withdraw'.

He is wrong to say that the United States' world role makes withdrawal impossible, though this is clear only in hindsight. In the article Kissinger underlines the loss of credibility that withdrawal would mean: in Europe, the Middle East and Asia any sign of weakness or unreliability by the United States would put stability at risk. This is not an unreasonable judgement at the time.

The fall of Saigon and the escape of the Vietnamese boat people are indeed a drama; but, as it turns out, the United States' allies prefer to see it out of a war it is losing, which has brought upheaval across the West.

These are the theories. In practice Nixon's Vietnam policy has three tracks: 'vietnamisation' – withdrawing US forces and replacing them with Vietnamese; military and diplomatic pressure on Hanoi; and negotiation with Hanoi. The first two reflect Nixon's instincts. The third is Kissinger's responsibility.

Vietnamisation is the most constant. Defense Secretary Melvin Laird supports it. For Nixon, reducing US forces is a visible step towards the peace he has promised; combine it with aid to Saigon and he cannot be accused of abandoning an ally. He announces this policy in July 1969 in Guam after discussions with Thieu. In these talks he has told Thieu what he is going to do – though not how far he is going to go. The 'Nixon Doctrine' says that the United States will support its allies, but 'we shall look to the country directly threatened to assume the primary responsibility of providing the manpower for its defence'.[42]

Thereafter Nixon makes further withdrawals known at regular intervals. On 16 September 1969 he announces the withdrawal of 60,000 troops by December, undercutting calls for a mass demonstration. On 3 November he confirms on television that withdrawals will continue as progress is made on the ground. In fact, withdrawals are linked to presidential appearances on US TV rather than to progress in Vietnam. On 20 April 1970, on TV again, he announces that he will withdraw a further 150,000 men in the next twelve months, so that the number of forces in Vietnam will have halved since he became president.[43] This is to pre-empt the spring campaign of the anti-war movement. And so on.

This goes on in spite of the mixed performance of the Vietnamese. In a broadcast in April 1971, Nixon refers to the success of operations by South Vietnamese forces in Cambodia and Laos and announces the withdrawal of another 100,000 men, bringing the numbers down to 180,000 (from 540,000 when he assumed office). The Laos operation has been a fiasco: South Vietnamese forces take a month to reach a village they are supposed to capture in five days. Thieu orders their withdrawal without consulting the United States. Soldiers are photographed clinging to the skids of the US helicopters sent to rescue them.[43] By spring 1972 US force levels are below 100,000. Only a small number of these are now front-line troops; the rest are there for training and support. In April Nixon is on TV again, promising more reductions. By now the risk of being drafted and sent to Vietnam is negligible; the mass demonstrations and the uproar on the campuses are coming to an end. In *Foreign Affairs*, Kissinger wrote that withdrawal was impossible; Nixon has proved him wrong.

Withdrawal is Nixon's way of pursuing peace. The purpose of pressure on the North is to ensure that it is 'peace with honour'. This reflects Nixon's personal instincts: from his days as Eisenhower's vice-president, he has been a hawk on Vietnam, as are many of his core supporters. They are not as vocal as the peace movement, but they will punish anyone who lets the United States or its armed forces down.

The pressure track begins in spring 1969, alongside the withdrawals. Nixon's first big foreign-policy decision is to bomb Cambodia. The aim is to disrupt supplies for Hanoi's forces and to destroy their headquarters in the South. This is supposed to be in Cambodia, but it probably never existed in the form imagined in Washington. It is difficult to identify Hanoi's guerrilla forces in the South; so cutting off their supplies is a sensible strategy. Bombing violates Cambodian neutrality, but Hanoi has been violating it for years. Kissinger supports this decision: pressure gives Hanoi an incentive to negotiate. With Nixon withdrawing forces, the negotiations have to make progress quickly. Also this is spring 1969, and he needs to win Nixon's confidence. Rogers is against the Cambodian operation; he warns of a domestic reaction, and complications in the negotiations.

The real debate on Cambodia is about secrecy. A good reason for secrecy is to avoid embarrassing Prince Sihanouk, the Cambodian head of state; a less good reason is to avoid domestic trouble in the USA. Those in favour of secrecy – Nixon and Kissinger – win, and an elaborate procedure for concealment is developed. Sihanouk knows, but does not object; in fact he resumes diplomatic relations with the United States while the bombing is going on. Nevertheless, secrecy does not work: the bombing raids are reported in *The New York Times* a few weeks after they begin.

Nixon and Kissinger assume this is from a leak. The FBI tap the telephones of Kissinger's staff and others in the White House with his knowledge. Then the 'plumbers' unit is created - to stop the leaks. This begins a path that leads eventually to Watergate.* The press story that starts it all does not, in fact, come from a leak; it is from the old-fashioned methods of a reporter on the ground, who looked up and saw the B-52s going over.

In the following year, 1970, Nixon orders large-scale ground operations in Cambodia, putting the interdiction of supplies at the heart of US strategy. Kissinger is his strongest supporter. By now Lon Nol has deposed Prince Sihanouk, and Cambodia is aligned with the United States. This time secrecy is impossible and Nixon makes a broadcast explaining the reasons for the operation. The news raises the protests to a new level. It is against this background that the National Guard kills protesters at Kent State University.

* A June 1972 break-in at the Democratic National Committee headquarters in the Watergate complex in Washington DC led to an investigation that revealed multiple abuses of power by the Nixon administration. On 9 August 1974, facing likely impeachment for his role in covering up the scandal, Nixon became the only US president to resign.

These operations have negative side effects. Some of Kissinger's staff resign. Beyond the protests, the most important impact is in Cambodia itself. The bombing and incursions push the North Vietnamese further into the interior of Cambodia, and the refugee population of Phnom Penh doubles. Prince Sihanouk, exiled in Beijing, declares an alliance with the Khmer Rouge. They receive support from both the Chinese and the North Vietnamese, but it is Sihanouk's backing that gives this unknown group legitimacy. The disaster that comes to Cambodia cannot be blamed solely on the policies of Nixon and Kissinger, but their actions play a big part.

Had these policies been effective, they might have been excusable. But at each stage the military overestimate what they will achieve. The bombing of Cambodia – more than 3,000 sorties – and the ground campaign by US and Southern forces in Laos as well as Cambodia fail to stop the supplies. The bombs and ground war cause damage, but never enough to cripple Hanoi's effort in the South. Kissinger has reason to support Nixon's efforts to bring Hanoi to the negotiating table; but he has forgotten his scepticism of the military, learned on the ground in Vietnam.

The final proof of failure comes on 30 March 1972. Hanoi launches a three-pronged attack in South Vietnam: in the north, in the central highlands and in the Mekong Delta. The massive quantities of materiel that support this have all come in along the Ho Chi Minh Trail.

This is the largest spring offensive the North has launched, a pre-election special. US forces are now below 100,000. The South Vietnamese bear the brunt of the attack and almost collapse. Nixon reacts with intensive bombing in the south, to support Vietnamese forces, and also in and around Hanoi, to interdict supplies for the south. Haiphong harbour is mined and four Soviet ships are hit.

This makes an impact. The rout in South Vietnam is halted. No less important, the government in the South replaces corrupt and ineffective generals. A stalemate is achieved, suggesting that Vietnamisation plus US airpower might work.

Alongside the four years of military pressure, Kissinger has tried to apply diplomatic pressure through Hanoi's two allies, the Soviet Union and China. Kissinger sees international relations through a great-power lens and attributes more influence to the Soviet Union and China than either exercises on Hanoi. He exploits differences between Moscow and Beijing skilfully; but he is less good at understanding lesser powers. The defining memory for Hanoi is of the Geneva Conference of 1954, convened to settle outstanding issues resulting from the Korean and First Indochina Wars: they see this as a joint betrayal by the Soviet Union and China. Hanoi got half a country when they wanted it all. The North trusts neither the Soviet Union nor China, the more so if they seem to be working together. Bad relations between China and the Soviet Union in the early 1970s are a blessing for Hanoi.

In 1972, as diplomacy between Washington, Moscow and Beijing gets going, Kissinger tries to exploit the diplomatic triangle to secure their help in getting out of Vietnam. The effort is large, the results are meagre. Moscow and Beijing are both more committed to Hanoi than to Washington. They compete with each other in supplying arms and in 1972 each sends a record quantity to North Vietnam.

The third strand of policy is negotiation. This should turn military and diplomatic pressure into an agreement enabling the United States to leave: peace with order, if not with honour. Nixon is sceptical of negotiations; but without an agreement, a unilateral end to the war will look like a defeat.

For three years the negotiations make no progress. Kissinger is dealing with a government that perfectly matches his description of a revolutionary power in *A World Restored*. Napoleon was interested only in victory; he did not negotiate settlements, he imposed them. The North Vietnamese are the same. Sure of their anti-imperialist creed, they see victory as the only way to realise it. The only reason for doing business with the United States is to receive its surrender.

Le Duc Tho, the North Vietnamese negotiator, is a negotiator's nightmare. Why should he negotiate what he intends to win on the battlefield? Out of office, Kissinger has written that the North sees war and negotiation as a single whole. Le Duc Tho embodies this: he is responsible for the military campaign in the South; he has political control of Hanoi's allies there; and he is in charge of the negotiations with the United States. Kissinger represents only the diplomatic dimension; military strategy is in the hands of Nixon and the Pentagon; Thieu commands the government and the military in the South. As revolutionaries, the North Vietnamese believe history is on their side. Speaking of the 1972 spring offensive, General Giap says: 'The battle that will decide the future of our people began more than twenty-five years ago. A battle, no matter how important it may be, whether Issus or Hastings, Philippi or Belle-Alliance*, can only represent the high point of a developing situation.'[45] He too thinks in political and historical terms.

It takes Kissinger time to understand what he is dealing with. In the first round of negotiations (August 1969 to April 1970) he follows the ideas in his *Foreign Affairs* article. He proposes a mutual withdrawal of forces, separating the military and political issues. Le Duc Tho demands the removal of President Thieu, as he has done all along. At the end of the April session Le Duc Tho notes that they have made no progress at all: polite but tough, with no hint of Oriental subtlety.

In the next round of talks in summer 1971 Kissinger offers a date for the United States to complete withdrawal (no longer mutual) in exchange for a standstill ceasefire. He has consulted Thieu, who has agreed this, even though it leaves Northern forces in his country. Thieu assumes that Hanoi will reject these proposals. He is right, and the talks break down again on the question of Thieu's departure. Echoing the argument in Kissinger's article, Le Duc Tho says: 'There is no war without political goals. . . . Military means are only the instruments to achieve political ends'[46]† – a change of regime in the South, that is.

So far the talks can hardly be called negotiations. The Vietnamese show no interest in give-and-take. Le Duc Tho proposes further talks for the end of 1971, but then pulls out. With the re-election campaign coming into view Nixon decides, in January 1972, to make the secret

* A French name of Waterloo.
† Kissinger comments: 'Clausewitz was alive and well and living in North Vietnam.'

talks public. For a moment this quietens his domestic critics; but it does not last. Those who want to get out of Vietnam do not do so because of the US negotiating position. They just want to get out. Increasingly, this applies to Congress too.

In spring 1972 things change. This is the year that the Nixon-Kissinger overtures to China come off. After the Beijing summit in February the North launches its spring offensive, the United States responding, as noted earlier, with massive bombing of Hanoi. In spite of this the Moscow summit goes ahead. This makes US political leverage visible just as its bombs and Thieu's forces are halting the North's offensive.

For all these reasons, and because of the presidential election, 1972 is the year when the talks with Le Duc Tho become serious. It is now clear that the United States as well as Hanoi has the ear of Beijing and Moscow. The effect of this should not be exaggerated. Both continue to provide Hanoi with arms and other support; Chinese minesweepers reopen Haiphong harbour so the arms can be delivered. But Moscow's readiness to hold a summit with Nixon while the United States is raining bombs on the North makes an impact.

For both the Soviet Union and China the war is an embarrassment. They want it to end. Neither reduces arms deliveries, but the Chinese message changes: now is the moment to make a deal, 'with a view to letting North Vietnam recover, thus getting stronger while the enemy is getting weaker'.[47] The Chinese suggest a pause of six months or a year before the North takes Saigon. They and the Soviets repeat Kissinger's increasingly explicit line that the US aim is to withdraw from Vietnam, and that what it needs is a 'reasonable interval' before the North takes over. The constant stream of suggestions along these lines registers with Hanoi, which cannot ignore China; meanwhile, the troop withdrawals show that the United States may really be leaving.

The failure of Hanoi's spring offensive helps too. When it begins, US combat forces have already all left. The North invades with large numbers of regular forces. But after initial success their progress is halted; then it is reversed by Southern forces with US logistic support

– mobility is critical – and by massive US bombing. This has a sobering effect in Hanoi. In the Tet Offensive of 1968, initial military gains were also followed by ground being retaken; but then US forces had played a large role. Equally significant is the lack of political impact in the United States (since, as always, Hanoi wages a political war). Two months after the Tet Offensive, Johnson announced that he would not seek a second term, and initiated a bombing pause. In 1972 Nixon is bombing the North more than Johnson ever did, and is on the way to an election victory. If you are fighting a political war, this begins to look like a defeat.

As the election approaches Nixon is not even sure he wants success at the negotiating table. He does not want anything that looks like an election stunt. He has demonstrated his toughness in the war; now he has told the public the story of Kissinger's secret talks, and shown his readiness to end the war on honourable terms. But he allows Kissinger to continue 'largely for [the negotiations'] utility in confusing his domestic opponents'.[48]

Hanoi watches US politics closely enough to know that Nixon will win a second term, and guesses it will get a better settlement before the election. It is an autocratic regime and does not understand the power of Congress, nor how hostile it will be to Nixon and the war. The Senate already has a majority for withdrawal from Vietnam in exchange for the return of prisoners of war.

Kissinger wants to finish the job he has started; unlike China, or the Moscow summit, he has done this on his own. And it will be difficult for Nixon to replace him if he succeeds in the Vietnam negotiations.

When Kissinger meets Le Duc Tho in Paris in July 1972 he smells, for the first time, a readiness to negotiate. The other person with a sensitive nose is Thieu. He smells betrayal. He understands what drives policy in Hanoi at least as well as Kissinger does. When Kissinger visits Saigon following this round of negotiations, Thieu questions him on the US position, point by point. By now the United States has withdrawn most of its forces; Thieu fears they are going to withdraw politically too. He rejects any compromise, however harmless. What Thieu is really objecting to is the idea of any agreement at all between the United States and Hanoi. Kissinger, however, persuades Nixon that he should make a deal with Le Duc Tho, even if Thieu's government is 'not on board in the last detail'.[49]*

Four weeks before election day in the United States, Kissinger and Le Duc Tho reach an agreement that meets all the US objectives. Kissinger gets what he has sought from the start: the political and military tracks are not linked. Le Duc Tho drops the demand that Thieu should step down; the committees that are supposed to bring North and South together – the last vestige of the coalition government to end the civil war – are designed to be unworkable and irrelevant. The problem is that, by now, the content of the agreement is very limited. There are no political concessions by the South and no military concessions by the North. A standstill ceasefire means that Northern forces remain in place in the South; and there is little to stop their resupply and reinforcement. This is far from the mutual withdrawal of forces that Kissinger started out with. Instead the United States has withdrawn its forces unilaterally, and the North's army, larger than ever, remains in place.

In exchange for its unilateral withdrawal the United States will get its prisoners of war back† – as soon as the last of the US forces leave Vietnam. This is the structure of the agreement. It is about withdrawal, not about peace. In theory there will be a ceasefire, an end to infiltration, a withdrawal of foreign forces from Laos and Cambodia. An international commission will monitor implementation. Both sides know it will be ineffective. Traditionally the winner of a battle is the one who remains in possession of the field. That is also how Thieu sees it. The withdrawal of the last US forces means the end of the United States' commitment.

Kissinger has negotiated in accordance with his instructions, and with political reality. After Le Duc Tho's endless stonewalling, it seems like a miracle. Everyone in Washington, including Nixon and those who have been excluded from the process, agrees that the deal is better

* In 1965 Kissinger, as a consultant, avoided the question of negotiations in his report because he thought they would undermine the government in Saigon. He was right.
† A lesson of the Korean War.

than they had expected. Nixon opens some Château Lafite to celebrate. No one in Washington seems to notice how far their objectives have changed in the course of the negotiation.

Saigon notices. If its interests were going to be an important factor in the negotiations, its representatives would have been in Paris, if not in the conference room. Kissinger is negotiating for the United States, not for South Vietnam. In Washington everyone persuades themselves that, because the agreement meets the latest version of the US government position, it ought also to be acceptable to Thieu.

It is not. Thieu refuses to go quietly. He demands changes to the agreement. In order not to wreck the election, it is put on hold. After Kissinger's over-enthusiastic statement on TV that 'Peace is at hand', everything goes quiet. When Nixon's election triumph is secure, Kissinger restarts talks with Le Duc Tho in Paris. He asks for sixty-nine changes in the document that he and Le Duc Tho agreed before the election. It is no surprise that he gets nowhere. He reminds Le Duc Tho that the October agreement 'required the concurrence of both Washington and Saigon'. But for a negotiator this is a humiliation; Le Duc Tho is justified in telling him that this is not serious. Kissinger has been in touch with Washington every day. He could have been in contact with Saigon too, had he chosen.

Kissinger seeks help from Moscow and Beijing, without success. Nixon's instructions are that he should reach an agreement; but Le Duc Tho thinks that is what they already did six weeks before. The talks break down in mid-December.

Unable to rewrite the agreement, Nixon and Kissinger send B-52s to bomb Hanoi with renewed intensity. Haldeman's diary for 6 December (while the talks are still going on) records: 'Both of K's options really lead to the same conclusion, which is that we start bombing'. Nixon makes him continue the futile negotiations for another week. From 18 December to the end of the year US aircraft fly 3,000 more sorties, dropping 40,000 tons of bombs.

Kissinger writes in *White House Years*: 'My description of the December negotiations can leave little doubt that Hanoi had in effect made a strategic decision to prolong the war'. In fact, Kissinger's description of the negotiations is convoluted and opaque, unlike his sharp, simple analyses everywhere else. It is the United States that reopens the agreement, and presents a long list of changes. And it is the United States that resumes military action.[50]

With Thieu, Nixon mixes pressure and reassurance. He promises 'swift and severe retaliatory action' on Hanoi, should the agreement be violated; but he also deals with Thieu in a brutal fashion: 'I have decided to . . . sign the Agreement on January 27 in Paris. I will do so, if necessary, alone. In that case I shall have to explain publicly that your government obstructs peace. The result will be an inevitable and immediate termination of military and economic assistance'.[51] This message, like almost all the others, is drafted by Kissinger and his team. Meanwhile Nixon bombs the North as it has never been bombed before.

This combination of browbeating and bombing brings agreement. The logic of the bombing is strange. Why bomb Hanoi when the problem is with Saigon? Yet it works. Perhaps the message is that Nixon is not somebody to trifle with. Whatever the answer, nothing of substance changes between the October agreement and the one that Rogers signs in Paris on 27 January 1973 – his only role in the negotiations. Kissinger goes to Hanoi, but never again to Saigon. He accepts the Nobel Peace Prize; Le Duc Tho refuses it.

The agreement that matters to the United States – the return of prisoners of war – is fulfilled in March. The war continues at a lower intensity. South Vietnamese forces retake some territory; the North instructs its forces in the South, some 150,000 men, to quieten things down and attack only where they have local superiority. Meanwhile it rebuilds its supply route – metalled roads and a pipeline – through Cambodia. Everyone complains of violations of the agreement. The United States continues bombing the Ho Chi Minh Trail until August 1973, when Congress puts a stop to it.

With the United States gone, the weakness of the South Vietnamese government is ever more apparent. The US presence sustained the economy; now it is no longer there, soldiers go unpaid at the bottom, while corruption continues at the top. At the end of 1974 the North begins its final assault. Le Duc Tho arrives in the South by motorcycle, to be with his army when it happens. The last Americans are evacuated by helicopter from the embassy roof on 29 April. The Saigon government surrenders the following day. Two weeks earlier the Khmer Rouge have taken control of Cambodia.

Kissinger often refers to Vietnam as a tragedy. It was indeed a tragedy for the people of Vietnam and Cambodia, as it was, in a lesser degree, for the United States. The word, however, has the ring of inevitability about it. But nothing is inevitable. This, like other wars, came from political decisions. On the US side there were many bad decisions, starting with John Foster Dulles in Geneva in 1954. He acted in the spirit of the times, and few questioned his judgement. Richard Nixon, vice-president at the time and influential in policy, supported military intervention in Southeast Asia more strongly even than Dulles. Only Eisenhower's scepticism about military solutions held them back.

Fifteen years later, Nixon and Kissinger's role is to clean up the mess; it is a dirty job. Nothing can justify the deaths on all sides during the last years of a lost war. In the four years following Nixon's election some 20,000 US servicemen are killed, and about three times as many wounded. The figures for Vietnamese casualties on either side are many multiples of this. The United States betrays the South; the South betrays its people; the North breaks all the agreements. The war was a mistake by the US government; those who get the United States out deserve more credit than those who got them in. It is Nixon who orders the unilateral withdrawal, and Congress that stops funding the war. Kissinger's job is to deliver the agreement. This is about prisoners, withdrawal and a ceasefire, which neither side observes. You cannot negotiate with a revolution.

Kissinger's persistence in the negotiation deserves admiration, and one can sympathise with his relief when he brings it to a conclusion. What sticks a little in the throat is his reiteration of the 'anguish' he felt at the decisions he made about Vietnam during this period. There is no sign of this in the documents of the time. Kissinger nicknamed those on his staff who argued against the intervention in Cambodia 'the bleeding hearts': this sounds more like scorn for those who do not understand the reality of power politics than it does like anguish.

And yet that is not the whole story. Kissinger is too complicated to be pigeonholed. As Saigon falls in April 1975, in a chaos of refugees and evacuation, and while Kissinger is wrangling with the Pentagon about evacuation flights and with the Justice Department about visa waivers for refugees, two State Department officials who served in Vietnam travel to Saigon on their own initiative to help the people they worked with. They do not ask permission, since they know it will be refused. This is a breach of discipline. On their return Kissinger has a senior official read them the riot act. Then they are brought to his office. There, after a formal word of disapproval, he tells them that there is little in the last months that anyone can be proud of, but that they are a credit to their country and to the Foreign Service. No disciplinary action is taken; after a decent interval they are each given an award.[52]

The Middle East

Following the signature of the Vietnam agreement, Haldeman records in his diary (6 February 1973) a discussion with Nixon about Kissinger. After the *annus mirabilis* of 1972 – the Beijing summit, the Moscow summit, the Vietnam agreement – Nixon

> feels he's [Kissinger] running down and getting bored, and so for that matter is the P[resident]. There's a real letdown and psychological depression after that type of accomplishment . . . Henry's not interested in taking the time to work out the details of the agreement etc., which must be done, but doesn't really interest him . . . Especially he is reluctant to move into the Middle East, which the P feels has got to be settled now.[53]

For the first four Nixon years, the Middle East is consigned to Rogers, so that he is not entirely humiliated. This means that neither Nixon nor Kissinger is interested. Sometimes the Middle East is mentioned as a generic foreign-policy issue – the kind that may be left to the State

Department because there is a lot of diplomacy and little result. The big game is the Cold War. China matters, as it rebalances the Cold War. If the Middle East has any importance it is as a proxy Cold War conflict: Israel with US support against Egypt and Syria with Soviet backing. The 1967 Six-Day War against Egypt, Syria and Jordan demonstrated Israel's strength, and there is no reason to fear for its safety. The Russians talk about the risks of renewed conflict, but neither Nixon nor Kissinger takes them seriously. The communiqué on the Middle East at the Moscow summit is notably bland, deliberately so on Kissinger's part: the Soviet Union aligns itself with unrealisable Arab demands and there is nothing to be gained from working with it.

During the first term, therefore, neither Nixon nor Kissinger sees much point in engaging on the Middle East: Nixon does not believe he will ever get a decent share of the Jewish vote; Kissinger thinks a period of stalemate might make the Arab states more flexible. (The State Department is a good instrument for stalemate.) They are wrong; something is happening in the Middle East but Nixon and Kissinger are too busy to notice, and they do not take seriously what Rogers, the State Department and Moscow are all saying.

Anwar Sadat has been President of Egypt since Nasser's death in 1970. He is not expected to last long; nor do his policies seem different from Nasser's. Both judgements are wrong: Sadat understands that he will need US support if he is to make progress with Israel. In 1971 he purges the most important Nasser supporters, including those close to the Soviet Union. At the same time he signs a twenty-year Treaty of Friendship with the Soviet Union; outsiders, including the United States, which has broken relations with Egypt, understand the treaty but not the purge.

Sadat makes tentative overtures to Washington, but these get nowhere. In April 1972 he proposes that his security adviser should meet Kissinger in secret – yet another back-channel. The meeting has not yet taken place when, in July, Sadat announces he is asking 15,000 Soviet military advisers to leave Egypt, taking both Moscow and Washington by surprise. At this moment Kissinger is up to his neck in Vietnam. A meeting with Sadat's adviser is finally arranged for February 1973, early in Nixon's second term. The adviser (Hafiz Ismail) brings a letter from Sadat warning of an explosion if nothing changes in their situation, and the Israeli occupation of Sinai continues. This seems like the standard Arab-Israel routine. He and Kissinger talk for two days in secret but nothing comes of it.

Then, the explosion: on 6 October Egyptian forces cross the Suez Canal and attack the Israeli army; they take them by surprise and win a series of stunning victories. Syria attacks the Golan Heights at the same time. Israel and the United States have examined such scenarios and dismissed them: there have been too many false alarms over the past year. Besides, why should an Arab state attack Israel when it is sure to be defeated? After 6 October, even the assumption of an Arab defeat looks questionable.

The only people who have seen this coming are in Moscow. Brezhnev and Gromyko have warned of an explosion, but neither Kissinger nor Nixon have taken notice, assuming, as superpowers do, that they know best. This is imprudent: the United States has only a limited presence in Cairo; the Russians have had thousands of military advisers in Egypt.

For practical purposes Kissinger runs US policy during and after the Yom Kippur War (named for the Jewish holy day on 6 October that year) on his own. Nixon is occupied with Watergate – and at one stage also with the resignation of Vice-President Spiro Agnew. (The one exception is the air lift for Israel, where Nixon's support is essential to get the Pentagon's co-operation.) From the start Kissinger is clear about US aims. These are to ensure that it is the United States that emerges as the peacemaker – that is, as the dominant outside power.

Kissinger's preoccupation during the conflict is to delay a ceasefire until Israel has recovered the ground it has lost in the first days of the war; anything else would be a defeat for Israel. When the Soviet Union invites him to Moscow to discuss a Security Council resolution Kissinger accepts but does not hurry. He tries at one point to suppress a Nixon letter to Brezhnev giving him full powers to agree a UN resolution – as this limits his scope for delay. He ignores Nixon's instruction for joint action with Moscow to stop the conflict. This is not the only time Kissinger disregards instructions, but here he follows a course opposite to the one Nixon proposes. From Moscow Kissinger flies to Israel, where his objective is to have Israel observe the ceasefire, but not too soon. He encourages Israel to fight on, beyond the Security Council's deadline – which the United States itself has proposed. Having urged the Israelis to behave in this cavalier fashion, he then has to rein them in before they destroy the Egyptian 3rd Army, surrounded and with its back against the Suez Canal.

When he succeeds, the United States is in the position that Kissinger has been aiming at: 'We could begin our peace process with the Arabs on the proposition that we had stopped the Israeli advance and with the Israelis on the basis that we had been steadfastly at their side in the crisis.'[54] This contradicts the conventional idea of a neutral mediator. Neutrality is one way to make peace, but power is better.

The negotiations are a personal triumph for Kissinger. But the hero in this story – as Kissinger himself acknowledges – is Anwar Sadat. Until the war Kissinger has not taken him seriously. The day after the Egyptian attack begins he receives a message from Sadat's office; from then on, there is almost daily contact with Cairo. In the course of this Kissinger comes to understand Sadat and his strategy:

> Until this message [on the second day of the conflict] I had not taken Sadat seriously. Because of the many threats to go to war that had not been implemented I had dismissed him as more actor than statesman. Now I was beginning to understand that the grandiloquent gestures were part of a conscious strategy. They had guaranteed surprise . . . The expulsion of Soviet advisers in 1972 suddenly took on a new significance. Then I had had trouble understanding why Sadat had not sought to negotiate their departure with us, instead of giving it to us for nothing. But Sadat was right . . . Sadat wanted to be rid of the Soviets to remove an encumbrance both to the war he was planning and to his projected move towards the United States. Acts of historic magnitude must not be mortgaged by petty manoeuvres.[55]

The letter from Sadat's office is itself a striking event. Egypt and the United States have not had diplomatic relations for several years. To contact Kissinger with their terms for ending the war is an invitation for the United States to become involved. The terms proposed are unrealistic, but they are for the record. The letter explains that the Egyptian objective is 'to show that we were neither afraid nor helpless'. Sadat's war aims are political: to change the psychological balance between Egypt and Israel, making it possible for the two sides to negotiate a peace.

The key moment in the negotiation is at the start. This is Kissinger's first visit to Egypt, one of his first to any Arab country. He arrives on 7 November, a month after the start of the war, a week after its end. Alone with Kissinger, the Egyptian president suggests 'a Kissinger Plan' and outlines it: Israeli forces are to pull back two-thirds of the way across the Sinai, etc. The sands of the Middle East are littered with over-ambitious peace plans: Sadat's is no better. Kissinger has had to pull out all the stops just to get the Israelis to observe the ceasefire, days after the UN Security Council has demanded it unanimously.

Kissinger does not reply to Sadat's proposal. Instead he asks him how he was able to surprise the world on 6 October. This is a way to flatter Sadat – everyone likes recounting successes. More important, it reminds Sadat of his goals: not military victory but to shock Israel into awareness of its vulnerability – a few months before, Golda Meir has told Nixon that Israel is militarily impregnable – and to restore Egypt's self-confidence so that the two can negotiate peace. The discussion is then framed by Sadat's strategy, which is about minds not maps. This also reminds Sadat that he has decided to bet on the United States to help him achieve his goals.

Having recalled Sadat to his purposes, Kissinger can speak frankly. He tells him that the most he can expect at that moment is to stabilise the ceasefire. In practice Kissinger dictates the terms: his six points ask so little of the Israelis that he is sure they will accept them. Israeli forces will stop where they have finished – well beyond the line of 22 October demanded by UN Security Council Resolution 338. Instead of insisting on the UN resolution, Sadat accepts a formula saying that the two sides will begin discussions to 'settle the question of the return to the 22 October positions';[56] thus the principle of the 22 October line is recognised. In practice no agreement will be reached and nothing will change. And it will not matter.

This takes the negotiation out of the UN's hands. If the two sides are talking to each other (through the United States), there is no need for the UN – and thus the Soviet Union – to be involved. Insisting on the line of 22 October would bring argument and delay, neither of which helps Egypt's aim of building confidence with Israel. Kissinger will work instead on the two things that need to be settled first: an exchange of prisoners – a key Israeli objective – and supply arrangements for the 3rd Egyptian Army in its precarious position.

Sadat finishes his conversation with Kissinger by underlining that his agreement is with the United States, and that he trusts Kissinger to deliver more later. The terms Sadat accepts depend not on UN resolutions, the Arab mantra over a long period, but on Kissinger's promise to obtain a more substantial Israeli withdrawal later. It takes Kissinger forty-eight hours of negotiations to persuade the Israelis to accept the stabilisation agreement, with various side letters and statements interpreting his six points. He asks nothing from them, except that they do not starve the Egyptian 3rd Army. In exchange they get their prisoners back, and the first direct dialogue between Israel and Egypt begins: the so-called 'kilometre 101 talks' between the two militaries about practical arrangements for the 3rd Army. The first Israeli and Egyptian prisoners are exchanged on 15 November, and arrangements for supplying the 3rd Army are already coming into place less than a week after the six points have been agreed. The Soviets are not involved at any stage.

The beauty of this arrangement is that it leaves everything as it is. Nothing is so easy to negotiate as the status quo. And the great merit of this particular status quo is that it is unsustainable. An Egyptian army is isolated on the east bank of the Suez Canal, Israeli forces on the west. To maintain its forces west of the canal, Israel would have to keep its army mobilised, which would be economically ruinous; and leaving its troops so close to Egyptian cities would be politically explosive. By not trying to solve problems, Kissinger forces the parties to do so. A more sustainable arrangement has to be found. There are tensions and difficulties, but among all the negotiations in the Middle East this one is remarkable for its speed and smoothness.

The second phase is more complicated. It is conducted by shuttle diplomacy:* disengagement of forces means drawing new lines, agreeing limitations on equipment, machinery for verification – which the United States provides. But the rapid negotiation of the first phase has bred the expectation of a rapid follow-up; and the lack of wrangling over details when consolidating the ceasefire has itself been a confidence-building measure.

Agreement is reached on 18 January 1974. The date is testimony: the negotiations cannot start until after the Israeli general election of 31 December 1973. For Sadat it is a major success: Israel, for the first time, gives up territory it has acquired by force, including some won in the Six-Day War. Sadat sticks to his objective of building confidence. Having insisted that Egypt be allowed 300 tanks on the west bank of the Suez Canal, he does not deploy them. Confidence is more valuable than capability. The ultimate fruit of this remarkable exercise comes four years later in the Camp David Accords. For these credit goes to President Carter, but the process begins with Sadat's strategic vision, Kissinger's appreciation of it, and his tactical skill. Sadat is the sort of man Kissinger had in mind when he wrote in *A World Restored* of the importance of the intangible in diplomacy.

In the spring, Kissinger spends a month in a shuttle between Damascus and Jerusalem negotiating a disengagement agreement between Israel and Syria. Hafiz Assad is not Anwar Sadat: his country does not have the history and identity of Egypt, nor is his domestic position so secure. And the Golan Heights are a gateway to Israel, whereas the Sinai is a barrier. The effort and the eventual success are the more remarkable. Here, too, Israel agrees to withdraw from some territory occupied after the Six-Day War. The agreement, on 31 May, ends an astonishing six months of diplomacy.

* The term comes from Joe Sisco, assistant secretary for the Middle East. He greeted passengers on Kissinger's plane, including journalists, with: 'Welcome to the Egyptian-Israeli shuttle' as they boarded for the return to Aswan on 13 January 1974.

Success comes at a price. Détente with the Soviet Union is damaged. This brief account has omitted the Geneva Conference on the Middle East of December 1973, for the good reason that it is irrelevant. The conference brings together representatives of Israel, Egypt, Jordan, the United States, the Soviet Union and the UN secretary general. Syria does not attend. After opening speeches the conference peters out, and the US shuttle takes over. This show of US-Soviet co-operation fools nobody, especially Moscow.

Kissinger regards this as a prize, not a price. His objective is to get the Soviet Union out of the Middle East. He started the process, half unwittingly, by insisting on an ultra-bland statement at the Moscow summit, triggering Sadat's decision to send the Soviet military advisers home. The process is completed with Kissinger's monopoly of the peacemaking after the October war.

The high point of non-détente comes on the night of 24–25 October. The Israelis, with encouragement from Kissinger, are in violation of the ceasefire demanded three days earlier by UN resolution 338 – the only piece of US-Soviet co-operation in this story. Brezhnev sends Nixon a message proposing that US and Soviet forces should go to Egypt to ensure implementation of the resolution. If the United States is not willing to act jointly, 'we should be faced with the necessity urgently to consider the question of taking appropriate steps unilaterally'.[55]

Kissinger's reaction is that the United States is not ready to send forces to Egypt, nor to accept Soviet forces going there: 'We had not worked for years to reduce the Soviet military presence in Egypt only to co-operate in reintroducing it'.* Alexander Haig† has told Kissinger not to wake Nixon, who is distraught with Watergate. A WSAG‡ meeting chaired by Kissinger agrees to a message to Brezhnev (in Nixon's

* *Years of Upheaval*, p. 579. In fact, the elimination of Soviet forces in Egypt is the result of Sadat's decision rather than years of work by the US.

† Kissinger is now both secretary of state and national security adviser; Al Haig is his deputy for the White House half of his job. While Kissinger is dealing with the Middle East he is looking after Nixon.

‡ Washington Special Action Group: a smaller, less formal version of the National Security Council.

name) saying that the United States would not agree a UN resolution sending US or Soviet forces, but it would participate with non-combat personnel in a UN mission to supervise the ceasefire. Unilateral Soviet action would be unacceptable, and a violation of the Basic Principles.[57] (The United States has been acting throughout the crisis to gain unilateral advantage, while the Soviets have been proposing collaboration, so this reference to the Basic Principles is remarkable.)

WSAG also agrees, on Kissinger's advice, to put US forces on high alert (DEFCON 3).* This is an instruction to the military to be ready for war; there is no obvious reason for it. Brezhnev accepts Nixon's reply. Nothing suggests that the alert played a role in this. Why Kissinger reacted so strongly is not clear: 'We were determined to resist by force if necessary the introduction of Soviet forces into the Middle East'.[58] Moscow's frustration is understandable; and Brezhnev is suggesting a joint approach. The language in his message – 'faced with the necessity urgently to consider the question'[59] of acting unilaterally – is mildly threatening, but also very cautious. If you are going to act unilaterally, why announce it in advance?

Probably both sides are bluffing. If so, Kissinger overreacts: in the phone transcripts† he is the more agitated of the actors. Or the alert is a way of asserting that the United States is now the master in the Middle East. Or it may be to get the attention of the Israelis, who finally start observing the ceasefire.‡

The alert is cancelled the following morning. The best commentary is Dobrynin's question to Kissinger a few days later: 'What kind of a relationship is this, if one letter produces a [nuclear] alert?'[60]

The medium-term consequence of Moscow's defeat in the Middle East is that it ceases to trust Kissinger, and stops taking political détente

* Nixon is in Camp David, having drunk heavily and asleep, when the decision is made. The journalist Elizabeth Drew named this 'Strangelove Day', after a scene in the film where the Russian leader is drunk. DEFCON 3 is rare: Kennedy put forces on this level of alert during the Cuban Missile Crisis; an air force commander raised the level for nuclear forces on DEFCON 2 without political authority.

† In Kissinger's blow-by-blow account in *Crisis*.

‡ Kissinger's explanation in *Years of Upheaval* is that Brezhnev was proposing that US and Soviet military forces impose not just a ceasefire but a final settlement. His message can be read this way, but it is not obvious.

seriously. In *White House Years* Kissinger refers to the Soviet strategy of 'selective détente'.[61] By the time of *Years of Upheaval* this has become US strategy. The Soviets' response to exclusion from one part of the Middle East is to turn their attention to others: Syria, Iraq and the Palestine Liberation Organisation. And then to Africa – Angola and the Horn. Five years later, one motive for the Soviet action in Afghanistan is the fear that Hafizullah Amin was going to 'do a Sadat' to them.[62] Meanwhile, the Yom Kippur War has another side-effect: Arab oil sanctions and the consequent rise in energy prices help pay for the increased Soviet activity in the Third World.

A longer-term consequence is that the Middle East becomes an area of predominant US influence. In foreign policy this counts as a success. Forty years on it is legitimate to ask what good this has done the United States or the Middle East. Total supremacy in any case rarely lasts. A few years after Kissinger's success, the Shah of Iran is overthrown. He is an American creation, though not a puppet; the forces that depose him begin an era of religious nationalism that has since changed the Middle East and the place of the superpowers in it.

Might it have been different if the superpowers had tried to work together, as Brezhnev wished? It is difficult to imagine co-operation between two such different countries, the one slow and bureaucratic, the other partly driven by public opinion and given to sudden changes of direction. Sovereign states, and especially superpowers, are not well designed for sustained co-operation. Perhaps it is a pity that Kissinger did not try, and that Nixon was by then drowning in Watergate. Co-operation would have been a challenge. But competition did not work well either: the competition in Africa that followed the United States' success in the Middle East was destructive and wasteful.[63]

Sideshows

This chapter is organised around the big themes of Kissinger-Nixon policy; as a result it gives a false picture of how a secretary of state spends his or her time in office. Normally he or she handles five or six major issues at the same time. To illustrate this, here is a sample of some of the other things going on in autumn 1970.*

Chile

The Marxist, Salvador Allende, is elected President of Chile on 4 September 1970, despite covert attempts by the Nixon administration to prevent this. Nixon decides that the CIA should continue to try to undermine Allende and help his enemies. The Chilean military are successful in a coup in 1973. It is not clear how far US help is instrumental in this.

Interference in Chile is difficult to justify on grounds of national interest. This and the administration's subsequent support for the dictator Augusto Pinochet's regime damage the United States' reputation and that of Henry Kissinger. The mistake begins when Chile is identified as 'another Cuba'. Kissinger's earlier *bon mot*, that Chile was 'a dagger pointed at the heart of Antarctica', was nearer the mark.

The Nixon administration and Kissinger were not different from their predecessors – Eisenhower, Kennedy and Johnson – when it came to interfering in Third World countries. But times were changing. Nixon and Kissinger, through Vietnam, Chile and Watergate, were themselves catalysts of this change.

Soviet Union-Cuba

Cuba is on Kissinger's mind in late 1970. Intelligence shows Soviet moves to build a submarine base there. Kissinger spots a soccer pitch in one of the photographs: Cubans don't play football; Russians do. When they look, it turns out that the Kennedy-Khrushchev understandings in the Cuban Missile Crisis were never put into a written agreement.

Kissinger tells the Soviet ambassador – in one of his regular calls to postpone the summit – that if the construction continues the United

* This period includes a number of significant events – Kissinger calls a chapter in *White House Years* 'The Autumn of Crises'. But there is always something. During the Cuban Missile Crisis, for example, India and China fought a war in the Himalayas.

States will take action to stop it. It does not matter whether or not this is a violation of the 1962 agreement: Kennedy acted not because an agreement had been broken but because of the threat to the United States. Nixon will do the same.

Moscow, sensibly and silently, stops the work.

Middle East

Following a spate of hijackings and an assassination attempt on his life, King Hussein of Jordan declares martial law and orders his army to disband the Palestinian guerrilla groups in Jordan, bringing something close to a civil war to Jordan. (This is where the name 'Black September' comes from.) As this action begins Kissinger agrees with Nixon to move three aircraft carriers and other military assets, including 1,200 Marines, close to Lebanon.

Three days later Syria invades Jordan with a mass of tanks. The United States continues to say nothing to the Soviets (Syria's sponsors), except that the Syrian forces should withdraw; but it also continues military movements and makes sure that these are noticed by Soviet intelligence. Israel, too, puts its forces on alert and moves them to the border. Meanwhile, Jordan begins to win the tank battles against the Syrians.

At this point the Soviets start saying that all countries should refrain from intervention; the Syrians withdraw.

This is a textbook example of preventive action, carried out in line with Kennan's dictum that actions speak louder than words. Kissinger notes in passing that diplomats too often relax at the first sign of goodwill. The time for reconciliation is when the crisis is over, not before. As usual, he has a point.

India-Pakistan

It is, as we have seen, in late 1970 that that the first contact is made between the White House and the government in Beijing, with the help of the President of Pakistan, Yahya Khan. His own country is meanwhile falling apart. In December 1970 the Awami League, which wants independence for Bengal, wins 98 per cent of the votes in East Pakistan and a majority in the National Assembly. The government sends its forces into East Pakistan; the result is shocking violence, plus a flood of refugees into India. In 1971 the Indian army attacks the forces in East Pakistan.

Nixon and Kissinger see this as a Cold War question: India is friendly to Moscow, which supplies its arms; Pakistan is a US ally. Nixon sends a carrier group to the Bay of Bengal to discourage India from launching a full-scale war against Pakistan: a courageous decision, says Kissinger, 'to preserve the world balance of power'.[64]

There are no signs of Mrs Gandhi wanting such a war. Pakistan is coming apart without her help. She acts with sensible restraint, and is mildly puzzled by the US naval deployment.

Berlin

Willy Brandt becomes Chancellor of Germany in October 1969. A year later his version of détente is beginning to show results: the treaty with Poland is signed in December 1970. This is examined in detail in the next chapter. Here it is enough to note that Kissinger follows the subject closely, especially as it concerns Berlin. The question is highly complicated. (His explanations in *White House Years* are a model of clarity.) For once, although he remains fully engaged, he delegates, in this case to Kenneth Rush, the US ambassador in Germany.

Kissinger and Nixon may profit more than they understand from Brandt's work. For a land power like the Soviet Union, with historical memories of invasion, nothing is more vital than its borders; Brandt's offer is as vital to Brezhnev as détente with the United States.

These are no more than a small sample of the issues Kissinger dealt with alongside the grander themes of his time in office. Each was intricate and complicated, sensitive and, for those directly concerned, of vital importance. All of them occupied large numbers of officials full-time.

Two conclusions might be drawn. Nixon and, especially, Kissinger saw foreign affairs as a single whole. This has merits, but also drawbacks; the Cold War framework was sometimes a distorting lens when it came to Third World questions. That is the lesson of Chile and India-Pakistan, and above all of Vietnam – though not necessarily of the Middle East.

Second, the State Department has its uses. Rush and the embassy in Bonn managed the Berlin negotiations well, though Kissinger's involvement was necessary and helpful. A stronger role for the State Department would have been useful in India-Pakistan and Chile too. As Kissinger's period in office as secretary of state shows, not all bureaucrats are bureaucratic.

No ordinary diplomat

Nothing about Henry Kissinger is ordinary. No one else in US diplomacy excites admiration and hostility to the same degree. Few would deny that he is an outstanding foreign-policy intellect; everything else is disputed.

Nixon and Kissinger were made for each other. Both believed in diplomacy backed by force, with a single mind in control. Both disliked bureaucrats: Nixon because he thought they looked down on him, Kissinger because he looked down on them. Bureaucrats do routine; diplomacy needs intuition, imagination and creativity. Nixon and Kissinger provided both. Nixon gave direction and authority; Kissinger turned these into policy.

The relationship was too close to be healthy. Both, says William Safire in *Before the Fall*, had elements of vulnerability and of paranoia; both were ready to bear any burden and pay any price in their personal cause. This was also because they wanted not just to go through the motions, but to *do* something.[65] Both were 'loners', though in Kissinger's case this did not exclude being gregarious, especially with the media, whom he dazzled with his clarity, wit and originality. Nixon had no interests except politics and was shy in personal relations, though he could be masterly in a small group or with an audience. As president, and at the peak of his power, he still needed reassurance. After an important speech White House staff were expected to telephone and tell him how wonderful he had been. When Nixon announced on TV that ground forces were going into Cambodia,[66] the White House telephone log shows fifty calls to the president, half from his staff. Seven were from Kissinger, whose flattery hit absurd levels of hyperbole. Nixon probably didn't believe it, and either knew or assumed that Kissinger bad-mouthed him in private. But he still needed the reassurance.

Kissinger's vulnerability was that of the servant to the master; and Nixon went out of his way *not* to reassure Kissinger, for example by keeping open as long as possible the question of who would make the secret visit to China. Nothing suggests that they liked each other. Nixon resented Kissinger's easy relations with the media, his growing stardom and his Nobel Prize. Meeting at Hubert Humphrey's funeral in 1978, when both were out of office, Nixon greeted him: 'You as mean as ever?' 'Yes,' said Kissinger, 'but I don't have as much opportunity.'[67]

Nobody questioned Nixon's views or told him that he might be wrong. The normal response to the president was to agree and reinforce. Experienced staff like Haldeman protected Nixon by *not* following some of his instructions. As time went by, Kissinger also made up his own mind on when to obey his instructions and when to follow his own judgement. When Nixon made a decision, he left the execution and tactics to Kissinger. As Nixon became more tangled in Watergate, Kissinger made more decisions without consulting him, the Yom Kippur alert being the outstanding example.

There was little debate on policy. In the first few months of the administration policy issues were discussed in the National Security Council – with Kissinger in control of the papers and Nixon in control of the proceedings. Six months into the job, on 4 June 1969, Haldeman's diary records: 'Decided no more NSC meetings. . . . Will make decisions privately with K.'[68] No other post-war president governed with so little discussion. This was an unhealthy way to make policy, though for Kissinger it was the job of his dreams.

It brought an extraordinary burden of work and responsibility. The work alone would have been too much for a normal man. Apart from the everyday job of briefing the president – and only Kissinger saw the president every day on foreign policy – Kissinger was running a full-time back-channel with Dobrynin, mostly about the negotiations on nuclear weapons, holding secret talks on Vietnam, providing personal instructions for Rush on Berlin and preparing for the secret visit to China. Keeping these operations hidden from the rest of the government added to the work.

Each of these was a major undertaking; on top of them Kissinger gave advice on all the ordinary, everyday crises we have forgotten about. He had a high-quality staff, but only he dealt with the president (until Haig was established as his deputy). All papers for the president went through him. The pressures were enormous. Larry Eagleburger, his first deputy and no softy, collapsed with nervous exhaustion after ten weeks (with Kissinger standing over him and shouting, 'Where's the paper?' until he realised what was happening).* Nine months after he started, Kissinger had lost ten of his twenty-eight staff.[69]

The White House was an unpleasant place to work. The telephones of Kissinger's staff were tapped.† He has expressed regret that he acquiesced in this. The taps went longer than any possible justification. The Pentagon, in turn, spied on Kissinger, correctly suspecting that he was not telling them everything. When Nixon got used to Haig briefing him in Kissinger's absence, Haig showed signs of a readiness to undermine Kissinger's position. Nixon, who was a friend of Israel and ran an administration packed with Jews, often used anti-Semitic language, and liked doing so with Kissinger. Probably he sensed that this was a point of vulnerability. An incident to illustrate the atmosphere in which Kissinger worked: after US forces had gone into Cambodia, Kissinger (whose staff were in revolt on the issue) received a phone call from the president; after a few minutes Nixon put his drinking companion, Bebe Rebozo, on the line: 'The president wants you to know, Henry, that if it doesn't work, it's your ass.'

* But working for Kissinger was exciting: Eagleburger returned as deputy under-secretary to Kissinger at the State Department in 1975.

† William Safire, Nixon's speech writer and a victim of phone tapping, makes the case that Kissinger was personally involved in the decisions. (*Before the Fall*, pp. 209-215).

It never was. Kissinger was the only one who could do the job that he and Nixon had invented. But he remained insecure up to the moment when Nixon, wounded by Watergate, appointed him secretary of state. By then Kissinger was a star. China made his name; the Vietnam negotiations seemed to give the United States the exit most of its citizens longed for; in the Middle East he achieved what seemed to be a miracle. Rogers was regularly humiliated, but while he remained, he was a source of anxiety for Kissinger.

Professionally, it was no contest. When the waters were lapping around Nixon and he was thinking of asking Haldeman to resign (April 1973), Nixon told John Ehrlichman: 'Haldeman is more important to me than Adams was to Ike: for example, the K situation, which only he can handle. I can handle the rest probably, but I can't do that.' Thus Haldeman was vital to Nixon because only he could handle Kissinger. Whatever problems he created, Kissinger was indispensable.

And he did create problems. Wherever you open *The Haldeman Diaries* a Kissinger problem pops up.* Often it is the Kissinger-Rogers question: which would fall on their sword for Nixon? Kissinger probably, but he would do it with maximum histrionics (March 1971). Or it is his ego – wanting the president to announce his (secret) trip to Moscow; this too is certain to upset Rogers (April 1972). Or it is Kissinger seeking military action in Vietnam when the negotiations are going wrong (December 1972).

The Nixon-Kissinger story is a drama of power. It is a pity that Harold Pinter (who hated both) never had the opportunity to write a screenplay: two men sacrificing all for power, including power over each other. As one sank, the other rose. From start to finish, for Kissinger it was a high-wire act. He deserves respect just for surviving. But he did not just survive: he did more – good or bad – than anyone who has held either of his two jobs.

How might Kissinger have been without Nixon? The question is partly absurd, since only Nixon would have given so much responsibility to one man. A couple of glimpses, however, suggest that at least

* The author came upon these passages by opening Haldeman's diaries at random.

his style might have been different (and style means a lot). In 1974, with Nixon drowning in Watergate, Kissinger was on his own. In this position he had the time to understand and admire Sadat, and the space to handle him as he felt right. His sympathetic approach gave Sadat the confidence to carry through his plan and to bet Egypt's future on the United States, and on Kissinger personally. Another glimpse comes in a small scene with Mrs Gandhi. In 1971, discussing a visit she was to make, Kissinger and Nixon competed in insulting her: 'bitch', said Kissinger; 'witch', said Nixon. Three years later, after India's 'peaceful nuclear explosion', Kissinger met Mrs Gandhi. The advice from the State Department was that pressure would produce the wrong reaction; Kissinger opened the conversation saying something like, 'Congratulations. You did it, you showed you could build nuclear weapons. Now what do we do to keep from blowing up the world?'[70]

The Nixon-Kissinger moment was one when the stars were aligned on several separate fronts. China's awakening to the threat from the Soviet Union and its own vulnerability – both the threat and the vulnerability were China's fault – coincided with Nixon's arrival, the one president who could change course on China without fear of attack from Richard Nixon, who for years had been the acceptable face of McCarthyism.* Kissinger and Nixon saw their coup mainly as a tactical gain for their handling of Moscow; and so it was until Mao died. Almost half a century later, the consequences are still working themselves out. In the Middle East it was Sadat's arrival that brought change; but Kissinger's sympathetic understanding of him was the key that turned opportunity into reality. Jimmy Carter completed the success, illustrating Kissinger's point that peace usually comes over a long period, from a series of steps, and not from a grand settlement.

The missed opportunity was with Moscow, the focus of both Nixon and Kissinger's greatest attention. Here too the stars were aligned. Brezhnev was never going to transform the Soviet Union as Gorbachev would try to. But his personal commitment to peace and his

* 'Nixon in China' has become a metaphor: the least likely person may be best for the task.

credentials as a hardliner (won by invading Czechoslovakia) made him a perfect partner for Nixon. To turn this opportunity into the basis of a long-term relationship would have needed a domestic campaign in the United States – similar to the one that Dean Acheson mounted to explain the Cold War and the Marshall Plan – to go with the work Nixon and Kissinger put into negotiating with Moscow.

Instead Kissinger used détente as a tranquilliser for the Soviet Union while the United States made competitive gains against it.[71] The price of the gain in power was loss of trust, the great intangible. Along with the opening to China, détente became another variant of the balance-of-power game. By the end of the Ford administration in 1977, Kissinger was describing US policy as designed 'to contain Soviet power'. This was back to square one. SALT and the ABM treaty might have laid the foundations for a common co-operative legitimacy; to develop that would have been the work of decades. It was not what either Kissinger or the United States wanted: power was still preferred to legitimacy. Nevertheless, Nixon and Kissinger were the ones who took the first steps.

Most of Kissinger's time was spent dealing with three very different revolutionary powers. In *A World Restored*, France has to be defeated before a common legitimacy can be created. This was not going to happen with the Soviet Union, but the revolution there was now old and bureaucratic, and steps towards a limited international co-operation looked possible. China was ready to come in from the cold, not to join the system but not to oppose it either. Vietnam was a true revolutionary power. It could neither be defeated nor reconciled; but it was not an essential part of the global order. Getting out and leaving it alone was a solution.

How was it that, in action, the brilliant thinker does not live up to the depth of his thought? One answer is that the best-conceived strategy still has to cope with the real world; and reality is always recalcitrant. That is not enough. A better answer is to be found in Kissinger's remark (in 'Central Issues of American Foreign Policy') that the massive increase in military strength had eroded its relationship to policy – that is, to diplomacy.[72] This thought was still in his mind when he wrote in *White House Years*: 'treating force and diplomacy as discrete phenomena caused our power to lack purpose and our negotiations to lack force'.[73] But in practice he never quite managed to bring military power and diplomacy together: not in Cambodia, nor in bombing North Vietnam. Vietnam was a political problem. In the absence of a political strategy, everything became military and, consequently, failed. Kissinger understood this when he was in Vietnam as a consultant. What the United States needed at this point was honesty. Peace with honour was not available; peace with honesty would have been the next-best thing. That was Nixon's problem more than Kissinger's. It would have been punished electorally but rewarded by history.

Kissinger's other attempts to use military assets politically had mixed success: the carrier group in the Bay of Bengal during the India-Pakistan War and the alert in the Yom Kippur War were probably not needed; but the military movements when Syria invaded Jordan in 1970 were a textbook operation. The best opportunity to bring military and political objectives together was with the Soviet Union, starting in the field of arms control. On his first visit abroad as president, Nixon spoke to an informal gathering in London about using arms control to create trust and a platform for wider political settlements. Both sides were right that co-operation in just one area would not work, but neither the United States nor the Soviet Union found the way to widen it. On the US side it is not clear that Kissinger wanted to. Using military strength for anything other than military victory is not easy. Few others have achieved this.*

The other part of the answer is more mundane. Kissinger and Nixon's belief that bureaucratic government cannot be creative imposed a limit on their own creativity. Bureaucracies also have imaginative people: give them a chance and they can do great things. The one certainty is that anyone who tries to do everything single-handed will not have the calm of mind to use their creative powers to the full.

Finally, Kissinger had a blind spot on economic questions. Trade had

* Sadat was one; Acheson, who used military power to build an alliance of mutual reassurance and influence in Europe, was another.

a part to play in détente, but it was mishandled. Exchanges of goods and people on a balanced basis are a starting point for a sound political relationship and for building a common legitimacy. That is true everywhere, and urgent with China today. Economic relations are integral to global order.

In foreign policy, as in history, everything flows. The Vietnam peace failed, but it got the United States out. Détente withered, but the roots did not die; it has borne fruit from time to time since, and may yet again. The opening to China was a beginning; its consequences are yet to come. The Israel-Egypt shuttle was Kissinger's masterpiece. That too has not fulfilled its potential. There, Kissinger succeeded not by threats or by manipulation, but by empathy and reassurance. Great powers are at their most powerful when they are most generous.

10

German Diplomacy: Adenauer, Brandt and Kohl

'What is won by force is as transient as the colours of a sunset. . . . What the allied soldiers won in Germany was . . . an opportunity for a fresh start.'

(Dean Acheson, *Sketches from Life*)[1]

Adenauer

Konrad Adenauer is seventy-three years old when he becomes the first chancellor of the Federal Republic of Germany (FRG) in 1949. Born in Bismarck's Germany, he embodies the dependable virtues of the middle classes. He has lived through two world wars and two revolutions. As governing mayor from 1917 to 1933, he organised Cologne's recovery from the First World War, through occupation, French-sponsored separatism and financial crisis. The Nazis dismissed him for refusing to fly their flag from the city hall. The years that followed were precarious: some were spent in hiding, some in a Gestapo prison; the same for his wife, who died soon after as a result. Adenauer was lucky to survive.

Then, in 1945, reappointed mayor by the Americans, he is dismissed again, this time by the British. The officer who does this keeps him standing while he reads out a list of complaints. He is also banned from Cologne and from political activity. He returns to his home on the Rhine, where a stream of political figures visit him. The result of these talks is the Christian Democratic Union (CDU), bringing together Catholics, Protestants and Christian socialists.* When the ban on political activity is lifted, he is elected leader of the CDU in the British zone.†

Don Cook of *The New York Herald Tribune* wrote of his dignity and old-fashioned courtesy: 'Dignity was rare in Germany in those days, when attitudes often varied from sullen arrogance to insufferable obsequiousness.'[2] Acheson, meeting him in 1949, recalled 'his conservation and prudent use of energy . . . He moves slowly, gestures sparingly, speaks quietly, smiles briefly'.[3] Adenauer is preserving himself: he will govern Germany for fourteen more years.

In 1945, seeing what is happening in the Soviet zone, he guesses that Germany and Europe are going to be divided. He concludes that the 'free part' of Germany must build ties with the neighbouring democracies: France, the Netherlands, Britain. His design is for Germany in Europe.

In 1948, after the breakdown of the Four-Power Conference on Germany, the occupation authorities in the West establish a Parliamentary Council, chosen by the *Länder* to propose a constitution for the western part of Germany. The CDU and the Social Democrats (SPD) reach an agreement that Adenauer will preside over the council's debates in Bonn.

As the council's work begins, the Soviet Union imposes a blockade on Berlin. Germany will be faced repeatedly with pressure on Berlin. At this moment it serves to remind the members of the Parliamentary Council that German security depends on its Western allies. Later the SPD will mock Adenauer as 'the chancellor of the Allies'. They are not wrong: he believes that German democracy can survive only if it is anchored in the West. His aims are freedom, peace and national unity; but in that order. Freedom means being part of the West. He chooses

* Before the war Adenauer was a leader of the Centre Party, which campaigned for rights for Catholics. The CDU was a new kind of party built on values rather than on social milieu.

† Asked much later whether he would have become chancellor had the British not dismissed him, Adenauer replied: 'Certainly not.'

a divided Germany in the West over a united but unattached, neutral Germany.

The Korean War (1950–53) is a reminder that force cannot be ruled out; it raises the question of German rearmament. The first attempt at a solution, as we have seen, is the European Defence Community (EDC), suggested by Jean Monnet, proposed in October 1950 by the French prime minister and confirmed in the Treaty of Paris (1952). The Treaty of Bonn, which restores German sovereignty, will come into force only when the Treaty of Paris is ratified. While the fate of the EDC is in doubt, Moscow proposes a return to Four-Power co-operation to discuss a united and neutral Germany (the Stalin Note of 1952). Adenauer dismisses this. He does not want Germany in a no-man's-land between two alliances; he wants a sovereign state that can choose its alliance partners.

In 1953 Stalin dies, raising hopes of change; but three months later Soviet tanks kill protesting workers in East Germany, and the hopes of change too. A flurry of activity follows, led by Britain and Churchill – who wants a summit. In 1954 the four foreign ministers meet in Berlin, the first such meeting since the pro-forma event in 1949. The Western three propose free elections as the path to unification, the Soviet side a confederation to bring the two states together. Both are impossible: how can you confederate a democracy and a Communist dictatorship? As for free elections, they do not exist in the GDR. The western part of Germany is three times as big as the east, and the Soviets can guess what the result would be if they took place. All the four ministers can agree is to reconvene later in the year to discuss Korea and Indochina. Germany is too difficult.

Every effort is put into the EDC. Britain agrees to be associated with it; John Foster Dulles, the US secretary of state, announces that if the treaty is not ratified the United States will be obliged to make an 'agonising reappraisal of its position in Europe'.[4] The next Four-Power meeting, in Geneva, chaired by the British and Soviet foreign ministers, Anthony Eden and Vyacheslav Molotov, is a success as far as Indochina is concerned: it enables the French to withdraw from Vietnam. Pierre Mendès-France then does what no previous prime minister has dared, and puts the EDC treaty to the National Assembly in Paris, which rejects it.

This brings a long-expected crisis. Eden has a fallback plan. He tours European capitals and then calls a meeting in London. The outcome is a complicated set of agreements. At its heart are US and British commitments to maintain forces in Europe, and German assurances not to pursue nuclear, chemical or biological weapons; plus German membership of the Western European Union (WEU) and NATO. This is a tour de force by Eden, who also wins credit for the way he has chaired the Geneva Conference – where Dulles was conspicuously rude to the Chinese representative, Zhou Enlai. And after four years of frustration, the problem of German rearmament is resolved in a month.

A part of the bargain with France is a referendum in the Saarland on whether it should be a part of France or Germany. Adenauer accepts, though he dislikes referendums, and he is criticised at home for agreeing. The Saarlanders choose Germany, just as they did after the First World War.

Adenauer gives way on all fronts except for Article 1 of the new *Deutschland Vertrag*: 'The Federal Republic shall have, accordingly, the full authority of a sovereign state.' For this he has worked since 1945.

The problem of East Germany does not go away. The Austrian State Treaty of 1955 – Soviet withdrawal in exchange for neutrality – is greeted with joy in Vienna. The idea of German neutrality is still not dead; but with the Eden package, West Germany is sovereign and inside NATO; its future is no longer in the hands of the Four Powers.

In response to Germany joining NATO, the Soviet Union creates the Warsaw Pact and gives the GDR more (theoretical) sovereignty. The new Federal Republic, in turn, adopts the Hallstein Doctrine, named after Walter Hallstein, Adenauer's key foreign-policy aide: the Federal Republic represents Germany as a whole; it will therefore not open diplomatic relations with any state that recognises the GDR.

Berlin is not part of German sovereignty; it is now the main focus of Soviet pressure. The western half of Berlin is an island in the GDR; for the West it is vulnerable; for the East it is an eyesore, a confirmation of the failure of socialism. Khrushchev believes that his missiles in the

GDR strengthen his leverage on the West (in theory they can hit Paris and London). He delivers a series of ultimatums on Berlin in 1958, demanding it be unified as a 'free city'.

No one believes that, surrounded by the GDR, the 'free city' of Berlin would remain free for long. Plans for a renewed air lift are drawn up again. The British prime minister, Harold Macmillan, who fought in the First World War and dislikes ultimatums, visits Khrushchev in Moscow in February 1959; Adenauer sees this as a breach of Western solidarity (and it is). Khrushchev backs down, but tries again in June, bullying Kennedy in Vienna. Everyone finds Khrushchev disagreeable, but nobody takes his threats seriously enough to act on them.

Nobody, that is, except for the East Berliners. The repeated threats raise their fears that their door to the West will close permanently. The number of those leaving accelerates: 10,000 in June 1961, 30,000 in July; 2,500 on one single day, 12 August.

On the next day, 13 August, East German soldiers start to close the border, first by stopping traffic, then with barbed wire, then with concrete. When the work is finished there will be mines, tripwires and automatic firing devices. The United States reinforces its presence in Berlin, and tanks confront each other at Checkpoint Charlie. The dogs bark on either side of a fence. But no one does anything to stop the division of the city.

The Adenauer years are those of the *Wirtschaftswunder* – the economic miracle. The credit for this begins with George Marshall; then General Clay, who sets the currency reform in motion; and then the economic policies of Ludwig Erhard, who succeeds Adenauer as chancellor. Adenauer provides stability and confidence.

The German people should not be forgotten. They choose to get on with the present and forget the past. They survive, recover and rebuild. Adenauer says little, but his actions speak louder: none more than when he agrees, without consulting his Cabinet or negotiating with the Israelis, to meet their request for $1.5 billion in compensation, an unheard-of sum, equivalent to two years' receipts from Marshall aid.

Adenauer explained himself to Acheson in 1949: it is not good for people to become isolated, he says. 'It accentuates their least desirable characteristics.'[5] He is thinking of Germany, as he has been for many years. But who can he trust? Not the Soviet Union, of course. Britain is disappointing; France is unreliable. Above all, not Germany. That leaves the United States.

But when the Berlin Wall goes up, Adenauer is absent. What everyone remembers is Kennedy, in 1963, speaking to a crowd that stretches as far as the eye can see: 'All free men wherever they may live are citizens of Berlin, and therefore, as a free man, I take pride in the words, "Ich bin ein Berliner."' By then a new era is in preparation.

Brandt

The Berlin Wall is a defeat for all sides; Khrushchev gives up the idea of uniting Berlin under the control of the East; Walter Ulbricht, leader of the Socialist Unity Party (SED) and de facto ruler, admits, by his actions, that East Germany is viable only as a prison; the West, confronted by the reality of East Germany in concrete, finds that it can do nothing about it. Kennedy's words are inspiring for Berliners in the West, but they offer nothing for those in the East. The wall divides families and friends throughout the city. This is the backdrop for a second generation of diplomacy.

When the Berlin Wall goes up, Willy Brandt is mayor. Brandt is a Berliner by adoption. Born Herbert Frahm in Lübeck in 1913 to a single mother, he grew up in a working-class world where Social Democracy was a natural part of life. He won a scholarship to a *Gymnasium*, which boys of his class would not normally attend. He was politically active and became radical (a master who admired his gifts said, 'What a pity. Politics will ruin him.').[6] Too radical for the SPD, he joined a splinter group, the Socialist Workers' Party, and became the head of its youth wing. In 1933 the party was banned, and Herbert Frahm gave himself the *nomme de guerre* 'Willy Brandt' to evade arrest. The party sent him as its representative to Oslo. There, and in Sweden, he learned the practical merits of moderate Social Democracy.

From exile in Norway, Brandt travelled: to France, to Spain in the civil war, briefly to Germany undercover; then he moved to Sweden after the German invasion of Norway – twelve years of politics and writing, with Germany as the central theme.

At the end of the war he returned to the ruins of Germany, working for a Norwegian newspaper, and then for the Norwegian embassy as press attaché. In 1948 he became the SPD's liaison officer in Berlin. Thus he settled into Berlin and the SPD under Ernst Reuter, the great mayor of Berlin, ex-Communist and anti-Communist, during the blockade. Reuter, and with him Brandt, saw the world from the front line. Salvation depended on the firmness of the Western allies. Ideas of reunification and neutrality were an illusion.

Brandt is outside Berlin, campaigning to become chancellor, when the GDR starts building the wall. He is woken in the early morning of 13 August 1961 with the news from Berlin. He gets off his train at Hanover and flies in to Tempelhof, the airport of the air lift. In Berlin he holds a special session of the Senate and visits the military headquarters. There he finds that the Allies still keep a place at the table for the Soviet commander, who has not used it since 1948. Nobody can think of anything to do about the wall, except to express outrage and counsel prudence. Brandt, too, does both. But he does one thing more: he writes to President Kennedy. The letter infuriates Kennedy; Brandt is usurping the chancellor's role (during an election campaign too). Kennedy finds the tone impertinent, and many of the suggestions it makes unwise. Brandt refers to the letter at an election rally even before Kennedy receives it, annoying him still more.

In spite of his irritation, Kennedy decides he has to do something, if only for domestic reasons. He sends General Clay, the former military governor and a hero in Berlin, and Vice-President Lyndon Johnson, who needs some persuading to go. This is nevertheless well judged. The president cannot go himself; and to send the secretary of state would suggest the United States had a policy to discuss. The vice-president is a symbol of US commitment; that is all the policy that the people of Berlin want. Johnson arrives on 19 August, the weekend after the wall goes up; the Berliners give him a welcome such as he has never seen before. He loves the visit; the crowds roar approval when he tells them that US military reinforcements are rolling up the autobahn. He stays longer than intended to greet the arriving troops, who the citizens of Berlin shower with flowers.

With the wall comes the first chink in Adenauer's armour. Brandt, and now Kennedy too, are reacting, but Adenauer is nowhere to be seen. He responds with studied calm. This may be right diplomatically – no one wants to start a war – but it is wrong for a chancellor whose citizens in Berlin want reassurance and solidarity. He chooses instead to make a personal attack on Brandt, referring to him as 'Brandt alias Frahm', drawing attention either to Brandt's illegitimacy or to his time in exile during the war. Then he somehow excludes himself from Johnson's visit to Berlin. Ten days after the wall goes up, he arrives in Berlin. As the placards inform him, he is late. His misjudgements cost the CDU its absolute majority in the Bundestag election. It is the beginning of the end.

Brandt does better than Adenauer in terms of symbols; but he knows that symbols are not enough. This, for many people, is a personal crisis. Someone needs to get to grips with the situation. East Germany and East Berlin are unpleasant; but they are realities that have to be dealt with in a practical way. The only way to do that is to deal with those who hold power.

Two weeks before he visits Berlin in 1963, Kennedy delivers a commencement address at the American University in Washington. The speech distils some of the president's reflections after the Cuban Missile Crisis. It attracts Brandt's attention: 'What kind of peace do we seek? Not a *pax Americana* enforced by American weapons of war. Not the peace of the grave or the security of the slave.'[7] It is time, Kennedy says, to rethink the United States' relationship with the Soviet Union, to rethink the Cold War, to focus on the practical and attainable rather than the grand, or the search for a magic formula. 'Genuine peace must be the product of many nations, the sum of many acts.' It should be possible to 'seek a relaxation of tension without relaxing our guard'. As practical steps, Kennedy speaks of non-proliferation and of banning or limiting nuclear tests.

As president, Johnson takes these projects forward, but he is entangled in Vietnam, part, as he saw it, of a global struggle against Communism; besides, his real project is domestic: the big society. But for Willy Brandt and for Egon Bahr – Brandt's closest collaborator, almost his alter ego, though Bahr is a thinker, not a politician – Kennedy's speech shows them the direction they want to take.

In July 1963 Bahr delivers a speech at the Political Academy of Tutzing University that develops these themes. The speech has been written for Brandt, but they decide it is too controversial for the party leader. Probably they are right. As it is, Bahr's remarks become the main focus of press attention, though Adenauer has spoken at the same conference.

The American strategy for peace, Bahr says, 'can also be defined by the formula that Communist rule should be changed, not ended. The US approach . . . helps change the status quo by first attempting not to change it.'[8] This is dialectic, too clever, too German, not the language you use in a commencement address. It is Bahr/Brandt's translation of Kennedy – though Kennedy does say it is not the business of the United States to change how other countries are governed. Brandt and Bahr see the rigidity of the East as a symptom of its weakness. Later in the speech Bahr refers to reunification not as a one-time act, coming through a historic decision, but as a process involving many steps, like Kennedy's approach to peace. The thesis of the speech is summed up in the phrase, 'Wandel durch Annäherung' (change through getting closer).*

Brandt and Bahr have themselves succeeded in one such step, the *Passierscheinabkommen* (permit agreement), painfully negotiated with the East German authorities,† that enabled West Berliners to visit the East over the Christmas holiday of 1963–4; 790,000, one-third of the population, took the opportunity to see relatives and friends in the East. Photographs show thousands queuing in the snow.[9] Behind *Ostpolitik* lies the hope that actions like this can ease the cruelty of the divided city and the divided country.

* The usual translation, 'Change through rapprochement', is too formal and diplomatic. Literally, *Annäherung* means getting closer. An *Annäherungsversuch* can be an advance, in the sense of seduction.

† In theory the Allies are in charge in Berlin; Brandt's negotiators recognise the reality that decisions are made by officials of the GDR, and work with them.

It takes two election cycles to give Brandt the opportunity to put the Tutzing speech into practice. He does well in the 1961 elections after the Berlin crisis and the wall, but not well enough to beat Adenauer, who remains chancellor until he retires, reluctantly, in 1963, handing over, also reluctantly, to Erhard. Brandt remains mayor of Berlin, coping with the divided city. The CDU stays in power, but increasingly in conflict with its coalition partner, the Free Democratic Party (FDP). In 1966 the coalition falls apart and Erhard loses power, suffering from the problems that afflict the successors of great men. A CDU-SPD 'grand coalition' then takes over with Kurt Kiesinger as chancellor and Brandt as vice-chancellor and foreign minister.

The grand coalition takes the transition further: the SPD shows it is competent to govern, and Brandt gets to know the machinery of government from the inside. As mayor of Berlin he is already well known abroad. Meanwhile, a new leadership and a new generation are taking over in the FDP, so that by the federal elections in 1969 its policies towards the East are closer to Brandt's than to those of its long-standing partner, the CDU. Thus, although the CDU wins the largest share of the vote in 1969, a coalition government of the SPD and the FDP is a natural development. Brandt becomes chancellor.*

His policies are based on the philosophy outlined at Tutzing. They are a radical change, but one that fits the international scene. The United States is talking about recognising post-war borders; NATO has agreed the Harmel Report: not just deterrence but dialogue too. In Germany many find the Hallstein Doctrine – that you cut off relations with any country that recognises the GDR – too rigid. Adenauer himself has twice spoken with Brandt about it in ways that suggested his commitment has grown less absolute.[10] The grand coalition prepares the way: it has recognised that Communist states in Eastern Europe have little choice, and exempted them from the doctrine. This allows it to establish relations with Romania and Yugoslavia. Kiesinger also breaks precedent by replying to letters from the GDR

* Nixon, seeing that Kiesinger had the largest number of seats, thought that he had won and telephoned to congratulate him.

government, though he will not use 'German Democratic Republic'.

Willy Brandt's commitment to the West and his anti-Communist credentials are strong, but so is his desire for change. He will not use force; that leaves negotiation as the only route to improving people's lives. His goals are human rights, including the right of self-determination for all Germans. The path to these goals is defined by power politics.

The grand coalition has given him the chance to turn his ideas into proposals to put to governments in the East. Brandt has had command of the resources of the Foreign Ministry, and has found people there he can trust. He makes Bahr head of the Planning Staff, which for once deserves the name: its business over the years 1966–9 is to test the ideas worked out in opposition and turn them into a plan for the next government. This is to establish relationships with the countries to the East, including the GDR, on the basis of the post-war territorial status quo while leaving the question of reunification open. Bahr's objective is to be ready so that, whatever Gromyko brings up in the talks, there is 'no single issue which we had not thought through beforehand'.[11]

Normally, after a war borders are settled in the peace treaty. This did not happen in 1945 because relations among the Second World War Allies broke down. The form that Brandt and Bahr propose to give to *Ostpolitik* is that of treaties renouncing the right to use force to settle disputes, including disputes about the existing borders. These treaties would have the same effect as a peace treaty in which the parties recognised the post-war borders. It sounds clumsy, but it is an imaginative and clever construction. Probably no government has ever come to power with a policy thought out in such detail as this one.

In the four years from January 1970, when Brandt becomes chancellor, the *Ostpolitik* negotiations bring treaties normalising relations with the Soviet Union (August 1970), Poland (December 1970), a renewed Four-Power Agreement on Berlin (September 1971), supported by an agreement between the FRG and the GDR on transit to and from Berlin (September 1971), and the Basic Treaty between the FRG and the GDR (December 1972). With this is an agreement on traffic, and another on membership of the UN (September 1973). Finally, the Prague Treaty restores relations with Czechoslovakia (December 1973). This is a comprehensive reversal of Adenauer's policy.

Brandt's goals are in the Wilsonian idealist tradition: a European peace order, built on self-determination. The strategy to implement it is impeccably realist. The starting point is Moscow, since that is where power lies. This was visible in Berlin in 1953, or 1958–62, in Budapest in 1956, in Prague in the spring of 1968 and in Warsaw on and off through the whole Cold War. In the course of Brandt's negotiations to change relationships in the East, Moscow demonstrates its power by changing the leaders in Warsaw and East Berlin.

The German ambassador in Moscow has begun exploratory exchanges in 1968, under the grand coalition. These are frozen following the Soviet intervention in Prague. They resume under the new government for a final session. After that, Bahr, now State Secretary at the Federal Chancellery, takes over.

Bahr begins in January 1970, not by putting papers on the table, nor with a formal statement. Instead he makes an oral presentation from notes. Behind this lie three years' thought and discussion. He sets out the whole programme. The treaty with the Soviet Union will be the centrepiece; but he also lays out Brandt's plans for agreements with the East European countries, including the GDR. He explains the renunciation of force as a way of recognising existing borders; in the case of the GDR this does not exclude change by peaceful means.

The discussion of concepts continues for three sessions. Gromyko contests some points, notably those relating to the GDR: he wants formal recognition of the Oder-Neisse line – the GDR's border with Poland – and West Berlin's status as separate from the Federal Republic. On the last, Bahr replies that he does not want West Berlin to become a third German state. Gromyko says these issues should be separated from the question of a European Security Conference; Bahr replies that a conference will make sense only if the German-Soviet issues are resolved. After five meetings over three weeks, including one with Prime Minister Alexei Kosygin – to show that the Soviet side is taking the negotiations seriously – Bahr offers to put the results on paper so the two governments can decide whether there is material for a treaty. They agree that each side should do this, with a view to turning the results into a common text.

This style of negotiation suits the radical nature of the proposals. Better to explain the ideas before putting them in writing: a written document brings the risk that misunderstandings get baked in. Beginning orally shows that Bahr is the master of his material, not a messenger, that he has authority to explore and to invent. In this way the negotiations become a collaborative process where the two sides seek a common understanding.

Two weeks later Bahr returns. Discussion is now about bringing together the papers that the two sides have written: then, a break for each side to go through the work done with their authorities. Then, in May, the moment that occurs in every negotiation when one side threatens to break off. In this case it is Bahr who thinks they are going nowhere. The Soviet side hastens to explain that the delay is because they have gone so far and so fast that they need new political authority. On 22 May Gromyko gets the instructions he is seeking from the Politburo. He and Bahr finish with ten agreed 'theses'. Some of these will go into the treaty; others – such as the Federal Republic's goal of reunification – will be in unilateral statements; others describe the way forward with other Eastern-bloc countries or at the European Security Conference.

Formal negotiations on the treaty are concluded between Gromyko and the Federal foreign minister, Walter Scheel, on 6 August 1970. The most sensitive point is the Soviet insistence that the treaty should refer explicitly to the Oder-Neisse line. Brandt agrees to this, subject to a side letter noting that the border (though inviolable) is still subject to a formal peace treaty. Six days later Brandt and Scheel on the one side, Kosygin and Gromyko on the other, sign the treaty, with Brezhnev taking centre-stage for the photograph. Three years' preparation followed by six months' negotiation end a fifteen-year blockage in relations between Moscow and Bonn. This sets the scene for treaties throughout Eastern Europe.

The Moscow Treaty ends the Federal Republic's claim to be the sole representative of the German people, and the Hallstein Doctrine.

A 'Scheel Doctrine' now asks third countries to put relations with the GDR on hold until the Federal Republic can finish its own negotiations with the GDR. The Moscow Treaty, tacitly, and Bahr's negotiating programme implicitly, acknowledges a Soviet sphere of influence in Eastern Europe. Bahr has begun the negotiations in Moscow, and he has agreed the whole programme there. Now, for the first time since the war, Germany is dealing with the Soviet Union on its own, as a normal European power – which to some degree it still is not.

Germany is once more Europe's largest economy; its history and Russia's are intertwined; now, as before, it will become Russia's most important economic partner, and the country that Russia will look to when it wants to modernise.* They are still on different sides; but the treaty opens new possibilities. It is this image of Germany, once again between East and West, that awakens historical memories in Henry Kissinger, so that, commenting on *Ostpolitik* to Richard Nixon, he recalls Bismarck and the Treaty of Rapallo (1922).[12]

The core of the Moscow Treaty is about borders. Germany accepts the frontiers negotiated by Stalin at Potsdam. Everyone assumed this would come sooner or later; but uncertainty stimulates the imagination. Twice in the century Germany has invaded Russia. Potsdam was as much a *diktat* as Versailles. One day an unratified border might again be made a *casus belli*. Everyone knows this issue is important for the Soviets; it is only as the process goes on that they understand how important.

Crushing the Prague Spring has secured Brezhnev's control of the party and given him the authority to take bold steps in relations with the West. The West, as a protest against Prague, has cancelled meetings and cooled relations. This makes Moscow all the more receptive to Brandt's initiative.

As described in the previous chapter, the one effect of the events in Prague, and the Brezhnev doctrine, is to alarm Beijing. For Moscow,

* The one exception is Peter the Great, who enlisted help from the Netherlands. The other giant of Russian history, Catherine the Great, was born German.

the clashes with China make it more urgent to settle the borders in the West. Soviet intelligence, as usual, sees a conspiracy: it is 'not a coincidence', they conclude, that a Chinese attack took place 'just at the same time' as Germany held its presidential elections in Berlin.[13] The United States is aware of the China factor, but imagines a link could be made to Berlin.

Warsaw

The negotiations with Warsaw, foreseen in the talks with Gromyko, begin while Bahr is in Moscow. They are launched by State Secretary Georg Duckwitz.* The content is similar to the Moscow Treaty: a renunciation of the use of force, the functional equivalent to recognition of the border. Like the Soviet government, Warsaw's interest is overwhelmingly in the borders. The agreement at Potsdam gave Poland 'provisional administrative responsibility' for a large part of the territory, not ownership. This was to await a peace treaty. Much of the land had been German for centuries.

Because their priority is the border, the Poles do not press for compensation for war damage. The Polish government renounced claims to reparations in 1953, but claims by individuals are still possible. This is true on the German side too: there are claims against German property taken over by Poles. The German side has another issue it prefers to keep out of the treaty: this is emigration for the 60,000 ethnic Germans who remain in Poland. The treaty says nothing on this; but the Polish government makes a statement of its readiness to work with the Polish Red Cross on 'the question of resettlement'. In the end two subjects come together: the German government agrees loans on generous terms, in theory to enable the Polish state to replace skilled Germans by mechanising the economy.

Focusing on these issues misses the point. This, more than any of the other *Ostpolitik* treaties, has an emotional content. Willy Brandt thinks of reconciliation with Poland as the Eastern equivalent of reconciliation

* The same Duckwitz who appears in Chapter Three, thirty years younger.

with France. Germany has participated in four partitions of Poland. The last was the Molotov-Ribbentrop Pact; after this the Polish state again disappeared from the map.*

The image of Brandt, and of *Ostpolitik*, that remains in the collective memory of Europe is that of the chancellor falling to his knees on the wet pavement of the monument to the Warsaw Ghetto. The official press in Poland chooses to interpret this as a gesture towards the Jewish victims of Nazi Germany – and the photograph is placed only in the Yiddish newspaper – but Brandt's thoughts go wider. In his memoirs he writes:

> I discussed it with no one. Oppressed by memories of Germany's recent history, I simply did what people do when words fail them. . . . My gesture was intelligible to those willing to understand it, and they included many in Germany and elsewhere. The tears in the eyes of my delegation were a tribute to the dead. As one reporter put it: 'Then he knelt, he who has no need to, on behalf of all who ought to kneel – but don't because they dare not, or cannot.' That was what it was, an attempt . . . to build a bridge to the history of our nation and its victims.[14]

His hosts, Brandt notes, say nothing that day. Perhaps his action disconcerts them. The next day the premier, Józef Cyrankiewicz – who he describes as having a faint aura of Austria-Hungary about him – tells Brandt that his wife telephoned a friend in Vienna to tell her about it, and the two wept.

Diplomacy should not be without emotion. Brandt's gesture is an act of remembrance and a plea for forgiveness – something easier done than said; it is a statement of how Germany should remember the war, and how it should live with its neighbours. This is still a time when most people in Germany choose not to think about the past – a continuation of the Adenauer era. After the visit to Warsaw, opinion polls

* The eastern border of Poland today remains roughly that of the Molotov-Ribbentrop Pact.

show that 48 per cent of Germans find Brandt's gesture 'excessive'. The new generation will view the past differently. Brandt is a turning point.

The emotion of Brandt's visit leaves a mark on Germany's relations with Poland; something of the special quality he brought to the relationship lives on, in spite of the ups and downs of business between difficult neighbours.

The German Democratic Republic

The Moscow negotiations set the political framework. The Warsaw visit is the emotional heart of *Ostpolitik*. But *Ostpolitik* begins with Brandt's experience as mayor of Berlin. In an interview in the *Frankfurter Allgemeine Zeitung* in 2005 Bahr says: 'The decisive point in the change in mentality was that wall. We understood in 1961 that everybody was content, that nobody was going to help us to make holes in it, or to make it permeable. So it began. Since we could not get travel permits from Bonn or America or Moscow, we had to negotiate with those who were authorised to issue them' – namely the GDR. The question of Berlin is at the root of *Ostpolitik*: an agreement with the GDR is the original goal, though the 'Moscow first' strategy is the essential means.

Negotiating with a state that you do not recognise, and for whom recognition is a great prize, means endless quibbling about words. By the end, the Federal Republic has recognised its ugly sister as a state in every practical sense, except that it deals with it through the Federal Chancellery instead of the Foreign Ministry since it is not a foreign country. For this reason it opens not an embassy in East Berlin but a 'liaison office', though there is no practical difference. Erich Honecker makes a state visit to Bonn in all but name, but the Federal Republic has never recognised the GDR. The German courts and German history have confirmed this.

The GDR, like the FRG, has practical concerns. Other countries such as Poland can relax tension, increase contacts, free up travel with the Federal Republic and prosper. The GDR wants as much recognition and as little contact as it can get. It knows that if it opens up, its population will emigrate to the West; if there is too much contact they may catch the virus of freedom; if they get freedom they might even choose reunification. The GDR is a weak state, held together by barbed wire and informers.

These risks are visible in another emotional moment. This is Willy Brandt's visit to Erfurt in March 1970, before any of the treaties are proposed, before he goes to Moscow or Warsaw. The visit is almost comically mismanaged by the GDR. The venue is changed to Erfurt at the last minute, probably because they fear that Brandt is too well known in East Berlin. It turns out he is well known in Erfurt too; and security there is less prepared. Plans are made late and then changed at the last minute. The authorities do not have time to organise their supporters. Instead, the people of Erfurt organise themselves: they gather hours before Brandt arrives. When, at the last minute, the police move one of the barricades – to block the view of Brandt's arrival – the crowd gets loose and the police never regain control.

It is a mistake, too, to give Brandt a hotel room with a window on a public square. The crowd gathers there, shouting, 'Willy Brandt to the window', drowning out those assembled by the state to shout for Willi Stoph, the GDR prime minister. Brandt goes to the window, gesturing to the crowd not to become too excited. In Moscow this brings him credit – it shows he is not trying to create a popular revolt. This is true: the last thing he wants is a repeat of 1953. But in Erfurt it is too late. The crowd is not demonstrating against their government, nor for unification; the people are showing their appreciation for a German leader who appeals to them.

Bahr has told the Soviet negotiators a month earlier that the Federal Republic is ready to negotiate with the GDR, but that they need to be aware of the 'special character' of relations between the two.[15] In a televised interview after the visit Brandt refers to the common history that Erfurt embodies – Luther presented his doctoral dissertation there – and quotes Napoleon's statement to Goethe, in Erfurt, that 'Politics is fate.' He is probably thinking how politics has determined the different lives of Germans in the GDR and the Federal Republic.*

Willy Brandt's talks in Erfurt with Willi Stoph show how barren negotiation will be.† Willi Stoph talks theory: recognition and history – the division of Germany is the fault of the West and the Federal Republic; both have pursued militaristic policies. The GDR's measures to 'safeguard its frontier' are a humanitarian act; reunification will happen only when socialism is victorious in the Federal Republic. Willy Brandt talks about practical matters, contact and communication, especially for West Berlin, and hears in return that West Berlin is not part of the FRG. Stoph shows some interest in improving commercial relations, but the Federal Republic, he insists, has robbed East Germany by unfair trade while the border was open. Both sides find the talks disappointing.

They meet again in Kassel in May. This time extremists from the right and left, exercising freedom of speech, provide less pleasant crowd scenes. The dialogue of the deaf continues. Willy Brandt sets out twenty points agreed by his Cabinet as a basis for a treaty: renunciation of force; 'internal' sovereignty; two states but one nation; the rights of the Four Powers in Berlin; more freedom of contact and of movement; exchange of 'plenipotentiaries' (ambassadors in all but name); membership of the UN. What divides them is the division of Germany: is it real and permanent? In the GDR this is a matter of Marxist theory, and it is difficult to discuss with people who do not share the faith. Willi Stoph concludes that Willy Brandt is refusing relations based on equal rights. Willy Brandt replies that contact has been established; but more goodwill will be needed for it to be productive.

Berlin

If the Cold War were an examination, Berlin would be a special paper. Berlin is the last remnant of the occupation, the last place still under

* Napoleon's remark recalls Rousseau's (in the *Confessions*): 'I had come to see that, at the root, everything was connected to politics, and that . . . no nation could be other than what the nature of its government made it' (Gallimard, *Pléiade*, vol. 1, p. 404).

† Many East Germans with houses along the railway line that brought Willy Brandt's special train to Erfurt placed 'Y's in their windows, to show which Willy they preferred.

the control of the Four Powers. The paradox of West Berlin is that it remains free because it *is* under occupation. The position of the West, however, is precarious. Since the blockade ended in 1949, co-operation among the Four Powers has been unreliable. On top of this, the GDR has a natural instinct for obstruction, and Berlin remains a tempting pressure point for Moscow.*

With the Moscow Treaty the balance changes. The Bundestag will not ratify it unless it is accompanied by an agreement on Berlin. The Soviet Union now needs the Berlin dimension of *Ostpolitik* to succeed. From autumn 1970 it instructs the GDR – through Party links – to engage directly with the FRG.

In Washington at this time, Kissinger notes the disturbances in Warsaw and Władysław Gomułka's fall; he concludes that *Ostpolitik* may bring instability. He decides to involve himself personally in the question of Berlin; this is where the United States has leverage.

Kissinger's attitude to *Ostpolitik*, and to Brandt and Bahr, is mixed. Of Bahr he writes: 'As for his alleged deviousness, I tended to share Metternich's view that in a negotiation the perfectly straightforward person was the most difficult to deal with.'[16] Kissinger follows this remark with a description of how, after a meeting with Bahr in his office accompanied by a State Department official, Bahr leaves the White House by the front door, and then returns through the basement to see Kissinger on his own. There they set up another 'back-channel' together.†

Thereafter Bahr briefs Kissinger on his most important meetings. It is Bahr's report of his talks that alerts Kissinger to the importance the Russians attached to the Moscow Treaty. He concludes that ratification by the Bundestag means there will have to be an agreement on Berlin. Hence:

* Khrushchev, with his instinct for colourful metaphor, described it as 'the testicles of the West'. If you want a reaction, you squeeze.

† Bahr too had a back-channel to Moscow set up by the KGB. Kissinger's back-channels were to cut out the State Department; Brezhnev and Gromyko set up Bahr's to cut out Kosygin.

> Bahr's talks had brought home to me that the linkage to Berlin was our ace in the hole. Bahr assured me that he had pressed Gromyko to agree to undisturbed civilian traffic to Berlin, an essential quid pro quo for German public opinion. Bahr wanted to make sure the Berlin negotiations did not lag behind the German talks. I had the opposite view; once the German talks [i.e. the Moscow Treaty] were completed our bargaining position would be vastly improved because the Soviets would be eager to see the Eastern Treaties ratified.[17]

Kissinger is right; but there is no policy difference between them. After signing the treaty in Moscow, Brandt tells Brezhnev how important it will be to have a good agreement on Berlin. Moscow's initial approach is to have the FRG and the GDR talk to each other; this serves the goal of recognition for the GDR. But in January 1971, Brandt publicly links ratification of the Moscow Treaty to an agreement on Berlin; from that point on Moscow takes an active interest in the Berlin talks.

Kissinger handles Berlin through another back-channel, this time to the US ambassador in Bonn, Kenneth Rush, a political appointee but a good one. Rush was Nixon's law professor at Duke University, competent and not tainted by association with the State Department. Kissinger finds ways to bring Bahr and Rush to Washington,* and sets up direct and secret communication with both. 'I insisted we keep each other informed about every contact with the Soviets or East Germans over Berlin . . . Bahr and Rush together would formulate propositions in three areas and sound out allied reactions; I would explore them Dobrynin; and then Rush or Bahr would put them into regular channels'.[18]

The three areas Kissinger refers to are: access, entry and status. Access (*Zugang*) means reliable arrangements for people and goods to transit East German territory to and from West Berlin. Entry (*Zutritt*) means that West Berliners should be able to visit the GDR, including East Berlin. Status (*Zuordnung*) concerns West Berlin's status as a part of the

* Bahr was invited to a space launch, Rush by his legal partner, John Mitchell.

Federal Republic. The first two are clear. Status is harder to pin down: the FRG makes its point, from time to time, by holding Federal events in Berlin, for example the Federal presidential election; this policy brings with it a series of small crises.

Initially the Soviet approach is to link Berlin to progress in FRG-GDR relations, and it encourages talks: Bahr for the FRG, Michael Kohl for the GDR (they worked together on the permit agreement, years before). When the Soviet side realise that the Berlin Agreement is critical to ratification of the Moscow Treaty they change their approach. M. E. Sarotte quotes Marcus Wolf, the East German spymaster: 'Nothing could be more inconvenient for him [Brezhnev] than independent, hard to oversee, contacts between the GDR and the FRG.'[19]

A similar thought seems to have occurred to Kissinger. In February 1971 he suspects that the Soviets are using the German-German talks to evade the Four-Power format (and the United States); he warns Bahr against this. Rush takes it up in a more dramatic fashion: Bahr is summoned late at night to a formal meeting of the three Western ambassadors, accompanied by their deputies. They tell him not to discuss transit with Michael Kohl until the Four Powers have reached agreement among themselves. After this the German-German talks pause.

From mid April the pace quickens. Kissinger and Anatoly Dobrynin, agree that Rush, Bahr and Valentin Falin (the top Soviet expert on Germany, now ambassador in Bonn) should work together to push the Four-Power talks along. Kissinger again finds a way to bring Bahr to the United States and meets him in Vermont. It seems that with this encounter he begins to appreciate Bahr: he approves Bahr's proposal to simplify the treaty by omitting explanations and instead simply stating the rights and obligations of the parties. Kissinger then tries out the idea on Dobrynin, who 'accepted with an alacrity that suggested he was not hearing it for the first time'. Kissinger comments: 'It was not always absolutely clear how many channels were operating and who the principal negotiator was.'[20] He evidently suspects that Bahr is negotiating behind his back. If so, he is doing it skilfully: and the Rush-Bahr-Falin group becomes the place where problems are solved.

This group meets first in May; from June, work moves forward at an undreamed-of pace. A month later Falin takes the draft agreement to Moscow for approval. By then, the Soviets are making the Berlin Agreement a condition for the US-Soviet summit, which they know Nixon wants. In fact, they all want the Berlin Agreement: Brezhnev to ensure ratification of the Moscow Treaty; Kissinger because it is the US that defends Berlin; Bahr because Berlin is where he and Brandt come from. The agreement is signed on 3 September 1971.

The remarkable thing about this complicated, multi-party, multi-layered negotiation is that, after preliminary skirmishing, it is all done by three people in one month. The lesson is that if you get the key people together – those whose interests are at stake, and who have the authority to decide – problems can be solved quickly. Of the three, only Rush is a member of the formal negotiating body. (The Russian in the Four-Power talks is not Falin but Peter Abrassimov, the ambassador to the GDR.) The agreement satisfies everyone except Ulbricht. Moscow, which for some time has found Ulbricht too independent, arranges for Honecker to replace him.

The Berlin Agreement gives Soviet (not GDR) guarantees to the West on access and visits – a sign of who is trusted and who is not; it makes some concessions on Federal activities in West Berlin, and allows the Soviets to open a consulate there. The Soviet concessions in this agreement are the price of ratifying the Moscow Treaty.

The last hurdle is the inability of the FRG and the GDR to agree on a German translation of the Berlin Agreement. This delays work on the implementation of the agreement. The French ambassador solves the problem by insisting that there should be no official German translation.*

The Berlin Agreement is one part of a three-part deal. It has to be accompanied by an FRG-GDR agreement to implement the principles

* Kissinger and Timothy Garton Ash (in *In Europe's Name*) find it odd that a treaty about Germany, where the recipients of rights and obligations are Germans, is not in the German language. But it is not about Germany. Berlin is in occupied Germany. Allied Directive no. 1 (1945) states that the official languages in occupied Germany will be English, French and Russian. The French ambassador is right.

agreed by the Four Powers. The foreign ministers of the Four will then sign a Final Act bringing the two agreements into force.

Thus, when Rush finishes his work and collapses with exhaustion, Bahr takes up the negotiations with Michael Kohl again. He begins by saying he knows nothing of customs and border procedures, and will leave them to experts. He and Michael Kohl deal with the principles. These are difficult enough. As a police and informer state the GDR does not like 'foreigners' travelling freely in its country; for access to Berlin, it insists that only certain routes can be used: there can be no stopping except at approved locations, including for 'comfort breaks'. Second, it objects to negotiating this with the FRG rather than the Berlin Senate: Berlin is not a part of Federal territory. Third, the GDR haggles about how much money will be paid – in theory, a contribution to highway maintenance – and who will pay, Berlin or Bonn.

Moscow, wanting the treaty ratified, helps with all three. On the second and third points Gromyko, visiting Berlin in October 1971, and Brezhnev later that month, express deep sympathy for the GDR's concerns; but ratification of all the treaties is too important. They will have to sign an agreement with the FRG on Berlin, and accept a lump-sum payment from Bonn covering both Berliners and West Germans. That is that. (The haggling over the sum is left to Bahr.) This means that both the Soviet Union and the GDR accept that West Berlin is a part of the FRG, in practice if not in theory, a perfect result for the West's objective on status (*Zuordnung*) in the quadripartite talks.

The conditions for travel imposed by the GDR are evidently unreasonable, and the three Western powers threaten to reject them. Bahr can do nothing about the conditions; but he enlists Falin to convince Rush that the agreement is as good as can be negotiated, and Rush persuades the other two. The Transit Agreement between the FRG and the GDR is signed in December 1971.

The first months of 1972 are occupied with domestic politics in the Federal Republic, ahead of the ratification debate. In the East, the GDR allows West Berliners to visit East Berlin over the weekends of Easter and Pentecost. A million do so, for the first time since 1966. This is to help Moscow's campaign for ratification in the Bundestag, but it is also as a dry run to help the Stasi work out how to deal with an influx of Westerners.

Brandt has been awarded the Nobel Peace Prize in 1971. This does not prevent an attempt to replace him as chancellor through a vote of no confidence in the Bundestag. The CDU is so confident of victory that its candidate, Rainer Barzel, has booked tickets to Moscow for two days after the vote, with a view to renegotiating the treaty.

In the event the opposition fails by two votes*, but the CDU shows its power by refusing to pass the budget of the Federal Chancellery the following day. To prepare for ratification, Brandt proposes the Bundestag make a statement interpreting the treaties. This incorporates elements from the opposition, and becomes part of the law ratifying the treaties. When it comes to the vote the opposition abstains, and the treaties are ratified on 17 May. Nine days later, in Moscow, Nixon and Brezhnev sign SALT 1. They welcome the Moscow Treaty and the Quadripartite Agreement, the first among the Four since the Cold War began in 1947.

Bahr and Michael Kohl move on to the traffic agreement between the GDR and the FRG. This is dense and technical, and also political. The Traffic Treaty refers to 'normal good neighbourly relations' and 'mutual exchange', but it means nothing of the sort. Normality is the last thing the GDR wants: everything is restricted and supervised. The work on this treaty ends during the ratification process and the no-confidence vote crisis. It is signed on 26 May, the first treaty between the two Germanies, unthinkable a few years before.

Bahr then negotiates the Basic Treaty with the GDR. This is another depressing experience, reflecting the dialogue of the deaf between Willy Brandt and Willi Stoph a year earlier. The problems are all theoretical: is there a German nation? Did the Second World War end without a peace treaty? The treaty changes little, though a side agreement enables both the GDR and the FRG to join the UN. The

* The East German spymaster, Markus Wolf, later explained: 'I bribed one Bundestag member and blackmailed another.' (Gordon Barrass, *The Great Cold War*, p. 175.)

GDR gets a little more recognition: West Germans can visit the GDR, but have to pay through the nose via an artificial exchange rate. For East Germans going to the West the price is higher: first persecution at home, second a long negotiation, third a large ransom paid by the FRG. Few of those wanting to leave get to stage three. Meanwhile, more West Germans visiting the GDR means more Stasi and more informers, making the GDR even more of a police state.

Kissinger writes that much of Germany was critical of Brandt because he 'foreswore its national claims in return for an improvement of atmosphere', plus the Berlin agreements.[21] Perhaps some on the right felt like that. But anyone who had asserted the 'national claims' would have provoked uproar, including in the United States. Some in the Bundestag complained, rightly, that the Soviet concessions on Berlin represented the 'return to the West of rights that had been pilfered in the past years'. But the result was not just a better atmosphere; it was that the era of Berlin crises was over.

Atmosphere also matters. Adenauer persuaded the West to trust Germany; Brandt persuaded the East that Germany was no longer to be feared. The German-Soviet relationship became more normal; that is another reason why the Berlin crises come to an end.

At Tutzing, Bahr has said that pressure from the West produced counter-pressure from the East. A less threatening Germany might bring fluidity in the East. The Soviet Union justified its sphere of influence as protecting Eastern European countries from a resurgent Germany. Moscow invoked the Second World War and the liberation of Eastern Europe when it supressed reform in Hungary and Czechoslovakia. Thus, over time, a change of atmosphere impacts on Soviet relations with its satellites as well as with Germany. A more normal Germany leads to a more normal Eastern Europe. A change of atmosphere is one of those 'intangibles' whose value can only be understood with the passage of time.

More normal also meant more sovereign. Adenauer detested Four-Power meetings: they were a symbol of Germany's powerlessness. Willy Brandt delivered a new agreement on Berlin that made life better and more secure for Berliners; this was negotiated not by the Four

Powers, but by three: the United States, the Soviet Union and the Federal Republic.

The failure of the Tutzing programme is the concept of 'small steps' and 'change by getting closer'. The one thing that does not change in the next two decades is the GDR.

Brandt was unusual in German politics: an international figure who brought ideas, charm and imagination. With Egon Bahr he formed one of the great diplomatic partnerships: Brandt open and emotional, Bahr cynical, but in his own way idealistic too. Brandt seems, in retrospect, an un-German figure, a comet in the night sky that visits and then is gone. While he executed them, his policies were fiercely contested. When they were done, they became common ground for all political actors. That is one definition of diplomatic success.

Kohl

The man behind Rainer Barzel's attempt to replace Brandt as chancellor in 1972 was said to be Helmut Kohl. Brandt remains in place, but Kohl replaces Barzel as leader of the CDU shortly after. In 1982 he becomes chancellor through a vote of no confidence: many Free Democrats desert their coalition with the SPD (then led by Helmut Schmidt) and vote for Kohl. In March 1983 the electorate gives a working majority to a CDU-FDP coalition, with Kohl as chancellor.

Kohl is known in political circles as 'Adenauer's grandson'. He joined the CDU in 1946, at the age of sixteen; he grew up in Adenauer's party and wrote his doctoral thesis at Heidelberg University on it. He was elected a CDU member of the Rheinland-Pfalz Landtag at the age of thirty, and nine years later became its minister-president.

In the early 1980s Germany is consumed by the debate on NATO's 'twin-track' decision. Track one is the deployment of Cruise and Pershing II missiles to offset Soviet SS-20s aimed at Europe; track two is the offer to give up all medium-range missiles on both sides. This policy is strongly defended by Helmut Schmidt. But his party is divided: many on the left do not want to deploy any missiles ever.

A Soviet-sponsored campaign against the deployment attracts massive support across Europe, above all in Germany. It brings the largest demonstrations in the post-war period, civil disobedience and a reference to the Constitutional Court. It divides the SPD and is one of the reasons that the FDP switches sides.

Kohl defeats this campaign. Important support comes from President François Mitterrand, who addresses the Bundestag on a first visit in January 1983: 'The missiles are in the East; the pacifists are in the West,'[22] he tells them. Kohl's victory in the election, six weeks later, confirms his line on the missiles and the Bundestag authorises deployment in Germany. Kohl's commitment to NATO and his co-operation with France both echo the Adenauer legacy.

The defeat of its campaign on the missiles is one of the failures of the Soviet Union of the 1980s that leads it to rethink its strategy. The peace movement ceases to matter in West Germany, but its idealism lives on in East Germany, where it will play a part in the events of 1989.

Kohl's memoirs, published in 1996, are entitled *Ich Wollte Deutschlands Einheit* (*I Wanted German Unity*). So he did. In his first speech commemorating the 1953 workers' rising in East Germany he says: 'Today, we return once more to the true purpose of this address. It concerns Germany. It concerns self-determination, human rights, the unity of our divided nation.'[23]

Through the 1980s the signs of change become more visible. In 1980 the ship workers of Gdansk create an independent trade union, Solidarity, under Lech Wałęsa; and the Supreme Court in Poland decides that it is not illegal. By then it has 10 million members. A year later General Jaruzelski declares martial law – a very un-Communist action. Solidarity is banned and Wałęsa imprisoned. But then he is released; and in summer 1983 martial law ends.

The arrival of Mikhail Gorbachev is usually seen as the turning point in the Cold War, but its precursor is the decision not to intervene in Poland. Yuri Andropov, then head of the KGB, supports this – 'The quota of interventions abroad has been exhausted' – as does Brezhnev.[24]

Brezhnev dies in 1982. He is replaced by Andropov, who dies of kidney failure just over a year later; his replacement, Konstantin

Chernenko, starts off almost as sick as Brezhnev in his final years, and lasts only a year. In March 1985 Gorbachev becomes General Secretary of the Communist Party. In July Gromyko, foreign minister since 1957, is kicked upstairs as president. Gorbachev chooses Eduard Shevardnadze to replace him.

Gorbachev is different: younger but no less tough; bolder, talking of disarmament and change.

In 1985, Hungarian elections permit and elect independent candidates. On 25 December that year, late at night, the doorbell rings in the Gorky apartment where Andrei Sakharov, the Soviet Union's best-known dissident, lives in exile. Outside are two electricians and a man from the KGB. They install a telephone. The next morning Gorbachev phones Sakharov to tell him personally that he and his wife are to be released.[25]

In 1986, the explosion of the nuclear reactor at Chernobyl and the attempts to keep it secret mean that the smell of failure and decay is unmistakable.

In 1987, the world hears Gorbachev speak of 'the common European home'. By the end of the year Shevardnadze and Secretary of State George Shultz have signed a treaty abolishing all intermediate-range nuclear missiles: Cruise, Pershing and the SS-20s. That is to say, against all the odds, NATO's twin-track policy has been won by track two. In 1988 the Soviet withdrawal from Afghanistan begins; and at the end of the year Gorbachev announces troop withdrawals from Eastern Europe.

It is in October 1988 that Kohl visits Gorbachev in Moscow for the first time. They had met before, but neither has made an impression on the other. After his first contact with Kohl, Gorbachev describes him to the Politburo as anxious to talk, but fearful that other Europeans are stealing a march on him in their relations with Moscow.[26] Yet he always sees the FRG as a crucial partner. He shocks Honecker in October 1986 by referring to the USSR-GDR-FRG triangle as key for world peace, putting the GDR, a fellow socialist country, on the same footing as the Federal Republic.[27] Just after this, however, Kohl says in an interview in *Newsweek* (27 October) that while Gorbachev seems promising, he is still a Communist – though he has a flair for propaganda. He adds that this had been true of Goebbels too.* Gorbachev is insulted by the comparison and decides to 'teach Kohl a lesson' by ignoring him. He receives the German president, Richard von Weizsäcker, instead of Kohl in 1987. Weizsäcker, like Mitterrand, appeals to the intellectual side of Gorbachev; he brings with him a personal message from Kohl apologising for the Goebbels remark; this paves the way for Kohl's visit the following year.[28]

Early in his visit, Kohl speaks personally about the war to Gorbachev: the two of them are the same age, he says, and lived through the war. Gorbachev's father was wounded; Kohl lost his brother. This is both calculated and sincere on Kohl's part. According to Anatoly Chernyaev, it has a remarkable effect: from that moment they are able to deal with each other 'without a hint of hostility or distrust'.[29]

This is an exaggeration. There is no doubt that Kohl admires Gorbachev and wants him to succeed; but there are also moments when the national interest will come first. Not only Kohl and the political class respect Gorbachev, but ordinary Germans do too. They are more aware than any other Western nation of what is happening in Eastern Europe. When he visits Bonn in June 1989, Gorbachev is greeted with unparalleled enthusiasm. Besides, both he and Kohl want change in East Germany, though not, Kohl underlines, instability.[30] By Kohl's account, at one point they speak privately about their war experiences and about German unification: Kohl points to the Rhine and says you cannot stop it flowing to the sea. It is the same with German unity. This is about history, not timetables.

In February 1989 the Polish Round Table talks begin. They agree on limited free elections. When they are held in June, Solidarity wins with every seat up for election in the lower house, and 99 out of 100 in the upper house. In September the first non-Communist government takes power in an Eastern European country. In the GDR's local elections, by contrast, the regime claims that 98.85 per cent voted for the SED. This is normal. What is new is that the elections are monitored

* Clumsy, but not ill intentioned: Kohl did admire Goebbels's skill as a propagandist and said so on other occasions, though not in the press.

by dissidents. They say they can prove that the results are false. Hungary legalises non-Communist parties; but even before the elections it changes its policies. After secret talks with the German government it opens the border in September, to allow the growing number of East Germans in Hungary to cross into Austria; from there they go to the Federal Republic. The GDR responds with restrictions on travel to Hungary; its citizens go instead to Prague, where they take refuge at the West German embassy. The square outside the embassy is filled with people: many of them young couples with a suitcase and a baby; nearby streets are blocked with abandoned Trabants.* Hans-Dietrich Genscher, Kohl's foreign minister, negotiates with the GDR for them to travel to West Germany in a special train, passing through East Germany. A large crowd gathers to watch the train go through Dresden station.

In the summer of 1989 Shevardnadze, on holiday on the Black Sea, hears from his staff that Nicolae Ceauşescu is calling for a Warsaw Pact intervention in Poland, but that Moscow has rejected this. He tells his (surprised) assistant that Moscow will lose control of the Warsaw Pact; ultimately this could lead to the break-up of the Soviet Union too.[31]

Gorbachev believes that socialism can be reformed and given a human face. This will prove more difficult than he thinks. But on one point he is consistent at every stage: his refusal to use force. On this he has the support even of the hardliners in the Politburo. In July the Warsaw Pact summit confirms that member countries have the right to take their own political position without outside interference. The 'Sinatra Doctrine' replaces the Brezhnev Doctrine: every country can do it their way.

Gorbachev, who is embarking on experiments with democracy in the Soviet Union, sees no reason to stop others doing the same. The Hungarian government has warned him of its plan to open the border to Austria, and he has not objected. He does not foresee all the consequences; but it is not clear that he would have changed his policies if he had.[32]

* A particularly cheap and awful GDR car.

Five events mark the path to German unity. The first is Gorbachev's visit to East Berlin in October for the fortieth anniversary of the state.

Gorbachev dislikes Honecker. He agrees to join the celebrations only if he can meet the whole Politburo. The visit is macabre. Gorbachev views a torchlight parade alongside Honecker. He hears East German youths, hand-picked for loyalty, march by shouting, 'Perestroika' and 'Gorbi, help us'. It is not clear whether Honecker, who is stone-deaf, also hears. The next day Honecker lectures Gorbachev on the regime's achievements. Talking to Honecker, he later tells Willy Brandt, is like throwing peas at a wall.[33]

Unification is not a topic. At home Gorbachev agrees that 'under no circumstances can we lose the GDR'. But in Berlin, in a speech at the grave of the unknown soldier, he quotes a poem by Fyodor Tyutchev:

The oracle of our times has proclaimed unity,
Which can be forged only with iron and blood.
But we will try to forge it with love;
Then we shall see which is more lasting.

This, as Philip Zelikow and Condoleezza Rice say in their book *Germany Unified and Europe Transformed*, is strange. It is hard to imagine a speechwriter suggesting it. It is reasonable to guess that this is Gorbachev speaking personally, saying that he is not in sympathy with Bismarck's methods: he will not see force used in the GDR.

Gorbachev does not instruct the GDR Politburo to dismiss Honecker. And Honecker takes his remark that life punishes those who are too late as self-criticism by Gorbachev – suggesting his deafness runs deep. At the end of the visit Egon Krenz, later to be the last Communist leader of East Germany, says to Falin, who is travelling with Gorbachev: 'Your man said all he needed to say. Ours didn't understand anything.' Falin replies, 'The rest is up to you.'[34]

Gorbachev is dedicated to law and to non-violence, but the system he operates in is essentially lawless. The Krenz-Falin exchange could have taken place in the world of the mafia. Krenz drew the right conclusion. At the next Politburo meeting he and his ally, Günter

Schabowski, propose a communiqué critical of the situation in the GDR and so, implicitly, of Honecker. This acts as a catalyst; at the meeting after that, the Politburo members line up to plunge the knife into Honecker. Willi Stoph (still prime minister, ten years after his meeting with Brandt) interrupts Honecker's opening statement to propose he step down; everyone else joins in. Two days later, on 18 October, Honecker resigns, suggesting to the Central Committee that Krenz succeed him.

The Soviet embassy is informed, but, in accordance with instructions from Moscow, it takes no position. Except on one point: the Soviet ambassador, Vyacheslav Kochemasov, gives 'categorical advice' against the use of force in dealing with demonstrators.[35] He instructs the local commander that Soviet troops should remain in barracks.

The most urgent issue for the new leaders in the GDR is travel abroad. This is now the theme of the weekly demonstrations in Leipzig and Berlin. After pleas from the Czechs, a further 23,000 East Germans are allowed to cross to the West in the first weekend of November 1989. The government now proposes to allow citizens out (if they have visas) through a new gate near the Czech border. This proposal is rejected by the Volkskammer. Willi Stoph and his government resign; the Politburo is reshaped, bringing in Hans Modrow, a reformist.

The second event comes on 9 November. On this day the Politburo and Central Committee agree new arrangements for travel to the West. When the government spokesman, Schabowski, begins a press conference that evening he is given a piece of paper with a sentence about the decision on travel. He was not present when it was discussed and he says nothing on the subject, hoping to avoid questions. He is about to leave when someone asks about travel. Using the paper, he gives a confused reply, seeming to say that all citizens will be able to leave. Asked when this comes into force, he replies: 'Immediately, right away.' With that the press conference ends.

At 7.03 p.m. some news wires report that the Berlin Wall is open. This is not yet true; but shortly after the press conference a crowd of East Berliners begins to gather at the Bornholmer Strasse crossing point. Emboldened by the regular demonstrations and the absence of a violent response to them, they press to be let through. The guards are reinforced by armed police; but they have no instructions. To relieve pressure they let a few people through the gate; but the crowd continues to grow, and the pressure is becoming dangerous. Still unable to find anyone able to tell them what to do, the guards open the gate. Thousands cross. By the end of the night the same has happened at several more crossing points. By Stasi estimates, some 80,000 East Berliners visit the West that night, most returning by morning. West Berlin gives itself over to a three-day street party.

The next day the Party insists that people wishing to visit the West should still apply for visas. Demand overwhelms bureaucracy, and two days later it gives up on visas. The government has opened the Berlin Wall by accident; but the context for the accident is the change in Eastern Europe, the growth of peaceful protest in the GDR, and the refusal of the authorities – above all, Moscow – to use force. Authority has rested on force since 1953. It never recovers.

German unification has not been on people's minds. It is no more than a theoretical possibility. Everyone watches Eastern Europe with a sense of wonderment. They wonder at Gorbachev too: is this real? Or is he a skilled publicist and a clever tactician whose goals are unchanged?

Helmut Kohl has spoken from time to time of unification as a goal of German policy, but neither he nor anyone else has suggested it might come in the foreseeable future. In Moscow, when Weizsäcker mentioned the subject, Gorbachev said it might take a hundred years; Weizsäcker suggested fifty. One person who is ahead of the game is the US president, George Bush. In Mainz early in 1989 he has spoken of 'Europe whole and free'; more recently he has picked up Gorbachev's phrase 'the common European home' and said that for this to be taken seriously people ought to be free to move from room to room, starting with Berlin. In October, in response to a request from Kohl, he has given an interview, saying: 'I don't share the concerns that some European countries have about a reunified Germany . . . Germany's commitment to and recognition of the Alliance is unshakeable.' This is on the front page of *The New York Times* on 25 October 1989, but it does not receive much attention.

Gorbachev neither desires nor expects German unification. He has grown up with the GDR as a part of the European scene. He may believe, as others do, that an East German socialist identity has grown over the years.* He also knows or guesses that Margaret Thatcher, François Mitterrand, Giulio Andreotti, Jaruzelski, plus Kissinger and Zbigniew Brzezinski do not want to see Germany unified.[36] But this list omits the two men who count most: Bush and Kohl. They, with Gorbachev, are the ones who will take the decisions.

In the next days the world watches, stunned, as the Berliners take over. More than half the population of the GDR visit West Berlin. Kohl flies in from Poland, where he was on his first official visit. Nothing will be the same again; but no one knows exactly how.

Leaders begin to feel their way forward. Mitterrand brings the twelve European heads together for a dinner in Paris on 18 November. Mrs Thatcher is the most outspoken. She says that the Helsinki Final Act has confirmed that there can be no question of changing Europe's borders.† Any attempt to change the status of the two Germanies will undermine Mr Gorbachev's position and open a Pandora's box of border changes in Eastern Europe. Others say little, but the atmosphere is not one of enthusiasm for dramatic change. Kohl uses the occasion to persuade Mitterrand that in return they should go together to a session of the European Parliament. This passes a resolution recognising the right of East Germans to be part of a united Germany.[37]

The third event is Kohl's Bundestag speech of 28 November and his ten-point plan. This is the first time anyone addresses the question of how the two Germanies should live together. Kohl works on his speech with his adviser, Horst Teltschik, but discusses it with no one else in the government. Relations with the GDR are the responsibility

* German unification was discussed at a conference of academics and officials that the author attended in the summer of 1989. No one regarded it as likely. Some West Germans suggested that the GDR, Protestant, socialist, disciplined, was a modern version of Prussia. Only one person, Jonathan Carr, a former correspondent of *The Economist* in Germany, got it right. He said he did not know what would happen, but if the idea of unification took hold it would spread like a forest fire.

† This was incorrect. A provision included at German insistence and backed by the West allows peaceful changes to borders when the parties concerned agreed.

of the Federal Chancellery, not the Foreign Ministry, since it is not a foreign country.

By the standards of what happens next, Kohl's proposals are modest and his timetable is measured. He promises assistance for the GDR, but only if there is fundamental political and economic change; then a 'treaty partnership', common institutions in economy, transport, health, environment; and after free elections in the GDR, 'confederative structures'. All this within a European framework.

This is not a plan for reunification. 'Confederative structures' – the last stage mentioned – implies that two separate German states would remain, but share institutions in some areas. (The phrase even echoes some of Moscow's early proposals on unification.) Kohl's speech speaks of education, health, economy, science, environment, but not defence. The ten points mention the European Community and the Conference on Security and Co-operation in Europe, but are silent on NATO. Kohl arranges that while he is speaking a message is sent to Bush – the one person he has informed – underlining his unshakeable commitment to the alliance.

With this, Kohl takes centre-stage. Nothing happens as he suggests; but nothing happens without him. The path to unification is now shaped by domestic politics in the two Germanies, by Kohl and Bush working together, and by their relationships with Gorbachev. From this day on, Bush and Kohl are in continuous contact.

The fourth event is Kohl's visit to Dresden. Kohl hears that Mitterrand is planning a state visit to Krenz in East Berlin on 21 December. He decides he should visit the GDR himself.* He goes to Dresden on 19 December. Here the vision in the ten points, of a slow, structured process evaporates. For Kohl, this is a political moment:

> We had hardly landed when it hit me: this regime is finished. It's going to be unification. The whole airport, especially the terminal, was covered with thousands of people, a sea of black-red-gold flags

* Krenz had been replaced by Modrow even before Kohl got there. Mitterrand maintained his state visit.

> waved in the cold December air. . . . As I stood on the bottom step of the steps, Modrow waiting for me ten metres away with a stony face, I turned round to Rudi Seiters and said, 'It can't be stopped'.[38*]

The scene as he arrives in the town centre resembles Brandt's visit to Erfurt, except that now there are no Stasi to prevent the crowds getting close. They chant 'Helmut, Helmut' and 'Deutschland, Deutschland' or 'Wir sind ein Volk' ('We are one people').[†] Kohl speaks to an enthusiastic crowd by the ruins of the Frauenkirche. Then his political instinct kicks in. He understands what the people want: not a better version of the GDR, as reformers in the SED do, nor a new socialist state, as the idealists in the protest movement do. The people he sees in front of him want something real and solid, and they want it quickly. Only unity with West Germany can give it to them.

German unification is both a democratic and a diplomatic process. The fifth defining event is the election in the GDR. But before that, some order has to be brought to the diplomatic process. In December, Shevardnadze, prompted by Gorbachev, calls for a meeting of the Four Allied Powers in West Berlin. Thatcher and Mitterrand agree that a meeting would be useful; the United States, having consulted Bonn, says they will agree to a meeting but only to discuss Berlin. This takes place at ambassadorial level. The Soviet ambassador raises German issues but his Western colleagues do not respond. Shevardnadze tries again in January 1990; this time the other three all say they are not in favour of a meeting – Bonn having made its views clear.

Gorbachev meets Bush in Malta just after Kohl's speech and suggests a pan-European conference on the Helsinki model; but this is not going to fill the diplomatic vacuum in a meaningful way. Technically correct, but even worse, would be a (much delayed) peace conference to bring the Second World War to a formal conclusion. By 1945, 110

* In German, 'Die Sache ist gelaufen'. Literally, 'It has run away'.

† Protesters in the GDR had begun with the slogan 'Wir sind das Volk' – 'We are the people' – denying the Party's claim to represent the people. As unification began to seem possible, this changed to 'Wir sind ein Volk' – 'We are one people'.

countries were at war with Germany; in theory they would all have the right to be present.

Meanwhile the GDR is collapsing. A thousand or more GDR citizens are leaving every day. In January protesters get into the headquarters of the Stasi, secure what files have not been destroyed and uncover the Stasi's store of luxury goods. The moral bankruptcy of the regime becomes clearer every day.

In theory, the future of the GDR is in the hands of a 'round table', constructed on the Polish model. But, unlike the Polish case, those at the table are from narrow constituencies: on the one side Modrow and the SED 'reformers', a small group inside a hated party; on the other dissidents, courageous, left-wing idealists who want to build socialism without a secret police. Neither represents the citizens who welcomed Helmut Kohl in Dresden. Nor do they look likely to provide reform quickly. Unification offers a ready-made alternative.*

In the course of January 1990 the State Department's planners come up with the '2+4' format as a way to satisfy form – 4 because a peace treaty is technically for the Four Powers – plus 2 to include the two Germanies. James Baker, US secretary of state, finds it a neat solution. He agrees with Genscher that the question of unification is for the Germans themselves, the 2; but the Four Powers can join them to discuss the external implications. He takes up the idea with the British and French foreign ministers – in practice the format is designed to satisfy them. In Moscow Gorbachev accepts it without difficulty; his collaborator Chernyaev had come up with a similar idea earlier. Baker puts it on the record at the press conference for a multilateral meeting in Ottawa, and it is too late for anyone to protest.[39] This puts paid to the idea of an all-Europe meeting to deal with Germany – which the Soviets have proposed and the EU agreed.

The supporting cast in the 2+4 group, France and Britain, are led by formidable characters, François Mitterrand and Margaret Thatcher, both of whom dislike the idea of a united Germany. Mitterrand says

* An excellent analysis is to be found in Mary Elise Sarotte, *1989: The Struggle to Create Post-Cold War Europe*, pp. 88–118.

this in private, including to Thatcher. But he realises early on that he is not going to stop it and the attempt would damage Franco-German relations. Instead he sells his agreement to Kohl in exchange for a promise of European Economic and Monetary Union.*

Thatcher neither compromises nor changes her mind. No one of consequence in her government shares her views. Douglas Hurd records that she 'delivered her last tirade against German unification in a Cabinet meeting on 8 February'.[40] She fails to persuade George Bush later in February.[41] Without allies either at home or abroad, she gives up.

The most important question raised by German unification is that of Alliance membership. Without Germany's integration in NATO, its central position might compel it to maintain an army large enough to fight a war on two fronts: large enough, that is, to terrify everyone. NATO membership enables Germany to keep modest force levels; all its neighbours are comfortable with this. It is 1914 rather than 1939 that many in Europe fear. Douglas Hurd records: 'I was hearing at No. 10 about the parallel with the years 1904–14.'[42] Mitterrand says to Bush in 1989, 'there has to be a new Europe or Europe will be back where it was in 1913'.[43] Manfred Wörner, the NATO secretary general, agrees that without Germany in the Alliance 'the old Pandora's box of competition and rivalry in Europe would be reopened'.[44]

Bush and Kohl have instinctively seen the Alliance as the solution to these fears. Bush's first statement on German unification mentions Germany's loyalty to the Alliance. Kohl, in the tradition of Adenauer, rejects the idea of neutrality from start to finish. Every US paper puts Alliance membership at the centre of policy on German unification.

What do you do when two states which belong to opposing alliances decide to unite? Should the new state be in one or other of the alliances, or both, or neither? Neutrality seems the obvious answer. This was what the Stalin Note of 1952 put forward. Falin suggests to Gorbachev that he propose 'a neutral, democratic and basically

* This was intended to curb German economic power.

demilitarised Germany'.[45]* Gorbachev by this time is taking little notice of his officials; the Federal Republic has succeeded in ensuring that discussion takes Germany's NATO membership as the starting point. In the end the only person to propose a neutral Germany is Markus Meckel, GDR foreign minister during its brief life as a democratic state.

The debate on Germany's Alliance status becomes one about whether its membership of NATO should be abated in some way. At different times Baker and Genscher seem to have contemplated Germany in the Alliance, but with the territory of the former GDR outside it.[46] In February 1990, Gorbachev buys Baker's argument that Germany should not be left alone to defend itself, but they also seem to agree that any extension of the 'NATO jurisdiction' to the East is unacceptable. It is difficult, however, to see how a united, sovereign state can be half in and half out of an alliance. Bush is now talking about Germany in NATO, but with the territory of the GDR having 'a special military status'. Baker then adjusts his language and speaks of guarantees that 'NATO forces would not be moving eastwards'.[47]

Gorbachev discusses the question of Germany in NATO with different leaders on several occasions. Kohl raises it with him in Moscow shortly after Baker's visit, but using a formula closer to Bush's. Gorbachev says only that he will think further. Briefing the press, Kohl and Teltschik portray this as a historic moment and a 'green light'. This is stretching things somewhat, though it is true that Gorbachev has discussed the NATO question without obvious qualms. Soviet officials make sure that their press reports that German membership of NATO has been categorically rejected.

Gorbachev discusses it with Baker again on his visit to Moscow in May to prepare Gorbachev's state visit to Washington. Baker finds him continuing to question the need for a united Germany to be in NATO.[48] Baker gives nine reasons for seeing NATO, and Germany in NATO, in a more positive light. These include: limitations on Germany – no

* The Germany of the Byrnes Treaty of 1946, disarmed and subject to inspection by the Four Powers, seems to be neutral but also not fully sovereign.

nuclear, chemical or biological weapons, a review of NATO's tactical nuclear weapons,* a transition period for Soviet troops to withdraw, no NATO forces in the old East Germany, and arrangements to ensure that the Soviet Union does not lose economically from unification. He also mentions the Helsinki Final Act, which says that a sovereign state has the right to belong or not belong to an alliance. Gorbachev mentions the idea of a united Germany belonging to both alliances – which makes no sense to anyone on the US side. Baker leaves the meeting with the problem unresolved.

Before Gorbachev leaves for Washington and Camp David, he has another visitor. This is Mitterrand. Gorbachev repeats to him the idea of Germany belonging to both alliances – as the two halves of Germany do at that moment – and acting as 'a bridge'. Mitterrand says this would be preposterous and delivers two more realistic messages. First, German unification is already under way in the minds of German people. Kohl intends to make it happen, and he has US support. Second, he does not see how he or anyone else could oppose Germany's wish to remain in NATO. 'What can I do? Send a division?' Gorbachev replies that he already has a division in Germany. (In fact, he has a third of a million men there – an army, not a division.) But Mitterrand has put the problem in plain terms. The only way to stop Germany choosing its alliance would be by war or the threat of war. This message comes from a credible messenger. Mitterrand has been in the GDR and is a reliable witness to what was happening there; he is one of those who has opposed German unification, and now he is no longer doing so. Gorbachev may have noticed that Thatcher too has fallen silent.[49]

In Camp David at the end of May, Gorbachev changes his position. Bush makes the same point as Baker about the Helsinki Final Act.[50] This time Gorbachev agrees that it applies to Germany, causing consternation among his advisers; but when Condoleezza Rice gives the Soviet ambassador a draft of the president's press statement, he raises no objection to the words: 'we are in full agreement that the matter

* Until German unification came up, the big debate in NATO had been about a successor to the short-range Lance nuclear missile. Short-range missiles, like the Soviet Luna, are the way in which a conventional exchange is most likely to become a nuclear war.

of alliance membership is, in accordance with the Helsinki Final Act, a matter for the Germans to decide'. Bush reads this out at the press conference, but without drawing attention to it.[51] Zelikow and Rice record that Chernyaev later confirmed that it was at this summit that the Soviet Union agreed to a united Germany in NATO, and that Baker's nine points played a part in changing his mind.[52]

A final discussion on NATO takes place between Kohl and Gorbachev, first in Moscow and then in the Caucasus, where they fly to visit Gorbachev's home territory, Stavropol, and the Caucasus mountains. Here the bargain is made explicit. In return for Soviet agreement to Germany inside NATO, the Alliance will be transformed to make it more political – it will, for example, accept diplomatic representatives from non-members; and the NATO summit will agree a package signalling a readiness for big arms reductions. Second, they agree that Russian forces will remain for three to four years in the GDR, and that Germany will pay a (somewhat inflated) sum to cover the costs of their return to the Soviet Union. (Haggling about timetables and money is still to come.) Kohl puts the decision on NATO on the record in the presence of Gorbachev at a nearby sanatorium which is serving as the press centre.

The Soviet position in the 2+4 negotiations lags some way behind that of their leaders. Eventually the two come together, with visible splits in the Soviet delegation, between the civilians and the military, and between new civilians like Shevardnadze and old ones like Falin.

The fifth and final event defining German unification is the election in the GDR on 18 March 1990, the only free election ever held there. The result confirms Kohl's intuition. For ordinary people, unification is the solution to the problems of their failing state; and a vote for the CDU is the way to make it happen. The CDU's eastern affiliate, the Alliance for Germany, finishes within a few votes of an absolute majority in the Volkskammer. It forms a coalition government with the Eastern version of the SPD; but its main role now is to co-operate with Bonn in the dissolution of the state. The foreign minister, Markus Meckell, a pacifist pastor from the SPD – he has refused to serve in the GDR military and was punished for it – speaks in the 2+4 talks for a neutral Germany, but no one takes any notice. The prime minister, Lothar de Maizière, then takes over himself, and does what Bonn instructs and Washington urges. The German Democratic Republic is dissolved into a Germany that remains a full member of NATO.

The 2+4 Agreement is signed in Moscow on 12 September 1990, seven months after this forum was invented. The agreement includes provisions that limit the stationing of NATO forces in the Eastern *Länder*. The Eastern *Länder* join the Federal Republic on 3 October 1990. This is a takeover, not a merger.* In consequence, existing treaty obligations remain in force, including those regarding the Polish border. As usual the real negotiations take place in bilateral meetings, only a few of which have been mentioned here. The 2+4 talks are a tidy way to bring it all together.

The speed of these events is breathtaking. From the opening of the barriers on Bornholmer Strasse to the unification of West and East Germany, less than a year has passed. The collapse of the GDR is an avalanche that gathers pace as it goes. Kohl's sense of politics and of timing shapes its course. The elections in the GDR create an incentive to move even faster. If unification comes quickly, then the election due in the old West Germany in January 1991 can be an all-German election. This offers the prospect of a big win for the CDU. Both diplomacy and domestic electoral politics point to speed. On Kohl's mind, as well as elections, is the question of what is going to happen in the Soviet Union. Lithuania has already declared itself independent, but has been persuaded by Bonn and Washington not to rush; the other Baltic States are heading in the same direction. Kohl wants to finish the German question while Gorbachev, and indeed the Soviet Union, are still there.

Kohl was both a straightforward local politician, very good at his job, and also a great European statesman. He took on the legacy of Willy

* Unification took place under Article 23, by which new *Länder* could join the Federal Republic, as the Saarland did in 1955. Article 146 was provided for a merger of the two states, but it proved unnecessary. After unification it was removed from the constitution, another way of making clear that Germany's borders were final.

Brandt. He knew what he wanted, and he knew how to get it; when the moment came he acted with instinct, opportunism and ruthlessness; and he acted with the United States.

Both were conscious of Germany's past and expressed their feelings about it: Brandt in his emotional gestures, Kohl in every speech and in half his conversations.

Both built on what Adenauer left behind. Three generations, two parties but a constancy of aim: freedom, peace, unity – and in that order. Or, to put it in Woodrow Wilson's language: democracy, multilateral institutions and self-determination. Germany, absent from the negotiations at the end of the First World War, is the main actor in the 1991 settlement ending the Second World War.

This is also a story about Germany and the United States: Adenauer, Acheson and Dulles, Brandt and Kennedy, Bahr and Kissinger, Kohl and Bush. On this base NATO and the European Union are built.

II

Two Diplomats and the Holocaust

The diplomats in this book are mostly foreign ministers, occasionally senior officials like Henry Kissinger or George Kennan. The officials in this chapter are low down in the pecking order; both are consular officers rather than diplomats. Consuls deal with 'low politics'; they help businessmen, merchant seamen or members of the public who are in trouble – visiting citizens in prison in foreign countries is one of their duties. They also issue visas on behalf of their home country, according to the rules laid down in their capitals.

Frank Foley

For those of us who live secure, ordinary lives, some scenes are almost impossible to imagine.

You are a prisoner in one of the worst places in the world: Sachsenhausen, north of Berlin. You are alive because of a determination to survive – maybe because of the young son that you have not yet seen. This determination keeps you alive when they are beating you and you would prefer to die; it is an instinct that tells you to hide on the day when everyone else in your hut is killed. You are thin, weak from the latest beating, when you are called out from the brick factory. For what? They tell you to take a shower; someone treats some of your wounds – which has never happened before. 'What's happening?' you ask. The SS guard tells you to shut up and throws a greatcoat over your shoulders to hide the bruises and the bleeding. There is a visitor for you. What does it mean? Who is there who knows that I'm here?

They take you into an office. On the other side of the desk is a small, ordinary-looking man with glasses. You have never seen him before. 'My name is Foley,' he says, 'I am from the British consulate in Berlin.'

Frank Foley, born in 1884, in Somerset. His father, an engine-fitter for the Great Western Railway, is ambitious for himself – he qualifies as a civil engineer – and for his family. Foley's mother is a devout Catholic. She sends her son and his sister to a Roman Catholic school, run by a French order. For a period, Frank talks of entering the priesthood; his sister eventually becomes mother superior of a convent school in Bristol. Frank attends a Jesuit school in Lancashire, and then goes to the Catholic University in Poitiers. But after that, changing his mind about the priesthood, he travels in Europe, studying here and there, paying his way by teaching. He is studying philosophy in Hamburg when war breaks out in 1914.

To avoid being interned, Foley borrows a German military uniform – he speaks near-perfect German as well as French – and finds his way back to Britain, discarding the uniform in favour of civilian clothing when he crosses into neutral Holland. He teaches in Britain for a year and then joins the army via the Inns of Court Officer Training Corps.

He is commissioned and sent to France with the North Staffordshire Regiment as a second lieutenant in February 1917. His first and last time on the front line comes a year later during the big German offensive of 1918. His regiment is in the line between Arras and Cambrai, at the heart of the fighting. The first day of the battle involves a massive artillery barrage, followed by waves of hand-to-hand fighting. By the end of the day, twenty-two officers and 500 men are killed or missing, two-thirds of the battalion. Foley is wounded – a bullet through the lung – on the first day. He is carried back behind the lines. This does not happen to all officers, suggesting that he is liked by the men. Captain Foley, as he is by then, is mentioned in dispatches; his unit is far from being an elite formation and it has no experience of battle, but it does its duty and more. Foley recovers in England but he is no longer fit for action. Then, by accident, someone spots his language skills and, just before the armistice, he is posted to the Intelligence Corps.

Foley goes briefly to France, then to Cologne, joining the Allied Control Commission, which takes over there after the armistice. The intelligence work is as much about French plans to set up a separatist state in the Rhineland as about Germany itself. One of his colleagues in Cologne, Henry Landau, who has run a successful operation tracking railway movements in Belgium, is sent to set up the post-war intelligence station in Berlin. But he finds peacetime intelligence work tame; and the cover job is even more tedious. Landau decides to quit and suggests Foley as his successor.

Foley goes to Berlin in April 1920. He is there until Britain declares war in 1939. The cover job is director of the Passport Control Office of the embassy. This is a good location for the intelligence operation: it is a low-profile role but it brings contact with people wishing to visit Britain. In normal times it is not too time-consuming, and most of the work consists of supervising a competent staff, of whom one or two may also be intelligence officers.

Foley has two advantages: his office, and the passport work he does, are separate from the embassy; and while ambassadors and diplomats come and go, he is a fixture. He is not supposed to deal with Germany or to recruit agents to report on Germany. In those days British intelligence officers did not spy on the country where they were accredited. His main target is the Soviet Union, and Berlin is a big centre for Bolshevik activity. The downside of this position is that he has no diplomatic immunity. He is potentially at risk of arrest, something to bear in mind when the SS and the Gestapo come to play a large role in the state apparatus.

After a year in Berlin Foley returns to England to marry Kay Lee. He brings her back to his apartment in a Jewish district of Berlin. Every country in Europe experiences turbulence after the First World War, but Frank and Kay Foley live through its most extreme version: strikes, foreign-sponsored separatism, political assassination, the separation of Silesia, the endless difficulties over reparations, the hyperinflation and the mass unemployment. Even as things seem to settle in the late 1920s, the shadow of the radical right and the contested Versailles Treaty never goes away. The economic crash brings the return of political chaos and, in 1933, the Nazi seizure of power.

Hitler becomes chancellor on 30 January; on 5 February an emergency decree enables him to take over Communist property; on 28 February, the day after the Reichstag fire, he has powers of arbitrary arrest. In March, groups of storm troopers attack Jews in the streets, beating them severely. In the same month Dachau, the first concentration camp, is established. From the beginning of April a boycott of Jewish shops begins; storm troopers paint Stars of David on the windows to identify them.

It goes on. Sometimes there is a remission – the shop boycott is called off when counter-boycotts of German goods abroad are started – but it is reintroduced later, step by step, alongside other measures. The law becomes an instrument of persecution: when people kill Jews, the courts decide that the victims have committed suicide; sexual relations between a Jew and a Gentile are classified as 'racial defilement'. Bullying of Jewish children is encouraged in schools; later they are excluded from education altogether.

'Aryanisation' starts with the civil service; the professions follow – Jews are forbidden to practise as doctors, dentists and lawyers. Then Jewish-owned companies are driven out of business, bringing the ruin and sometimes the suicide of their owners. The Nuremberg Laws make discrimination into a legally enforced system. Yellow Stars are imposed, bans on using park benches and swimming pools, all accompanied by gratuitous acts of violence against Jews and their shops or homes, and by the arrest of Jews and those who defend them.

In 1933 some 60,000 Jews leave Germany; but many of them do not go far enough away. For those who want to escape, Britain is particularly important. Frank Foley's passport operation covers the British Empire as well as Britain itself. That means it is responsible for emigration to Palestine, where Britain holds the League of Nations mandate. By the time the persecution begins Foley already knows many members of the Jewish community. He has helped the father of Wilfred Israel, the owner of a large Berlin department store, get a visa to visit a dying relative in London, and they become friends. Israel plays a large part in the *Hilfsverein der deutschen Juden*, which gives advice and practical assistance on emigration. He is in regular contact, partly in his intelligence capacity, with Hubert Pollack, also of the *Hilfsverein*. Pollack acts as a go-between with Palestine, and has experience in handling the German police and bureaucracy. He knows how to buy documents, permits, occasionally release from prison – though not from concentration camps. He knows who to bribe and how much, for the administration is corrupt as well as brutal.

Foley does both his jobs well – the passports and the intelligence. He plays a key part in recruiting 'Jonny X', a Comintern agent who works for Britain through the 1930s and the war, and he establishes relationships of confidence in London.

This chapter is concerned with his job as the head of the Passport Control Office in Berlin. Nazi officials have an ambiguous attitude to Jewish emigration: on the one hand they want to be rid of the Jews; on the other they don't want to make life easy for them. They may issue exit permits, but they also take as much of their property as they can, requiring deposits in special accounts and changing any payments abroad at punitive exchange rates – if they can be exchanged at all.

The anecdotes that follow illustrate how Foley operates. They are the tip of the iceberg. They come from those he helped or their children. Foley is a modest man to whom self-promotion is alien.

For many Jews the most attractive option is to escape to Palestine, and the only way to get there is with a 'capitalist visa'. For this they have to transfer the equivalent of £1,000 to the Templar Bank in Palestine (a substantial sum – more than Foley's annual salary). This can be done only after paying an exit tax, 25 per cent of the value of their property, and placing the rest in a blocked Reichsbank account. The exchange rate for the transfer is extortionate, and the transfer can be made only when its owner is in Palestine – and sometimes not then either, because of the shortage of foreign exchange. Foley solves this Catch-22 situation for one applicant, Wolfgang Meyer-Michel, by suggesting that a letter promising to provide the funds could be counted as a sufficient guarantee. Foley issues the visa, though the promise is transparently an empty one. By late 1935 he is issuing visas to people who do not even pretend to have the money.[1]

Shanghai is the one place in the world where Jews can go without a visa. The consul general there begs the Foreign Office to stop the flow of destitute Jews – this is their position by the time they are able to get out of Germany. Foley comments: 'It might be considered humane on our part not to interfere officially to prevent Jews choosing their own graveyards. They would rather die as free men in Shanghai than as slaves in Dachau.'[2]

A young Jewish woman has spent two years in prison as a Communist. While she is there she has given birth to a baby. She wants to join her boyfriend in Southern Rhodesia. The *Hilfsverein* sends her to the Passport Control Office. The instructions on visas are that anyone with a criminal record or 'unacceptable politics' should not be given a visa for Britain, Palestine or the empire. The passport examiner notes that she does not seem to qualify; but because of the child, he passes the case on to Foley. He asks her age, and notes that she was only seventeen when she was arrested as a Communist; this might therefore be ascribed to the folly of youth. He meets her the next day and gives her a visa to join the child's father in Southern Rhodesia.[3] She sails from Bremen a few hours before her Gestapo exit permit expires (the Gestapo make it clear that they are tracking her).

Leopold Wertheimer is imprisoned after a business rival accuses him of taking trade away from him. Fearful that he will be moved straight from prison to a concentration camp – the day of release is always the moment of greatest danger – his wife, Adele, tries at the British consulates in Frankfurt and Munich; she is turned down. She turns to the *Hilfsverein*, and they send her to Foley. She goes with her sister, waits all day but finally sees him. Foley calms her down, listens, tells her of the restrictions on visas and the waiting lists. He also tells her to return two days later. When he gives her the visa, he says it is for the child (and it is through the child, as in many other cases, that this story comes to us). They are there with the visa when Leopold is released from prison, and they all leave for Palestine.[4]

In 1938 tension is rising and the difficulties for Jews are getting worse.

The *Anschluss* with Austria means that the accumulated anti-Semitic laws of Germany are imposed on 190,000 Jews in Austria overnight, and there is an explosive rush for emigration. The Passport Control Office there is overwhelmed; Thomas Kendrick, Foley's opposite number in Vienna, also an intelligence officer, is arrested and badly treated. Foley is recalled to London for his own safety.

The tension eases with the Munich Agreement at the end of September, and Foley returns to Berlin. Shortly after he gets back, one of Foley's agents in the Jewish community, Willi Preis, a furrier, is arrested. (The fur trade is a useful source of information, fur being the favourite gift of senior Nazi Party members for their mistresses.)

Preis manages to contact his wife and tells her to see Foley. By this time the Passport Control Office is crammed with applicants, but Frau Preis brings one of Foley's visiting cards with her and gets to see him quickly. He in turn goes straight to the Gestapo headquarters in Alexanderplatz, taking with him a visa for Willi Preis, his wife and their two children. They leave for Holland the same night.[5]

At this time a British business contact, Cobden Turner, comes to Foley about a case that a friend has brought to him. This concerns a young girl who is half Jewish, Martyl Karweik. Her mother, wholly Jewish, has been divorced by her husband, a Nazi who does not want the marriage to damage his career. She is expelled from Germany and is able to reach the United States; but she has not been able to take her daughter with her because she is half Aryan. Not only is Martyl now separated from her mother, but she has no future in Germany except, probably, death in a labour camp. Foley solves the problem by giving her a passport as Cobden Turner's daughter. He takes her to England and she lives with his family until she is able to join her mother at the end of the war. On Foley's part this is not so much bending the rules as breaking them.[6]

The 9th of November 1938 is *Kristallnacht* (the night of broken glass). It is open season for those who want to attack Jews and Jewish shops, or what is left of them. Many Jews are arrested and taken to camps. Foley drives around Berlin with his wife to report to London on the frenzy and atrocities but also, as recounted by Ohmiel, one of the children of Willi Preis, to help Jews where he can. Following *Kristallnacht*, Foley gives a number of Jews refuge in his apartment when they fear to go home at night.

Richard Lachs loses his job when the company he works for is 'Aryanised'. He has a permit to enter the United States, but the quota is full. After *Kristallnacht* he goes into hiding. He has relatives in Britain but they do not have enough money to give the financial guarantees required. With nothing else to do he applies for a British visa anyway, with no expectation of receiving one. His son later recalled the Sunday morning when a letter from the Passport Control Office arrives asking his parents to send their passports so that the visas could be put in. He and his sister literally jump for joy. His parents assume it is a clerical error; but realise later that it is not when they find their children are included. With no money the family live on the edge of poverty in Manchester, but they survive and make their lives in Britain.[7]

From January 1939 the British government allows the Council for German Jewry to open a transit camp in Kent for refugees. The British doctrine of visa-issuing is that it is the responsibility of the man on the spot. Foley and Pollack work out together who to take. Many of those given visas are not really in transit, unless it is to the British armed forces. While the home secretary is expressing concern at 'this stagnant pool of refugees', Foley continues to issue Home Office letters guaranteeing them temporary asylum in Britain. The last group of 300 leave Germany at the end of August 1939, reaching Britain as war is declared.

Gunter Powitzer is imprisoned for eighteen months for 'racial defilement': his Aryan girlfriend becomes pregnant and a Nazi relative tells the Gestapo. His brother, a radio engineer already in Palestine, manages to get word to Foley. But it is now 1939 and Powitzer, having finished his sentence, has been moved to Sachsenhausen. He is the man at the beginning of this chapter. Foley's intervention saves his life. He and the child are able to travel to Palestine a few days later.

Nobody knows how many lives Foley saved. He started by treating his instructions from London in a liberal fashion, and ended up ignoring them more or less completely. There were limits to what he could do, but he had collaborators in London and Jerusalem who understood what he was doing and did not draw attention to it. The best estimate comes from Benno Cohn, co-chairman of the German Zionist Association, who, in his evidence at the trial of Adolph Eichmann, said: 'There was one man who stood out above all others like a beacon, Captain Foley, a man who in my opinion was one of the greatest among the nations of the world. . . . He rescued thousands of Jews from the jaws of death.' (From his evidence at the trial of Adolf Eichmann, 1961.) This was also what Hubert Pollack thought: 'the number of Jews saved from Germany would have been tens of thousands less, yes, tens of thousands less, if an officious bureaucrat had sat in Foley's place'.[8]

There was a limit to what he could do, set by his calculation of what he could get away with. The British government was trying to limit the number of Jewish refugees coming to Britain: by 1939 Foreign Office guidance listed as 'unsuitable' for refugee status small businessmen, traders, shopkeepers, musicians, artists and the 'rank and file' of the professions – all areas in which Jews often work. (The professions, medicine, dentistry and the law, were already closed.)

Frank Foley never told his story. It has been pieced together from those he helped, and is far from complete. The picture that emerges is one of a decent, modest man. Physically small, he had a personality that commanded respect. When the Gestapo took too close an interest in the Jews queuing outside his office, he would ask them if they were there to apply for visas. When they said they were not he would suggest they leave; and it seems that they usually did. Later, as the numbers grew, he recruited porters from the embassy to supervise. They were all ex-servicemen, and he had them wear their medals. (And in the winter when people were queuing outside he gave them tea to help them keep warm.)

Those who worked for him describe him as extraordinarily hardworking, but also good-tempered, kind and tolerant. The fact that he was primarily an intelligence officer, and that passport control was not the main purpose of his work, may have given him more distance from his job than most full-time passport officers would have.

Religious conviction played a part. This was the view of Benno Cohn. He spoke of the consulate as virtually a place of refuge. 'Foley was humane. . . . He told us he was acting as a Christian and that he wanted to show how little the Christians who were in power in Germany had to do with real Christianity.'[9]

When the Palestine commissioner for migration sent him 1,000 blank certificates, for visas for young unaccompanied children, Foley responded with a cable saying, 'God bless you. Foley.' He used the same formula when someone in London gave him a positive response on a difficult case.[10] Even so, not many Christians behaved as he did. It seems that over time he persuaded some of those in London to share his view on what should be done and to collaborate with him.

It is striking, too, how many of the anecdotes involve children. It is as though, having sometimes to make a terrible choice – whom to help and whom not – he did his utmost in cases where children were involved.

On Foley's last day in Berlin he hands over his remaining eighty blank permits for settlement in Palestine to the *Hilfsverein* and tells them to use them as they think best.

Chiune Sugihara

In July 1940 Chiune Sugihara is the Japanese vice-consul in Kaunas in Lithuania, a one-man diplomatic post established primarily to report to Tokyo on military developments. This is a busy time for such work. In August 1939 Molotov and Ribbentrop have divided the Baltic region into German and Soviet spheres of influence. In the follow-up negotiation they have agreed that the Soviet Union will get the three Baltic States, with the Polish border adjusted to enlarge Lithuania. None of this is public. Japan is a member of the Anti-Comintern Pact; and it has been in an undeclared war with the Soviet Union (on the border between Mongolia and Manchuria). It has major interests at stake in relations between Germany and the Soviet Union, hence the need for someone to observe what is going on at the border.

Sugihara arrives in Kaunas in late 1939, after the German invasion of Poland but before the Soviets take over Lithuania completely. In

June 1940 large numbers of Soviet forces move into Lithuania; in July, following new elections, the Lithuanian parliament votes to join the Soviet Union.

On 27 July, Sugihara awakes to find more than a hundred people, men, women and children, outside the consulate, which is his home as well as his office. As the day goes on the numbers grow. Some try to climb over the railings to get into the consulate. He learns from his staff that they are refugees from Poland, fleeing from the Germans who have begun to round up Jews. This is not a situation for which he is at all prepared. After some hesitation he asks the crowd to choose five representatives to explain their situation to him.

The five, led by Zorach Wahrhaftig, come into the consulate. They tell him what is happening to Jews in Germany and Poland, and of the journey they have made, on foot mostly, to Kaunas. They have heard rumours that it may be possible to get transit visas for Japan. The Dutch honorary consul, Jan Zwartendijk, who is ready to issue visas for Curaçao, joins the meeting. But the only way to get there is through Japan.

Sugihara tells the five that he will have to consult Tokyo about issuing such a large number of visas. The next morning, after a sleepless night, he sends a cable copied to the Japanese ambassadors in Riga and Berlin (his wife, Yukiko, makes the copies for him). The telegrams explain that he is being asked for transit visas, and concludes: 'As a fellow human being, I cannot refuse their requests. Please permit me to issue visas to them.' The reply, as expected says, no, in the plainest language possible: 'NO EXCEPTIONS STOP NO FURTHER ENQUIRIES EXPECTED STOP.'

In Tokyo they may have guessed from the tone of the first cable where Sugihara's instincts pointed. After a couple of days he sends another message, setting out in more detail how long the journey would take, and the possibilities this would provide for solving the question of the final destination. Same reply.

Then a third cable: a last attempt to avoid making a decision himself. Same reply. This is a one-man post; he has no colleague he can consult. So instead he turns to the people who matter most to him and who will share the consequences of his decision: his family. They are unanimous, children too. His wife and her sister, Setsuko, understand that it means an uncertain future for them – if he disobeys instructions he may lose his job in the Foreign Ministry. But if he obeys the instructions, he condemns the refugees outside his office to imprisonment, probably death – though there is no guarantee that the visas will save them. He is grateful for his family's support: it is what he has wanted to do all along.

The next morning he goes to the Russian embassy and persuades the officials there to issue the permits needed for the Jews to cross Siberia. In her account of these events Yukiko says that the officials concerned may have made money on the transactions. This is possible, but Japanese will say the same of Sugihara himself, and that is not true. We do not know. Sugihara's near-native command of Russian is an asset in putting the case for helping the Jews. As he tells the story, the Soviet consul decides on the spot. His motives may not have been so different from Sugihara's.

Then he tells the refugees. In Yukiko's account, 'an electricity . . . flowed through the crowd . . . they hugged and kissed one another. Others looked up and reached towards the sky . . . Mothers picked up their children to share the joy with them.'[11]

Then begins the work. Sugihara issues each of them with a number. He has to examine their cases one by one, their final destinations, the availability of funds and much else. The consulate has been set up to track military movements, not to issue visas, and he doesn't have all the forms he needs. He writes them by hand, from eight in the morning until late in the evening. His target is 300 a day, but the process is too complicated for that. His fountain pen breaks and he has to revert to an old-fashioned pen which he dips in ink. Then the ink begins to run out, and he has to water it down to make it go further. Yukiko offers to help, but that would not be legally correct, and he does not want to risk her getting into trouble. To save time, he stops numbering the visas or keeping a record or charging the small fee.

Meanwhile he is under pressure from both Japan and the Soviets to close the consulate: Lithuania has ceased to exist as an independent state. Eventually Sugihara does so on 28 August, moving into a downtown hotel; but he leaves the address on the consulate gates, and continues to write out visas in the hotel lobby. He no longer has the consulate stamp, but it turns out later that at least some of those to whom he gave these visas are able to escape. As the train pulls out of the station in Kaunas he hands out the remaining blank visa forms to people on the platform. These too, it turns out, enabled one or two to escape.

Many of those who did not escape were taken and killed the following year when the German invasion of the Soviet Union began. By the end of the war more than 90 per cent of Lithuania's Jews had been killed.

When these events took place, Chiune Sugihara was forty years old. He was born in 1900 in central Japan, into a middle-ranking samurai family, in the last generation when such things mattered. As a boy he spent some years in Korea (then a colony of Japan) with his family. He wanted to study abroad and teach English. In deference to his father's wishes he sat the examination for medical school, but failed since he did not answer a single question. Then he returned to Japan and worked his way through Waseda University doing part-time jobs.

While at Waseda, in 1919, he responded to an advertisement from the Japanese Foreign Ministry for people who wanted to study abroad, with a view to a possible career in the Diplomatic Service. Either his enthusiasm or his abilities impressed, since he was accepted and sent to Harbin University in northern China to study Russian. Sugihara was a remarkable linguist, picking languages up both by ear and by studying texts. The story is that when he was learning Russian he carried a dictionary with him, tearing out each page as he memorised the words on it. While at Harbin University he lived with a (White) Russian family, and converted to the Greek Orthodox Church. By the time he finished his university course his Russian was sufficiently impressive that he was asked to teach there part-time while working for the Foreign Ministry.

In 1932 Sugihara moved to work for the Foreign Ministry of the (puppet) government of Manchukuo, as Japanese-occupied Manchuria was called. There he was responsible for negotiations with the Soviet Union on the purchase of the Northern Manchurian Railway. The agreement he reached was regarded on the Japanese side as highly successful, rather less so on the Soviet side. As a result Sugihara was promoted to be number two in the Foreign Ministry. This was less important than it sounds, since the state was entirely under Tokyo's control.

In 1934, disturbed by the way that the Japanese occupation forces treated the Chinese, he resigned and returned to Tokyo in a subordinate position. It was there that, in 1935, he met and married Yukiko, some thirteen years his junior. Two years later he was sent to Helsinki. The railway negotiations still rankled in Moscow and the ministry was unable to obtain a visa for him to serve there, or even a transit visa. He therefore travelled east across the United States to Helsinki. Yukiko accompanied him, taking Setsuko to help with the children.

From Helsinki, Sugihara had been scheduled to transfer to Turkey, but the Molotov-Ribbentrop Pact changed that. The Japanese government, by then dominated by the military, decided they needed someone in Lithuania to watch developments around the border between the two spheres of influence. Sugihara was close by; he spoke both Russian and German – he was one of those people to whom languages stuck like flies to flypaper; and he was a reserve officer in the army from his time in Manchukuo.

He has been at Kaunas less than a year when the events described earlier change his life, and also the lives of many others.

To Sugihara's relief, when he arrives in Berlin from Kaunas he is neither reprimanded nor dismissed. Yukiko's memoir speculates that he may have been protected by the military: they had arranged his appointment in Kaunas; and while they knew of his pacifist disposition they also appreciated his work. It is also possible that the Foreign Ministry had not yet understood the scale of Sugihara's disobedience. Kaunas to Berlin is a day's journey by rail; and the Jews to whom he has given visas are still far from Japan. Though he has sent records of visas and visa fees to Japan, this is wartime, and there is no reason why these should come to the attention of senior officials immediately.

Sugihara is sent first to Prague as consul general and then, when Germany completes its takeover there, to Königsberg, as before to observe what was happening around the border – at this time, the preparations for Operation Barbarossa. In the autumn of 1942 he is posted to Bucharest as head of mission. (The war makes it impossible for his predecessor to leave, so he stays on too.)

Sugihara is still in Bucharest when the war ends. When the Soviet army arrives the whole family is interned. A Japanese officer has announced that he will kill them all rather than permit the disgrace of surrender, but he does not go through with this. (Yukiko, meanwhile, has spent a week caught between the front lines, first with the Germans and then with Romanian partisans; but she emerges unscathed.) Their internment lasts nearly two years; they move from camp to camp across Siberia in miserable conditions. Eventually, in April 1947, they arrive in Japan, happy to have survived and to be home, even though Japan is in ruins.

After a period for recovery Sugihara is asked to report to the Foreign Ministry. He arrives home forlorn: the events of Kaunas have caught up with him and he has been dismissed. He receives a small severance payment, but it does not go far; nor do their savings when they are able to retrieve them. He is not able to find work, and for a time sells light bulbs door to door. The misery of the family is made worse by the death of their youngest son, and then a year later by that of Yukiko's sister Setsuko. Sugihara manages to get a job at an American PX – his language skills still have a market; and though Yukiko finds it disgraceful for him to work for Japan's conquerors, the family finances improve.

When the PX closes down, he gets a job with an American company doing business between Japan and the Soviet Union. The president of the company, though American, is a Russian speaker. Sugihara discovers that he is Jewish, and is reminded of Kaunas. Now he is working in Moscow, this time leaving Yukiko behind – without diplomatic status Moscow is less secure, and besides the children are at school. In Moscow he is the doyen of the Russian-speaking Japanese, many of whom were his pupils. He does not speak about Kaunas. Once, he tries to find out if any of the people for whom he issued visas survived. Nobody knows.

By chance he is back in Tokyo from Moscow in August 1968 when a call comes from the Israeli embassy. Could he possibly go and see them? When he arrives there he is greeted by the new economic attaché, Mr Nishri. He was one of the five representatives Sugihara met on the first day of the refugees. He still has the visa thirty years later. Many of the refugees who survived have tried to find Sugihara, but they have never succeeded. This may be because he told them that his given name was 'Sempo' – easier, he thought, for foreigners than Chiune. In response to enquiries the Foreign Ministry said that it had no one of this name in its records. This is true. On the other hand, it would not have been difficult to identify the Sugihara who had served in Kaunas. He is the only Japanese diplomat ever to have done so.

But at some point, Sugihara made an attempt to find out what had happened to the visa recipients. The Israeli embassy could tell him nothing; but he left his phone number, and they kept it.

After this, bit by bit, the story gets out. A good number of those to whom he gave visas survived. The Japanese government, though an ally of Germany, was not anti-Semitic, and the Japanese quarter of Shanghai was a refuge for many. Others were able to get to the United States or to Canada. How many Sugihara helped cannot be known precisely; often a whole family managed to travel on one visa. Yukiko calculated that he might have issued more than 2,000 visas. After he departed from Kaunas, one of those left behind copied the consulate stamp and forged more. The total number Sugihara helped may be over 6,000.

Sugihara and his family – who played their part in the rescue – are welcomed and honoured in Israel, and later in the United States. The story reaches the Japanese media, and he is celebrated there too. Finally, even the government and the Foreign Ministry honour him.

Why did he act as he did? Sugihara was a kind man. He treated his wife as an equal; in Manchuria he made friends with Chinese and Koreans, and resigned because he did not like the way they were treated. His religious beliefs may be part of the story; but equally he may have chosen his religion because it matched his view of life. He did what he thought was right; he and Yukiko never doubted that they made the right choice.

Many others, from all walks of life, hid victims of the Holocaust or helped them escape or survive. Sometimes that even included the people who were supposed to be persecuting them.

The stories told here are only two of a number of diplomats who deserve to be remembered. Another was the Portuguese consul general in Bordeaux, Aristides de Sousa Mendes. Like Sugihara he ignored explicit instructions from his government and worked day and night, with the help of his sons and some of the refugees, to help Jews escape from France. He was ordered to return to Lisbon and an escort was sent to take him back. On the way, in Bayonne, he saw a crowd similar to the one that had gathered outside his Bordeaux consulate. Disregarding his escort, he ordered the consul there, who was still under his authority, to give them visas too. When he reached Lisbon he was dismissed from the ministry. He died a few years later in poverty.

Another was Ho Feng-Shan, the Chinese consul general in Vienna. He disobeyed instructions from the ambassador in Berlin, under whose authority he was. He issued uncounted numbers of visas for Shanghai from the *Anschluss* in 1938 onwards. Visas were not required to enter Shanghai; but they were needed to leave Germany/Austria. On some occasions Ho's visas, like those of Frank Foley, enabled the release of Jews from concentration camps.

These further two examples are mentioned as an indication of the variety of people who used their position as diplomats to save lives. Their number includes honorary appointees as well as career officers. The largest and most systematic effort was that mounted by Raoul Wallenberg in Budapest on behalf of the Swedish government, with assistance from other diplomats in Budapest at the time. All of these were exceptional people. Unfortunately, they were also exceptions: the majority followed the rules and their instructions.

Conclusion: Putting the Fragments Together

> 'Men are not tied to one another by papers and seals. They are led to associate by resemblances, by conformities, by sympathies. It is with nations as with individuals. Nothing is so strong a tie of amity between nation and nation as correspondence in laws, customs, manners and habits of life. They have more than the force of treaties in themselves. They are obligations written in the heart.'
>
> *Edmund Burke, Letters on a Regicide Peace, 1796*

A piece of paper makes the difference between life and death. That is what the Foley visas and the Sugihara visas did. They did it when the signatures were not authorised and sometimes when the documents were half forged.

This book is about pieces of paper that save lives. Its heroes are the diplomats who solve problems by negotiation or co-operation. The treaties that made up the Peace of Westphalia resolved enough of the conflicts of the Thirty Years War to end the state of general war in Europe. The Congress of Vienna brought peace and order, for a period, following the Napoleonic Wars. The final treaty of this era, the product of Talleyrand's last negotiation, was the Treaty of London which guaranteed Belgian neutrality: 'A scrap of paper', the German chancellor, Bethmann-Hollweg called it in 1914.

The Soviet-Finnish Treaty of Friendship, Co-operation and Mutual

Assistance for once lived up to its title: the friendship was limited, but the treaty gave Finland peace and independence; and the Soviet Union gained some security though co-operation with its neighbour. Diplomacy saved Denmark too: not treaties but skilful handling of an enemy, backed by the solidity of Denmark's democratic society and government. The North Atlantic Treaty establishing NATO, and the Treaty of Paris setting up the European Coal and Steel Community, were not peace treaties in the normal sense. They were better than that; they created a living society of states. The treaties negotiated by Willy Brandt and Egon Bahr were also not called peace treaties, but they might have been, since they foreswore the use of force. None of these documents is as dramatic or as direct as the Sugihara visas; but they have brought order and security in a continent where war once seemed to be a way of life.

Peace treaties have not always brought peace. Sometimes, as Bevin noted, they have contained the seeds of the next conflict. Probably he was thinking of Versailles. That is not the only case: negotiations among the victors may break down over division of the spoils. This almost happened at the Congress of Vienna: the allies who had been united against France nearly came to blows over Saxony-Poland, and were called to order by France. After the First Balkan War in 1912, when Slavs had driven Turkey out of much of the Balkans, the victors fought the Second Balkan War to settle the new borders.* At Potsdam, the Second World War Allies agreed on the division of Germany; but in the conferences that followed they could agree on nothing else. Out of this grew the Cold War.

Through much of history, war has been a normal part of life: civil wars to establish states; and then wars between states. Machiavelli is a starting point for modern Europe. The state is there to provide security. That means being stronger than potential enemies. Strength comes from size and from internal cohesion; alliances, in the nature of things, are temporary. The task of the prince is therefore to conquer

* The treaty that ended this war included a large Albanian-speaking population in Serbia. Out of this, almost a century later, came the Kosovo War of 1999.

and to absorb the conquered state into his own. War was constant in Machiavelli's Europe; so it has remained until the mid-point of the last century.

The balance of power was to preserve the state system, not the peace. But even before the Peace of Utrecht made balance a principle, the seeds of failure had been planted. The Dutch revolt began with religion; but it brought with it the beginnings of nationalism and democracy. The printing press reinforced the idea of the nation by creating national languages. With the French Revolution nationalism became a political force. At the Congress of Vienna, this new world was only dimly discernible. Talleyrand, looking ahead, saw that peoples could no longer be passed around, like a dairy herd, as territory was won and lost; Castlereagh spoke of self-determination for Poland, but did not think of applying it in Ireland, much less in the British Empire.

The Industrial Revolution reinforced the idea of the nation. Railways needed national time (for timetables); industry needed national languages. As the state became the nation state, democracy grew. Liberals dreamed that nation and democracy would bring peace. To begin with, they brought the opposite. Democracies do not fight limited wars for concepts such as the balance of power. They fight as the nation in arms; and they fight to the end. In victory they are vengeful; in defeat they are unstable. In this world, the free competition of power no longer delivered equilibrium, much less peace. As the idea of self-determination grew, empires fell apart. But wars still ended with pieces of paper and ink.

Denmark, Finland and Belgium were products of self-determination, and of great-power politics. Denmark's national democratic enthusiasm started a war that was disastrous for the Danes.* Bismarck used it to achieve national unification under Prussia, and without democracy: power politics at home and abroad. Finland found its way to self-determination as the First World War ended in revolution and the collapse of great-power empires.

* Self-determination was proposed by the British in 1864, as a way to settle the frontier in Schleswig. The Danes rejected it, along with all other proposals. It was eventually applied in1920, successfully.)

Bethmann-Hollweg's 'scrap of paper', originally negotiated by Talleyrand, played a role: Belgian neutrality brought together conservatives in Britain who believed in the balance of power and liberals who believed in the sanctity of treaties. The First World War buried the old system, along with millions of dead. It was natural to look for new solutions.

Woodrow Wilson's was to embrace democracy and self-determination, and to safeguard peace through law and institutions. The League of Nations would settle disputes and enforce rules. Collective security proposed an alliance against aggression. It was a new version of the old system, but one that had never worked; not in the Peace of Lodi,* nor in the Peace of Westphalia. No one in the 1930s wanted to fight another war to end all wars. Besides, the exclusion of Germany, the Russian Revolution and, above all, the absence of the United States doomed the League. You cannot run the world if three great powers are missing – and two important ones, China and Japan, are alienated. This piece of paper was empty. After that, the 1930s seemed to prove the Marxist-Leninists right: first the collapse of capitalism, then war among the capitalist states.

Yet after the Second World War, Europe has enjoyed a peace that no one imagined. The world of Machiavelli and Hobbes is forgotten. How did this happen? How do words, spoken or written, save lives?

The answer is in what lies behind the words. Sometimes it is simple. The Foley visas were a legal document for a part of the world where the rule of law was strong. They gave a right to enter the UK or Palestine, and that was that. The Sugihara visas were similar. But there were also visas written after Sugihara had left that were not legal. And the statements signed by Jan Zwartendijk, that the holder did not need a visa to enter Curaçao, had no legal value. But to make Sugihara's transit visa valid the holder needed to show they had a visa for somewhere else; the Dutch stamp gave border officials an excuse to let the holder

* The Peace of Lodi (1454) obliged Italian states to take up arms against any of their number who attacked another; and to join together in opposing any non-Italian state invading Italy. Neither happened in 1494. For Westphalia see Chapter Two.

through. Some may have taken it at face value; others acted out of human sympathy.

After the Second World War the words that mattered came from Harry Truman and George Marshall. Truman was heir to Wilson's ideas, but he implemented them in his own way. He had fought in the First World War and understood what had gone wrong after it. In a speech to the American Legion in 1938, as the storm gathered, he called for an air force second to none; he told his audience that isolationism had been the worst of all mistakes, that America had erred in refusing to ratify the Treaty of Versailles and to join the League of Nations: 'we did not accept our responsibilities as a great power . . . . In the coming struggle between democracy and dictatorship, democracy must be prepared to defend its principles'. As the fog began to clear in 1946 and 1947, these memories governed his decisions.[1]

The first step was the Truman Doctrine. The United States announced that it was going to be a European power, something it had never been before; it had not yet given up on the United Nations, but that did not look likely to save Europe any more than the League of Nations had. The United States would take responsibility in the Eastern Mediterranean, the place where three continents met; and it was prepared to do so more widely too.

The second step was to protect democracy in Europe. Italian fascism in the 1920s, grounded in violence without law or limits, heralded Italian aggression in the 1930s; the takeover of political life by the military in Japan opened the path to war in China. In Germany the Nazi seizure of power meant the end of peace in Europe. The origins of the Second World War were in part domestic. To protect the peace you had to protect democracy. The economic crises of the 1920s and 1930s had brought the ruin of democratic politics. Reparations, debt, currency collapse, banking crises, exchange rate instability, trade restrictions, the ruin of the middle classes by inflation, the impoverishment of the working classes in the depression – it is a surprise that democracy lasted as long as it did.

The Marshall Plan tackled the threat to democracy from economic dislocation. Without action by the United States, Europe would have been easy prey for Communism. National policies for workers' rights and welfare complemented Marshall aid by dealing with social problems. The New Deal was already doing this in the United States; Truman added a civil rights dimension. In Britain, the Labour government's programme had free health care (the NHS) as its centrepiece; General MacArthur gave Japan a constitution with equal rights for women, and a land reform that ended rural poverty. Many European governments were coalitions of the left with policies for a more equal society. Liberty and equality go together. Growing inequality today is one more reason to worry about the future of democracy.

The idea of democracy as a cornerstone of peace is associated with Wilson, and is part of a long liberal tradition. Some liberals have emphasised national self-determination, some free trade, some institutions. All have their role, but many imagined a world from which military power had disappeared. Machiavelli's insight that republics could live together 'as brothers' is significant since it comes from one whose thinking was rooted in power.

The third step was multilateral institutions; but this time they were not the result of a single blueprint. In the late 1940s it was becoming clear that the United Nations was not going to be the cornerstone of world peace that many, including Roosevelt, had dreamed of.

Meanwhile the democratic world needed to defend itself. Bevin spoke to Marshall of 'not a formal alliance', but a 'sort of spiritual federation of the West'. Like Friedrich von Gentz, writing of the Concert of Europe as 'not an alliance, properly so called',* he could not escape the language of war that still shaped European thinking on foreign relations. Soviet actions in Eastern Europe and the scares over Finland and Norway made the organisation that grew from Bevin's idea more military than he may have intended. The Korean War reinforced this. Even so, the 'spiritual' dimension – today we would say 'values' – is not wholly absent from NATO.

The commitment in NATO Article 5 is not that of a classical alliance at all. The key phrase – 'an attack on one or more . . . shall be

* See the passage from his letter quoted at the end of Chapter Three.

considered an attack against them all' – was copied and pasted from the Rio Treaty, setting up the Organization of American States, not usually seen as an alliance. This in turn was probably borrowed from the League of Nations Covenant, which contains almost identical language, but with mandatory sanctions. A similar obligation can be found in the Westphalia treaties. NATO Article 5 is the weakest of them all: the only obligation is for each to 'take such action as it deems necessary'.

This prompts the question: how it is that in NATO, this weak principle has become the foundation of a strong alliance and lasting security?

NATO

One answer is that NATO is multilateral, with an open-ended timeframe* and an open-ended agenda. It is not directed at a specific country or a specific problem. That makes it different from the alliances of Europe's history, a list that ends with those that led to the First World War. More important, and unlike the alliances of the past, NATO is not just a treaty, it is an institution: there is a council, a military staff and daily contact among its members. And while NATO has a distinct military flavour, it also has the character of a society of states.

The second factor is democracy, not because democracies are inherently peaceful, but because an association of democracies is more likely to work – for the reasons Burke gives in the quotation above. It is easy to work with countries when you share habits and institutions. Democracies are used to discussion and debate. When NATO meets at the political level its members are of unequal size, but they all have elections, parliaments, a free press (or most of them do) and similar styles. There is a cultural affinity. The Concert of Europe worked while memories of the Napoleonic Wars were strong, and while those who had worked together then were in office. It broke up as divisions grew between the relatively liberal Britain and France, and the conservative autocracies of Austria, Prussia and Russia.

* The original treaty was for twenty years; when this ended its members made the duration indefinite.

The third, indispensable, factor is US leadership. There is no American guarantee in the treaty, but it is a defining feature of NATO. With the United States committed to defending Germany against a Soviet attack, Germany does not have to keep forces at a level that would terrify France and everyone else. Because of this, for the first time in history, European countries do not measure their defences against those of their neighbours. The possibility of a US role in Europe after the Second World War began with the Atlantic Charter and Lend-Lease; but it remained uncertain until George Marshall became secretary of state. The United States dominates; but NATO's multilateral character leaves space for debate; even the USA has to persuade. In the Cold War, NATO strengthened America's power as well as Europe's security. This is still true in the more complicated post-Cold-War world.

Alan Brooke foresaw the need for a 'super foreign secretary' to bring Germany into a Western system to resist the Soviet Union. Bevin played a part in the creation of the West; but the role that Brooke foresaw for a British foreign secretary belonged to a wider circle including Marshall, Acheson, Schuman and Monnet, and especially Adenauer. The rebirth of German as a democracy was essential in the reversal of the alliances.

The purpose of military power is to produce political effects. History is littered with failures to do this: Vietnam, Iraq and Libya are recent examples. NATO gave Europe confidence in the future and built trust among its members. As a political use of military power it is an outstanding success.

The European Union

Konrad Adenauer identified the problem: being alone brings out the worst in countries. Further back, von Gentz's pregnant remark that 'not one of the states [of Europe] . . . could remain isolated' suggests that the path to ending Europe's wars might lie in finding the right way to bring them together.

That is what Monnet did. The Coal and Steel Community never

functioned as he imagined it would. But it solved the problem of the Ruhr and persuaded its six members that civil collaboration among sovereign states could work.

To be sustained, collaboration has to be useful. The Customs Union and the Single Market – copied from the Benelux Union, and then driven by that remarkable duo, Margaret Thatcher and Jacques Delors – brought prosperity as they removed barriers. Eliminating border controls and sharing regulatory authorities reduces bureaucracy. The Customs Union gives the EU power in trade negotiations, where size matters. The Single Market brings it influence in global regulation: if your standards are high and are widely used, others adopt them. The EU is not a great power in the normal way; but it has the making of a regulatory superpower. Good regulation – environmental protection, fair treatment of workers, safety in food and medicine – is a mark of civilisation. It is something to be proud of.*

The point of the European project was never just a bigger, better market. What Monnet, Schuman, Adenauer and Dean Acheson wanted was simple to formulate: good political relations among European states. But for 500 years it seemed impossible. Monnet's insight was that the affinities that join men and states, of which Burke writes, could be created. He was not the first to see that a common task can bring people of different backgrounds together: Herman Melville's accounts of life at sea are full of examples, but Monnet was the first to apply this thought to the problem of the sovereign state.

The density of EU business means that national governments are in continuous negotiation. One consequence is that you never know whose help you may need tomorrow. You can never break with anyone, no matter how bad the quarrel. Tonight you may not be on speaking terms about Iraq; but tomorrow you will be shoulder to shoulder on milk quotas. It is a regime of compulsory friendship.†

For most of the nineteenth century, and right up to the 1950s if not

* This is explained in detail in Anu Bradford's *The Brussels Effect: How the European Union Rules the World*.

† The author witnessed these two sides of the British-German relationship at a European Council just after the invasion of Iraq in 2003.

later, the states of Western Europe regarded each other with distrust. Historically, fear has been the dominant motive in foreign relations. A. J. P. Taylor's study of nineteenth-century diplomacy, *The Struggle for the Mastery in Europe 1848–1918*, tells us in its first sentence that Hobbes's 'state of nature', in which violence was the only law, had never existed for individuals; but this was how the great powers of Europe had always lived: in a state of continual fear, where life was 'nasty, brutish and short'. A fuller quotation from *Leviathan reads*: 'and the life of man, solitary, poore, nasty, brutish and short'. The first word, 'solitary', is the most important.

What is it that lies behind the EU treaties that makes them work? As with NATO, democracy is important: this is a brotherhood of republics such as Machiavelli imagined. If both Kant and Machiavelli see republican constitutions as essential to peace, there must be something in it. Third, there is Monnet's simple but powerful insight. Finally, a precondition of this leap in the dark was the defeat in war of all the original members. That is also part of the explanation of Britain's late entry and unnecessary exit.

The men who built the post-war Western order saw themselves as Wilson's heirs. They chose, differently from Wilson, to use US power, including financial power, not to dominate but to protect.

The continuing puzzle: dealing with those who may be enemies

The first task of any country or group of countries is to look after itself, its institutions and its friendships. That is what most post-war diplomacy has been about. With a liberal order established – though still in need of care, since nothing is permanent in politics – the difficult question remains: how to deal with countries that do not belong to it, and do not want to belong to it, and that may be its enemies.

In Henry Kissinger's terms these are still revolutionary times. In spite of peace, stability and progress, at least two major powers do not accept the liberal order, do not trust it and would like to undermine it. Russia expresses its resentment by trying to destabilise its neighbours and by interfering in the West when it sees an opportunity. China's aims are less certain but may be more far-reaching. Both see the world as a struggle for power: those whom you do not dominate are your enemies, or will be one day.

George Kennan's message in the Long Telegram still holds good today: don't think the government in Moscow thinks or operates as we do. It applies to Beijing even more strongly. The Russian Federation and the People's Republic of China are not seeking a world revolution; but they are not satisfied with their position in the international order, nor with the order itself. Instead of the traditional *cordon sanitaire* or sphere of influence, Russia today aims at a *cordon insanitaire* of neighbours off-balance through Russian-sponsored separatist movements. Further afield it uses cyberspace to undermine the liberal world. China is more integrated in the world economy than the Soviet Union ever was. This gives it opportunities for co-operation, but also for manipulation. Its claims on territorial seas, on Taiwan and the way in which its diplomacy has become harsher as its strength has grown – for example, in taking foreigners hostage – are all warning signs. No one believes any longer that China's participation in the world economy will, on its own, turn it into a liberal state and part of the liberal order.

Lesser powers can also be disruptive: North Korea's nuclear weapons mean that it meets one of the criteria for being a great power. The United States would add Iran to the list: some parts of that state, though not all, remain committed to revolution and disruption.

There is no single formula for dealing with such countries; but Kissinger's three rules for engagement are a good starting point: first, concreteness – do business with them, but agreements should have substance; dialogue for dialogue's sake too easily becomes self- deception. Second, reciprocity or 'linkage' – advantages in one field should be balanced in another; third, restraint – both sides should avoid provocative actions.*

* The agreement reached by the five permanent members of the Security Council and Germany with Iran on its nuclear programme, the JCPOA, subsequently wrecked by the Trump administration, met all these criteria.

Restraint means that you have to understand the other side. It requires people who understand their language, history and culture, who can guess at their ambitions and apprehensions. You need them on the ground, and you need to take them seriously. It was harmful to the United States that it was absent from China at critical moments; it is regrettable that it is absent from Iran.

Kissinger failed partly because he did not build domestic support – he and Nixon were innovating, so this would have been sensible – but also because he forgot the principle of restraint. This is easily done when your partners are people you do not understand well, whose instinct is to see your actions in a hostile light.

NATO would have done well to recall this principle when it discussed membership for Georgia and Ukraine in 2008. Bill Burns, one of the great professionals of the modern State Department, warned against. It might have been avoided had Britain joined Germany and France in opposing it at the Bucharest summit. What followed has harmed Ukraine, Russia and the West.

It is wise not to expect too much. Ambitious powers do not become friends overnight. Autocratic systems run on orders from the top, 'the vertical of power', as it is called in Russia. Autocracy neither teaches nor values the skills that are needed for co-operation: persuasion and compromise, for example. The pure autocrat, Napoleon or Stalin, is more comfortable with conquest than with co-operation. Autocrats still like peace by separation. This is Alexander and Napoleon at Tilsit, the Molotov-Ribbentrop Pact and Stalin at Yalta: agreements on spheres of influence. After the Second World War, the only agreements that stuck were those on boundaries.

Brezhnev's wish to set borders in stone was the reason for the Helsinki Conference. Thirty-five European states met from November 1972 (to agree the agenda) to July 1975 (to sign the Final Act). In between they agreed ten principles for relations among states in Europe (plus 600 steps to give effect to them!).* The principles include inviolability of

* The Helsinki Principles are admirable, but they recall Napoleon's remark to Talleyrand: 'I like principles, they don't commit me to anything.'

frontiers and territorial integrity of states – as Brezhnev wished. But the principle of sovereignty also states that borders may be changed by agreement and in accordance with international law; and that sovereign states have the right to belong or not to belong to alliances. Both were invoked to support German unification within NATO.

After Helsinki there was more dissent in the East, and more suppression of dissent: there was more trade with the West and also ballooning debts in the East. But the Soviet Union never again intervened militarily.

We should notice that while Kissinger's project of working with an enemy failed, Brandt's succeeded. Most remarkable of all, perhaps, was Paasikivi's success. But these are exceptions: thirty years from the end of the Cold War, relations with Russia are no better than those with the Soviet Union.

The only thing we know about the future is that it is not like the past. Today there is one big certainty. This is climate change. The consequences of global heating are clearer every day, and the need for action more urgent. The logic of tackling a global problem through co-operation – joint development and ownership of technology, agreed rules and transparency on emissions – is compelling. Our first concern should be the climate itself; but we should bear in mind that action in this area could be a catalyst for co-operation and trust in other areas. The environment is a global public good that needs global management. This could be an opportunity to build common ground. Or it could be another area for wasteful competition.

The liberal order

First there was peace by empire; then peace – or rather limits to war – by balance; then there was peace by separation.

The liberal order brings peace by co-operation: a system of consent and consensus that offers freedom as well as peace. We cannot force it on others: that is not the nature of liberalism. Countless examples have shown that it is easier said than done. But if liberalism defends itself, it could spread slowly, by example.

The multilateral order changes everything. One state on its own is isolated. Two states, and relations will be transactional –'the art of the deal' – or they may be a conspiracy against a third. Three is the magic number. When three or more states are gathered together, there is transparency and very likely rules, written or unwritten. At the least, there will be rules of procedure. This is what von Gentz saw at work in the Concert of Europe, though he had no name for it; this is what Grey wanted before the First World War, what Wilson tried for after it.*

Liberal ideas were born in the sciences and in the arts; the idea that we should seek the truth, not from doctrine but by examining the world, is as old as Aristotle. This is the beginning of liberal culture. A second strand is found in literature; Montaigne's essay describing his personal repugnance at torture was a starting point. Shakespeare's politics were conservative, and his plays are about the need for order. But in *Troilus and Cressida*, those who preach order and hierarchy end in a waste of blood and betrayal. And in *King Lear* it is not the high-born but the servants, the fool, a blind man and the mad king, who speak the truth.

John Donne's 'Any man's death diminishes me, because I am involved in mankind'† puts the idea of a shared humanity into words. Rousseau, in *The Social Contract* (1762), turns the words into politics: 'Man is born free, but he is everywhere in chains.' Voltaire tells us that at the London Stock Exchange, 'the Jew, the Mahometan, and the Christian do business together, as if they were of the same religion' (and the name of infidel is reserved for the man who is bankrupt).‡ Here is another clue – liberalism is connected to business: Talleyrand preferred commerce to conquest; Monnet was a banker; the Marshall Plan was to support democracy by restarting trade. Markets like freedom, but they also need regulation and the rule of law.

Today's liberal order is more a thing of patches than an order. The

* Voltaire, writing when political questions wore religious clothing, remarks that a country with only one religion will be despotic; with two there will be conflict; with many there will be religious freedom.

† From *Devotions upon Emergent Occasions* (1624).

‡ *Lettres Philosophiques* (1733), sixth letter.

UN does not govern the world, as Roosevelt and Truman had hoped it would. The IMF and the World Bank do their job, but both need the backing of the US government. The WTO is less than it might have been, and will become less still, if US policy continues its present course. Regional bodies like the EU, ASEAN, Mercosur and the African Union are a part of this patchwork too: they are imperfect, but all stand for co-operation, and the world is better off for them. In fact, looking at the world as it is, the idea of it being under a single supreme authority is somewhere between implausible and undesirable.

The great diplomats understood that they were dealing not just with foreign relations, but also with the future of the state itself – which is inseparable from its relations with its neighbours. Talleyrand lived through a crisis of legitimacy and saw how the style of government had to change to meet the shifting currents of legitimacy. For Machiavelli, Monnet and Marshall legitimacy was the hidden heart of policy.

Talleyrand's only equal as a diplomat was Bismarck* – equal in clarity of mind, in calculation and in readiness to take risks. But Bismarck was blind on legitimacy. As a result, the legacy of his diplomatic success was poisoned. It would prove fatal for Germany and a calamity for Europe.

The United States is the creator and protector of the liberal order. Europe is its most important success; and both are in trouble. Hungary and Poland are causes of concern, and they are not the only ones. Democracy and the rule of law are difficult – more difficult than we thought in 1989. If they fail, or decay, or become corrupted, this too is poison for Europe. The solutions lie in politics and diplomacy. The external system of diplomacy and the internal systems of the state are two parts of one whole.

If the liberal order dies, the sickness will begin in domestic politics. It is domestic systems of government that make us what we are. Security depends on a country's military and economic strength; on its friends and relationships; but also on the strength of its internal resilience. This is a lesson from Denmark and Finland, and it is one that matters all the

* Not included in this book, partly because I dislike him, partly because I could not match Henry Kissinger's portrait in his essay for *Daedalus*, 'The White Revolutionary: Reflections on Bismarck', or in *Diplomacy*, pp. 103–36.

more in an age of information warfare. That is why the Afterword looks at two problems of liberal democracy in Britain that need attention.

I have not tried to draw lessons about diplomacy from the stories in this book. Its heroes and the problems they tried to solve are too various. It is right that diplomacy is conducted with patience, courtesy and calm; because not far below the surface lie conflict and emotion. The greatest diplomats engage with emotions as well as with reason. The ends of diplomacy – Henry Kissinger's 'intangibles' – are emotions: reconciliation or revenge, hope or fear? Empathy and imagination matter as much as clarity and precision. Indeed, they matter more. Diplomacy is an art, not a science.

Afterword: Two Problems in British Democracy

'I had come to see that, at the root, everything was connected to politics, and that . . . no people could be other than the nature of its government made it.'

Jean-Jacques Rousseau, The Confessions, Book Nine

Rousseau is right. Our lives are shaped by the political systems in which we live. Life in a dictatorship, or a country where political authority is collapsing, is different from life under the rule of law in a democratic country.

It is also true that some democracies work better than others. This may be the result of factors such as education; but these in turn are determined by politics. It all starts with the political system: get this right and you are more likely to get the rest right.

The United Kingdom is admired for its long democratic tradition; but it has weaknesses. The strength of its traditions may even be one of them. As society changes, democracy needs to change too.

Many things suggest that something is wrong in Britain. The most obvious is the Brexit referendum. A flawed process has delivered an irreversible result. Opinion polls in the last three years show a growing majority who think that the decision to leave the EU was a mistake. But nothing can be done.

It is time to re-examine the institutions that got us into this mess. Two elements of British democracy are particularly undemocratic.

The first undemocratic element is the electoral system

Voters in Britain elect Parliament by a system known as 'first past the post' (FPTP): one person, one vote, in single-member constituencies; the candidate who gets the most votes is elected. What could be wrong with that?

The answer is: several things. First, this method produces different results according to the geographical distribution of votes. In the last general election (2019), the Scottish National Party (SNP) won forty-eight seats in Parliament (7.4% of those available) with 3.9% of the vote. This was because their votes were, not surprisingly, concentrated in Scottish seats. At the other extreme, the Liberal Democrats won eleven seats, less than a quarter of the SNP's total, although about three times as many people voted for them (11.6%). The Greens did even worse: their vote was just under half that of the SNP, but they won only one seat. It is reasonable to ask whether this is fair.

A second result of this system is that a party can win a majority in Parliament without having a majority of the votes. In 2019, the Conservative Party did exactly this: 365 seats out of 650 – a landslide majority – although it had the support of only 43.6% of the electorate. A government cannot represent everybody; but should it not have the backing of the majority of voters?

Third, we should look at FPTP from the voter's point of view. I have voted in every election for the last forty years. Until recently, I knew that my vote did not matter: I lived in a 'safe seat' – one with an unassailable Conservative majority. Many, if not most, voters in the UK are in this position. It is not healthy.

Recently the constituency boundary changed, and it ceased to be a safe seat. My vote now mattered more. In 2019, I voted for the Liberal Democrat candidate. The Conservative candidate won. Her majority over the Labour candidate was tiny – 150 votes. Had I known this in advance, I would have voted Labour. Others might have done so too. But we knew how to vote only when it was too late.

Thus, FPTP is unfair for individual voters, for the parties and for the country as a whole.

Australia and the Republic of Ireland inherited FPTP when they separated from the UK. Over time they concluded it was unfair and switched to a system known as the Single Transferable Vote (STV).

Under STV, constituencies each elect three or more MPs. On the ballot paper voters indicate their order of preference among the candidates. When the first preferences have been counted, votes are transferred down from candidates at the top, who have won more votes than they need to be elected, and up from candidates at the bottom as they are eliminated.* Every vote contributes to the result. This is a system that allows voters to indicate whom they are against as well as whom they are for. (In the UK this system is already used for elections to the Assembly in Northern Ireland and for local elections there and in Scotland.)

Under STV every vote counts. An MP for a safe seat in first-past-the-post Britain can afford to ignore a voter who belongs to another party. Under STV, he or she may need that voter's second or third preference to beat rivals from their own party. With STV, every candidate has reason to listen to every voter. Isn't that how elections should be?

STV makes it more difficult for a single party to win a majority in Parliament. Instead of the drama of the loser packing their bags and leaving No. 10 the morning after the election, there may be times when coalition negotiations delay the change of government. If the result is a government that better reflects opinion in the country – that is to say, a more democratic, more legitimate government – it is a price worth paying.

Both at the level of the voter and at the level of Parliament, STV is a system that encourages people to work across party lines. Those in the

* To give a simplified example: in a four-seat constituency, to be elected a candidate needs a quarter of the votes. If one candidate receives 50 per cent of the first-preference votes, he or she has twice as many votes as are needed; half a vote is therefore transferred to the second preferences on each ballot paper. This is repeated until only four candidates remain, each with 25 per cent of the vote.

UK who regret the divisions caused by the referendum, or who think politics should be about bringing people together – as well as about fighting for every vote – ought to support STV.

FPTP crushes new parties and small parties (unless they have a regional base). This was visible in the 2019 UK election results. In a market economy any decent competition authority would reject such a system. Open competition is important in politics, just as it is in the economy. It brings new faces and new ideas.

One-party politics is tyranny. Two-party politics is oligarchy. Multiparty politics is healthy. In the real world, few choices are entirely binary. Politics should be about cooperation as well as competition.

The second undemocratic element is the House of Lords

The House of Lords is a survivor of the medieval Estates – the Lords Spiritual and Temporal. The great landowners are now only a token presence. Today's lords are mainly nominated in recognition of service in different walks of life, but especially in politics. ('Service to politics' may include donations to party funds). In wisdom and decency, the Lords has few equals. Its debates are civilised and well informed. It does good work in improving the quality of the legislation sent it by the Commons.

But it is not democratic. As a result it is only rarely able to stand up to a government that has a solid majority in the Commons. A check of this kind would be useful in Britain, where there is little separation of powers, and where the prime minister has been well described as an elected dictator.*

Reform of the Lords has been discussed for decades; its composition has changed, but not yet in ways that enable it to challenge the Commons. It is understandable that the parties in the Commons do not want this; but it would be healthy for democracy.

* By Lord Hailsham, a former Lord Chancellor, in the Richard Dimbleby Lecture on the BBC in 1976.

Some advocate a second chamber elected by the regions. This would be similar to the upper house in Germany (the Bundesrat). German experience is not encouraging. If the Bundesrat has the same majority as the lower house (the Bundestag), there seems little point in it. If it has a different majority it blocks and delays. It is a check of sorts, but not a very useful one.

If we want a second chamber that does not copy the first, one way would be to choose it, as juries are chosen, by lot. This would take us back to the origins of democracy in Greece. An experiment on such radical lines would require debate, perhaps some trial and error. Many questions would need to be answered: the method of selection, the term of office, procedures and support. We would also have to look at what we would lose if we changed the House of Lords in this way, and consider how to compensate for it, and at how to make the best use of the knowledge and experience that the current house offers.

We should look at the attractions too. A house chosen by lot would reflect the diversity of Britain's people; it would be a place in which every citizen could imagine him- or herself a member. The result would be two chambers, each representative but in different ways: one because it is elected, the other because it is a representative sample of the people.*

A body of ordinary people, chosen at random, reflecting the whole population, serving their country rather than seeking a career, might win more respect than the House of Commons and more legitimacy than the present House of Lords. The populist accusation that they are 'in it for themselves' could not be made.

In the past, selection by lot and election by vote were thought of as alternative methods of democracy. The first is associated with Athens, the second with Rome. Rousseau and Montesquieu both saw selection by lot as more democratic. Such a house would, for once, come close to the government 'by the people' that Abraham Lincoln spoke of in the Gettysburg address.

* Anyone wishing to know more about this should turn to *Against Elections: The Case for Democracy* by David Reybrouck.

The process that led to constitutional change in the Republic of Ireland included an assembly, most of which was chosen by lot, to reflect the Irish population as a whole. Their debates informed the vote in the referendum that supported constitutional change.

Experience suggests that such assemblies make sensible choices. They are preferable to referendums because they can hold debates in depth. The tendency in a group of strangers brought together in this way seems to be to seek consensus. This would provide a contrast to the House of Commons, where contention is inbuilt.

Populist upsurges are often a signal that something is wrong. That is true in Britain today. The best way to deal with populism is to see to it that government is respected and legitimate.

I am sceptical of magic solutions. I do not claim that these proposals would provide instant perfection. I insist only that we can do better than we do now. We need change; and we need a debate about the form it should take.

Bibliographical Note

Histories, memoirs and biographies each have their place. Biographies tell us things the memoir writer omits. Histories give us the context. But memoirs are special. The best tell you how the writer thought and felt: who they were, as well as what they did.

Diplomatic and political memoirs go back two millennia; they became a large phenomenon in the twentieth century, led by Lloyd George and Winston Churchill, who wanted the first draft of history to be theirs.

Machiavelli left no memoirs, but *The Prince*, written from hope, anger and personal experience, is a memoir of the mind. Reading it requires the help of an editor: each page has references that need explaining. *Machiavelli, The Prince* (Cambridge Texts in the History of Political Thought), edited by Quentin Skinner and Russell Price, is all you could wish for: footnotes answer questions before you ask them; short biographies explain the people mentioned. To know Machiavelli more personally, go to *Between Friends*, his letters to Francesco Vettori, edited by John Najemy; they show the private man, vulnerable as well as brilliant. A new biography by Alexander Lee gives us his life as a diplomat, riding across Europe in all weather, studying men and politics, and short of money. For the Italian Renaissance, I have long admired Jack Plumb's labour of love. The (not so) *New Cambridge Modern History* volume on the Renaissance, edited by G. R. Potter, is useful, particularly Cecilia Ady's chapter on the invasions of Italy. For Machiavelli's ideas start with Philip Bobbitt's

The Garments of Court and Palace, and see where that leads.

Richelieu left behind a political testament: advice for his successors and for the king, reflecting his sense of duty, his fear that the king would do poorly without him, and his wish to control all things, even after death. There are many biographies: from Carl Burckhardt's four volumes to Jean-Vincent Blanchard's racy *Eminence*, and Françoise Hildesheimer's thoughtful *Richelieu*. Richelieu himself is elusive: he knows everything, calculates and controls all. He succeeded so well in controlling his image that we may never find the private man. Two books with a wider focus helped me: J. H. Elliott's *Richelieu and Olivares* compares Richelieu with his great Spanish rival; A. Lloyd Moote's biography of Louis XIII shows a king who is all too human. For the background of the Thirty Years War, Peter Wilson's *Europe's Tragedy* is inexhaustible and indispensable.

Mazarin left behind not a political testament but a young king who knew how to govern – perhaps too well. Geoffrey Treasure is the authority in Britain and his *Mazarin* is a pleasure to read; in France it is Claude Dulong (in French), who has also written on Anne of Austria, Louis XIII's long-suffering queen, and regent in Louis XIV's minority. Derek Croxton's *The Last Christian Peace* is a guide to the age, as well as to the Congress of Westphalia.

Talleyrand's memoirs are 'full of gossip', he says, but 'with as little as possible of his life and relationships'. In fact, they are a series of episodes – the revolution, Napoleon with the tsar in Erfurt, the restoration and the Congress of Vienna – with gaps in between; but with a constancy of vision and telling observations throughout. Talleyrand tells the story of his betrayal of Napoleon to Alexander I directly; the Congress of Vienna is recounted through his correspondence with Louis XVIII. For the rest, Emmanuel de Waresquiel's biography is as fascinating as the man himself. (*Le prince immobile* in French; with the *Memoirs* in the second volume). In English, Duff Cooper's biography of 1932 is still in print: excellent, accurate and a pleasure to read.

The Congress of Vienna has a great literature (and Napoleon has even more). The best narrative history today is *Rites of Peace* by Adam Zamoyski. Henry Kissinger, in *A World Restored*, makes the case for his heroes, Metternich and Castlereagh. He takes the story on through the short-lived Concert of Europe. This book also contains profound comments on the methods and purposes of diplomacy.

This is the place to mention Andreas Osiander's *The States System of Europe 1640–1990*. Osiander examines the historic congresses of Europe: Westphalia, Utrecht, Vienna and Paris. His chapter on Vienna is illuminating (and he shares my partiality for Talleyrand); so is his ability to pick out key documents from these events.

There are no English-language biographies or memoirs of Paasikivi or Scavenius. For Finland, I have relied heavily on Max Jakobson's *Finland Survived* (about the war) and *Finland in the New Europe* (about the rest). The context – independence and civil war – are part of the story too. See the histories by Jussila, Hentilä and Nevakivi and by Kirby, listed in the Bibliography. For Denmark, Bo Lidergard's *A Short History of Denmark in the 20th Century* is the best English-language book. The same author's *Countrymen* tells the story of the rescue of the Jews. It is also worth looking at either Tom Buk-Swienty's book *1864*, or the TV drama taken from it. This war appears in European history books as a minor event, opening Bismarck's road to German unification. For Denmark it was a national disaster whose effects lasted into the next century.

George Kennan's memoirs are special. They are 'primarily an intellectual autobiography': memoirs not of his deeds, but of his thoughts. These tell us how poorly the Soviet Union is understood in America, and how empty and misguided US policy is. The result is 293 pages of frustration. Kennan writes of the Soviet Union almost in passing, but his occasional sentences on Stalin are still memorable. On page 294, it all changes. Kennan's voice is heard. Marshall arrives as secretary of state, and for four years Kennan is at the heart of policy. When I was a student, Kennan's *Memoirs* were on every reading list. They should be still, not least because they tell you what it is like to be a diplomat. Kennan's memoirs are completed by John Lewis Gaddis's fine biography, *George F Kennan: An American Life*. This fills the gaps: what Kennan is doing, what he is writing, what is going on around him.

The other great memoir of the period is Acheson's. Leaving office under a hail of abuse from Senator McCarthy, he did not want his memoirs to seem a self-justification. The passage of time and the success of his *Sketches from Life* persuaded him that a new generation should hear about Truman and Marshall. *Present at the Creation* is more than a memoir. Acheson had researchers work on State Department papers, while he studied his own. This is history in the first person, serious, sometimes thrilling. Whether he is responding to the attack on Korea or handling an angry Churchill, Acheson always knows what to do. Robert Beisner's biography shows that the perspective of four decades enhanced Acheson's achievement. In the twentieth century, his was the hour of the diplomat.

Alongside these belong the memoirs of Chip (Charles) Bohlen, *Witness to History 1929–1969*. Kennan's friend, Roosevelt's interpreter and Marshall's counsellor, later ambassador in Moscow and Paris, Bohlen was at Tehran, Yalta and Potsdam. The title is too modest: Bohlen is more conventional then Kennan, but he too was an exceptional diplomat.

Two other memoirs of the period are worth reading. Robert Murphy was a vice-consul in Munich at the time of the beer-hall putsch; then he was Roosevelt's man in Vichy France. He prepared the way for the US landings on the ground in North Africa, where he knew and admired Monnet. After the war, he was General Clay's adviser in Berlin. *Diplomat Among Warriors* is about the rougher side of diplomacy, sharply observed. Frank Roberts's *Dealing with Dictators* gives a view of the same great events from a brilliant British diplomat. He was private secretary to Bevin, ambassador in Khrushchev's Soviet Union, and much else besides.

Bevin did not tell his own story. Alan Bullock's biography (vol. 3 for Bevin as foreign secretary) will not be surpassed in its grasp of both detail and strategy. Acheson's *Sketches from Life* tells how it felt to work with Bevin; Francis Williams's memoir of Bevin as a trade unionist adds a human touch. Douglas Hurd's essay on Bevin and Eden in *Choose Your Weapons*, a book comparing foreign secretaries from Castlereagh to Eden, catches what is unique in Bevin (and Eden too) with remarkable brevity. Anne Deighton's *The Impossible Peace* is a study of Bevin's diplomacy in action, how his approach to Germany evolved and how it shaped the post-war world. Peter Hennessy's *Never Again: Britain 1945–51* gives Bevin a context and adds insights even to Alan Bullock's monumental volume.

Marshall was too modest ever to think of writing memoirs. Forrest Pogue's biography fills the gap. The private man remains private, but he left an impression on all who worked for him, Bohlen and Acheson among them. David McCullough's biography of Truman is a great work. I also like Stephen Graubart's *The Presidents*: the discipline of limited space makes his portrait of Truman vivid.

François Duchêne, Jean Monnet's biographer, tells us: 'He [Monnet] could not write himself and was deeply suspicious of anyone doing it for him.' François Fontaine, his assistant, wrote the *Memoirs* at Monnet's instruction – except for one paragraph – but it is Monnet's voice you hear. Duchêne's biography is a perfect complement.

Cuba is the crisis that launched a thousand books. The first was Robert Kennedy's *Thirteen Days*, partly a memoir, since he was a participant. Michael Dobbs's *One Minute to Midnight* tells the story hour by hour, like a thriller. Fursenko and Naftali's *'One Hell of a Gamble'* goes deeper into the background and what is going on in the Kremlin; Allison and Zelikow's *Essence of Decision* adds intellectual rigour on the decision-making. Personally, I value Sheldon Stern's *The Cuban Missile Crisis in American Memory*. He writes from a study of the tapes. His account of the debate in Washington demolishes Robert Kennedy's, and takes the reader through all the confusions and contradictions of real life. Those who want more real life can find it in May and Zelikow's *The Kennedy Tapes*: three volumes, each hundreds of pages long.

Henry Kissinger's *White House Years* might be given to students as a textbook on the practice of diplomacy. Kissinger tells us what he said, what he did, why he did it and what he was thinking. For some his account is too good to be true: Seymour Hersch's investigative work *The Pursuit of Power* and Raymond Garthoff's professional *Détente and Confrontation* cast doubt on parts of Kissinger's story and his motives. Jussi Hanhimäki in *The Flawed Architect* is low-key and factual. Mario del Pero examines Kissinger's ideas in action in *The Eccentric Realist*, a beautiful, short essay. Of the biographies, it is clear from the first volume that Niall Ferguson's will set a new standard. All Kissinger's writings, especially from the pre-power period, are worth reading. His essay on Bismarck, 'The White Revolutionary', is unsurpassed. The drama of the Nixon period is recorded in many great books: Stephen Ambrose's biography of Nixon and Margaret MacMillan's *Nixon and Mao* are just two of them.

The best English-language guide to German diplomacy in the Cold War is Timothy Garton Ash's *In Europe's Name*. Marie Elise Sarotte tells the eastern side of the German stories of both Brandt (*Dealing with the Devil*) and of reunification (*1989*) readably and accurately. 1989 is an American as well as a German story; Zelikow and Rice (*Germany Unified and Europe Transformed*) are both academics and insiders, with an eye for detail and an understanding of process.

For the stories of Frank Foley and Chiune Sugihara, I have relied heavily on Michael Smith's biography *Foley*, which covers Foley's intelligence work, too, and Yukiko Sugihara's memoir of her husband, *Visas for Life*. Those who want the full stories should turn to these.

Two less usual items merit a special mention: first, *The American Encounter* by James Hoge and Fareed Zakaria, a collection of *Foreign Affairs* articles. It includes several mentioned in this book, and others that made history as well as describing it; second, the website of the State Department's Office of the Historian – Foreign Relations of the United States – FRUS. No other country has anything like it: a symbol of how far the United States and its State Department are ahead of the rest of the world.

Beyond the books and articles mentioned here, or referenced in the different chapters, lies a sea of works on foreign policy: memoirs and biographies, books on the development of the states, books on the evolution of the state system; books on political philosophy, books on the history of regions, on the history of international relations, on the development of diplomacy, on the theory of diplomacy, books on wars, and a few on peace too.

I will mention a few of those that influenced me, or that I return to. The list is not that of scholar but of a diplomat who wanted to understand what he was doing.

The beginning is history. *The Penguin History of Europe* is a good starting point. No European country can be understood on its own. See under Blanning, Evans and Greengrass. There is much to be said for reading the history of our wars, since, as Charles Tilly says, 'The state made war; and war made the state.' The late Sir Michael Howard's *War in European History* is a book everyone interested in history or in Europe should read. The same goes for his last short book, *The Invention of Peace*. One book that remains in my memory is Roger Knight's *Britain Against Napoleon* for its account of how the Napoleonic Wars helped modernise the British state. To bring things up to date: Mary Kaldor's *Old and New Wars* describes the wars of the late twentieth and twenty-first century. Rupert Smith's *The Utility of Force* looks at the political nature of war: how to fight wars that are not a struggle to the death, as the world wars were.

One personal preoccupation is the changing nature of the state: Ernest Gellner's *Nations and Nationalism* is the book that started me thinking about this. Another is Karl Polyani's *The Great Transformation*, which tells how regulation became a core function of the liberal state – as it is today of the European Union. In spite of what others say, I like Francis Fukuyama's *The End of History and the Last Man*, as well as his works on the origin and decay of political order.

As a general diplomatic history, there is nothing to match Henry Kissinger's *Diplomacy*; but one should also look at A. J. P. Taylor's *The Struggle for the Mastery of Europe* – to remind ourselves that each of the events Kissinger whizzes through was infinitely complicated.

Diplomacy is best understood through a close examination of key events. I like books such as Lawrence Wright's *Thirteen Days in September* on Camp David, or Margaret MacMillan on *Nixon and Mao* or *The Peacemakers* (about Versailles). David Reynolds's *Summits* is not at the same level of detail, but it provides a good entry point. Not quite in this micro-category, but close, is Kori Shake's *Safe Passage*, on how the United States and the United Kingdom avoided the (so-called) Thucydides trap. To understand the EU as a political animal, the best account is Luuk van Middelaar's *Alarums and Excursions*, which looks at how policy is made in crisis.

On the history of diplomacy itself, Harold Nicolson's short books have an old-fashioned charm; Hamilton and Langhorne's *The Practice of Diplomacy* is a useful guide; I also like G. R. Berridge, Maurice Keens-Soper and T. G. Otte, *Diplomatic Theory from Machiavelli to Kissinger.* Diplomacy itself is an elusive subject. Kissinger's most interesting comments are in *A World Restored* rather than *Diplomacy*.

Finally, I mention two books that relate not to any of the chapters in this book but to the seminal events of the present age: the beginning and aftermath of the First World War. There are many fine books on both, but I particularly admire T. G. Otte's *The July Crisis*, which traces the diplomatic exchanges of the last month until the war begins. It gives a sense of the 'incalculable complications' foreseen by von Gentz. On the aftermath, Adam Tooze's *The Deluge* tells us of those that followed; it is a book so dense and so interesting that it needs reading more than once.

Bibliography

Acheson, Dean, *Sketches from Life: Of Men I Have Known* (Hamish Hamilton, 1961)

Acheson, Dean, *Present at the Creation: My Years in the State Department* (W. W. Norton, 1987)

Adenauer, Konrad, transl. Beate Ruhm von Oppen, *Memoirs 1945–53* (Weidenfeld & Nicolson, 1966)

Alanbrooke, Field Marshal Lord, ed. Alex Danchev and Daniel Todman, *War Diaries 1939–1945* (Weidenfeld & Nicolson, 2001)

Allison, Graham and Zelikow, Philip, *Essence of Decision: Explaining the Cuban Missile Crisis* (Longman, 1999)

Ambrose, Stephen, *Nixon*, vol. 2: *The Triumph of a Politician 1962–1972* (Simon & Schuster, 1989)

Baker, James A., with Defrank, Thomas M., *The Politics of Diplomacy: Revolution, War and Peace, 1989–1992* (Puttnam, 1995)

Ball, George W., *The Past Has Another Pattern: Memoirs* (W. W. Norton, 1982)

Bark, Dennis L. and Gress, David R., *A History of West Germany 1945–1989*, 2 vols (Blackwell, 1993)

Barrass, Gordon, *The Great Cold War* (Stanford University Press, 2009)

Beisner, Robert L., Dean Acheson: A Life in the Cold War (Oxford University Press, 2006)

Bergin, Joseph and Brockliss, Laurence (eds), *Richelieu and His Age* (Oxford University Press, 1992)

Berlin, Isaiah, *The Proper Study of Mankind: An Anthology of Essays* (Pimlico, 1998)

Berridge, G. R., Keens-Soper, Maurice and Otte, T. G., *Diplomatic Theory from Machiavelli to Kissinger* (Palgrave Macmillan, 2001)

Bidault, Georges, *Resistance: The Political Autobiography of Georges Bidault* (Weidenfeld & Nicolson, 1957)

Black, Robert, *Machiavelli* (Routledge, 2013)

Blanchard, Jean-Vincent, *Eminence: Cardinal Richelieu and the Rise of France* (Walker and Company, 2011)

Blanning, Tim, *The Pursuit of Glory: Europe 1648–1815* (Allen Lane, 2007)

Blumberg, Rhoda, *What's the Deal? Jefferson, Napoleon and the Louisiana Purchase* (Scholastic, 1998)

Bobbitt, Philip, *The Garments of Court and Palace: Machiavelli and the World that he Made* (Atlantic Books, 2013)

Bohlen, Charles E., *Witness to History 1929–1969* (Redwood Press, 1973)

Boucher, David, *Political Theories of International Relations* (Oxford University Press, 1998)

Braithwaite, Rodric, *Armageddon and Paranoia: The Nuclear Confrontation* (Profile Books, 2017)

Brandt, Willy, transl. J. Maxwell Brownjohn, *People and Politics* (Collins, 1978)

Brinkley, Douglas, *Dean Acheson: The Cold War Years, 1953–71* (Yale University Press, 1992)

Brinkley, Douglas and Hackett, Clifford (eds), *Jean Monnet: The Path to European Unity* (St Martin's Press, 1991)

Buk-Swienty, Tom, *1864: The Forgotten War that Shaped Europe* (Profile Books, 2015)

Bullock, Alan, *Ernest Bevin: Foreign Secretary 1945–1951* (Oxford University Press, 1985)

Bundy, McGeorge, *Danger and Survival: Choices about the Bomb in the First Fifty Years* (Random House, 1988)

Burckhardt, Carl J., transl. and abridged by Edwin and Willa Muir, *Richelieu: His Rise to Power* (Vintage, 1964)

Burns, William J., *The Back Channel: American Diplomacy in a Disordered World* (C. Hurst, 2019)

Buruma, Ian, *Year Zero: A History of 1945* (Atlantic Books, 2013)

Cadogan, Sir Alexander, ed. David Dilks, *The Diaries of Sir Alexander Cadogan, OM 1938–1945* (Faber & Faber, 1971)

Chen, Jian, *China's Road to the Korean War: The Making of the Sino-American Confrontation* (Columbia University Press, 1994)

Churchill, Winston, *The Gathering Storm*, vol. 1 of *The Second World War* (Penguin Classics, 2005)

Cohen, Eliot A. and Gooch, John, *Military Misfortunes: The Anatomy of Failure in War* (First Free Press, 2006)

Cooper, Duff, *Talleyrand* (Phoenix, 1997)

Cradock, Percy, *Know Your Enemy: How the Joint Intelligence Committee Saw the World* (John Murray, 2002)

Croxton, Derek, *The Last Christian Peace: The Congress of Westphalia as a Baroque Event* (Palgrave, 2013)

Dallek, Robert, *Nixon and Kissinger: Partners in Power* (HarperCollins, 2007)

Dallek, Robert, *John F. Kennedy: An Unfinished Life* (Penguin, 2013)

Dannenberg, Julia von, *The Foundations of Ostpolitik: The Making of the Moscow Treaty Between West Germany and the USSR* (Oxford University Press, 2008)

Deighton, Anne, *The Impossible Peace: Britain, the Division of Germany and the Origins of the Cold War* (Clarendon Press, 1990)

Del Pero, Mario, *The Eccentric Realist: Henry Kissinger and the Shaping of American Foreign Policy* (Cornell University Press, 2010)

Djilas, Milovan, transl. Michael B. Petrovich, *Conversations with Stalin* (Harcourt Brace, 1990)

Dobrynin, Anatoly, *In Confidence: Moscow's Ambassador to America's Six Cold War Presidents* (Times Books, 1995)

Dobbs, Michael, *One Minute to Midnight: Kennedy, Khrushchev and Castro on the Brink of Nuclear War* (Vintage, 2008)

Duchêne, François, *Jean Monnet: The First Statesman of Interdependence* (W. W. Norton, 1994)

Dulles, John Foster, *War or Peace* (Harrap, 1950)

Dulong, Claude, *Mazarin* (Perrin, 2010)

Elliott, J. H., *Richelieu and Olivares* (Cambridge University Press, 1984)

Erlanger, Philippe, *Richelieu: L'ambitieux, Le revolutionnaire, Le dictateur* (Perrin, 2006)

Evans, Richard, *The Pursuit of Power: Europe 1815–1914* (Allen Lane, 2016)

Ferguson, Niall, *Kissinger 1923–1968: The Idealist* (Penguin Random House, 2015)

Fink, Carole and Schaefer, Bernd (eds), *Ostpolitik, 1969–1974: European and Global Responses* (Cambridge University Press, 2009)

Freedman, Lawrence, *Kennedy's Wars: Berlin, Cuba, Laos, and Vietnam* (Oxford University Press, 2000)

Fukuyama, Francis, *The End of History and the Last Man* (Free Press, 1992)

Fukuyama, Francis, *The Origins of Political Order: From Prehuman Times to the French Revolution* (Profile Books, 2011)

Fukuyama, Francis, *Political Order and Political Decay* (Profile Books, 2014)

Fursenko, Aleksandr and Naftali, Timothy, *'One Hell of a Gamble': The Secret History of the Cuban Missile Crisis 1958–1964* (John Murray, 1997)

Fursenko, Aleksandr and Naftali, Timothy, *Khrushchev's Cold War: The Inside Story of an American Adversary* (W. W. Norton, 2006)

Gaddis, John Lewis, *Strategies of Containment* (Oxford University Press, 1982)

Gaddis, John Lewis, *George F. Kennan: An American Life* (Penguin, 2011)

Galbraith, John Kenneth, *Name Dropping: From FDR On* (Houghton Mifflin, 1999)

Garthoff, Raymond L., *Détente and Confrontation: American-Soviet Relations from Nixon to Reagan* (Brookings Institution, 1985)

Garton Ash, Timothy, *In Europe's Name: Germany and the Divided Continent* (Jonathan Cape, 1993)

Gellner, Ernest, *Nations and Nationalism* (Cornell University Press, 2008)

Gilbert, Martin, *Road to Victory: Winston S. Churchill 1941–1945* (Guild Publishing, 1986)

Graubart, Stephen, *The Presidents: The Transformation of the American Presidency from Theodore Roosevelt to George W. Bush* (Penguin, 2004)

De Grazia, Sebastian, *Machiavelli in Hell* (Vintage, 1994)

Greengrass, Mark, *Christendom Destroyed: Europe 1517–1648* (Allen Lane, 2014)

Hackett, Clifford P. (ed.), *Monnet and the Americans: The Father of a United Europe and his US Supporters* (Jean Monnet Council, 1995)

Hackett, Clifford P., *A Jean Monnet Chronology: Origins of the European Union in the Life of a Founder, 1888 to 1950* (Jean Monnet Council, 2008)

Halberstam, David, *The Coldest Winter: America and the Korean War* (Hyperion, 2007)

Haldeman, H.R., *The Haldeman Diaries: Inside the Nixon White House* (Putnam's, 1994)

Hamby, Alonzo L., *Man of the People: A Life of Harry S. Truman* (Oxford University Press, 1995)

Hamilton, Keith and Langhorne, Richard, *The Practice of Diplomacy: Its Evolution, Theory and Administration* (Routledge, 1995)

Hanhimäki, Jussi M., *Containing Coexistence: America, Russia, and the 'Finnish Solution', 1945–1956* (Kent State University Press, 1997)

Hanhimäki, Jussi M., *The Flawed Architect: Henry Kissinger and American Foreign Policy* (Oxford University Press, 2004)

Hastings, Max, *The Korean War* (Michael Joseph, 1987)

Hastings, Max, *Armageddon: The Battle for Germany 1944–45* (Macmillan, 2004)

Henderson, Sir Nicholas, *The Birth of NATO* (Weidenfeld & Nicolson, 1982)

Hennessy, Peter, *Never Again: Britain 1945–51* (Penguin, 1992)

Hersch, Seymour M., *The Pursuit of Power: Kissinger in the Nixon White House* (Summit Books, 1983)

Hildesheimer, Françoise, *Richelieu* (Flammarion, 2004)

Hinsley, F. H., *Power and the Pursuit of Peace* (Cambridge University Press, 1967)

Hoge, James F. Jr and Zakaria, Fareed (eds), *The American Encounter:*

The United States and the Making of the Modern World (Basic Books, 1997)

Holsti, Kalevi J., *Peace and War: Armed Conflicts and International Order 1648–1989* (Cambridge University Press, 1991)

Hoopes, Townsend, *The Devil and John Foster Dulles* (André Deutsch, 1974)

Howard, Sir Michael, *The Invention of Peace: Reflections on War and International Order* (Profile Books, 2000)

Howard, Sir Michael, *War in European History* (Oxford University Press, 2009)

Hurd, Douglas, *Memoirs* (Abacus, 2003)

Hurd, Douglas and Young, Edward, *Choose Your Weapons: The British Foreign Secretary: 200 Years of Argument, Success and Failure* (Phoenix, 2010)

Jackson, Julian, *A Certain Idea of France: The Life of General de Gaulle* (Penguin, 2019)

Jakobson, Max, *Finnish Neutrality: A Study of Finnish Foreign Policy Since the Second World War* (Hugh Evelyn, 1968)

Jakobson, Max, *Finland Survived: An Account of the Finnish-Soviet Winter War 1939–1940* (Otava, 1984)

Jakobson, Max, *Finland in the New Europe* (Praeger, 1998)

Jenkins, Roy, *Winston Churchill* (Macmillan, 2001)

Jespersen, Knud J. V., transl. Christopher Wade, *A History of Denmark* (Palgrave Macmillan, 2011)

Jones, Joseph Marion, *The Fifteen Weeks: An Inside Account of the Genesis of the Marshall Plan* (Viking, 1955)

Jussila, Osmo, Hentilä, Seppo and Nevakivi, Jukka, transl. David and Eva-Kaisa Arter, *From Grand Duchy to a Modern State: A Political History of Finland since 1890* (Hurst, 1999)

Kaldor, Mary, *New & Old Wars: Organized Violence in a Global Era* (Polity Press, 2012)

Karnow, Stanley, *Vietnam: A History* (Penguin, 1991)

Kennan, George, *Russia, the Atom and the West* (Oxford University Press, 1958)

Kennan, George, *Memoirs 1925–1950* (vol 1.) and *1950–1963* (vol. 2) (Random House-Pantheon, 1967 and 1971)

Kennan, George, *The Decline of Bismarck's European Order: Franco-Russian Relations 1875–1890* (Princeton University Press, 1979)

Kennan, George, *American Diplomacy* (University of Chicago Press, 1984)

Kennedy, Robert, *Thirteen Days: A Memoir of the Cuban Missile Crisis* (W. W. Norton, 1969)

Kirby, David, *A Concise History of Finland* (Cambridge University Press, 2006)

Kissinger, Henry, 'The White Revolutionary: Reflections on Bismarck', *Daedalus*, vol. 97, no. 3 (Summer 1968), pp. 888–924.

Kissinger, Henry, *American Foreign Policy: Three Essays* (Weidenfeld & Nicolson, 1969)

Kissinger, Henry, *White House Years* (Little Brown, 1979)

Kissinger, Henry, *Years of Upheaval* (Little Brown, 1982)

Kissinger, Henry, *Diplomacy* (Simon & Schuster, 1994)

Kissinger, Henry, *A World Restored: Metternich, Castlereagh and the Problems of Peace 1812–1822* (Weidenfeld & Nicolson, 1999)

Kissinger, Henry, *Years of Renewal* (Simon & Schuster, 1999)

Kissinger, Henry, *Crisis: The Anatomy of Two Major Foreign Policy Crises* (Simon & Schuster, 2003)

Knecht, R. J., *Richelieu* (Longman, 1991)

Knight, Roger, *Britain Against Napoleon: The Organization of Victory 1793–1815* (Allen Lane, 2014)

Kohl, Helmut, *Ich Wollte Deutschlands Einheit* (Propyläen, 1996)

Kuklick, Bruce, *Blind Oracles: Intellectuals and the War from Kennan to Kissinger* (Princeton University Press, 2006)

Lee, Alexander, *Machiavelli: His Life and Times* (Picador, 2020)

Lidergaard, Bo, *A Short History of Denmark in the 20th Century* (Gyldendal, 2009)

Lidergaard, Bo, transl. Robert Maas, *Countrymen: How Denmark's Jews Escaped the Nazis* (Atlantic Books, 2014)

Lippman, Walter, *The Cold War: A Study in US Foreign Policy* (Harper, 1947)

Lloyd Moote, A., *Louis XIII, the Just* (University of California Press, 1989)

Machiavelli, Niccolò, transl. Allan Gilbert, *The Chief Works and Others*, vol. 1 (Duke University Press, 1989)

Machiavelli, Niccolò, ed. Quentin Skinner and Russell Price, *The Prince* (Cambridge University Press, 2019)

Macmillan, Margaret, *Peacemakers: The Paris Peace Conference of 1919 and Its Attempt to End War* (John Murray, 2001)

Macmillan, Margaret, *Nixon and Mao: The Week That Changed the World* (Random House, 2007)

McCullough, David, *Truman* (Simon & Schuster, 1992)

McNamara, Robert S., *In Retrospect: The Tragedy and Lessons of Vietnam* (Times Books, 1995)

Maier, Charles S., *Dissolution: The Crisis of Communism and the End of East Germany* (Princeton University Press, 1997)

Mallaby, Christopher, *Living the Cold War: Memoirs of a British Diplomat* (Amberley, 2017)

Mansfield, Harvey C., *Machiavelli's New Modes and Orders: A Study of the Discourses on Livy* (University of Chicago Press, 2001)

Maresca, John J., *To Helsinki: The Conference on Security and Cooperation in Europe, 1973–1975* (Duke University Press, 1985)

Marshall, Barbara, *Willy Brandt* (Cardinal, 1990)

Mattingly, Garrett, *Renaissance Diplomacy* (Forgotten Books, 2018)

May, Ernest R. and Zelikow, Philip D. (eds), *The Kennedy Tapes: Inside the White House during the Cuban Missile Crisis* (W. W. Norton, 2002)

Metternich, Prince Clemens von, *The Autobiography 1773–1815* (Ravenhall, 2004)

Van Middelaar, Luuk, transl. Liz Waters, *Alarums & Excursions: Improvising Politics on the European Stage* (Agenda Publishing, 2019)

Monnet, Jean, transl. Richard Mayne, *Memoirs* (Doubleday, 1978)

Murphy, Robert, *Diplomat Among Warriors* (Collins, 1964)

Najemy, John M., *Between Friends: Discourses of Power and Desire in the Machiavelli-Vettori Letters of 1513–1515* (Princeton University Press, 1993)

Najemy, John M. (ed.), *The Cambridge Companion to Machiavelli* (Cambridge University Press, 2010)

Nicolson, Sir Harold, *The Evolution of Diplomatic Method* (Cassel, 1954)

Nicolson, Sir Harold, *Diplomacy* (Oxford University Press, 1969)

Osiander, Andreas, *The States System of Europe, 1640–1990: Peacemaking and the Conditions of Stability* (Clarendon Press, 1994)

Otte, T. G., *July Crisis: The World's Descent into War, Summer 1914* (Cambridge University Press, 2014)

Palmer, Alan, *Metternich: Councillor of Europe* (Weidenfeld & Nicolson, 1972)

Parker, Geoffrey (ed.), *The Thirty Years' War* (Routledge, 1987)

Del Pero, Mario, *The Eccentric Realist: Henry Kissinger and the Shaping of American Foreign Policy* (Cornell University Press, 2010)

Plumb, J. H., *The Italian Renaissance* (American Heritage Books, 1961)

Pogue, Forrest C., *George G. Marshall 1945–1959* (Viking, 1987)

Polyani, Karl, *The Great Transformation: The Political and Economic Origins of Our Time* (Beacon Press, 2001)

Potter, G. R. (ed.), *The New Cambridge Modern History, Volume 1: The Renaissance 1493–1520* (Cambridge University Press, 1957)

Van Reybrouck, David, transl. Liz Waters, *Against Elections: The Case for Democracy* (Bodley Head, 2016)

Reid, Escott, *Time of Fear and Hope: The Making of the North Atlantic Treaty* (McClelland & Stewart, 1977)

Reynolds, David, *Summits: Six Meetings that Shaped the Twentieth Century* (Penguin, 2007)

Richelieu, Armand Jean du Plessis, *Maximes d'état, ou testament politique d'Armand du Plessis, cardinal duc de Richelieu, Nouvelleed Augmentée des observations de monsieur l'abbé de Saint Pierre, & Charles duc de Lorraine & Bar v 2 of 2* (reproduction from Library of Congress)

Richelieu, Cardinal, transl. Bertram Hill, *The Political Testament: Significant Chapters* (University of Wisconsin Press, 1961)

Richie, Alexandra, *Faust's Metropolis: A History of Berlin* (HarperCollins, 1998)

Roberts, Frank, *Dealing with Dictators: The Destruction and Revival of Europe 1930–1970* (Weidenfeld & Nicolson, 1991)

Rousseau, Jean-Jacques, transl. and intro. by Maurice Cranston, *The Social Contract* (Penguin, 1968)

Rousseau, Jean-Jacques, ed. Michel Launay, *Les Confessions*, 2 vols (Flammarion, 1968)

Safire, William, *Before the Fall: An Inside View of the Pre-Watergate White House* (Ballantine, 1977)

Salter, Arthur, *Allied Shipping Control: An Experiment in International Administration* (Clarendon Press, 1921)

Sarotte, Mary Elise, *Dealing with the Devil: East Germany, Détente & Ostpolitik, 1969–1973* (University of North Carolina Press, 2001)

Sarotte, Mary Elise, *1989: The Struggle to Create Post-Cold War Europe* (Princeton University Press, 2009)

Schwartz, Hans-Peter, transl. Louise Wilmott, *Konrad Adenauer: A German Politician and Statesman in a Period of War, Revolution and Reconstruction*, 2 vols (Berghahn Books, 1995)

Shake, Kori, *Safe Passage: The Transition from British to American Hegemony* (Harvard University Press, 2017)

Sherwood, Robert E., *Roosevelt and Hopkins: An Intimate History* (Harper, 1948)

Sked, Alan, *Metternich and Austria: An Evaluation* (Palgrave Macmillan, 2007)

Skinner, Quentin, *Machiavelli: A Very Short Introduction* (Oxford University Press, 2000)

Smith, Michael, *Foley: The Spy Who Saved 10,000 Jews* (Hodder & Stoughton, 1999)

Smith, Rupert, *The Utility of Force: The Art of War in the Modern World* (Penguin, 2006)

Stern, Sheldon M., *The Cuban Missile Crisis in American Memory: Myths Versus Reality* (Stanford University Press, 2012)

Strauss, Leo, *Thoughts on Machiavelli* (University of Chicago Press, 1978)

Stueck, William, *Rethinking the Korean War: A New Diplomatic and Strategic History* (Princeton University Press, 2002)

Sugihara, Yukiko, transl. Hiroki Sugihara, *Visas for Life* (Holocaust Oral History Project, 1993)

Talleyrand, *Mémoires et correspondances du Prince de Talleyrand: Édition*

intégrale présentée par Emmanuel de Waresquiel (Robert Laffont, 2007)
Talleyrand, Charles-Maurice de, *Mots, Propos, Aphorismes 1754–1838*,
Présentation et choix d'Eric Schell, Préface d'Emmanuel de Waresquiel (Albin Michel, 2016)
Taubman, William, *Khrushchev: The Man, His Era* (Simon & Schuster, 2005)
Taubman, William, *Gorbachev: His Life and Times* (Simon & Schuster, 2017)
Taylor, A. J. P., *The Struggle for the Mastery in Europe, 1848–1918* (Oxford University Press, 2001)
Thomas, Daniel C., *The Helsinki Effect: International Norms, Human Rights, and the Demise of Communism* (Princeton University Press, 2001)
Thomas, Hugh, *Armed Truce: The Beginnings of the Cold War 1945–46* (Sceptre, 1988)
Tooze, Adam, *The Deluge: The Great War and the Remaking of Global Order* (Allen Lane, 2014)
Treasure, Geoffrey *Mazarin: The Crisis of Absolutism in France* (Routledge, 1997)
Treasure, Geoffrey, *Richelieu & Mazarin* (Routledge, 1998)
Voltaire, *Lettres philosophiques* (Garnier-Flammarion, 1964)
De Waresquiel, Emmanuel, *Talleyrand: Le prince immobile* (Fayard, 2006)
Westad, Odd Arne, Chen Jian, Stein Tonnesson, Nguyen Yu Tung, and James G. Hershberg, eds. '77 Conversations Between Chinese and Foreign Leaders on the Wars in Indochina, 1964-1977', *CWIHP* Working Paper No. 22 (Wilson Center, 1998)
Westad, Odd Arne, *The Global Cold War* (Cambridge University Press, 2011)
Westad, Odd Arne, *The Cold War: A World History* (Allen Lane, 2017)
Williams, Francis, *Ernest Bevin: Portrait of a Great Englishman* (Hutchinson, 1952)
Wilson, Peter H., *Europe's Tragedy: A New History of the Thirty Years War* (Penguin, 2010)
Wright, Lawrence, *Thirteen Days in September: Carter, Begin and Sadat at Camp David* (Vintage, 2015)

Young, Hugo, *This Blessed Plot: Britain and Europe from Churchill to Blair* (Macmillan, 1998)

Zamoyski, Adam, *Rites of Peace: The Fall of Napoleon and the Congress of Vienna* (Harper Perennial, 2007)

Zelikow, Philip and Rice, Condoleezza, *Germany Unified and Europe Transformed: A Study in Statecraft* (Harvard University Press, 1997)

Zubok, Vladislav M., *A Failed Empire: The Soviet Union in the Cold War from Stalin to Gorbachev* (University of North Carolina Press, 2009)

Notes

Chapter 1: Niccolò Machiavelli

1 Philippe de Commynes, a French diplomat, attributes this *bon mot* to Pope Alexander VI. It was made famous by *The Prince* (Chapter XII).
2 Florence is a republic, but not a democracy. The election is by the Eighty, one of the committees that run the republic.
3 Francis Bacon, the father of the scientific method, cited him with approval in *The Advancement of Learning*: John N. Najemy (ed.), *The Cambridge Companion to Machiavelli* (Cambridge University Press, 2010), p. 249.
4 The full title is 'Discourses on the First Ten Books of Titus Livy'.
5 This is in Chapter III, the point where the prince comes alive, as Machiavelli makes it clear that he is not going to present the usual collection of platitudes.
6 Victoria Kahn, 'Machiavelli's Afterlife and Reputation to the Eighteenth Century', in Najemy (ed.), *The Cambridge Companion to Machiavelli*, p. 252
7 Isaiah Berlin, *The Proper Study of Mankind: An Anthology of Essays* (Pimlico, 1998), pp. 269–325.
8 Quoted in J. H. Plumb, *The Italian Renaissance: A Concise Survey of its History and Culture* (Harper and Row, 1965), p. 190.

Chapter 2: Richelieu and Mazarin: the Making of the State

1 A. Lloyd Moote, *Louis XIII, the Just*, p. 215.
2 Carl J. Burckhardt, *Richelieu: His Rise to Power*, transl. and abridged by Edwin and Willa Muir (Vintage, 1964), p. 310.
3 R. J. Knecht, *Richelieu* (Longman, 1991), p. 19.
4 Ibid., p. 45.
5 Knecht, *Richelieu*, p. 13.
6 Knecht, *Richelieu*, p. 14.
7 Hermann Weber in Joseph Bergin and Laurence Brockliss (eds), *Richelieu*

and His Age (Oxford University Press, 1992), p. 46.

8 J. H. Elliott, *Richieu and Olivares* (Cambridge University Press, 1984), p. 135.

9 Ibid., p. 60.

10 R. J. Knecht, *Richelieu* (Profiles in Power) (Longman, 1991), p. 76.

11 Richelieu, *Traité pour Convertir*, in Elliott, *Richelieu and Olivares*, p. 30.

12 Burckhardt, Richelieu, p. 155.

13 Geoffrey Parker, *The Thirty Years' War* (Routledge, 1987), p. 97.

14 Geoffrey Treasure, *Mazarin: The Crisis of Absolutism in France* (Routledge, 1997), p. 19.

15 Burckhardt, *Richelieu*, p. 109.

16 Françoise Hildesheimer, *Richelieu* (Flammarion, 2004), p. 147.

17 Ibid., p. 153.

18 Parker, *The Thirty Years' War*, p. 129.

19 Treasure, *Mazarin*, p. 54.

20 Ibid., pp. 56–7.

21 Ibid., p. 57.

22 Ibid., p. 63.

23 Derek Croxton, *The Last Christian Peace: The Congress of Westphalia as a Baroque Event* (Palgrave, 2013), pp. 143–55.

24 Ibid., pp. 228–32.

25 Treasure, *Mazarin*, p. 246.

26 Kalevi J. Holsti, *Peace and War: Armed Conflicts and International Order 1648–1989* (Cambridge University Press, 1991), p. 35.

27 Ibid., p. 25.

28 Elliott, *Richelieu and Olivares*, p. 58.

29 Ibid., p. 43.

30 Andreas Osiander, *The States System of Europe, 1640–1990: Peacemaking and the Conditions of Stability* (Clarendon Press, 1994), p. 41.

31 Treasure, *Mazarin*, pp. 247–8.

32 Osiander, *The States System of Europe*, p. 132.

33 Ibid., p. 138.

34 Ibid., p. 141.

Chapter 3: Talleyrand: the Uncorrupted Mind

1 Emmanuel de Waresquiel, *Talleyrand; le prince immobile* (Fayard, 2006), p. 401.

2 Andre Suarès, 'De Napoléon', published in *Les Cahiers de la Quinzaine*, 23 Juillet 1912, pp. 66-68 (quoted in de Waresquiel, *Talleyrand*, p. 401).

3 Talleyrand, *Mémoires et correspondances du Prince de Talleyrand: Édition intégrale présentée par Emmanual de Waresquiel* (Robert Laffont, 2007), p. 186 (my translation).

4 Ibid., p. 194.

5 Ibid., p. 191.
6 Ibid., p. 192.
7 De Waresquiel, *Talleyrand*, p. 169 (my translation).
8 William Hague, *William Pitt the Younger* (Harper Press, 2005), p. 495.
9 Letter of Thomas Jefferson to Robert Livingston, his representative in France. Rhoda Blumberg, *What's the Deal? Jefferson, Napoleon and the Louisiana Purchase* (Scholastic Inc., 1998), p. 77.
10 Metternich, Prince Clemens von, *The Autobiography 1773–1815* (Ravenhall, 2004), p. 88.
11 De Waresquiel, *Talleyrand*, p. 281.
12 Ibid., p. 351.
13 Ibid., p. 341.
14 Quoted by Duff Cooper, *Talleyrand* (Phoenix, 1997), p. 126.
15 Ibid., p. 390.
16 Alan Sked, *Metternich and Austria* (Palgrave Macmillan, 2007), p. 298.
17 Talleyrand, *Mémoires*, p. 335.
18 Jean-Jacques Rousseau, *The Social Contract*, transl. Maurice Cranston (Penguin Classics, 2003), p. 32.
19 De Waresquiel, *Talleyrand*, p. 432.
20 Ibid., p. 426.
21 Henry Kissinger, *A World Restored: Metternich, Castlereagh and the Problems of Peace 1812–1822* (Weidenfeld & Nicolson, 1999), p. 136.
22 De Waresquiel, *Talleyrand*, p. 442.
23 Ibid., p. 434.
24 Ibid., p. 463.
25 Talleyrand, *Mémoires*, p. 439.
26 De Waresquiel, *Talleyrand*, p. 472; his endnote cites a note by Von Gentz dated 12th February 1815.
27 Ibid., pp. 479–80.
28 Adam Zamoyski, *Rites of Peace: The Fall of Napoleon and the Congress of Vienna* (Harper Perennial, 2007), pp. 282–3.
29 Ibid., p. 290.
30 Talleyrand, *Mémoires*, p. 503.
31 Zamoyski, *Rites of Peace*, p. 291.
32 Ibid., p. 28.
33 Talleyrand to Louis XVIII, 20 December 1814; *Mémoires*, p. 602.
34 Zamoyski, *Rites of Peace*, p. 390.
35 Kissinger, *A World Restored*, p. 166.
36 Talleyrand to Louis XVIII, 28 December 1814; *Mémoires*, pp. 606–10.
37 Zamoyski, *Rites of Peace*, p. 391.
38 Talleyrand to Louis XVIII, 4 January 1815; *Mémoires*, pp. 612–15.
39 Zamoyski, *Rites of Peace*, p. 395.
40 Kissinger, *A World Restored*, p. 168.

41 Zamoyski, *Rites of Peace*, p. 442.
42 Talleyrand, *Mémoires*, pp. 711–27.
43 De Waresquiel, *Talleyrand*, p. 501.
44 Ibid., p. 502.
45 Ibid., p. 522.
46 Duff Cooper, *Talleyrand* (Phoenix, 1997), p. 316.
47 De Waresquiel, *Talleyrand*, p. 576.
48 Ibid., p. 583.
49 From de Waresquiel, Introduction, *Mots, propos, aphorismes: Charles-Maurice de Talleyrand* (Éditions Horay, 2016).
50 *Memoirs of Madame de la Tour du Pin* (Harvill Press, 1960), pp. 245, 247.
51 Talleyrand, *Mémoires*, p. 457.
52 Ibid., pp. 711–27, especially pp. 722–3.
53 De Waresquiel, *Talleyrand*, p. 506.
54 Cooper, *Talleyrand*, p. 220.
55 Richard Evans, *The Pursuit of Power: Europe 1815–1914* (Allen Lane, 2016), p. 1.
56 Osiander, *The States System of Europe*, p. 232.
57 Ibid., pp. 248–9, memorandum of November 1818; original in Metternich, *Nachgelassene Papiere*, ed. Prince Richard Metternich and A. von Klinkowström, 8 vols (Vienna, 1880–84), vol. 3, p. 168. Like Osiander, I have made some small changes to the translation in the hope that it will be easier to follow.

Chapter 4: Two Small Countries: Denmark and Finland

1 From Erik Scavenius, *Forhandingspolitiken unter Besöttelsen* (Hasselbalch, 1948), p. 9. Jespersen, Knud J. V. transl. Christopher Wade, *A History of Denmark* (Palgrave Macmillan, 2004) p. 26.
2 Bo Lidergaard, *A Short History of Denmark in the 20th Century* (Gyldendal, 2009), p. 129.
3 Ibid., p. 150.
4 Ibid.
5 Albert Camus, *Le mythe de Sisyphe* (Folio essais, 2013), p. 166.
6 Bo Lidergaard, transl. Robert Maas, *Countrymen: How Denmark's Jews Escaped the Nazis* (Atlantic Books, 2014), pp. 71–2.
7 Ibid., p. 50.
8 Ibid., p. 213.
9 Max Hastings, *Armageddon: The Battle for Germany 1944–45* (Macmillan, 2004), p. 490.
10 Max Jakobson, *Finland Survived: An Account of the Finnish-Soviet Winter War 1939–1940* (Otava, 1984), p. 20.
11 Ibid., p. 10.
12 Ibid., p. 135.

13 Ibid., p. 139.
14 William Taubman, *Khrushchev: The Man, His Era* (Simon & Schuster, 2005), p. 141.
15 Jakobson, *Finland Survived*, p. 210.
16 Charles E. Bohlen, *Witness to History 1929–1969* (Redwood Press, 1973), p. 418.
17 Jussi M. Hanhimäki, *Containing Coexistence: America, Russia, and the 'Finnish Solution', 1945–1956* (Kent State University Press, 1997), p. 11.
18 Max Jakobson, *Finland in the New Europe* (Praeger, 1998), p. 54.
19 Ibid., p. 59.
20 John Foster Dulles, speaking at Iowa State College, 9 November 1956. Eisenhower was in hospital at the time, and Dulles spoke to counter his recent defence of military neutrality. See Townsend Hoopes, *The Devil and John Foster Dulles* (André Deutsch, 1974), pp. 216–17.
21 Jakobson, *Finland in the New Europe*, p. 60.
22 Hanhimäki, *Containing Coexistence*, p. 186.
23 Bohlen, *Witness to History*, p. 150.
24 Martin Gilbert, *Road to Victory: Winston S. Churchill 1941–1945* (Guild Publishing, 1986), p. 1022.
25 Kissinger, *A World Restored*, p. 329.
26 David Kirby, *A Concise History of Finland* (Cambridge University Press, 2006), p. 242.

Chapter 5: George Kennan: the Foot Soldier

1 John Lewis Gaddis, *George F. Kennan: An American Life* (Penguin, 2011), p. 182.
2 Ibid., p. 203.
3 George Kennan, *Memoirs 1925–1950* (Random House-Pantheon, 1967), p. 290.
4 Ibid., p. 291.
5 Ibid., p. 293.
6 David Reynolds, *Summits: Six Meetings that Shaped the Twentieth Century* (Penguin, 2007), p. 141.
7 Alonzo L. Hamby, *Man of the People: A Life of Harry S. Truman* (Oxford University Press, 1995), pp. 317–18.
8 Reynolds, *Summits*, p. 142.
9 Kennan, *Memoirs 1925–1950*, p. 83.
10 Hamby, *Man of the People*, p. 341.
11 Gaddis, *George F. Kennan*, p. 227.
12 Robert L. Beisner, *Dean Acheson: A Life in the Cold War* (Oxford University Press, 2006), p. 36.
13 Kennan, *Memoirs 1925–1950*, p. 557.

14 Ibid., p. 559.
15 Gaddis, *George F. Kennan*, p. 68.
16 Kennan, *Memoirs 1925–1950*, p. 67.
17 Ibid., p. 70.
18 Ibid., p. 72.
19 Gaddis, *George F. Kennan*, p. 97.
20 Kennan, *Memoirs 1925–1950*, p. 90.
21 Ibid., p. 133.
22 Ibid., p. 136.
23 Ibid., p. 145.
24 Ibid., p. 159.
25 Ibid., p. 161.
26 Ibid., p. 166.
27 Gaddis, *George F. Kennan*, p. 168.
28 Kennan, *Memoirs 1925–1950*, pp. 530–31.
29 Ibid., p. 541.
30 Bohlen, *Witness to History*, p. 160.
31 Kennan, *Memoirs 1925–1950*, pp. 191–2.
32 Ibid., p. 274.
33 Ibid., p. 195.
34 Ibid., p. 559.
35 Ibid., p. 310.
36 John Lewis Gaddis, *Strategies of Containment* (Oxford University Press, 1982), p. 49.
37 Henry Kissinger, *White House Years* (Little Brown, 1979), p. 135.
38 James F. Hoge Jr and Fareed Zakaria (eds), *The American Encounter: The United States and the Making of the Modern World* (Basic Books, 1997), p. 168.
39 Kennan, *Memoirs 1925–1950*, p. 408.
40 Ibid., p. 258.
41 Gaddis, *Strategies of Containment*, pp. 189–90.
42 Kennan, *Memoirs 1925–1950*, p. 440.
43 Ibid., p. 496.
44 Walter Lippmann, *The Cold War: A Study in US Foreign Policy* (Harper, 1947).
45 George Kennan, *Russia, the Atom and the West* (Oxford University Press, 1958), p. 47.
46 Gaddis, *Strategies of Containment*, p. 668.
47 Robert S. McNamara, *In Retrospect: The Tragedy and Lessons of Vietnam* (Times Books, 1995), p. 322.
48 Kennan, *Memoirs 1925–1950*, p. 212.
49 Ibid., p. 229.

Chapter 6: All the Olympians: Bevin, Marshall, Acheson

1 Francis Williams, *Ernest Bevin: Portrait of a Great Englishman* (Hutchinson, 1952), pp. 74–81.
2 Ibid., p. 192.
3 Ibid., p. 195.
4 Ibid., p. 196.
5 Amery's speech is in the *Penguin Book of Twentieth-Century Speeches*, ed. Brian MacArthur (Penguin, 1999), pp. 181–3, as well as Hansard for 7 May 1940. A full account of the events is in *Six Minutes in May: How Churchill Unexpectedly Became Prime Minister* by Nicholas Shakespeare (Vintage, 2017).
6 Williams, *Ernest Bevin*, p. 219.
7 Ibid., pp. 215–33.
8 Douglas Jay, quoted in Peter Hennessy, *Never Again: Britain 1945–51* (Penguin, 1992), p. 68.
9 Williams, *Ernest Bevin*, p. 272.
10 David McCullough, *Truman* (Simon & Schuster, 1992), p. 415.
11 Robert Murphy, *Diplomat Among Warriors* (Collins, 1964), pp. 316ff.
12 McCullough, *Truman*, p. 451.
13 Field Marshal Lord Alanbrooke, ed. Alex Danchev and Daniel Todman, *War Diaries 1939–1945* (Weidenfeld & Nicolson, 2001), p. 575.
14 Bohlen, *Witness to History*, p. 240.
15 Hugh Thomas, *Armed Truce: The Beginnings of the Cold War 1945–46* (Sceptre, 1988), p. 296.
16 Alan Bullock, *Ernest Bevin: Foreign Secretary 1945–1951* (Oxford University Press, 1985), pp. 130–37; see also Bohlen, *Witness to History*, p. 246.
17 John Foster Dulles, *War or Peace* (Harrap, 1950), p. 28.
18 Bullock, *Ernest Bevin*, p. 311.
19 Bohlen, *Witness to History*, p. 248.
20 Ibid., p. 250.
21 National Archives, Kew, FO 945/16 and FO 371/55586.
22 *Foreign Relations of the United States* (FRUS) 1946, vol. 4, p. 261.
23 FRUS 1946, CMF 4, doc. 266.
24 Murphy, *Diplomat Among Warriors*, p. 371.
25 Bullock, *Ernest Bevin*, p. 352.
26 FRUS 1947, vol. 2, p. 40.
27 Dean Acheson, *Present at the Creation: My Years in the State Department* (W. W. Norton, 1987), p. 218.
28 Beisner, *Dean Acheson*, p. 57.
29 Milovan Djilas, transl. Michael B. Petrovich, *Conversations with Stalin* (Harcourt Brace, 1990), p. 106.
30 Bullock, *Ernest Bevin*, p. 482.
31 Anne Deighton, *The Impossible Peace: Britain, the Division of Germany and the Origins of the Cold War* (Clarendon Press, 1990), p. 156; FO 800/447.

32 Forrest C. Pogue, *George G. Marshall 1945–1959* (Viking, 1987), p. 195.
33 Georges Bidault, *Resistance: The Political Autobiography of Georges Bidault* (Weidenfeld & Nicolson, 1967), p. 144.
34 Radio address by George Marshall, 28 April 1947, www.Marshall Foundation.org.
35 Bohlen, *Witness to History*, p. 253.
36 www.Marshall Foundation.org.
37 FRUS 1947, vol. 3, doc. 180, quoting Bevin's account of the discussion.
38 Bullock, *Ernest Bevin*, p. 422.
39 Vladislav M., Zubok, *A Failed Empire: The Soviet Union in the Cold War from Stalin to Gorbachev* (University of North Carolina Press, 2009), pp. 72–3.
40 FRUS 1947, vol. 3, p. 198.
41 FRUS 1947, vol. 3, ERP 233.
42 FRUS 1947, vol. 3, p. 148.
43 Bullock, *Ernest Bevin*, pp. 498–9.
44 Ibid.
45 Ibid., p. 499.
46 FRUS 1947, vol. 2, pp. 271–301, 315–320.
47 Bullock, *Ernest Bevin*, p. 517.
48 FRUS 1948, vol. 3, p. 6.
49 11 March FRUS vol. 3, p. 37.
50 Ibid.
51 Bullock, *Ernest Bevin*, p. 537.
52 Ibid.
53 Henry Wallich, quoted in Alexandra Richie, *Faust's Metropolis: A History of Berlin* (HarperCollins, 1998), p. 660.
54 Murphy, *Diplomat Among Warriors*, p. 389.
55 FRUS 588.
56 FRUS 662.
57 FRUS 1948, vol. 3, pp. 83 27/4
58 Escott Reid, *Time of Fear and Hope: The Making of the North Atlantic Treaty* (McClelland & Stewart, 1977), p. 63, quoted in Beisner, *Dean Acheson: A Life in the Cold War*, p. 129.
59 FRUS 1949, vol. 3, p. 50.
60 Acheson, *Present at the Creation*, p. 287.
61 Ibid., p. 385.
62 Williams, *Ernest Bevin*, p. 152.
63 Bullock, *Ernest Bevin*, p. 774.
64 JLG pp. 377–81, Bullock, *Ernest Bevin*, pp. 229–35, Acheson, *Present at the Creation*, pp. 346–9.
65 Bullock, *Ernest Bevin*, p. 233.
66 Acheson, *Present at the Creation*, p. 422.
67 Max Hastings, *The Korean War* (Michael Joseph, 1987), p. 119.

68 Acheson, *Present at the Creation*, p. 452.
69 Ibid., p. 15.
70 Bullock, *Ernest Bevin*, p. 196.
71 Ibid., p. 361.

Chapter 7: Jean Monnet: the Practical Imagination

1 Acheson, *Present at the Creation*, p. 342.
2 Clifford P. Hackett, *A Jean Monnet Chronology: Origins of the European Union in the Life of a Founder, 1888 to 1950* (Jean Monnet Council, 2008), p. 243.
3 François Duchêne, *Jean Monnet: The First Statesman of Interdependence* (W. W. Norton, 1994), p. 190.
4 Jean Monnet, *Memoirs*, transl. Richard Mayne (Doubleday, 1978), pp. 285–6.
5 Ibid., p. 287.
6 Ibid., pp. 289–93.
7 Ibid., p. 295.
8 Ibid.
9 Hackett, *A Jean Monnet Chronology*, p. 251.
10 Acheson, *Present at the Creation*, p. 383.
11 Monnet, *Memoirs*, p. 303.
12 Ibid., p. 52.
13 Ibid., pp. 58, 59.
14 Ibid., pp. 67–8.
15 Duchêne, *Jean Monnet*, p. 37.
16 Ibid., p. 70.
17 Duchêne, *Jean Monnet*, p. 55.
18 Monnet, *Memoirs*, p. 117.
19 Ibid., p. 28.
20 Duchêne, *Jean Monnet*, p. 88.
21 Monnet, *Memoirs*, p. 160.
22 Ibid., p. 166.
23 Robert E. Sherwood, *Roosevelt and Hopkins* (Harper, 1948), p. 64.
24 Monnet, *Memoirs*, p. 177.
25 Clifford P. Hackett (ed.), *Monnet and the Americans: The Father of a United Europe and his US Supporters* (Jean Monnet Council, 1995), p. 199.
26 Ibid., p. 174.
27 Duchêne, *Jean Monnet*, p. 109.
28 Monnet, *Memoirs*, pp. 186–9.
29 Ibid., p. 186.
30 Ibid., p. 187.
31 Ibid., p. 188.
32 Duchêne, *Jean Monnet*, p. 113.

33 Monnet, *Memoirs*, p. 221.
34 Ian Buruma, *Year Zero: A History of 1945* (Atlantic Books, 2013), p. 295.
35 Duchêne, *Jean Monnet*, p. 132.
36 Douglas Brinkley and Clifford Hackett (eds), *Jean Monnet: The Path to European Unity* (St Martin's Press, 1991), pp. 93–9.
37 Written in an essay by Wall, quoted in *Jean Monnet*, Brinkley and Hackett (eds), p. 98 and p. 101.
38 Hugo Young, *This Blessed Plot: Britain and Europe from Churchill to Blair* (Macmillan, 1998), p. 60.
39 Ibid., p. 67.
40 Monnet, *Memoirs*, p. 316.
41 Ibid., p. 280.
42 Ibid., p. 310.
43 Ibid.
44 Hackett (ed.), *Monnet and the Americans*, p. 264.
45 Beisner, *Dean Acheson*, p. 142.
46 Ibid., p. 370.
47 Monnet, *Memoirs*, p. 359.
48 Duchêne, *Jean Monnet*, pp. 229 and 231.
49 Ibid., p. 259.
50 Monnet, *Memoirs*, p. 195.
51 Brinkley and Hackett (eds), *Jean Monnet*, p. 187.
52 Monnet, *Memoirs*, p. 76.
53 Ibid., *Memoirs*, p. 126.
54 Murphy, *Diplomat Among Warriors*, p. 227.
55 Monnet, *Memoirs*, p. 373.

Chapter 8: The Cuban Missile Crisis

1 Aleksandr Fursenko and Timothy Naftali, *'One Hell of a Gamble': The Secret History of the Cuban Missile Crisis 1958–1964* (John Murray, 1997), p. 171.
2 John Kenneth Galbraith, *Name Dropping: From FDR On* (Houghton Mifflin, 1999), p. 105.
3 Michael Dobbs, *One Minute to Midnight: Kennedy, Khrushchev and Castro on the Brink of Nuclear War* (Vintage, 2008), p. 88.
4 Fursenko and Naftali, *'One Hell of a Gamble'*, p. 206.
5 Anatoly Dobrynin, *In Confidence: Moscow's Ambassador to America's Six Cold War Presidents* (Times Books, 1995), pp. 74–7.
6 McGeorge Bundy, *Danger and Survival: Choices about the Bomb in the First Fifty Years* (Random House, 1988), p. 198.
7 FRUS 1961–3, vol. 2, doc. 18.
8 Fursenko and Naftali, *'One Hell of a Gamble'*.

9 Ibid., p. 348.
10 Robert Dallek, *John F. Kennedy: An Unfinished Life* (Penguin, 2013), p. 290.
11 Dobbs, *One Minute to Midnight*, p. 15.
12 Ibid., p. 79.
13 Taubman, *Khrushchev*, p. 541.
14 Ibid., p. 408.
15 Dobbs, *One Minute to Midnight*, p. 250.
16 George W. Ball, *The Past Has Another Pattern: Memoirs* (W. W. Norton, 1982), pp. 286–310.
17 Sheldon M. Stern, *The Cuban Missile Crisis in American Memory: Myths Versus Reality* (Stanford University Press, 2012), p. 155.
18 Lawrence Freedman, *Kennedy's Wars: Berlin, Cuba, Laos, and Vietnam* (Oxford University Press, 2000), p. 139.
19 FRUS, 1961–3, vol. 6, Kennedy-Khrushchev exchanges no. 63, letter dated 24 October 1962.
20 Dobbs, *One Minute to Midnight*, p. 85.
21 FRUS 1961–3, vol. 6, Kennedy-Khrushchev exchanges no. 63, letter dated 24 October 1962.
22 FRUS 1961–3, vol. 6, Kennedy-Khrushchev exchanges no. 65, letter dated 25 October 1962.
23 Rodric Braithwaite, *Armageddon and Paranoia: The Nuclear Confrontation* (Profile Books, 2017), p. 327.
24 Taubman, *Khrushchev*, p. 567.
25 Freedman, *Kennedy's Wars*, p. 219.
26 Dobbs, *One Minute to Midnight*, p. 229.
27 Taubman, *Khrushchev*, p. 557.
28 Dobbs, *One Minute to Midnight*, p. 290.
29 FRUS 1961–3, vol. 6, no. 65.
30 Ibid.
31 Kissinger, *A World Restored*, p. 329.
32 Stern, *The Cuban Missile Crisis in American Memory*, p. 15.

Chapter 9: Henry Kissinger: Theory and Practice

1 Kissinger, *A World Restored*, p. 1.
2 Ibid., p. 326.
3 Ibid., p. 15.
4 Ibid., p. 180.
5 Ibid., p. 329.
6 Kissinger, 'Reflections on American Diplomacy', *Foreign Affairs*, October 1956.
7 Niall Ferguson, *Kissinger 1923–1968: The Idealist* (Penguin Random House,

2015), p. 174.
8 Ibid., p. 126.
9 Ibid., p. 664.
10 Ibid., p. 681.
11 Seymour M. Hersch, *The Pursuit of Power: Kissinger in the Nixon White House* (Summit Books, 1983), pp. 18–21.
12 Ibid., p. 39.
13 Ferguson, *Kissinger 1923–1968*, p. 854.
14 Kissinger, *White House Years*, pp. 10–16.
15 Hanhimäki, *Containing Coexistence*, p. 63.
16 Kissinger, *White House Years*, p. 141; see also H. R. Haldeman, *The Haldeman Diaries: Inside the Nixon White House* (Putnam's, 1994), p. 30.
17 The final paragraph of 'Central Issues of American Foreign Policy', published by the Brookings Institution in a collection called *Agenda for the Nation* (1968) and later by Weidenfeld & Nicolson in *American Foreign Policy: Three Essays* (1969).
18 Kissinger, *White House Years*, pp. 128–9.
19 Zubok, *A Failed Empire*, p. 200.
20 Hersch, *The Pursuit of Power*, p. 147.
21 Raymond L. Garthoff, *Détente and Confrontation: American-Soviet Relations from Nixon to Reagan* (Brookings Institution, 1985), pp. 158–69.
22 Henry Kissinger, *Diplomacy* (Simon & Schuster, 1994), p. 744.
23 Stephen Ambrose, *Nixon*, vol. 2: *The Triumph of a Politician 1962–1972* (Simon & Schuster, 1989), p. 549.
24 Zubok, *A Failed Empire*, p. 242.
25 Kissinger, *White House Years*, p. 1230.
26 Henry Kissinger, *Years of Renewal* (Simon & Schuster, 1999), p. 7.
27 Henry Kissinger, *Years of Upheaval* (Little Brown, 1982), p. 983.
28 Garthoff, *Détente and Confrontation*, p. 459.
29 Zubok, *A Failed Empire*, p. 220.
30 Garthoff, in *Détente and Confrontation*, pp. 290–96, provides an excellent guide.
31 H. R. Haldeman, *The Ends of Power* (Times Books, 1978), p. 91.
32 Zubok, *A Failed Empire*, p. 210.
33 Margaret MacMillan, *Nixon and Mao: The Week That Changed the World* (Random House, 2007), p. 144.
34 Ibid., p. 178.
35 Kissinger, *White House Years*, p. 710.
36 Ibid., pp. 733–87.
37 Ibid., p. 748.
38 Macmillan, *Nixon and Mao*, p. 304.
39 Odd Arne Westad, *The Cold War: A World History* (Penguin Random House, 2017), p. 369.

40 Ambrose, *Nixon*, vol. 2, pp. 190–91.
41 Ambrose, *Nixon*, vol. 2, p. 213.
42 Haldeman, *The Ends of Power*, p. 54.
43 Ambrose, *Nixon*, vol. 2, p. 339.
44 Ibid., p. 113.
45 Stanley Karnow, *Vietnam: A History* (Penguin, 1991), p. 654.
46 Kissinger, *The White House Years*, p. 1029.
47 Zhou Enlai to Le Duc Tho 12/7/72 in '77 Conversations Between Chinese and Foreign Leaders on the Wars in Indochina, 1964-1977.', *CWIHP* Working Paper No. 22 (Wilson Center, 1998)
48 Kissinger, *White House Years*, p. 1311.
49 Haldeman, *The Ends of Power*, p. 238.
50 Kissinger, *White House Years*, p. 1446.
51 Ibid., p. 1469.
52 Kissinger, *Years of Renewal*, p. 533.
53 Haldeman, *The Haldeman Diaries*, pp. 574–5.
54 Kissinger, *Years of Upheaval*, p. 487.
55 Ibid., p. 482.
56 Ibid., p. 641.
57 Ibid., p. 583.
58 Ibid., p. 591.
59 Ibid., p. 580.
60 Ibid., p. 580.
61 *Hanhimäki*, *The Flawed Architect*, p. 316.
62 Kissinger, *The White House Years*, p. 416.
63 Zubok, *A Failed Empire*, p. 241.
64 See Westad, *The Global Cold War.*
65 Kissinger, *White House Years*, p. 911.
66 William Safire, *Before the Fall: An Inside View of the Pre-Watergate White House* (Ballantine, 1977), p. 566.
67 Ibid., p.258.
68 Robert Dallek, *Nixon and Kissinger: Partners in Power* (HarperCollins, 2007), p. 618.
69 Haldeman, *The Haldeman Diaries*, p. 63.
70 Dallek, *Nixon and Kissinger*, p. 100.
71 George Perkovich, *India's Nuclear Bomb: The Impact on Global Proliferation* (University of California Press, 1999), p. 183.
72 Garthoff, *Détente and Confrontation*, p. 548.
73 'Central Issues of American Foreign Policy', p. 59.
74 Kissinger, *White House Years*, p. 64.

Chapter 10: German Diplomacy: Adenauer, Brandt and Kohl

1 Acheson, *Sketches from Life*, pp. 165–6.
2 Dennis L. Bark and David R. Gress, *A History of West Germany 1945–1989*, 2 vols (Blackwell, 1993), p. 108.
3 Dean Acheson, *Sketches from Life: Of Men I Have Known* (Hamish Hamilton, 1961), p. 161.
4 Dulles's speech at the NATO Council meeting, 14 December 1953.
5 Acheson, *Sketches from Life*, p. 162.
6 Barbara Marshall, *Willy Brandt* (Cardinal, 1990), p. 7.
7 Commencement Address at the American University, 10 June 1963, JFK Library.
8 Speech at the Evangelical Academy in Tutzing by Egon Bahr, 15 July 1963.
9 Timothy Garton Ash, *In Europe's Name: Germany and the Divided Continent* (Jonathan Cape, 1993), p. 262.
10 Willy, Brandt, *People and Politics*, transl. J. Maxwell Brownjohn (Collins, 1978), p. 129.
11 Julia von Dannenberg, *The Foundations of Ostpolitik: The Making of the Moscow Treaty Between West Germany and the USSR* (Oxford University Press, 2008), p. 128.
12 Kissinger, *White House Years*, p. 409.
13 Mary Elise Sarotte, *Dealing with the Devil: East Germany, Détente & Ostpolitik, 1969–1973* (University of North Carolina Press, 2001), p. 26.
14 Brandt, *People and Politics*, p. 399.
15 Sarotte, *Dealing with the Devil*, p. 40.
16 Kissinger, *White House Years*, p. 411.
17 Ibid., p. 531.
18 Ibid., p. 809.
19 Sarotte, *Dealing with the Devil*, p. 86.
20 Ibid., p. 828.
21 Ibid., p. 534.
22 Speech in the Bundestag, 21 January 1983.
23 Speech in Berlin, 17 June 1983.
24 Zubok, *A Failed Empire*, p. 267.
25 William Taubman, *Gorbachev: His Life and Times* (Simon & Schuster, 2017), p. 251.
26 Ibid., p. 277.
27 Charles S. Maier, *Dissolution: The Crisis of Communism and the End of East Germany* (Princeton University Press, 1997), p. 219.
28 Taubman, *Gorbachev*, pp. 388–9.
29 Ibid., p. 390.
30 Zubok, *A Failed Empire*, p. 324.
31 Dobrynin, *In Confidence*, p. 632.
32 Taubman, *Gorbachev*, pp. 481–4.

33 Ibid., p. 486.
34 Ibid., p. 485.
35 Maier, *Dissolution*, pp. 136–8.
36 Taubman, *Gorbachev*, p. 490.
37 Mary Elise Sarotte, *1989: The Struggle to Create Post Cold War Europe* (Princeton University Press, 2009), pp. 64-65.
38 Helmut Kohl, *Ich Wollte Deutschlands Einheit* (Propyläen, 1996), p. 215.
39 James A. Baker, with Thomas M. Defrank, *The Politics of Diplomacy: Revolution, War and Peace, 1989–1992* (Putnam's, 1995), pp. 193–216.
40 Douglas Hurd, *Memoirs* (Abacus, 2003), p. 424.
41 Philip Zelikow and Condoleezza Rice, *Germany Unified and Europe Transformed: A Study in Statecraft* (Harvard University Press, 1997), p. 207.
42 Hurd, *Memoirs*, p. 422.
43 Zelikow and Rice, *Germany Unified and Europe Transformed*, p. 142.
44 Ibid., p. 195.
45 Sarotte, *1989*, p. 121.
46 Zelikow and Rice, *Germany Unified and Europe Transformed*, p. 175.
47 Baker with Defrank, *The Politics of Diplomacy*, p. 184.
48 Sarotte, *1989*, p. 164.
49 Ibid., p. 166.
50 Zelikow and Rice, *Germany Unified and Europe Transformed*, pp. 275-278.
51 Ibid., pp. 281-283
52 Taubman, *Gorbachev*, p. 550.

Chapter 11: Two Diplomats and the Holocaust

1 Michael Smith, *Foley: The Spy Who Saved 10,000 Jews* (Hodder & Stoughton, 1999), p. 94.
2 Ibid., p. 151.
3 Ibid., pp. 109–10.
4 Ibid., pp. 112–13.
5 Ibid., p. 118.
6 Ibid., p. 119.
7 Ibid., p. 159.
8 Ibid., p. 171.
9 Ibid., p. 132.
10 Ibid., p. 133.
11 Yukiko Sugihara, transl. Hiroki Sugihara, *Visas for Life* (Holocaust Oral History Project, 1993). p. 21.

Conclusion: Putting the Fragments Together

1 McCullough, *Truman*, p. 262.

Index